MW00675015

Design, Implementation, and Evaluation of Virtual Learning Environments

Michael Thomas
University of Central Lancashire, UK

Managing Director: Lindsay Johnston
Senior Editorial Director: Heather A. Probst
Book Production Manager: Sean Woznicki
Development Manager: Joel Gamon
Acquisitions Editor: Erika Gallagher
Typesetter: Jennifer Romanchak
Cover Design: Nick Newcomer, Lisandro Gonzalez

Published in the United States of America by
Information Science Reference (an imprint of IGI Global)
701 E. Chocolate Avenue
Hershey PA 17033
Tel: 717-533-8845
Fax: 717-533-8661
E-mail: cust@igi-global.com
Web site: http://www.igi-global.com

Library of Congress Cataloging-in-Publication Data

Design, implementation, and evaluation of virtual learning environments /Michael Thomas, editor.
p. cm.
Includes bibliographical references and index.
Summary: "This book highlights invaluable research covering the design, development, and evaluation of online learning environments, examining the role of technology enhanced learning in this emerging area"--Provided by publisher.
ISBN 978-1-4666-1770-4 (hardcover) -- ISBN 978-1-4666-1771-1 (ebook) -- ISBN 978-1-4666-1772-8 (print & perpetual access) 1. Web-based instruction--Design. 2. Computer-assisted instruction. I. Thomas, Michael, 1969-
LB1044.87.D475 2012
371.33'44678--dc23
2012002478

British Cataloguing in Publication Data
A Cataloguing in Publication record for this book is available from the British Library.

Kieron Sheehy, *Open University, UK*
Leslie Shield, *Open University, UK*
Sukunesan Sinnappan, *Swinburne University of Technology, Australia*
Sandra Sutton Andrews, *University of Northern Arizona, USA*
Hagit Tal, *Open University of Israel, Israel*
Ricardo Torres, *Citilab-i2Cat, Spain*
Tracy Villareal, *University of Texas at Austin, USA*
Charles Wankel, *St. John's University - New York, USA*
Peter Worrall, *Media Consultant, UK*

Table of Contents

Preface xvi

Section 1
Key Concepts

Chapter 1
The Centralisation Dilemma in Educational IT 1
Martin Weller, The Open University, UK

Chapter 2
eLearning in the Cloud 10
Niall Sclater, The Open University, UK

Chapter 3
Toward a Personal Learning Environment Framework 20
Mohamed Amine Chatti, RWTH Aachen University, Germany
Mohammad Ridwan Agustiawan, RWTH Aachen University, Germany
Matthias Jarke, RWTH Aachen University, Germany
Marcus Specht, Open University, The Netherlands

Section 2
Design

Chapter 4
Designing Effective Spaces, Tasks and Metrics for Communication in Second Life Within the Context of Programming LEGO NXT Mindstorms™ Robots 42
Michael Vallance, Future University Hakodate, Japan
Stewart Martin, Teesside University, UK
Charles Wiz, Yokohama National University, Japan
Paul van Schaik, Teesside University, UK

Chapter 5
Homo Virtualis: Virtual Worlds, Learning, and an Ecology of Embodied Interaction 58
Leslie Jarmon, The University of Texas at Austin, USA

Chapter 6
Second Life as a Surrogate for Experiential Learning 77
Michael N. DeMers, New Mexico State University, USA

Chapter 7
An Interdisciplinary Design Project in Second Life: Creating a Virtual Marine Science Learning Environment 93
Riley Triggs, University of Texas at Austin, USA
Leslie Jarmon, University of Texas at Austin, USA
Tracy A. Villareal, University of Texas Marine Science Institute, USA

Chapter 8
Virtual Speed Mentoring in the Workplace - Current Approaches to Personal Informal Learning in the Workplace: A Case Study 112
Chuck Hamilton, IBM Center for Advanced Learning IBM, Canada
Kristen Langlois, IBM Canada Ltd., Canada
Henry Watson, IBM Canada Ltd., Canada

Section 3
Implementation

Chapter 9
Communication and Education in a Virtual World: Avatar-Mediated Teaching and Learning in Second Life 121
Lorri Mon, Florida State University, USA

Chapter 10
Mechanics Simulations in Second Life 137
Kelly Black, Clarkson University, USA

Chapter 11
Development of an Interactive Virtual 3-D Model of the Human Testis Using the Second Life Platform 153
Douglas R. Danforth, Ohio State University, USA

Chapter 12
Affective Load and Engagement in Second Life: Experiencing Urgent, Persistent, and Long-Term Information Needs 168
Diane Nahl, University of Hawaii, USA

Chapter 13
Investigating Modes of Student Inquiry in Second Life as Part of a Blended Approach 184
Sheila Webber, University of Sheffield, UK

Chapter 14
Low-Cost Virtual Laboratory Workbench for Electronic Engineering 201
Ifeyinwa E. Achumba, University of Portsmouth, UK
Djamel Azzi, University of Portsmouth, UK
James Stocker, University of Portsmouth, UK

Section 4
Evaluation

Chapter 15
The Development of a Personal Learning Environment in Second Life 219
Sandra Sutton Andrews, Arizona State University, USA
Mary Stokrocki, Arizona State University, USA
Angel Jannasch-Pennell, Arizona State University, USA
Samuel A. DiGangi, Arizona State University, USA

Chapter 16
A Framework for the Assessment of Wiki-Based Collaborative Learning Activities 237
Hagit Meishar-Tal, Open University of Israel, Israel
Mat Schencks, Open University, UK

Chapter 17
Evaluating Games-Based Learning 250
Thomas Hainey, University of the West of Scotland, Scotland
Thomas Connolly, University of the West of Scotland, Scotland

Chapter 18
Challenges Facing the Semantic Web and Social Software as Communication Technology Agents in E-Learning Environments 265
Bolanle A. Olaniran, Texas Tech University, USA

Compilation of References 279

About the Contributors 307

Index 316

Detailed Table of Contents

Preface xvi

Section 1
Key Concepts

Chapter 1
The Centralisation Dilemma in Educational IT 1
Martin Weller, The Open University, UK

The trend with organisational adoption of virtual learning environments (VLE) seems to be cyclical. Initially, a decentralised approach was adopted, wherein each department implemented different learning environments or mixtures of technology, often developed in-house. The last five years have seen an increased centralisation of learning environment implementation, with most universities adopting a single VLE. However, in more recent times the proliferation of free, easy-to-use third party tools that fulfil a range of functions has seen a desire amongst some educators to return to a more decentralised model of technology provision, by supporting Personal Learning Environments (PLE). This paper examines the issues surrounding both a centralised and decentralised model. These include pedagogic, support, financial, reliability, data and technical issues. The conclusion is that although the fully individualised PLE may not be possible or desirable in higher education, maintaining separate, often inferior versions of commonly available software is not a sustainable position.

Chapter 2
eLearning in the Cloud 10
Niall Sclater, The Open University, UK

Elearning has grown rapidly in importance for institutions and has been largely facilitated through the "walled garden" of the virtual learning environment. Meanwhile many students are creating their own personal learning environments by combining the various Web 2.0 services they find most useful. Cloud computing offers new opportunities for institutions to provide dynamic and up-to-date Internet-based, e-learning applications while ensuring high levels of service, and compliance with institutional policies and legislation. The cloud is rapidly evolving in its architecture, the services offered and the logistics of deployment. It brings with it risks but also possibilities for learners and for educational institutions to reduce costs and enhance services. It is likely to severely disrupt the business model developed by existing vendors of VLEs who provide an integrated suite of e-learning tools, installed and maintained by the institution's IT services department.

Chapter 3
Toward a Personal Learning Environment Framework 20
Mohamed Amine Chatti, RWTH Aachen University, Germany
Mohammad Ridwan Agustiawan, RWTH Aachen University, Germany
Matthias Jarke, RWTH Aachen University, Germany
Marcus Specht, Open University, The Netherlands

Over the past decade, it has been argued that technology-enhanced learning (TEL) could respond to the needs of the new knowledge society and transform learning. However, despite isolated achievements, TEL has not succeeded in revolutionizing education and learning processes. Most current TEL initiatives still take a centralized technology-push approach in which learning content is pushed to a predefined group of learners in closed environments. A fundamental shift toward a more open and learner-pull model for learning is needed. Recently, the Personal Learning Environment (PLE) concept has emerged to open new doors for more effective learning and overcome many of the limitations of traditional TEL models. In this paper, the authors present theoretical, design, implementation, and evaluation details of PLEF, a framework for mashup personal learning environments. The primary aim of PLEF is to help learners create custom learning mashups using a wide variety of digital media and data.

Section 2
Design

Chapter 4
Designing Effective Spaces, Tasks and Metrics for Communication in Second Life Within the Context of Programming LEGO NXT Mindstorms™ Robots 42
Michael Vallance, Future University Hakodate, Japan
Stewart Martin, Teesside University, UK
Charles Wiz, Yokohama National University, Japan
Paul van Schaik, Teesside University, UK

Science education is concerned with the meaningful pursuit of comprehension, knowledge and understanding of scientific concepts and processes. In Vygotskian social constructivist learning, personal interpretation, decision-making and community cooperation fosters long-term understanding and transference of learned concepts. The construction of knowledge requires learners to be actively involved in the process of learning. For effective science learning to take place an instructor's pedagogical approach must be anchored in meaningful contexts so that students have actual opportunities to experience science. This paper presents the early stages of a research project that attempts to assess and define effective measurements for evaluating strategies for communicating science by using LEGO robots and Mindstorms™ RCX controllers that are collaboratively constructed and programmed by students using virtual technologies while physically situated in different locations.

Chapter 5
Homo Virtualis: Virtual Worlds, Learning, and an Ecology of Embodied Interaction 58
Leslie Jarmon, The University of Texas at Austin, USA

This article previews the emergence of homo virtualis. Drawing on data from seven research studies, peer-reviewed published research articles, and selected excerpts of 30 months of field notes taken in Second Life, the article examines virtual learning environments and embodiment through the lens of interactions of avatars with other avatars, virtual objects, landscapes, sounds, and spatial constructs. Analysis is grounded in the polyvocal evidence provided by select participants who experienced a sense of embodied co-presence and connection with others across geo-physical distances. The discourse ranges from that of high school girls, professional retirees, toxicology and design undergraduates, interdisciplinary graduate students, to educators and researchers from K-12 through university full professors collaborating in SL. In an ecology of virtual contexts, learners inhabit a broader landscape of their own and others' making that allows them to be teachers, designers, researchers, communicators, and collaborators.

Chapter 6
Second Life as a Surrogate for Experiential Learning.. 77
Michael N. DeMers, New Mexico State University, USA

Second Life is increasingly being used as a venue for education, especially for delivery of online instruction where social presence and community building are essential components. Despite its robust 3-D modeling tools and powerful scripting language, many educational uses of Second Life are limited to passive forms of content delivery that often mimic some variety of Victorian style lecture setting. This article demonstrates a series of exercises designed around a more active learning model for my geography courses based on Kolb's (2005) theory of experiential learning. Active class exercises encourage hands-on interaction with components of the virtual world, but are linked explicitly to real subject matter content. By providing fun pre-exercise training and promoting learning by discovery, the exercises are designed to encourage the four fundamental components of the experiential learning environment: involvement, reflection, analysis, and problem solving. Beyond providing an excellent educational environment, such approaches can act as surrogates for real-world experiences that are either impossible or logistically problematic.

Chapter 7
An Interdisciplinary Design Project in Second Life: Creating a Virtual Marine Science Learning Environment... 93
Riley Triggs, University of Texas at Austin, USA
Leslie Jarmon, University of Texas at Austin, USA
Tracy A. Villareal, University of Texas Marine Science Institute, USA

Virtual environments can resolve many practical and pedagogical challenges within higher education. Economic considerations, accessibility issues, and safety concerns can all be somewhat alleviated by creating learning activities in a virtual space. Because of the removal of real-world physical limitations like gravity, durability and scope, virtual space allows for an expansion of possibilities and approaches to knowledge transfer and discovery learning and becomes an "environment for information" rich with collaborative possibilities. Experimentation and participation in conceptual as well as applied projects is encouraged for both students and instructors. One of these virtual environments, Second Life, was used in a cross-disciplinary project for the creation of a Marine Science virtual class environment as an assignment for design students at a major southwestern research university in the United States. This paper reports on the findings from a project that utilized Second Life as a medium for enhancing and extending design education using a process of interdisciplinary collaboration.

Chapter 8
Virtual Speed Mentoring in the Workplace - Current Approaches to Personal Informal Learning in the Workplace: A Case Study.. 112
Chuck Hamilton, IBM Center for Advanced Learning IBM, Canada
Kristen Langlois, IBM Canada Ltd., Canada
Henry Watson, IBM Canada Ltd., Canada

Informal learning is the biggest undiscovered treasure in today's workplace. Marcia Conner, author and often-cited voice for workplace learning, suggests that "Informal learning accounts for over 75% of the learning taking place in organizations today" (1997). IBM understands the value of the hyper-connected informal workplace and informal learning that comes through mentoring. This case study examines a novel approach to mentoring that is shaped only by virtual space and the participants who inhabit it. The authors found that virtual social environments can bridge distances in a way that is effective, creative and inexpensive. Eighty-five percent of virtual speed mentoring attendees reported that this approach achieved their learning objectives. Participants also reported that virtual social spaces like Second Life® are suitable delivery vehicles for mentoring, and that connecting with people was much easier than via telephone or web conferencing.

Section 3
Implementation

Chapter 9
Communication and Education in a Virtual World: Avatar-Mediated Teaching and Learning in Second Life 121
Lorri Mon, Florida State University, USA

Education within Second Life frequently recapitulates the "sage on the stage" as students sit their avatars down in chairs in the virtual world and listen to or read an instructor's lecture while watching a slideshow. This conceptual article explores alternative active learning techniques supporting independent and collaborative learning within virtual worlds. Within Second Life, educators can utilize a variety of scripted tools and objects as well as techniques of building and terra-forming to create vibrant virtual personal learning environments and learning experiences that are engaging and responsive to individual learners. Issues of embodiment in an avatar are discussed in terms of social presence, and student learning styles are considered as well as approaches to problem-based learning, games, role play, and immersive virtual world environments.

Chapter 10
Mechanics Simulations in Second Life.. 137
Kelly Black, Clarkson University, USA

This paper examines the use of the 3-D virtual world Second Life to explore basic mechanics in physics. In Second Life, students can create scripts that take advantage of a virtual physics engine in order to conduct experiments that focus on specific phenomena. The paper explores two particular examples of this process: 1) the movement of an object under the influence of gravity, and 2) the movement of an object using simple forces. Findings suggest that Second Life offers a flexible and wide range of possibilities for simulations in mechanics; paradoxically, however, the environment also presents challenges for effective use by instructors and learners. Any implementation making use of the Second Life application requires technical knowledge of the system and a wide range of pedagogical and learner skills related to building, scripting, and educational design.

Chapter 11
Development of an Interactive Virtual 3-D Model of the Human Testis Using the Second Life Platform.. 153
Douglas R. Danforth, Ohio State University, USA

One of the strengths of a virtual environment is the ability to immerse the occupant into an environment that would otherwise be impossible. The primary focus of the author's project in Second Life is to take advantage of this opportunity to explore novel approaches to medical education. Second Life can be used to model doctor-patient interaction, clinical diagnosis skills, and three dimensional molecular and cellular modeling of objects from individual molecules to whole organ systems, both healthy and diseased. Using the powerful building and scripting tools of the Second Life platform, the author has created a model of the human testis that students can fly through and interact with to understand how the anatomy and physiology of the testis work together to regulate sperm production. The anatomical and physiological interactions occurring during these processes are described in accompanying audio and text. The development of educational tools within the Second Life context is in its infancy. As the technology matures, the opportunities for education within Second Life will continue to expand as an important adjunct to traditional pedagogical approaches.

Chapter 12
Affective Load and Engagement in Second Life: Experiencing Urgent, Persistent, and Long-Term Information Needs 168
Diane Nahl, University of Hawaii, USA

New users of virtual environments face a steep learning curve, requiring persistence and determination to overcome challenges experienced while acclimatizing to the demands of avatar-mediated behavior. Concurrent structured self-reports can be used to monitor the personal affective and cognitive struggles involved in virtual world adaptation to specific affordances while performing particular tasks and activities with avatars. Examination of user discourse in self-reports reveal that participants focus on micro-management concerns about how to proceed in an activity, replete with intense emotions and uncertainty over how to operate affordances. Concurrent structured self-reports engage users in meta-affective and meta-cognitive reflection and facilitate coping with confusion and negative emotions. As Second Life is a complex virtual world with hundreds of affordances, people experience a continuous stream of information needs. Urgent, persistent, and long-term information needs are associated with differing qualities and intensities of affective load, such as impatience, irritation, anxiety, and frustration. When a particular information need is met, affective engagement results in intensity proportional to the affective load. Constructing user discourse during virtual activities serves as a coping mechanism that facilitates adaptation by raising meta-cognitive and meta-affective awareness.

Chapter 13
Investigating Modes of Student Inquiry in Second Life as Part of a Blended Approach 184
Sheila Webber, University of Sheffield, UK

This article discusses activities carried out in the virtual world of Second Life (SL) as part of a compulsory class in the first year of an undergraduate programme. The paper identifies the contribution of SL to the students' learning environment and an Inquiry Based Learning (IBL) approach to programme design. The reasons for taking an IBL approach are explained in relation to institutional and disciplinary goals. The paper reflects on the contribution of the three key learning environments—the classroom, WebCT and SL—to students' learning. SL is evaluated in relation to a conceptual framework of IBL. It is concluded that SL has made a contribution to students' achievement of learning outcomes from the class, and has facilitated the development of students' inquiry skills. In conclusion, further avenues for developing research and teaching are identified.

Chapter 14
Low-Cost Virtual Laboratory Workbench for Electronic Engineering 201
Ifeyinwa E. Achumba, University of Portsmouth, UK
Djamel Azzi, University of Portsmouth, UK
James Stocker, University of Portsmouth, UK

The laboratory component of undergraduate engineering education poses challenges in resource constrained engineering faculties. The cost, time, space and physical presence requirements of the traditional (real) laboratory approach are the contributory factors. These resource constraints may mitigate the acquisition of meaningful laboratory experiences by students, which is especially true in developing countries. Virtual laboratories can be used to complement the traditional laboratory to enhance students' laboratory experience. In extreme cases of lack of resources, the virtual lab can be used as an alternative laboratory . Although some research on the implementation of virtual laboratories has occurred, more efforts are required because of the diverse experiential needs and requirements of the engineering curriculum. This paper presents a low-cost, web-based virtual laboratory workbench for use as part of undergraduate electronic engineering courses. Some distinguishing features of the virtual workbench are that students can undertake curriculum-based laboratory activities in a realistic manner; it integrates a Bayesian Network-based assessment structure for the assessment of students' performance; and it affords the instructor flexibility in designing laboratory exercises.

Section 4
Evaluation

Chapter 15
The Development of a Personal Learning Environment in Second Life 219
Sandra Sutton Andrews, Arizona State University, USA
Mary Stokrocki, Arizona State University, USA
Angel Jannasch-Pennell, Arizona State University, USA
Samuel A. DiGangi, Arizona State University, USA

In this qualitative pilot study, the authors report on curriculum field trials within a personal learning environment (PLE) designed by a collaboration of academic researchers and nonprofit volunteers working together in the virtual world of Second Life. The purpose of the PLE is to provide learners less likely to have access to educational opportunities with a means to create a 'new life' in the real world, through a basic web-based curriculum and an advanced Second Life curriculum. Field trials of the Second Life curriculum were held with youth from underserved populations (n=6) to identify participant characteristics that facilitate success with the curriculum. Performance on instructional outcomes was examined in addition to a participatory action research methodology (PAR) that was employed with participants as co-researchers. To protect identities, the authors use a case study approach to track one composite participant/co-researcher through the curriculum.

Chapter 16
A Framework for the Assessment of Wiki-Based Collaborative Learning Activities 237
Hagit Meishar-Tal, Open University of Israel, Israel
Mat Schencks, Open University, UK

This paper discusses the pedagogical and technological aspects of assessing wiki-based collaborative learning activities. The first part of the paper presents a general framework of collaborative learning assessment. The framework is based on four aspects of assessment, characterized by four questions: who, what, how and by whom. The second part of the paper concentrates on the analysis of the applicability of the assessment framework in wikis. A systematic analysis of MediaWiki's reports is conducted in order to discuss the requisite information required for a well-balanced and effective assessment process. Finally, a few suggestions are raised for further improvements of the wiki's reports.

Chapter 17
Evaluating Games-Based Learning.. 250
Thomas Hainey, University of the West of Scotland, Scotland
Thomas Connolly, University of the West of Scotland, Scotland

A highly important part of software engineering education is requirements collection and analysis, one of the initial stages of the Software Development Lifecycle. No other conceptual work is as difficult to rectify at a later stage or as damaging to the overall system if performed incorrectly. As software engineering is a field with a reputation for producing graduate engineers who are ill-prepared for real-life software engineering contexts, this paper suggests that traditional educational techniques (e.g. role-play, live-through case studies and paper-based case studies) are insufficient in themselves. In an attempt to address this problem we have developed a games-based learning application to teach requirements collection and analysis at the tertiary education level. One of the main problems with games-based learning is that there is a distinct lack of empirical evidence supporting the approach. This paper will describe the evaluation of the requirements collection and analysis process using a newly developed framework for the evaluation of games-based learning and will focus on evaluation from a pedagogical perspective.

Chapter 18
Challenges Facing the Semantic Web and Social Software as Communication Technology Agents in E-Learning Environments.. 265
Bolanle A. Olaniran, Texas Tech University, USA

The semantic web describes the process whereby information content is made available for machine consumption. With increased reliance on information communication technologies, the semantic web promises effective and efficient information acquisition and dissemination of products and services in the global economy, in particular, e-learning. Despite the semantic web's promises, certain challenges face the realization of these goals. In this paper, the author addresses key challenges, including technological and socio-cultural issues, in addition to discussing specific implications relating to the direction of the semantic web.

Compilation of References 279

About the Contributors 307

Index.. 316

Preface

Over the last decade virtual learning environments (VLE) have become increasingly prominent across all stages of the education system from primary schools to higher educational institutions, as well as professional and adult training contexts, all around the world (Siemens, 2004; Weller, 2006). As they have been adopted in different contexts, there has inevitably been some transformation in the terminology used and while the acronym VLE persists in the UK, they are sometimes referred to as learning management systems (LMS) in North America and learning platforms (LP) or course management systems (CMS) in professional training environments. Though initially designed mainly for facilitating distance and online learning environments, such has been the widespread adoption and success of VLEs that they have also been quickly adopted by administrators as a vital component in the delivery of face-to-face education. Moreover, in this context, they have become an important gateway for a new vision of an integrated student experience, in which as well as allowing access to standard learning modules, they also incorporate tools for managing information resources in libraries and accessing electronic databases and other important communication tools for learners, faculty and administrators. VLEs have achieved such a state of normalisation and ubiquity that it is indeed difficult to imagine a time when access to a set of learning materials, particularly in higher education, did not involve logging on to the institutional VLE in order to read the course syllabus, weekly lectures and materials, or contribute to discussion boards or chat rooms.

Beginning from around the year 2000, VLEs started to replace the *ad hoc* web pages that had typically been designed by educators who dabbled in HTML on their often multi-coloured and multi-functional pages. On another level, the shift has been symptomatic of the increasing role of technology in education as well as of the increasing need for educational institutions to present a unified and standardised corporate brand image to stakeholders and customers. It is no accident then that the rise of the VLE occurred against the background of a new environment for educational institutions within more competitive national and international markets. Although VLEs promised changes in pedagogy, they were typically related to the need to provide a solution that could produce savings in terms of the costs involved with instruction; be used by educators who had no specialist knowledge of programming or technical equipment in order to add content across all courses and disciplines; enable instruction at different locations and at different times by using standardised learning materials; and facilitate more effective ways of assessing and grading students as well as the rich flow of such information across the different administrative services and departments of an educational institution.

During this period, a number of prominent VLEs have been developed by commercial providers to realise these goals, with first WebCT and then Blackboard being the major players in the market. Following Blackboard's takeover of WebCT in 2006, its estimated share of the market stood at just over

50% in 2010. At the same time, open source virtual learning environments such as Moodle and Sakai have also risen to prominence, with the former in particular becoming a beacon of the spirit of freedom and non-commericialism that had been among the most important structuring principles behind the emergence of the World Wide Web in its first iteration.

This tension between the centralising and commercial tendencies of VLEs such as Blackboard and open source alternatives like Moodle, the latter with its international array of developers, users, and enthusiasts, is a tension that can be found throughout the history of educational technology (Cuban, 2001). Rather than being peripheral to debates about the future of education and learning then, the role and design of the VLE is significant in that it also frames important questions about the nature and direction of pedagogy today and for the decades ahead (Conole, 2008). Along with debates about the marketisation of education and the potential of technology to promote a transformation of learning in the digital age, they also include timely discussions about copyright of information and educational resources; the role of administrators and teachers in designing curricula; the changing landscape of presence-based and distance education; and current debates about open access, to name but a few influential topics.

As implied by those in the open source camp, though intended for use by educators and students, commercially available VLE applications have often been imposed as top-down solutions by educational managers and administrators, and have often been criticised as inflexible tools that emphasise control rather than the ability to foster learner autonomy, creativity, or collaboration as a result (McDonald, 2003; Meishar-Tal & Tal-Elhasid, 2008).

It is from this context that the idea of a personal learning environment (PLE) or personal learning network (PLN) is derived (Siemens, 2007; Wilson et al., 2007). Both terms emerge as a reaction to the interpretation of the VLE as a somewhat stifling administrative repository for course materials rather than a truly learner-centred learning environment. Though rather ambiguous, the PLE has been increasingly advocated as a decentralized alternative, aimed at providing learners with the opportunity to acquire greater control of their own learning progression, goal setting, and personal development planning. While the definition of a PLE has remained rather amorphous, more research is beginning to be done on the area and efforts to define the potential role of such an environment in contemporary education are being made. PLEs are often connected with a group of personal tools associated with one particular learner thus supporting a more learner-centric and constructivist approach to learning. Rather than being associated with a particular application or being overly technical in orientation, a personal learning environment relates to an aggregate of tools that learners (or indeed faculty members) have chosen and are able to access anywhere. Writing in 2007, Siemens captures this focus:

PLEs aren't an entity, structural object or software program in the sense of a learning management system. Essentially, they are a collection of tools, brought together under the conceptual notion of openness, interoperability, and learner control. As such, they are comprised of two elements – the tools and the conceptual notions that drive how and why we select individual parts. PLEs are a concept-entity. ... My PLE may consist of an entirely different combination and set of tools than a colleague's. (Siemens, 2007)

With the advent of Web 2.0 applications, some commentators argue that many of the characteristics of a PLE stand their best chance to date of being realized. These features include, for example, the ability to enable learners to communicate more easily with one another, manage the process of learning more effectively, and take a larger stake in their ownership of content. When stated in these terms, it is difficult to oppose the intent to place the learner and his/her unique needs at the center of the educational process, rather than assuming that learning must always be the result of a transmisison or "push" strategy in which learners are vessels to be filled with content controlled by external curriculum designers, managers, or instructors.

Moreover, given the emergence of so-called digital natives, advocates of PLEs argue that practitioners are closer than ever to being able to realize a form of rich personalized learning initiated by learners themselves, as the students currently entering schools and universities are already familiar with their own group of Web-based social networking and communication tools in their social lives (Prensky, 2001). While the digital native concept is not without its problems and limitations and today's learner's are far less competent in the sophisticated use of digital technologies than this myth would have everyone easily believe (Bennett, Maton & Kervin, 2008), many more of today's learners are at least familiar with the importance of social software for communication and collaboration. Indeed, in the context of Web 2.0 and the read/write Web, the PLE embodies the possibility of learners balancing the traditional transmission or *push* strategy of education with a *pull* strategy in which they can access the learning materials they want, whenever they want, and wherever they are (O'Reilly, 2007).

As desirable as this vision of a transformation in education may appear, the current prominence of personalized learning is nevertheless fraught with a number of technological, pedagogical and cultural issues that also need to be addressed in order to make progress toward its realisation. These include providing solutions to support a large group of learners with a multiplicity of different tools at their disposable; balancing student choice and learner centrism with institutional standards for assessment, quality assurance, and instructor expertise; and enabling the use of common tools for communication, collaboration, and the shared construction of knowledge. In addition, advocacy of personalized learning and personal learning environments is in danger of being supported by the same kind of evangelical rhetoric of educational transformation evident in the history of learning technologies, from educational radio and television to interactive whiteboards and tablet computing. Pushed forward by government policy makers in search of something new rather than learning technologies based on sound pedagogy and educational research, the philosophy of personalized learning risks repeating the same errors and aporias if it is not grounded in a carefully articulated pedagogy that is realistic rather than utopian or merely a reaction to the perceived centralising tendencies of VLEs.

At ALT 2009 (the Association of Learning Technologists Conference) a lively panel debated the topic "The VLE is Dead" (Weller, 2007). A number of the arguments cited above were discussed, including in particular the idea that the VLE is a rather incidious force representing everything that is wrong with the new managerialism and spirit of commodifcation in higher education. While the word *learning* may be limited by the sole use of a VLE as nothing more than a repository for course documents, the author of this introduction would prefer to emphasise that this capacity depends on the imagination and creativity of the instructor as well as the learners who inhabit it. At the very least, the notion of a VLE as a repository has brought a much-needed sense of structure to educational spaces, albeit at times one that was rather cumbersome and prone to rely on too many individual mouse clicks. Rather than being dead, the VLE is (has always been) in a state of transition. Out of these negotiations and transitions, understanding of the VLE and the PLE will continue to develop over the next five to ten years alongside trends in Web 2, the personalisation and customisation of learning brought about in part by the popularity of mobile digital devices, as well as developments in open educational resources and the virtualisation of the Web. It is far from clear how these centripetal and centrifugal influences will continue to interact and shape educational technology but trends in three dimensional worlds, augmented reality, the semantic Web, and

4G broadband technologies seem set to change the rather flat experience currently on offer in VLEs into one based on enhanced social presence for all involved in the delivery and consumption of education.

The eighteen chapters collected in this volume have been written by leading international academics, researchers, and instructors engaged in the design, implementation, and evaluation of virtual and personal learning environments over the last decade. Contributors derive from a range of professional and educational contexts in seven countries, including Canada, Germany, Israel, Japan, the Netherlands, the UK and the USA. The volume intends to reflect on current areas of research in the field by incorporating a range of studies, many of which are related to the 3D virtual world of Second Life in particular, as well as by examining a number of tools and applications from the wider Web 2.0 educational context. Following an opening section which sets the scene identifying some of the key themes, terms and concepts related to virtual learning environments, the succeeding sections focus on design (Section 2), implementation (Section 3), and evaluation (Section 4). The aim of the book is to promote further discussion on these topics and to engage in debate that is critical in orientation rather than idealistic, research-based rather than merely descriptive, and committed to exploring the most appropriate forms of pedagogy to engage learners and faculty in online and virtual environments.

OVERVIEW OF THE CHAPTERS

Section 1: Key Concepts

Weller's chapter, "The Centralisation Dilemma in Educational IT," identifies a cycle of decentralization and centralization in the adoption of educational technologies that has been particularly in evidence in the adoption of virtual learning environments. During the early phases of the World Wide Web, a more dispersed strategy was influential in which individual departments or educational institutions developed their own platform. This approach has been largely surpassed by a more centralized approach often organized by central governments or regional authorities. In turn this centralized focus has led to a reaction that has produced the idea of the personal learning environment (PLE). While there is often dissatisfaction with centralized models which imply control and surveillance, Weller speculates that a fully realized personal learning environment may not be achievable. In order to pursue this line of research, Weller argues that it may be necessary to examine how it is possible to maintain the centralized system but build in a series of diversified personal elements in addition.

The tension identified by Weller is also explored in the second chapter by Sclater, which looks forward to the implications of cloud computing in an educational context. As Weller implied, e-learning has progressed mainly as a result of the highly centralized and secure virtual learning environment. The PLE is being developed particularly by students as an alternative which gives them increased freedom via the use of Web 2.0 tools such as blogs, wikis, social networking, and podcasting. Sclater's chapter is one of the first to examine these opportunities, showing how institutions can harness the power of dynamic Web-based content within their existing policy and regulatory frameworks. At the same time it is necessary for institutions to examine the associated risks to security and data protection in order to balance the *sin qua non* argument that the cloud will inevitably lead to decreased costs. Sclater argues that while this may indeed be the case, cloud computing will also pose significant threats to existing business models within education.

The chapter by Chatti, Agustiawan, Jarke, and Specht entitled, "Toward a Personal Learning Environment Framework," discusses in more detail the argument that PLEs are a reaction to the *centralized technology-push approach* that has characterized many of the developments in technology-enhanced learning over the last two decades. In order to produce the shift that is required for a more learner-centred or *learner-pulled* form of pedagogy, the authors consider a detailed framework for developing a personal learning environment, arguing that it is important to integrate perspectives such as design and evaluation in the process.

Section 2: Design

Having established a number of key contextual factors in the opening chapters, Section 2 considers in more detail the importance of design in the development of virtual learning environments. In the first of five contributions, Vallance, Martin, Wiz, and van Schaik's chapter, "Designing Effective Spaces, Tasks, and Metrics for Communication in Second Life within the Context of Programming LEGO NXT Mindstorms™ Robots," reports on the initial stages of research examining the use of a virtual environment underpinned by constructivist principles with science students in the UK and Japan. Participants in the study utilise virtual technologies while situated in physically dispersed locations and explores the assumptions of a Vygotskian social constructivist learning framework. Such a pedagogical framework supports a range of skills based on fostering personal responsibility and decision-making while emphasising the active role learners have to play in contributing to their acquisition of knowledge. Moreover, in terms of science education, the use of a virtual world coupled with a task-based approach founded on social constructivist principles attempts to locate learning within meaningful and authentic contexts in which learners are presented with what the authors refer to as *real opportunities to experience science* first hand.

Continuing the focus on 3D worlds, Jarmon's chapter, "Homo Virtualis: Virtual Worlds, Learning, and an Ecology of Embodied Interaction," provides a highly detailed report on a series of seven research studies in which field note data was collected over a period of two and a half years in Second Life. The main focus of the chapter is the interaction of avatars – their sense of what Jarmon calls their *embodied co-presence* – with the virtual world and objects around them which mediate and structure their presence online via the spatial, visual, and auditory landscapes found in Second Life. A wide range of participants' voices are found in the research presented here including high school and university students as well as academics. Findings suggest that the virtual world presents participants with opportunities to occupy a range of subject positions which transform the traditional learner/instructor relationship, enabling them to be as Jarmon suggests, "teachers, designers, researchers, communicators, and collaborators" in the process.

In "Second Life as a Surrogate for Experiential Learning," DeMers continues this focus on the use of virtual worlds to explore their potential for allowing individuals to experience online forms of social presence and community (de Freitas, 2008). DeMers points out that the initial investment by educators in virtual worlds like Second Life have more often than not merely reproduced the pedagogical context found in traditional face-to-face educational contexts. This in turn tended to produce passive learning environments rather than exploit the full potential of virtual worlds to encourage learners to actively engage in the reflective skills and tasks required by experiential learning. Based on Kolb and Kolb's (2005) model of active learning in the context of geography courses, DeMers describes how his research stimulates a hands-on and interactive approach coupled with a 'learning by discovery' orientation. Consequently, his research of virtual environments is aimed at realizing what he calls the four main aspects of an experiential learning environment, namely, involvement, reflection, analysis, and problem-solving. His findings suggest that such an approach presents perhaps the best opportunity educators have of using online worlds to simulate real-world contexts which may not be realizable either because of geographical or logistical constraints.

A further example of research on virtual worlds is presented in "An Interdisciplinary Design Project in Second Life: Creating a Virtual Marine Science Learning Environment," by Triggs, Jarmon, and Villareal. Virtual spaces are again deployed to overcome many of the logistical and pedagogical barriers presented by traditional forms of education. Virtual environments in this research study are harnessed to overcome a range of economic, physical, safety, and accessibility barriers to promote discovery based knowledge transfer. This particular research project was based on a cross-disciplinary approach in the area of Marine Science at a US university in which a virtual world was used to produce a collaborative and interdisciplinary pedagogy.

In the final chapter in this section, Hamilton, Langlois, and Watson from IBM Canada describe a fascinating case study of how their multinational organization uses Second Life to create a personal learning environment based on the important notion of mentoring in "Virtual Speed Mentoring in the Workplace - Current Approaches to Personal Informal Learning in the Workplace: A Case Study." The research is based on the idea as the authors suggest that, "Informal learning accounts for over 75% of the learning taking place in organizations today" (Conner, 1997). IBM utilises Second Life as a virtual social environment and as alternative to telephone and video conferencing in order to enable effective collaborative spaces which promote creativity while also being inexpensive to produce and maintain.

Together the chapters in this section have identified insightful examples of research studies that allow for highlighting a number of key aspects necessary for the design of effective virtual and personal learning environments. Section 3 turns to exploring examples that build on these frameworks to examine how these collaborative social spaces may be effectively implemented.

Section 3: Implementation

In "Communication and Education in a Virtual World: Avatar-Mediated Teaching and Learning in Second Life," Mon further deconstructs the *sage on the stage* metaphor of traditional face-to-face education and the way it is often adopted in ill thought-out pedagogical approaches in virtual worlds. Mon rejects the idea that virtual spaces should merely reproduce pedagogical spaces with traditional seating arrangements that enable learners to watch passively as slideshows or videos are displayed. The chapter explores an alternative vision based on the principles of good design in online worlds identified above in which learning techniques are identified to stimulate and support a range of autonomous and collaborative learner interaction. Examples of how educators can use tools and techniques to build and contribute to the virtual landscape are identified as well as how best to approach strategies focused on problem-based learning, the utilization of gaming and simulated role-playing tasks (de Freitas & Griffiths, 2008; Gee, 2007).

In "Mechanics Simulations in Second Life," Black describes a further example of this approach in the specific disciplinary area of physics where a virtual physics engine has been designed to explore specific experiments in simulated environments. The findings from the study importantly underline both the challenges and opportunities presented by the virtual world, in that the environment enables a wide range of chances for scientists to simulate the real-world in a controlled environment, while at the same time presenting a series of technical barriers that designers need to master in order to produce optimised learning contexts.

Continuing with specific examples of online environments, which otherwise would be difficult or impossible to replicate in the lab or real-world, Danforth's chapter, "Development of an Interactive Virtual 3-D Model of the Human Testis Using the Second Life Platform," examines a number of original ways to teach medical education. Three main areas of potential are identified, including opportunities for modeling doctor-patient discussion and interaction, developing three dimensional models and simulations of organs and objects, and developing students' clinical diagnosis skills. In this particular case study, the researchers developed a model of the human testis that medical students could explore in detail by flying through it, thereby gaining detailed first hand anatomical and physiological experience. Findings suggest that learners benefited in particular from the interactions between the three dimensional models which are supported with audio and video narratives and the style and mode of delivery which appeals to learners across the educational spectrum from high school to university level. The chapter speculates how the maturation of these capabilities will be able to aid students in the future.

Related to the environments that described above is an important understanding of the role of learners' virtual identities in the form of their avatars. Nahl pursues these issues in her chapter, "Affective Load and Engagement in Second Life: Experiencing Urgent, Persistent, and Long-Term Information Needs." She examines the learning curve required of learners and instructors in acclimatizing themselves to the virtual world and the types of support they will need in participating in task and problem-based learning activities in a three dimensional context. The research draws on data from self-reports written during learner task engagement and identifies a range of learner emotions (such as learner irritation, anxiety and frustration vis-à-vis their virtual selves) related to their cognitive skills in the midst of a constant stream of complex information streams. The chapter is important in focusing on the complex challenges faced by learners in adjusting to their virtual selves and for not taking for granted the unproblematic transition from their real-world to virtual identity. The research gives rise to knowledge about how learners can develop coping strategies for dealing with this virtual transition process.

A number of these above-mentioned case studies have focused on developing pedagogical approaches that fit with the virtual environment. In this next chapter, "Investigating Modes of Student Inquiry in Second Life as Part of a Blended Approach," Webber continues this theme by turning to consider an Inquiry Based Learning (IBL) approach, which has been integrated into a mandatory undergraduate programme in a UK university. Using Second Life alongside WebCT and a traditional classroom environment within a blended learning format, the chapter discusses how Second Life in particular facilitated learner achievement and aided autonomous modes of inquiry. The research concludes by discussing further aspects of this blended framework and how the virtual environment can be utilized in future.

The emphasis on the potential role of virtual learning environments in science education is further emphasized in the chapter by Achumba, Azzi, and Stocker in "Low-Cost Virtual Laboratory Workbench for Electronic Engineering." The research reports on how requirements related to costs, physical presence, time, and space often prohibit the use of lab-based environments for undergraduate engineering students. These resource constraints and scarcity of equipment may be felt in particular in developing countries. The research explores the use of a virtual lab that can be used as a rich and viable alternative within which learners and instructors can model experiments and conduct research in an authentic manner regardless of time and place. The virtual solution examined in this chapter incorporates a Bayesian Network-based assessment structure in order to promote an integrated assessment strategy and is especially attuned to allowing instructors the flexibility required in order to produce and replicate a wide range of realistic lab-based experiments.

Section 4: Evaluation

In the final section of the book, four chapters consider issues related to the evaluation of virtual and learning environments. In "The Development of a Personal Learning Environment in Second Life," Andrews, Stokrocki, Jannasch-Pennell, and DiGangi discuss findings from qualitative research on the use of the virtual world as a personal learning environment. The study was designed by a joint collaboration of researchers and volunteers from nonprofit organisations in order to provide disadvantaged learners with opportunities to explore their own creativity and negotiate new virtual identities. Utilising a participatory action research methodology (PAR) the research examined the learner characteristics which may enable curriculum achievement and success in these new environments.

Developing a framework for the evaluation of Web 2.0 tools and their use in educational contexts is a particularly important area in need of further elaboration. Meishar-Tal and Schencks' chapter, "A Framework for the Assessment of Wiki-Based Collaborative Learning Activities," articulates a strategy of assessment that could be used in a collaborative environment based on the use of wikis. Issues related to both the technological and pedagogical perspectives of evaluating wikis are examined, with the first part of the study exploring the key characteristics of the framework, and the second part analyzing the applicability of the framework in relation to MediaWiki reports.

In addition to wikis and blogs, digital game-based learning has emerged as another area of research in the last few years that builds on many of the components of virtual environments. Hainey and Connolly consider existing research in this area in their discussion of software engineering education entitled, "Evaluating Games-Based Learning." The chapter explores how traditional educational strategies such as role-play and case studies may be inadequate in classroom and lab contexts due to the lack of more highly developed authentic contexts (Lave & Wenger, 1991). Simulation and games-based approaches may provide one area for potential solutions to these challenges, though as yet few sustained empirical studies have been published. This chapter attempts to map future directions in the field by considering an appropriate pedagogical framework concerned with evaluating gaming environments.

In the final contribution to the book, Olaniran's chapter, "Challenges Facing the Semantic Web and Social Software as Communication Technology Agents in E-Learning Environments," looks forward to the impact of developments associated with the next generation of the internet, the so-called Semantic Web. In this environment it is assumed that the three-dimensional virtualisation of the web has become more commonplace through its assimilation into the everyday browsing experience. While it is often assumed that the Semantic Web will lead to enhanced opportunities for ever greater information management, Olaniran indentifies a number of integral socio-cultural and technological barriers to entry, which will need to be understood and overcome if its full potential is to be realised effectively.

At this point in the history of VLEs it is clear that they have passed through a series of independent but overlapping stages in their development. These include: 1) Early attempts by independent instructors and faculty members to construct their own Web sites to manage their course materials and facilitate learning, largely independent of administrator control; 2) The emergence and large-scale success of centralised and standardised VLEs such as Blackboard for which sophisticated programming skills are not required; 3) The growing importance of open source solutions such as Moodle and the reaction against commercial alternatives that are considered to be less focused on pedagogy, primarily constructivist pedagogical approaches; and 4) An increasing concern with personalised and customised learning, a trend captured but not fully developed in the use of the acronym PLE or PLN, which draws on the growing importance of mobile digital devices and social software. To some extent, the final stage in this unofficial brief history returns to the start, with individual faculty and learners taking greater control of the technologies and communicative mediums available to them.

A decade ago in 2002, the author of this preface remembers ignoring the comments of a fellow faculy member who protested against ceding control of his own self-developed course web site in the face of impending *Blackboardisation*. His argument was that he simply could not trust administrators to reliably deliver the flexible solution he required or keep up with the speed of change needed to integrate new and innovative Web-based tools. Ten years later, having come full circle, the author finds himself having greater understanding of and sympathy for his arguments. In the years ahead the problem remains how best to resolve what Cuban (2001) identified as the technology hype cycle and Weller (this volume) has called the decentralisation/centralisation dilemma, in order to produce an effective and workable balance of these competing interests.

Michael Thomas
University of Central Lancashire, UK

REFERENCES

Bennett, S., Maton, K., & Kervin, L. (2008). The 'digital natives' debate: A critical review of the evidence. *British Journal of Educational Technology*, *39*(5), 775–786.

Conole, G. (2008). New schemas for mapping pedagogies and technologies. *Ariadne*, *56*, Retrieved from http://www.ariadne.ac.uk/issue56/conole/

Conner, M. L. (1997). *Informal learning*. Retrieved from http://www.marciaconner.com/intros/informal.html

Cuban, L. (2001). *Oversold and underused: Computers in the classroom*. Cambridge, MA: Harvard University Press.

de Freitas, S. (2008). *Serious virtual worlds: A scoping study*. JISC publications. Retrieved March from http://www.jisc.ac.uk/publications/publications/seriousvirtualworldsreport.aspx

de Freitas, S., & Griffiths, M. (2008). The convergence of gaming practices with other media forms: What potential for learning? A review of the literature. *Learning, Media and Technology*, *33*(1), 11–20.

Gee, J. P. (2007). Are video games good for learning? In de Castell, S., & Jenson, J. (Eds.), *Worlds in play* (pp. 323–336). New York, NY: Peter Lang.

Kolb, A. Y., & Kolb, D. A. (2005). *The Kolb learning style inventory—version 3.1: Technical specifications*. Boston, MA: Hay Resources Direct.

Lave, J., & Wenger, E. (1991). *Situated learning: Legitimate peripheral participation*. New York, NY: Cambridge University Press.

MacDonald, J. (2003). Assessing online collaborative learning: Process and product. *Computers & Education*, *40*(4), 337–391.

Meishar-Tal, H., & Tal-Elhasid, E. (2008). Measuring collaboration in educational wikis: A methodological discussion. *International Journal of Emerging Technologies in Learning*, *3*, 46–49.

Prensky, M. (2001). Digital natives, digital immigrants. *Horizon*, *9*(5). Retrieved from http://www.marcprensky.com/writing/Prensky%20-%20Digital%20Natives,%20Digital%20Immigrants%20-%20Part1.pdf

O'Reilly, T. (2007). What is web 2.0? Design patterns and business models for the next generation of software. *International Journal of Digital Economics*, *65*, 17–37.

Siemens, G. (2004). Learning management systems: The wrong place to start learning. *Elearnspace*. Retrieved from http://www.elearnspace.org/Articles/lms.htm

Siemens, G. (2007). *PLEs – I acronym, therefore I exist*. Retrieved from http://www.elearnspace.org/blog/2007/04/15/ples-i-acronym-therefore-i-exist/

Weller, M. (2006). *Virtual learning environments: Using, choosing and developing your VLE*. London, New York: Routledge.

Weller, M. (2007). *The VLE/LMS is dead*. Retrieved from http://nogoodreason.typepad.co.uk/no_good_reason/2007/11/the-vlelms-is-d.html

Wilson, S., Liber, O., Johnson, M., Beauvoir, P., Sharples, P., & Milligan, C. (2007). Personal learning environments: Challenging the dominant design of educational systems. *Journal of e-Learning and Knowledge Society*, *3*(2), 27-38.

Section 1
Key Concepts

Chapter 1
The Centralisation Dilemma in Educational IT

Martin Weller
The Open University, UK

ABSTRACT

The trend with organisational adoption of virtual learning environments (VLE) seems to be cyclical. Initially, a decentralised approach was adopted, wherein each department implemented different learning environments or mixtures of technology, often developed in-house. The last five years have seen an increased centralisation of learning environment implementation, with most universities adopting a single VLE. However, in more recent times the proliferation of free, easy-to-use third party tools that fulfil a range of functions has seen a desire amongst some educators to return to a more decentralised model of technology provision, by supporting Personal Learning Environments (PLE). This paper examines the issues surrounding both a centralised and decentralised model. These include pedagogic, support, financial, reliability, data and technical issues. The conclusion is that although the fully individualised PLE may not be possible or desirable in higher education, maintaining separate, often inferior versions of commonly available software is not a sustainable position.

INTRODUCTION

The proliferation of free online services, many of them part of the social media, Web 2.0 culture has led many educators to suggest that decentralised, loosely coupled learning environments would be superior to the centralised, integrated VLEs currently deployed in most higher education institutions. For example, Weller (2007 para 8):

If a service can be disintermediated then it will be. In this case the central VLE system is disintermediated as academics use a variety of freely available tools. On balance then, I think this shift to loosely coupled, freely available third party systems will happen.

And similarly Leslie (2005), argues for the use of social media back in 2005 (para 2):

DOI: 10.4018/978-1-4666-1770-4.ch001

I've been really disappointed with the vision of learning... too many talks on eportfolios that see them solely as a way to create a resume, or just another way to squish students into an artificial assessment framework, too many talks on more and better ways to generate reams of metadata and remove the humans from that sticky operation of sharing and reusing learning resources.

...We need software that is obvious in the value it offers its end users so we aren't forcing them to do things they don't want to already do. We need software that recognizes users not just as the 'operators' of software, but also as having identities that are important, identities that are the basis for rich connections and enabling possibilities. We need software that notices and records these connections and interactions in order to add even more value to those users and to other people trying to do similar things.

CENTRALISATION AND VLES

VLEs can be interpreted as an attempt to bring order to a previously chaotic situation with regards to educational technology. And this is itself a reflection on the growing significance of educational technology within higher education. With the advent of the internet, and the interest in elearning at the end of the 1990s, there was an initial *ad hoc* phase whereby individual educators, and then departments adopted their own solutions. Initially these were bespoke Web sites, and later commercial offering were adopted, which combined a number of basic tools, such as navigation, text forums, roles, etc. These were the early VLEs.

By 2004 the shift to centralisation was well under way. As elearning had moved into the mainstream, so universities felt a need to centralise their elearning systems. This entailed a rationalisation of existing systems into a single, centrally hosted and supported environment. The OECD looked at e-learning in tertiary education in thirteen countries in 2004 (OECD, 2005) and found that all institutions had a VLE of some description, but only 37 percent of respondents had a single institution wide VLE, while the remainder had a mixture of systems. However, 90 percent expected to have an institution-wide system in next five years.

The arguments for a centralised VLE can be summarised as:

1. Uniformity of student experience
2. Centralised support
3. Quality assurance
4. Efficiency
5. Robustness
6. Integration of different tools
7. Staff development
8. Platform for expanding elearning offering

In essence, the VLE saw learning technology move from being individual offerings in the hands of educators, to enterprise systems under the control of central IT services. A'Herran (2000) suggests that there are four perspectives from which a VLE is analysed (para 12):

- **Administrators:** Scalability, value for money and integration with existing systems are important for these users
- **Technicians:** Robustness, user base, technical support and ease of maintenance will be significant.
- **Course developers or teachers:** Customisability, flexibility and the integration of legacy materials will be paramount.
- **Learners:** Consistency, accessibility and quality of design will be the main concerns.

Thus the decision-making process for selecting and deploying a VLE needed to take into account these various stakeholders. A proliferation of decision-making methods were proposed as all higher education establishments went through a similar process of deciding upon a main VLE (e.g. Chohan 2001; Alvardo 2004; Liber & Holyfield 2006; Weller 2006).

THE DECENTRALISED MODEL

The eight justifications given above for centralised models are reasonably compelling, so what are the main arguments for those who favour a decentralised model? Behind the move to a less centralised model has been the proliferation of free to use tools and services, which could broadly be categorised under the Web 2.0 banner. There is thus a wide range of tools available to everyone, and crucially, these are relatively easy to use. The arguments for a decentralised model can be summarised as:

1. Quality: The individual components of an integrated system will not be as good as specialist tools performing any one of these functions
2. Flexibility
3. Pedagogic suitability
4. Relevance
5. Educator control
6. Personalisation

The proposition then is that we move away from a centralised learning environment to a more distributed personal learning environment, which is constituted from a variety of existing third party tools. Many people have created a personal learning or working environment, without the explicit intention of doing so, simply by accruing a number of tools they use regularly. An example of one is in Figure 1.

Terminology and the PLE Continuum

Before examining some of the conflicts between the centralised and decentralised model in detail, it is worth setting out some of the different terminology, and what these reveal about the beliefs and values around the issues.

- **VLE/LMS (virtual learning environment/learning management system):** A centralised system that gives a consistent user experience to everyone.
- **TLE (teacher learner environment):** Less centralised than a VLE, the educator determines the range of tools, e.g. a blog with specific widgets, but all students use the same.
- **DPLE (default PLE):** In this novice users are given a default set of applications to constitute their PLE, but they have the freedom to switch them out over time. A common example might be users switching to email providers of their choice from the default institutional system.
- **PLE/PWE (personal learning/work environment:** The collection of tools an individual accrues over time, and continues to evolve.
- **PLN (personal learning network):** This term is preferred by many over PLE (e.g. see http://educationaltechnology.ca/couros/1156), and it emphasises the people that constitute a network. For example, your PLE may contain the microblogging service Twitter, but if you moved to a different tool (e.g. FriendFeed) you would presumably transfer many of the contacts who constitute the network, which is the valuable component for learning.

We can think of these interpretations of learning environments as being part of a continuum of personalisation, with conventional VLEs at one end and the personally configured PLE at the other.

Figure 1. A PLE consisting of different tools

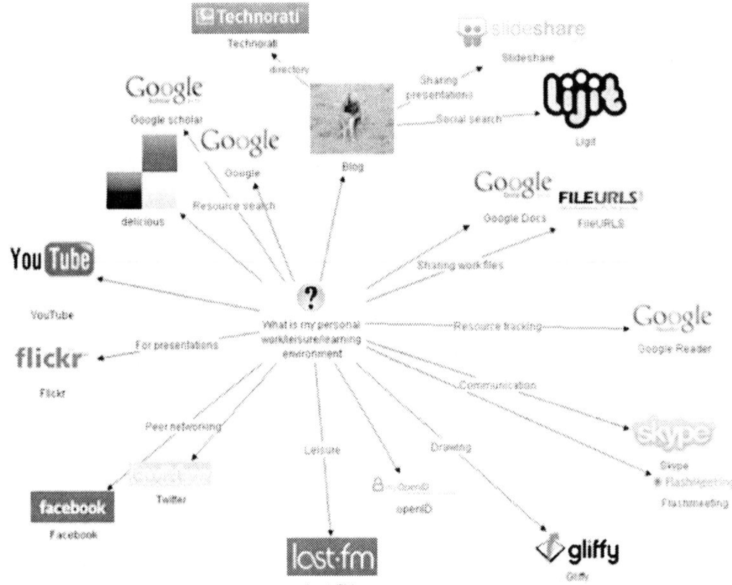

THE CENTRALISATION–DECENTRALISATION DEBATE

There are a number of objections raised against the decentralised model, and also advantages given for it. By considering these in turn the core issues around the centralisation debate can be explored.

Support

One of the arguments often put forward by the proponents of VLEs is that many young people use a wide range of technologies in everyday life, and then encounter inferior technology when then come to university. This is partly related to the digital natives debate (Prensky, 2001). As several recent research studies have demonstrated (e.g. British Library 2008, Bennett et al., 2008) the digital natives arguments may be somewhat overblown. Bennett et al. (2008, p. 778) say they found little evidence for the two main arguments of the digital natives debate, namely that:

1. Young people of the digital native generation possess sophisticated knowledge of and skills with information technologies.
2. As a result of their upbringing and experiences with technology, digital natives have particular learning preferences or styles that differ from earlier generations of students.

So the suggestion that new students are all experienced users of technology is not borne out. The role of support is still an important one then, both in terms of being able to use the technology and using it effectively for learning. Much of this type of support is most conveniently realised for the institution if it can focus on core technologies, rather than on a vast range. However, there is an argument that this focus teaches students how to use a specific technology rather than develop the generalised communication and technology skills they will require beyond their studies.

Student Confusion

Following on from the issue of support is that of student convenience. Learning about their chosen subject is the main focus of students and the technology used should be subservient to that aim. The argument is therefore that it should be as seamless and uniform as possible. Using multiple sites often requires multiple identification names and for the user to switch to different sites for different functions. For example, this student at Simon Fraser University (The Peak, 2009, para 7) bemoaned the proliferation of sites he was required to use:

Here is a list of the Web sites of which I must (must) make regular use, for this semester's four courses, alone: go.sfu.ca, my.sfu.ca, Webct.sfu.ca, loncapa.sfu.ca, gradebook.com.

These are supplemented by three separate official course homepages, and by the personal Web sites of two other professors. That's 10 Web sites, in one semester, for four courses.

To receive or hand in assignments, to interact with professors and TAs, to check grades, to find lecture notes, I must use each and every one of these sites.

This is not to mention sites like turnitin.com, firstclass.com, masteringphysics.com, and any number of other faculty-specific Web sites, which all basically do the exact same thing.

And from a teacher's perspective, Fisher (2006) comments how he used a loosely-coupled approach comprising:

- Blog accounts at learnerblogs (free)
- Two wikis at pbwiki.com (free)
- Podcasts and vlogs posted at Ourmedia and Archive.org (both free)
- A suprglu page (free)
- Bloglines accounts for each students in the class (free)
- A flickr account (could be free, but we've gone with a pro account)
- Every student has an email account and most have an IM (both free as well)

Although these tools were all free, and ideally suited to his purposes he worries that: "In the past I felt I was able to build a solid structure for learning to occur within, but sometimes this year, I feel like I'm building a tower held together by duct tape" (para 7).

There is clearly a balance to be struck between using pedagogically appropriate tools, giving students experience of a range of tools while also ensuring the proliferation of technologies do not become a barrier to learning.

The response to this from the proponents of a decentralised approach is that there is a form of loose integration that allows these separate tools to be easily aggregated in one place. We will look at this in the next section, but even with technical integration the user experience will be different in each tool. The debate then, is the extent to which we feel that technology is pervasive enough and the range of tools around now are sufficiently easy to use.

Integration

One advantage of centralised systems is that they provide readily integrated packages. This offers three main advantages:

- **Convenience:** The default set of tools and educator would require are readily available without them needing to locate and choose.
- **Monitoring:** The integration of tools allows administrators and educators to monitor usage, so for example they can track the overall access of a resource, or the use of tools by an individual.

- **Authentication:** Single sign-on means that users only need one user ID name, and also that the system can allocate roles and functions to individual users.

The challenge for decentralised systems is how they can address these three advantages. This is probably the key obstacle to the adoption of a collection of third party tools. The first issue, that of convenience could be overcome relatively easily with a default set of tools provided to the educator. These could be integrated within a single portal in the manner in which iGoogle and Netvibes use iframes to incorporate several tools. The tools though, are essentially ignorant of each other, which brings us onto the issue of monitoring. The availability of third party statistical services (for example Google Analytics, Compete.com) can offer detailed analysis of usage. This would cover some of the more general usage, but without integration of tools at the user level it is difficult to track any individual's progress. And because the applications are not reporting back activity, they act as a black box, so what happens within these various tools is not reported. For example, if you have a discussion forum tool, there is no standard means of passing back data regarding activity (for example, number and date of posts or replies).

There are a number of attempts to address this issue. Norman (2008) coined the term 'eduglu' to describe the means of stitching together different tools. He describes it thus (para 1):

The problem is on one hand very simple - a person publishes a bunch of stuff, and all they need to do is pull it into a course-based resource. On the other hand, it's really quite hard - how can software provide what appears to be a centralized service, based on the decentralized and distributed publishings of the members of a group or community, and honour the flexible and dynamic nature of the various groups and communities to which a person belongs?

One of his solutions is to use simple methods already available: "The magic combination of features for EduGlu are: Aggregation of feeds + Groups + Social Rating + Tagging." There are other more rigorous approaches such as the IMS Global Tools Interoperability Guidelines (http://www.imsglobal.org/ti/index.html), which aim to address "the growing demand for a reusable mechanism for integrating third-party tools with core LMS platforms. Tools can add specialist functionality to the LMS such as assessment or discipline-specific teaching aids."

None of these possible methods of integration have really achieved the easy assembly of portals such as Netvibes and Pageflakes, and thus, even if they are effective, their uptake would be limited. However, the advent of open APIs as evidenced by Facebook and Twitter has created more interest in data portability, with Google's OpenSocial claiming to define "a common API for social applications across multiple Web sites" so that "developers can create apps that access a social network's friends and update feeds" (Google, 2009, n.p.). While none of these solutions offer the sort of ready integration that matches a purpose built integrated system, the general trend seems to be towards data portability.

The last advantage of the centralised system was that of authentication. Having to remember a number of user IDs and passwords, and having to log in to each application separately creates a barrier to the use of technology. But students are using multiple external sites on a daily basis with little difficulty. As with data integration there is a trend towards interoperability in authentication also, with the advent of openID, a single ID and password that can be used across multiple sites. The data integration techniques mentioned above would also address authentication to a degree.

Robustness and Complexity

A common reservation regarding decentralised systems is that they may not be as reliable or robust as centrally hosted systems. For example, when the site Slideshare was down, Sclater (2007) commented that (para 1):

afficionados of small pieces will argue that services are improving all the time and such things are a temporary hitch but what happens when you've recommended a service to a student who needs it for an assignment and the service is down for maintenance?

Centrally hosted systems can also go down, but the argument is that the university can make accommodation for this, for instance in terms of assessment deadlines. In a widely distributed model this becomes more difficult. Some universities are moving to an outsourced model for basic services, for instance, by adopting Google Apps for Education or Microsoft's Live@edu. However, they can have a service level agreement and with large organisations such as Google and Microsoft there is some guarantee of robustness not found with many smaller sites.

An alternative view is that a decentralised model distributes risk, since there are many different sites and the loss of any one will not compromise the whole learning experience.

This debate, like much of that in educational technology, comes down to quality assurance. Being able to monitor and control central IT services means that remedial action can be taken if problems arise, for example if a core service is affected, then marks in assessment can be adjusted accordingly. This is not possible with a widely distributed system. But this interpretation of quality is then offset against one which considers the quality of the individual components of any system, which are likely to be superior in any distributed system.

Pedagogic Suitability

The suitability of technology to support the demands of educators should be paramount. However, it is rarely the case that there is a clear pedagogic demand for a particular tool consistent across a university. Rather it is the case that some individuals have requirements, or want to experiment.

Centralised VLEs, although ubiquitous, are not particularly popular. For instance, in a 2008 survey of the favourite tools of elearning professional (Hart, 2008) Moodle was ranked 12th, while Blackboard was not in the top 100. However, this may give a distorted view, since many educators are not interested in technologies, and will use the main university system. Conole (2008) argues that there is a close affinity between the pedagogical theory inherent in Web 2.0 tools (the sort that would be adopted in a decentralised model):

What is striking is that a mapping to the technologies shows that recent trends in the use of technologies, the shift from Web 1.0 to Web 2.0 echoes this; Web 2.0 tools very much emphasise the collective and the network. (para 13)

A centralised system will always struggle compete with a decentralised one in terms of diversity, and thus pedagogic suitability. A proprietary system will require the company to develop a particular tool, which has to compete with other requests for priority. It then needs to be rolled out as part of a scheduled release. Even open source systems will require negotiation, development and integration into the core code.

One alternative is to have an extendable central system, which uses an open integration method, such as an open API that other tools can use to be integrated within the core set. This requires a smaller degree of technical development, however, the debate about centralisation of IT services is, as we have seen, not restricted to technical issues. Even if easy integration is possible, as A'Herran (2000) suggests, that is only one dimension of a VLE. Other issues such as centralised support, staff development and service level would still be relevant, so it is likely that the integration of any third party applications into an open VLE would be highly regulated through central IT services. The result is a system that, although open in principle, is still reasonably closed in practice.

CONCLUSION

Having looked at some of the issues surrounding centralised and decentralised educational IT services, we can see that there is dissatisfaction with the current centralised model, but also problems with the implementation of a decentralised model. What this may signify is that we are in a transition point as educational IT services evolve from a tightly controlled and deployed set of systems to a broader continuum of tools.

There is an analogy with the process of plant succession here. When there is a new environment, for example barren rock, a few pioneer species, such as lichens begin to grow. The acid from these decomposes some rock particles, and their own death creates a coarse soil. This is suitable for mosses, which require little soil, and in turn these decompose to enrich and deepen the soil, until it is suitable for some grasses to grow. The process ends with the establishment of a stable, climax community. In education terms, the initial decentralised model of tools acted as the pioneer species, creating slight changes which made the habitat suitable for secondary colonizers. In this case, the centralised VLE, which required the initial phase of individual, or departmental level tool deployment to occur. The kind of environmental changes wrought by VLEs include general acceptance of the elearning approach, integration with administrative systems, staff development, recruitment of enthusiasts, changes in assessment practice, acknowledgement of tools already used by students, and so on. This then establishes an environment for the next wave.

This next succession of IT services is likely to see an attempt to retain some of the benefits of a centralised system with the diversity of a decentralised one. This will see the easy, open integration of third party applications into an existing hub of central, core services.

However, this approach is still unlikely to satisfy those in the decentralisation camp, because the implementation of educational technology can also be seen as a metaphor for how the institution itself operates. The primary benefit of a centralised system is that it facilitates control – this enables universities to perform their duty of care, both pastoral and educational, to their students by controlling the environment. In order to realise a decentralised model it would necessitate a good deal of relinquishing control. But for those who favour a decentralised model, this control is both restrictive in terms of the technologies they use, but also what they do with them.

There is thus a tension between those educators who want a more liberal technological policy and the institutional response which wants to be able to control the technological environment. This tension is not necessarily a negative force however, since it creates a dialogue between the two camps. It forces the 'centralists' to engage with new technologies and to improve existing offerings, while making the 'decentralists' aware of many of the subtle issues around institutional responsibility and support.

REFERENCES

A'Herran, A. (2000, June 12-17). Research and evaluation of online systems for teaching and learning. *AusWeb2k-The Sixth Australian World Wide Web Conference*, Rihga Colonial Club Resort, Cairns. Retrieved April 30, 2009, from http://ausWeb.scu.edu.au/aw2k/papers/a_herran/paper.html

Alvardo, P. (2004, January). Seven steps to selecting a learning management system. *Chief Learning Officer*. Retrieved April 30, 2009, from http://www.clomedia.com/content/templates/clo_Webonly.asp?articleid=365&zoneid=78

Bennett, S., Maton, K., & Kervin, L. (2008). The 'digital natives' debate: A critical review of the evidence. *British Journal of Educational Technology, 39*(5), 775–786. doi:doi:10.1111/j.1467-8535.2007.00793.x

British Library. (2008). *Information behaviour of the researcher of the future*. Retrieved April 30, 2009, from http://www.bl.uk/news/pdf/googlegen.pdf

Chohan, N. (2001). VLE procurement. *JISC briefing paper, 2*. Retrieved April 30, 2009, from http://www.jisc.ac.uk/mle/reps/briefings/bp2.html

Conole, G. (2008). New schemas for mapping pedagogies and technologies. *Ariadne, 56*. Retrieved April 30, 2009, from http://www.ariadne.ac.uk/issue56/conole/

Fisher, C. (2006). *Small pieces versus Moodle*. Retrieved April 30, 2009, from http://remote-access.typepad.com/remote_access/2006/10/small_pieces_ve.html

Google. (2009). *OpenSocial: The Web is better when it's social.* Retrieved May 25, 2009, from http://code.google.com/apis/opensocial/

Hart, J. (2008). *Top 100 Tools for Learning 2008.* Retrieved April 30, 2009, from http://www.c4lpt.co.uk/recommended/top100.html

Leslie, S. (2005). *The good thing about bad presentations, or how I came to love social software.* Retrieved April 30, 2009, from http://www.edtechpost.ca/wordpress/2005/11/17/the-good-thing-about-bad-presentations-or-how-i-came-to-love-social-software/

Liber, O., & Holyfield, S. (Eds.). (2006). Creating a managed learning environment. *JISC InfoNet.* Retrieved April 30, 2009, from http://www.jiscinfonet.ac.uk/InfoKits/InfoKits/creating-an-mle/index_html

Norman, D. (2008). *On eduglu – part 1: Background.* Retrieved April 30, 2009, from http://www.darcynorman.net/2008/02/16/on-eduglu-part-1-background/

OECD. (2005). E-learning in tertiary Education: Where do we stand? *Education & Skills, 4*, 1–293.

Prensky, M. (2001). Digital natives, digital immigrants. *On the Horizon, 9*(5). NCB University Press. Retrieved April 30, 2009, from http://www.marcprensky.com/writing/Prensky%20-%20Digital%20Natives,%20Digital%20Immigrants%20-%20Part1.pdf

Sclater, N. (2007). *Downside of the small pieces model.* Retrieved April 30, 2009, from http://sclater.com/blog/?p=45

The Peak. (2009). *Opinions: Editor's voice: SFU online voice sucks, 132*(4). Retrieved May 25, 2009, from http://www.the-peak.ca/article/18222

Weller, M. (2006). *Virtual learning environments: Using, choosing and developing your VLE*. London, New York: Routledge.

Weller, M. (2007). *The VLE/LMS is dead.* Retrieved April 30, 2009, from http://nogoodreason.typepad.co.uk/no_good_reason/2007/11/the-vlelms-is-d.html

This work was previously published in International Journal of Virtual and Personal Learning Environments, edited by Michael Thomas, Volume 1, Issue 1, pp. 1-9, copyright 2010 by IGI Publishing (an imprint of IGI Global).

Chapter 2
e-Learning in the Cloud

Niall Sclater
The Open University, UK

ABSTRACT

Elearning has grown rapidly in importance for institutions and has been largely facilitated through the "walled garden" of the virtual learning environment. Meanwhile many students are creating their own personal learning environments by combining the various Web 2.0 services they find most useful. Cloud computing offers new opportunities for institutions to provide dynamic and up-to-date Internet-based, e-learning applications while ensuring high levels of service, and compliance with institutional policies and legislation. The cloud is rapidly evolving in its architecture, the services offered and the logistics of deployment. It brings with it risks but also possibilities for learners and for educational institutions to reduce costs and enhance services. It is likely to severely disrupt the business model developed by existing vendors of VLEs who provide an integrated suite of e-learning tools, installed and maintained by the institution's IT services department.

INTRODUCTION

Of increasing importance to educational institutions for managing elearning content and functionality are their virtual learning environments (VLEs), also known as learning management systems (LMSs). There is no single definition of a VLE and the systems themselves are continuously evolving and adopting new tools such as blogs and wikis as these emerge on the Internet. Some VLEs incorporate eportfolio functionality, for example, while others keep this outside the conceptual boundary of the VLE.

A major criticism levelled at VLEs is that they are not good at enabling the generation and storage of user-generated content or the fostering of social networks. Some educators bypass their institutional systems to avoid the restrictions placed on users. They find tools which are freely available on the Internet and provide more up-to-date, "fun" facilities for students to collaborate and to create, store and share their own content. In the context of formal learning this is arguably only possible with small groups of students, facilitated by educators with high levels of IT skills. There are also many problems with every student

DOI: 10.4018/978-1-4666-1770-4.ch002

building their own personal learning environment (PLE), particularly where the elearning elements of a course are collaborative or assessed.

One feature common to all VLEs (and not easy to replicate by piecing together various applications hosted elsewhere on the Internet) is the ability to provide specific content and functionality to closed groups of students who are taking a particular course for a defined period. This is necessary in the context of formal learning for a number of reasons as outlined in Sclater (2008). The institution may have invested substantially in the development of learning content and may feel that its market is threatened if it makes the content available freely to anyone on the Internet (though many universities report business benefits from their open content initiatives). Secondly there are advantages to learning within a "walled garden" where a sense of community and common purpose can be developed with fellow students, keeping out spammers and disruptive users, which is particularly important if the learners are children. Thirdly there are elements of the environment which the institution may wish to control for legal, ethical or business reasons such as accessibility for disabled learners, availability and robustness, security of personal data and branding. Finally there are advantages in the institution owning user access data so that services and content can be enhanced, leading to a better learning experience and higher levels of student retention.

If the institutionally-hosted VLE is at one extreme of elearning provision and the personal learning environment comprised of multiple Web 2.0 sites controlled by the learner is at the other, a third potentially disruptive model has recently emerged. Two companies, Google and Microsoft, have begun to offer services to university staff and students which replace or complement functionality hosted by institutional systems such as email, instant messaging, calendaring, the creation, storage, sharing of personal documents and Website creation. Google's Apps for Education and Microsoft's Live@edu systems package together a range of tools which can be customised and branded to some extent for institutions but are hosted externally by the companies in what has come to be known as "the cloud".

THE CLOUD HOVERS OVER THE ELEARNING LANDSCAPE

Google's cloud is a network made of perhaps a million cheap servers distributed in data centres across the World, storing numerous copies of the World Wide Web. This massive, distributed architecture makes searching extremely fast and provides a high degree of resilience, enabling individual servers to be replaced with faster machines after a few years with no impact on overall performance (Baker, 2007). Google and a few other companies with very large high speed distributed networks of computers, notably Microsoft and Amazon, realized that their computing resources were of value to other organisations and could be made available to them for a wide range of applications.

As with the term "VLE", Cloud Computing has various definitions. Vaquero et al. (2009) examined more than twenty of them and proposed the following:

Clouds are a large pool of easily usable and accessible virtualized resources (such as hardware, development platforms and/or services). These resources can be dynamically re-configured to adjust to a variable load (scale), allowing also for an optimum resource utilization. This pool of resources is typically exploited by a pay-per-use model in which guarantees are offered by the Infrastructure Provider by means of customized SLAs. (p. 51)

Apart from being able to benefit from economies of scale, providers of cloud computing are increasingly operating from locations where electricity is cheaper than in regions where organisations currently host their data centres. Prices vary dramatically between states in the US and elsewhere in the World – currently from 5.91 cents per kilowatt-hour in Idaho to 23.35 cents in Hawaii (Energy Administration Information, 2009). Situating a data centre next to a hydroelectric power station makes sense fundamentally because it is easier to transport photons than electrons, or data over fibre optic cables than electricity over high-voltage lines (Armbrust et al., 2009). If this location also combines the availability of skilled labour, low taxes and low property costs then the financial advantages can be even greater (Katz, Goldstein & Yanosky, 2009).

There are three main categories of cloud computing services which utilize the distributed hardware infrastructure (Johnson, Levine & Smith, 2009). At the lowest level are computing resources such as Amazon's Elastic Compute Cloud where organisations can effectively run their own Linux servers on virtual machines and scale up usage as required extremely quickly. At the next level up developers can write applications for proprietary architectures such as the Google Apps Engine in the Python language. This is currently free to use though there are limits to storage and monthly traffic (Buyya, Yeo & Venugopal, 2008). The final type of cloud computing service, of most interest to educational institutions, involves applications which are hosted in the cloud and accessed through a Web browser. Not only is the data stored in the cloud, but the application is too, changing the computing paradigm to a more traditional client-server model where minimal functionality resides on the user's machine. This leaves the responsibility for software upgrades, virus checking and other maintenance with the cloud service provider. It also means that because everything is accessed and held on the Internet, sharing, version management and collaborative editing are much easier than when the applications and data reside on individuals' computers. Additionally, it allows the vendor to provide applications on the platform of their choice (though they must still ensure they work on a variety of browsers) (Hayes, 2008).

The primary attraction for institutions signing up for cloud services such as Apps for Education or Live@edu is because it is cheaper to do this than to provide the services themselves; in fact there are currently no charges at all. There is no longer any need for purchasing and maintaining in-house the hardware and software to run these services. Such facilities are inevitably under-utilized anyway; server usage in data centres is estimated to range from 5% to 20%. However for many services the peak workload is a factor of up to ten greater than the average (Armbrust et al., 2009). Such peaks can occur at universities for instance when exam results are released online. Cloud computing offers the illusion of infinite scalability, allowing rapid temporary escalations of usage for institutions. The idea is that the cloud is able to handle sudden spikes in usage by distributing the requests across its multiple servers.

In the cloud organisations do not have to plan usage levels in advance to cope with rapid or longer-term increases or falls in levels of business. They simply pay for the computing resources used. This is likely to have positive environmental impacts as well which may add an ethical argument for a shift towards the cloud. Another claimed advantage of cloud computing is that organisations can mix and match the various components they require without being bound to a rigid computing infrastructures (Jigsaw Networking, 2009). In the educational sphere, a university may decide to use Google Apps for Education for hosting student email, but withhold the other features. At a later stage an institution might decide to provide Google Docs, the online word processor and spreadsheet application to students.

Another major advantage of cloud computing is the reduction in staff costs and the removal of the requirement to support certain applications by the organisation or to maintain staff skills in that area. One university estimates a saving of $450,000 per year by decommissioning its self-hosted email system (Barlow & Lane, 2007). The conclusion reached by some commentators is that services of this sort will pave the way for commodified computing where organisations no longer host their own data centres with expensive hardware, power bills, rarely used computing power and staff salaries (Weiss, 2007). Costs are not reduced completely however as the educational institutions still need to maintain the systems which feed student registration data into the cloud systems. Universities retain control over the data, and are responsible for dealing with cases of misuse and frontline user support.

One cloud application which has begun to embed itself in universities by stealth is Second Life. Few institutions are seriously considering hosting Second Life (or other virtual worlds) in-house when Linden Labs will maintain the hardware and software for them at minimal cost. So what are the advantages to Microsoft and Google of offering their services for free to universities? The services are offered advertisement-free so there is no revenue generated in that way. Software is generally heavily discounted for those in education so it is part of a long tradition. The companies hope however to increase brand awareness and if the students continue to use the services after graduation they are then presented with advertising. Google also offers Apps for companies so some alumni may consider introducing the services which they have become used to as students in their workplace.

A GRADUAL MIGRATION OF ELEARNING SERVICES TO THE CLOUD

Email is likely to be the catalyst for an increasing shift of educational service provision from university data centres to the cloud. Many students opt to use their own email account already, often using Microsoft's Hotmail or Google's Gmail, so will be unaffected or may simply switch to a university account on the same cloud-based system they are used to. Already more than 1,000 educational institutions have signed up with Microsoft or Google to give their students an email account branded with the institution's domain name (Carnevale, 2008). The companies also offer to host staff and alumni accounts for free and the case for moving these to the cloud as well may become increasingly compelling. Many faculty and staff at Arizona State University, for example, were keen to follow their students in moving to Gmail and take advantage of the other Google applications (Barlow & Lane, 2007).

Email is a relatively easy service to make the case for migrating as it is a simple technology, standards-based, has minimal bespoke institutional adaptations, and incurs a variety of institutional costs. One institution reported 97% of email being spam or suspected spam and an "unquenchable" demand for additional storage by users (Sanders, 2008). The benefits of having experts elsewhere dealing with issues such as spam removal and software upgrades, and the large amounts of storage space available freely to users are clear. However even the introduction of cloud-based email has proved difficult for some institutions. At the University of Idaho, students protested vehemently and inundated their help desk when Microsoft Live@edu email was introduced. They felt that the university was forcing them to use a particular product from a vendor which was not universally liked. The biggest complaint was the lack of access to email through POP or IMAP. Microsoft accelerated the development of POP functionality, and the release of this together with better communications alleviated the situation. A year later the majority of the students were finding the system easy to use (Kearney & Miller, 2008).

Email is just one of a whole host of online services currently provided by the educational institutions themselves. Table 1 shows some of the most common elearning services and under which systems they can be found.

The table compares the two most widely used VLEs, Blackboard and Moodle, with Microsoft and Google's educational cloud offerings. It also

Table 1. Elearning services offered by different systems

	Blackboard	Moodle	Microsoft Live@edu	Google Apps for Education	Google Groups
Communications					
Forum	•	•	•		•
Instant Messaging	•	•	•	•	
Email			•	•	
Blog	•	•	•		
Wiki / collaborative editing	•	•	•	•	
Polling / surveys	•	•		•	
On demand group collaboration areas		•	•		•
Audio/video conferencing					
Shared whiteboards					
Assessment					
Quiz	•	•		•	
Assignment upload	•	•			
Gradebook	•	•			
Content					
Group document storage	•	•	•		•
Personal document storage	•	•	•	•	
Glossary		•	•		
Newsfeeds		•	•		

includes Google Groups, a system available to anyone which could easily be added to Google Apps for Education to provide spaces for group collaboration. It should be noted that this is a rapidly changing landscape and features are being continually added to all of the systems listed. Some of the tools such as personal document storage may not be part of the VLEs themselves but can be provided through plug-ins while others such as the synchronous facilities of videoconferencing and shared whiteboards are generally provided by commercial systems such as Elluminate or Webex. Also the different systems implement these facilities in different ways, VLEs tending to provide tools which are customized for education, while the cloud systems are for more general usage.

What is interesting about the table is that the cloud applications already provide the majority of the functionality of a virtual learning environment. A notable exception however is around assessment. While Google Apps allows the creation of surveys which could be used for assessment – and the automatic collation of student input in a spreadsheet for the assessor – the system would have none of the sophistication of the quiz tools in Moodle and Blackboard which is required for any serious use of e-assessment. There is of course no gradebook functionality either in the cloud applications. This is hardly surprising as they have not been designed with education specifically in mind. However it is unlikely to be long before both Microsoft and Google begin to add education-specific applications to these suites. Educational users have already been suggesting to Google that the company builds a VLE together with Google Apps (Google, 2009a). If this functionality continues to be offered for free, the case for institutions to host their own copies of Moodle or Blackboard will become considerably weaker.

In the meantime Google has introduced integration between Google Apps and Moodle, enabling single sign-on. This was developed by MoodleRooms, a company which, along with others, already hosts Moodle "in the cloud" for educational institutions who do not want the expense of internal hosting (Shanbhag, 2008).

One educational application which may be a prime candidate for movement to the cloud is the eportfolio. There are some commercial eportfolio applications such as PebblePad and open source equivalent, Mahara, which integrate with Moodle. The concept of the eportfolio is still evolving but it is primarily a storage area, enabling the user to share content with others and compile different components of their work into collections of documents for assessment purposes. Eportfolio systems often commonly include learning journals and blogs. Boundaries between eportfolio systems and VLEs are fluid.

Barrett (2009) shows how various Google applications can be combined to create an eportfolio system. Students can set up a portal using iGoogle with links to their files and applications. They can discuss their work with other students and their tutor using Google Groups. Textual documents, spreadsheets and presentations can be stored in Google Docs, while videos and images can be uploaded to other Google applications. Google Sites (one of the applications with Google Apps for Education) can be used to compile the various documents into a submission for assessment purposes. A current limitation of this approach is that there is no way to "freeze" a Google site at a particular point, something which may be necessary for assessments. If it was possible to submit an entire Google site to an assignment handling system that might be one way forward.

The affordances of cloud applications (or lack of them) as with any system used in an educational context can have major implications for the design of learning activities and assessments, and the resulting student experience. A vendor may for example remove user accounts which have not been used for a specified period. If an eportfolio is to be potentially a record of lifelong learning then such a system would clearly not be usable in that context.

RISKS OF MIGRATING TO THE CLOUD

Moving elearning services to the cloud is not without risk to the institution. While companies such as Google and Microsoft are unlikely to go bankrupt in the foreseeable future, leaving customers without essential services, there are risks in becoming heavily dependent on a single company. Both organisations offer a service level agreement to universities, lasting for several years. There is of course no guarantee that the service will remain after that period or that it will remain free of charge. Significant changes to the service could result in major costs for institutions who have relinquished control over the software, if not the data. Even minor upgrades to the cloud software which are released regularly could make documentation obsolete or subtly change a carefully crafted learning activity.

It has already been seen how in one university there was resistance to the imposition of Microsoft's Hotmail service. Google may in the future suffer from similar adverse publicity and associating an institution's brand too closely with Google may be inadvisable. The "Googlization" of universities through increasing dependence on Google Search, Google Scholar, Google Maps and other Google applications could provoke a backlash among students. Issues such as Google's submission to Chinese censorship laws and recent objections to the Google Street View camera car have impacted on the company's image.

Students and staff may have legitimate concerns about the storage of their data, particularly if it is located in the US where data protection laws are less strict than in the EU. Google however claims that European student data will be held in compliance with EU law. Both companies have privacy policies which state that student data is not shared with third parties or mined to gather information on individuals (Carnevale, 2008).

Even Google and Microsoft with the vast resources and skills available to them are not immune from service disruptions such as denial of service attacks. The management of cloud computing by a single company is a single point of failure, even if the company is using data centres distributed geographically. This has led one institution to suggest that the soundest strategy would be to use more than one cloud provider (Armbrust et al., 2009), though the logistics of this in the context of elearning are currently daunting. More fundamentally, cloud computing is still a new phenomenon and technical implementation issues remain. There are concerns that existing networks may not be ready yet to handle the implied massively increased traffic and that client machines are almost useless when network access is unavailable (Weiss, 2007). Google Gears allows users to continue working in several Google applications when disconnected and it does seem likely that future applications will combine limited functionality on the client with computing power in the cloud.

The Google and Microsoft systems do not function equally well on all browsers and recent tests at the Open University have shown that they are not fully accessible, particularly to users with screen readers. Usability remains an issue: operating systems based on multiple windows have been fine-tuned over many years and it is difficult to duplicate this functionality within a Web browser (Hayes, 2008). HTML still does not incorporate the ability to drag a document from the desktop to a Web browser window, for example, though this is promised in future versions of the language.

CONCLUSION

Does the cloud offer a way forward in the debate between protagonists of personal learning environments and those in institutions responsible for hosting virtual learning environments? Cloud applications provided under service level agreements with reputable vendors will give university IT departments the reassurances they need about availability and robustness, protection of minors, accessibility and data protection. It will also mean that they retain access to valuable "clickstream" data, allowing them to monitor usage and enhance services accordingly. PLE advocates on the other hand want students and themselves to be able to select the best tools from the Internet to carry out their learning. They would like to be free from restrictive institutional policies and have flexible, highly available tools. Cloud-based elearning services are likely to be more up to date than those provided within VLEs and might satisfy some of the innovators' desires for better user generated content creation tools and social networking software. Greater personalization is also possible with tools such as iGoogle. In fact Arizona State University built systems to feed course content, news headlines etc. to a Google Personal Start Page (Barlow & Lane, 2007).

Google has opened up Apps for Education with an API allowing institutions to customize the applications and integrate other software. Even if Google does not create functionality specifically for learners, another provider may choose to develop elearning applications which effectively turns Google Apps into a VLE. Universities themselves are experimenting with making their services available as "pluggable objects" that can be incorporated in systems where students might prefer to be (Hermans & Verjans, 2009). The Open University has provided an application in Facebook which allows students to "find a study buddy" for example. One suggested way forward is for a flexible architecture where widgets (typically small HTML files incorporating JavaScript libraries) for services such as timetabling and tutor messaging are provided by the institution in their VLEs and also in the Web 2.0 application of the student's choice (Wilson, Sharples & Griffiths, 2009). Both the VLE and the other applications may reside on the cloud but the widget would be delivered from the University's internal systems. Google Wave (Google, 2009b), a collaboration system merging concepts from email, instant messaging, forums and social networking sites may prove to be a good model for such a widget residing in the cloud but integrated into various applications running on multiple platforms including mobile devices.

From a university's point of view the cloud enables certain parameters to be much more controllable than where students are pointed to the Websites of a variety of providers on the Internet with whom the institution has no contractual arrangement. The service level agreement offered by Microsoft and Google for several years guarantees a level of service that the institutions are unlikely to provide themselves. The Open University's computing service for example aims for 99.5% availability of elearning services and sometimes does not meet that target. Google offers 99.9% availability for Apps for Education and anecdotal reports from the University of Westminster are that the service provided is nearer to 99.99%. The impact of service disruptions on students who rely on the VLE for learning and assessment cannot be underestimated.

IT services departments can also hope that users who have their needs fulfilled from cloud applications will be less likely to set up an insecure server under their desk and that the overall complexity of university networks can be reduced. On the other hand, staff will find it increasingly easy to bypass central services and take decisions without reference to policies which have been designed to protect the institution (Yanosky, 2008). Will IT services therefore resist a movement to the cloud which may ultimately reduce the power and authority associated with controlling large budgets and numbers of staff? Goldstein (2008) suggests that the rise of the cloud could actually increase the influence of the chief information officer, moving the focus to how the institution can make best use of the technology rather than merely how to implement it. Younger staff (and students) who barely remember a world without Google search, broadband and Facebook may be considerably less resistant to embracing cloud-based services (Katz, Goldstein & Yanosky, 2009).

Much has been written about the commodification of IT (e.g. Carr, 2003), drawing parallels with the infrastructure developed for railways and electricity provision. The case for moving low level computing infrastructure to the cloud is convincing. Generic applications in widespread use outside education such as wordprocessing, spreadsheets, image editing software and email also make sense to be delivered increasingly this way. It remains to be seen whether all educational applications can be made generic enough to be delivered from the cloud however. Many institutions have unique requirements due to their teaching methodologies, examination regulations, funding regimes and government policies, and national or regional legal frameworks. It is likely that large institutions with diverse or specific requirements will move to the cloud more slowly than smaller organisations (Goldstein, 2008). The inertia in higher education and previous financial commitments will also militate against a sudden paradigm shift to cloud computing (Jigsaw Networking, 2009), particularly for those with significant amounts of content and learning activities embedded in existing VLEs and large numbers of staff who have developed skills with particular elearning systems.

The full costs of delivering IT services are rarely taken into account by universities and there are justified concerns such as avoiding adverse publicity which may mean a slower migration to the cloud than in industry. On the other hand, cloud zealots may underestimate the real costs of moving services outside the institution, both for the migration itself and any ongoing maintenance required (Katz, Goldstein & Yanosky). The vision of true commoditization for elearning services where institutions can switch providers with ease is unlikely to materialize as this would require universally agreed standards. The minimal interoperability between existing content and applications in learning management systems such as Blackboard and Moodle suggests that being able to move an entire university's elearning provision from one system in the cloud to another would be a highly complex and expensive task.

Implementations of Blackboard and Moodle are themselves increasingly likely to migrate to the Cloud. The question remains whether institutions will make use of integrations of these VLEs with other cloud applications or whether systems such as Live@edu and Google Apps for Education will adopt more specific elearning functionality and make the more traditional VLEs obsolete.

REFERENCES

Armbrust, M., Fox, A., Griffith, R., Joseph, A. D., Katz, R. H., Konwinski, A., et al. (2009). *Above the clouds: A Berkeley view of cloud computing.* University of California at Berkeley. Retrieved May 25, 2009, from http://www.eecs.berkeley.edu/Pubs/TechRpts/2009/EECS-2009-28.html

Baker, S. (2007). Google and the wisdom of clouds. *Business Week*, , 4064.

Barlow, K., & Lane, J. (2007). Like technology from an advanced alien culture: Google Apps for education at ASU. In *Proceedings of the 35th Annual ACM SIGUCCS Conference on User Services* (pp. 8-10). New York: ACM.

Buyya, R., Yeo, C. S., & Venugopal, S. (2008, September). Market-oriented cloud computing: Vison, hype, and reality for delivering IT services as computing utilities. In *Proceedings of the 10th IEEE International Conference on High Performance Computing and Communications*. Los Alamitos, California: IEEE CS Press.

Carnevale, D. (2008). Colleges get out of e-Mail business. *The Chronicle of Higher Education, 54*(18).

Carr, N. G. (2003). IT doesn't matter. *Harvard Business Review, 81*(5), 41–49.

Energy Information Administration (2009). *Average retail price of electricity to ultimate customers by end-use sector, by state.*

Goldstein (2008). The tower, the cloud, and the IT leader and workforce. In R. Katz (Ed.), *The tower and the cloud* (pp. 238-260). Boulder, CO: Educause.

Google (2009a). *LMS and Google Apps – first comes love... Official Google enterprise blog.* Retrieved May 29, 2009, from http://googleenterprise.blogspot.com/2009/02/lms-and-google-apps-first-comes-love.html

Google (2009b). *Google wave*. Retrieved May 29, 2009, from http://wave.google.com/

Hayes, B. (2008). Cloud computing. *Communications of the ACM, 51*(7). New York: ACM.

Hermans, H., & Verjans, S. (2009). *Developing a sustainable, student centred VLE: The OUNL case*. Retrieved May 29, 2009, from http://dspace.ou.nl/bitstream/1820/1894/1/Hermans_Verjans_ICDE2009_V4.pdf

Jigsaw Networking. (2009). *Cloud computing.* Retrieved May 29, 2009, from http://www.jigsawnetworking.com/articles/cloud-computing-for-creatives.aspx

Johnson, L., Levine, A., & Smith, R. (2009). *The 2009 horizon report*. Austin, TX: The New Media Consortium.

Katz, R., Goldstein, P., & Yanosky, R. (2009). *Research Bulletin (Sun Chiwawitthaya Thang Thale Phuket)*, 2009.

Kearney, D. J., & Miller, D. C. (2008). VandalMail live: Bringing a campus into the Microsoft @EDU program. In *Proceedings of the 36th Annual ACM SIGUCCS Conference on User Services* (pp. 107-112). New York: ACM.

Sanders, C. A. (2008). Coming down the e-mail mountain, blazing a trail to Gmail. In *Proceedings of the 36th Annual ACM SIGUCCS Conference on User Services Conference* (pp. 101-106). New York: ACM.

Sclater, N. (2008). Web 2.0, personal learning environments and the future of learning management systems. Boulder, CO: Educause Center for Applied Research. *Research Bulletin (Sun Chiwawitthaya Thang Thale Phuket)*, 13.

Shanbhag, R. (2008). *Open source Moodle heads to the Amazon cloud*. Retrieved May 29, 2009, from http://asterisk.tmcnet.com/topics/open-source/articles/34257-open-source-moodle-heads-the-amazon-cloud.htm

Vaquero, L., Rodero-Merino, L., Caceres, J., & Lindner, M. (2009). A break in the clouds: Towards a cloud definition. New York: ACM. *Computer Communication Review*, *39*(1), 50–55. doi:10.1145/1496091.1496100

Weiss, A. (2007). Computing in the clouds. *netWorker, 11*(4), 16-25. New York: ACM.

Wilson, S., Sharples, P., & Griffiths, D. (2009). Distributing education services to personal and institutional systems using Widgets. In *Proceedings of the First International Workshop on Mashup Personal Learning Environments* (pp. 25-32). Maastricht, Netherlands.

This work was previously published in International Journal of Virtual and Personal Learning Environments, edited by Michael Thomas, Volume 1, Issue 1, pp. 10-19, copyright 2010 by IGI Publishing (an imprint of IGI Global).

Chapter 3
Toward a Personal Learning Environment Framework

Mohamed Amine Chatti
RWTH Aachen University, Germany

Mohammad Ridwan Agustiawan
RWTH Aachen University, Germany

Matthias Jarke
RWTH Aachen University, Germany

Marcus Specht
Open University, The Netherlands

ABSTRACT

Over the past decade, it has been argued that technology-enhanced learning (TEL) could respond to the needs of the new knowledge society and transform learning. However, despite isolated achievements, TEL has not succeeded in revolutionizing education and learning processes. Most current TEL initiatives still take a centralized technology-push approach in which learning content is pushed to a predefined group of learners in closed environments. A fundamental shift toward a more open and learner-pull model for learning is needed. Recently, the Personal Learning Environment (PLE) concept has emerged to open new doors for more effective learning and overcome many of the limitations of traditional TEL models. In this paper, the authors present theoretical, design, implementation, and evaluation details of PLEF, a framework for mashup personal learning environments. The primary aim of PLEF is to help learners create custom learning mashups using a wide variety of digital media and data.

INTRODUCTION

There is a wide agreement that the new era is defined by rapid knowledge development, and that traditional learning initiatives failed to cope with the increasing complexity and fast-paced change of the new knowledge society. For example, Brown and Adler (2008) note:

DOI: 10.4018/978-1-4666-1770-4.ch003

In the twentieth century, the dominant approach to education focused on helping students to build stocks of knowledge and cognitive skills that could be deployed later in appropriate situations. This approach to education worked well in a relatively stable, slowly changing world in which careers typically lasted a lifetime. But the twenty-first century is quite different. The world is evolving at an increasing pace (p. 30)

In order to align with the rapid change of the new knowledge intensive era, a new vision for learning is required. Learning is fundamentally personal, social, distributed, ubiquitous, flexible, dynamic, and complex in nature. Thus, a fundamental shift is needed toward a more personalized, social, open, dynamic, emergent and knowledge-pull model for learning, as opposed to the one-size-fits-all, centralized, static, top-down, and knowledge-push models of traditional learning solutions (Chatti et al., 2007). In this paper, we discuss critical factors that must be addressed to ensure that future learning models will endure, analyze why traditional technology-enhanced learning (TEL) initiatives have failed, and present an alternative TEL model based on the concept of the Personal Learning Environment. This paper also describes some initial theoretical steps towards a Personal Learning Environment Framework (PLEF) that can support learners in taking control over their learning experience by creating and managing their own PLEs. Mashups that refer to a reuse and combination of services stemming from different sources to create entirely new services, build the cornerstone of PLEF. Furthermore, we present, design, implement, and evaluate details of a first prototype of PLEF, around the concept of mashups by aggregation.

TEL CHALLENGES

There are several critical challenges, opportunities, and movements in learning that must be considered in the development and implementation of TEL environments. These include encouraging lifelong learning, valuing both informal and formal learning, and recognizing the different contexts in which learning takes place, as well as the fundamental changes in the perception, technology and use of the Web in the past (Attwell, 2007a, 2007b).

Lifelong Learning

Lifelong learning refers to a society in which learning possibilities exist for those who want to learn (Aspin & Chapman, 2000). Learning is not restricted to the classroom and to formal learning inside learning institutions; rather it is an activity that happens throughout life, at work, play and home. In the modern knowledge-intensive era, lifelong competence development has become a major challenge to our educational systems that have not changed their educational policies and pedagogical models to support lifelong learning. There is an increasing demand for new approaches toward fostering lifelong learning perspectives (Klamma et al., 2007).

Informal Learning

An important theme in learning is the nature of informal and non-formal learning: "Once you step beyond traditional institutional boundaries you can find learning, which is driven by and for, 'you, the learner' " (Klamma et al., 2007, p. 73). Cross (2006) argues that at work we learn more in the break room than in the classroom. We discover how to do our jobs through informal learning, observing others, asking the person in the next cubicle, calling the help desk, trial-and-error and simply working with 'people in the know'. Formal learning is the source of only 10% to 20% of what we learn at work. Informal learning is however not restricted to a corporate context. Much of our academic learning happens beyond the formal institutional educational systems. It comes from different informal channels; for example, through games, simulations, experiments, story-telling and discovery. Outside the classroom boundaries, we use Google, communicate with peers, join online communities, work on problems together, and share learning resources (Chatti et al., 2007).

Personalized Learning

Learning is personal in nature. Tobin (2000), for example, states: "All learning is self-directed ... The learner may not have control over what is taught, but the learner always has control over what is learned" (p. vii). Thus, one of the core issues in learning is the personalization of the learning experience. Learners have a variety of learning styles, which are mirrored in the way they learn. By personalization we mean the ability on the part of the learner to learn the way she deems fit. In general, learners tend to resist the one-size-fits-all learning approaches that often fail to address their individual differences, expectations, preferences, and needs. Attwell (2007b) stresses that central to learning is "placing control of learning in the hands of learners themselves and providing learners with the skills and competences to manage their own learning" (p. 40). Jafari et al. (2006) note that learners "need to have a system that is centered on what they want and need. This requires a system that is adaptive and responsive" (p. 58). Carmen and Haefner (2003) also write "management by the learner is often key to learning" (as cited in Jafari et al., 2006, p. 58).

Network Learning

Learning is fundamentally social in nature (Lave & Wenger, 1991; Nonaka & Takeuchi, 1995; Polanyi, 1967; Wenger, 1998) and it resides in networks (Downes, 2006; Siemens, 2006). The notion of network learning is even more supported by a more social and connected Web that has arisen over the past few years. Nowadays, Web users absorb knowledge very quickly across different channels and they prefer random on-demand access to all kinds of knowledge disseminated over the Internet. They are in close contact with their friends using networks to share and create new knowledge. This new Web generation is often termed Web 2.0 (O'Reilly, 2007, p.17).

The changes in the perception, technology and use of the Web in the past few years are leading to a new generation of learners, who are not merely seen as consumers, but also as active producers of knowledge. The openness of knowledge resources and the social nature of Web 2.0 through participation, voting, collaboration, sharing, aggregation and distribution are leading to a new generation of TEL. TEL via Web 2.0 technologies has been referred to as E-Learning 2.0 (Downes, 2005). From the learner's perspective the Web evolves into a rich pool of knowledge, demanding learner-centric models which put the control over learning itself into the hands of the learners. Downes (2005) points out that learners are more active and the roles of learner and teacher switch. This implies that changing roles makes the distinction between teachers and learners more difficult, as both sides are able to learn from one another.

Virtual Learning Environments

Current technology-enhanced learning (TEL) approaches are following a static and predefined representation of knowledge and are mainly focusing on content delivery and technology. In fact, TEL has always been connected to computer-based delivery of learning objects and a strong emphasis has been placed on how to centralize and standardize the learning experience. Most TEL today is designed, authored, organized, and delivered via centralized Virtual Learning Environments (VLE) as statically packaged online courses and modules, following the pattern of modularization of courses and the isolation of learning into discrete units (Wilson et al., 2007). Examples include Learning management Systems (LMS), Learning Content Management Systems (LCMS), Course Management Systems (CMS) or Content Management Systems (CMS) such as CLIX, WebCT, Blackboard, Moodle, ATutor, ILIAS, Plone or Drupal (Baumgartner et al., 2004). In most of the cases, an initially paper-based learning resource is just converted into a digital form and a classroom training event is transformed into an online course where learning objects are assembled and managed via central standards-conformant learning management systems. As Downes (2005) writes: "The learning management system takes learning content and organizes it in a standard way, as a course divided into modules and lessons, supported with quizzes, tests and discussions, and in many systems today, integrated into the college or university's student information system" (Where We Are Now section, para. 4).

The view of learning as course delivery and learning resources as learning objects has led to the implementation of large and centralized learning object repositories (LOR) of context-free and reusable content described by metadata. Complex standards have emerged to make learning objects shareable and learning object repositories interoperable. Learning providers often try to deliver SCORM (SCORM, 2009) compliant content. In order to achieve interoperability among learning repositories, different communication frameworks for querying have been proposed, such as the universal interoperability layer Simple Query Interface (SQI) (Van Assche et al., 2006).

Obviously, the LMS-centric model of learning has failed to achieve performance improvement and innovation. A major reason of the failure is that learning is more than static content, and technology is only a secondary issue. Moreover, LMS- driven TEL solutions follow a one-size-fits-all approach and suffer from an inability to satisfy the heterogeneous needs of many learners. Furthermore, LMSs have been designed with the primary focus on management and control. All learning materials and services in an LMS-based course are organized and managed by and within a centrally managed, often complex system, which is driven by the needs of the educational institution and consequently often not adopted by the learners. Siemens (2004), among others, argues that LMS is the wrong place to start learning. In Siemens' words "beginning learning with an LMS is often a matter of wrong tool for wrong purposes" (Introduction section, para. 3). Siemens further notes that "the more feature-rich an individual tool becomes, the more it loses its usefulness to the average user" (Drawbacks to Learning Management Systems section, para. 1).

In short, the LMS-controlled, top-down management of learning activities conflicts with how we are actually learning. Learning is personal and social in nature, and most of it is informal. This requires a change in focus from content/technology-push to learner-pull models of learning that put the learners at the center and respect their unique needs.

Personal Learning Environments

Recognizing the failures of traditional LMS-driven TEL initiatives to achieve performance improvement, we need to rethink how we design new TEL models that can meet the challenges of lifelong, informal, personalized, and networked learning in the new knowledge intensive world, and mirror the characteristics of learning which is fundamentally personal, social, distributed, ubiquitous, flexible, dynamic, and complex in nature. In this section, we discuss a new learning model characterized by the convergence of lifelong, informal, and personalized learning within a social context. This learning model is based on the concept of Personal Learning Environment.

A common idea behind LMS-based TEL solutions is that different tools are pushed by the educational institution and pre-packaged into a centralized system. A Personal Learning Environment (PLE), however, is a more natural and learner-centric model to learning that takes a small pieces, loosely joined approach, characterized by the freeform use of a set of learner-controlled tools and the bottom-up creation of knowledge ecologies.

In contrast to LMSs, PLEs have the following characteristics:

- **Personalization:** A LMS follows a one-size-fits-all approach to learning by offering a static system with predefined tools to a set of many learners around a course. A PLE, by contrast, is responsive and provides a personalized experience of learning. It considers the needs and preferences of the learner and places her at the center by providing her with a plethora of different tools and handing over control to her to select and use the tools the way she deems fit.
- **Informal learning and lifelong learning support:** A LMS is not supportive of informal or lifelong learning. It can only be used in a formal learning setting, managed and controlled by the educational institution. And, in a LMS, learning has an end. It stops when a course terminates. As Jafari et al. (2006) put it: "Current L/CMSs, in their conception as management system, shut the learners and the instructor out after the semester ends, as if learning, teaching, and reflecting have symbiotically ended" (p. 58). A PLE, however, can connect formal, informal, and lifelong learning opportunities within a context that is centred upon the learner. Attwell (2007a) writes: "the PLE purports to include and bring together all learning, including informal learning, workplace learning, learning from the home, learning driven by problem solving and learning motivated by personal interest as well as learning through engagement in formal educational programmes" (p. 2). A PLE allows the learner to capture her informal and lifelong learning accomplishment and develop her own e-portfolio (Anderson, 2006). In a PLE learning is fluid. It continues after the end of a particular course.
- **Openness and decentralization:** Unlike a LMS, which stores information on a centralized basis within a closed and bounded environment, a PLE goes beyond the boundaries of the organization and operates in a more decentralized, loosely coupled, and open context. A PLE offers an opportunity to learners to make effective use of diverse distributed knowledge sources to enrich their learning experiences. As Downes (2006) states: "the heart of the concept of the PLE is that it is a tool that allows a learner (or anyone) to engage in a distributed environment consisting of a network of people, services and resources" (A Network Pedagogy section, para. 10).
- **Bottom-up approach:** Within a LMS there is a clear distinction between the capabilities of learners and teachers, resulting in to a one-way flow of knowledge (Wilson et al., 2007). In contrast to a hierarchical top-down LMS, shaped by command-and-control and asymmetric relationships, a PLE provides an emergent bottom-up solution, driven by the learner needs and based on sharing rather than controlling.
- **Knowledge-pull:** A LMS adopts a knowledge-push model and is concerned with exposing learners to content and expecting that learning will then happen automatically. A PLE, however, takes a knowledge-pull model. Learners can create their very own environments where they can pull knowledge that meets their particular needs from a wide array of high-value knowledge sources.
- **Ecological learning:** A PLE-driven approach to learning is based on personal environments, loosely connected. A PLE is not only a personal space, which belongs to and is controlled by the learner, but is also a social landscape that offers means to connect with other personal spaces for effective knowledge sharing and collaborative

knowledge creation. Rather than belonging to hierarchical and organization-controlled groups, each learner has her own personal environment and network. Based on their needs and preferences, different learners come together for a learning experience. They work together until the learning goal is achieved and thereby do not have a permanent relationship with a formal organization or institution. The distributed PLEs can be loosely connected to build a knowledge ecology. Unlike LMS-driven groups/communities, which are closed, bounded, structured, hierarchical, and organization-controlled, a PLE-driven knowledge ecology is open, distributed, diverse, emergent, self-organized, and learner-controlled.

DEVELOPMENT OF PERSONAL LEARNING ENVIRONMENTS

There is still no agreement on what mechanisms can underpin the development of PLEs. Wilson et al. (2007) note that the PLE pattern suggests several very different strategies may be feasible. The authors state "a single PLE application may be possible, or on the other hand, the coordinated use of a range of specialized tools may achieve a satisfactory result" (p. 33). In the same direction, Jafari et al. (2006) point out that some envision a PLE "as a portal or portfolio, whereas others see a self- generated and self-determined point through which the learners (and the instructor) select how and where they access the functions that are needed to achieve their goals and outcomes" (p. 58).

There have been some attempts to define approaches to developing PLEs. Attwell (2007a), for example, asserts that a PLE is not an application; it is rather a collection of all the different tools we use in our everyday life for learning. Lubensky (2006) discusses different ways of PLE development. According to the author, PLEs can be realized as WebTops, desktop applications, e.g. PLEX (Wilson et al., 2007); content management systems, e.g. plone and drupal; or in terms of mashups. PLEs can also exist in an ad-hoc manner, for instance through blogs.

Personalized start pages such as iGoogle, My Yahoo, Netvibes, or Pageflakes were not designed as educational technology, but their design strategies match parts of the characteristics discussed in the previous section. These services, for instance, provide a means to facilitate the aggregation of different services into a personalized space, through RSS feeds and widgets.

In this work, we go for the development of a PLE as a flexible entry point that enables a learner-controlled integration of different learning tools and services into a personalized place. A PLE in that sense is not a multifunction Swiss Army Knife with special-purpose tools, rather it is a self-designed toolbox used to collect a range of single-purpose tools based on learner desires. This personalized entry point would then represent a knowledge home, e-portfolio, and identity for learners.

In the next sections, we present theoretical issues, requirements, design, implementation details, and an evaluation of the PLEF; a conceptual framework that can support learners in taking control over their learning experience by creating and managing their own PLEs.

The Personal Learning Environment Framework

We believe that it is unrealistic to imagine a single Personal Learning Environment that can be adopted by all learners, given their very heterogeneous desires and different contexts. However, a systematic conceptual framework is needed that can guide the design of PLEs.

A PLE is a learner's gate to knowledge. It can be viewed as a self-defined collection of services, tools, and devices that help learners build their Personal Knowledge Networks (PKN), encompassing tacit knowledge nodes (i.e. people) and

Figure 1. Mashup personal learning environments

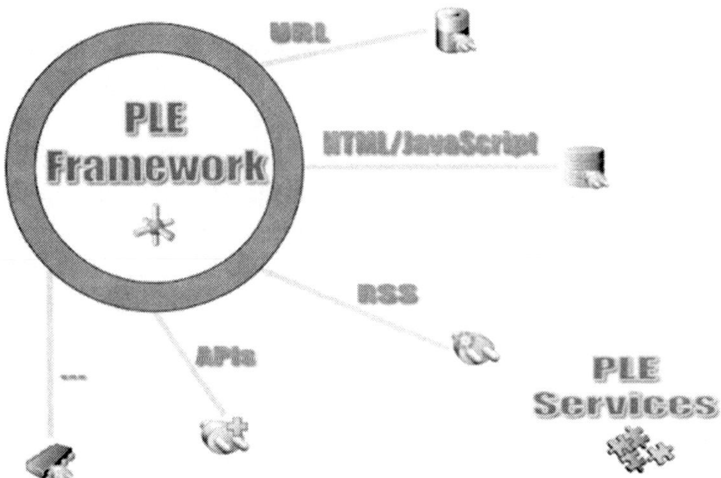

explicit knowledge nodes (i.e. information). Thus, mechanisms that support learners in building their PLEs become crucial. Mashups provide an interesting solution to developing PLEs.

In Web terminology, a mashup is a Web site that combines content from more than one source (from multiple Web sites) into an integrated experience. We differentiate between two types of mashups:

- **Mashups by aggregation:** simply assemble sets of information from different sources side by side within a single interface. Mashups by aggregation do not require advanced programming skills and are often a matter of cutting and pasting from one site to another. Personalized start pages, which are individualized assemblages of feeds and widgets, fall into this category.
- **Mashups by integration:** create more complex applications that integrate different application programming interfaces (APIs) in order to combine data from different sources. Unlike mashups by aggregation, the development of mashups by integration needs considerable programming expertise.

The Personal Learning Environment Framework (PLEF) provides a framework for mashup personal learning environments. A conceptual view of PLEF is depicted in Figure 1. PLEF leverages the possibility to plug learning components from multiple sources into a learner-controlled space. This ranges from simply juxtaposing content from different sources (e.g. feeds, widgets, media) into a single interface (mashup by aggregation), to a more complex remixing of different APIs into an integrated application, in order to create entirely different views or uses of the original data (mashup by integration).

PLEF Requirements

At the heart of PLEF lie mashups. PLEF should have a flexible architecture enabling learners to enrich their PLEs with a heterogeneous set of services. A learner should be able to easily aggregate, integrate, and mash-up different learning services (e.g. feeds, widgets, media, Web Services based on lightweight communications technologies such as REST and AJAX), according to her needs and interests. Furthermore, PLEF should meet the challenges and reflect the PLE characteristics outlined in the previous sections. It thus needs to address the following attributes:

- **Personalized:** PLEF should provide the learner with the ability to incorporate a myriad of tools and services; and the ability to determine and use the tools and services the way she deems fit to create her own PLE, adapted to her own situation and needs. It is crucial to provide access to a wide range of tools and services that support different learning activities such as production, distribution, reflection, and discussion. It is also important to enable customized search across the collection of learning items in one's own PLE as well as in peer PLEs. PLEF should also offer learner-defined access control mechanisms for each PLE item, as well as support for multi-views of the PLE, enabling the learner to filter the mass of available knowledge sources based on her needs, and switch between multiple learning contexts.
- **Social:** PLEF should support the building of interactive environments by offering a means to connect with other personal spaces, such that learners can engage in knowledge sharing and collaborative knowledge creation. Social features such as social tagging, commenting, and sharing have to be supported.
- **Open:** PLEF should be based on open standards (e.g. RSS, OpenID, OAuth, OpenSocial) to ensure interoperability and communication with other services. It should also provide a public API that can be used by third-party services.
- **Ubiquitous:** PLEF should provide a means for flexible delivery and ubiquitous access to PLEs from multiple channels and a wide variety of platforms and (mobile) devices.
- **Filter:** One concern with knowledge-pull approaches is information overload. Therefore, PLEF should provide powerful filters, that tap the wisdom of crowds (Surowiecki, 2004) (e.g. recommendations, ratings, rankings, reviews, votes, comments) to help learners find quality in the Long Tail (Anderson, 2006).
- **Easy to use:** PLEF should provide rich experience with e.g. AJAX support. A learner should be able to copy-and-paste and drag-and-drop elements to personalize and manage her PLE with minimum effort.

Parts of these requirements have been achieved in a first prototype of PLEF, which only addresses the first type of mashups, i.e. mashups by aggregation. A key requirement for mashups by aggregation is that content should be available in standardized formats that can be reused easily in other contexts, such as Web feeds, widgets (i.e. JavaScript source code), and image/video formats. Driven by mashups by aggregation, PLEF enables learners to easily combine different learning resources and services (e.g. feeds, widgets, and different media) from multiple learning platforms and service providers within a personalized space. The design, implementation, and evaluation of this prototype are discussed in some detail in the next sections.

PLEF Design

This section presents the software architecture pattern behind PLEF and the detailed architecture of PLEF. We have endeavored to structure this section according to the requirements specified in the previous section.

Model-View-Controller (MVC)

Model-View-Controller (MVC) is a software architecture that separates an application's data model, user interface, and control logic into three distinct components so that modifications to the view component can be made with minimal impact to the data model component (Eckstein et al., 1998). The MVC paradigm breaks the application's interface into three parts: the model, the view, and the controller.

PLEF Architecture

This section presents the architecture of the PLEF. This architecture was previously presented in an abstract manner in Figure 2. PLEF is intended to provide a framework which supports personalized, informal, lifelong, and network learning experiences and helps learners to create their very own PLEs. A PLE created by PLEF consists of a personal collection of a myriad of learning services in different formats, such as media, feeds, and widgets. These learning elements can be pulled from different third party service providers on the Web and then structured into several pages and organized according to particular tags. A learner can manage (add, edit, delete), search, and view the learning elements in her PLE. A learner can also visit other PLEs and give comments. A PLEF also provides the learner with the possibility to share a specific learning element with peers.

While the abstract architecture was for a personal learning environment framework geared towards the TEL community in general, the following detailed architecture, is specific to the PLEF, with an eye on how the concepts talked of previously, have been translated into functions. Core requirements identified in previous sections served as input into the design of the PLEF's architecture. What follows, is a discussion of the PLEF's detailed architecture with subsequent discussions on the various modules present therein. Figure 3 depicts the global class diagram of the PLEF. The class diagram roughly defines how the application would appear, and how the individual components communicate with each other, as well as their responsibilities. Following the MVC architecture pattern, classes in PLEF

Figure 2. Abstract view of PLEF

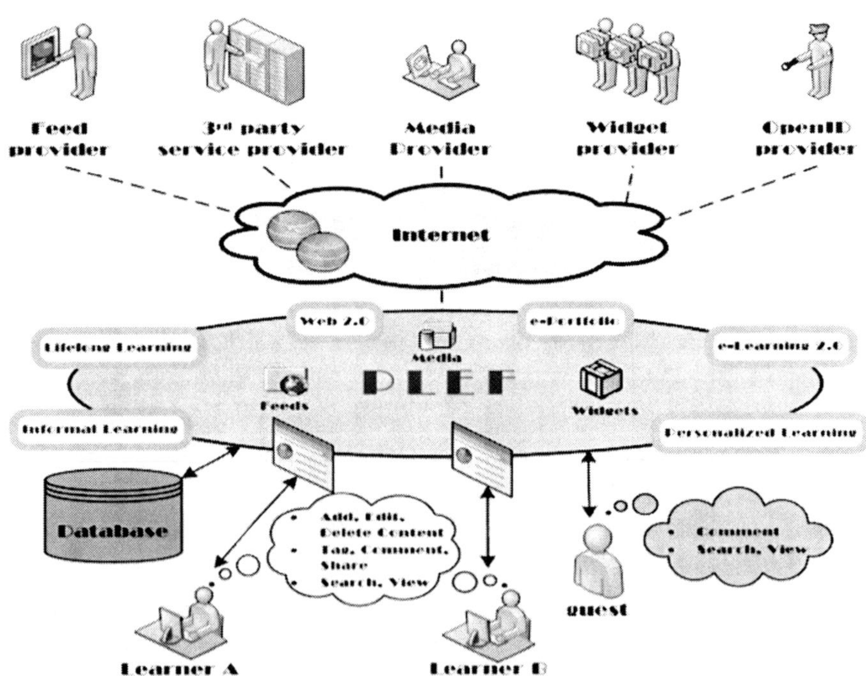

are classified into *model*, *view* and *controller* modules. The model module is represented by *PlefModel* class. The view module is represented by *UI class*. The controller module consists of four classes: *MainController*, *SessionHandler*, *DatabaseHandler* and *Authentication*.

The model module is depicted in Figure 4. The *PlefModel* class is responsible for handling the available content in a PLE. The *PlefContent* class is specialized into *PlefPage* and *PlefElement* classes.

The *UI* class generates the PLEF user interface and captures any input from the user's side. The user interface is generated in HTML and JavaScript code. Each interaction between the user and PLEF is captured by an Ajax script, which, based on the input, determines what kind of request data will be sent to the *UI* class.

The *MainController* class is responsible for controlling all processes and data in the PLEF. After receiving an input from the user, the *UI* class will determine the input type and then pass it to the *MainController*. In the case of a valid input, the *MainController* class invokes some actions, e.g., instantiates other classes, calls other classes' methods, determines authorization for particular users, or changes the view of a PLE. The *SessionHandler* class is responsible for handling session data, e.g., storing, getting and deleting session data. The *DatabaseHandler* class is responsible for storing, updating, and deleting data in the PLEF database. The *Authentication* class is used for OpenID authentication.

PLEF Implementation

We now follow up on the architecture presented in the previous section with the actual working of the PLEF. The implementation details will be presented and illustrated by screenshots of the PLEF in action. This section presents the various features and functionalities discussed in the previous section, in complete implementation detail.

Front-End Implementation

- **Interface:** The PLEF interface consists of north, west, east and center panels, as

Figure 3. Global class diagram of PLEF

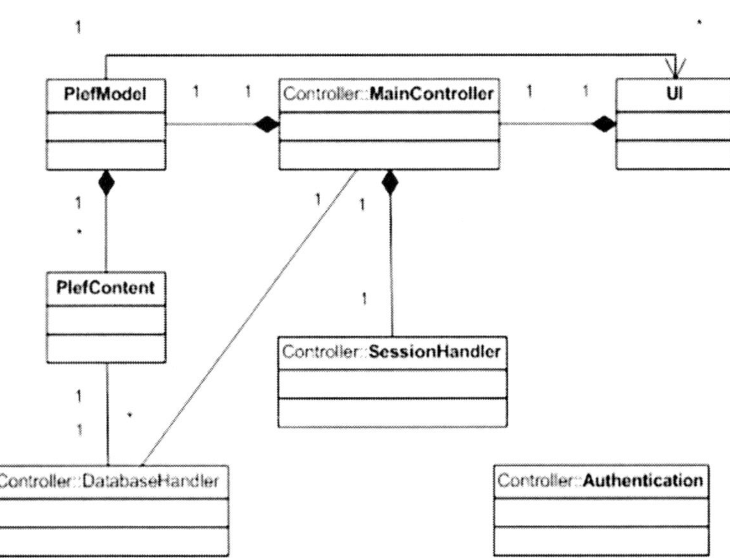

Figure 4. Model module in PLEF

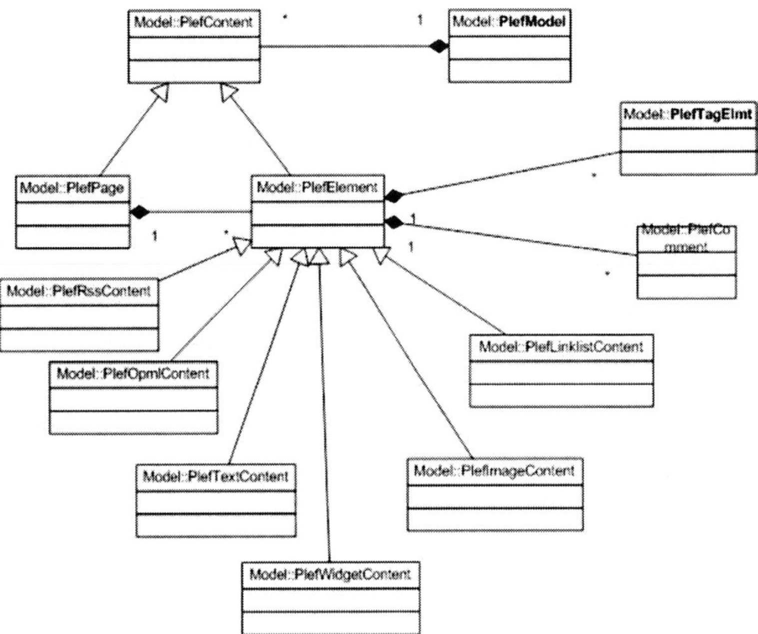

shown in Figure 5. The north panel enables the learner to login/logout, add new PLE pages, and show the element insertion panel in the west panel, which is used to insert new elements into a PLE. The east panel is used for viewing and searching of the PLE elements. The center panel shows the elements either organized in pages or grouped based on tags. Drag-and-drop action is supported in both center and east panels. In the center panel, it enables the learner to change the position of elements within pages. In the east panel, it enables users to move elements between pages and to change their order within a PLE.

- **Authentication:** PLEF uses OpenID for authentication. The learner is requested to enter her OpenID either to access/create her PLE or comment on a specific PLE element. PLEF verifies the given OpenID by sending a request to the associated OpenID provider and enables the required action if the OpenID is valid.
- **Pages and Elements:** PLEF enables a learner to organize her learning resources into pages. A page panel in PLEF consists of three parts: tab, toolbar and body (Figure 6). The page tab contains the page title and icon. The page toolbar includes a page settings menu, a share page button, a private/public button, and a delete page button. The page settings menu contains four items: title, number of columns, background color, and icon of the page. A page in PLEF encompasses several elements. Currently, PLEF supports the following element types: feed, OPML, text, image, link list, and widget. An element panel in PLEF consists of three parts: header, body and footer. The element header contains the element title and icon and the collapse-expand button. A different element icon is associated with each element type. The element footer consists of several buttons, which are edit, tag, share, private/public, comment and delete buttons. The element

body differs according to the type of the element it shows.

- **Social Tagging, Commenting and Sharing:** Social features supported by PLEF include social tagging, commenting, and sharing of PLE pages and elements. Each element in PLEF can be associated with different tags. And, learners are able to provide comments on each element. Thereby, they can login as anonymous users or via their OpenIDs. PLE pages and elements can be shared via email. If a learner receives and opens a link to a shared page or element, she will be redirected into the PLEF. Once logged in, she will receive a panel showing the shared content that can then be added automatically into her PLE.
- **Views:** Besides a traditional page view, PLEF provides a tag view of all elements in a PLE. Once a tag view is preferred, all tags will appear as nodes of a tree in the east panel. A tag can then be selected and its associated elements will be shown in the center panel (Figure 7).
- **Search:** PLEF enables full-text and tag-based search of all elements in a PLE. Search is performed in the page/tag view of the east panel. If a sequence of characters is detected by the search field's listener, deep first search will be performed on the tree in the page/tag view to find all pages and elements which contain the exact string. The title of the nodes containing the exact string will then be shown as bold, as shown in Figure 8.
- **Access Control:** PLEF enables access control at both PLE page and element levels. Newly inserted elements or pages are automatically set as private and can then be made as public by clicking the private/public button which is located at the element footer or the page toolbar.

PLEF Evaluation

The PLEF is a learning mashup service that aims at not only providing learners with extendible personal spaces, which belong to and are controlled by them, but also providing the means to connect to other personal spaces for effective knowledge sharing and collaborative knowledge creation.

Figure 5. PLEF interface

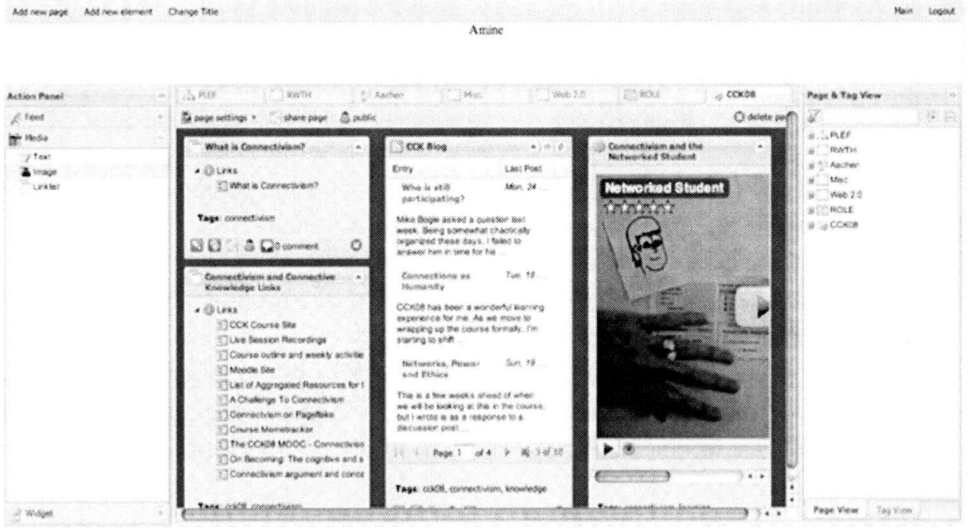

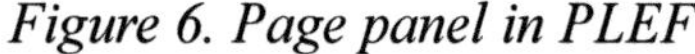

Figure 6. Page panel in PLEF

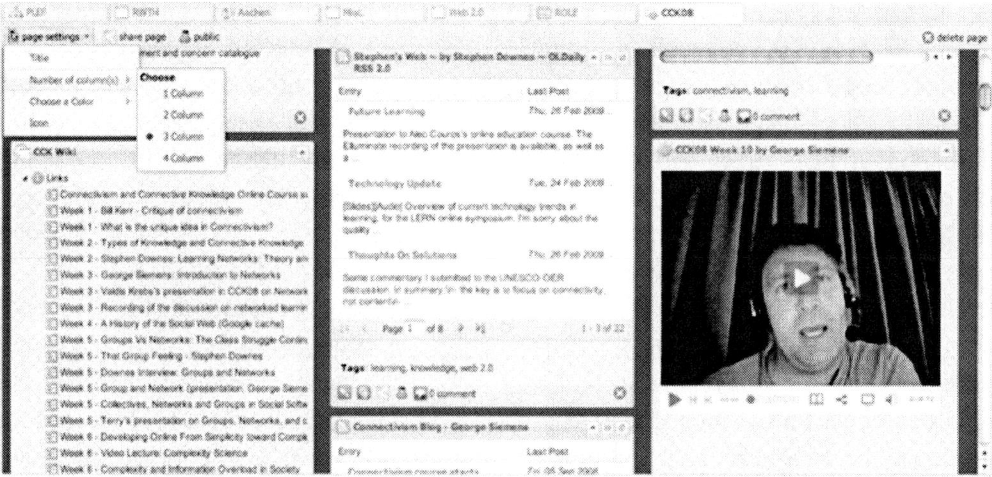

These aims were the basic guiding principles behind the design and implementation of the PLEF. To check the efficacy of our solution, we aim to evaluate the service developed to understand whether the PLEF succeeds in delivering personalized learning experiences and making managing a PLE a much more intuitive and simpler task. We designed and distributed a questionnaire to learners at the academic level to facilitate this process. We set up PLEF in a public website (http://eiche.informatik.rwth-aachen.de:3333/PLEF/) and allowed learners to freely interact with the service and report their impressions on the feedback form provided at the beginning of the process.

Feedback Form

Distributed in the form of a questionnaire with a number of multiple-choice questions (MCQs), the feedback form was designed to be user-friendly. The questionnaire was distributed into various subsections dealing with the general background of the evaluator, different aspects of the PLEF and its impact. Open-ended questions, which require much thought, were either left out, or framed as MCQs to allow the evaluator to quickly peruse the questions and fill in answers.

The first section of the questionnaire deals with finding out the specific background of the evaluators. These are general questions regarding the evaluators experience with TEL and her familiarity with existing Learning Management Systems and Personalized Start Pages.

The overall system evaluation is the focus of the next section. It is related to the evaluator's experience with the system as a whole, without paying attention to the individual modules.

The evaluators' opinion of the different personalization and collaboration features implemented in the PLEF is gauged next with a series of questions which aim to identify the authentication, views, search, access control, and social features of the PLEF.

The final section attempts to summarize the evaluators' impression of PLEF, and whether such a service has the potential to support collaborative learning and self-directed learning activities.

Results of Feedback

Feedback forms were sent to 25 evaluators from varied backgrounds. Out of the 25 questionnaires, 23 answers were received. The results of

Figure 7. Tag view in PLEF

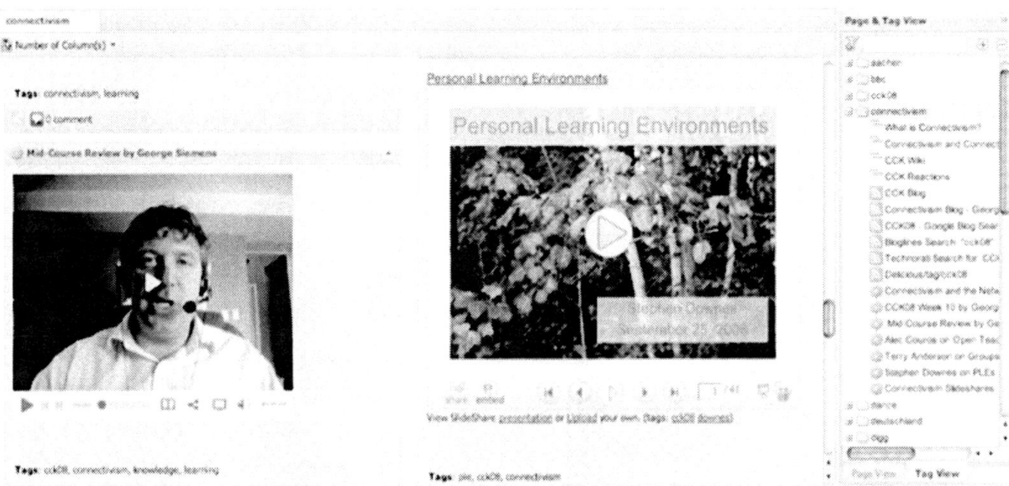

the feedback are discussed in some detail in the following subsections.

- **Learner Profiles and General Questions:** Altogether, 8 females and 15 males tested the service, all of them currently students in the age range 19-28 years. For the most part, the evaluators were academic learners in Europe. Out of 23 feedback forms returned, only 4 evaluators came from outside Europe, more specifically Egypt, Indonesia and Australia. The evaluators included students enrolled at the RWTH Aachen University in various disciplines, Cairo University, TU Delft, and the Institute of Technology Bandung. The evaluators also came from different backgrounds. 13 Evaluators came from a Computer Science background and the rest from other majors (e.g. Electrical Engineering and Mechanical Engineering) (see Figure 9).

All evaluators have had prior experience in TEL. While only 8 of the evaluators are familiar with LMSs, 15 of them have had experience with Personalized Start Pages, especially iGoogle and MyYahoo!, and 14 admitted that they indulge regularly in blogging. Out of the 8 evaluators who were familiar with LMSs, 5 of them use the Lehr- und Lernportal (L2P) (L2P, 2008) at RWTH Aachen University and the rest use Blackboard and Moodle at the Cairo University eLearning Center (CUELC, 2008). We also found out that almost all evaluators who use LMSs also have prior knowledge of Personalized Start Pages. Another finding was that out of 14 evaluators who have their own blogs, only 3 make use of blogs to facilitate their learning.

- **Overall User Evaluation:** The overall system evaluation section includes 20 questions, which are a subset of the 50-question database of the Software Usability Measurement Inventory (SUMI) – a rigorously tested and proven method of measuring software quality from the end user's point of view (SUMI, 2008). The SUMI database embraces the user's opinion vis-à-vis the usability of the system, including measures such as learnability and understandability, the reliability of the system, such as fault tolerance and recoverability, the maintainability of the system, such as

Figure 8. Search in PLEF

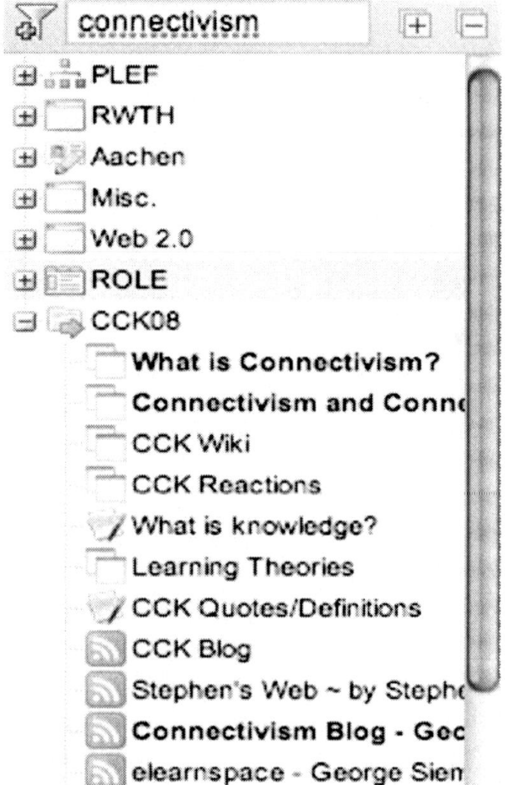

stability, the efficiency of the system such as time and resource behavior, and the functionality of the system, such as accuracy and suitability.

For the evaluation of the results of the SUMI questionnaire, the System Usability Scale (SUS) (Brooke, 1996), which is based on a 5-grade scale and yields a single number in the range from 0 to 100, was used.

Out of a total population of 23, only 22 evaluator feedback forms can be calculated since 1 evaluator did not answer this section. The final scores for the overall satisfaction of 22 evaluators of PLEF turned out to be in the range from 32.5 to 95 points. 5 of them are below 50 points, more precisely 32.5, 38.75, 45, 41.25 and 46.25. 12 of them are between 50 and 60 points. 2 of them are between 60 and 70 points. The other 3 are above 70 points, more precisely 65, 66.25 and 95 points respectively. This results in an average user satisfaction of 46.318 points out of 100 points, or approximately 46.32%.

From the results in this section, we derived three statements, which contributed the relatively low score achieved. These are "This system has helped me overcome any problems I have had in using it", "I prefer stick to other systems that I know best" and "I sometimes don't know what to do next with this system" and have values 33, 35 and 36, respectively. By dividing each of these values by the number of evaluators, we get 1.5, 1.59 and 1.63. This means that evaluator opinions for the first statement lie between "generally disagree" and "undecided", while for the second and third statements, the opinions lie between "generally agree" and "undecided".

This result shows that:

- PLEF still does not provide adequate error messages, (input) validations and error prevention mechanism to support learners.
- PLEF still needs improvements in terms of system learnability and understandability.

We also noticed that there are two statements which had the highest score, i.e., "The system has at some time stopped unexpectedly" and "If this system stops, it is not easy to restart/reload it". Respectively, these statements are given a total score 70 and 67, which means that most evaluators averagely chose between "generally disagree" and "strongly disagree". This shows that most of the evaluators were quite satisfied with PLEF in terms of system reliability, stability, and recoverability.

- **Functionality Questions:** The functionality questions attempted to gauge the evaluators' impression of the features provided by PLEF. These include authentication, social features, support for multi-views, search, and access-control.

Figure 9. Evaluator profiles

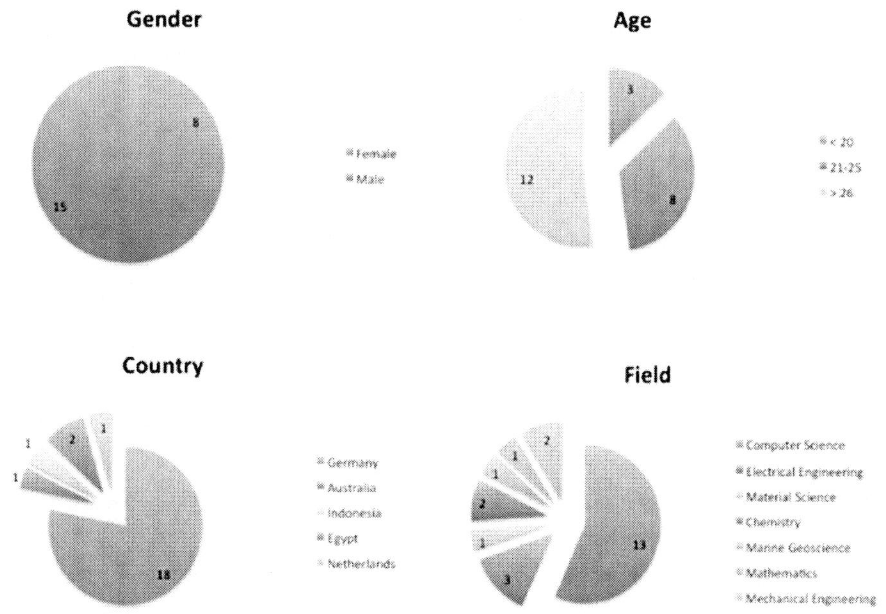

- **Authentication:** Out of 23, 16 evaluators reported that they encountered problems when logging into their PLEs. This was mainly due to their unfamiliarity with the OpenID authentication procedure.
- **Social Features:** The evaluators were asked if they encountered any problems while using the social features in PLEF. These currently include social tagging, commenting and sharing of PLE elements and pages. A majority of the evaluators found the social features in PLEF to be satisfactory indeed and did not report problems in using them (Figure 10). Almost all the evaluators recognized the importance of being able to tag elements in their PLEs, in order to classify, categorize, search and re-find their PLE elements at a later time.
- **Multi-views Support:** The next questions dealt with the evaluators' impression of the multi-views support in PLEF. Almost all the evaluators (22 out of 23) did not encounter problems while switching between the two different views currently implemented in PLEF, i.e. the page-view and the tag-view. There was a general agreement on the necessity of a tag-view in order to present and filter the amount of available PLE elements according to the current learning context.
- **Search:** The next questions attempted to gauge the evaluators' impression of the search feature in PLEF. A majority of the evaluators (20 out of 23) indicated that they did not face any problems, and found the use of full-text as well as tag-based search of PLE elements and pages to be very productive and a feature that made PLEF much more intuitive to use.
- **Access Control:** There was unanimous agreement amongst all evalu-

ators on the efficacy of this feature. Without exception all evaluators saw the benefit of such a solution where access control is defined at both PLE page and element levels. Almost all evaluators did not encounter any problems when granting access to their PLE pages and elements. Opinions, however, were divided on the sufficiency of this feature. 12 of the evaluators found the current granularity level of the access control (public vs. private) to be enough. However, 11 of the evaluators believed that it would be better if the PLEF adopted a more flexible level of access control granularity, such that the learner could determine who would have access to the PLE elements and pages.

- **Concluding Remarks from the Evaluators:** The evaluators were asked to summarize the efficacy of PLEF in its original intent of being used for learning in general, collaborative learning, as well as self-directed learning (Figure 11). One evaluator did not answer at all in this section. From the answers given in this section, we noted the following:
    - 14 out of 22 evaluators agreed that the PLEF has the potential to be used for learning purposes.
    - The 3 evaluators who answered this question with "no" are Chemistry and Mechanical Engineering students. And, 3 out of 5 evaluators who answered this question with "not sure" are not Computer Science students.
    - Only 2 out of 7 female evaluators (one female evaluator didn't answer at all in this section) could not see the potential of using PLEF in a learning context (i.e. answered with "no" or "not sure"). Both of them are Chemistry students.
    - 14 of the evaluators found that PLEF can support collaborative learning experiences. To note here that 3 of them, however, answered the first question with "no" or "not sure".
    - 13 of the evaluators found PLEF to be generally suitable for self-directed learning purposes. 11 of them also answered "yes" to the previous question, that is, 11 evaluators agreed that PLEF could support both collaborative learning and self-directed learning.
    - 6 out of 8 evaluators, who could not see the potential of PLEF to support collaborative learning (i.e. answered there with "no" or "not sure"), could not see its potential to support self-directed learning either.
    - 9 out of 22 evaluators answered all three questions with "yes". All of them are Computer Science students.
    - 5 evaluators (2 Mechanical Engineering, 1 Material Science, 1 Electrical Engineering, and 1 Chemistry students) answered all three questions in this section with "no" or "not sure". One question that can be raised here and needs to be further tested is whether students from different disciplines have different learning styles that impact their choice of the learning method.
    - We were not able to see any pattern concerning the impact of age and location variables on the evaluation results.

The evaluators were also asked to summarize their likes and dislikes about PLEF. Evaluators were nearly unanimous in their evaluation of PLEF as having the potential to create an environment customized to learners' needs. They were also satisfied with the fact that they could easily

Figure 10. Social features

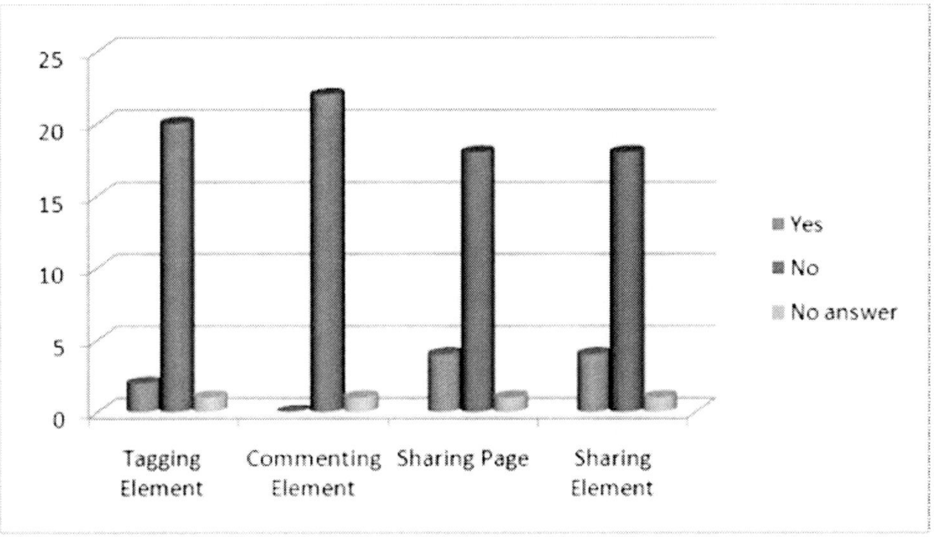

extend their environments with different elements, especially feeds and widgets. Several evaluators, however, point out that the user interface is not simple for a novice user and that more help messages and a manual should be provided, in order to guide the users in their interaction with the PLEF. Moreover, many evaluators stressed again that they were not familiar with the OpenID authentication procedure, and as a consequence faced some difficulties to login to the PLEF.

CONCLUSION AND FUTURE WORK

In this paper, we addressed how the growing complexity and constant change of knowledge, and the increasing need to bridge the worlds of lifelong, informal, personalized, and network learning, require a new approach to learning. We stressed that a radical revision of the traditional pedagogical principles and policies imposed by formal educational institutions is required to align with the needs and challenges of the new knowledge landscape. In the new knowledge intensive era, the one-size- fits-all, centralized, static, top-down, and knowledge-push models of traditional learning initiatives need to be replaced with a more personalized, social, open, dynamic, emergent, and knowledge-pull model for learning. We then discussed a new learning model characterized by the convergence of lifelong, informal, and personalized learning within a social context. This learning model is based on the concept of a Personal Learning Environment, which offers a learner-centric view of learning. A PLE-driven approach to learning gets beyond centralized learning management systems and supports a wide variety of learning experiences outside the institutional boundaries. A PLE suggests the freeform use of a set of lightweight and loosely coupled tools and services that belong to and are controlled by individual learners. Rather than being restricted to a limited set of services within a centralized institution-controlled system, the idea is to provide the learner with a plethora of different services and hand over control to her to select, use, and remix the services the way she deems fit. We presented the theoretical details of PLEF; a conceptual framework for mashup personal learning environments that can support learners in taking control over their learning experience by creating and managing their own

Figure 11. Concluding remarks

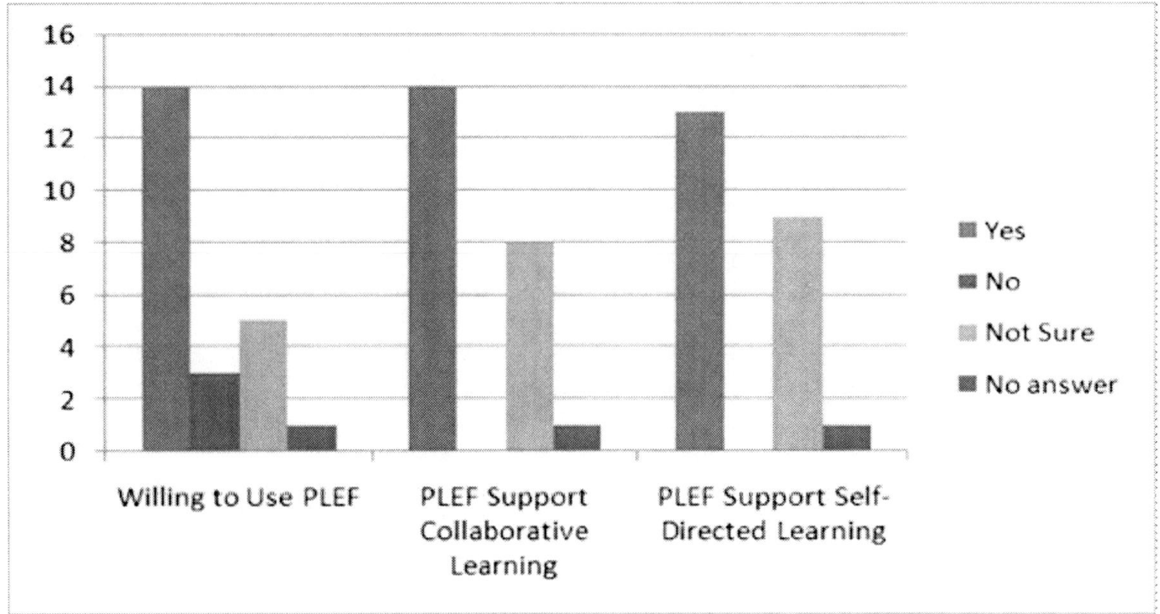

PLEs. At the heart of PLEF lie mashups that help learners take existing services coming from different sources and combine these to create new customized services. We then presented the requirements, design, and implementation details of a first prototype of PLEF, based on the concept of mashups by aggregation. Finally, we discussed the evaluation procedure that was adopted and the results of the aforementioned evaluation. A questionnaire was designed and a cross section of users was chosen to evaluate and provide their feedback on the framework. The feedbacks were sampled and graphs generated to give a clearer view of user's likes and dislikes with regard to PLEF. This feedback reflects the general level of satisfaction of the user community with the PLEF as providing the requisite solution for a mashup personal learning environment that can help learners reuse services coming from different sources and remix them within a personalized space.

There is, however, a couple of perspectives, in which PLEF could be further improved to meet the requirements of a personal learning environment framework, discussed previously. The first one is related to the usability and learnability of the currently developed framework. The second is associated with the potential technical enhancements of the framework. The third is concerned with the broadening of the functionality spectrum of the framework.

Regarding the usability of PLEF, an improvement is possible through providing more input validation and error prevention mechanisms as well as a thorough documentation of the framework.

Regarding the technical aspects of PLEF, it can be further improved to support more open standards, such as OAuth and OpenSocial and provide a public API that can be used by third-party services, platforms and devices.

Regarding the functionality spectrum of PLEF, future work will include an enhancement of PLEF to include mashups by integration. This can be achieved through an intelligent semantic mashup engine that enables learners to automatically mash-up JSON/REST Web services from a standard semantic description of them (e.g. SMD or SA-REST). Further improvement is also envisioned in the extendibility of the system with a social filtering engine that can tap the wisdom of crowds to help learners find quality in the Long Tail.

Future work will also include the evaluation of an enhanced prototype of PLEF in real learning settings. We plan to use PLEF in association with open courses provided at Cairo University eLearning Center and Open University Netherlands. To achieve this, we plan to further enhance PLEF with a widget, that, at the same time, can act as a dashboard for the learner in a self-directed learning setting, a monitoring tool for the teacher in a formal learning setting, and an activity tracking service for the researcher performing an experiment with PLEF. This widget would then enable us to track the usage of the PLEF by collecting important information, such as the number of pages and elements created by a learner, the number and type of services (e.g. widgets, feeds, media, REST Web services) plugged into the PLE; the number of comments and shares; and number of tags and elements tagged with the same tag. We also plan to evaluate PLEF from a cultural point of view. The main aim will be to study the impact of different cultures on the adoption of a self-directed learning approach.

REFERENCES

L2P. (2008). *Lehr- und Lernportal (L2P)*. Retrieved April 1, 2010, from http://www.cil.rwthaachen.de/L2P.htm

Anderson, C. (2006). *The long tail: Why the future of business is selling less of more*. Hyperion.

Anderson, T. (2006). *PLEs versus LMS: Are PLEs ready for prime time?* Retrieved April 1, 2010, from http://terrya.edublogs.org/2006/01/09/ples-versus-lmsare-ples-ready-for-prime-time/

Aspin, D. N., & Chapman, J. D. (2000). Lifelong learning: Concepts and conceptions. *International Journal of Lifelong Education, 19*(1), 2–19. doi:doi:10.1080/026013700293421

Attwell, G. (2007a). The personal learning environments - the future of elearning? *eLearning Papers, 2*(1). Retrieved April 1, 2010, from http://www.elearningeuropa.info/files/media/media11561.pdf

Attwell, G. (2007b). Personal learning environments for creating, consuming, remixing and sharing. In *Proceedings of the 2nd TENCompetence Open Workshop* (pp. 36-41). Bolton, UK: Institute of Educational Cybernetics.

Baumgartner, P., Hfele, H., & Maier-Hfele, K. (2004). *Content Management Systems in e-Education. Auswahl, Potenziale und Einsatzmglichkeiten*. Innsbruck-Wien, Germany: StudienVerlag.

Brooke, J. (1996). SUS: a "quick and dirty" usability scale. In Jordan, P. W., Thomas, B., Weerdmeester, B. A., & McClelland, A. L. (Eds.), *Usability Evaluation in Industry*. London: Taylor and Francis.

Brown, J. S., & Adler, R. P. (2008). Minds on fire: Open education, the long tail, and learning 2.0. *EDUCAUSE Review, 43*(1), 16–32.

Carmean, C., & Haefner, J. (2003). Next-generation course management systems. *EDUCAUSE Quarterly, 26*(1), 10–13.

Chatti, M. A., Jarke, M., & Frosch-Wilke, D. (2007). The future of elearning: A shift to knowledge networking and social software. *International Journal of Knowledge and Learning, 3*(4/5), 404–420. doi:doi:10.1504/IJKL.2007.016702

Cross, J. (2006). *Informal learning: rediscovering the natural pathways that inspire innovation and performance*. Pfeiffer.

CUELC. (2008). *Cairo University eLearning Center*. Retrieved April 1, 2010, from http://elearning.eng.cu.edu.eg

Downes, S. (2005). E-learning 2.0. *eLearn, 10*(1). Retrieved April 1, 2010, from http://elearnmag.org/subpage.cfm?section=articles&article=29-1

Downes, S. (2006). *Learning networks and connective knowledge*. Retrieved April 1, 2010, from http://it.coe.uga.edu/itforum/paper92/paper92.html

Eckstein, R., Loy, M., & Wood, D. (1998). *Java Swing*. Sebastopol, CA: O'Reilly Media.

Jafari, A., McGee, P., & Carmean, C. (2006). Managing courses, defining learning: What faculty, students, and administrators want. *EDUCAUSE Review*, *41*(4), 50–71.

Jennex, M., Olfman, L., Panthawi, P., & Park, Y. (1998). An organizational memory Information Systems success model: An extension of DeLone and McLean's I/S success model. In *Proceedings of the Thirty-First Annual Hawaii International Conference on System Sciences* (p. 157).

Klamma, R., Chatti, M. A., Duval, E., Hummel, H., Hvannberg, E. H., & Kravcik, M. (2007). Social software for life-long learning. *Journal of Educational Technology & Society*, *10*(3), 72–83.

Lave, J., & Wenger, E. (1991). *Situated learning: Legitimate peripheral participation*. New York: Cambridge University Press.

Lubensky, R. (2006). *The present and future of Personal Learning Environments (PLE)*. Retrieved April 1, 2010, from http://members.optusnet.com.au/rlubensky/2006/12/presentand-future-of-personal-learning.html

Nonaka, I., & Takeuchi, H. (1995). *The knowledge-creating company: How Japanese companies create the dynamics of innovation*. New York: Oxford University.

O'Reilly, T. (2007). What is Web 2.0: Design patterns and business models for the next generation of software. *International Journal of Digital Economics*, *65*, 17–37.

Polanyi, M. (1967). *The tacit dimension*. New York: Anchor Books.

SCORM. (2009). *The Sharable Content Object Reference Model (SCORM), Advanced Distributed Learning*. Retrieved April 1, 2010, from http://www.adlnet.org/Technologies/scorm/default.aspx

Siemens, G. (2004). *Learning management systems: The wrong place to start learning*. Retrieved April 1, 2010, from http://www.elearnspace.org/Articles/lms.htm

Siemens, G. (2006). *Knowing knowledge*. Retrieved April 1, 2010, from http://ltc.umanitoba.ca/KnowingKnowledge/index.php/Main_Page

SUMI. (2008). *SUMI-The de facto industry standard evaluation questionnaire for assessing quality of use of software by end users*. Retrieved April 1, 2010, from http://sumi.ucc.ie/

Surowiecki, J. (2004). *The wisdom of crowds: Why the many are smarter than the few and how collective wisdom shapes business, economies, societies, and nations*. New York: Doubleday.

Tobin, D. R. (2000). *All learning is self-directed: How organizations can support and encourage independent learning*. ASTD Press.

Van Assche, F., Duval, E., Massart, D., Olmedilla, D., Simon, B., & Sobernig, S. (2006). Spinning interoperable applications for teaching & learning using the simple query interface. *Journal of Educational Technology & Society*, *9*(2), 51–67.

Wenger, E. (1998). *Communities of practice: Learning, meaning, and identity*. Cambridge, UK: Cambridge University Press.

Wilson, S., Liber, O., Johnson, M., Beauvoir, P., Sharples, P., & Milligan, C. (2007). Personal learning environments: Challenging the dominant design of educational systems. *Journal of e-Learning and Knowledge Society*, *3*(2), 27-38.

This work was previously published in International Journal of Virtual and Personal Learning Environments, edited by Michael Thomas, Volume 1, Issue 4, pp. 66-85, copyright 2010 by IGI Publishing (an imprint of IGI Global).

Section 2
Design

Chapter 4
Designing Effective Spaces, Tasks and Metrics for Communication in Second Life Within the Context of Programming LEGO NXT Mindstorms™ Robots

Michael Vallance
Future University Hakodate, Japan

Stewart Martin
Teesside University, UK

Charles Wiz
Yokohama National University, Japan

Paul van Schaik
Teesside University, UK

ABSTRACT

Science education is concerned with the meaningful pursuit of comprehension, knowledge and understanding of scientific concepts and processes. In Vygotskian social constructivist learning, personal interpretation, decision-making and community cooperation fosters long-term understanding and transference of learned concepts. The construction of knowledge requires learners to be actively involved in the process of learning. For effective science learning to take place an instructor's pedagogical approach must be anchored in meaningful contexts so that students have actual opportunities to experience science. This paper presents the early stages of a research project that attempts to assess and define effective measurements for evaluating strategies for communicating science by using LEGO robots and Mindstorms™ RCX controllers that are collaboratively constructed and programmed by students using virtual technologies while physically situated in different locations.

DOI: 10.4018/978-1-4666-1770-4.ch004

INTRODUCTION

Science education is concerned with the meaningful pursuit of comprehension, knowledge and understanding of scientific concepts and processes. The effective science educator's pedagogical approaches are anchored in meaningful contexts so that students 'experience' science and develop their 'craft' (Thornburg, 2002). Such 'experiential learning' provides learners with opportunities to engage with problems that require the retrieval of prior knowledge, offer multiple perspectives of problems and solutions, and facilitate a challenging process which leads to an achievable outcome. Learning does not occur in isolation but involves communication, cooperation and collaboration with fellow learners and experts (Kolb, 1984). In this Vygotskian social constructivist learning perspective, personal interpretation, decision-making and community cooperation fosters long-term understanding and transference of learned concepts. The construction of knowledge requires learners (of science or other subjects) to be actively involved in shaping the learning process.

Research in the informed use of technology for educational purposes highlights the need to go beyond replication of traditional, didactic practices to an appropriation of digital communication (Warschauer, 1999) facilitated by a constructivist pedagogy (Jonassen & Land, 2000) to support purposeful tasks (Martin & Vallance, 2008). The convergence of instructivism, constructionism, social and collaborative learning towards a 'Conversational Framework' (Laurillard, 2002) provides opportunities for learners to take, "a more active role in learning and for tutors to support learning activities in multimodal ways" (deFreitas & Griffiths, 2008, p. 17). Of course, all of this is not a revelation. Piaget, Dewey and Bruner all advocated the learner being an active participant in the learning process. In a study of the future of work, Thornburg (2002) concluded that today's Digital Age learners will need to become active learners, effective collaborators who seek and contribute knowledge, and proficient users of online collaboration tools.

One class of collaborative tools gaining traction in Higher Education is virtual worlds. Virtual worlds are persistent computer-simulated environments that allow for three-dimensional representations of individuals and objects that can be manipulated and modified. Usually, individuals are represented through avatars that have varying degrees of similarity to human appearance. Some virtual worlds such as Second Life allow for extensive modification of avatars and enable users to build a wide variety of virtual objects. Avatars can walk, fly, sit down, dance, teleport throughout the virtual world and interact with those of other human participants. Users can utilize their avatars to communicate with other avatars using text, voice and gesture. Virtual worlds are increasingly evident in Higher Education courses, and yet the enthusiastic adoption and economic investment in virtual worlds such as Second Life often results in a mirror world; a world that mimics our physical state. For instance, many universities and other educational institutions are establishing a presence in Second Life and have begun to conduct classes and provide other services for students. However, they attempt to replicate the real world through the virtual building of traditional classrooms and activities that do not utilize the uniqueness of the virtual space and its tools. Innovative virtual collaboration requires a uniqueness of contribution by participants (personally or anonymously), synchronously and/or asynchronously (whichever is the most comfortable for the user) with a democratization of the process leading to a sum product greater than the individual contributions (Vallance & Wiz, 2007). This represents a move from the commonly seen replication of existing practice towards the exploitation of the unique pedagogical affordances offered by emerging technologies – a move from first to second order change (Cuban, 1992).

However, pragmatically and pedagogically, it would be a mistake for practitioners using technology to only consider educational opportunities in virtual spaces. For instance, working with the internet (e.g. broadcast World Wide Web, social networking) and virtual spaces (e.g. interactive Second Life) can represent an amalgamation of real world activities and virtual world activities from which the combined way of working will result in the development of a personal and group artifact that can be imported, modified and exported (e.g. printed out or posted to a Website). Such multiple media artifacts (documents, spreadsheets, slide-shows, images, movies) can therefore maintain an independent existence in the virtual space thereby allowing for continued modification at any time (synchronously or asynchronously). Moreover, the artifact may not necessarily reside solely in the virtual space but can be additionally downloaded to a computer's hard drive as a virtual collaborative artifact for presentation or archival purposes (Vallance & Wiz, 2007).

In science education researchers have shown interest in using virtual worlds as they provide a number of benefits: making science relevant to the learner; incorporating current research into the curriculum; providing a means to present opportunities to engage students in authentic scientific inquiry; and giving learners real examples of career possibilities in science (Niemitz et al., 2008). However, de Freitas (2008) in her detailed study of serious virtual worlds for the UK Joint Information Systems Committee (JISC) confirmed the need for, "developing better metrics for evaluating virtual world learning experiences" and also "developing better techniques for creating virtual learning experiences (e.g. frameworks, approaches and models)" (p.11). Perhaps understanding virtual worlds is especially necessary because, "we increasingly live in a world in which opting out of technology systems is more and more difficult and yet participation within those systems pushes us to accept structures we might oppose" (Taylor, 2006, p. 135).

The challenge proffered by de Freitas and others is for educational researchers to develop valid, reliable and transferable metrics for assessing the teaching and learning effectiveness of virtual worlds. The metrics need to relate to student engagement in science-based, collaborative tasks that have quantitatively and qualitatively measured outcomes. In the design and implementation of the constructivist learning experiences, tasks should encourage students to take responsibility for their own learning, including what and how they learn, provide them with opportunities to find solutions and meaning using multiple perspectives, create self awareness of their learning process, make learning relevant and authentic, make learning a collaborative and interactive social experience, and use multiple modes of representation and rich media (Honebein, 1996). In science education, programming a robot to undertake discrete physical movements provides a clear representation of success. LEGO Mindstorms, for instance, enable students to build a robot, input instructions via the NXT Mindstorms software, program the robot to follow the instructions, and subsequently view the physical movements of the programmed robot. In a collaborative environment the robot design and Mindstorms program can then be communicated and taught to another student remotely located. The degree of success of the transfer of process and information can be measured by the physical movements of the 'taught' robot. Reviewing the research on teaching robotics Barker and Ansorge (2007) found that: 1) it is an effective tool for teaching science, engineering, and technology; 2) students who have engineered and programmed robots are exposed to other disciplines that are important for robotics, science and engineering; 3) there is exposure to real world conditions with multiple possible solutions; 4) effective teamwork is a significant outcome; and 5) that female students respond positively to working with robots. Combining the teaching of robotics with collaborative technologies and task-based design has potential for increasing university students' science and technological skills. However, this potential can only be realized if clear objectives are established and if educators know how to understand and measure the most effective ways to do this. Researching effective quantitative metrics to evaluate strategies for teaching robotics to university students using collaborative technologies provides a needed foundation for future research and academic staff development. One outcome of this research is designed to provide a valid, reliable and viable framework for assessing and evaluating outcomes in the fields of science education, robotics, programming, virtual and augmented reality environments, and collaborative technologies. Working in a virtual world can also introduce unforeseen affective factors so using digital capture and facilitating follow up reflection activities by students may reveal new information about the process and product of science related tasks conducted in a virtual world.

To summarize, the research project discussed here has been designed to asses and define effective measurements for evaluating strategies for teaching programming using robots (with reflective and touch sensors, independently driven wheels and a LEGO Mindstorms RCX controller) collaboratively constructed and programmed by students using virtual technologies while physically situated in different locations. The research compares different collaborative processes and the effectiveness of each of these in producing specific learning outcomes of remotely located science students who are using collaborative technologies to program robots to follow basic instructions. It is further posited that the research can provide a framework that can be developed for successful implementation of collaborative tasks undertaken in emerging virtual worlds.

METHODOLOGY

Standardized metrics for measuring the effectiveness of autonomous robots is not universally recognized by those in the field of robotics. An expert in neural networked robotics was interviewed to seek clarification about robot metrics. Our presumption was that engineers working in this field have access to established algorithms and metrics which enable the superiority of one program over other competing designs to be established and that agreed standards exist against which these can be benchmarked. The analogy might be with motor transport, where different engineering solutions can be compared and evaluated for fuel consumption, braking distance, road holding, acceleration or load-carrying. It was explained that this was not the situation in robotics, because each project tended to be built for a specific purpose. Different purposes created different solutions and approaches and because there is no common agreement about the kinds of desirable features of robotic systems in general, unlike with cars or lorries, no common metrics exist to allow engineers to compare different solutions in terms of effectiveness, appropriateness or efficiency. This is not dissimilar to the situation found in the use of technologies to support learning. There are many and sometimes competing desired outcomes for education: in our students we seek subject mastery and recall but also value higher order thinking and reflective and collaborative learning. The means to produce and measure the outputs of one are not necessarily useful for the others. Given this predicament the challenge for educators is to establish the conditions and circumstances that make best use of new technologies.

Our adopted methodology was developed with consideration of Olsen and Goodrich's (2003) quantitative instrument and Martin and Vallance's (2008) qualitative instrument. The participants programmed robots to navigate courses designed by others, and subsequently modified the program to improve navigation on successive attempts. The metrics proposed for assessing the experiment were Task Effectiveness (TE), Interaction Effort (IE), frequency of course navigation, and the time requirement for successful course completion. Communication between groups was carried out using synchronous interactive virtual technologies and all communication was digitally captured, transcribed and analyzed using the approach described in Vallance (2007). The quantitative data set (i.e. Task Effectiveness (TE) - the number of commands successfully programmed into the robot, and Interaction Effort (IE) – the amount of time required to interact with the robot (Olsen & Goodrich, 2003)) were merged with personalized 'meaning' of data collected via a qualitative data set; i.e. the follow up interviews and digital capture of participants on task. Combining both quantitative and qualitative data sets reduces bias (Brown, 1992). Tasks which employ the virtual world condition need to be considered in terms of whether they will facilitate a meaningful process for producing a challenging but achievable outcome. Prior to implementing the tasks, communication and robot programming, a virtual learning space was designed using a futures studies method. The futures studies method supports the development of possible, probable and preferable futures through the use of scenarios. This involves an analysis, a critique and a panoramic view of present designs in order to facilitate a discussion and an ownership of the change process (Groff & Smoker, 1997).

Finally, it is recognized that as an intervention this research may be, "fleeting and fragile, not readily transportable to settings outside the innovator's control" (Brown, 1992, p. 171). However, the research is designed to observe the iterative process of successful, science related tasks for learning in a virtual world which will in turn support the development of transferable metrics and a framework for meaningful education with tangible, quantifiably measured outcomes.

IMPLEMENTATION

This section summarizes six tasks conducted in a virtual world by students in Japan whilst physically distant at the time of implementation. The tasks discussed in this paper were iteratively developed in two phases. Phase 1 consisted of two tasks with the aim of designing and building a learning space within Second Life. Phase 2 consisted of four tasks with the aim of communicating a LEGO NXT Mindstorms program within the learning space. The two participants involved in this research project had no prior experience of virtual worlds or LEGO NXT Mindstorms programming. The remit for Taro (the name of student 1; avatar name - Hotaru Kurmin) was to design a learning space within leased land in Second Life. The remit for Toshi (student 2; avatar name - Soka Naidoo) was to teach LEGO NXT Mindstorms programming by communicating in the designed Second Life learning space. Phase 3 of the research, not discussed in this paper, will consist of further tasks of increasing navigational complexity for robot transit and Mindstorms programming conducted by students from Japan and the UK.

To begin the design process, a class of design students taught by one of the researchers were asked to digitally create a classroom of the future that could then be built within a virtual world. To implement this process a 'futures studies' method (Groff & Smoker, 1997) was employed. In education contexts, futures studies is systematic learning to create, process and communicate new insights. Cognitive theories of learning can be broadly categorized using a dichotomy of convergent and divergent thinking. Convergent thinking involves bringing material from a variety of sources to produce solutions using description, observation, prioritization and deduction (a process is most easily recognized in fields such as mathematics and science). Divergent thinking is exemplified by the creative elaboration of ideas prompted by a stimulus (Iversen, n.d). Educational contexts often feature learning within the continuum from convergent to divergent thinking. In recognition of this continuum, futures studies employs a number of techniques such as triangulation (push-pull-weight) and scenarios in order to succinctly contextualize, illustrate and communicate new designs. Iversen posits that the use of scenarios allows for a mix of convergent and divergent thinking thereby facilitating the rich interpretations of scenarios as they develop. Although beyond the scope of this paper it is important to indicate the use of these systematic processes that were involved in all stages of this research project. Towards the end of the design course all futures scenarios were presented to Taro (student 1) who then selected a 'classroom of the future' design to build in Second Life.

Meanwhile, Toshi (student 2) constructed and duplicated a LEGO robot. One was given to Taro who had to program the robot to follow a pre-determined circuit as instructed by Toshi through synchronous communication in Second Life. The LEGO related tasks further enabled Taro to modify the design of the learning space resulting in the desired tools (i.e. media viewer, presenter, and options wall) to support text and voice communication, plus moveable and copiable NXT program blocks within the Second Life learning space (see Figures 1 to 3).

The designed Second Life learning space consisted of two levels with transparent walls. The lower level space was used as a sandbox (the term used in Second Life for avatars to learn how to construct and modify objects). A media viewer or presenter with images previously uploaded was also available for avatars to use. The media presenter is essentially a presentation screen connected to a virtual laptop. Pressing the keyboard on the laptop changes the image on the presenter. Avatars can upload images from their own inventory. The second level provided tools for the LEGO experiments. Again, a media presenter was available. Next to the media presenter was a video streaming screen. This enabled live video to be streamed from a student's physical working area (via a video camera connected to a networked computer). The screen also displayed fixed images in a similar way to the aforementioned presenter. On the sides (named Options walls by the students) of the second level were images of the NXT configuration panels (see Figure 1). These were displayed so that students could point and focus on specific configurations that needed to be inputted in order to replicate the operation of the assembled robots. On the floor were the customizable objects representing the NXT software programming blocks. During the implementation the avatars would meet on the second level and together reconstruct their NXT program. Figure 3 illustrates a NXT program circuit being constructed. The avatars used both voice and text

Figure 1. LEGO NXT Mindstorms in Second Life

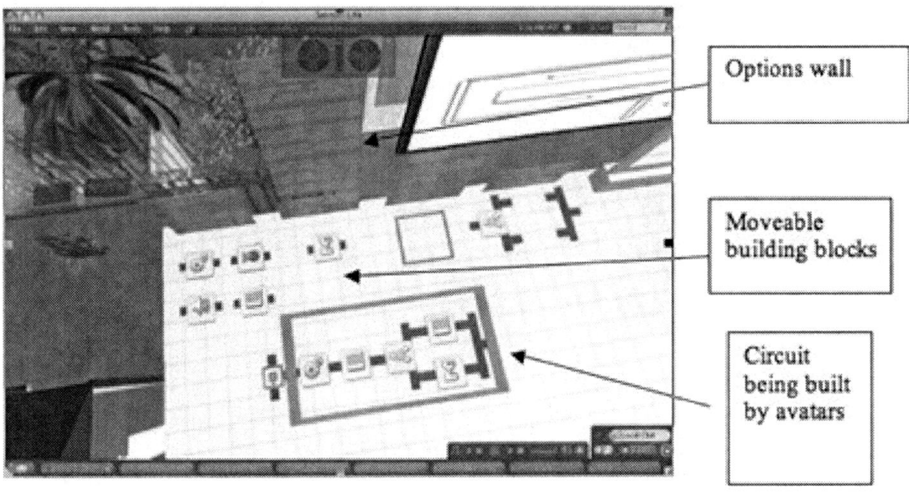

Figure 2. Avatars collaborating in Second Life

to communicate, made reference to the Options wall by pointing and zooming in to specific configuration panels, constructed new NXT objects (using the 'Shift and drag' computer operation), and moved the NXT objects (see Figures 2 and 3) to construct the program required to upload to the LEGO robot (see Figure 4).

Once the learning space had been built, six tasks were implemented. Each task required avatars to communicate and collaborate to create a successful outcome. The initial intention was for students to become active and engaged in the experience of working and learning within the virtual world. The initial tasks aimed to familiar-

Figure 3. Manipulating LEGO NXT Mindstorms blocks in Second Life

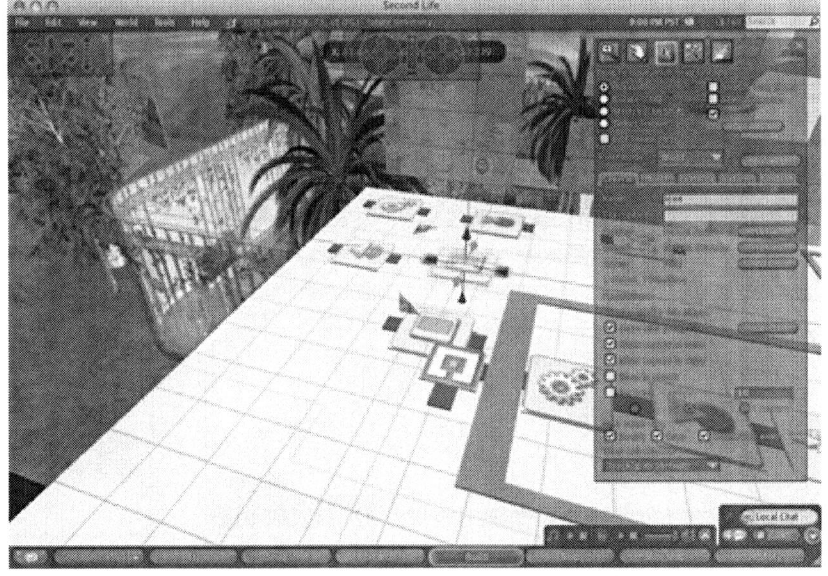

Figure 4. LEGO NXT Mindstorms interface

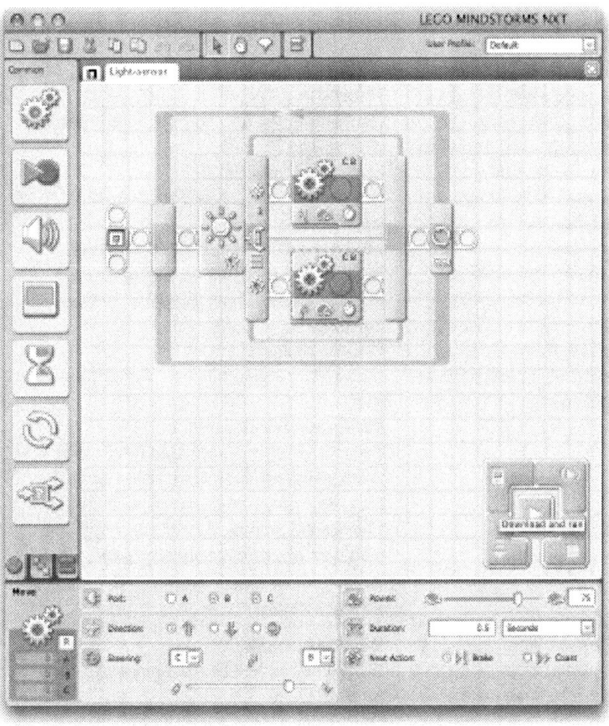

ize students with the communication and navigation tools within Second Life (see Table 1).

In tasks 3 to 6 the use of NXT program blocks as manipulative, interactive images was included on the horizontal floor of the learning space while NXT block variables were represented as vertical images. Students were remotely located and used avatars in Second Life for communication. The activities were conducted using voice and text. Student A (avatar: Soka Naidoo) re-arranged the NXT blocks in Second Life (see Figure 2) to replicate the Mindstorms program (see Figure 4). Student B (avatar: Hotaru Kurmin) simultaneously programmed NXT as instructed. He later uploaded the resultant program to the LEGO robot via a physical USB cable and tested the robot on a classroom floor. The students also printed the interface images so that they could record their information. The students reported that they felt more comfortable when blending familiar analog tools with the new digital collaboration. All the images of the Mindstorms interface and target circuit were uploaded and viewable on a screen within the Second Life learning space (see Figure 1). Both students could switch images on the viewable screen at any time, if desired. The communication was thus augmented by the synchronous display of the images in the virtual space. The synchronous, multimodal communication provides an advantage over asynchronous forms of digital communication. For instance, in tasks 5 and 6 the NXT building blocks were moved around forming the program that had to be replicated in the actual NXT software. This presented a visual image that could be altered in real time through negotiation between the two avatars. Finally, Soka Naidoo's and Hotaru Kurmin's robots were then operated and evaluated for comparison. For ease of checking the Task Effectiveness (TE) and Interaction Effort (IE), the students were located together in real life. Moreover, all actions, text and voice data

Table 1. Initial task reflections by participants

Task number	Task	Reflection (+/-)	Implementation for subsequent task
1	The students were provided with two pictures of a town centre. However, picture B contained missing information. The purpose was to find the location of a number of buildings such as the law courts, hospital, post office, etc. The students were then provided with print outs of two spreadsheets containing prices of hardware components. The purpose was to share information and determine the most economical shop at which to purchase particular components	**What was difficult?** Confirming the task was difficult because of English. Only text chat used. Did not look at each avatar so did not know other's actions. I did not check the text while chatting. We did not know that we had different information. I did not check or confirm the task. **What was easy?** Using SL is enjoyable, visual, comfortable. **Moderator's comment.** Two activities in 30 minutes were too intense. Although basic gap filling activities, they were quite tough for the students. The second activity flowed smoothly and would be a good introductory activity for those students being familiarized with, and communicating in, SL.	**What would you like to do next time?** Use Japanese. Use pictures.
2	Two images of a town were uploaded to the SL space presenter and viewable on the big screen. The students had to determine 10 differences between the 2 images.	**What was difficult?** We did not look at the two pictures simultaneously. One avatar did not teleport immediately so we did not know what was happening (technical problem in SL). Took a long time. English text. **What was easy?** We used picture screen. Text chat was easier. Lots of checking in text chat. All sentences were short. **Moderator's comment.** Students were remotely located so used avatars for communication. They had to use text only. Language was English only. The two images were viewable on the SL presenter. Both students could switch images at any time, if desired.	**What would you like to do next time?** Japanese. Want two projector/image screens on same level (not two levels and fly). Prior check of SL connection and bandwidth.

were digitally captured. The voice data was transcribed and analyzed using language function codes in TAMS analyzer (see Results section). Table 2 highlights the reflections made by the students in follow up interviews.

To summarize, in the development of tasks and metrics for communication in newly conceptualized and designed virtual spaces, we have identified a number of characteristics which contributed to the students' successes in completing synchronous tasks involving the programming of LEGO robots:

- The use of voice for interaction, use of text for confirmation;
- Use of arrow and zoom function in Second Life to focus upon details within images;
- Use of two presenters for displaying images;
- Use of customizable and moveable blocks;

Table 2. Task reflections

	Task	Reflection (+/-)	Implementation for subsequent task
3	Two images of the LEGO NXT Mindstorms software were uploaded to the SL space presenter. Student A had to teach student B.	**What was difficult?** Used text took a long time. Some information was misunderstood because the expert explained the incorrect use of interface (it should have been What is it called? but was taught as What does it do?). Did not know what the student was doing. **What was easy?** Japanese. We understood difficult contents because used Japanese text. Felt natural. Printout plus SL use for activity. One avatar was the expert. So felt easy. Student looked at the pictures in the presenter. **Moderator's comment.** Students covered most of my observations. I wish they used the presenter more effectively though. In this task it became evident that having an avatar as an expert 'felt easy' (see students' comment above) despite the unusual (for Japanese students) roles adopted (i.e. one expert, one non-expert). Jumping into these roles without prior formalities of status acknowledgment is culturally difficult for the Japanese students. This was confirmed in a much later follow up interview when one student remarked that when talking to a teacher he would feel tense and this was felt also in Second Life.	**What would you like to do next time?** Expert student must confirm or check understanding. Use voice.
4	Two new images of the LEGO NXT Mindstorms software were uploaded to the SL space presenter. Student A had to teach student B.	**What was difficult?** Voice level up and down so difficult to listen. Voice was fast but had to write on printout when expert was talking. Technical issue – surrounding noise heard by other avatars. Recommend using headphones and microphones. No voice chat log so cannot see previous communication (but can in text chat). **What was easy?** Voice is better than text. Easy to ask questions. Very quick – 10 to 15 mins. Efficient use of time unlike text which takes too long. **Moderator's comment.** I felt they did not use the function of the presenter (i.e. switching images) which would have been useful. Students used text communication to structure difficult interactions (e.g. they used text for confirming and providing NXT configuration details) but preferred voice communication for most interactions as it was faster and felt natural.	**What would you like to do next time?** Student must ask to wait. Expert must check understanding by using text chat – not voice.
5	Images of the LEGO NXT Mindstorms software were previously uploaded to the SL space presenter and Options wall. Student A had to teach student B to program the robot to follow specific instructions. No specific circuit was required so no circuit image uploaded. This open-ended task may be construed as increasing the cognitive load required to conduct the task. However, it was felt that student B needed to become more familiar with the NXT objects.	**What was difficult?** Voice was unclear today so had to revert to text. **What was easy?** Japanese usage. Previous familiarity with NXT interface (Activities 3 and 4) essential. **Moderator's comment.** The activity lasted 20 minutes and went smoothly. The communication process this time was much more effective (see Table 3 for an analysis). The two robots were identically programmed successfully. The implementation of the innovation to create three dimensional representations of the NXT objects (as opposed to the two dimensional view of the NXT software) in SL was undertaken. The 3D representation of NXT software objects allowed the users to physically move the objects around and create the program which was then replicated quickly into the actual NXT software.	**What would you like to do next time?** Create NXT software objects as 3D objects in SL.

continued on following page

Table 2. Continued

	Task	Reflection (+/-)	Implementation for subsequent task
6	Student A (avatar: Soka Naidoo) to teach student B (avatar: Hotaru Kurmin) how to program the LEGO NXT Mindstorms software so that the robot would traverse a particular circuit: forward/ stop/turn 90 degrees left/forward/ stop/turn 90 degrees left/forward/ stop/turn 90 degrees left/forward/ stop. Return to original position.	**What was difficult?** Nothing in particular today. Maybe the final USB connection to the physical robot as it failed first time but tried again and succeeded. **What was easy?** Japanese usage. Previous familiarity with NXT interface. The building blocks helped very much. **Moderator's comment.** The activity lasted 20 minutes and was successfully completed. NXT building blocks were moved around forming the program that had to be replicated in the actual NXT software. Program 'building blocks' were manipulated. On the walls were the various options for each block. The blocks were moved by both avatars. The options were communicated by voice and text. A thick blue arrow allowed avatars to point for physical direction and focus. A picture of the robot was also uploaded so that ports could be identified (this was for the USB connector).	**What would you like to do next time?** Teacher (Soka Naidoo) did most of the actual building. Need to allow student (Hotaru) to move building blocks too. Add more pictures to image presenter **during** the programming process. This will be more applicable as the program becomes more sophisticated.

- The need for structured exchanges, and promotion of confirmatory exchanges;
- Blend familiarity such as use of print-based materials.

RESULTS AND DISCUSSION

The remaining section of this paper will interpret the process of designing effective spaces, tasks and metrics for communication in Second Life within the context of programming LEGO robots using NXT Mindstorms software. First, an explanation of the tasks' processes and observations will be offered. Then an analysis of the communication involved in the tasks' discourse will be summarized. This analysis will then be coupled with an informed, initial proposal for effective metrics when conducting educational tasks in virtual worlds such as Second Life.

The design of the virtual space in Second Life followed a prescribed form that, we argue, provides credibility and functionality over commercial designs that often emphasize aesthetics. This was important as it provided ownership of the space to the participants. The next step involved the implementation of tasks developed iteratively (six in total at this stage of the research). The aim of each task was to communicate the programming of a LEGO robot. The quantitative measure of amount of success was Task Effectiveness (TE) - the number of commands successfully programmed into the robot, and Interaction Effort (IE) – the amount of time required to interact with the robot. Upon reflection, the tasks at this stage of the research were quite straightforward; possibly less challenging than anticipated but certainly with achievable outcomes. Given the innovative application of such educational practices, this cautious approach resulted in rich qualitative data. All multiple media actions and communication (text and voice) were digitally captured and after transcribing the communications, the text was tagged for communicative functions using TAMS Analyzer. The functions were: independently providing information (22%); asking questions (21%); confirming information previously provided (18%); answering a question with an affirmative statement (15%); expressing an observation (8%); making a suggestion (4%); giving a direct instruction (3%); praising (3%); making a request (2%); answering a question with a negative statement (1%); apologizing (1%); greeting (1%).

The complexity of the linguistic code was quite low although the interpretive density (i.e. the complexity of the operations which need to be carried out (Candlin, 1987) may be considered high, as illustrated in Table 3.

As the students progressed through the tasks there was a familiarity and continuity of the process as the learners related more to the task. Such cognitive familiarity reduces communicative stress and increases cognitive processing (Skehan, 1998) evidenced by better organization of the information being communicated, a clarity of information through question and confirmation discourse, a greater amount of information being communicated in later tasks, and the type of information being more specific, concrete and contextualized to the task objectives (see Table 4).

There is also evidence of a change of the Japanese students' construction process in considering how they are learning in the virtual world. This is revealed in a post-task reflection interview with the participants:

Toshi could know through his Graduate Study that before starting this project he just learned by doing assigned work and not seriously think about the way of learning. But he found he had to do everything by himself and think about a 'way' of learning at each step. He had not been aware of this kind of learning before. So there are many ways to learn. He realized the traditional way of learning is just one way of learning. Note that this is a translated report of Toshi's Japanese comments.

There is further evidence of change as students reflected on their prior experiences as 'learning by body' whereas being involved in the research introduced these students to the concept of 'learning by theory'.

Participating in the Second Life research the students commented that experiential learning was difficult and required more time than anticipated. The students had also never experienced this approach to learning where they were expected to reflect upon each of their actions. Kendo fencing was used as a Japanese analogy. In practicing kendo, students 'do' many times (repetition and practice) and this would be considered 'learning by body'. In addition, prior to the samurai age, Japanese scholars learned classical Chinese theory of ethics or politics 'by memory'. Therefore, traditionally in Japan, learning has been 'learning by body' and 'learning by memory'. Learning by theory is considered relatively new to Japanese society. However, the students stated that they were positive about this 'new way of learning' and that it became easier to learn throughout the duration of the research. Note that this is a translated report of a science academic and Taro's Japanese comments.

This is the first stage of a longer research project involving international collaboration and communication to develop much-needed metrics for informed, meaningful and effective educational practices within virtual worlds. Designing worthwhile tasks that engage students and support learning through inductive and deductive reasoning is challenging enough. When immersed in virtual worlds good task design is essential if students are to meet the intended aim. Tasks are primarily constructed to facilitate a challenging and meaningful process which draws upon students' prior knowledge and transference to new contexts with the intention that these will ultimately lead to achievable outcomes. The iterative task design and implementation employed here draws upon the work of Vygotsky (1986) and Kolb (1984). The results reveal that successful tasks must encourage students to communicate using prominent tools of the environment that are there to use.

The development of these metrics will therefore enable the identification and quantification

Table 3. Interpretive density

Task	Communication	Operation being undertaken
3	[19:07] SoKa Naidoo: 8番は、「スイッチ」を意味します。No. 8 means “switch”. [19:07] SoKa Naidoo: 分岐の動作を行えます。It enables you to activate branching behavior. [19:08] Hotaru Kurmin: 例えばどのような分岐があるのですか? Could you give me examples of the types of branching? [19:08] SoKa Naidoo: 光センサーを用いて、明るさで条件を付けて分岐出来ます。By using the light sensor, setting conditions on brightness, you can branch. [19:09] SoKa Naidoo: 他にも色んなセンサーでも行えます。In addition to that, branching can be done by various sensors, too. [19:10] Hotaru Kurmin: 光センサーは暗さ明るさの加減で分岐するのですか?Does the light sensor branch depending on light intensity? [19:10] SoKa Naidoo: そうです。具体的な数値を入力して条件を付けます。That’s right. You need to attach conditions to it by entering concrete numbers. [19:11] Hotaru Kurmin: わかりました。I understand.	At this stage of task 3 avatar Soka Naidoo is explaining the basic functions of the light sensor in the NXT program.
4	[00:02:15] SoKa Naidoo: 2番いってよろしいですか。Can I start talking about No.2 now? Hotaru Kurmin: はい、お願いします。 Yes, please. SoKa Naidoo: はい、次に2番は、場合分けでセンサーを OK. The No.2 button [00:02:30] SoKa Naidoo: 選んだので、制御に使うセンサーを、決めるボタンです。[cont’] decides which sensor needs to be used for control, since the sensor is selected based on the situation. Hotaru Kurmin: 場合分けで、セン、セン、センサーを選、選んだので Did you just say “since the sensor is selected based on the situation”? [00:02:45] SoKa Naidoo: はい。Yes, I did. Hotaru Kurmin: んと、その制御を決める Um, I am not so clear on the function of the button to decide the control. SoKa Naidoo: はい、つまり、あの、制御を、制御に使うセンサーを決めるボタンです。 Yes, I mean, you use this button which is applied to fix the sensors to control the controls. Hotaru Kurmin: あ、なるほど。I see. [00:03:00]Hotaru Kurmin: 例えば、あの、光センサーだとかタッチセンサーみたいなことですね。For instance, it is similar to optical sensors or touch sensors, isn’t it? SoKa Naidoo: はい、そうです。That’s right. SoKa Naidoo: え、次よろしいですか。Shall we move on to the next? Hotaru Kurmin: わかりました。Of course.	At this stage of task 4 avatar Hotaru Kurmin is checking his understanding of the functions of the light sensor as he knows he will need this information for programming the robot later.
5	[21:09] SoKa Naidoo: 緑の歯車のアイコンをドラッグしてください。Could you drag the green gear wheel shaped icon? [21:10] Hotaru Kurmin: [21:10] Dafydd Beresford: i am observing [21:10] SoKa Naidoo: 持続時間を4回転にします。You have to make the “persistence time” [last] for 4 revolutions. [21:11] Hotaru Kurmin: しました I did. [21:11] Hotaru Kurmin: 単位はなにでしょうか? What is the unit? [21:12] SoKa Naidoo: 文字は全て英語になってますか Are all the characters written in English? [21:12] Hotaru Kurmin: 現在はrotationsになっています Currently, it is the “rotations”. [21:12] Hotaru Kurmin: はい Over to you. [21:13] Hotaru Kurmin: degreesです It is the “degrees”. [21:15] Hotaru Kurmin: 一番最初のrotationsですね It is the first “rotations”, isn’t it? [21:15] SoKa Naidoo: はい。Yes, that’s right. [21:15] SoKa Naidoo: 次に Next...	At this stage of task 5 avatar Hotaru Kurmin is fine tuning one of the program blocks. He is following avatar Soka Naidoo’s directions being displayed in the Second Life learning space.

continued on following page

of learning activities, educational outcomes and pedagogical practice which replicates but does not develop existing practice even when this may initially be obscured within a visually rich and unfamiliar interactive virtual environment. Being able to make these distinctions clearly will be important in using these metrics to design tasks within immersive virtual spaces which do create effective new relationships between learner and teacher to facilitate second order change (Cuban, 1992).

Table 3. Continued

Task	Communication	Operation being undertaken
6	Soka Naidoo:で、次に..Next... [00:01:45] Soka Naidoo:左に曲がります。You have to turn left. Hotaru Kurmin:はい。 OK. Soka Naidoo:で、それはこの半分くらいです。And, it is half the size as the last time. Hotaru Kurmin:はい、は、半分と言いますと?What do you mean by half the size? Soka Naidoo:その、1.5センチくらいでいいです...I mean the distance to proceed..... [00:02:00] Soka Naidoo:その進む距離は。[cont'] is about 1.5cm. Hotaru Kurmin:はい、わかりました。I see. Soka Naidoo:で、次にまた左に曲がります。Then, you need to turn left again. Hotaru Kurmin:はい。 OK. Soka Naidoo:で、次はさっき最初に書いたのと同じ長さです。3センチくらいです。This time, the length is as same as the first time. It's about 3 cm. [00:02:15] Hotaru Kurmin:はい。OK. Soka Naidoo:で、ここから左に曲がります。Now, can you turn left from this point? Hotaru Kurmin:はい。OK. Soka Naidoo:で、最初の位置に戻った感じですか?Have you reverted to the position where you had started? [00:02:30] Hotaru Kurmin:あ、はい。最初の位置に戻るように矢印を書けばいいんですね?Yes, I have. I just need to draw an arrow so that it comes back to the starting point, right? Soka Naidoo:はい。That's correct. Hotaru Kurmin:はい、書きました。I finished drawing it. Soka Naidoo:で、最後にその位置でまた左に曲がります。 Good. Finally, you've got to turn left one more time. Hotaru Kurmin:あ、はい、わかりました。OK, no problem.	At this stage of task 6 avatar Hotaru Kurmin is adjusting one of the program blocks in Second Life and also adding the co-ordinates as explained by avatar Soka Naidoo. Both avatars are questioning and confirming completion of each step.

Table 4. Example of familiarity of programming process in latter stages of Task 6

Communication	Operation being undertaken
[00:06:30] Soka Naidoo:次の2個目のブロックに移動してください。Can you move to the second block? Hotaru Kurmin:はい。OK. Soka Naidoo:で、ステアリングってありますか?And, do you see a steering wheel there? Hotaru Kurmin:ステアリング、はい。A steering wheel..... Yes, I do. [00:06:45] Soka Naidoo:ステアリングをCですね、左いっぱいにしてください。左端です。Can you set the steering wheel to C until it doesn't turn left anymore? It is on the extreme left. Hotaru Kurmin:はい、左いっぱいにしました。Yes, I had it turn left until it can't be moved anymore. Soka Naidoo:はい。で、持続時間の単位を...Good. Then, can you make the unit of the "persistence time"... Hotaru Kurmin:はい。Uh huh. [00:07:00] Soka Naidoo:度、度にしてください。[cont'] degree? Hotaru Kurmin:度、はい。度にしました。The degree... All right, I have set the unit to degree. Soka Naidoo:で、数値は180です。Currently, the number needs to be set to 180. Hotaru Kurmin:はい。あ、180にしました。Right. I have just set it to 180. [00:07:15] Soka Naidoo:はい。で、次、3つ目いいですか? Excellent. Now, may I move on to the third one?	At this stage of task 6 the turning coordinates are being finely tuned in the NXT program within Second Life. The communication has become more specific to the details required by both avatars and subsequently displays an understanding of the communicative and programming processes.

The next phase of the research will involve tasks with more challenging circuits. Task effectiveness and interaction effect will be measured along with coded communicative functions. A framework of informed task design for conducting science-based tasks in virtual worlds will be developed that, in addition to quantitative metrics, will involve students' perceptions of interactions, teamwork, use of prior knowledge, information seeking behavior and problem solving skills. The framework will be linked to learning outcomes and academic competencies as described in Martin and Vallance (2008). In addition, a technical challenge will be to develop a software translator that will transfer the information in the NXT block images in the Second Life learning space to NXT program commands for the Mindstorms software so that a direct transference of the program code can be undertaken when the associated icons are invoked.

CONCLUSION

Currently, measurements used to assess the pedagogical effectiveness and associated knowledge uptake of a given science skills curriculum is measured using standardized achievement tests. Such tests commonly measure changes in acquired basic knowledge but are often incapable of measuring critical thinking ability, task effectiveness, and the contribution of collaborative interactions when engaged in tasks. This research is investigating metrics that can be applied to general and focused science, technology, and engineering learning environments. Controlled experiments with a purposive select group of participants can help establish a framework for effective and successful implementation of a science-based task within virtual collaborative environments. This research limits the virtual word context to the familiar Second Life space. It is anticipated that other virtual worlds will become available to educators in the near future and that our resultant framework and protocols for effective collaborative tasks will still apply. The research is not simply an intellectual pursuit within a novel educational technology environment, but rather an attempt to further the effective and informed use of ICT and the necessary considerations of task design processes and outcomes, teaching pedagogies, and measurements of actual learning. During and after this research period the analysis will be used to implement international collaborative tasks with a more generalized audience of science students. It is anticipated that collaboration with and in virtual immersive interactive environments will become more prominent in mainstream Higher Education within the next five years, and this research aims to provide educators with a framework upon which to construct their curricula, design effective tasks, and assess learning outcomes within such environments.

ACKNOWLEDGMENT

The research is supported by the UK Prime Minister's Initiative (PMI2) and the Japan Advanced Institute of Science and Technology (JAIST). Many thanks to Taku Suto, Tatsuya Nishi, Hiroshi Numata and Dr. Hartono Pitoyo of Future University Hakodate, Japan, and to ISTE for leasing their SL land.

REFERENCES

Barker, S. B., & Ansorge, J. (2007). Robotics as means to increase achievement scores in an informal learning environment. *Journal of Research on Technology in Education*, *39*(3), 229–243.

Brown, A. L. (1992). Design experiments: theoretical and methodological challenges in creating complex interventions in classroom settings. *Journal of the Learning Sciences*, *2*(2), 141–178. doi:10.1207/s15327809jls0202_2

Candlin, C. (1987). Toward task-based learning. In C. Candlin & D. Murphy (Eds.), *Language Learning Tasks* (pp. 5-22). Englewood Cliffs, N.J: Prentice Hall.

Cuban, L. (1992). Curriculum stability and change. In P.W. Jackson (Ed.), *Handbook of research on curriculum* (pp. 216-247). New York: Macmillan.

de Freitas, S. (2008). *Serious virtual worlds: A scoping study*. JISC publications. Retrieved March 14, 2009, from http://www.jisc.ac.uk/publications/publications/seriousvirtualworldsreport.aspx de Freitas, S., & Griffiths, M. (2008). The convergence of gaming practices with other media forms: what potential for learning? A review of the literature. *Learning, media and technology, 33*(1), 11-20.

Groff, L., & Smoker, P. (1997). *Introduction to futures studies*. Retrieved October 1, 2007, from http://www.csudh.edu/global_options/IntroFS.HTML

Honebein, P. C. (1996). Seven goals for the design of constructivist learning environments. In B. Wilson (Ed.), *Constructivist learning environments: Case studies in instructional design*. (pp. 3-8). Englewood Cliffs, NJ: Educational Technology Publications. Iversen, J. S. (n.d). *Futures thinking methodologies – Options relevant for "schooling for tomorrow"*. Retrieved March 14, 2009, from http://www.oecd.org/dataoecd/41/57/35393902.pdf

Jonassen, D. H., & Land, S. M. (2000). *Theoretical foundations of learning environments*. Mahwah, N.J: Lawrence Erlbaum Associates.

Kolb, D. A. (1984). *Experiential learning: Experience as the source of learning and development*. Englewood Cliffs, N.J: Prentice-Hall.

Martin, S., & Vallance, M. (2008). The impact of synchronous inter-networked teacher training in information and communication technology integration. *Computers & Education, 51*, 34–53. doi:10.1016/j.compedu.2007.04.001

Niemitz, M., Slough, S., Peart, L., Klaus, A. D., Leckie, R. M., & St. John, K. (2008). Interactive virtual expeditions as a learning tool: the school of rock expedition case study. *Journal of multimedia and hypermedia, 17*(4), 561-580.

Olsen, D. R., & Goodrich, M. A. (2003). *Metrics for evaluating human-robot interactions*. Retrieved March 14, 2009, from http://icie.cs.byu.edu/Papers/RAD.pdf

Skehan, P. (1998). *A cognitive approach to language learning*. UK: Oxford University Press.

Taylor, T. L. (2006). Play between worlds: exploring online game culture. MIT Press: Cambridge, MA. In T. Boellstorff (2008). *Coming of Age in Second Life*. NJ: Princeton University Press.

Thornburg, D. (2002). *The new basics: Education and the future of work in the telematic age*. Virginia: ASCD.

Vallance, M. (2007). An information and communications technology (ICT)-enabled method for collecting and collating information about pre-service teachers' pedagogical beliefs regarding the integration of ICT. *ALT-J, 15*(1), 51–65. doi:10.1080/09687760601129851

Vallance, M., & Wiz, C. (2007, March). *Virtual collaborative spaces*. Keynote paper and Podcast presented at North Zone Online ICT Symposium, Singapore. Retrieved March 14, 2009, from http://www.mshs.moe.edu.sg/symposium2007/keynote.htm

Vygotsky, L. (1986). *Thought and language*. Cambridge, MA: MIT Press.

Warschauer, M. (1999). *Electronic literacies: language, culture, and power in online education*. Mahwah, N.J: Lawrence Erlbaum Associates.

This work was previously published in International Journal of Virtual and Personal Learning Environments, edited by Michael Thomas, Volume 1, Issue 1, pp. 20-37, copyright 2010 by IGI Publishing (an imprint of IGI Global).

Chapter 5
Homo Virtualis:
Virtual Worlds, Learning, and an Ecology of Embodied Interaction

Leslie Jarmon
The University of Texas at Austin, USA

ABSTRACT

This article previews the emergence of homo virtualis. Drawing on data from seven research studies, peer-reviewed published research articles, and selected excerpts of 30 months of field notes taken in Second Life, the article examines virtual learning environments and embodiment through the lens of interactions of avatars with other avatars, virtual objects, landscapes, sounds, and spatial constructs. Analysis is grounded in the polyvocal evidence provided by select participants who experienced a sense of embodied co-presence and connection with others across geo-physical distances. The discourse ranges from that of high school girls, professional retirees, toxicology and design undergraduates, interdisciplinary graduate students, to educators and researchers from K-12 through university full professors collaborating in SL. In an ecology of virtual contexts, learners inhabit a broader landscape of their own and others' making that allows them to be teachers, designers, researchers, communicators, and collaborators.

This article addresses some of the emergent questions regarding embodiment, social presence, sensory ortho-prosthetics, improvisation, and other dimensions of the extension of ourselves into 3-D virtual world learning environments. Online virtual world platforms such as Second Life have generated a public-private space that is already being used as an effective personal learning environment (PLE) across many sectors. New developments and designs are appearing rapidly, including new technologies for how we interface with computers as well as new input devices. It seems clear, however, that 3-D virtual worlds in whatever form will be increasingly used as knowledge and social interaction management tools in the foreseeable future, and as such, we might more accurately refer to them as *social* learning environments (SLEs).

This article explores how the affordances of the 3-D virtual world environment known as Second Life (SL) are impacting ways of knowing and ways of learning in an emerging ecology of

DOI: 10.4018/978-1-4666-1770-4.ch005

embodied interaction that now extends into online computer-mediated virtual spaces (see Jarmon 1996). In his review of learning environment research, Mayer (2003) called for evidence-based practice and issue-driven research. Drawing on data from seven different research studies, from peer-reviewed published research articles, and from selected excerpts of 30 months of field notes taken in Second Life, this article explores learning environments and 'embodiment' through the lens of actual virtual interactions of avatars with other avatars, virtual objects, landscapes, sounds, and spatial constructs. Analysis and discussion are grounded in the polyvocal evidence provided by those select participants who report having experienced a sense of embodied co-presence and connection with others across geo-physical distances. Participants whose discourse is presented here range from high school girls, professional retirees, toxicology and design undergraduates, interdisciplinary graduate students, and educators and researchers from K-12 through university full professors who are collaborating in SL.

The complex virtual contexts built by and for users in SL allow learners to be teachers, designers, researchers, communicators, and collaborators. Learners inhabit a broader landscape of their own and others' making. In this article, therefore, I preview the emergence of *homo virtualis*.

For purposes of illustration, I begin with a composite case of a virtual learning *experience* that, although partially fictional, has been crafted from actual learning activities already at play in SL. The case is followed by a brief description of the seven research studies from which I am drawing exemplars. Selected excerpts are quoted at length throughout the remainder of the article to foreground the voices of those who have had embodied experiences in SL and are attempting to articulate those experiences using language, e.g., text chat, focus group, or survey response. Next, I examine embodiment as part of a sociotechnical system and explore the mechanics of the online virtual platform as a *digital-sensory extension* of experience that, as is the case with many tools, becomes an extension of our "body." Then we move into an analysis that highlights social interaction and the improvisational nature of our foray as humans into new virtual spaces. Finally, using selected voices from the data, I formulate some concluding observations about the emergence of *homo virtualis*.

A COMPOSITE VIRTUAL SOCIAL-LEARNING-ENVIRONMENT CASE

Drawing from numerous and already existing learning activities in SL, and for the purposes of concrete illustration, what follows is an example of a complex, multi-party virtual learning *experience*. Although partially fictional, every element in this case has been crafted from similar virtual learning experiences that are already occurring in SL and are characteristic of *homo virtualis*.

Julia and the Mars Living Module Station in Second Life

Julia, a sophomore in a civil engineering class in her university in El Paso, Texas, is working with her class team on a homework project to build a mockup of a room in the Mars Living Station module in their 'sandbox' area in Second Life (SL). Julia (her avatar's name is *Julieta Canta*) and her team are applying the stress equations they've been studying in class. She's at home working from her laptop while her team members are dispersed, with 2 at a campus computer lab, 1 at the public library, and 1 at Starbucks). They IM (instant message) two friends from NASA's CoLab community in SL to review their structure-in-progress and to give feedback, and the two experts teleport over to the team's sandbox (one is on a computer in Houston, the other in Germany). Because now working in SL they can create visualizations and models so easily, Julia and her teammates can *see the impact immediately* when their equations are not accurate.

Over time, through trial and error, and with everyone pitching in ideas from their class notes, Julia's student team is finally pleased with their homework project and are ready to give a 'virtual tour' of their module to their classmates to demonstrate just how their equations are working. Joining the virtual tour will be 15 students from a State University TeleCampus Health Services Technology class who will be taking a 'field trip' in SL to collect data on how health issues are being addressed in diverse environments; their data collection is part of an IRB-approved faculty research project and part of the statewide Undergraduate Research Initiative.

Julia is especially proud because, on the one hand, she is very confident that she really understands the homework because she had to actually build an important structure and test it. On the other hand, she knows that pictures of their Mars module will be used by a SL non-profit organization whose mission is to inspire young women to take engineering and other STEM courses (her younger sister, Angela, went to a virtual STEM summer camp on the Teen Grid in SL led by non-profits Girlstart and the Educators Coop).

Because it's so easy to collaborate in the virtual world, Julia's engineering professor decided to also connect with a medical science class at the University Health Science Center in San Antonio and with an undergraduate design class in the United Kingdom, taking advantage of the distributed knowledge dimension of SL. Julia enjoys hearing those students' different accents when they visit and ask questions or offer ideas.

Although Julia is feeling a bit tired, she's also feeling a sense of accomplishment. She takes a few final snapshots in SL of herself (*Julieta*) and her teammates learning and building the module. Then she opens up her class blog, reflects on her learning experiences, and shares insights with her class about how these days she feels like she's connecting to people and systems of knowledge that actually matter. She uploads the photos from her team's work-and-learning-in-progress for the final Class Report. Her class will be submitting a paper to an international virtual engineering conference with participation by undergraduates and sponsored by Engineers Without Borders in SL. She thinks, "School's not what it used to be. I feel like I'm part of something important."

BRIEF DESCRIPTION OF SEVEN RESEARCH SOURCES

In this examination of embodiment and *homo virtualis*, exemplars presented in the rest of the article are drawn from selected data from seven research studies (some are on-going), from peer-reviewed published research papers, and from 30 months of field notes taken in SL (excerpts marked as Field Notes). This section briefly describes the seven studies, the subjects, and the students' level of participation in SL for each.

A Word about Degrees of Participation in SL

A user's experience of embodiment is not in any way a foregone conclusion. It is important for researchers and instructional designers to make some distinctions between various participation levels regarding SL. The experience of embodiment is in many ways driven by the degree of a person's active use of the affordances of the virtual platform and the degree of personal agency a person chooses or is allowed to assume. Furthermore, much of the discussion about education in virtual worlds frequently fails to describe the degree of students' active entry in the virtual world in terms of personal agency, duration, and frequency.

For now, however, first, at one end of the spectrum and speaking generally, some learners may only read or hear about SL but never actually log in to the online program, and this level of participation can be considered to be minimal at best, because their understanding of a 'virtual world' is not actually based on first-hand experience or personal agency.

Second, as may be the case for a number of educators and students, virtual activities in a class may be mediated through the instructor and his/her avatar in SL by way of projecting the scene on the instructor's monitor onto a large screen in the classroom. Although students may be able to watch and hear interaction with others in SL through an instructor's avatar, these students have no personal agency themselves; however, they may have experienced some minimal degree of co-presence or participation with the virtual world through, for example, virtual guest speakers in SL and virtual question-and-answer interactive sessions with those guests.

Third, in many virtual learning activities, students log into the SL program on their own and may began to experience participation levels with a fuller sense of personal agency. However, as seen with the results from one research study used here (Pena et al., 2009), the students' actual freedom to use the affordances of the virtual platform was severely constrained. Fourth, depending on both the duration of time spent in SL and the frequency of students' visits to SL, the probability increases that they may experience a sense of fuller participation, agency, and co-presence with others, if they are allowed greater personal agency.

This discrepancy of degrees of participation in SL can influence how users respond to survey questions and can impact educational research findings accordingly. The level of participation for each of the seven research studies described below is indicated, as well as a notation for how learners' observations from that study will be identified throughout the rest of the discussion. In all cases, only subjects who reported some sense of embodied experience are included in this article's exploration of *homo virtualis*.

Study 1: The Educators Coop: Developing A Community of Practice in the Shared Virtual Environment Of Sl (2007 – On-Going)

This on-going IRB-approved research project being conducted in SL focuses on collaboration and interactions in virtual worlds, specifically among the members of the Educators Coop. The Educators Coop is a virtual non-profit residential community of university faculty, librarians, and K-12 teachers actively teaching or conducting research in SL. Participants volunteered to join the community and are from 32 different educational institutions. The majority first met in SL and most have only known one another virtually. Preliminary results indicate that these researchers and educators are using the virtual world in very practical and concrete ways to carry out their work (Jarmon & Sanchez, in press, 2008a, 2008b).

During the last 24 months, we have collected hundreds of chat logs, conducted five online surveys, held four virtual focus group sessions, and conducted 46 in-depth virtual interviews in SL with members of the Educators Coop. Later in the article, selected excerpts from these data will be presented as illustrations of embodiment experiences where users have complete freedom of activity in SL. (Excerpts will be identified using the following abbreviations: Ed Coop Chat, Ed Coop Interview, or Ed Coop Focus Group).

Study 2: The Influence of Virtual Self-Representations on Language Use, Test Performance, and Perceptions of Embodiment (Pena et al., 2009)

This 2009 study on the automaticity model of priming effects extends research on the Proteus effect (Yee & Balilenson, 2007) to investigate the relative influence of avatar appearance and role labels in a virtual setting. Ninety-seven students enrolled in communication courses in a large Southwestern university volunteered to participate in exchange for course credit. In contrast to Study 1, the design for the priming effects experiment was very austere and used only the objects required for the experiment, including a mirror in which the test avatar could 'see' itself reflected. Significantly, the virtual situation was highly constrained in terms of participant choice and personal agency. Students' avatars were pre-created and assigned, no modifications were permitted, movement was restricted to walking, and there was no interaction with other avatars.

After completing the priming effects portion of the experiment, subjects were prompted to elaborate on their experience, if any, of embodiment during the experiment. While the majority reported none, even under these highly restricted conditions, some students did report a feeling of embodiment, and their descriptions are included in the discussion. (Excerpts marked as JP Survey).

Study 3: Girlstart IT Summer Academy in SL for Social Change and Gender Equity (2008)

Girlstart, an educational non-profit organization (girlstart.org), sponsored an Information Technology Summer Academy in Teen Second Life during the summer of 2008 for 40 high school girls and their 8 counselors. In addition to STEM literacy activities, the camp curriculum included sessions on gaming, career pathways, social change, and gender equality. Although not the focus of the virtual camp, online survey data regarding embodiment were collected. Campers were allowed to explore many of the affordances of SL, and their insights on embodiment will be used in the discussion. (Excerpts marked as GS Survey).

Study 4: Exploring Learning in SL in an Interdisciplinary Communication Course (Jarmon et al., 2008; Jarmon et al., 2009)

This two-part study (Jarmon et al., 2008; Jarmon et al., 2009a) provided initial and final research findings of how SL was used in a graduate interdisciplinary communication course offered at a large Southwestern university in 2007. Preliminary results indicated strong experiential benefits from using SL to learn strategies of interdisciplinary communication. A project-based emphasis in the curriculum was recommended to fully accommodate student experiential learning in SL.

Importantly, as an unexpected and concrete measure of their enduring learning and of the perceived relevance of this course, the student team remained intact and continued their work in SL 18 months after the semester ended. The students were allowed to take full advantage of the affordances of the virtual environment, and their voices will join those of the other learners throughout this article. (Excerpts marked as LJ Survey, LJ Focus Group, or LJ Class Data).

Study 5: OLLI: Aging, Lifelong Learning, and the Virtual World of SL (Jarmon, et al., in press)

Contributing to our understanding of the potential for SL to provide a framework for establishing virtual lifelong learning environments, this study examined how SL is perceived and understood by older adults in a classroom setting. The study was conducted during a six-session introductory course on SL offered to older adults participating in the Osher Lifelong Learning Institute (OLLI) program at a large Southwestern research university. The OLLI program provides intellectual enrichment for mostly retired individuals, and the seminar presented a wide-ranging introduction to SL using virtual guest speakers and virtual fields trips. Participants had widely varying degrees of participation in the virtual world, ranging from no actual individual immersion to full immersion, and the comments of those who reported having embodied experiences appear in the discussion. (Excerpts marked as OLLI Survey or OLLI Focus Group).

Study 6: Exploring Problem-Based Experiential Learning in a Pharmacology and Toxicology Course in SL (on-going 2009)

This study investigates how using SL in an upper division undergraduate Pharmacy and Toxicology course offered at a large Southwestern university influences student learning through scenario role-playing and problem-based activities. Students were challenged to solve clinical toxicology mysteries *ala* the popular television series, *CSI*, in four virtual interactive scenarios designed to increase retention of material learned in class. The simulations provided an opportunity for students to test their skills and knowledge in an interactive safe zone, in their own time, without risk to others. Specific survey questions addressed embodiment, and excerpts from the data will be presented as illustrations of embodiment in a context where students had a large degree of agency, where the task was directly tied to course learning objectives, and where the completion of each of the four tasks in-world was of short duration (approximately 30 minutes). (Excerpts marked as AC Survey).

Study 7: Exploring Experiential Learning and Interdisciplinary Collaboration in Design Courses in SL (on-going 2009)

This study examines interdisciplinary collaboration and how SL was used in an undergraduate Design course, *Introduction to the microcomputer as an integrator of visual information: Its applications to organizational systems in the design process*. The students planned and implemented a semester-long project in SL to design and build a marine science research center that would be used as a total virtual classroom the following semester for an online *Oceanography: Human Exploration / Exploitation of the Sea* course. These learners' descriptions of their embodied experiences will contribute to the analysis in this article. (Excerpts marked as RT Survey).

As we explore the emergence of *homo virtualis* in the following sections, it will be through the lens of these learners who have had embodied experiences and who are attempting to articulate those experiences using language, e.g., text chat, focus group, interview, or survey response. The analysis presented here is grounded in their evidence, and their efforts to communicate the nature of their experiences will be quoted at length.

HOMO VIRTUALIS: EMBODIMENT IN A SOCIOTECHNICAL SYSTEM

I felt I was actually in there myself. (GS Survey)

It feels like I have the freedom to walk around the Internet. I can see everything visually. (JP Survey)

When other classmates could see my avatar **I felt like they could see me or like we were in the same place together.** *(AC Survey 2; bold added)*

In this section, I examine embodiment as part of a sociotechnical system with the intention to better understand personal and social learning environments. I explore the mechanics of the online virtual platform as a digital-sensory extension of experience where the tool becomes an extension of our 'body.' Three critical elements for engagement in learning in the digital age are interactivity, connectivity, and access (Dresang & McClelland, 1999), and these are three key elements of the online virtual world environment of SL. Research has suggested that such a learning environment can enhance student engagement through a sense of shared experiences, offer opportunities for collaboration, and provide access to information about the virtual environment and user-created content (FitzGerald, 2007). As we have seen above in the composite case with Julia/*Julieta*, users of SL are represented through their virtual avatars, and research on pedagogical agents has found that the presence of avatars can increase engagement and learning beyond computer-mediated communication without such agents (Atkinson et al., 2005).

Importantly, research on shared virtual environments (SVEs) and on collaborative virtual environments (CVEs) is particularly relevant to our concerns because this research examines participants' sense of presence, co-presence, and place-presence. The four short excerpts that introduced this section of the article echo similar sentiments expressed by many across all seven of the studies, depending in part on the degree of participation allowed. Three-dimensional virtual worlds such as SL provide both synchronous and asynchronous collaborative environments and, compared to text-based online learning settings, create an enriched sense of place with the visual projection of oneself and other individuals. As we shall later observe, users report that collaboration can occur because the virtual technology provides conditions for an experiential, embodied, and social reality. This social reality, in turn, provides a virtual 'new space' wherein existing communication practices and social networking tools are converging.

Stahl et al. (2006) have argued that, "CSCL [computer-supported collaborative learning] requires a focus on the meaning-making practices of collaborating groups and on the design of technological artifacts to mediate interaction" (p. 409). In SL, since the participants themselves, as users, can become the creators of content, that is, of the virtual artifacts that mediate their own interaction and learning, they become the early vanguard of *homo virtualis*.

Suchman's research on human-machine communication has provided a useful framework whereby researchers can explore the relationships between everyday embodied communicative practices and the design of the *socio-technical systems* in which they can occur (Suchman, 1987, 2002). The concepts of embodiment and learning are of great interest to researchers when explored through the lens of users' actual lived experience and of instances of interactions of people's avatars with virtual objects, landscapes, and spatial constructs. Furthermore, the individual SL user's connectivity within the socio-technical system includes interaction among avatars as well as using a computer, monitor screen, keyboard, headset, and computer mouse with hands, body, and mind. All these elements also become part of an extended system of experience and interaction, and, following Lave and Wenger, they constitute what can be called a complex situated learning environment (Lave & Wenger, 1991).

In his study of hybrid games, Thomas (2006) uses a similar concept for describing what he calls pervasive learning games, and he suggests that what is most important is "not the use of so-called pervasive technologies but the social processes that connect learners to communities of devices, people, and situations (p. 42). Thus, as suggested in the introduction and in the following observations from users, we might more accurately claim that virtual PLEs are inherently SLEs, *social* learning environments.

OM: So one theme that emerged was why SL is different

DW: Space/time is a biggie. Also the idea that *this glass screen in front of me is permeable in both directions.* Yea. You're in Austin. I'm in Greely. We're talking. Now. You'd have to come to Greeley or I'd have to go to Austin to do this in RL [real life]. It's like a permanent Convention Site, the largest permanent floating crap game in Detroit. We come here and regardless of where we all sit, we can come here and meet, talk, build, bitch, create, be silly, be serious, whatever. *There's power in the ability to create, but there's power in the relationships we build.* (Ed Coop Interview 3/6/09; italics added)

- I think it's awesome seeing 'myself' in the 2nd world where I can do anything, build anything, meet anyone without being shy. It's very cool.
- It feels like I'm really there. (GS Survey)

Embodiment: A Sensory Ortho-Prosthetic Extension of Self

Changes in technology and materials science (new lightweight plastics, rugged carbon fiber, nanomaterials) have allowed us to create better fitting, more comfortable artificial limbs, and other orthotic and prosthetic devices. The term orthotics is derived from the Hellenistic Greek ορθωσνς, meaning *to make*, and ορθουν, *to set straight*. Prosthesis, derived from the ancient Greek προστιθεναι, carries the sense of *addition, to add*. Both terms are relevant to our discussion of embodiment.

For example, consider literacy as a cognitive prosthesis that, as a tool for symbolic representation, extends our potential to act, understand, create, and be in the world. With frequent and regular use, the prosthesis itself becomes increasingly transparent. Similarly, consider *online virtual literacy* – that extended landscape of *homo virtualis* that is still largely uncreated and unexplored – as a cognitive and sensory ortho-prosthesis of both the self and the community. According to the voices of experience presented here, with frequent and regular use, the SL ortho-prosthesis, too, can become increasingly transparent, and *homo virtualis* goes about the business of living life in, through, and across the ecology of an expanding landscape.

This construct of the *self* is contested territory (Di Paolo, 2009), but for the purposes of our discussion here, the *self* will be defined as that which experiences its own embodiment and can be mutable, extendible, and persistent. In his work on third cultures, Andy Clark has noted (2009) that: "More so than any other creature on the planet, we humans emerge as *natural-born cyborgs*, factory tweaked and primed so as to be ready to grow into extended cognitive and computational architectures: ones whose systemic boundaries far exceed those of skin and skull" (p. 5). We regularly "attach" tools to ourselves to extend our abilities beyond normal human-scale. A hammer attached to a hand leverages greater force than the hand alone, and a user "attached to" the Internet, thereby connecting virtually with others in an online course, leverages greater connectivity than could the individual without the tool.

I realized that I was the one controlling the avatar, thus it was an **extension of myself**. (RT Survey 2; bold added)

Vygotsky held that we use tools and signs to mediate the essence of our human behavior, and that our "tools orient outward, toward the transformation of the physical and social reality" (Moll, 1992, p. 45). In fact, this capacity to use tools to extend our intentions and abilities are affordances of the tools themselves, and a prescient Gibson (1979/1986) suggested that "the *boundary* between the animal and the environment is not □xed at the surface of the skin but can *shift*" (p. 41). When we frame online virtual technology as a tool, as a *sensory ortho-prosthetic extension* of our experience, then it becomes an extension of our "body" like any other tool. The virtual world is a constructed *continuation* of (and improvisation on) our constructed world. Significantly, it is also a continuation of our tacit knowing and being in and of that world (Polanyi, 1966). As such, the affordances of online virtual worlds like SL are impacting our ways of knowing and learning.

Therefore, listening to the observations of users, we come to understand that logging-in to the SL platform (attaching to it) provides them with a set of 3-D sensory ortho-prostheses that include robust visual controls, auditory fields, communication channels, navigation capabilities (e.g., flying, teleporting), and the ability to create completely new virtual objects and tools. These capabilities lead to embodied experiences for the users. Early on, in sometimes awkward and challenging ways, the perceived boundary of the embodied self begins to shift from skin-bound into the highly extendible and socially-constructed world within and with which users *dwell* (Polanyi, 1966; see *extensible self* in Adams, 2005). Hence, the emerging *homo virtualis*.

Most of the time it is frustrating because I try to see myself as the avatar but it's irritating to control my movements by hand and not by mind **as I am normally accustomed to.** *(JP Survey; bold added)*

- When walking around the island, **my visual and audible senses** have allowed me to perceive the expanse of the land, the depth of the water, and my location and distance from accurate representation of sound changes as a result of my avatar's position in SL.
- While in SL I found a strong connection with my avatar, like it was **an extension of me** - not just a video game character. I think this is because there isn't any set path, just like real life. *(RT Survey 2; bold added)*

Recent research in neuroscience and psychology has suggested that a network of mirror neurons in the human brain constitutes an experiential "simulation," and in interpersonal relationships they provide the basis for empathic understanding of one another and thus for collaboration (Gallese, Eagle & Migone, 2007). They write:

The neural circuits activated in a person carrying out actions, expressing emotions, and experiencing sensations are activated also, automatically via a mirror neuron system, in the observer of those actions, emotions, and sensations. It is proposed that this finding of shared activation suggests a functional mechanism of "embodied simulation" that consists of the automatic, unconscious, and noninferential simulation in the observer of actions, emotions, and sensations carried out and experienced by the observed. (p.131; see also Iacoboni, 2008)

Thus far, we have heard SL users declare their full identification with their avatars ("I *felt* I was actually in there myself"), and we have heard them note the new perspective of being able to observe their own movements as well as those of others. For *homo virtualis*, it may well be that mirror neurons continue to play a role as well, stimulated by new kinds of sensory input through the ortho-prosthesis of SL. This research is likely to have critical implications for some special needs populations as well as athletes and older adults. For example, stroke victims visiting the protected virtual area in SL for people with disabilities called SL Dreams have reported that the *experience of seeing themselves walking aided in their recovery* (Stein, 2007; italics added). The learners in our studies described their sense of identification explicitly:

- I think when you create your avatar and you start to get to know your avatar... you identify with that avatar. It's you.
- When I go in there I feel that's me. I don't feel the least bit different. (OLLI Focus Group)
- I feel like it is me since I looked in the mirror. I just feel like I have control over this person and it's weird.
- It makes me feel as though **I am watching myself.**
- It is kind of like being there because she does the motions like you would do. It

feels kind of weird because **it is almost like you start to think that it is thinking like you**. *(JP Survey; bold added)*

Now let us briefly look more closely at some specific sensory ortho-prosthetic affordances that our learners reference in their comments about experiencing embodiment. Within the virtual design infrastructure of SL, text chat is 'readable' out to a distance of 20 meters, and voice chat grows fainter even as one's avatar turns and faces away from the current speaker. An entirely new visual dimension to interaction has been provided in SL through the ortho-prosthesis of the virtual camera functions (essentially, an avatar's *vision*). For example, an adjustment allows users to center their eyes and ears on a specific speaker to hear more clearly, regardless of the spatial distance of one's own avatar from that speaker (within certain broader limits). Furthermore, a user can center their view on an avatar, on an object, or *behind, above, or below* one's own avatar, providing a 360 degree spherical range of vision, zooming in or out to a distance of many meters. For *homo virtualis*, virtual hearing and seeing are no longer tied to physical proximity nor to the sensory mechanisms, so to speak, of *homo sapiens*.

SD: There is always the camera trick.:)
BT: What's the camera trick?
QQ: There is no privacy in SL.
SD: You increase your draw distance and alt-zoom in. (Ed Coop Chat 3/6/09)
MN: Because of the chat circle construct in SL, circles are important to design of spaces. People can hear you in a 20m circumference from where you stand, a circle around you
NW: Like the one our avatars are sitting in right now
MN: Exactly! We *naturally* form into circles here. (Ed Coop Chat 3/9/09; italics added)

In explicitly education-related activities, people frequently integrate multiple technologies in the 3-D spatial domain that are visible to other co-present avatars. In fact, users often seamlessly *act under the assumption* that the people around them can see what they are seeing, what they are pointing to, and what they are referring to in the physical context around them. This can include, for example, virtual constructed objects, models, or imported presentation slides. For *homo virtualis*, the space has a sense of immediacy and becomes a highly flexible, shapeable, and shared palette, and this can have broad implications for discovery and learning because the sense of being co-present becomes pervasive and transparent:

MN: I have some slides so as we go along *I'll show some pretty pictures* from the study on *that whiteboard which is back behind me.* And please feel free to jump in anytime with questions, comments, thoughts – I'm happy to discuss. [WhiteBoard (e): Showing Image 2/13 - 7p-2-sl]. So *here's* one set of my research questions. There are some places which themselves ARE the answers. *That* is the immersive, experiential environment. *The top* is the Library of Alexandra at Roma. (Ed Coop Chat 3/9/09; italics added)

Virtual participants can also extend their awareness of another avatar's presence in SL using virtual proximity sensors. SL is a tool-making tool, and accordingly, because people will invent new virtual devices to meet their needs, a very common virtual ortho-prosthesis is a sensing device called a HUD (heads up display) that an avatar 'wears.' The device senses when an avatar approaches within a set number of meters and notifies the wearer by displaying that avatar's name on the monitor screen. Similarly, the SL Friends settings can be adjusted to notify users when a friend has logged-in to SL (indicating that they are now available for interaction) or has logged-out of SL (they are no longer available for interaction). Even when an avatar is logged out, instant messages may still be sent and inventory objects, information note cards, and other items may still be shared with that user, thereby affording a kind of virtual 'front porch' access to others.

These and other creative, temporal, spatial, and informational affordances in the ecology of SL's sociotechnical system challenge users to explore and to articulate the nature of their new *virtualness*. In the following excerpt, we hear members of the Educators Coop trying to tease out the meaning of the *Mesa* where they are gathered, a large plateau in the middle of an island used for community gatherings.

CP: Is the Mesa a place or a space? (or does it depend on who's asking?):-)
MN: I'm going to guess the Mesa is more of a space?
CP: The Mesa is certainly very mutable!
NW: Well, again it depends on how we use it and think of it. It is a place, a landmark, of course
SD: Home?
NW: But it is also a discursive space, for us. It "represents" the sharing of ideas (space) as much as it IS a place to share ideas
OM: *Right now it is a space between knowing and learning*
NW: Yep. *And a space OF knowing and learning*
SD: *Never really thought of it in those terms... I like it.*
MN: I like this whole issue of the use of space, what an "information architecture" is, and when is space/place necessary, how is it used. (Ed Coop Chat 3/9/09; italics added)

In their recent research on experiential learning and situated learning spaces, Kolb and Kolb (2008) remind us that learning spaces include "socialization into a wider community of practice that involves membership, identity formation, [and] transitioning from novice to expert" (pp. 24-25). Time and immersion are required to better understand and to attempt to characterize the *virtual* learning affordances and to progress from novice to expert:

DW: It takes time. They [teachers] are missing the part where you can't teach something you don't understand. But the experience is very different from teaching something that you LIVE. When you're *immersed* ... you become an expert. *But it takes practice, which takes time and focus*. That's why I started the real estate business, so I'd be IN the world instead of just looking at it. That's important - I think - *to help me understand how to use the space, to learn. Because I have to know how to learn here before I can begin to think about how to use it to teach.* (Ed Coop Interview 12/18/07; italics added)
HC: It is a place to work in quiet. *Mostly it is a place to work and be less rushed and able to explore different kinds of things.* In retrospect I learned the value of just giving myself *the freedom to play around and tinker.* (Ed Coop Interview 12/18/07; italics added)

Furthermore, the co-evolution of this extended ecology of embodied interaction is multi-directional. In other words, in iterative ways, while the technology provides a tool for the extension of human presence and intention into virtual domains, so to speak, at the same time, the experiences users have through their avatars have an effect on users and their behavior when not logged in. Yee and Balilenson (2007) have studied what they refer to as the Proteus effect:

Although most research in CMC has focused on the technical affordances of the medium (lack of social cues, social presence, anonymity, etc.), we argue that theoretical frameworks of self-representation cannot be ignored because choosing who we are is a fundamental aspect of virtual environments. More importantly, who we choose to be in turn shapes how we behave. Although avatars are usually construed as something of our own choosing—a one-way process—the fact is that our avatars come to change how we behave. (p. 287)

The following observations capture our users reflecting on the nature of this multi-directional ecology of effects. While users can create their avatars and construct the physical space around them in SL, *both* of these can in turn affect the users themselves.

- I can relate my feelings through her.
- **I was kinda sad** when I made my avatar fat, and people started **to make fun of me**. Just having my avatar be that way was allowing me to see **what people of a larger stature go through in real life.** *(GS Survey; bold added)*

  CP: HM has just started to show us his GIS materials

  HM: *geez I'm getting nervous now* (Ed Coop Chat 2/23/09; italics added)
- Well, with the way **that she is dressed**, it almost makes me feel that **I have to act proper and sophisticated.**
- Well it does make me feel like I'm there... **also I was scared when I almost made the avatar fall** *(JP Survey; bold added)*

  DW: So we wanted to have a get together and thought that the hot tub in the Geek Temple would be a cool way to get people to come and talk ... People coming and going. And exploring that whole issue of "embodiment," where *what you see on the screen really effects how you feel in your skin.* (Ed Coop Interview 3/6/09; italics added)

  JL: I have newb bod [newbie body] and hair and *feel otherwise out of body. Not myself today. Funny how that affects us,* or doesn't... Today when I see myself, I have weird hair, the wrong shape. *It changes how I handle myself, the same as RL clothes do*. In my robe vs. in a suit. Or with something wrong with my hair. (Field Notes – Chat 5/9/08; italics added)

  DW: I set out to find a new look and I had a heck of a time because *it just wasn't me.* Finally what hit me was that I wasn't bald, and *the bald head and bearded face was "me" in some way I don't understand.* (Ed Coop Chat 12/16/08; italics added)

Finally, we conclude this section on the sociotechnical system and embodiment with the following excerpts that illustrate an important characteristic of *homo virtualis*. In the earlier excerpts related to mirror neurons, where neurochemical reactions may be taking place in the locally-situated physical bodies of users observing the activities of themselves and of others, the experiences people have in the virtual world can affect their perceptions, feelings, and behaviors when they are *not* online but rather are acting in what used to be their 'real' world. *Homo virtualis* does not have to be in the virtual world to manifest new and embodied experiences that may have originated or been learned and even practiced there but that now can span across all dimensions of the ecology inhabited by us.

DW: One lesson SL has taught me is that *real life isn't as inelastic as I once thought*. (Ed Coop Interview 3/6/09; italics added)

In RT Survey 2, students were asked, "When you are NOT in SL, if you have ever found yourself noticing something differently or thinking about something in a different way because of your experiences in SL, please describe those instances." Their responses included these:

- I have noticed a greater interest in *observing others interacting in space*.
- I have noticed myself *analyzing physical spaces, objects, and architectures in the real world* and pondering how they could be translated into Second Life.

- I was in my history class thinking, *what would this look like in SL?*
- My interactions between the real environments *began to blur with the virtual*. While walking down the stairs, my perceptions often changed. I began to *make comparisons of people on the street as SL avatars interacting within a space.*
- It made me realize *the spatial interactions we experience every day.*
- Occasionally I will imagine how something would *look from a bird's-eye point of view.*
- Now often I find myself wishing that I could just click + option and *be able to move and zoom my view around without having to move my body/head/eyes.* (RT Survey 2; italics added)
- I do find myself twitching my mouse fingers to try and navigate my eyes behind the 2d image on a TV screen! (Field Note)
- Even the enlargement in perspective. If, say, I spent two hours walking around in SL, my frame of mind *now is more open to new ideas than when I just go to a book.* (LJ Focus Group; italics added)
- Anytime I look at a jpeg [in RL], I wish I could move the camera around, zoom in on instructions I can't read. (Field Note)

Having briefly examined the sociotechnical system and embodiment, complete with sensory ortho-prostheses and activated mirror neurons, through the words of participants in the seven research studies, let us now turn to the connections users experience through social interaction in SL and the improvisational and performative characteristics of those experiences.

SOCIAL INTERACTION AND IMPROVISATION

I liked how easy it was to interact with others. *(GS Survey)*

One approach for considering the development of the social system of SL is to view it as "constellations of interconnected practices," multiple communities of practice that are related depending on the perspective one adopts (Wenger, 1998; p. 127). Because of the co-evolution of both the technology and the social systems, SL is inherently a *learning organization* (Senge, 1994).

For example, let us look more closely at the Educators Coop, the virtual residential community of educators. Preliminary results from the study indicate that the members are using the virtual world in very practical and concrete ways to carry out research and educational projects collaboratively. In other words, the diverse community members, their students, and their guests have created what Gee has called "cross-functional affiliations" (2007, p. 327). They have their real lives and virtual areas of specialization, but they also collaborate and share their knowledge and resources across what may have been perceived as social boundaries in RL.

KE: I think there is a real sense that *we residents know each other*. That we are not only colleagues, *but neighbors and friends. The sense of place becomes very real*. I can look at the mini-map and say, "Oh, QQ is here. Somebody's on the Mesa. ST is here." And then wander around and say hi. For a while, I always saw MN on first thing in the morning, just like a regular neighborhood. But in fact, I actually have things in common with *these neighbors!* (Ed Coop Interview - 12/18/07; italics added)

Drawing on tacit behavioral patterns from RL, these *homo virtualis* users are improvising new forms of social interaction and are discovering new ways of *making sense of* and of *talking about* their embodied social experiences. Based on evidence provided by these learners, it is becoming increasingly evident that on-going iterations of new, repeated, and improvised experiences are beginning to dissolve some formerly solid distinctions between the experience of the 'virtual' and the experience of the 'real' (Burke 1935; Goffman 1959; Yee & Bailenson 2007). According to de Nood and Attema (2006), in open-ended online simulations such as SL, the:

... distinction between the physical (real) world and the virtual world tends to disappear. As the distinction between these two worlds fades in the experience of the visitors, one speaks of 'inter-reality.' When these virtual worlds continue to grow and develop, they would then seem to offer practically unexplored opportunities for our society, in economic, cultural and social terms. (p. 3)

Researchers examining collaborative virtual environments are particularly interested in the relationship between co-presence, the sense of being with other people, and place-presence, the feeling that a virtual environment is a place (Steed et al., 1999). *Homo virtualis* is emerging via its social interaction in socially constructed expanding landscapes of these inter-realities. For example:

CP: DW - we heard you and QQ actually met in RL!

DW: Last week in Orlando. Yes! It was... odd. But she's so obviously who she is. I've seen her pictures... I could pick her in a lineup. But I never knew how much her avatar really looks like her. But it was also so familiar, *like we stopped the conversation here and picked it up in Florida.* (Ed Coop – Chat 2/7/08)

OM: My class decided today that they would rather meet in SL than RL. They participate a lot more in SL. (Ed Coop - Chat 2/7/08)

MN: Zone of proximal development if you will - I have learned more, and faster, *because I'm together with others.* (Ed Coop Interview 12/18/07; italics added)

Another approach to co-presence based on the principles of embodied cognition (Riva et al., 2006) defines presence as the "non-mediated perception of successfully transforming an intention into action," rather than merely a notion that persons are physically occupying the same geographical space. In a 2009 study (Jarmon, et al., 2009a), some students reported that the three-dimensionality of the SL environment facilitated the sense of personal presence and tangible experiences as factors that enhanced learning.

Yeah, the embodiment of it [SL]. You generally somehow do feel more like a human being. The other thing about SL is that I think it can enhance learning, is that it's very evocative. Like, if you had to build the model of those Alley Flats [in the real world] you never would have been able to capture the alley with like those pigeons, the papers blowing in the wind and everything. And especially with those big screens [virtual images of Austin skyline]. **I just felt I was there. And so I had a very visceral connection to what was being built.** *I don't think you can get that in a model or anywhere except real life or virtual reality. (LJ Focus Group; bold added for emphasis).*

A theoretical framework used by interaction researchers and relevant for this discussion is that of *improvisation* (Goffman, 1956; Bateson, 1993). *Homo virtualis* learners are exploring the versatility of the building and modeling tools to discover and improvise new ways of visualizing information by creating interactive objects. Simultaneously, they must improvise new ways of making sense of an array of unfamiliar and challenging experiences confronting them.

QM: Well, for one thing... everyone is a learner. Big time. Everyone is out of their natural element. We have to learn from each other. We are not bound by space... and as people who've experienced SL seem to say, it IS different from a phone conference or video conference. We embody our avatars. We are to an extent physically present with each other. The idea of everyone is a teacher and everyone is a learner is one of the keys of Transformational Learning, learning that changes how people think and view the world. Not just how they do stuff. *So this environment is conducive to us learning how to examine even the very questions we ask when we approach an issue, which is really something...* (Ed Coop Interview; italics added)

In the toxicology research study, students role-played investigators solving mysterious deaths by drawing on lessons from class. They had to improvise problem-solving strategies, and after the class ended they reported these impacts of being in SL:

- I have learned to be observant and to pay close attention to surroundings.
- It enhanced my knowledge by allowing me to apply information learned in class to the scenarios. It was active learning versus passive.
- I learned how to be a better problem solver, and quickly look things up to solve a case.
- I will never forget the antidotes to the poisons that were presented in SL, or the symptoms that led to the deaths. *(AC Survey 2)*

Thus, people are improvising on pre-existing patterns of behavior and are re-interpreting those behaviors in virtual social spaces filled with new tools. Interactants connect, build relationships (Nardi, 2005), pursue objectives, and act with embodied purpose; in some cases, communities of practice are forming or re-establishing themselves in virtual spaces (Wenger, 1998). However, it can be difficult to put these experiences into words. The improvised discourse emerging from virtual social interactions in SL reflects the inventive, poetic, and pragmatic nature of people with a need to communicate. The new experiences and discoveries of *homo virtualis* lead to new utterances that reveal people's on-going attempts to negotiate meaning and its articulation. In the territory of *homo virtualis*, we note Suchman's observation that "a frame of artful integration emphasizes the ways in which new things are made up out of reconfigurations and extensions to familiar environments and forms of action" (2002, p. 144). In the following excerpts, we see users are improvising new discursive formations:

I tried to turn the sun to noon. (Field Note)

I'm gestating myself. I'll let you know how it goes. (Field Note, Notecard, 12/14/07)

Such utterances might have at one time understandably been characterized along the lines of Chomsky's (1957, 15) "*Colorless green ideas sleep furiously*" as syntactically correct but semantically nonsensical. However, for example, in this last instance ("I'm gestating myself"), the person is referring to a gestation script purchased in SL that animates one's avatar to reproduce the virtual impression of pregnancy, with special features ("Baby-in-Tummy"). The "baby" in this case was the person's alternate avatar form.

As we have heard from the voices of the users presented here, people are improvising on prior patterns and constructs, and they are languaging into being new discursive expressions to articulate, sometimes in forms that are poetic, that which is experientially and virtually new.

CONCLUSION

Following Latour's dictum (1990) that "what draws things together draws things together," we can say that the 3-D virtual world environment of SL allows users to *draw things together* in experiential ways with a convergence of mediated forms of social interaction by means of the embodied sensory extension of self. In fact, for *homo virtualis*, we might say:

What draws us together, draws us together.

Through the voices of the learners presented throughout this article, I have attempted to introduce *homo virtualis*, a human evolutionary form whose field of play entails a complex sociotechnical system increasing in territory hourly. The sensory ortho-prosthesis of the SL platform provided these users with clear and direct instances of embodied experience, even for some who were involved in research studies under highly constrained conditions and who were prohibited from using the affordances of the virtual environment. The sense of social connectivity and the improvisational nature of their experiences both point toward opportunities for engaged learning and enhanced retention. The composite case of Julia/*Julieta* which opened this discussion is an illustration of what is already emerging for *homo virtualis*.

A better understanding of virtual learning environments, embodiment, and co-presence has worldwide implications for humanity on this path to *homo virtualis*, and some researchers have begun to examine *presence engineering*. The European Community has appropriated funding for 2002 through 2013 for a research initiative aimed at continuing the study of presence but to also include:

... presence engineering: the deliberate manipulation of technological and non-technological factors to create those forms of presence that enhance users in primary activities. Moreover, it enlarges the scope and ambition to mixed realities, to social interaction, to persistent effects and to a wider range of technologies, including mobile and low-end ones... (Information Society Technologies, 2009)

In the short-term, user acceptance of 3-D virtual world environments will continue to be an important challenge to overcome (Fetscherin & Lattemann, 2007, p. 20). The fact that there is no predefined structure on how to use virtual worlds suggests how critical innovative instructional design can be to facilitate learning in such environments (Jarmon et al., 2009a; Mayrath et al., 2007; Sanchez, 2007). Lynch and Tunstall (2008) have suggested that projects attempting to develop educational simulation games require a development framework and design process that is *integrated* into course design, is engaging, relevant, useful for students, and is flexible, cost effective, and reusable (p. 383). More basic research is needed to demonstrate both how learning activities are being effectively designed in virtual spaces and how virtual spaces are influencing what we imagine *education* itself will become, regardless of age group. As Helen Fox asked educators almost two decades ago, "Are we ready to imagine knowledge differently?" (1994, p. 136).

Effective educational applications in SL will result from the larger learning community developing a deeper understanding of the special affordances of online virtual space accompanied by a spirit of openness, exploration, and improvisation. Active engagement in the virtual world will pull us into a broader landscape where 'real life' plus 'virtual life' yields an inter-reality that is rapidly growing vaster as it is simultaneously being created by and being inhabited by *homo virtualis*.

REFERENCES

Adams, P. C. (2005). *The boundless self: Communication in physical and virtual spaces*. NY: Syracuse UP.

Akrich, M. (1992). The description of technical objects. In Bijker, W., & Law, J. (Eds.), *Shaping technology/building society: Studies in sociotechnical change* (pp. 205–224). Cambridge, MA: MIT Press.

Atkinson, R. K., Mayer, R. E., & Merrill, M. M. (2005). Fostering social agency in multimedia learning: Examining the impact of an animated agent's voice. *Contemporary Educational Psychology, 30*(1), 117–139. doi:doi:10.1016/j.cedpsych.2004.07.001

Bateson, M. (1993). Joint performance across cultures: Improvisation in a Persian garden. *Text and Performance Quarterly, 13*(2), 113–121. doi:doi:10.1080/10462939309366037

Brouchoud, J. (2006). *The arch*. Retrieved May 1, 2009, from http://archsl.wordpress.com/2007/08/30/open-source-scripts-reflexive-virtual-architecture/

Burke, K. (1935). *Permanence and change: An anatomy of purpose*. NY: New Republic.

Chomsky, N. (1957). *Syntactic structures*. The Hague, Paris: Mouton.

Clark, A. (2009). *Natural born cyborgs? Edge: The third culture*. Edge Foundation, Inc. Retrieved February 21, 2009, from http://www.edge.org/3rd_culture/clark/clark_index.html

de Nood, D., & Attema, J. (2006). *Second Life: The second life of virtual reality*. The Hague: Electronic Highway Platform.

Di Paolo, E. A. (2009). Extended life. *Topoi, 28*, 9–21. doi:doi:10.1007/s11245-008-9042-3

Dresang, E., & McClelland, K. (1999). Radical change: Digital age literature and learning. *Theory into Practice, 38*(3), 160–167.

Fetscherin, M., & Lattemann, C. (2007). *User acceptance of virtual worlds: An explorative study about Second Life*. Rollins College: University of Potsdam.

FitzGerald, S. (2007). *Virtual worlds: What are they and why do educators need to pay attention to them?* Paper presented at the meeting of the E-learning Networks June Online Event. Retrieved February 20, 2009, from http://seanfitz.wikispaces.com/virtualworldsenetworks07

Fox, H. (1994). *Listening to the world: Cultural issues in academic writing*. Urbana, IL: National Council of Teachers of English.

Gallese, V., Eagle, M., & Migone, P. (2007). Intentional attunement: Mirror neurons and the neural underpinnings of interpersonal relations. *Journal of the American Psychoanalytic Association, 55*(1), 131–176.

Gee, J. P. (2007). Are video games good for learning? In de Castell, S., & Jenson, J. (Eds.), *Worlds in play* (pp. 323–336). New York: Lang.

Gibson, J. J. (1979/1986). *The ecological approach to visual perception*. Mahwah, NJ: Erlbaum.

Goffman, E. (1956). *The presentation of self in everyday life*. New York: Doubleday.

Gorini, A., Gaggioli, A., Vigna, C., & Riva, G. (2008). A Second Life for eHealth: Prospects for the use of 3D virtual worlds in clinical psychology. *Journal of Medical Internet Research, 10*(3): e21. Retrieved February 20, 2009, from http://www.jmir.org/2008/3/e21.

Iacoboni, M. (2008). *Mirroring people: The new science of how we connect with others*. New York: Farrar, Straus & Giroux.

Information Society Technologies. (2009). *Presence research pro-active initiative*. Retrieved February 20, 2009, from www.cordis.lu/ist/fet/pr.htm.

Jarmon, L. (1996). *An ecology of embodied interaction: Turn-taking and interactional syntax in face-to-face encounters*. Unpublished doctoral dissertation on CD-ROM, University of Texas at Austin.

Jarmon, L. (2009). Learning in virtual world environments: Social-presence, engagement, and pedagogy. In Rogers, P., Berg, G., Boettcher, J., Howard, C., Justice, L., & Schenk, K. (Eds.), *Encyclopedia of distance and online learning* (pp. 1610–1619). Hershey, PA: IGI Global.

Jarmon, L., & Sanchez, J. (2008a). The educators coop experience in Second Life: A model for collaboration. *The Journal of the Research Center for Educational Technology*, *4*(2), 66–82.

Jarmon, L., & Sanchez, J. (2008b, October 24-29). The educators coop: A virtual world model for real world collaboration. In *Proceedings of the 2008 Annual Convention of the American Society for Information Science and Technology (ASIS&T)*, Columbus, OH.

Jarmon, L., & Sanchez, J. (in press). The educators coop: A model for collaboration and LSI communication research in the virtual world. *Electronic Journal of Communication. CIOS.*

Jarmon, L., Traphagan, T., & Mayrath, M. (2008). Understanding project-based learning in Second Life with a pedagogy, training, and assessment trio. *Educational Media International*, *45*(3), 157–176. doi:doi:10.1080/09523980802283889

Jarmon, L., Traphagan, T., Mayrath, M., & Trivedi, A. (2009a). Virtual world teaching, experiential learning, and assessment: An interdisciplinary communication course in Second Life. Elsevier. *Computers & Education*, *53*, 169–182. doi:doi:10.1016/j.compedu.2009.01.010

Jarmon, L., Traphagan, T., Traphagan, J., & Jones-Eaton, L. (in press). Aging, lifelong learning, and the virtual world of Second Life. In Wankel, C., & Kingsley, J. (Eds.), *Higher Education in Second Life*. Charlotte, NC: Information Age Publishing.

Kolb, A. Y., & Kolb, D.A. (2008). The learning way: Meta-cognitive aspects of experiential learning. *Simulation & Gaming*, OnlineFirst, published on October 10, 2008 as doi:10.1177/1046878108325713.

Latour, B. (1990). Drawing things together. In Lynch, M., & Woolgar, S. (Eds.), *Representation of Scientific Practice* (pp. 19–68). Cambridge, MA: MIT Press.

Lave, J., & Wenger, E. (1991). *Situated learning: Legitimate peripheral participation*. New York, NY: Cambridge University Press.

Lynch, M. A., & Tunstall, R. J. (2008). When worlds collide: Developing game-design partnerships in universities. *Simulation & Gaming*, *39*(3), 379–398. doi:doi:10.1177/1046878108319275

Mayer, R. (2003). Learning environments: The case for evidence-based practice and issue-driven research. *Educational Psychology Review*, *15*(4), 359–366. doi:doi:10.1023/A:1026179332694

Mayrath, M., Sanchez, J., Traphagan, T., Heikes, J., & Trivedi, A. (2007, June). *Using Second Life in an English course: Designing class activities to address learning objectives.* Paper presented at ED-MEDIA World Conference on Educational Multimedia, Hypermedia & Telecommunications, Vancouver, Canada.

Moll, L. C. (1992). *Vygotsky and education: Instructional implications and applications of sociohistorical psychology*. UK: Cambridge University Press.

Nardi, B. A. (2005). Beyond bandwidth: Dimensions of connection in interpersonal communication. *Computer Supported Cooperative Work, 14*(2), 91–130. doi:doi:10.1007/s10606-004-8127-9

Peña, J., McGlone, M., Jarmon, L., & Sanchez, J. (2009). *The automatic effects of avatar appearance and role labels in language use in a virtual environment*. Paper to be presented at the November 2009 Annual Convention of the National Communication Association, Chicago, Ill.

Polanyi, M. (1966). *The tacit dimension*. Garden City, NY: Doubleday.

Riva, G., Anguera, M., Wiederhold, B., & Mantovani, F. (Eds.). (2006). *From communication to presence: Cognition, emotion and culture towards the ultimate communicative experience*. Amsterdam: IOS Press. Retrieved February 20, 2009, from http://www.emergingcommunication.com/volume8.html

Sanchez, J. (2007, June). *A sociotechnical systems analysis of Second Life in an undergraduate English course.* Paper presented at ED-MEDIA World Conference on Educational Multimedia, Hypermedia & Telecommunications, Vancouver, Canada.

Senge, P. (1994). *The fifth discipline: The art and practice of a learning organization*. New York: Doubleday Publishers.

Stahl, G., Koschmann, T., & Suthers, D. (2006). Computer-supported collaborative learning: An historical perspective. In Sawyer, R. K. (Ed.), *Cambridge handbook of the learning sciences* (pp. 409–426). UK: Cambridge University Press.

Steed, A., Slater, M., Sadagic, A., Bullock, A., & Tromp, J. (1999, March 13-17). Leadership and collaboration in shared virtual environments. In *Proceedings of the IEEE Virtual Reality*, VR. IEEE Computer Society, Washington, DC, 112.

Stein, R. (2007, October 6). Real hope in a virtual world. *Washingtonpost.com,* p. A01. Retrieved February 28, 2009, from http://www.washingtonpost.com/wp-dyn/content/article/2007/10/05/AR2007100502391.html

Suchman, L. (1987). *Plans and situated actions: The problem of human-machine communication*. New York: Cambridge University Press.

Suchman, L. (2002). Practice-based design of information systems: Notes from the hyperdeveloped world. *The Information Society, 18*, 139–144. doi:doi:10.1080/01972240290075066

Thomas, S. (2006). Pervasive learning games: Explorations of hybrid educational gamescapes. *Simulation & Gaming, 37*(1), 41–55. doi:doi:10.1177/1046878105282274

Wenger, E. (1998). *Communities of practice: Learning, meaning, and identity*. UK: Cambridge University Press.

Yee, N., & Balilenson, J. (2007). The Proteus effect: The effect of transformed self-representation on behavior. *Human Communication Research, 33*, 271–290. doi:doi:10.1111/j.1468-2958.2007.00299.x

This work was previously published in International Journal of Virtual and Personal Learning Environments, edited by Michael Thomas, Volume 1, Issue 1, pp. 38-56, copyright 2010 by IGI Publishing (an imprint of IGI Global).

Chapter 6
Second Life as a Surrogate for Experiential Learning

Michael N. DeMers
New Mexico State University, USA

ABSTRACT

Second Life is increasingly being used as a venue for education, especially for delivery of online instruction where social presence and community building are essential components. Despite its robust 3-D modeling tools and powerful scripting language, many educational uses of Second Life are limited to passive forms of content delivery that often mimic some variety of Victorian style lecture setting. This article demonstrates a series of exercises designed around a more active learning model for my geography courses based on Kolb's (2005) theory of experiential learning. Active class exercises encourage hands-on interaction with components of the virtual world, but are linked explicitly to real subject matter content. By providing fun pre-exercise training and promoting learning by discovery, the exercises are designed to encourage the four fundamental components of the experiential learning environment: involvement, reflection, analysis, and problem solving. Beyond providing an excellent educational environment, such approaches can act as surrogates for real-world experiences that are either impossible or logistically problematic.

INTRODUCTION

Online college and university courses are proliferating at a pace that far exceeds that of higher education in general. It is estimated that during the fall term of 2007, 3.9 million students were taking at least one course online, with roughly 20% of all United States higher education students taking an online class. This constituted a 12.9% growth in online courses compared to a 1.2% increase in higher education enrollment overall (Allen & Seaman, 2008). This trend is placing a renewed sense of urgency on educators who must satisfy often wildly different learning styles in a medium that places constraints on instructional design. Some see it as critical that we meet the needs of particular learning communities whose traditional styles of learning might not be obviously amenable to online delivery, such as those involving hand-on experiences. In fact, many disciplinary

DOI: 10.4018/978-1-4666-1770-4.ch006

specialists, especially those in the sciences, point out the limitations of online learning to address such experiences as an objection to online learning in the first place. Among these disciplines is my own field of geography, a field that, although becoming increasingly technological, is still rooted in field trips, first hand observation, data collection, analysis, description, and prediction. Kolb (1984) most often categorized such learners as "assimilators," whose learning is best facilitated by experiential forms of education. Research by Healy and Jenkins (2000) suggests that, by and large, geographers are assimilators, and that as such, they are best served by experiential forms of education.

Like many disciplines that rely on experiential learning, geography has developed a set of well-established forms of experience that have served the needs of the traditional learner. Such experiences include hands on map exercises, field trips, extended field camps, and various forms of strategy games that simulate planning scenarios or changes in the earth's environments. One might recall games such as SimCity and SimEarth – both of which have been used in the geography classroom. Instrumentation has also played a major role in geographic experiential education where students use thermometers, wind vanes, and sling psychrometers to measure weather variables, or collect soils, vegetation, tree core, pollen, water or other environmental variables for later laboratory analysis. Most recently, faculty have employed high-end statistics software (e.g., SAS and SPSS), CAD and other graphic software, GPS equipment, and remote sensing and Geographic Information Systems (GIS) software to analyze pre-selected study areas or even to pursue project-based learning exercises.

Developing meaningful experiential learning situations is often difficult even in the real world (Fuller et al., 2003), as exemplified by the logistics of providing vehicles and living accommodations during extended field courses (Haigh & Gold, 1993) or by the expense of using high end scientific instruments such as scanning electron microscopes for examining viruses, and mass spectrometers for performing chemical analyses. For some disciplines, such scenarios might prove impossible. Imagine, for example, trying to create an international business that students could operate including the development of products, marketing, capitalizing, etc. The financing alone would be prohibitive. Circumstances might also limit or even prohibit the development of experiential learning scenarios under normal conditions – for example where the experience might require the study of landforms that do not occur within a reasonable distance or where access to samples involves travel to ocean depths. The venue of education itself, most notably the online delivery of courses, often severely limits development of experiential content.

Perhaps because of the perceived difficulties of delivering experiential learning online, it is still a small portion of distance delivery despite the use of experiential learning modules in traditional postal forms of distance learning. This situation must be reversed in an age when both an aging workforce is being decimated through retirements, and where job skills change so quickly. If online education is going to be effective at providing students with real world working knowledge, and if it is going to adapt to the rapid changes in workforce skills and demands for teamwork, then incorporation of experiential forms of learning is essential.

Nearly a decade ago, Mclaughlin and Luca (2002) demonstrated the use of asynchronous communication tools to enhance professional management skills for multi-media developers. The formation of a collaborative learning community, focused on real-world problems, relied on the use of a listserve and a community website for sharing information. Students were able to develop relationships with a client online, create design problem solutions, and develop a project brief.

One critical factor in this successful experiential opportunity was the ability to work on large real-world or "real-world-like" problems in a project-based learning approach. Additionally, the workforce is increasingly demanding team formation and team-based collaboration as an integral part of everyday work. Despite the availability of an increasing array of online collaboration tools such as websites, shared documents, blogs, wikis, and many others, the formation of a true learning community relies on social presence that is largely lacking from such text-based tools or traditional learning management systems. While there are tools such as VoiceThread, SlideShare, Skype, Animoto, and many others that allow different forms of communication, the sheer numbers of such tools often overwhelms both the course designer and the learner. Each tool has its own user interface, its own hardware requirements, and its own limitations as a collaborative tool. Most, in fact are not designed for nor well adapted to educational settings. What is needed is a setting in which the experiences can be actively shared within an immersive environment in which the learners have a shared intellectual landscape, with a common user interface, that is adaptable to most modern computing environments. Such an environment must also provide an enhanced level of social presence than a loose collection of unrelated multi-media tools can provide.

ENTER SECOND LIFE

One possible solution to the online experiential environment is the multi-user virtual environment (MUVE), such as Second Life. Second Life provides a rich 3-D environment in which the students can collaborate with each other and where course designers are free from the bonds of the traditional classroom setting (Schneiderman, 2008). Course content can be incorporated into existing simulations for role-play or created for specific subject matter such as geography (DeMers, 2008). Virtually all forms of delivery and interaction are available from text-based chat, file sharing, voice chat, movies, and simulation and modeling; and deliver all of this in real time (Berg, 2008). Because the faculty and the learners create their own persona using an avatar (a computer rendition of themselves) they can convene meetings, collaborate on projects, explore simulated spaces, and learn in a community manner which is more engaging than typical Learning Management Systems-based online courses (Barab et al., 2007).

While Second Life is an intriguing environment for education, its strength is derived from its ability to augment and/or enhance the learning environment of online courses rather than as a means of replacing face-to-face courses (Hargis, 2006; Trotter, 2008). Among the most often cited enhancements are the impact immersion has on creating shared intellectual landscapes. Successful examples of such immersive settings include the simulation of the human testis developed by The Ohio State University Medical School or the simulation of the hallucinations associated with schizophrenia developed by faculty at the University of California at Davis (Yellowlees et al., 2006). Historians have used Second Life to recreate classic settings to enhance role-play to provide a more robust understanding of historical events by allowing the students to experience the same environment simultaneously.

A related enhancement is the ability of students to communicate and collaborate in a more natural manner than asynchronous online settings. Jarmon et al. (2008), for example, have employed Second Life to teach communication studies in a synchronous environment (McVey, 2008). Computer scientists, for example, have devised ways to use the shared intellectual landscape to provide for collaborative activities through shared visualizations (Bourke, 2008). Collaboration can also involve the use of in-world building tools in a collaborative environment to, for example, train architecture students and planners (Herwig & Parr, 2002). Another way that collaboration can easily be provided is through creating meeting places where students' avatars get together to discuss any number of group-based projects (Jarmon et al., 2008, 2009).

This latter approach to collaboration brings up yet another positive aspect of Second Life that is frequently cited as one of its advantages over traditional LMS-based online courses – that of social presence (Barab et al., 2007; Taylor, 2006; Ward, 2008). Social presence provides a sense of belonging, often associated with student success in face-to-face university programs (Johnson, 2000). The feeling that one is actually in the room with fellow students and the instructor, combined with the relative anonymity of using an avatar as a surrogate for the real person seems to contribute to a willingness to participate in the learning experience. Additionally, this participation contributes to a sense of "flow" in which the time passes quickly because the students are engaged in their own learning. A surrogate for time-on-task, this is often a good predictor of learning.

One often neglected, but extremely valuable, aspect of Second Life that may be of importance to its utility as a learning environment is its ability to act as a replacement for experiential learning. Based on the traditional proverb that promises "I do and I understand," and combined with Kolb's Experiential Learning Theory, one major missing element, especially for the group of learners called "Accommodators," is the hands-on experience (Kolb & Kolb, 2005). Students who study disciplines like commerce, demography, education, environmental studies, geography, political science, and public policy might well be served by using content within multi-user virtual environments like Second Life to provide an opportunity for online students of such disciplines to have the necessary simulated hands-on experiences. While some have shown how second life can incorporate experiential learning through the use of virtual worlds like Second Life for project based learning.

This paper demonstrates, with three simple examples, how such hands-on experiential activities can be developed within geography - identified as being one of a number of disciplines heavily populated by accommodators (Healy & Jenkins, 2000; Healy et al., 2005). While focusing on geography content other disciplines, especially those allied to the graphical and environmental sciences are easily adapted. In fact, Nulty and Barrett (1996) suggested that accommodators also dominate academic fields such as commerce, demography, education, public policy, and political science. According to Kolb's model "accommodators" have the following characteristics (Kolb & Kolb, 2005):

1. They like to carry out established plans;
2. They like action and results;
3. They adapt to changing circumstances;
4. They are comfortable with changing circumstances;
5. They like a trial and error approach to problem solving;
6. They are good at setting objectives;
7. They are good at setting schedules.

For this research I made the assumption, based on the results of Healy and Jenkins (2000) and Healy et al. (2005) that the students, all geographers, would likely be heavily oriented toward the "accommodator" learning styles. Rather than focusing on the degree to which each student's learning style fit within the "accommodator" category, and how this fit might affect the learning, this research was an initial attempt at content creation and a rapid prototype of the utility of creating surrogate experiential learning in immersive environments.

While immersive environments such as Second Life's Genome Island provide extremely rich environments for both shared intellectual landscapes and experiential learning (Lowe & Clark, 2008), they do not really provide much guidance for course designers who need smaller, less complex, and less time-consuming experiences to address the needs of experiential learners. For this reason, I have chosen a more modular approach where the experiences do not require elaborate simulations and extensive programming. For the course designer, this means that individual learning objects can be developed incrementally.

The following examples illustrate how content-related scenarios can be developed quickly, and how they can easily include effective learning objectives and behavioral indicators. I further demonstrate that such experiential surrogates cannot only replace experiential opportunities but that in some instances, these opportunities might actually be an improvement over their face-to-face equivalents. All of these experiential opportunities are developed in a retrievable package format called a gift box. Second life allows one to create primitive 3-D objects called prims that can hold content such as images (called textures), text (in the form of notecards), and other prims if needed.

Scenario One: Creating and Visualizing the Families of Map Projections (Substitute for Map Analysis)

Problem

Geographers deal with maps on a regular basis. Maps are 2-D representations of a spherical earth and so must undergo a dimensional transformation (3-D to 2-D). This process, called map projection, is often conceived of as occurring in one of three different families. The families are planar, conical, and cylindrical. There are generally two ways that this is represented and examined whether online or face-to-face; graphics or as a manipulation using map manipulation software. Both of these are 2-D representations of items that are in reality three-dimensional (3-D).

Solution

Map projection exercise in Second Life.

Lesson Purpose

Create an opportunity for students to actively create and manipulate the three families of map projections.

Materials

A gift box that includes the following:

1. An instructions notecard that includes learning objectives and behavioral indicators;
2. A notecard with an answer sheet for student responses;
3. A map image (texture) uploaded as a .jpeg file;
4. The following textures:
    a. Mercator-800, PLSS, Snapsots 001 through 006 (for your assistance), and UTM-zones;
5. These instructions;
6. An answer sheet.

The instructions notecard includes the following information:

Lab 02 has the following learning objectives:

1. Demonstrate that you can articulate graphically (3-D) and verbally what happens when a spherical Earth is projected on a flat surface;
2. Demonstrate that you can specifically articulate graphically and verbally the impact of implementing a cylindrical, conic, and planar projection.

Directions for Part 1: Projections

For Part One you are to visualize the three families of map projection using the building tools of second life.

Steps

- Rez a sphere;
- Convert the sphere to 3m x 3mTexture the sphere using the Mercator-800 (See Snapshot_001_Globe);
- Change the Horizontal (U) Repeats per Face to 0.995 to remove the seam;

- Call this object Lab02 Globe (save it to your inventory when you are done with the lab);
- Use "shift copy" to reproduce the Lab02Globe;
- Use the stretch utility (Ctrl-Shift) to flatten the copy so it is only 0.1 meters thick (See Snapshot_002_Planar);
- Call this object Lab02 Planar (save it to your inventory when you are done with the lab);
- Now create a flat prim (start with a cube) that is exactly 4 m wide, by 3m high, by 0.1 m thick;
- Texture only one side using Mercator-800 (See Snapshot_003_ Mercator included);
- Call this object Lab02 Mercator (save it to your inventory when you are done with the lab);
- Now create a cylinder with dimensions 2 m x 2 m wide by 3m high. Hollow the sphere to 95% (optional);
- Texture the outside of the cylinder using mercator-800 (See Snapshot_004_Cylinder);
- Call this object Lab02 Cylindrical (save it to your inventory when you are done with the lab);
- Now create a cone with dimensions 3 m x 3 m x 3 m;
- Texture the outside of the cone using Merator-800;
- Change the Horizontal (U) Repeats per Face to 0.995 to remove the seam (See Snapshot_005_Conical);
- Call this object Lab02 Conical (save it to your inventory when you are done with the lab);
- For each of the five objects you just created, answer the following on your answer sheet:
    - Describe (on the answer sheet) the differences in how the continents and geographic grid change when displayed as a globe, a Mercator projection on a flat map, and on the three families of map projection (planar, cylindrical, conical).Be sure to include the changes in size and shape of the continents and how the lines of latitude and longitude align.

Results and Learning Enhancement

This was one of my earliest Second Life experiential laboratories and still remains one of the most successful. The students were able to recreate the map on all five different forms of prim (Figure 1) with what seemed to be little difficulty forthem. Most began the exercise immediately after I taught them the procedures for building and texturing, which proved to be advantageous. Upon creating the 3-D models of the map projection families, the students were quick to voice their surprise at both their success for building maps and projection models in Second Life, but also at how easily they were able to create 3-D visualizations of their course content. The students' 'aha' reaction was identified by the text chat and instant message (IM) windows filling with statements such as "wow" and "cool" and many others coming from the students. Some students were still talking about the "wow factor" after two weeks. Such reactions are indicative of the excitement of discovery that I have not seen in students regarding the three map projection families. Any discipline that relies on visualization, especially 3-D visualization could benefit from exercises like these.

Figure 1. A 3-D visualization of flat maps, globes, and each of the three families of map projections (planar, cylindrical, and conical), showing how the earth's shape and grid change after projection. This Second Life approach allows the student to actually create their own visualizations and then walk among their creations.

Scenario Two: Spatial Distributions, Data Collection, and Analysis (Substitute for Spatial Analysis)

Problem

Spatial statistics – those that qualitatively or quantitatively describe distributions of point, line, and area objects – are becoming increasingly common and are therefore more common in geography courses. Statistics instructors have often pointed to the increased understanding afforded to statistical analysis of data collected by the students (Hogg, 1991). Gathering data on distributional patterns is often prohibitively costly and time consuming.

Solution

Because Second Life uses maps, and because each avatar in Second Life is plotted on the map (in real time with a green dot) as well as X, Y, and even Z coordinates relative to the Second Life Grid (Figure 2), it provides a convenient environment in which to collect spatial distributions. Moreover, the distributions can be evaluated for different regions, with different environments, during different periods of time if one wanted to have students perform analysis of spatio-temporal pattern changes.

Lesson Purpose

Create an experience in which students can collect distributional data and analyze those data.

Materials

1. The following note cards: These directions, Lab 09 answer sheet;
2. The following textures: Lab 9-1, Lab 9-2;
3. The following scripts: floating text (a small program that puts a set of text over the prims).

Figure 2. An example of a Second Life map showing how each avatar is identified by its X, Y, and Z coordinates. ("epione" in the upper right).

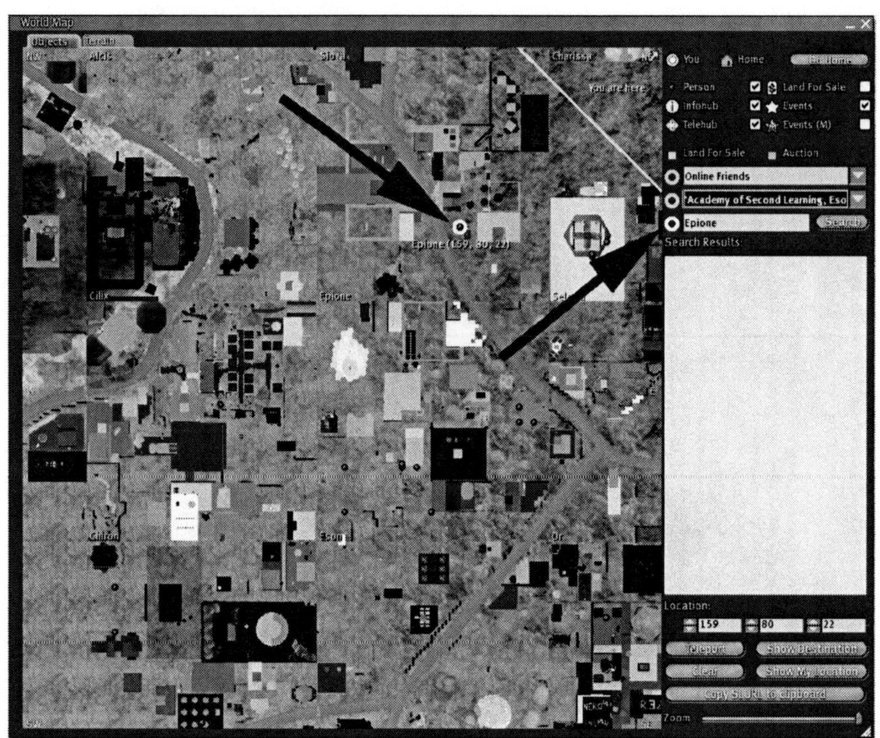

Lab 09: Spatial Arrangement (Density and Distribution)

Lab 09 has the following learning objectives

1. Find a study area within Second Life in which to conduct a spatial sample of avatars (surrogates for people);
2. Select a sample of at least 30 avatar locations (X and Y... the Z can be ignored for this exercise);
3. Take a snapshot of the study area with the avatars present to preserve the study area;
4. Calculate the density of avatars in your study areas (number of avatars per square meter);
5. Perform a "nearest neighbor" statistic on the dataset;
6. Discuss the relevance of the results.

Directions

Part I: Creating a sample point distribution dataset

- Use the "search" button on the bottom of your screen to search for locations of interest to you and that contain at least 30 avatars located within the world map of that area (See Texture 9-1);
- Take a snapshot of the map to be turned in with your assignment.
- Move your cursor over the four corners of your study area;
- Note and write down those four coordinates on a notecard;
- Count the number of avatars you see in the study area;
- Move your cursor over at least 30 randomly selected avatar locations and click on each. As you do, a small red circle will ap-

pear and their X,Y, and Z coordinates will appear in the window on the right (Texture 9-2);
- Record these coordinates for later analysis.

Part II: Analyzing the dataset

- Calculate the size of your dataset in meters;
- Calculate the density of your dataset (avatars / square meter);
- Number your avatar samples based on the order in which you are selecting them;
- On your note card, tabulate the X and Y locations of your samples;
- Calculate the nearest neighbor distance of each of your 10 or more samples;
- Calculate the average nearest neighbor distance of your sample set.

Part III: Discussing the results.

- Create a gift box called "My_Name_Lab09";
- Include the picture of your study area in the box (request reimbursement for the ten Linden dollars (L$10) charge);
- Complete the answer sheet and return it in the gift box.

Results and Learning Enhancement

Results from this exercise were mixed, but showed potential of virtual environments in education. The students collected their own data for their lab rather than relying on preset datasets. This resulted in a sense of ownership of the experiment and the analytical process. This sense of reality of the dataset was not as pronounced, based on anecdotal comments by the students. Many of them understood the concept, but were not always readily able to identify the green dots as belonging to people. The connection between analyzing avatar locations as a surrogate for people was not as strong as I expected. Part of this seems to be related to the sites the students chose. The activities in which the avatars were engaged varied greatly from student to student because each chose his or her own location. Some chose sites randomly, others based their sample selections on a pattern that they observed when they searched Second Life maps for sites, and others just took a first found approach.

To improve the effectiveness of this exercise, I will pre-define the study area for the students in the future. Moreover, I will identify the land use categories for the students, and provide a scenario of the types of activities that generally occur in the sim (Second Life terminology for a thematic simulation, e.g. shopping, dancing, etc.). This will give a common structure to the experience and provide a purpose for the data collection. The scenario seems the missing element here.

While this experience was not obviously exciting to the students, they were able to complete the exercise in a timely manner and were able to provide some reasons for distributions in at least two instances. The take-home message for this exercise is that, without having to create extensive teaching simulations such as the experimental setting of Genome Island, one can still obtain statistical data for analysis.

Scenario Three: Land Measurement and Survey (*Substitute for Field Work*)

Problem

Field measurements are common in geographic research, but require measurement instruments (e.g., survey equipment), field sites, transportation, and logistics that are unavailable in an online environment.

Solution

Create an environment in which students can measure virtual landscapes as surrogates for real landscapes.

Lesson Purpose

Provide an understanding of different aspects of distance measurement.

Lab 04 has the following learning objectives:

1. Demonstrate that you can create a 3-D visualization (surface drainage model) of how the drain function (least cost path) works in a raster database and relate it to the figure in your text(Figure 3);
2. Demonstrate that you can create a 3-D visualization of how cumulative cost surfaces work in a raster database;
3. Demonstrate that you can calculate least cost path using a small (5 X 5) grid;
4. Calculate Manhattan (on-edge) distance, area, and perimeter with a small (5 X 5) grid;
5. Calculate the planimetric, and non-planimetric distance and sinuousity ratio of a curved linear feature.

Materials

- The following objects: a 481 Lab 06 Least Cost Grid, a 481 Manhattan Distance Grid, and an upright-gridmaker v1.6 GPL;
- The following textures: Fundamentals Fig 09-18(textbook figure);
- The following note cards: these instructions, 481 Lab 06 Answer Sheet.

Directions

Parts 1 & 2: 3-D visualizations

For both parts, you will use the same surface model you create. Refer to textbook Figure 9-18 (included). You DO NOT need to reproduce this exactly. In fact, it will be easier if you make your own.

Part 1: Basic steps for making the raster surface model (textbook figure 9-18):

- Rez (create a digital version that appears apparently out of nowhere) a cube
- Rename the cube (surface drain model);
- Use the "shift copy" command to make four copies all in a line (resulting in a line of five cubes all touching);
- Select all five of these cubes and use the "cntrl-L" or "cmd-L" command (mac) to link these;
- Use the "shift copy" command to make four copies of the row of cubes (resulting in a set of 5 X 5 or 25 cubes;
- Select the entire grid and link all the parts using the "tools>link" command;
- In the edit menu, stretch the top of each of 25 cubes you have created. NOTE: first be sure you have the "edit linked parts" selected (ON), and be sure your "stretch both sides" option radio dial is turned OFF.

Create a surface of your own choosing:

- Determine the starting grid cell (the top);
- Determine the direction of flow (which grid cells will be used by a liquid as it flows downhill);
- Select these grid cells one by one and color code them with a single blue color representing flow (i.e. water);
- Leave the model where it is;
- Take a screenshot of your avatar standing next to your model;
- Place this picture in a giftbox called "481Lab06_your_real_name".

Part 2

- Create a cube (essentially an accumulation surface) that is 0.52 m high x 25.4 m x 25.4 m;
- Color code this a light blue. Set transparency to 50%;
- Place this grid on the ground and over your drainage model so it is exactly cen-

Figure 3. A 3-D model showing down-slope movement compared to its 2-D figure (figure 9-18 backdrop) from the course textbook. This is similar to the models the students will create.

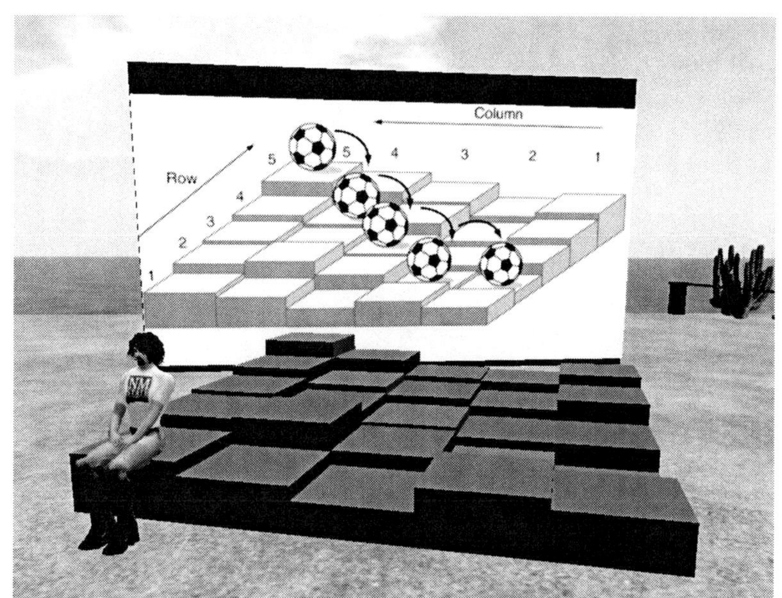

tered on the model. This should be just a little wider (X and Y) than the model so it shows through, and just a little higher than the first 0.5 meters of your model;

- Take a screenshot of your model and place it in your 481 lab 6 giftbox;
- Make your accumulation surface cube 1.02 or 1.52 or 2.02 (so it just goes over the 2nd, 3rd, or 4th level of your original model.18. Take a picture of this cumulative surface model and include it in your gift box.

Part 3 (4 points): Least Cost calculation

- Rez the 481 Lab 06 Least Cost Grid;
- Refer to pages 221 and 222 in your text;
- Assuming the yellow squares constitute a friction value of 2, and using the formulas on pages 221 and 222 in your book, you are going to move from the centroid of the white cell to a final destination at the center of the red cell;
- Determine the least cost value for the red cell (the lowest possible value you could get traveling from the white to the red cell);
- Place that value on your answer sheet, which you will eventually return in your gift box.

Part 4 (4 points): Manhattan Distance:

- Rez the 481 Manhattan Distance Grid;
- Moving from the outside corner of the bottom left red cell to the outside corner of the upper right red cell calculate:
    - The Manhattan Distance along the white cells;
    - The Manhattan Distance along the blue cells;
- Provide your answers on the 481 Lab 06 answer sheet that you will be turning in via your gift box.

Part 5: Vector Distance(Figure 4)

You will find a set of yellow stakes on the western portion of Aggie Island. The first of these

Figure 4. Topographic surface study area where students use instruments to measure straight-line versus sinuous distance, as well as planimetric versus elevational distance.

poles has floating text that says (Start Here) and the last has floating text that says (End Here).

- Rez the upright gridmaker;
- Measure the planimetric distance along the total length of these stakes (total planimetric distance);
- Measure the planimetric Euclidean distance (straight-line) from the first stake to the last stake;
- Measure the vertical distance (elevation) at the bottom of the last stake using the vertical part of your vertical grid);
- Calculate the actual distance, including adjustments for elevation from start to finish. *** Hint, you will need to make these adjustments for each segment using the Pythagorean Theorem (distance equation). You will also want to "slide" the vertical gridmaker so it is always at ground level;
- Based entirely on planimetric distances, calculate the sinuosity ratio of the line of stakes;
- Place your answers on the answer sheet and turn it in via your gift box with the rest of your materials;
- Request reimbursement for your L$30 costs (no reimbursements will be made for more than that so take care when you do your photographs).

Results and Learning Enhancement

This exercise had both the visualization elements of the first exercise and the data collection elements of the second. It also had the advantage of providing a field experience, which the others did not. Unfortunately, this experience was less successful than the other two. Only two of my volunteer students actually finished this laboratory although portions had been performed in an early incarnation of the exercise. One problem with this laboratory is that it took considerably longer to complete. It also experienced some initial logistical issues that are also part of the Second Life venue. In this instance, the original location I set out for the students to do the survey of the planimetric and topographic distances did not allow the students the permission to "rez" their instruments. I had to relocate the students and re-do the study site on a different part of the island where building and rezzing are allowed for non-owners.

Some students told me that they did not do this lab because they became frustrated with the inability to rez their instruments. Those who contacted me finished the exercise. Although I contacted all the students and indicated the change in study area location, they told me informally that they simply did other class-work. They admitted at that time that during mid-term exams the time required to do labs in Second Life was prohibitive.

The results of the exercise itself were acceptable, but the lessons learned from this experience have more to do with planning than with execution. One of the most important aspects of experiential learning is that it is well planned to elicit the required lesson. I believe the logistical issue, combined with timing issues, interfered with the lesson here. By shortening the exercise, timing it so it does not occur during mid-term exams, and assuring that the land rights are set properly will improve the likelihood for future successful implementation of the lesson.

The only comments I received had to do with the 3-D model of the textbook picture that seemed to help students understand the way the software operates. There were no comments about the land survey exercise so I have no indication of its effectiveness. I plan to make the suggested modifications and try this experiential learning object again. Additionally, I am currently creating an assessment rubric that will provide feedback on student understanding.

SUMMARY AND CONCLUSION

This article provided three concrete examples of experiential learning objects that require substantially less investment in Second Life skills, time, and computational resources than some of the more complex immersive environments being used for education in Second Life. There are still few examples of how experiences can be developed in Second Life by the online course designer, which provide some guidelines for them. In particular, these exercises were designed to work for the accommodators, the learners best adapted to experiential learning activities.

Each of the three examples demonstrated some signs of success based on observations, the results of the exercises themselves, and some unsolicited anecdotal comments provided by the students. The 3-D visualization seems to be one of the strongest aspects of these experiences, especially with regard to the map projection exercise and the stream model. Those who worked together in teams were more successful at both completing the laboratories in a timely manner and producing the most acceptable results.

The primary advantage of these exercises is that they provide an opportunity for experiential learning in an online environment. In this instance, they were surrogates for map work, field analysis, and statistical data collection and analysis. While the student reactions to these laboratories were not systematically examined, there is anecdotal information based on results, and on unsolicited student comments. This suggests that other disciplines whose learners are predominantly accommodators can potentially benefit from similar learning modules.

While there is potential for success, there are still lessons to be learned from both the successful and the unsuccessful aspects of these three examples. First, anything that relies on 3-D visualization seems to be a positive. The students responded with great enthusiasm when they were able to visualize the three projection families in three dimensions. For this to succeed, however, requires that the students have the requisite skills for developing the objects inside Second Life, thus suggesting the use of skills building exercises prior to each exercise. Another factor that seems important in the success of these exercises is that you have student buy-in and that they take ownership of the exercises they are performing. When students were able to make 3-D models of figures from the textbook, they seemed more engaged in the topic and demonstrated a sense of accomplishment not just because they understood the material, but that they were able to produce objects that clearly demonstrated that knowledge.

Another important aspect is that the students have a clear and thorough understanding of the purpose of the exercise. Additionally, because they are experiential, I believe it is vital that they also have a scenario that makes sense and is well spelled out. This was clearly a challenge with the second exercise on statistical data analysis. Rather than relying on the student to formulate the scenario and its attendant relationships, this needs to be carefully constructed so that students know what they are looking for.

One aspect of these exercises that is not present in their current form is a recommended opportunity for reflection. In their present state, the students perform the exercise, interact with each other during their completion, periodically ask for assistance from their instructor, and then turn the assignment in for grading. The time required to develop the exercises hampered my ability to spend time creating the reflection scenario. I have subsequently included a required "fireside chat" for each laboratory so we can talk about the results. I plan to have this experience around a pre-created chat setting with logs and a crackling fire to set an informal atmosphere to encourage discussion and reduce apprehension. I have also provided a bare space (an open place in the NMSU Aggie Island simulation) so the students can rez their own exercise so we can all view the results and discuss them with the object of the discussion presence.

These results, although mixed, are encouraging in that they demonstrate the potential of developing a large array of short, easy to construct, domain-specific learning experiences for online learners. They encourage ownership of learning, collaborative interaction, and often provide visualizations and approaches that are difficult or impossible in other online environments. My experiences suggest an incremental approach. I would also recommend that a teaching assistant perform the laboratory exercises in-world so that errors, time limitations, Second Life permissions settings and other potential pitfalls could be identified before implementation. I suggest that the opportunity for reflection be considered as a critical component of the laboratory design. These should provide the necessary fabric for the successful use of Second Life as a surrogate environment for experiential learning.

Beyond improving the exercise environment, future research needs to be considerably more systematic. There are several things that must be addressed. First, for this research I made an assumption, based on previous research, that all the students involved were "assimilators." This generalization is not sufficient to allow a detailed analysis of the relationship between either experiential learning and student success, much less surrogate experiential learning. Prior to any future research, an analysis of Kolb's learning styles must be performed. Related to this, is a need to develop instruments for measuring the degree to which the students gained additional insights over their peers who did not participate in the Second Life experiences. To do this will require not just grading rubrics, but a control group for comparison.

One important, and often neglected, aspect of learning in virtual worlds such as Second Life that must be addressed to determine its effectiveness for learning has to do with the steep learning curve and technical issues related to the Second Life environment. Second Life is both a cultural shock to some students, especially those who are not experienced gamers. More than that, however, Second Life is also a multi-tasking environment that requires the manipulation of an avatar, opening and closing several computer windows, operating pull-down menus, and orchestrating the creation and modification of three-dimensional objects – all at the same time. Such multi-tasking environments can be very disconcerting to some and must be accounted for by a pre-examination of multi-tasking skills to eliminate them as an impediment to learning. Finally, a pre- and post-assessment of student attitudes and perspectives regarding each exercise to ascertain its relevance and effectiveness to support the course content would also provide insights into the potential for student success.

REFERENCES

Allen, I. E., & Seaman, J. (2008). Staying the course: online education in the United States, 2008. *Sloan-C*. Retrieved June 22, 2009 from http://www.sloan-c.org/publications/survey/pdf/staying_the_course.pdf

Barab, S., Scott, B., Ingram-Goble, A., Goldstone, R., Zuiker, S., & Warren, S. (2007). Situative embodiment as a curricular scaffold: using videogames to support science education. In *Proceedings of the American Education Research Association*, Chicago, IL. Retrieved June 22, 2009 from http://inkido.indiana.edu/research/onlinemanu/papers/emb_lab_study.pdf

Berg, Z. (2008). Multi-user virtual environments for education and training? A critical review of Second Life. *Educational Technology Magazine: The Magazine for Managers of Change in Education, 48*(3), 27–31.

Bourke, P. (2008). Evaluating Second Life as a tool for collaborative scientific visualization. In *Proceedings of the Computer Games and Allied Technology*, Singapore. Retrieved June 30, 2009 from http://local.wasp.uwa.edu.au/~pbourke/papers/cgat08/index.html

DeMers, M. (2008). Inside the metaverse: A Second Life for GIS education. *GIS Educator*, Winter, 3. Environmental Systems Research Institute (ESRI), Redlands: California. Retrieved September 6, 2009 from http://www.esri.com/library/newsletters/giseducator/gised-winter08.pdf

Fuller, I., Gaskin, S., & Scott, I. (2003). Student perceptions of geography and environmental science fieldwork in the light of restricted access to the field, caused by foot and mouth disease in the UK in 2001. *Journal of Geography in Higher Education, 27*(1), 79–102. doi:10.1080/0309826032000062487

Haigh, M., & Gold, J. R. (1993). The problems with fieldwork: a group based approach towards integrating fieldwork into the undergraduate geography curriculum. *Journal of Geography in Higher Education, 17*(1), 21–32. doi:10.1080/03098269308709203

Hargis, J. (2008). Second Life for distance learning. *Turkish Online Journal of Distance Education, 9*(2), 57–63.

Healey, M., & Jenkins, A. (2000). Learning cycles and learning styles: the application of Kolb's experiential learning model in higher education. *The Journal of Geography, 99*, 185–195. doi:10.1080/00221340008978967

Healey, M., Kneale, P., & Bradbeer, J. (2005). Learning styles among geography undergraduates: an international comparison. *Area, 37*(1), 30–42. doi:10.1111/j.1475-4762.2005.00600.x

Herwig, A., & Parr, P. (2002). Game engines: tools for landscape visualization and planning. Trends in GIS and virtualization. In *Environmental Planning and Design* (pp. 161–172). Heidelberg, Germany: Wichmann Verlag.

Hogg, R. V. (1991). Statistical education: improvements are badly needed. *The American Statistician, 45*, 342–343. doi:10.2307/2684473

Jarmon, L., Traphagan, T., & Mayrath, M. (2008). 2009). Understanding project-based learning in Second Life with a pedagogy, training, and assessment trio. *Educational Media International, 45*(3), 157–176. doi:10.1080/09523980802283889

Jarmon, L., Traphagan, T., Mayrath, M., & Trivedi, A. (2008). Virtual world teaching, experiential learning, and assessment: an interdisciplinary communication course in Second Life. *Computers & Education, 53*(1), 169–182. doi:10.1016/j.compedu.2009.01.010

Johnson, J. L. (2000). Learning communities and special efforts in the retention of university students: what works, what doesn't, and is the return worth the investment? *Journal of College Student Retention: Research. Theory into Practice, 2*(3), 219–238.

Kolb, A. Y., & Kolb, D. A. (2005). *The Kolb learning style inventory—version 3.1: Technical Specifications*. Boston, MA: Hay Resources Direct.

Kolb, D. (1984). *Experiential learning: Experience as the source of learning and development*. Englewood Cliffs, NJ: Prentice-Hall.

Lowe, C., & Clark, M. A. (2008). Student perceptions of learning in a virtual world. In *Proceedings of the 24th Annual Conference on Distance Teaching and Learning.* Retrieved June 30, 2009 from http://www.uwex.edu/disted/conference/Resource_library/proceedings/08_13442.pdf

McLoughlin, C., & Luca, J. (2002, June 24-29). Experiential learning on-line: the role of asynchronous communication tools. In *Proceedings of the 14th ED-MEDIA World Conference on Educational Multimedia, Hypermedia & Telecommunications,* Denver, CO.

McVey, M. (2008). Observations of expert communicators in immersive virtual worlds: implications for synchronous discussion. *Research in Learning Technology, 16*(3), 173–180.

Nulty, D. D., & Barrett, M. A. (1996). Transitions in students' learning styles. *Studies in Higher Education, 21*(3), 333–345. doi:10.1080/03075079612331381251

Schneiderman, B. E. (2008). Creating a learning space that is virtual and experiential. *Journal of Aesthetic Education, 42*(2), 38–50. doi:10.1353/jae.0.0003

Taylor, K. (2006). Social networks and presence in Second Life. *Cyberpsychology & Behavior, 12*(1), 721–722.

Trotter, A. (2006). Educators get a "Second Life.". *Education Week, 27*(42), 1.

Ward, A. (2008). The power of connections. *The American School Board Journal, 195*(9), 52–54.

Yellowlees, P. M., & Cook, J. N. (2006). Education about hallucinations using an Internet virtual reality system: a qualitative survey. *Academic Psychiatry, 30*, 534–539. doi:10.1176/appi.ap.30.6.534

This work was previously published in International Journal of Virtual and Personal Learning Environments, edited by Michael Thomas, Volume 1, Issue 2, pp. 16-30, copyright 2010 by IGI Publishing (an imprint of IGI Global).

Chapter 7
An Interdisciplinary Design Project in Second Life:
Creating a Virtual Marine Science Learning Environment

Riley Triggs
University of Texas at Austin, USA

Leslie Jarmon
University of Texas at Austin, USA

Tracy A. Villareal
University of Texas Marine Science Institute, USA

ABSTRACT

Virtual environments can resolve many practical and pedagogical challenges within higher education. Economic considerations, accessibility issues, and safety concerns can all be somewhat alleviated by creating learning activities in a virtual space. Because of the removal of real-world physical limitations like gravity, durability and scope, virtual space allows for an expansion of possibilities and approaches to knowledge transfer and discovery learning and becomes an "environment for information" rich with collaborative possibilities. Experimentation and participation in conceptual as well as applied projects is encouraged for both students and instructors. One of these virtual environments, Second Life, was used in a cross-disciplinary project for the creation of a Marine Science virtual class environment as an assignment for design students at a major southwestern research university in the United States. This paper reports on the findings from a project that utilized Second Life as a medium for enhancing and extending design education using a process of interdisciplinary collaboration.

DOI: 10.4018/978-1-4666-1770-4.ch007

INTRODUCTION

Virtual environments allow for experimentation and participation in conceptual and applied projects by teachers and students together. In this paper, one of these virtual environments, *Second Life*, was used in a cross-disciplinary project for the creation of a Marine Science virtual class environment as an assignment for Design students at a major southwestern research university in the USA. The purpose of the study was to address five research questions:

1. Was there a change from before to after the course in terms of what the participants reported they knew or understood about the key course concepts as described in the course objectives? (see below under Objectives of the Design Class).
2. If participants reported prior gaming experience, did that prior experience play a role in participants' understanding of virtual worlds and their impression of *Second Life*?
3. How and during what kinds of situations and class activities does learning occur in *Second Life*?

Therefore, this paper reports on the findings of using *Second Life* (SL) as a medium for enhancing and extending Design education in an interdisciplinary and collaborative context.

PEDAGOGY OF A DESIGN PROGRAM

Design is an inherently heuristic pursuit which relies on processes that develop within the designer to generate solutions that are solved by intuition, or in other words, from a holistic reading of a situation using deductive and inductive reasoning concurrently to produce an optimal result (Gruson et al., 2000). In the Design program, a developed critical process of thinking and making is the desired result under examination in this study more than any single set of manual skills or mastery of a specific medium or particular tangible product. This approach equalizes the value of teaching of critical thinking with the teaching of content or product, and, since each faculty member has a background in a different design discipline (including graphic design, typography, industrial design, design writing and architecture), this approach also equalizes the exposure and practice of disciplines within Design.

The placement of equal emphasis in the program on 'design thinking' suggests that it is similar to a visual liberal arts program in that it produces well-rounded graduates with the ability to contextualize information and to communicate, or to make sense of that information visually with sophisticated complexity and appropriateness across various areas of engagement. This 'design thinking' is largely taught through a process of 'thinking through making' that encourages understanding to be achieved through the creative act or crafting process itself. The result of combining the critical thinking and 'thinking through making' components creates graduates who are able to operate across fields of inquiry with equal alacrity because they are able to approach the problem to be solved without the restrictions or burden associated with using a single medium. The application and practice of this skill, therefore, are incidental to the desired learning experience of the methodology itself, and because of this, the Design program's curriculum is inherently suitable for cross-disciplinary experiences.

VIRTUAL WORLDS AND *SECOND LIFE*

Three-dimensional virtual worlds such as *Second Life* (SL) are rapidly being accepted and used in instructional settings. Indeed, the New Media Consortium and the EDUCAUSE Learning initiative (2007) identified virtual worlds as an emerging technology that is likely to have a large impact on teaching and learning within higher education in the near future.

Thus far suggested positive instructional effects of virtual worlds include the common and uncommon benefits of games, such as accommodating learning preferences of Net Generation students, enhancing student motivation and engagement, providing opportunities for social interactions and facilitating collaboration. To this we can also add, increasing a sense of shared presence and experience, dissolving social boundaries, and allowing free exploration, creation, and use of the environment, data and media content (Craig, 2007; Dede et al., 2005; FitzGerald, 2007; Gee, 2003; Jarmon, 2009a; Jarmon et al., 2009; Jenkins, 2007, cited in Craig, 2007; Kirriemuir & McFarlane, 2003; Lamb, 2006; McGee, 2007; Prensky, 2006; The New Media Consortium, 2009).

In SL, users' *avatars* move around and interact with one another in virtual space. Users also can create buildings and materials in SL. Educators have used SL for a variety of learning activities, such as holding class sessions, simulations, experimenting with architecture or urban planning, role-plays, synchronous collaboration, presentations, and computer mediated communication (*Second Life* in Education, n.d.; New Media Consortium and the EDUCAUSE Learning Initiative, 2007).

The fact that there is no predefined structure on how to use virtual worlds suggests how critical instructional design can be to facilitate learning in such environments (Mayrath et al., 2007; Sanchez, 2007). Yet, to date there are still few empirical studies that inform instructional design and practices in virtual worlds, much less collaboration across disciplines. Our prior studies attempted to begin filling that gap, by exploring the nature and process of learning in SL in a context of an interdisciplinary communication course (Jarmon et al., 2009). This study, on the other hand, looks at how SL in an undergraduate Design course influences participants' learning, especially their experiential learning. The study was conducted in the course called DES 311K: Design Technologies II. Furthermore, it looks at how SL and the virtual environment impact collaboration across disciplines when the learning activities of one class (in the Design course) are directly connected to the design of a course in a different discipline, 'Oceanography: Human Exploration / Exploitation of the Sea' (to be taught in fall 2009).

A key element of this Design course for spring 2009 is its project-based organization wherein Design students must learn and assimilate information from Marine Science and integrate that information into their Design learning by using their spatial intelligence, one of the multiple intelligences explored by Gardner (1983). Students must learn to translate data into spatial form, and develop ways of communicating in three dimensions as they are developing their spatial intelligence. In this study, SL is used to help students learn by concentrating on the space in between the virtual and the physical, where the differences and similarities become more readily apparent and allow for a more informed, personal re-territorializing of design. Existing literature in three different fields suggest that SL would substantially facilitate such learning.

First, studies in computer-mediated communication (CMC) indicate that diverse people interacting via the Internet are more likely to experience positive contact and a shared understanding due to the elimination of geographical barriers and anxiety in contact, as well as control over the contact environment and the ease of disclosure (Amichai-Hamburger & McKenna, 2006). Soukup (2004) also states that people within virtual environments, having the ability to construct the environment, enhance the chances of building community and strengthening the cohesiveness of participants' interactions. Similarly, Steinkuehler and Williams (2006) argue that interacting within virtual worlds not only helps people build communities but also exposes them to a 'diversity of world views' through the development of these virtual social relationships (p. 21).

Second, literature on pedagogical agents implies that the presence of avatars enhances engagement and learning beyond CMC without such agents. Atkinson et al. (2005) state that life-like, animated agents 'prompt the social engagement of the learner, thus allowing the learner to form a simulated human bond with the agent' (p. 121). Moreno et al. (2001) found that such an emotional bond enhanced by agents led to increased scores on the transfer of botany knowledge and to increased motivation.

Third, literature on experiential learning suggests that elements of mediated communication in SL may serve students' experiential learning in new ways. To foster experiential learning, the activities designed for the course in this study take advantage of virtual worlds' affordances for rapid access to creative building tools and to social interactions with individuals from various fields. Experiential learning strategies have been used to inform the ways people engage with difficult social challenges, live in relation to one another, and explore different spaces and perspectives through praxis (Freire, 1976). Kolb and Kolb (2009) have updated their earlier theoretical framework and remind us that their experiential learning model includes 'socialization into a wider community of practice that involves membership, identity formation, [and] transitioning from novice to expert' (pp. 24-25).

This brief survey of literature suggests that the use of SL is well suited for facilitating experiential learning and in particular for the design of a visual information course. Furthermore, it suggests that such applications of SL provide fertile ground for continuing to explore the potential of virtual worlds as learning environments.

WHY SECOND LIFE IS SUITED TO DESIGN EDUCATION

The mission of the BFA degree in Design is to educate a new generation of designers who can adapt to the unique conditions of an information-rich, knowledge-based society. Because Design itself is a heuristic pursuit, the educational methodologies in the Design Division are, in turn, heuristic, and this encourages the curriculum to be flexible and reverberative both with the student and society as it evolves. While speaking about a desirable human-computer interaction (HCI) design curriculum, Faiola (2007) posits that a design curriculum, which produces 'knowledge domains that can account for understanding design, social context, and business' (p. 30), can only be achieved in a process 'by which students learn the theory and best practice of design as a unified approach to knowledge management' (p. 30).

One of the techniques supporting this heuristic approach, while fostering the core program value of critical thinking, is to transform the learning in the classroom into student-driven research and production that are not dependent on the instructor for prompting. This strategy transforms the instructor into coach and mentor, and encourages the learning-to-learn model rather than the authoritative master-apprentice studio model that can produce clones of the teacher. The environment of SL is well suited to provide a safe experimentation ground for student-initiated activities while allowing unanticipated results to emerge instead of predictable solutions to prescriptive prompts.

While most educational activities that currently take place in SL are focused on presenting content to a student, in Design education, the activities can become the creation and presentation of that content. What this offers BFA in Design students is the opportunity to approach multiple layers of learning areas simultaneously in one project while emphasizing the inter-connected nature of the different parts of the project to the central goals of the curriculum.

The imperative of Design education is to keep pace with the technologies and cultural evolution in which designers operate. The emergence of three-dimensional persistent online environments is the current trajectory of our move towards connectivity through the Internet. Corporations, learning institutes and individuals are creating new ways to connect and interact through these environments of information. Increased connectivity comes with a unique set of opportunities and new ways of making sense of the world, which designers are already exploring. The openness and free availability of SL allows currently unmatched student access to this new type of design environment.

INTERDISCIPLINARY OPPORTUNITIES

Undergraduate education is often restricted to existing silos of traditional academic areas because learning methodologies are entrenched in the history and traditions particular to each academic. Boundaries that have historically been set to enhance and to commodify education in a particular subject are now being seen in some instances as a hindrance. A goal of the Design program is to extend and enrich the education of students by opening up lines of inquiry that may benefit from advances and alternate methodologies in other disciplines.

Interdisciplinary studies have been one of the hottest trends in academia since the mid-1990s (Honan, 1994). One way to benefit from these opportunities is to have students participate in a cross-disciplinary project in which students and instructors benefit from both the uniqueness and similarities in the different disciplines.

The current trend in academia is to promote and encourage cross and interdisciplinary activities amongst academic areas, but in reality, these objectives are often impossible within the bounds of existing university structures. These established academic boundaries can be impenetrable working within the established university system, and interdisciplinary activities are often accomplished only through the efforts of instructors working individually below departmental-level involvement. With the use of the pervasive online virtual environment of SL, the traditional academic boundaries can easily be de-territorialized to provide the undergraduate with a unique and truly cross-disciplinary learning experience.

At the large, public university in the USA where our research is being conducted, this cross and interdisciplinary activity was established in the early 1990s in the Art Department with the creation of a new Design program. From the beginning, the Design program has looked to make connections across campus to other programs in order to provide an interdisciplinary context with which to broaden the learning experience for their students. This experience has been in the form of collaborative projects with architecture, interior design, engineering, marketing and business students, but for the first time, a project was undertaken to facilitate education and directly affect the coursework of a set of students in a science-oriented discipline, namely, Marine Science.

THREE DIMENSIONAL LEARNING ENVIRONMENTS AND DESIGN

The purpose of the course under examination in this research study, DES 311K Design Technologies II, is to explore issues of skills related to designing objects and space. This revolves around the technical skill of designing objects using three dimensional computer modeling software. Projects over the past several years have explored the need for designers to rectify the inherent disconnection between designing and modeling in a virtual world using two and three dimensional computer-aided design and drafting software where anything is possible, and the real world, where craft, tolerances, and budgets are paramount in determining the success of realizing a product. The facility to 'smooth' the space between the virtual design and the real product is essential in order to create successful designs for production. For the semester under examination in this research study, the activities capitalized on the free availability of the online environment of SL, and the coursework shifted focus from creating products to creating a 'smoothing' process between virtual and real environments.

METHODOLOGY FOR DESIGNING THE LEARNING EXPERIENCES

Deleuze and Guattari (1988) proposed the trans-historical relation between two conceptualizations of space: the 'smooth' and the 'striated'. The smooth space, the space of nomadic trajectories, is likened to the Japanese game of *Go* where individual pieces territorialize and deterritorialize fluid spaces, and striated space is likened to European chess, where pieces code and decode spaces.

According to Deleuze and Guattari, a striated space exists only in relation to an unstable smooth space, and that while striation seeks to encode the flows of people, goods (and desires) of this space with nomadic trajectories, the smooth space seeks simultaneously to de-territorialize the striated matrix of social order. This is not a policy, but a potential, as the volatile smooth space of desire can erupt anywhere in a striated space (Mical, 2002).

The intent of the class was to perform smoothing between the physical and virtual world in a three-dimensional virtual environment in order to actively engage spatial intelligence in the design process. Spatial intelligence is one of seven acknowledged human capabilities in which we operate in the world, and Van Schaik (2008) notes that linguistic, mathematical, kinetic, natural, inter/intra-personal intelligence and musical intelligence are all more consciously applied in our daily lives, and thus spatial intelligence is often underrated as a means for understanding the world (p. 8). It is, however, how we navigate our way through the world, and much can be communicated through how all of the other forms of intelligence are organized in our environment. The project concentrated both on how to develop spatial intelligence in the design student as well as on how to use it to communicate a deeper understanding of our physical world in a three-dimension environmental.

OBJECTIVES OF THE DESIGN CLASS

The ideas of smoothing real and virtual space were brought together with an exploration of spatial intelligence by learning the skills and tools required to create environments for understanding (or making sense) of the real world in a virtual world. This methodology focuses on environments and systems in an exploration of interactions and a (virtual) environment. The course objectives are shown in Table 1. The methodology used in this course is classified as third- and fourth-order design, which is currently transforming the Design profession as well as Design education (Buchanan, 1999).

THE SPECIFIC PROJECT: MODELING OCEANOGRAPHIC RESEARCH FROM A DESIGN PERSPECTIVE

The Design course instructor collaborated with the instructor of a Marine Science class and a faculty development specialist to negotiate what the interdisciplinary focus of the project would be. Eventually, it was decided that the Design students would attempt to create an alternative learning situation concerned with ocean data collection and sampling for the introductory oceanography class. Essentially, in demonstrating their understanding

Table 1. Objectives of the design class

Striated Objectives	To develop spatial design sensibilities related to the virtual and real.
	To engage in a design practice of moving between virtual and real creation.
	To acquire new technical and manual skills with which to communicate concepts and methods of making.
	To develop awareness and application of spatial intelligence.
Smooth (Overriding) Objectives	To develop spatial interventions that deterritorialize the virtual and the real worlds.
	To develop and communicate a refined understanding of the virtual and the real worlds.
	To deterritorialize, then smooth and reterritorialize the everyday.
	To explore possibilities for creating environments of information.

and assimilation of course concepts, the Design students were set the task of building a new virtual classroom in Second Life for the Marine Science students to use in the following semester.

DESCRIPTION OF THE PROJECT

Project NEREUS (Nautical Environment for Research, Exploration and Understanding of the Seas) is named after the Greek Titan who lived in the Aegean Sea and was known for his truthfulness and virtue. He was the eldest son of Pontus (the Sea) and Gaia (the Earth), and he is often referred to as the Old Man of the Sea. NEREUS was set forth to provide a bridge of knowledge between a land-bound campus and students and the oceanographic information and instructor based in the coastal research station.

The project for the Design students was to provide a virtual learning environment in which students of an undergraduate Marine Science class could experience the task of planning and executing an oceanographic expedition and charting ocean data. The task of charting the ocean is an important factor in understanding the condition of the world's seas at any given moment in history, and the class learns the different techniques that have been used throughout the history of ocean exploration. The SL simulation is then the culminating example of how modern expeditions sample and chart the ocean from data collected using modern instruments. Data samples are provided from actual data slices of the Pacific Ocean and translated into SL. The categories of data are salinity, temperature, fluorescence and oxygenation of the water. The Marine Science students then take the data provided in the simulation and create their own charts in software applications used by oceanographers. The Design students were tasked with framing the overall simulation and creating the objects and necessary coding.

PROCESS OF THE PROJECT

The eight-week long project began with a field trip by the Design students to a coastal research center in order to learn about the process of sampling that they were to recreate.

A trip aboard a research vessel into the bay on a sampling run by the instructor of the Oceanography class allowed the Design students to witness first-hand what the groups of Marine Science students were creating with the simulation (Figure 1). The Design students recorded sounds, photographed the ship and equipment, and noted the process and form of the data collected by the crew. The instructor then presented a lecture that he gives to his own class so that the students could contextualize how the simulation would fit into the course.

In the same trip, a visit was made to a large aquarium (Figure 2). A tour of the facilities was conducted by the lead exhibit designer, which aligned the project with trying to encapsulate a wilderness experience within a confined setting.

Figure 1. Marine data collection device on research vessel

Lessons of compression, simulation and scale were learned that directly applied to the SL project and prompted a discussion about the place of the aquarium as an interstitial space between the ocean and land. This experience thus acted much the same way as the SL project in its positioning between real and virtual space.

Upon return, the Design students were given a very basic introduction to SL including a simple overview of building, navigation and scripting actions. The intent was to give them enough to get started and then let them discover how SL worked both socially and technically. This also placed the responsibility for learning how to use the software with the students. They were encouraged to move at their own pace and ask questions as they encountered them. Their pre-existing familiarity with gaming and social networks allowed them to enter the SL world with some ease, but the newness of the environment was out of their normal comfort zone, which allowed for contextual discussions of virtual identity, persistent online environments and the technological structure that supports them.

The Design students then participated in a project management workshop given by a university instructional specialist that is a part of the support provided to instructors whose students work in SL. The students were organized as a single team and encouraged to form groups that were based around tasks that they, with help of the instructor, identified were necessary to complete the project. The groups were: Identity and Public Relations (ID/P) that was charged with creating the logo and other art work, gathering project updates and creating a manual for student end users; the Data group mated the real world data to SL; the Environment group created the ocean and land environments and populated them with flora and fauna; the Shack group built the meeting and display headquarters building; the HUD (Heads Up Display) group worked on the interface design and supporting visual materials; and the Ship group crafted and scripted the vessel and equipment for sampling.

Students were also largely involved in organizing project time lines, meetings and presentations. Update sessions uncovered needed elements and assisted students in prioritizing their own needs and efforts in relation to the project and other students in the class as a whole. These meetings were held in the computer lab and classroom, but they were also held in SL where presentations and tutorials were conducted with team members and specialists from several universities and locations around the United States. The inclusion of these experts would not have been possible otherwise due to cost and time constraints.

THE PRODUCT OF THE PROJECT

The culminating deliverable product for the semester was an island environment in SL to be used as a classroom, meeting place and simulation

Figure 2. Collecting data at aquarium

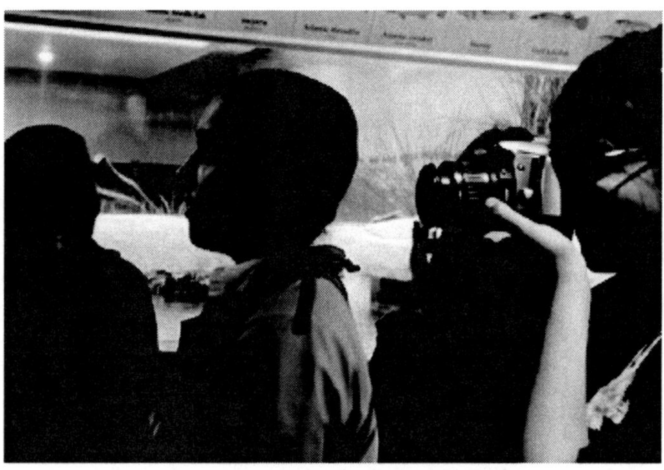

environment for the instructor and students of the oceanography class beginning fall 2009. Included in the approximately 16 acre SL sim is a Pacific island complete with beach, shack, flora, fauna, wooden docks, ships and non-player character guides (Figure 3).

The two-story shack serves as the headquarters for the island and is comprised of classroom, lounge and observation decks. A contemporary massing taking into account the ability in SL to fly is wrapped in distressed material textures associated with the sea: rusting corrugated metal roofing, faded and peeling gray paint of wood siding and heavy timber posts and detailing. Observation decks on the roof are outfitted with found and made objects including chairs, railings and telescopes.

Surrounding the island is animated water inhabited by dolphins, whales, schools of fish, coral, kelp and a variety of other environmental elements. A pair of wooden docks is the embarkation point for the simulation where the sampling ships will be 'rezzed' to start the simulation exercises. The ship is modeled after ocean vessels used for scientific research and include a sampling array, crane and A-frame that represent the tools of the oceanographer. Multiple ships may be rezzed allowing several Marine Science students to perform the exercise concurrently.

Once on the ship, the student directs the vessel to move to coordinates in the water where sampling data about the ocean, including temperature, salinity, fluorescence and oxygenation, is returned to the student for later charting using oceanographic visualization software. The data is from a collection of Pacific Ocean data and can be modified as desired to represent different eras and bodies of water as desired by the instructor. The assignment covers key sea exploration elements of expedition planning, charting and synthesis of gathered data that are impossible to perform in the physical world because of budgetary and time constraints.

DESIGN STUDENT EXPERIENCE AND DESIGN EDUCATIONAL RESULTS

Since the project was based in SL, Design students were exposed to a broad range of design-related activities throughout the project that called on skills already developed as well as first-time exposures. These included: developing interaction

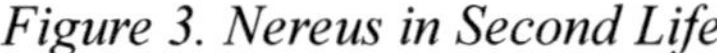

Figure 3. Nereus in Second Life

narratives for the overall simulation as well as non player character interactions (such as one would develop for gaming applications); designing and implementing graphic and typographic products for screen and print; diagrammatic visualizations of information; personal presentation skills; three-dimensional computer modeling; computer script coding; interaction design; three-dimensional spatial organization; service design; product design; and project management.

The experience of working with material from another discipline is typical of designers in the workforce, and the ability to approach new content areas with alacrity is important to a Design professional. The project exposed the Design students to an unfamiliar set of methodologies, language and objectives from another discipline, which could potentially inform their individual approach to their own discipline.

The students were also afforded an opportunity to interact with a client and developed associated skills such as relationship-building and expectation management. The act of shifting responsibility in terms of learning was complimented by a shift from trying to please only the instructor to trying to please the instructor plus a third party client. This service of multiple client figures (including one's self) is a common condition in Design practice. The students' awareness of what actions would please whom was evident in multiple verbalized instances of predicting who would like what solution in a given circumstance and why.

RESEARCH QUESTIONS AND METHODOLOGY

The purpose of the study was to address five research questions:

1. Was there a change from before the course to after the course in what the participants reported that they knew or understood about the key course concepts as described

in the course objectives? (see above under Objectives of the Design Class).

2. If participants reported prior gaming experience, did that prior experience play a role in participants' understanding of virtual worlds and their impression of *Second Life*?
3. How and during what kinds of situations and class activities does learning occur in *Second Life*?
   - Does being in SL where students are using their spatial understanding of the world have an impact on their learning course concepts?
   - In what ways do students characterize the impact of educational activities in *Second Life* on their learning (favorable, unfavorable)? What specific variables (class activities, instructor competence, project assignments, etc.) contribute to the students' assessment?
   - In what ways do instructors characterize the impact of educational activities in *Second Life* on their students' learning (favorable, unfavorable)? What specific variables (class activities, student engagement, instructor competence, project assignments, etc.) contribute to the instructors' assessment?
4. Does learning in *Second Life* transfer to real life?
5. To what extent and in what ways do participants experience a sense of being 'present' or embodied in their avatars?

The working hypothesis was that Second Life, as an online virtual world, provides an immersive environment that can facilitate opportunities for experiential learning (and teaching) and interdisciplinary collaboration.

DATA COLLECTION AND ANALYSIS

The study collected data from the participants (Design students) in the seminar by employing two participant surveys, a voluntary focus group, a qualitative analysis of their final projects in SL (based on the instructor's criteria for assessing the assignment and on the students' own reflections as elicited from the survey and focus group), and an in-depth interview with the instructor.

Surveys

Online surveys were conducted twice, at the beginning and at the end of the course. Both surveys took less than 15 minutes to complete.

Survey 1 addressed RQ 1 and 2, while Survey 2 addressed RQ 1 through 5. The two surveys contained both closed (Likert-scale) and open-ended items. Examples of survey items include 'I have heard of *Second Life* before,' with five-point scale response options and, 'If you have used *Second Life*, please describe what you have done in *Second Life*,' for the first survey. For the second survey, examples of survey items included Likert-item statements such as, 'The interactive style of this course helped me learn more about *Second Life*,' and 'I would like to try using *Second Life* or other related technologies on my own in the future,' with five-point scale response options, and 'How has the *Second Life* environment helped you understand the relationship between the 'virtual' and the 'real' world?' and 'How has the *Second Life* environment helped you understand how to use visual information to communicate ideas?' Another example of an open-ended question is, 'To what extent and in what ways have you experienced a sense of being "present" or embodied in your avatar?'

The survey results from the closed-ended items were summarized as descriptive statistics, and the results from the open-ended items were qualitatively analyzed for recurring themes.

Focus Group

A semi-structured focus group session of approximately one-hour in length was conducted with volunteer participants during the last class session, addressing participants' insights and perceptions about SL in particular, and whether they believe that they will use it in their own lives. The focus group provided an opportunity for them to articulate how they might consider using it. Examples of the questions include: 'What did you learn about SL in this course?'; 'If you are considering using SL yourself, please describe some possible ways that you imagine yourself using it'; 'How do you think the use of *Second Life* may affect your life?'; and 'To what extent and in what ways have you experienced a sense of being "present" or embodied in your avatar?'

Final Projects in *Second Life*

A qualitative analysis of the students' final projects in Second Life was conducted at the end of the semester for those who have volunteered to participate. The qualitative rubric evaluated three learning outcomes:

1. How well did the students succeed in assimilating the Design information?
2. How well did the students translate the information into three dimensions in *Second Life*?
3. How well did the students relate the different sets of science information to each other?

All three components are critical for communicating information in three dimensions effectively.

In-Depth Instructor Interview

After the end of the course, researchers conducted an in-depth interview with the instructor to address RQ3. Questions included: 'In what ways do instructors characterize the impact of educational activities in *Second Life* on their students' learning (favorable, unfavorable)?'; and 'What specific variables (class activities, student engagement, instructor competence, project assignments, etc.) contribute to the instructors' assessment?'

RESULTS

In this section we limit our report to the results of the 2 online surveys. There was continuity of participants in the data collection. 14 students completed Survey 1 and 15 students completed Survey 2. The entire class (16 students) participated in the hour-long focus groups session, and the instructor was interviewed for approximately 45 minutes.

A comparison of the results of Surveys 1 and 2 indicates a clear shift toward greater confidence in students' understanding of key course concepts based on the learning objectives of the Design course. For example, when given the prompt, 'I have spatial design sensibilities related to virtual and real' on a Likert scale (strongly agree, agree, neutral, disagree, and strongly disagree), students who strongly agreed moved from 28.6% to 40%. Three more dramatic examples of this trend toward increased confidence is how students responded to the prompts, 'I understand how to engage in a design practice of moving between virtual and real creation'; 'I have learned to develop spatial interventions that deterritorialize the virtual and the real worlds'; and 'I have developed and learned to communicate a refined understanding of the virtual and the real worlds'. The shift toward greater confidence can be seen in the contrast between Survey 1 and Survey 2 results, where in Survey 2 by the end of the semester no students disagreed with the statements and no students responded that they did not know what the questions meant (see Table 2, Table 3, and Table 4).

In Survey 2, when prompted with, 'The experience in Second Life was more process oriented than usual college-level classes,' 80% of the

Table 2. 'I understand how to engage in a design practice of moving between virtual and real creation.'

Response Survey 1 Survey 2
Strongly Agree 14.3% 46.7%
Agree 57.1% 53.3%
Disagree 21.4% 0.0%
Strongly Disagree 0.0% 0.0%
Do Not Know What This Is 7.1% 0.0%

Table 3. 'I have learned to develop spatial interventions that deterritorialize the virtual and the real worlds.'

Response Survey 1 Survey 2
Strongly Agree 21.4% 53.3%
Agree 42.9% 46.7%
Disagree 35.7% 0.0%
Strongly Disagree 0.0% 0.0%
Do Not Know What This Is 0.0% 0.0%

students responded with Strongly Agree and Agree. And 86.7% responded with Strongly Agree and Agree when prompted with, 'I now expect a class using Second Life to be a more immersive learning environment than usually found in traditional college-level courses.' Finally, when prompted with, 'I believe that my knowledge of virtual worlds will have some impact on my future life,' 93.4% of the students responded with Strongly Agree and Agree.

After the course was completed, students responded to the open-ended questions in Survey 2 that were designed to address their perceptions of having used Second Life for their semester-long team projects, and, again, there was an overall positive perception regarding the value of SL as an educational tool, even beyond the parameters of the course. For example, one question asked, 'What possible impacts might learning about virtual worlds have on your future life?' and the students responded by writing in the text box:

- Definitely interested in being involved in the development of virtual worlds and its theoretical impact on how we understand human nature.
- I see it as a potential job, and also as a forum for gaining knowledge or experience that I would otherwise not have access to.
- I will be able to experience and learn quicker in other virtual worlds and games.
- An understanding of how to go about programming and modeling virtual objects.
- Virtual worlds, like SL, that provide spaces and building tools have already begun to influence my creative thinking. I am beginning to think of space and objects as experimental with the use of visualization in virtual worlds. The virtual worlds that connect people all across the globe and create communities by providing tools to foster sharing of knowledge and creativity can be used to benefit many different interdisciplinary and disciplinary fields. Like the Architecture Engineering department using these virtual tools to explore environments and possible experimentations in the real world.
- In the future, I hope to use tools provided by virtual worlds in the field of design to allow for interdisciplinary projects and experimentations.
- Virtual worlds have already allowed me to look at things in a more three-dimensional format. To understand and know depth, and understand how an object would look differently at other angles. This will help me greatly because I intend to work in the animation or comic industry where understanding how objects would look at different angles makes whatever I create more realistic and life like.

Table 4. 'I have developed and learned to communicate a refined understanding of the virtual and the real worlds.'

Response	Survey 1	Survey 2
Strongly Agree	14.3%	60.0%
Agree	50.0%	6.7%
Disagree	35.7%	0.0%
Strongly Disagree	0.0%	0.0%
Do Not Know What This Is	0.0%	0.0%

- They provide tiny microcosms for learning. They might be ridiculous caricatures that can hopefully teach us something.
- I think that it will open up so many doors. It is a whole new avenue for design and communication. If you can't design something in person, SL might be a great way to present your ideas interactively. It removes a lot of limitations we have as students. Anything is possible.
- It increases my ability to communicate words and visual information more successfully than many real life instances.
- As someone interested in going into an art direction and visual development, knowledge about how virtual worlds operate may come in handy. Experience in developing environments in the virtual realm would also be useful in this field.
- I think it's brought up questions on how people interact for me, and just how much of a tool it can be for networking and group intelligence to be able to get things done. I know we wouldn't have been able to complete the project if we hadn't found other people on SL that knew what they were doing, knew how to answer the questions we had, and it wouldn't have been possible to find these people in the real world, not like we did in second life.
- I think our world it constantly becoming more 'virtual' so any knowledge of virtual worlds (even as little as how to move and interact in them) or just the general understanding of the concept of 'smoothing space' will help me in the future.
- I think it is going to be really relevant in the future. It's a relatively undiscovered outlet that I see becoming more and more integrated into real life.
- I'm more apt to creating future virtual experiences and think more about how people interact, engage with objects, immerse themselves in an experience, and learn.

In particular, this response from a student highlights the possibilities for how SL can enrich or enhance the quality of the learning experience: 'I know we wouldn't have been able to complete the project if we hadn't found other people on SL that knew what they were doing, knew how to answer the questions we had, *and it wouldn't have been possible to find these people in the real world, not like we did in Second Life*' (italics added for emphasis).

Finally, the students' responses to some of the other open-ended questions in Survey 2 are telling. When asked to 'Please describe the most significant learning event you experienced in this course because of Second Life,' the students responded with:

- I think that Second Life (and the internet in general) helps people overcome fears of new situations, fear of the unknown, because you can virtually explore new territories without having to put your real self on the line. It also helps people find their place in a community which may not exist as a true collective in the real world; in other words, I began to see how physical space can become meaningless and cease to be a restriction preventing congregation. I've realized the value of a free and open network that renders physical spatial separation meaningless, and puts the emphasis entirely on connections.

- I think the most significant thing I discovered over this course was learning how to think about interaction between creator and user. As the creator, it is sometimes easy to overlook how something you've created could be impractical or difficult for the user to interact with. Taking that step back and learning to see from a user perspective how the whole SL experience will turn out became a vital part of designing the NEREUS [marine science simulation].
- I think the possibility to be connected to anyone in the whole world and 'meeting' inworld creates a more personal relationship than if you just conversed by email or phone. I could this as tool for meeting future colleagues or just to gain information about different events/ cultures both in world and in the real world.

When asked, 'What additional thoughts and comments do you have about using Second Life for teaching and learning?' one student summed it up this way:

'I can't think of very many college courses that wouldn't be enriched by something like our Second Life project. While Second Life is certainly lacking many things that would make a virtual experience exactly like a real one, it's a lot closer than just reading a textbook or listening to a lecture.'

Overall, then, the results of the analysis of the data collected indicate a shift by the students toward greater confidence in their understanding of key course concepts based on the learning objectives of the Design course and a positive valence on their perception of SL as a useful, even important, educational resource.

NEXT STEPS FOR THIS ON-GOING PROJECT

In addition to the Design students' learning outcomes, the output from this exercise was a virtual ocean environment around a project center that focused attention on the oceanographic expedition. Undergraduate students in a marine science class, MNS 367k Human Exploration and Exploitation of the Sea, will use this virtual environment as a base of operation for their presentations in class as well as the starting point for the virtual oceanographic expedition. These learning activities will build on the lessons learned in the first part of the project, specifically with students acquiring knowledge by creating representations in Second Life, collaborating with their peers, and interacting with the Design students who created the simulation.

Finally, this general model will be used in the Marine Science class. Students will build and create in SL, and thereby assume a much more personal ownership of the information. In addition, the oceanographic expedition will demand acquisition of skills related to project planning, group organization, and hypothesis testing.

There were several value-added outcomes from this collaboration that were not initially planned:

- Increased scientific literacy in the design students.
- Increased appreciation of how valuable active learning in SL can be by the science instructor (TAV).
- The intellectual synergism that resulted from this interdisciplinary collaboration.

These products resulted in a state change in how the course was taught, and are the basis for a continued quantitative study on the role of virtual realities in science education. Amongst the team, there is a clear recognition that this outcome (specific tools for improved pedagogy) is extremely unlikely to have occurred without a collaborative effort.

FUTURE EXPANSIONS OF THE PROJECT

New Hypothesis: *A virtual environment can be an effective learning space for Marine Science students.*

The successful first stage implementation of Project Nereus provides a novel platform for expanding instructor/student interactions in the Marine Science course. The course is primarily taught over a video link, a technology that inherently distances the instructor from the student. The video link is a necessity due to the distance from the marine lab (340 km) to the main campus. The identification of self with avatar in SL provides a distinctly different way of teaching/learning through interaction in SL, and will be a major improvement over static lecture formats. The early, qualitative impressions from the course are that students are already deeply challenged by the novel environment in SL, and show an unprecedented excitement about the material they will be presenting in SL.

While there is no substitute for actually going to sea, it is impractical to take large groups of students to sea. Research vessels' costs range from $10,000 to over $30,000 per day, space is limited, and there are legal and institutional policies that severely constrain what can be done. Furthermore, the size of the ocean restricts what could be done, even should a vessel be available. However, a virtual research vessel, once created, has almost no overheads, no restriction on where it can go, and can be rapidly reprogrammed to take samples in both time and space within the short duration of one semester. Since students must plan their cruise to acquire data suitable for hypothesis-testing, the virtual learning activities capture the essence of the field's discipline in a low cost, low hazard environment. When linked to preparatory lectures, real-world examples, and the actual software used by practicing scientists to examine their data, this experience is designed to create an understanding both of the practice of oceanography and the nature of the oceans.

Future expansion of the project will be focused in creating more data options (biological data) as well as integrating the ocean database with dynamic models that permit a changing ocean environment. The ability to both conceal and then reveal data with the simulation provides unique ways to explore and compare regions that are normally invisible (the bottom) or difficult to represent graphically at the introductory level (spatial variability and patchiness). We anticipate that this project will continue to build on the unique interdisciplinary resources of this team, with design students learning skills necessary to developing practical, investigation-driven learning tools for science students.

CONCLUSION

Running a Design class in SL had benefits as well as risks for both instructor and students that often resulted from the same conditions. The open-ended nature of SL allowed and encouraged students to invest and to develop their own ideas, while at the same time the lack of inherent prescribed answers challenged the instructor to be flexible and more open to student interpretations as well as more involved in the development of each student's project. This approach appeared to be no more time consuming for the instructor than non-SL projects in the course because of the emphasis on student-initiated learning and encouragement of peer support. The dynamic nature of Project NEREUS removed much of the stability and structure usually found in a lower division undergraduate course, and this was initially disconcerting to students. Later in the semester, however, this dynamic nature was embraced, and it led to a much more rapid advancement in skills and understanding of course concepts because the students were able to assume responsibility for their own learning. The complexity and multi-faceted nature of the project provided opportunities for developing heuristic understanding and methodologies consistent with the curricular goals of the program.

The SL environment afforded an effective platform from which to explore the notions of smooth space and information environments. The accessible nature of the platform provided a relatively easy transition for students to operate in a virtual space, and this ease supported and highlighted the relevancy of the subject of the course. Students were left with a better understanding of the relationship of the physical world to the many virtual worlds we inhabit every day, and for the most part they were able to fully embrace the notion that they could be agents in the deterritorialization and smoothing of our physical and virtual worlds.

The collaborative and interdisciplinary nature of the project benefited students in several ways. They were afforded the opportunity to view the world through the lens of another academic discipline as well as to experience alternate methods and processes for development of ideas and projects in a scientific setting. This also highlighted the importance of the ability to negotiate unfamiliar territory using one's own methodologies to make sense of the journey. Since they were required to understand some of the material from the oceanography course for which they were developing the project, collateral learning also occurred as most Design students had never studied Marine Science. The collaborative framing also allowed the students to work *with* the instructor as opposed to performing *for* the instructor, which further imbued responsibility and increased motivation in the students.

Because of the positive feedback from students, the breadth of design topics engaged, and the affordances of a virtual setting, the instructor is planning to continue conducting classes in SL. In future classes, to speed the progression to more advanced work, more direct, practical support in the basic technical workings of the SL environment will be provided to the students while still maintaining the student-centered responsibility for pursuing the advanced techniques and applications.

Finally, science educators should also consider exploring virtual realities as learning platforms. It will be critical to use the platforms as active rather than passive learning tools. Interdisciplinary collaboration such as the one described in this study permit 'out of the box' discussion since inherent disciplinary assumptions are challenged, and personal boundaries are expanded tremendously.

REFERENCES

Amichai-Hamburger, Y., & McKenna, K. (2006). The contact hypothesis reconsidered: Interacting via the Internet. *Journal of Computer-Mediated Communication, 11*(3), 825–843. doi:doi:10.1111/j.1083-6101.2006.00037.x

Atkinson, R. K., Mayer, R., & Merrill, M. (2005). Fostering social agency in multimedia learning: Examining the impact of an animated agent's voice. *Contemporary Educational Psychology, 30*(1), 117–139. doi:doi:10.1016/j.cedpsych.2004.07.001

Buchanan, R. (1999). Design Research and the New Learning. *Design Issues, 17*(4), 3–23. doi:doi:10.1162/07479360152681056

Craig, E. (2007, June). *Meta-perspectives on the Metaverse: A blogsphere debate on the significance of Second Life.* Paper presented at ED-MEDIA World Conference on Educational Multimedia, Hypermedia & Telecommunications, Vancouver, Canada.

Dede, C., Clarke, J., Ketelhut, D., Nelson, B., & Bowman, C. (2005). *Fostering motivation, learning, and transfer in multi-user virtual environments*. Paper presented at the American Educational Research Association Conference, Montreal, Canada.

Deleuze, G., & Guattari, F. (1988). *A Thousand plateaus: Capitalism and schizophrenia*. Minneapolis: University of Minnesota Press.

Faiola, A. (2007). The Design enterprise: Rethinking the HCI education paradigm. *Design Issues, 23*(3), 30–45. doi:doi:10.1162/desi.2007.23.3.30

FitzGerald, S. (2007, June). *Virtual worlds - What are they and why do educators need to pay attention to them?* Paper presented at E-learning Networks June Online Event. Retrieved July 18, 2009, from http://seanfitz.wikispaces.com/virtualworldsenetworks07

Freire, P. (1976). *Education, the practice of freedom*. London: Writers and Readers Publishing Cooperative.

Gee, J. P. (2003). *What videogames have to teach us about learning and literacy*. New York: Palgrave Macmillan.

Gruson, E., Staal, G., & St. Joost, A. (2000). *Copy proof: A new method for design and education*. Rotterdam, The Netherlands: 010 Publishers.

Honan, W. (1994, March 23). Academic disciplines increasingly entwine, recasting scholarship. *New York Times*, 19.

Jarmon, L. (2009a). *Homo Virtualis*: Virtual worlds, learning, and an ecology of embodied interaction. *International Journal of Virtual and Personal Learning Environments, 1*(1), 38–56.

Jarmon, L. (2009b). Learning in virtual world environments: Social-presence, engagement & pedagogy. In Rogers, P., Berg, G., Boettcher, J., Howard, C., Justice, L., & Schenk, K. (Eds.), *Encyclopedia of distance and online learning* (pp. 1610–1619). Hershey, PA: IGI Global.

Jarmon, L., Lim, K., & Carpenter, S. (Eds.). (2009). *Special Issue*: Pedagogy, education and innovation in virtual worlds. *Journal of Virtual Worlds Research*. Retrieved July 18, 2009, from http://www.jvwresearch.org/v2n1.html

Jarmon, L., & Sanchez, J. (2009). The Educators Coop: A model for collaboration and LSI communication research in the virtual world. *Electronic Journal of Communication, 9*(1/2).

Jarmon, L., Traphagan, T., Mayrath, M., & Trivedi, A. (2009). Virtual world teaching, experiential learning, and assessment: An interdisciplinary communication course in Second Life. *Computers & Education, 53*, 169–182. doi:doi:10.1016/j.compedu.2009.01.010

KirriemuirJ.McFarlaneA. (2004).

Kolb, A. Y., & Kolb, D. A. (2009). The learning way: Meta-cognitive aspects of experiential learning. *Simulation & Gaming, 40*(3), 297-327. Retrieved July 26, 2009, from http://sag.sagepub.com/cgi/content/short/40/3/297

Lamb, G. M. (2006, October 5). Real learning in a virtual world. *The Christian Science Monitor*. Retrieved October 6, 2006, from http://www.csmonitor.com/2006/1005/p13s02-legn.html

Literature review in games and learning. Retrieved July 18, 2009, from http://www.futurelab.org.uk/research/lit_reviews.htm#lr08

Mayrath, M., Traphagan, T., Jarmon, L., Trivedi, A., & Resta, P. (2009). *Teaching with virtual worlds: Factors to consider for instructional use of Second Life*. Paper presented to 2009 Annual Convention of the American Educational Research Association, San Diego, CA.

McGee, P. (2007, June). *Extreme learning in a virtual (world) learning environment: Who needs pedagogy anyway?* Paper presented at ED-MEDIA World Conference on Educational Multimedia, Hypermedia & Telecommunications, Vancouver, Canada.

Mical, T. (2002). The stealth landscape of Tokyo. *NEH Summer Institute 2002*. Retrieved August 15, 2005, from http://www.usc.edu/dept/LAS/ealc/Mical.pdf

Moreno, R., Mayer, R., Spires, H., & Lester, J. (2001). The case for social agency in computer-based teaching: Do students learn more deeply when they interact with animated pedagogical agents? *Cognition and Instruction, 19*(2), 177–213.doi:doi:10.1207/S1532690XCI1902_02

New Media Consortium. (2009). *The Horizon Report.* Retrieved July 18, 2009, from http://www.nmc.org/publications/2009-horizon-report

Prensky, M. (2006). *Don't bother me, Mom, I'm learning! How computer and video games are preparing your kids for 21st century success and how you can help!* St. Paul, MN: Paragon House.

Life, S. in Education (n.d.). *Educational uses of Second Life.* Retrieved July 18, 2009, from http://sleducation.wikispaces.com/educationaluses

Soukup, C. (2004). Multimedia Performance in a Computer-Mediated Community: Communication as a Virtual Drama. *Journal of Computer-Mediated Communication, 9*(4). Retrieved July 26, 2009, from http://jcmc.indiana.edu/vol9/issue4/soukup.html

Steinkuehler, C., & Williams, D. (2006). Where everybody knows your (screen) name: Online games as 'third places.' *Journal of Computer-Mediated Communication, 11*(4). Retrieved July 26, 2009, from http://jcmc.indiana.edu/vol11/issue4/steinkuehler.html

Van Schaik, L. (2008). *Spatial intelligence.* Chichester, UK: John Wiley & Sons, Ltd.

This work was previously published in International Journal of Virtual and Personal Learning Environments, edited by Michael Thomas, Volume 1, Issue 3, pp. 17-35, copyright 2010 by IGI Publishing (an imprint of IGI Global).

Chapter 8
Virtual Speed Mentoring in the Workplace – Current Approaches to Personal Informal Learning in the Workplace:
A Case Study

Chuck Hamilton
IBM Center for Advanced Learning IBM, Canada

Kristen Langlois
IBM Canada Ltd., Canada

Henry Watson
IBM Canada Ltd., Canada

ABSTRACT

Informal learning is the biggest undiscovered treasure in today's workplace. Marcia Conner, author and often-cited voice for workplace learning, suggests that "Informal learning accounts for over 75% of the learning taking place in organizations today" (1997). IBM understands the value of the hyper-connected informal workplace and informal learning that comes through mentoring. This case study examines a novel approach to mentoring that is shaped only by virtual space and the participants who inhabit it. The authors found that virtual social environments can bridge distances in a way that is effective, creative and inexpensive. Eighty-five percent of virtual speed mentoring attendees reported that this approach achieved their learning objectives. Participants also reported that virtual social spaces like Second Life® are suitable delivery vehicles for mentoring, and that connecting with people was much easier than via telephone or web conferencing.

DOI: 10.4018/978-1-4666-1770-4.ch008

INTRODUCTION

IBM Virtual Speed Mentoring has been developed in Second Life to provide an online forum for employees to discuss issues relating to their careers with an expert. Speed Mentoring is an informal meeting in which mentors and protégés from every corner of the world dialogue in fifteen-minute bursts. In these calendared events, protégés, industry experts, managers and executives from all levels of the business converge in a virtual mentoring space. This intensity of skill mixing rarely occurs in day-to-day work, making such encounters both career and life changing for many participants.

Corporations have understood for many years that mentoring ensures experience and knowledge is shared and helps employees feel connected to one another. IBM employs approximately 398,000 worldwide (IBM, 2009), and in large companies it is difficult to create and maintain mentoring connections. IBM understands how this practice can impact career growth. But with increased travel costs and productivity demands, mentoring has become both more difficult and more important to sustain. An approach like virtual speed mentoring can reduce workplace connection barriers and increase productivity with a minimal investment (IBM, 2005).

BENEFITS OF VIRTUAL SPEED MENTORING

In October 2008, 50 IBM Canada and a few IBM global employees met in Second Life in the first IBM virtual speed mentoring event. An internal career planning website promoted the program, inviting participants to join based on either a manager recommendation or request generated from the site. About 20 experienced business leaders acted as mentors to roughly 30 more junior, less tenured employees. Participants included IT Specialists, IT Architects, Project Managers and Consultants. The approach to mentoring was simple: protégés could ask career planning questions of different mentors in a series of fifteen minute rotations.

Each speed mentoring session began with a main tent event offering an overview of the objectives and a description of mentoring at IBM program. The introduction was followed by two guest speakers who shared their mentoring and work life experiences with the group. Participants chose "mentoring pods" where up to three protégés could sit and speak with a mentor. After 15 minutes at one pod, the mentor moved to a different pod and continued to dialogue, through a 12-pod rotation. This rotation of pods gave protégés a variety of perspectives on career planning questions and opportunities across IBM.

Typically, participants described their current role and position to the group, highlighting latest directions, observations on their progress and their hopes for the future. Each mentor offered feedback, connections and possible new directions to the group based on his or her own experience in the company. Participants also exchanged ideas with each other, quickly expanding the mentoring options for each protégé. The 15-minute rotation allowed for many exchanges, while mentors quickly gained a feel for the concerns and career planning tactics applied across the company. Mentors often recommended connections to other protégés who shared concerns or career paths. This approach built new connections across the company and helped protégés to share best practices.

Speed mentoring is not intended to circumvent deeper, longer-term mentoring relationships. Instead, speed mentoring rapidly connected concerns and people in an informal manner. Although speed and breadth of topic outweighed depth of relationship in this application, virtual speed mentoring sessions often became the starting point for greater depth and longer-term mentor/protégé relationships. As an additional benefit, every participant learned more about the value of and practice of mentoring.

Each event concluded with a visit to a virtual resource center (hovering above the main event area) where protégés had access to IBM career planning tools and resources, followed by a satisfaction survey forwarded to each participant's email address.

The virtual speed mentoring facility was built and managed as a partnership between IBM's Global Business Services and IBM Learning. This team also taught protégés and mentors how to maneuver in a 3D virtual world. Some participants needed to learn the fundamentals, starting with basic navigation and tools while others needed a quick orientation and were ready to participate.

The entire project took under two months to complete. Its virtual space included 12-speed mentoring pods, an observation deck, a main tent meeting area and a floating resource center. Development, deployment and two pilot sessions cost approximately $40K. This business investment is low, considering the asset's reuse and scalability. Face-to-face mentoring normally takes place only at scheduled career events requiring travel for many of the participants. Typical per-participant costs for these events range from $300 to $2,000 depending on their location and duration. Even if mentoring is only one part of a larger career event, its portion can constitute one-third of the overall event cost. In contrast, the virtual speed mentoring space provides a greater return on investment. Now that the environment has been created and tested, individual events cost only a few dollars per person.

While reducing costs, virtual speed mentoring also breaks through geographical barriers and time constraints. Protégés learn rapidly from experts regardless of proximity, in a relaxed setting that feels surprisingly realistic. In fact, virtual speed mentoring space motivates protégés to grab expertise in burst sessions, quickly acquiring knowledge and best practices. One of the goals of the IBM Learning organization (operating within Human Resources) is to continuously develop and retain IBM's most important asset — its people — and virtual speed mentoring helps achieve this objective. As an added benefit, employees can collaborate in a familiar 3D place (similar to visiting an IBM conference facility, favorite restaurant or coffee house), meeting and connecting with fellow IBM employees around the world.

Figure 1. A virtual speed mentoring pod in Second Life

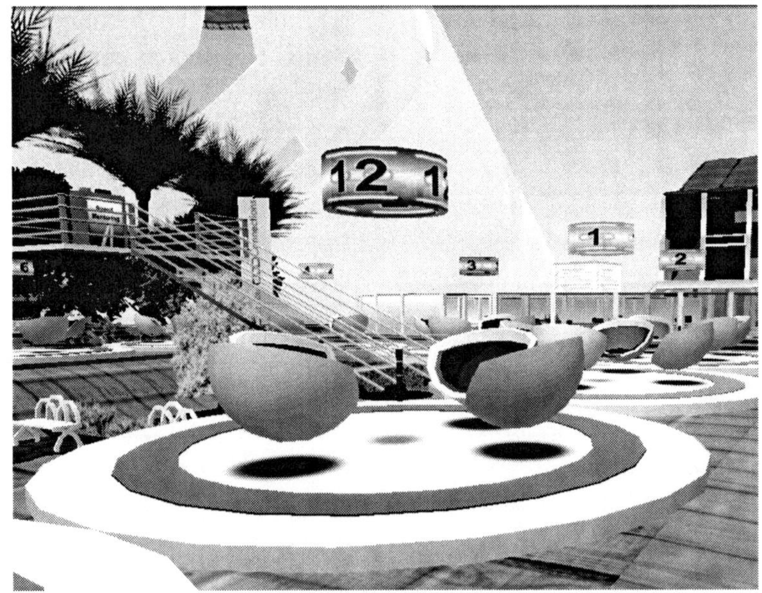

DESIGN AND EXECUTION CONSIDERATIONS

Creating effective virtual social environments for collaboration and learning requires a deep understanding of virtual social environment design. These environments are "converged spaces," where virtual world affordances, new collaboration and community tools, new measurement options, play, immersion, culture and presence collide in a rapidly evolving medium. It is difficult enough to create compelling and measurable learning experiences. Adding complexity to this emerging metaverse requires juggling several new languages and technologies at once.

Physical Design

Because IBM wants all participants to feel comfortable while discussing specifics about themselves, designers must pay special attention to security and privacy within this environment. To accomplish this, the design team developed circular mentoring pods with defined sound spaces that prevent conversations within one pod from being heard at another. By design, this allows individual avatars standing close to a pod (where they can easily be seen) to listen in without interrupting the dialogue. This helps protégés track a specific mentor or other protégés for follow-up discussions. Mentors are also given password-protected long-distance phone bridges for strictly one-on-one conversations. As a precaution, the entire IBM owned space is restricted to specific "IBM only" groups within Second Life.

By leveraging converged-presence tools such as voice, person-to-person messaging and open chat, IBM designers expanded the level of presence for all participants, while still protecting their anonymity.

Affordance Design

In addition to physical layout, the design team applied several affordances to the virtual speed mentoring environment. In this context the term affordance refers to perceived and actual properties of the virtual environment that maximize its value. Virtual world affordances are both native and constructed characteristics that have been observed to be core differentiators of virtual worlds for learning and collaboration (see Norman, 1990; Gibson, 1977).

After many trials IBM has learned to adopt different affordances for various applications. This case study discusses two learning design affordances (*the interplay of presence and reputation* and *the manipulation of space and scale*) in the context of the virtual speed mentoring model. Overall, IBM has identified ten affordances that show promise for the optimization of virtual spaces for learning. To fully exploit virtual learning spaces, learning designers should identify and leverage the affordances that best align to predefined learning goals. In addition to the affordances discussed later in the case study, consider the following native and constructed learning design affordances:

- Leveraging both native and constructed practice and simulation opportunities;
- Blending place across multiple geographies, organizations or time;
- Leveraging co-creation and collaboration with disparate individuals or groups;
- Monitoring observable behavior and performance for individuals and groups;
- Leveraging self and anonymity characteristics of avatars;
- Enriching the user experience through converged media;

- Creating opportunity for mass connected innovation;
- Leveraging both native and constructed universal visual language opportunities.

The first affordance that IBM designers applied to virtual mentoring is the interplay of presence and reputation. Users construct part of their virtual presence and reputation when they create their avatars' visible characteristics and names. They add depth with supplemental information such as interests, associated groups, real life photos and personal notes. Users tend to refine their avatar profiles as they spend time in the virtual environment, during which a visible and measurable identity emerges — a reflection of "the real you." However, the avatar identity is not an exact replica of the user and it is not, for example, as revealing as the image presented during video conferencing. Probably because of this, observation and participant surveys suggest that people represented as avatars are comfortable asking questions they might not ask in person. Although people start interacting and participating quickly in virtual spaces, they feel shielded and strengthened by their avatar representations.

The ability for participants to remain anonymous, to appear as either gender or even in non-human forms, is a core design element afforded by Second Life itself. This flexibility in describing oneself can have both advantages and disadvantages. While most participants in the speed mentoring project introduced themselves using their real names (as opposed to chosen avatar names), participants still benefitted from the self-image they created. Protégés described feeling less restrained and more able speak freely, with the whole event space feeling more playful and "easy going" than typical face-to-face meetings. This approach encouraged questions from protégés who might have been reluctant to ask questions in face-to-face situations—an improvement over mentoring by phone, video conferencing or face-to-face. However, some protégés adopted extreme adaptations of their avatar, which other participants sometimes found off-putting—a disadvantage in a mentoring setting. The interplay of self-image characteristics within persistent collaboration tools will require more research to understand it more effectively.

Two more affordances applied by IBM designers relate to space and scale. Space refers to the notion of being in an apparent physical location. Scale refers to size and shape constraints inherent to the space. Space and scale offer complimentary affordances that can be used for virtual activities taking place in apparent locales whose characteristics cannot be provided in the physical or online classroom. Using these affordances, participants can work at both microscopic and macroscopic levels, providing a transformational opportunity for learning.

Virtual Speed Mentoring in the workplace uses space and scale to accommodate numerous pods, a gathering area, observation spaces and an information center in a single navigable space. Similar services in the real world might have required several floors of a building with a large staff and support services. At the same time, individual mentoring pods are scaled for only four participants, providing apparently natural limits for voices and privacy.

Connected spaces with presence, reputation space and scale have already been formed in the Web for some time, usually without avatars or the artistic surroundings. However, more recent IBM virtual meeting trials suggests that people no longer want to be represented as a dot in a chat tool or a photo in a social space with a cryptic email address. Using the richer information communicated by avatars and location offers many benefits, including a common human "body language" that people understand everywhere in the world. If seeing is believing, then this richer communication helps to build trust and authenticity across virtual spaces, while still allowing anonymous connections when necessary.

Consider the text messages sent by new participants just entering a virtual space. "Wow this space is massive. How many people does this theatre hold? I was told that you can merge these four simulations for events holding up to two hundred people, is that true? Can I build a full-scale model here?" Such messages from participants describe the power of applying space and scale design affordances.

Once we understand native and constructed affordances, we are only limited by an environment's computational capacity and our imaginations. IBM learning designers are creating more virtual spaces optimized by affordances and while there is much more to learn about this approach, it is already clear that affordance-based design can increase the business value of virtual spaces.

SUMMARY

The virtual speed mentoring project successfully implemented a cost-effective and engaging approach to mentoring in the workplace. More important, this project can lead to the design of other new ways to connect across geographic and organizational boundaries, yielding greater business value over time. In this case study IBM has:

- Delivered a low cost, highly immersive experience in which mentors and protégés build strong career connections;
- Demonstrated a rare opportunity for skill-mixing in day-to-day work;
- Created engaging encounters with avatar-represented protégés who are comfortable asking questions they might not ask in person;
- Developed new environment design and software skills necessary for the virtual global enterprise. These new skills are valuable to both IBM and its customers;
- Developed a highly scalable and reusable asset that can be applied to ongoing work and innovation.

When survey participants were asked if they felt that Second Life was suitable for mentoring, the response was summarized by one participant as, "Surprisingly, yes! I think my expectations were not very high and this virtual environment certainly exceeded my expectations. I was pleasantly surprised at how effective this method of delivery can be and I think I came out of the session as a believer in this approach."

85% of the virtual speed mentoring attendees reported feeling that the event achieved their objectives. Those 85% also reported that virtual social spaces like Second Life are suitable for mentoring, and that connecting with people was easier than on the telephone or a Web conference. Participants reported that they were able to learn from each other and build relationships that might otherwise not have developed in their workplace.

Both email feedback and satisfaction survey results show that the virtual speed mentoring environments are easy to use, even for beginners. In fact, good design can remove the dependency on interface created by the virtual world creators, because in this application people only need to walk, sit, raise their hands and listen—actions that are familiar in real life and quickly learned in the virtual world. Participants described leaving the session with either a renewed interest in building a new mentoring relationship or a renewed passion for their current mentoring relationships. Most important, participants left feeling invigorated and excited to be IBM employees. This helps IBM retain employees while encouraging individual career development.

The overall results of the virtual speed mentoring in the workplace project parallel feedback from face-to-face speed mentoring sessions, suggesting that the novelty of the Second Life medium was

Figure 2. Virtual speed mentoring environment in Second Life

not a significant factor in people's rating of the experience. Furthermore, the results underscore the opportunity to consider taking virtual world spaces further, applying more affordances and designing even more engaging experiences in the future.

With over forty projects focused on learning and HR applications within virtual spaces, IBM is beginning to surface affordances that help define best practices in design. A team at the IBM Center For Advanced Learning is gathering all of this new knowledge and methodology into a central resource, to help internal and external customers leverage this emerging medium.

Building on this success, we will continue to study each virtual mentoring event and share best practices with IBM as a whole. According to Kristen Langlois, IBM HR Learning Program Manager, "It's all about making connections and whatever we can do to help people connect in our workplace is a win."

Jeffrey Gitomer (2006) writes about the importance of making connections, "All things being equal, people want to do business with their friends. All things being NOT so equal, people still want to do business with their friends" (p. 1). We cannot always meet our friends and co-workers face-to-face, and we understand that rich connections require more than a call or email. In our increasingly virtual and cross-geographical world, connecting grows more difficult. We can bridge these distances with engaging virtual social environments—and if it is fun, creative and inexpensive to do so, all the better.

ACKNOWLEDGMENT

IBM, the IBM logo, and ibm.com are trademarks or registered trademarks of International Business Machines Corp., registered in many jurisdictions worldwide. Other product and service names might be trademarks of IBM or other companies. A current list of IBM trademarks is available on the Web under "Copyright and trademark information" at www.ibm.com/legal/copytrade.shtml. Second Life is a trademark or registered trademark of Linden Research, Inc. The opinions expressed in this paper are those of the authors and not necessarily of the IBM Corporation.

REFERENCES

Conner, M. L. (1997). *Informal learning*. Retrieved September 15, 2009 from http://www.marciaconner.com/intros/informal.html

Gibson, J. J. (1977). The theory of affordances. In Shaw, R. E., & Bransford, J. (Eds.), *Perceiving, acting, and knowing*. Hillsdale, NJ: Lawrence Erlbaum Associates.

Gitomer, J. (2006). *Little black book of connections – 6.5 ASSETS for networking your way to RICH relationships*. Austin, TX: Bard Press.

IBM. (2005). *On demand learning: Blended learning for today's evolving workforce*. Retrieved September 15, 2009 from http://www935.ibm.com/services/uk/index.wss/executivebrief/igs/a1022918?cntxt=a1006794

IBM. (2009). *About IBM*. Retrieved September 9, 2009 from http://www.ibm.com/ibm/us/en/

Norman, D. A. (1990). *The design of everyday things*. New York: Doubleday.

This work was previously published in International Journal of Virtual and Personal Learning Environments, edited by Michael Thomas, Volume 1, Issue 2, pp. 59-66, copyright 2010 by IGI Publishing (an imprint of IGI Global).

Section 3

Implementation

Chapter 9
Communication and Education in a Virtual World:
Avatar-Mediated Teaching and Learning in Second Life

Lorri Mon
Florida State University, USA

ABSTRACT

Education within Second Life frequently recapitulates the "sage on the stage" as students sit their avatars down in chairs in the virtual world and listen to or read an instructor's lecture while watching a slideshow. This conceptual article explores alternative active learning techniques supporting independent and collaborative learning within virtual worlds. Within Second Life, educators can utilize a variety of scripted tools and objects as well as techniques of building and terra-forming to create vibrant virtual personal learning environments and learning experiences that are engaging and responsive to individual learners. Issues of embodiment in an avatar are discussed in terms of social presence, and student learning styles are considered as well as approaches to problem-based learning, games, role play, and immersive virtual world environments.

INTRODUCTION

Millions of distance students worldwide participate in online learning environments. In the United States alone, distance student enrollment increased from 1.6 million students in 1998 to over 3.9 million in 2007 (NCES, 1999; NCES, 2008; Sloan-C, 2008). Approximately 75% of distance courses in 2007 occurred within asynchronous Internet-based learning environments (NCES, 2008, p. 3).

Within asynchronous online learning environments, researchers observed high student attrition rates, with students citing frustration, isolation, and lack of social interaction (Weasenforth et al., 2002; Terry, 2001; Beard & Harper, 2000; Hara & Kling, 1999; Hiltz, 1997) However, students interacting with and more aware of the "social presence" of classmates and instructors reported experiencing greater satisfaction in online courses (Chou, 2001; Tu & Corry, 2001; Gunawardena, 1997). Perceived "social presence" increases

DOI: 10.4018/978-1-4666-1770-4.ch009

civility and trust, supporting willingness to share personal information and opinions with others. (Murphy & Cifuentes, 2001; Murphy & Collins, 1997).

Synchronous online teaching enables real time interaction between students and instructors in environments varying from text-based chat rooms to computer conferencing software and virtual worlds. While computer conferencing and virtual worlds both offer audio, video, text and image sharing, in virtual worlds teachers and learners are uniquely embodied as avatars synchronously co-present within immersive 3-dimensional surroundings, engendering a heightened sense of social presence (Warburton, 2009). The virtual world has physics – balls roll, or fall when dropped – and a social and economic milieu in which learners can build artifacts, join in marketplaces of goods or ideas, undertake simulated experiences (Dunleavy, Dede, & Mitchell, 2008), and interact with others beyond the classroom. Unlike conferencing environments, virtual worlds are persistent (Childress & Braswell, 2006), continuing to exist, evolve and change even while learners are offline. To leverage the unique qualities of virtual worlds, instructional designs can integrate these elements of immersion, simulation, and enhanced social presence in interpersonal interaction.

TEACHING IN VIRTUAL WORLDS

A long tradition of educational research exists within virtual worlds. In 2003, Delwiche (2006) taught ethnographic research to undergraduate students who formed "the Halfling Ethnographers Guild" within the virtual world of Everquest (http://www.everquest.com/). At Illinois State University, undergraduate education students undertook quests within World of Warcraft (http://www.worldofwarcraft.com/) (Mullen, Beilke, & Brooks, 2007). Within Quest Atlantis (http://atlantis.crlt.indiana.edu/), fourth graders completed quests to analyze environmental science problems. (Barab et al., 2007) In Active Worlds, Cornell University taught science to high school students, while the University of Colorado-Boulder taught a business accounting course (Damer, 2008; Corbit, 2002). In Second Life, courses ranged from English Composition at Ball State University to law at Harvard Law School, genetics at Texas Wesleyan University, sociology and criminology at Coventry University, computer science at Ohio University, and astrobiology at the University of Arizona (Grove & Steventon, 2008; Gollub, 2007; Ye, Liu, & Polack-Wahl, 2007; Boulous, Heatherington, & Wheeler, 2007).

Assessment of education in virtual worlds notes improvements in attentiveness (Mikropoulos, 2001), participation (Ketelhut, 2007), class attendance, and performance on exams (Blaisdell, 2006), although visually rich environments can distract students off-task (Omale et al., 2009). Assessment of satisfaction finds students responding positively to learning activities in Second Life (Jarmon et al., 2009; Good, Howland, & Thackeray, 2008; McVey, 2008) but with some criticisms over workload and ease of use (Wagner, 2008; Wang & Braman, 2009). DeLucia et al. (2009) found college students experienced a high level of social presence in Second Life.

Establishing relevance of virtual world activity to course learning is important for student satisfaction (Minocha & Tingle, 2008; Mayrath et al., 2007). There should be solid pedagogical reasons for visiting Second Life such as observing events, visiting relevant places, or participating in learning activities. Cost in both cognitive load and technical requirements should be considered to ensure sufficient time, training, and technical trouble-shooting for students to participate successfully in activities and assignments (Conrad, 2002; Guzdial, 2001). Since significant effort is required to use Second Life, basic skills orientation is a necessary first step.

ORIENTATION TO SECOND LIFE

Students begin by registering a free account at the Linden Lab's Second Life Web site (http://www.secondlife.com). There are several bits of useful advice for students at this point, as well as planning decisions for instructors to consider.

First, instructors should consider making activities optional. Students cannot participate via dial-up connections, and hardware/graphics card configurations required are not supported by all computers. In campus computer labs, the Second Life software must be installed and kept updated; alternatively, students may download and use the software on thumb drives.

During registration, students invent an avatar first name and select a surname from a list. This has two implications: 1) student avatar names are not immediately recognizable to instructors, and 2) some students use school IDs as a first name - not always a good choice ("Hello, jsb022!"). Instructors must maintain lists of student avatar names. Some instructors purchase a single surname for all students, as with Elon University computer science professor Meg Conklin's surname "Radiks" for her students conducting cyber-culture research (Foster, 2005); this requires a basic cost plus an annual fee.

Some instructors find that when an entire class registers simultaneously from the same domain (such as 'fsu.edu'), registrations are blocked. To avoid this, students can complete registrations in advance from school or home; alternatively, instructors can establish registered accounts and distribute logins and passwords. Linden Labs can assist by 'whitelisting' domains for simultaneous registrations.

Registration gives students various starting location options in Second Life; thus, students do not begin together in the same location and no instructor is present at their arrival, although strangers may be present. Some educational organizations have established alternative registration pages and starting locations, such as the New Media Consortium (http://sl.nmc.org/create.php) and Virtual Ability (http://virtualability.org/signup.aspx). Alternative registration pages allow students to avoid more crowded 'main' orientation areas, assembling in one starting place where the instructor can join them.

Upon arrival, students learn to walk, fly, and change avatar appearance. However, instructors may need to teach additional skills (see Table 1).

Not all of these skills are needed for every activity, but for those needed, a variety of teaching methods can be used. Useful training resources include Second Life's Quick Start Guide (http://www.scribd.com/doc/14427744/Second-Life-Quickstart-Guide) and help videos (http://secondlife.com/video).

Second Life classes are limited by "lag," slowed-down graphical rendering when locations become overloaded with too many avatars and objects. Lag can be reduced by removing unnecessary objects and having avatars use less-bandwidth-consuming clothing choices; an "avatar rendering cost" setting can be enabled showing contributions to lag by each avatar. For best results, groups should be limited to 25-30 avatars, subdividing larger classes into smaller groups for in-world activities.

LECTURES

The most commonplace teaching method recapitulates the traditional "sage on the stage" in which instructors use whiteboards to show slide images ("textures"), and deliver lectures by typing into text chat, or speaking using voice chat. Some instructors use devices such as the Speakeasy HUD (a 'Heads Up Display' control panel) which preloads text lectures in a note card, enabling instructors to deliver voice audio and a line-by-line text chat simultaneously. Dual-mode delivery helps auditory learners as well as those with visual or hearing disabilities, and text chat doubles as class notes for students.

Table 1. Second Life skills

Presenting the Self	customizing avatar appearance, opening boxes, changing clothes, saving appearance, updating a profile, using animations (avatar movements), using sounds
Wayfinding	walking, flying, teleporting, using landmarks (location links), using camera controls, searching for places, using maps, setting 'home' locations, finding and using SLURLs (Second Life URLs for locations)
Communicating	using text chat and IM, using voice chat, playing audio and video, making and giving note cards, uploading and giving textures (images), giving and receiving objects
Managing Keepsakes	copying chat logs, taking snapshots, making landmarks, obtaining free items, making purchases, searching and organizing inventory
Socializing	offering friendships, offering teleports, searching for groups, joining and leaving groups, making notes about people, culture and etiquette
Building and Creating	creating and linking prims (the Second Life basic 'building blocks'), applying textures, setting permissions, making machinima (in-world movies), scripting (programming), terraforming (sculpting the landscape), land management (e.g. setting access permissions)
Troubleshooting	adjusting environmental settings, changing draw distance (distance at which visuals are shown), accessing advanced menu and settings

(Calogne, 2008; Neustaedter & Fedorovskaya, 2009; Johnson & Levine, 2008)

To 'hear' text chat, student avatars must stand within 20 meters. The audible range increases to 60 meters using voice chat, and 96 meters with text "shout." Marking a circle or seating area helps demonstrate where students should stand. While group chat instant messaging has no distance limitations, instructors pay a fee to create the group and then must ensure that all students accept invitations to join. Written "handouts" can be distributed as note cards, or by having students touch objects to receive note cards, textures, or open Web pages.

Cheal (2007) warns that "passive viewing is boring in a world that promises action" (p. 209); popular pastimes among students include experimenting with avatars, exploring the virtual world, and participating in events. Instructors might therefore supplement lectures with events, discussions, and demonstrations.

EVENTS, DISCUSSIONS AND DEMONSTRATIONS

A common Second Life complaint is the 'empty world' syndrome. Newcomers do not know where to go or what to do upon arriving in-world, but experienced users generally spend their initial moments reading 'group notices' about activities, events, and places to visit. Joining groups helps instructors learn where students can participate in events, or observe experts giving demonstrations. Truelove and Hibbert (2008) prepared students for building activities by first giving them an opportunity to watch a master builder at work, thus demonstrating what was possible to achieve.

Avatars represent an opportunity for exploring identity, self representation, and gender issues. Modifying avatar appearance can be an 'icebreaker' activity, giving students a shared experience to discuss (Lamont, 2007). At Ball State University, Sarah Robbins' English undergraduates wrote about their avatar and non-avatar 'selves' (Mullen, Beilke, & Brooks, 2007). Delwiche (2006) facilitated discussions of gender and identity in which undergraduate students created avatars of different genders, and other students questioned them to determine which students matched their avatar's projected gender identity.

Findings of greater satisfaction among learners who interact with fellow distance students (Beffa-Negrini, Miller, & Cohen, 2002; Swan, 2001;

McAlpine, 2000) suggests the potential value of collaborative learning assignments. Minocha and Tingle (2008) recommended following activities with discussions for shared reflection and debriefing. Besides using text or voice chat for student responses, activity-based feedback allows students to use kinesthetic responses. Pitcher (2007) described an activity at Massachusetts Institute of Technology in which students moved their avatars to appropriate spots on a 'hot or cold' feedback grid, noting that color-coded circles on the ground or colored flags could also be used. Other tools for helping students express opinions include 'voting platforms' such as Esme Quinha's 'Likert Scale Floor Mat' (Minocha & Tingle, 2008, p. 222) and Entropy Hax's "Opinionator" in which students move their avatars to spaces representing Likert scale choices ("agree"/"disagree"), with results aggregated in a colorful pie chart. Angrybeth Shortbread's "hand-show chairs" enable hand-raising for volunteering or voting.

Vygotsky (1978) described the "Zone of Proximal Development" as the distance between potential for personal independent learning compared to increased learning possibilities in collaboration with others. Creelman, Petrakou, and Richardson (2008) demonstrated this type of collaborative learning in intercultural discussions between Swedish students at University of Kalmar and American students at the University of Central Missouri. Text chat universal translation tools facilitate multilingual and multi-cultural discussions. Since Second Life is used worldwide, opportunities abound for international and cross-university collaborations.

EXHIBITS AND REPLICATIONS

Virtual exhibits and replications demonstrate sights and sounds of unfamiliar places, helping students to conceptualize unfamiliar surroundings and time periods. Bryan Carter at University of Central Missouri has taught English within a 1920's-1930's 'Harlem Renaissance' replication to help students better understand the literature of the time period (Peters, 2007). Visual and kinesthetic learners walk Virtual Harlem's streets, visiting the Cotton Club and Apollo Theater. At National Oceanic and Atmospheric Administration (NOAA)'s Meteroa, visitors fly through a hurricane or witness a tsunami, while at Second Life's International Spaceflight Museum, visitors can inspect 50 different spacecraft and rockets (Cochrane, 2006). At Vassar College's island, Steve Taylor recreated the Sistine Chapel (Kelton, 2007). Students can fly up to the chapel's ceiling to examine fine architectural and artistic details.

Internal landscapes, the microscopic world, and individual personal perceptions are also replicable. Winn (2002) referred to the "umwelt" or individual perceptions of the environment, such as the world seen through the eyes of a bird, fish, or insect. When the entire learning environment conveys the world as others see it, surroundings reinforce personal learning. At the University of California at Davis, Dr. Peter Yellowlees and Dr. James Cook used Second Life to show medical students how the world looks to schizophrenic patients experiencing visual and auditory hallucinations (Yellowlees & Cook, 2006). Hilde Hullabaloo's Cancerland takes visitors into her thyroid cancer experiences using visuals and audio to convey her medical treatment as well as her feelings and fears, rendered both realistically and metaphorically.

Exhibits can offer instructional guidance on performing specific tasks via posters, models and other replicas. At Elon University's site, an exhibit demonstrated proper focusing of a telescope (Kemp & Livingstone, 2006). At the University of St. Andrews, film students could observe how to set up and connect video equipment (Ryan, 2008). Some exhibits go beyond replication, incorporating interactive experiences. Don Bickley's giant human anatomy models at Northern Michigan University's Speech Language and Hearing Science Island are scripted with quizzes (Bickley, 2009).

Learners fly up into a giant larynx and attempt to identify different anatomical parts, receiving running totals on their correct and incorrect answers. Students not only closely examine 3-D models, but also test and practice their knowledge.

GAMES

Games introduce fun and challenge into the virtual personal learning environment. In interviewing students, Hollins and Robbins (2008) found key elements of successful games were "action, unpredictability, strong characters, good narrative, multiple paths, progressive difficulty, and an immersive environment" (p.176). Good game design motivates players to continue, for example by rewarding accomplishments with desirable goods (Jeffery, 2008). In Whyville's virtual world, kids play science games to earn Whyville's in-world money, known as "clams" (Feldon & Kafai, 2008, p. 578), which they use to buy new adornments and features for their avatars. In Second Life, rewards could include clothing and tools as well as "Linden dollars," the in-world currency. When using gift items to reward and motivate students, Ramondt (2008) observed that typically in quest-style games, each reward is slightly better than the last.

Games can teach basic Second Life skills, or subject knowledge such as English, nutrition or genetics. In English Village, treasure hunts teach English as a second language (ESL) (Derrington & Homewood, 2008). At Fontys University of Applied Sciences, student avatars are asked quiz questions and must scramble to the next location before answering (Ryan, 2008), gaining practice in moving their avatars as well as practicing their subject knowledge. On Genome Island, students play "the Mating Game" created by Mary Anne Clark of Texas Wesleyan University (Boulous, Heatherington, & Wheeler, 2007), running botany experiments on genetic inheritance by collecting and analyzing data. A nutrition game created by Dr. Chang Liu, Christopher Keesey, and Tessa Cooper at Ohio University's site challenges students to visit several restaurants and eat three meals without exceeding recommended daily calories, fat or cholesterol (Boulous, Heatherington, & Wheeler, 2007). Students can test the impact of food choices based on their avatar's size, or their own height and weight.

Treasure hunts, quests, and games during orientation can teach basic skill proficiencies. For example, Truelove and Hibbert (2008) gave students a 'hide and seek' challenge teaching them to use Second Life's map features (p. 365). Minocha and Tingle (2008) assigned pairs of students to treasure-hunt for note cards with relevant learning information; they further suggest integrating rewards such as Linden dollars, gift items, or points earned.

Virtual worlds such as Quest Atlantis and Runescape integrate automated "non-player characters" to give players key information for solving quests. Grove and Steventon (2008) suggest that in Second Life, learners could interact with chatbots as non-player characters. Chatbots would answer questions and provide key information to teach skills and solve challenges. Jeffery (2009) recommends a visible title floating above the chatbot non-player character's head to clearly signal students to interact with that character. Chatbot non-player characters might prompt students to look for their "Library" inventory folder to discover clothes, tools, and other items, or might give students note card instructions for quests teaching them how to fly, teleport, search, or join a group.

Beyond skills training, games create an opportunity for distributing "gifts" of supplies useful for future activities. Examples include: whiteboards for class presentations, landmarks of recommended places to visit, clothes, avatar shapes, skins, animations, scripts, informational note cards, and other items. Instructors sometimes pay students Linden dollars for class-work use (Minocha & Tingle, 2008; Jeffery, 2008), since building projects may require students to pay in Linden dollars to upload images. As individually paying students can be time-consuming, integrating payments as game rewards could more efficiently manage distribution.

PROBLEM-SOLVING SCENARIOS

Problem scenarios or case studies place students into situations where they must diagnose and solve problems. Ideally scenarios should require shared cognitive efforts of students working together for a successful conclusion (Notar et al., 2002; McLoughlin, 2001). A challenge scenario can be set for the entire class, with smaller groups completing sub-parts of the challenge that contribute toward the larger solution.

At Idaho State University, Play2Train engages first responders and health personnel in emergency preparedness scenarios such as biohazards and flu pandemics (Taylor, 2009). Trainees work with replicas of expensive equipment, avoiding costs and risks of running a biohazard scenario in the real world. Medical and nursing students similarly undertake simulations of medical cases. In the Heart Murmur Sim created by Jeremy Kemp (Boulos, Hetherington, & Wheeler, 2007), students listen to patients with different heart rhythms, examine medical charts, and then diagnose a patient's mystery heart ailment.

In a Coventry University community safety scenario, undergraduate Criminology students walked through a simulated neighborhood, discussing their observations on lighting, graffiti, and litter (Grove & Steventon, 2008). At St. George's University, students worked within paramedic scenarios, treating an injured motorcyclist and a woman experiencing cardiovascular problems (Burden et al., 2008). In small groups, students assessed patients, decided on actions, and wrote case notes on a note card which was dropped into an in-world mailbox for instructor evaluation.

ROLE-PLAY

Role-play immerses students in unfamiliar viewpoints, settings, and activities. While many institutions replicate classrooms within Second Life, learning can occur outside of classroom settings. Childress and Braswell (2006) described class discussions within a café where the instructor served as barista and discussion topics appeared on the menu board. In Coventry University's community safety scenarios (Grove & Steventon, 2008), students created and assumed the roles of characters living in the community. Students discussed safety issues from the perspectives of role-play characters such as an elderly widower with asthma, or an Indian doctor who had experienced a racial attack.

Role-play allows students to gain insights into personal viewpoints on various sides of an interaction. At University of Kansas, medical students role-played clinic scenarios from the perspectives of doctor, patient, nurse and family member, then discussed and reflected on what they learned (Childress & Braswell, 2006; Antonacci & Modaress, 2005). At Harvard University's Berkman Island, law students role-played different participants in litigation scenarios (Ryan, 2008).

Role-play can draw upon literary classics, or recreate famous historical figures. In a text-based MOO virtual world environment, Arver (2007) assigned 9th graders to role-play characters in William Golding's *The Lord of the Flies*. Students joined teams such as "Hut Builders" and "Food/Fruit Finders," (p.39), wrote journals, stories and poems, and learned relevant vocabulary. In Teen Second Life, Ramapo middle school students role-played the courtroom scene from John Steinbeck's *Of Mice and Men* (Calogne, 2008). In a world literature and rhetoric course in Second Life, undergraduate students wrote about historical figures that they admired such as Mother Teresa and Malcolm X, then modified their avatar to appear as that historical character during class discussion and debate (Mayrath et al., 2007).

Role-play also enables learners to practice skills in context. Phillips (2008) described how Asperger's autism patients role-played social skills in Second Life, practicing asking another person out on a date and participating in a job interviews. Derrington and Homewood (2008) described actors in Language Lab's 'English City' engaging students in English language conversations by posing as street musicians or poets in the public park.

Research suggests that computer-mediated virtual participation in which students collaborate as someone other than themselves enables "disinhibition," encouraging greater risk-taking in participation (Dede, 1995; Bonk & Reynolds, 1997). Surroundings conveying a sense of being 'elsewhere' heighten immersion into role-play. At St. George's University, student avatars donned paramedic uniforms during scenarios (Burden et al., 2008). Immersive role-play can be enhanced not only by modifying avatar appearance and terra-forming the landscape, but even by changing ambient sounds and lighting to simulate a dark night with howling wolves, or bright sunshine with twittering birds.

EXPERIENTIAL LEARNING

Beyond imaginative learning activities, students have participated in experiential and community service learning projects by working with in-world organizations. Sanchez (2009) described a community service learning assignment at the University of Texas-Austin in which undergraduate students planned and conducted fundraising events for nonprofit charitable organizations such as the American Cancer Society. At Ohio University, computer science and engineering students participated in design teams creating software for real clients (Ye, Liu, & Polack-Wahl, 2007). Students learned skills while gaining hands-on experience with potential future employers.

Universities and colleges, libraries, museums and nonprofit organizations are among the many communities of practice that exist in Second Life. Opportunities exist for students to observe and learn from these communities of experts. Brown, Collins, and Duguid (1989) emphasized "situated learning" in which learners observe experts performing skills in context. On Second Life'sInfo Island, librarians and graduate students observe practitioners at the Community Virtual Library reference desk. Learners have also gained skills through a process of gradually increasing responsibility that Lave and Wenger (1991) term "legitimate peripheral participation," attending meetings and participating in other ways such as helping run in-world events. At Florida State University in 2007 and 2008, library graduate students worked on collection-building projects, attended events, and observed at the reference desk as peripheral participation in Info Island library community of practice.

Second Life offers a rich virtual learning laboratory for investigative research. At Ball State University, Sarah Robbins assigned English undergraduate students to conduct research within Second Life (Mullen, Beilke, & Brooks, 2007). Students formulated research questions, designed and conducted the research, and wrote reports, just as Dr. Meg Conklin's computer science students had done in a cyber-culture class at Elon University (Foster, 2005). Such experiential learning assignments move students beyond reading about theory to applying it directly in solving problems.

Just as students can use virtual settings in observing the work of professionals, experts can likewise observe and comment on student projects (Guzdial, 2001). Virtual science fairs, poster sessions, and other in-world showcases allow students to share their work and receive feedback from both professionals and peers.

CREATION AS A LEARNING ACTIVITY

Second Life's popularity as a virtual world derives in no small part from the freedom to build and create afforded to its users. Any Second Life user can create an in-world object, coloring, shaping, sizing and imbuing it with material properties, such as rubber or stone. Landowners can terraform at will, raising mountains and carving out rivers, building under the ocean or in the sky. This flexibility is well-suited to educational activities of building and creating, which Camilleri and Montebello (2008) described as "allowing learners to build their own 'learnscapes' " (p. 75). Students can create individual or group projects, make movies, write programs ("scripts") and publish books.

Among student-created builds is Virtual Morocco, a collaboration between students at Johnson and Wales University and Morocco's Ministry of Tourism (Johnson & Levine, 2008). At University of Texas-Austin, graduate students in Dr. Leslie Jarmon's communication course collaborated with architecture students to build a Second Life version of "Alley Flats," a proposed East Austin community building project (McCarthy & Crossette, 2007). OpenSimulator ("OpenSim"), the open-source virtual world platform, has similarly hosted student building projects. Truelove and Hibbert (2008) described assignments allowing undergraduate students in a Graphic Arts and Design course at Leeds University to experiment with the OpenSim environment, as for example building "a tower as tall as possible" (p. 364); in another task, students created a shrine to their avatars as a way of exploring identity.

In-world movie-making, or "machinima," captures on-screen activity using keyboard commands within Second Life's interface, or through third-party video capturing software such as Fraps. At Anglia Ruskin University, students in small groups created Second Life machinima videos, first storyboarding and designing objects for the videos and then filming and acting in the movies (Brown, Gordon, & Hobbs, 2008). Students were evaluated on their group video and storyboard, individual contributions such as objects created, and final group presentations of their work. Brown, Gordon, and Hobbs (2008) found machinima projects well-suited to group work, since one student records video while others provide the on-screen action (p. 42).

Programming, or "scripting" can be assigned using 'Linden Scripting Language' (LSL) as programming code within Second Life. At Colorado Technical University, students designed and tested Second Life computer games for a software design class (Calogne, 2008). In an undergraduate communications class, Delwiche (2006) taught game design fundamentals, game aesthetics, and cyber-culture. Student teams designed, built and scripted the games, then tested the games and wrote reflective papers. These assignments not only give practice in creative design but also in teamwork and project management.

Books are valued within Second Life, and students can create books by designing 'pages' in Powerpoint and then converting each page into an image which is uploaded into Second Life. Resulting page images can be applied as 'textures' to objects, such as flat surfaces; in-world book publishing devices also can be purchased, such as Toneless Tomba's THiNC books and printing press. Books can be created in collaborative group writing projects, or by producing a class 'library' of individually student-written books.

TOURS

Since students are motivated to explore Second Life, educators should offer interesting and relevant places for students to visit. Ideally, opportunities should be offered for visiting some sites together as well as links for additional places that students can visit independently (see Appendix I: "Touring Second Life").

In group tours, the major challenge is keeping the group together; the larger the group, the greater the challenge. Students wandering out of range may not hear instructions, and if the leader walks or flies away, may miss seeing which direction the leader went. For students, it is frustrating to become 'lost' in a strange world. To prevent this, instructors leading a tour group can use a variety of techniques:

- **Landmarks:** giving students a collection of landmarks as clickable teleporting links to tour destinations.
- **Note cards:** giving students clickable tour links in a note card, including help information.
- **Group instant messaging:** establishing a class 'group' and inviting all students to join. When touring, instant messages can be sent to the group.
- **Friending:** exchanging friendship with students allows them to more easily 'instant message' instructors, and helps instructors offer students a teleport or give needed items (landmarks, note cards).
- **Visual cues:** 'real world' tour guides sometimes carry big umbrellas, balloons, or other objects visible at a distance; Second Life tour leaders might likewise use visible signals (big hat, large sign, bright colors).
- **Map usage:** students should be shown use of map features; 'green dots' indicate other avatars, to help lost students rejoin the group.
- **Gadgets:** some tools for purchase allow group transports. For example, MystiTool HUD has a feature that brings other avatars along in 'follow chairs.' Teleport systems exist that can teleport avatars in groups; or if students are teleporting around on one site, teleportation devices can be strategically placed for students traveling to the next location.

Because tour logistics can be challenging, no more than a few destinations should be planned per class session. Tours may be combined with other activities, such as traveling to a guest lecture or exhibit.

SUMMARY AND CONCLUSION

Second Life as a virtual personal learning environment offers a variety of learning experiences that are engaging and responsive to learners' needs. While the traditional classroom lecture can be replicated, alternative teaching options include games, problem-solving scenarios, experiential and service learning, role-play, tours, guest speakers, events, and creative activities such as building, programming/scripting, movie-making, and publishing.

Second Life's steep learning curve requires significant effort from both students and instructors. Beyond a well-planned orientation process, establishing pedagogical relevance of in-world activities to course learning goals is essential for student satisfaction. Activities should be followed by time for reflection and discussion, ideally with opportunities for student avatars to learn together as distance students highly value interactions with classmates and instructors.

Because virtual world teaching is still relatively new, more research is needed on the effectiveness of pedagogical approaches. Integrating research assessment of student satisfaction and success in achieving learning outcomes within virtual world courses is essential to developing guidelines for best practices in education beyond 2-dimensional class Web pages into 3-dimensional virtual learning environments, where teaching and learning can be visual, textual, auditory and kinesthetic, and where teachers can move mountains and students can fly.

REFERENCES

Antonacci, D., & Modaress, N. (2008). Envisioning the educational possibilities of user-created virtual worlds. *AACE Journal, 16*(2), 115–126.

Arver, C. (2007). Are you willing to have your students join Ralph, Jack, and Piggy? *English Journal, 97*(1), 37–42.

Barab, S., Sadler, T., Heiselt, C., Hickey, D., & Zuiker, S. (2007). Relating narrative, inquiry, and inscriptions: Supporting consequential play. *Journal of Science Education and Technology, 16*(1), 59–82. doi:10.1007/s10956-006-9033-3

Beard, L., & Harper, C. (2000). Student perceptions of online versus campus instruction. *Education, 122*(4), 658–664.

Beffa-Negrini, P., Miller, B., & Cohen, N. (2002). Factors related to success and satisfaction in online learning. *Academic Exchange Quarterly, 6*(3), 105–114.

Bickley, D. (2009). *NMU Speech-Language & Hearing Virtual Clinic: Project news/updates.* Retrieved June 23, 2009 from http://www.donbickley.com/nmuspeechpathPN.html

Blaisdell, M. (2006). All the right MUVEs. *T.H.E. Journal, 33*(14), 28–38.

Bonk, C., & Thomas, H. (1997). Learner-centered web instruction for higher-order thinking, teamwork, and apprenticeship. In Khan, B. H. (Ed.), *Web-Based Instruction* (pp. 167–178). Englewood Cliffs, NJ: Educational Technology Publications.

Boulos, M., Hetherington, L., & Wheeler, S. (2007). Second Life: an overview of the potential of 3-D virtual worlds in medical and health education. *Health Information and Libraries Journal, 24*(4), 233–245. doi:10.1111/j.1471-1842.2007.00733.x

Brown, E., Gordon, M., & Hobbs, M. (2008). Second Life as a holistic learning environment for problem-based learning and transferable skills. In *Proceedings of the Researching Learning in Virtual Environments International Conference* (pp. 39-48). Retrieved May 8, 2009 from http://www.open.ac.uk/relive08/documents/ReLIVE08_conference_proceedings_Lo.pdf

Brown, J., Collins, A., & Duguid, P. (1989). Situated cognition and the culture of learning. *Educational Researcher, 18*(1), 32–42.

Burden, D., Conradi, E., Woodham, L., Poulton, T., Savin-Baden, M., & Kavia, S. (2008). Creating and assessing a virtual patient player in Second Life. In *Proceedings of the Researching Learning in Virtual Environments International Conference* (pp. 49-62). Retrieved May 8, 2009 from http://www.open.ac.uk/relive08/documents/ReLIVE08_conference_proceedings_Lo.pdf

Calongne, C. M. (2008). Educational frontiers: Learning in a virtual world. *EDUCAUSE Review, 43*(5), 36-48. Retrieved June 1, 2009 from http://net.educause.edu/ir/library/pdf/ERM0852.pdf

Camilleri, V., & Montebello, M. (2008). SLAVE – Second Life assistant in a virtual environment. In *Proceedings of the Researching Learning in Virtual Environments International Conference* (pp. 72-82). Retrieved May 8, 2009 from http://www.open.ac.uk/relive08/documents/ReLIVE08_conference_proceedings_Lo.pdf

Cheal, C. (2007). Second Life: hype or hyperlearning? *Horizon, 15*(4), 204–210. doi:10.1108/10748120710836228

Childress, M., & Braswell, R. (2006). Role-playing games for online learning. *Distance Education, 27*(2), 187–196. doi:10.1080/01587910600789522

Cochrane, K. (2006). Case study: International Spaceflight Museum. In D. Livingstone & J. Kemp (Eds.), *Proceedings of the Second Life Education Workshop at the Second Life Community Convention 2006* (pp. 2-5). Retrieved May 5, 2009 from http://www.simteach.com/SLCC06/slcc2006-proceedings.pdf

Conrad, D. (2002). Engagement, excitement, anxiety, and fear: Learners' experiences of starting an online course. *American Journal of Distance Education*, *16*(4), 205–226. doi:10.1207/S15389286AJDE1604_2

Corbit, M. (2002). Building virtual worlds for informal science learning (SciCentr and SciFair) in the Active Worlds Educational Universe (AWEDU). *Presence: Tele-operators & Virtual Environment*, *11*(1), 55–67. doi:10.1162/105474602317343659

Damer, B. (2008). Meeting in the ether: A brief history of virtual worlds as a medium for user-created events. *Journal of Virtual Worlds Research*, *1*(1). Retrieved June 5, 2009 from http://journals.tdl.org/jvwr/article/view/285/239

De Lucia, A., Francese, R., Passero, I., & Tortora, G. (2009). Development and evaluation of a virtual campus on Second Life: the case of SecondDMI. *Computers & Education*, *52*(1), 220–233. doi:10.1016/j.compedu.2008.08.001

Dede, C. (1995). The evolution of constructivist learning environments: Immersion in distributed, virtual worlds. *Educational Technology*, *35*(5), 46–52.

Delwiche, A. (2006). Massively multiplayer online games (MMOs) in the new media classroom. *Educational Technology & Society*, *9*(3), 160–172.

Derrington, M., & Homewood, B. (2008). Get real - this isn't real, it's Second Life: Teaching ESL in a virtual world. In *Proceedings of the Researching Learning in Virtual Environments International Conference* (pp. 106-120). Retrieved May 8, 2009 from http://www.open.ac.uk/relive08/documents/ReLIVE08_conference_proceedings_Lo.pdf

Dunleavy, M., Dede, C., & Mitchell, R. (2009). Affordances and limitations of immersive participatory augmented reality simulations for teaching and learning. *Journal of Science Education and Technology*, *18*, 7–22. doi:10.1007/s10956-008-9119-1

Feldon, D., & Kafai, Y. (2008). Mixed methods for mixed reality: Understanding users' avatar activities in virtual worlds. *Educational Technology Research and Development*, *56*(5/6), 575–593. doi:10.1007/s11423-007-9081-2

Foster, A. (2005). The avatars of research. *The Chronicle of Higher Education*, *52*(6), A35.

Gollub, R. (2007). Second Life and education. *Crossroads: The ACM Student Magazine, 14(1).* Retrieved June 12, 2009 from http://www.acm.org/crossroads/xrds14-1/secondlife.html

Good, J., Howland, K., & Thackray, L. (2008). Problem-based learning spanning real and virtual worlds: a case study in Second Life. *ALT-J*, *16*(3), 163–172. doi:10.1080/09687760802526681

Grove, P., & Steventon, G. (2008). Exploring community safety in a virtual community: using Second Life to enhance structured creative learning. In *Proceedings of the Researching Learning in Virtual Environments International Conference* (pp. 154-171). Retrieved May 8, 2009 from http://www.open.ac.uk/relive08/documents/ReLIVE08_conference_proceedings_Lo.pdf

Gunawardena, C., & Zittle, F. (1997). Social presence as a predictor of satisfaction within a computer-mediated conferencing environment. *American Journal of Distance Education*, *11*(3), 8–26. doi:10.1080/08923649709526970

Guzdial, M., Jochen, R., & Kehoe, C. (2001). Beyond adoption to invention: Teacher-created collaborative activities in higher education. *Journal of the Learning Sciences*, *10*(3), 265–279. doi:10.1207/S15327809JLS1003_2

Hara, N., & Kling, R. (1999). Students' frustrations with a web-based distance education course. *First Monday, 4*(12). Retrieved June 1, 2009 from http://www.uic.edu/htbin/cgiwrap/bin/ojs/index.php/fm/article/view/710/620

Hiltz, S. (1997). Impacts of college-level courses via asynchronous learning networks: Some preliminary results. *Journal of Asynchronous Learning Networks, 1*(2). Retrieved May 3, 2008 from http://www.aln.org/alnweb/journal/issue2/hiltz.htm

Hollins, P., & Robbins, S. (2008). The educational affordances of multi user virtual environments (MUVE). In *Proceedings of the Researching Learning in Virtual Environments International Conference* (pp. 172-180). Retrieved May 8, 2009 from http://www.open.ac.uk/relive08/documents/ReLIVE08_conference_proceedings_Lo.pdf

Jarmon, L., Traphagan, T., Mayrath, M., & Trivedi, A. (2009). Virtual world teaching, experiential learning, and assessment: an interdisciplinary communication course in Second Life. *Computers & Education, 53*(1), 169–182. doi:10.1016/j.compedu.2009.01.010

Jeffery, C. (2008). Using non-player characters as tutors in virtual environments. In *Proceedings of the Researching Learning in Virtual Environments International Conference* (pp. 181-188). Retrieved May 8, 2009 from http://www.open.ac.uk/relive08/documents/ReLIVE08_conference_proceedings_Lo.pdf

Johnson, L., & Levine, A. (2008). Virtual worlds: Inherently immersive, highly social learning spaces. *Theory into Practice, 47*(2), 161–170. doi:10.1080/00405840801992397

Kelton, A. J. (2007). Second Life: Reaching into the virtual world for real-world learning. *Educause Center for Applied Research (ECAR) Research Bulletin*, (17), 1-13. Retrieved May 12, 2009 from http://net.educause.edu/ir/library/pdf/ERB0717.pdf

Kemp, J., & Livingstone, D. (2006). Putting a Second Life 'metaverse' skin on learning management systems. In D. Livingstone & J. Kemp (Eds.), *In Proceedings of the Second Life Education Workshop at the Second Life Community Convention 2006* (pp. 13-18). Retrieved May 5, 2009 from http://www.simteach.com/SLCC06/slcc2006-proceedings.pdf

Ketelhut, D. (2007). The impact of student self-efficacy on scientific inquiry skills: an exploratory investigation in "River City," a multi-user virtual environment. *Journal of Science Education and Technology, 16*(1), 99–111. doi:10.1007/s10956-006-9038-y

Lave, J., & Wenger, E. (1991). *Situated learning: Legitimate peripheral participation*. Cambridge, UK: University of Cambridge Press.

Mayrath, M., Sanchez, J., Traphagan, T., Heikes, J., & Trivedi, A. (2007). Using Second Life in an English course: Designing class activities to address learning objectives. In *Proceedings of the World Conference on Educational Multimedia, Hypermedia and Telecommunications* (pp. 4219-4224). Retrieved June 5, 2009 from http://research.educatorscoop.org/EDMEDIA07.proceeding.pdf

McAlpine, I. (2000). Collaborative learning online. *Distance Education, 21*(1), 66–80. doi:10.1080/0158791000210105

McCarthy, S., & Crossette, A. (2007). *University of Texas at Austin unites project in East Austin with virtual reality world.* Retrieved June 5, 2009 from http://www.utexas.edu/news/2007/12/03/architecture_alley_flat/

McVey, M. (2008). Observations of expert communicators in immersive virtual worlds: implications for synchronous discussion. *ALT-J, 16*(3), 173–180. doi:10.1080/09687760802526673

Mikropoulos, T. (2001). Brain activity on navigation in virtual environments. *Journal of Educational Computing Research, 24*(1), 1–12. doi:10.2190/D1W3-Y15D-4UDW-L6C9

Minocha, S., & Tingle, R. (2008). Socialisation and collaborative learning of distance learners in 3-D virtual worlds. In *Researching Learning in Virtual Environments International Conference Proceedings* (pp. 216-227). Retrieved May 8, 2009 from http://www.open.ac.uk/relive08/documents/ReLIVE08_conference_proceedings_Lo.pdf

Mullen, L., Beilke, J., & Brooks, N. (2007). Redefining field experiences: Virtual environments in teacher education. *International Journal of Social Sciences, 2*(1), 22–28.

Murphy, K., & Cifuentes, L. (2001). Using web tools, collaborating, and learning online. *Distance Education, 22*(2), 285–305. doi:10.1080/0158791010220207

Murphy, K., & Collins, M. (1997). Communication conventions in instructional electronic chats. *First Monday, 2*(11). Retrieved June 1, 2009 from http://www.uic.edu/htbin/cgiwrap/bin/ojs/index.php/fm/article/view/558/479

National Center for Education Statistics (NCES). (1999). Distance education at postsecondary education institutions: 1997-1998. *U.S. Department of Education, NCES 2000-013*. Retrieved June 1, 2009 from http://nces.ed.gov/pubs2000/2000013.pdf

National Center for Education Statistics (NCES). (2008). Distance education at degree-granting postsecondary institutions: 2006-07. *U.S. Department of Education*. Retrieved June 1, 2009 from http://nces.ed.gov/pubsearch/pubsinfo.asp?pubid=2009044

Neustaedter, C., & Fedorovskaya, E. (2009). Capturing and sharing memories in a virtual world. In *Proceedings of ACM CHI 2009 Conference on Human Factors in Computing Systems* (pp. 1161-1170). Retrieved June 4, 2009 from http://portal.acm.org/citation.cfm?doid=1518701.1518878

Notar, C., Wilson, J., & Ross, K. (2002). Distant learning for the development of higher-level cognitive skills. *Education, 122*(4), 642–648.

Omale, N., Hung, W., Luetkehans, L., & Cooke-Plagwitz, J. (2009). Learning in 3-D multiuser virtual environments: exploring the use of unique 3-D attributes for online problem-based learning. *British Journal of Educational Technology, 40*(3), 480–495. doi:10.1111/j.1467-8535.2009.00941.x

Peters, T. (2007). *A report on the first year of operation of the Alliance Second Life Library 2.0 project also known as the Alliance Information Archipelago*. April 11, 2006 through April 18, 2007. Retrieved June 8, 2009 from http://www.alliancelibrarysystem.com/pdf/07sllreport.pdf

Phillips, A. (2008, January 15). Asperger's therapy hits Second Life: Experts express concern about applying online actions to real life. *ABC News*. Retrieved June 8, 2009 from http://abcnews.go.com/Technology/OnCall/story?id=4133184&page=1

Pitcher, J. (2007). *Class management*. Retrieved June 4, 2009 from http://jpitcher.edublogs.org/2007/11/14/class-management/

Ramondt, L. (2008). Towards the adoption of Massively Multiplayer Educational Gaming. In *Proceedings of the Researching Learning in Virtual Environments International Conference Proceedings* (pp. 258-268.) Retrieved May 8, 2009 from http://www.open.ac.uk/relive08/documents/ReLIVE08_conference_proceedings_Lo.pdf

Ryan, M. (2008). 16 ways to use virtual worlds in your classroom: Pedagogical applications of Second Life. In *Proceedings of the Researching Learning in Virtual Environments International Conference* (pp. 269-277). Retrieved May 8, 2009 from http://www.open.ac.uk/relive08/documents/ReLIVE08_conference_proceedings_Lo.pdf

Sanchez, J. (2009). Student Second Life event: under water fun. Retrieved June 9, 2009 from http://educatorscoop.org/blog/?p=171

Sloan-C. (2008). *Staying the course: Online education in the United States, 2008*. Retrieved May 8, 2009 from http://www.sloan-c.org/publications/survey/pdf/staying_the_course.pdf

Swan, K. (2001). Virtual interaction: Design factors affecting student satisfaction and perceived learning in asynchronous online courses. *Distance Education*, *22*(2), 306–331. doi:10.1080/0158791010220208

Taylor, A. (2009). Virtual worlds, social networks provide brave new world for emergency training. *Idaho State University Magazine, 39*(2). Retrieved June 10, 2009 from http://www.isu.edu/magazine/spring09/play2train.shtml

Terry, N. (2001). Assessing enrollment and attrition rates for the online MBA. *Technological Horizons in Education Journal*, *28*(7), 64.

Truelove, I., & Hibbert, G. (2008). Learning to walk before you know your name: Pre-Second Life scaffolding for noobs. In *Proceedings of the Researching Learning in Virtual Environments International Conference* (pp. 362-368). Retrieved May 8, 2009 from http://www.open.ac.uk/relive08/documents/ReLIVE08_conference_proceedings_Lo.pdf

Tu, C., & Corry, M. (2001). A paradigm shift for online community research. *Distance Education*, *22*(2), 245–263. doi:10.1080/0158791010220205

Vygotsky, L. S. (1978). *Mind and society: The development of higher mental processes*. Cambridge, MA: Harvard University Press.

Wagner, C. (2008). Learning experience with virtual worlds. *Journal of Information Systems Education*, *19*(3), 263–266.

Wang, Y., & Braman, J. (2009). Extending the classroom through Second Life. *Journal of Information Systems Education*, *20*(2), 235–247.

Warburton, S. (2009). Second Life in higher education: Assessing the potential for and the barriers to deploying virtual worlds in learning and teaching. *British Journal of Educational Technology*, *40*(3), 414–426. doi:10.1111/j.1467-8535.2009.00952.x

Weasenforth, D., Biesenbach-Lucas, S., & Weasenforth, C. (2002). Realizing constructivist objectives through collaborative technologies: Threaded discussions. *Language Learning & Technology*, *6*(3), 58.

Winn, W. (2002). Learning in artificial environments: Embodiment, embeddedness and dynamic adaptation. Retrieved March 12, 2009 from http://depts.washington.edu/edtech/ticl.htm

Ye, E., Liu, C., & Polack-Wahl, J. (2007). Enhancing software engineering education using teaching aids in 3-D online virtual worlds. In *Proceedings of the 37th ASEE/IEEE Frontiers in Education Conference* (pp. T1E-8-T1E-13).

Yellowlees, P., & Cook, J. (2006). Education about hallucinations using an Internet virtual reality system: a qualitative survey. *Academic Psychiatry*, *30*(6), 534–539. doi:10.1176/appi.ap.30.6.534

APPENDIX I: TOURING SECOND LIFE

Replicas and Exhibits

International Spaceflight Museum (http://slurl.com/secondlife/Spaceport%20Alpha/47/77/24)
Cancerland (http://slurl.com/secondlife/Kula%203/197/86/21)
Sistine Chapel (http://slurl.com/secondlife/vassar/165/91/24)
Virtual Harlem (http://slurl.com/secondlife/Virtual%20Harlem/119/82/30)
Virtual Morocco (http://slurl.com/secondlife/Casablanca/141/89/26/)
Virtual Alamo (http://slurl.com/secondlife/ISTE%20Island%204/245/183/30)
NMU Giant Larynx (http://slurl.com/secondlife/Second%20Earth%207/70/181/48)
NOAA (http://slurl.com/secondlife/Meteora/176/160/27)
UC Davis' Virtual Hallucinations (http://slurl.com/secondlife/sedig/27/45/22/0

Games for Learning

'Splo / The Exploratorium (http://slurl.com/secondlife/Sploland/183/78/26/)
Genome Island (http://slurl.com/secondlife/Genome/127/128/49/)
Heart Murmur Sim (http://slurl.com/secondlife/Waterhead/130/50)
Ohio University Fast Food game (http://slurl.com/secondlife/Ohio%20University/190/177/27)

Role-Play

ROMA (http://slurl.com/secondlife/ROMA/214/25/22/)
Caledon (http://slurl.com/secondlife/Caledon/190/190/23)

Learning Locations

English Village (http://slurl.com/secondlife/English%20Village/136/117/108)
ICT Library (http://slurl.com/secondlife/Info%20Island/56/201/33)
Ivory Tower of Prims (http://slurl.com/secondlife/Natoma/204/70/25/)

Second Life Help and Information

New Citizens Incorporated (http://slurl.com/secondlife/Kuula/55/168/29)
Virtual Ability (http://slurl.com/secondlife/Virtual%20Ability/132/129/23)
Second Life Library Info Island (http://slurl.com/secondlife/Info%20Island%20International/116/237/34)

This work was previously published in International Journal of Virtual and Personal Learning Environments, edited by Michael Thomas, Volume 1, Issue 2, pp. 1-15, copyright 2010 by IGI Publishing (an imprint of IGI Global).

Chapter 10
Mechanics Simulations in Second Life

Kelly Black
Clarkson University, USA

ABSTRACT

This paper examines the use of the 3-D virtual world Second Life to explore basic mechanics in physics. In Second Life, students can create scripts that take advantage of a virtual physics engine in order to conduct experiments that focus on specific phenomena. The paper explores two particular examples of this process: 1) the movement of an object under the influence of gravity, and 2) the movement of an object using simple forces. Findings suggest that Second Life offers a flexible and wide range of possibilities for simulations in mechanics; paradoxically, however, the environment also presents challenges for effective use by instructors and learners. Any implementation making use of the Second Life application requires technical knowledge of the system and a wide range of pedagogical and learner skills related to building, scripting, and educational design.

INTRODUCTION

This paper examines the use of Second Life as a way for students to explore basic mechanics and kinematics. Second Life includes an integrated physics engine, Havoc 4, which can be used to simulate the motion of objects. Additionally, the platform allows people to create objects with scripts that can interact with the physics engine directly and indirectly. A number of computational environments are available for focused studies of mechanics. They range from predefined applets such as those created by Phet (2009) to the Open Source Physics project that provides a comprehensive software suite for designing your own applets. Another option that is widely available is VPython (Scherer, 2009). These are all computational engines that allow students to set up computational based experiments. Our focus here, however, is to examine environments that provide an experience that allows for more interaction between participants within the environment itself, and we examine the teaching of mechanics within a virtual environment.

DOI: 10.4018/978-1-4666-1770-4.ch010

Investigators have constructed virtual environments specifically designed to explore diverse physical phenomena including Newtonian mechanics, electrostatics, and molecular interactions (Dede et al., 1996a). Other virtual environments have been considered for a wide range of activities (Dede et al., 1996b; Mason, 2007), but our focus is on the use of Second Life for mechanics.

One of the goals is to place students in situations that allow for rich exchanges between one another and to explore a wide variety of options. This goal is motivated by the challenge of creating an environment that supports active engagement by the students. As an example, the idea is to support the student's "basic habits of mind." The students should seek diverse representations of the phenomena of interest. They should compare and contrast their results to what they expected, and then be able to describe the results in a variety of ways (Dufresne et al., 2005).

The construction and use of a virtual environment can be a difficult task. One goal of the design of such environments is to explicitly define relationships between the concepts and concrete representations (Barab et al., 2001). The difficulty is that the visualizations that are created should be consistent with the way students internalize the ideas (Gilbert et al., 2008). At the same time the students are expected to be placed into contexts that allow them to be active and create enhanced learning situations (Barab et al., 2001).

A virtual environment provides additional tools to the instructor to place the students in situations that support such efforts. In the specific case of mechanics the tool allows students to focus on situations that emphasize ideas that are associated with common misunderstandings. For example, many students have an Aristotelian view that the direction of motion determines the direction of force (Gilbert et al., 1982). Student misconceptions can be confronted in effective ways by examining relevant contexts and fostering active learning environments coupled with careful assessment (Guidugli et al., 2005).

When implemented appropriately, computer simulations can change the conceptions held by students (Tao & Gunstone, 1999). Computer simulations offer one more way to engage the students and can make abstract ideas more concrete (Pena & Alessi, 1999). The use of such tools offers an advantage in that students' preconceptions are not easily changed in traditional settings (Jimoyiannis & Komis, 2001). The use of more familiar contexts (Guidugli et al., 2005) and efforts to require students to explore the material more fully such as making use of prediction, observation, rich comparisons and multiple representations (Dufresne et al., 2005) provide ways to confront student misconceptions.

Multiple representations offer more ways for students to see and experience the ideas in different ways. Some representations provide exploratory models that allow simulation of physical laws. Other representations provide explicit models that allow the students to define the important relationships. The use of multiple representations, however, is not a magic bullet. Instructors must be careful in that misconceptions can be constructed on the spot (Rowlands et al., 2007).

The focus in this paper is on the use of one particular activity: the use of virtual environments for mechanics simulation. The importance of "immersion" within the virtual environment has been a focus of many studies. For example, some have examined the use of a head mounted display for a more complete immersion. The idea is that the level of interaction between the students and the virtual world are vital (Dede et al., 1996a; Dede et al., 1996b). The level of immersion is important with respect to the students to "trigger" a stronger reaction (Dede, 2009).

A less technically intensive approach is to focus more on the interactive aspects (Jimoyiannis & Komis, 2001) which is the approach discussed here. In particular the goal is to create an environment that allows students to change the parameters of an experiment and see the phenomena of interest in a variety of situations. This is more in line with the experiences of Byrne (2009) and Byrne and Bricken (2009). Their experience is that the ability to alter a situation and change parameters is more important than immersion.

Additionally, an approach requiring less obtrusive technical apparatus provides more flexibility in the way that students can devise and explore an experiment. For example, Byrne and Meredith observed some gender differences for different age groups. For example, some younger girls were less likely than other groups to sit quietly and work by themselves on their projects (Byrne & Bricken, 1992; Byrne, 2009). Flexible environments can be easily adapted to a wide range of group learning styles.

In addition to the student activities, the role of evaluation is another important aspect of any project. This is a difficult topic with a wide array of considerations. It is beyond the scope of this paper, but educators should keep in mind that evaluation and assessment should be carefully integrated throughout any project using multiple approaches (Andrews & Schwarz, 2002).

The use of Second Life to explore mechanics has received minimal attention. Our goal is to explore the software for greater use as a tool to engage students in an interactive, three dimensional simulation environment. Other software platforms exist, but Second Life offers a number of advantages. It requires relatively minimal hardware costs. It is widely available on all major operating systems. It also offers a platform that students can use to work with one another with minimal configuration and software updates. Most importantly students can work together in a wide variety of circumstances allowing them to interact with team members in the same room or across the globe in real time.

Our focus here is on how to use Second Life to explore basic mechanics. We first provide a brief overview of Second Life itself. Next we discuss the scripting language and provide an overview of some of the features that can be exploited by students exploring the movement of objects. We then examine two problems that students commonly examine in the first year, college level mechanics course. The first problem revolves around an examination of how an object moves under the influence of a simple force. The second problem is a projectile problem and requires students to determine the velocity required to hit an object with a projectile.

SECOND LIFE

Second Life is a product developed by Linden Labs and is freely available. It is a virtual world that is defined on a large set of servers maintained by Linden Research, and a special viewer is required in order to visualize the creations. The vast majority of virtual objects that have been defined have been created by the people making use of the system and not Linden Research. (The people using the system are referred to as "residents"). Here we briefly describe what the world is. We then briefly describe the user interface to the viewer and then discuss how to create and interact with objects.

The world is defined as a set of "sims" that are arranged on a two dimensional grid. Each sim is defined to be a 256 m by 256 m square, and the sim can be divided into smaller rectangles. Each rectangle is rented to a resident which is one of the ways Linden Research generates revenues. Linden Research provides space at reduced cost to educational institutions, and a wide variety of options are available for educators including free trial periods and there are also organizations who make space available for free.

The collection of sims are distributed on the set of servers operated by Linden Research. The requirements to access the grid are an Internet connection, a computer, and the Second Life viewer. The Second Life Viewer is freely available and the source code is available through the GPL (Free Software Foundation, accessed 17 Aug 2009). People can make use the viewer from any location and interact in real time with other people who are logged in at the same time.

The user interface to the viewer is shown in Figure 1. Each resident is represented by a customizable avatar. The "objects" that are found in the world offer a range of options for personal interaction. Avatars can bump into the objects with options to treat the objects as a solid or to simply pass through them. Scripts allow the objects to react when a user moves their mouse cursor over the object and clicks on the object.

An object can be created and then modified to take on a wide range of appearances. There are multiple ways to do this, and one way is shown in Figure 2. With this method a person moves their mouse cursor over a spot on the ground, clicks on the ground using the mouse, and then chooses "create" from a list of options. (The method of how a user clicks on an object depends on which operating system is being used).

Once the object has been created a special editing window is available for changing the object, see Figure 3. A number of basic shapes are available, and each shape can be altered in a number of different ways. For example, the object can be sliced into cross sections or twisted around different axes.

Each object also includes an inventory in which other objects can be stored within it. Scripts can also be stored in an object's inventory. An example of a newly created script is given in Figure 4. When a new script is created it consists of a default set of commands. An editor window is available to allow you to edit the script from the viewer.

The Linden Scripting Language

Within the Second Life platform a set of basic objects can be constructed which in turn can be combined in novel ways to create more complex objects. The objects can be modified by applying images (textures) and also by embedding scripts within them.

The scripting language that is used is called the Linden Scripting Language (LSL). The language

Figure 1. The basic interface and window into Second Life

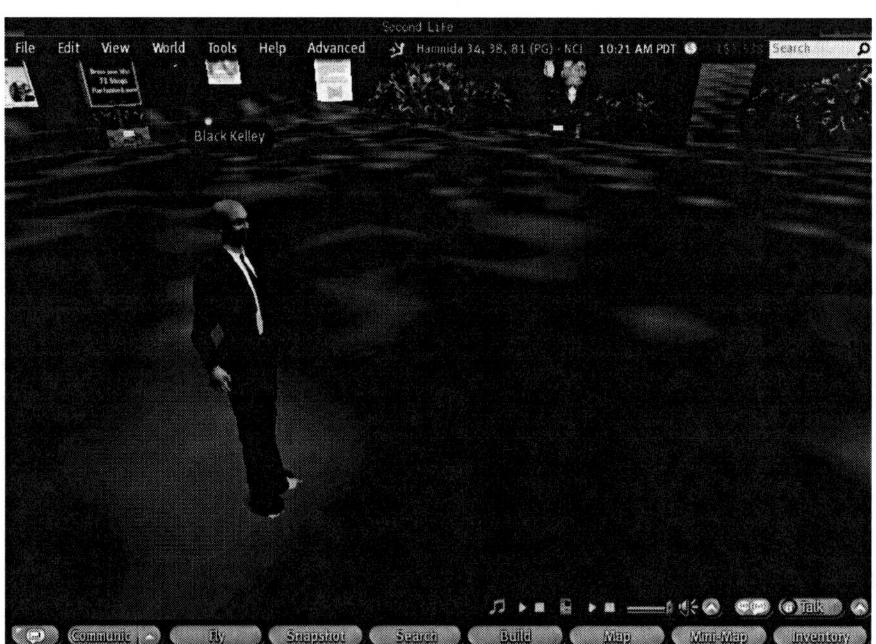

Figure 2. One way to create an object is to point to a location on the ground, right click and choose "create"

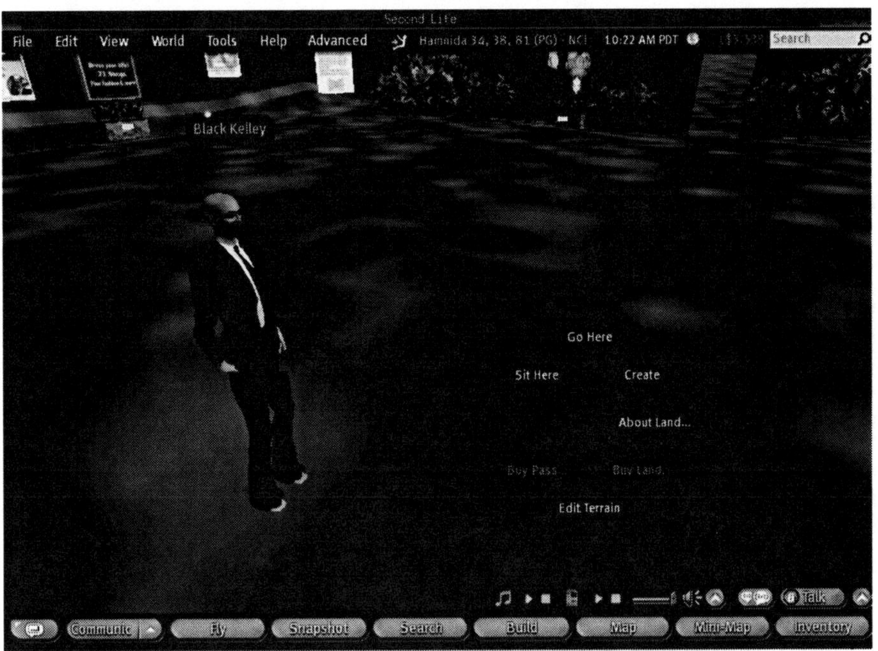

is an event based language. Libraries are included that allow for interaction by moving an object, detecting other objects, reacting to predefined events, and providing a connection with the physics engine built into the system. Here we focus on using the scripting language in conjunction with the physics engine.

We do not provide a detailed introduction into the language. Linden Research has made more detailed documentation available at their website (Linden Research Inc., 2009g). We first focus on the basic routines that can define how scripts react for predefined events. Next the routines that provide access to the physics engine are explored. Finally, the events that allow for the detection of the physical state of another object are examined.

Events

Programs in LSL are constructed to react to a set of predefined events. Scripts automatically begin to wait for events without requiring explicit definitions or explicitly entering a loop polling for events. A script will react to a set of events if a subroutine with a predetermined name happens to exist in the script.

A wide range of routines define the basic events. For example, there are a number of events that can detect when a collision occurs between other objects or the ground, but the event that we will be interested in is when someone moves their mouse pointer over the object and clicks on it. This is referred to as a "touch" event and an example is shown in Listing 1.

When the script in Listing 1 is running it waits until someone touches the object in which it is embedded. When someone first moves their mouse pointer over the object and clicks then the routine touch_start is called. The subroutine checks to see if the person clicking on it is the owner of the object. If the person is the owner then it prints out a message that only the owner can see.

Figure 3. A new object has a default size and shape which can be altered

Physics

Objects within Second Life have a number of different settings and options. One of the options is to change the position or momentum using the internal physics engine. When an object is set to physical its position and velocity are simulated using the system's physics engine and can be moved in a number of ways.

One way to change the object's position and momentum is through a script. Two of the relevant commands influence the object by applying an angular impulse or angular acceleration. The other two commands apply a linear impulse or linear acceleration. We focus on the latter two commands.

The two commands are llSetForce (Linden Research Inc., 2009e) and llApplyImpulse (Linden Research Inc., 2009a). Both functions require two arguments, a vector and a Boolean variable indicating whether or not the vector is a local or global coordinate system. For our purposes in this paper we refer to a global coordinate system.

The llSetForce command is used to apply a continual force to the center of mass of the object that holds the script. It represents the total force acting on the object. The resultant force is specified using this command. The llApplyImpulse command is used to apply a one time impulse to the object which holds the script. The llApplyImpulse command is the most useful in terms of moving an object in a prescribed manner. In terms of the educational aspect we focus on the llSetForce command.

The script given in Listing 2 demonstrates how to apply a force to an object. When the owner touches the object a constant 1 Newton force is applied in the global x-direction. The subroutine state entry (Linden Research Inc., 2009i) is called when the script is reset. The script will execute the commands in this subroutine and then wait until someone clicks on it. The state entry subroutine is used to turn off the physical properties of the object.

When someone clicks on the object the script tests to see if the person is the owner of

Figure 4. A script can be created by adding it to an object's inventory. A new script has a default set of statements.

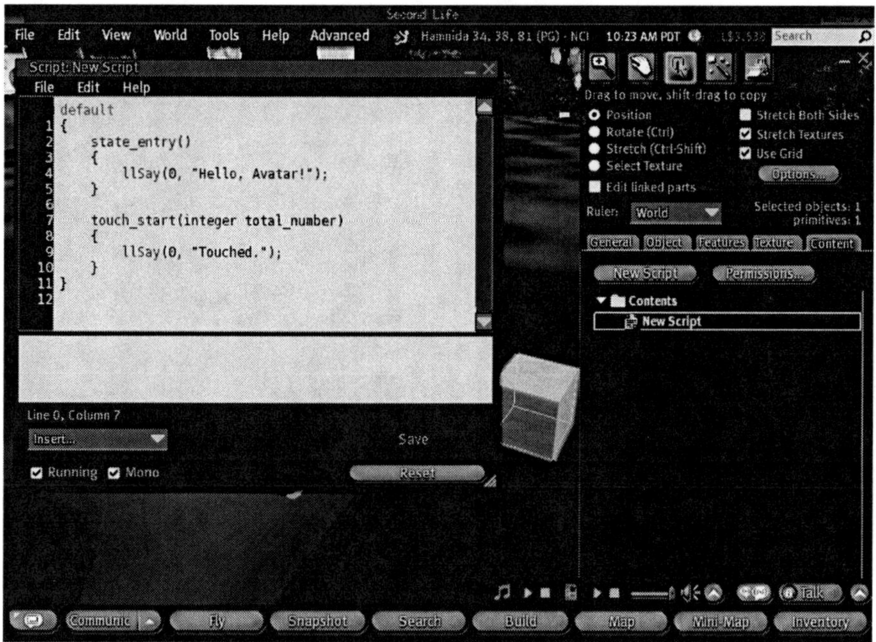

the object. If it is, then the script indicates that it should be treated as a physical object. Next, a new command is used, llSetBuoyancy (Linden Research Inc., 2009d). This command is used to indicate that the object should not be influenced by gravity. Finally, a constant 1 Newton force in the *x*-direction is applied.

Timers

The final element needed to perform a basic physics experiment is to implement a timer. A new event is defined that calls a subroutine at predefined intervals. The subroutine is named timer (Linden Research Inc., 2009j). The llSet-TimerEvent (Linden Research Inc., 2009f) command is used to indicate that the script's timer routine should be called at regular intervals, and

Listing 1. The touch start event

```
state default {

   touch start(integer number) {                    \\React when clicked.
      if ( llDetectedTouch (0)==llGetOwner ()) { \\If this is my owner
          llOwnerSay("Hello World. " );            \\ say "hello world."
      }
   }

}
```

Listing 2. Setting a Force

```
state default {

    state entry () {                              \\ On start of the script.
       llSetStatus (STATUS PHYSICS, FALSE); \\ Turn off physical setting.
    }

    touch start(integer number) {                      \\ React when clicked.
      if ( llDetectedTouch (0)==llGetOwner ()) { \\ If this is my owner
          llSetStatus(STATUS PHYSICS, TRUE);       \\ Turn on physical set-
ting.
          llSetBuoyancy (1.0);                       \\ Turn gravity off.
          llSetForce (<1.0 ,0.0 ,0.0 >, FALSE ); \\ Apply the force.
      }
    }

}
```

the command defines the length of time between calls to the subroutine.

For our example we will need to keep track of the current time. This requires that a variable be defined that retains its value despite which subroutine the script happens to be executing. A global variable is defined outside of the main code. The language recognizes a variety of different data types, and the types used here are vectors, integers, and floating type variables.

The script given in Listing 3 is used to set a timer. When the owner touches the object which contains the script, the script sets a counter to zero and then begins a timer that calls the timer event every 0.2 seconds. When the timer event is executed it increments the global variable number, and it then calculates the total time that has elapsed since the timer was initiated.

NEWTON'S SECOND LAW

The scripting techniques detailed in the previous section can be put together to perform an experiment to explore Newton's Second Law:

$$\frac{d}{dt}mv = \sum_i F_i.$$

The quantity m is the mass of the object, the vector $\vec{v}$ is the velocity of the object, and the vectors F_i represent each of the forces acting on the object. In our case the mass of the object is constant, and the relationship can be reduced to the more familiar form of:

$$m\vec{a} = \sum_i \vec{F}_i.$$

where the vector $\vec{a}$ is the acceleration of the object.

We first discuss the motivations for exploring Newton's Second Law in a variety of ways. We then discuss the advantages for making use of Second Life. Finally, we focus on how to adapt the script to a range of scenarios.

Motivations

Newton's Second Law is an idea that is subject to a wide array of treatments in the curriculum and is subject to many misconceptions. The idea here

Listing 3. Timer Event

```
integer number;
float timeStep = 0.2;
state default {
   touch start(integer number) {                    \\ React when clicked.
      if ( llDetectedTouch (0)==llGetOwner ()) { \\If this is my owner
         number = 0;                                \\then initialize and
         llSetTimerEvent(timeStep);                 \\ start the timer.
      }
   }
   timer () {                                           \\ Timer event.
      float currentTime ;                               \\Variable for the
                                                        \\ current time.
      number += 1;                                      \\ Increment the counter.
      currentTime = timeStep. (( float ) number ) ; \\ Set the current time.
   }
}
```

is to construct an experiment that will challenge the student's perceptions using more concrete representations (Gilbert et al., 2008).

When designing activities the teacher must recognize that students come into the class with a wide range of experiences and should consider them when designing curriculum (Gilbert et al., 1982). At the same time students are not necessarily engaged when dealing with alternate media. The structure, questions and activities should be carefully constructed (Choi1 et al., 2005).

The simulations that are integrated into the activities must also be carefully considered. The simulations may be met with some skepticism from students even when they are correct (Thaden-Koch, 2003). The students view the simulations based on their own expectations and small variations in the way they alter a situation can have a large impact on how they perceive the simulation (Thaden-Koch, 2003).

The whole range of activities must be considered, and making use of a virtual world is not enough. Any approach must be carefully constructed, and it is not adequate to simply provide interactive situations. Students can use interactive media in superficial ways (Yeo et al., 2004). In fact, providing realistic scenarios can be counterproductive. Making things too familiar may work against the goal of challenging assumptions.

An important goal is to allow the students to explore the phenomena in a meaningful way. Students should be able to explore a wide variation and feel free to interact with the experimental setup. For example, students should be able to explore various initial conditions and try different values for the parameters. Direct student control and appropriate feedback is an important consideration in the design of student activities (Beichner, 1990). Additionally, considering alternate and multiple solutions is also important (Tao, 2001; Dufresne et al., 2005). The activities should allow students to examine the phenomena over a range of parameters and situations (Jimoyiannis & Komis, 2001).

Advantages

One of the advantages of using the Second Life viewer is that it is portable over a wide range of computing environments. It also requires relatively moderate technological resources. The software mitigates some of the issues of using microcomputer based labs which can be difficult because they can be highly dependent on the hardware (Pena & Alessi, 1999). The same considerations are also required when developing the supporting documentation (Di Nitto et al., 2006).

The technology associated with some virtual environments can be considerable. For example, other environments make use of head mounted displays with the goal of more complete immersion (Dede et al., 1996a). The advantage is more extreme sensory input, but there is a cost to the use of such technologies. There is also another disadvantage. Students who are susceptible to motion sickness tend to be negatively impacted when using more immersive technologies (Dede et al., 1996a). Additionally, virtual technologies are not perceived the same way by every student. The extent of the student's spatial abilities does have an impact on the efficacy of the use of a virtual environment (Trindade et al., 2002).

Despite the problems there is an advantage over more traditional science laboratories. First, the use of dynamic presentations can enable students to better identify the question that is posed (Dancy & Beichner, 2006). Additionally, traditional labs have a dual goal of establishing lab practice and techniques that compete with the conceptual goals. For example, computer simulations take away some of the drudgery of data collection. The use of computer based labs allows the students to focus on one idea and can be more effective at challenging preconceived ideas (Pena & Alessi, 1999).

Second Life

The construction of a virtual experiment allows students to focus on a few specific ideas. The specific idea we examine is Newton's Second Law and how an object moves under the influence of a single force. In our case the force will act solely in the x-direction. The value of the mass can be determined from within a script using the llGetMass (Linden Research Inc., 2009b) command. An example of a script that will apply a constant 1 N force in the x-direction for 4 seconds is given in Listing 4.

The force used in the script can be adapted to change in time. The timer event can be altered, and an example is given in Listing 5. At each time step the current time is calculated. If the time is less than the prescribed end time the force is updated. In this case the force is set according to a sine function. Note that the script makes use of a predefined constant, PI (Linden Research Inc., 2009h).

The previous script allows for a convenient way to create an object that has a force acting on it that changes in time. In this particular case the force is a sine function, and because the object starts from rest the result is that the object ends nearly where it started from. This result may seem intuitive to the students since the area under the curve is zero. For some students this may be misleading since a common misconception is that the area under the curve represents the displacement rather than the change in momentum (McDermott, 2001).

The area does not represent the displacement, but rather the change in momentum of the object. Once the object and script have been set up and manipulated within the Second Life environment

Listing 4. Constant Force

```
integer number;       // The number of time steps that have elapsed
float timeStep = 0.2; // The time between time steps.
float endTime = 4.0;  // The time to stop the experiment.
vector initialPos ;   // The initial position of the object.

state default {

 state entry () {                                // When the script starts
    llSetStatus(STATUS PHYSICS, FALSE);          // Set to not physical.
    llOwnerSay("Move the object to its " +       // Give the owner
        "starting position and click on it."); // a short message.
 }

 touch start(integer number) {                   // When touched check
    if ( llDetectedTouch (0)==llGetOwner ()) { // to see if this is the
      number = 0;                                // owner. If so then
      llSetTimerEvent(timeStep);                 // initialize the counter
                                                 // and start the timer.
      llSetStatus(STATUS PHYSICS, TRUE);         // Set the object to physical.
      llSetBuoyancy (1.0);                       // Turn off gravity.
      llSetForce ( <1.0 ,0.0 ,0.0 > , FALSE);    // Set a constant force.

      initialPos = llGetPos ();                  // Record the initial SOS.

    }
 }

 timer () {                                      // Each time the timer is
                                                 // called execute this routine.
   number += 1;                                  // Increment the counter.
   if (timeStep*((float)number)>=endTime) {      // Check how long it has been.
       llSetForce(<0.0,0.0,0.0>,FALSE);          // If the time is past then
       llSetStatus(STATUS_PHYSICS,FALSE);        // turn off the force and turn
       llOwnerSay("Displacement: " +             // off the physical setting.
             (string)(llGetPos()-initialPos)); // Give a brief message.
       llSetTimerEvent(0.0); // Turn off the timer.
   }

 }


}
```

Listing 5. Non-constant force, sine

```
28   timer () {                                 // Each time the timer is
29                                              // called execute this rou-
tine.
30     float currentTime;                       // The time since the start.
31
32     number += 1;                             // Increment the counter.
33     currentTime = timeStep*((float)number);  // Set the current time.
34     if (currentTime>=endTime) {              // Check how long it has been.
35        llSetForce(<0.0,0.0,0.0>,FALSE);      // If the time is past then
36        llSetStatus(STATUS PHYSICS, FALSE);   // turn off the force and turn
37        llOwnerSay(.Displacement:. +         // off the physical setting.
38            (string)(llGetPos()-initialPos )); // Give a brief message.
39        llSetTimerEvent(0.0);                 // Turn off the timer.
40     } else {
41       llSetForce(<llSin(PI*currentTime),0.0,0.0>,FALSE); // Set the new
force.
42     }
43
44 }
```

the force can easily be altered and a new set of experiments can be conducted. For example, if line 41 is changed to a cosine function as shown in Listing 6 then a new force can be tested.

The change from a sine to a cosine results in a different displacement. The change in momentum is still zero, but the displacement is not zero. The task of finding the displacement is not to simply find the area under the force curve, but it requires finding the solution to a second order differential equation. In this case a second integral can be used to evaluate the displacement, and the constant term from the first integral results in a nonzero displacement.

KINEMATICS

Another common set of problems found in the introductory mechanics course are those associated with kinematics. By default, a physical object in Second Life acts under the influence of a simulated gravity. It is possible to create an object at a specified location with a predefined velocity using the llRezAtRoot command (Linden Research Inc., 2009c).

The implementation of a script to create an object requires some knowledge of the Second Life inventory system that we do not discuss here. We briefly discuss two possible examples that can be

Listing 6. Non-constant Force, cosine

```
41 llSetForce(<llCos(PI*currentTime),0.0,0.0>,FALSE); // Set the new force .
```

explored using the Second Life viewer. The first is the problem of hitting a target with a projectile, and the second is the "falling monkey" problem.

The projectile problem comes in many forms. One common way to pose a problem is to ask the students to determine the angle or the velocity necessary for an object to hit a target using a cannon. For example, a common situation is to give a student the location of a target and a cannon that will shoot an object at a given angle. The goal is to hit the target, and the student must calculate the velocity necessary.

The "falling monkey" problem is similar. In this problem the projectile will fire directly toward a monkey sitting in a tree. At the exact same moment that the projectile moves toward the monkey, the monkey drops. The goal for the students is to show that the projectile will strike the monkey as it is falling.

These examples are common textbook problems but can be difficult to implement reliably in a laboratory experiment. Within an environment such as Second Life, however, an experiment can be constructed which will provide the correct initial conditions in a safe, reliable manner.

These experiments are different from the discussion in previous section in that the object has a non-zero initial speed and is only influenced by a constant gravity. Fortunately, the force due to gravity is a built in aspect of the physics engine, and it only requires that a "physical" object be given the right initial velocity at a specific location.

The activities for the students are different as well. In these exercises the students must break up the movement into different components for each of the different directions. It also requires that the students work with system of equations. The result is that scripts require more technical constraints and can be more difficult for the students.

DISCUSSION

The use of virtual environments to explore physical phenomena is not new. The technology required has varied widely (Dede et al., 1996a; Dede et al., 1996b) with different goals for the level of immersion (Dede, 2009). Here we explore an approach with a focus on interactivity (Jimoyiannis & Komis, 2001; Byrne & Bricken, 1992; Byrne, 2009) and technology that is portable and relatively inexpensive (Pena & Alessi, 1999).

The primary motivation for exploring this approach is that concrete representations can help students think about the basic ideas in new ways (Barab et al., 2001; Gilbert et al., 2008) and challenge their conceptions of the phenomena (Tao & Gunstone, 1999; Pena & Alessi, 1999; Jimoyiannis & Komis, 2001). Our focus here is on the use of Second Life as a way to explore Newton's Second Law. The flexibility of the software allows the approach to also be adapted to explore kinematics.

Other types of physics are possible to simulate within Second Life. Such simulations would require greater complexity and are not discussed here. For example, electrical fields would require the use of sensors that could determine relative distances and charges. Such methods require a greater degree of computational sophistication and are not discussed here.

CONCLUSION

The Second Life software is flexible and offers a wide range of possibilities. Paradoxically this is also a difficult obstacle for its use. Any implementation making use of the software requires technical knowledge of the system and a wide range of skills for building, scripting, and educational design. Bringing all of these things together for an effective learning experience can be a difficult task (Rowlands et al., 2007).

The implementation of a system to explore physical phenomena in Second Life requires a wide range of technical abilities and has a steep initial learning curve. Despite the disadvantages the open nature of the platform allows for a great deal of flexibility. Additionally, the relatively inexpensive technical requirements of the environment offers ways to explore fundamental physical principles in a wide variety of contexts.

REFERENCES

Andrews, T., & Schwarz, G. (2002). Preparing students for the virtual organisation: An evaluation of learning with virtual learning technologies. *Educational Technology and Society*, *5*(3), 54–65.

Barab, S. A., Hay, K. E., Barnett, M., & Squire, K. (2001). Constructing virtual worlds: Tracing the historical development of learner practices. *Cognition and Instruction*, *19*(1), 47–94. doi:10.1207/S1532690XCI1901_2

Beichner, R. J. (1990). The effects of simultaneous motion presentation and graph generation in a kinematics lab. *Journal of Research in Science Teaching*, *27*(8), 803. doi:10.1002/tea.3660270809

Byrne, C. (2009). *Water on tap: The use of virtual reality in education*. Retrieved June 30, 2009 from http://www.hitl.washington.edu/publications/dissertations/Byrne/

Byrne, C., & Bricken, M. (1992). *Summer students in virtual reality: A pilot study on educational applications of virtual reality technology*. Retrieved June 30, 2009 from http://ftp.hitl.washington.edu/projects/education/psc/psc.html

Choi, I. L., & Turgeon, A. J. (2005). Scaffolding peer-questioning strategies to facilitate metacognition during online small group discussion. *Instructional Science*, *33*(5-6), 483–511. doi:10.1007/s11251-005-1277-4

Dancy, M. H., & Beichner, R. (2006). Impact of animation on assessment of conceptual understanding in physics. *Physical Review Special Topics-Physics Education Research*, *2*(1), 010104. doi:10.1103/PhysRevSTPER.2.010104

Dede, C. (2009). Immersive Interfaces for Engagement and Learning. *Science*, *323*(5910), 66. doi:10.1126/science.1167311

Dede, C., Salzman, M., & Bowen Loftin, R. (1996a). ScienceSpace: Virtual realities for learning complex and abstract scientific concepts. In *Proceedings of the Virtual Reality Annual International Symposium* (pp. 246-252, 271). Washington, DC: IEEE.

Dede, C. J., Salzman, M., & Loftin, R. B. (1996b)... *Lecture Notes in Computer Science*, *1077*, 87.

Di Nitto, E., Mainetti, L., Monga, M., Sbattella, L. M., & Tedesco, R. (2006). Supporting interoperability and reusability of learning objects: The virtual campus approach. *Educational Technology & Society*, *9*(2), 33–50.

Dufresne, R. J., Gerace, W. J., Mestre, J. P., & Leonard, W. J. (2005). *Ask-it/a2l: Assessing student knowledge with instructional technology*. Retrieved June 30, 2009 from http://www.citebase.org/abstract?id=oai:arXiv.org:physics/0508144

Free Software Foundation. (2009). *The gnu general public license*. Retrieved June 30, 2009 from http://www.gnu.org/copyleft/gpl.html.

Gilbert, J. K., Reiner, M., & Nakhleh, M. (Eds.). (2008). *Visualization: Theory and practice in science education*. New York: Springer Verlag. doi:10.1007/978-1-4020-5267-5

Gilbert, J. K., Watts, D. M., & Osborne, R. J. (1982). *Physics Education*, *17*(2), 62. Retrieved June 30, 2009 from http://stacks.iop.org/0031-9120/17/62

Guidugli, S., Gauna, C. F., & Benegas, J. (2005). *The Physics Teacher, 43*(6), 334. Retrieved June 30, 2009 from http://link.aip.org/link/?PTE/43/334/1

Jimoyiannis, A., & Komis, V. (2001). Computer simulations in physics teaching and learning: A case study on students' understanding of trajectory motion. *Computers & Education, 36*(2), 183–204. doi:10.1016/S0360-1315(00)00059-2

Linden Research Inc. (2009a). *llapplyimpulse*. Retrieved June 9, 2009 from http://wiki.secondlife.com/wiki/LlApplyImpulse

Linden Research Inc. (2009b). *llgetmass*. Retrieved June 9, 2009 from http://wiki.secondlife.com/wiki/LlGetMass

Linden Research Inc. (2009c). *llrezatroot*. Retrieved June 9, 2009 from http://wiki.secondlife.com/wiki/LlRezAtRoot

Linden Research Inc. (2009d). *llsetbuoyancy*. Retrieved June 9, 2009 from http://wiki.secondlife.com/wiki/LlSetBuoyancy

Linden Research Inc. (2009e). *llsetforce*. Retrieved June 9, 2009 from http://wiki.secondlife.com/wiki/LlSetForce

Linden Research Inc. (2009f). *llsettimerevent*. Retrieved June 9, 2009 from http://wiki.secondlife.com/wiki/LlSetTimerEvent

Linden Research Inc. (2009g). *Lsl portal*. Retrieved June 9, 2009 from http://wiki.secondlife.com/wiki/LSL Portal

Linden Research Inc. (2009h). *Pi*. Retrieved June 9, 2009 from http://wiki.secondlife.com/wiki/PI

Linden Research Inc. (2009i). *State entry*. Retrieved June 9, 2009 from http://wiki.secondlife.com/wiki/State entry

Linden Research Inc. (2009j). *timer*. Retrieved June 9, 2009 from http://wiki.secondlife.com/wiki/Timer

Mason, H. (2007, August 24-26). *Experiential education in Second Life*. Paper presented at the Second Life Education Workshop at Second Life Community Convention, Chicago Hilton, Chicago, USA.

McDermott, L. C. (2001). Students knowledge and learning. In Tiberghien, A., Jossem, E. L., Barojas, J., & Deardorff, D. (Eds.), *Connecting research in physics education with teacher education*. Melville, NY: American Institute of Physics.

Pena, C. M., & Alessi, S. M. (1999). Promoting a qualitative understanding of physics. *Journal of Computers in Mathematics and Science Teaching, 18*(4), 439–457.

Phet. (2009). *Interactive simulations*. Retrieved June 30, 2009 from http://phet.colorado.edu

Rowlands, S., Graham, T., Berry, J., & McWilliams, P. (2007). Conceptual change through the lens of Newtonian mechanics. *Science & Education, 16*, 21–42. doi:10.1007/s11191-005-1339-7

Scherer, D. (2009). Vpython. Retrieved June 30, 2009 from http://vpython.org/

Tao, P. K. (2001). Developing understanding through confronting varying views: The case of solving qualitative physics problems. *International Journal of Science Education, 23*, 1201–1218. doi:10.1080/09500690110038602

Tao, P. K., & Gunstone, R. F. (1999). Conceptual change in science through collaborative learning at the computer. *International Journal of Science Education, 21*, 39–57. doi:10.1080/095006999290822

Thaden-Koch, T. C. (2003). *A coordination class analysis of college students: Judgments about animated motion* (Tech. Rep. No. AAI3104628). Nebraska, USA: ETD collection for University of Nebraska -Lincoln. Retrieved June 20, 2009 from http://digitalcommons.unl.edu/dissertations/AAI3104628

Trindade, J., Fiolhais, C., & Almeida, L. (2002). Science learning in virtual environments: a descriptive study. *British Journal of Educational Technology, 33*(4), 471–488. doi:10.1111/1467-8535.00283

Yeo, S., Loss, R., Zadnik, M., Harrison, A., & Treagust, D. (2004). What do students really learn from interactive multimedia? A physics case study. *American Journal of Physics, 72*(10), 1351–1358. doi:10.1119/1.1748074

This work was previously published in International Journal of Virtual and Personal Learning Environments, edited by Michael Thomas, Volume 1, Issue 2, pp. 31-44, copyright 2010 by IGI Publishing (an imprint of IGI Global).

Chapter 11
Development of an Interactive Virtual 3-D Model of the Human Testis Using the Second Life Platform

Douglas R. Danforth
Ohio State University, USA

ABSTRACT

One of the strengths of a virtual environment is the ability to immerse the occupant into an environment that would otherwise be impossible. The primary focus of the author's project in Second Life is to take advantage of this opportunity to explore novel approaches to medical education. Second Life can be used to model doctor-patient interaction, clinical diagnosis skills, and three dimensional molecular and cellular modeling of objects from individual molecules to whole organ systems, both healthy and diseased. Using the powerful building and scripting tools of the Second Life platform, the author has created a model of the human testis that students can fly through and interact with to understand how the anatomy and physiology of the testis work together to regulate sperm production. The anatomical and physiological interactions occurring during these processes are described in accompanying audio and text. The development of educational tools within the Second Life context is in its infancy. As the technology matures, the opportunities for education within Second Life will continue to expand as an important adjunct to traditional pedagogical approaches.

INTRODUCTION

Data from several sources suggest that approximately 65% - 80% of adults are "visual learners", with the remainder distributed between auditory learners and kinesthetic/tactile learners (Felder & Silverman, 1988; Felder, 1993; Valkoss, 2005). Educational theory also suggests the advantages of active learning and participation in small groups over traditional lecture based approaches (Bonwell & Eison, 1991; Mayer, 2004). One of the strengths of virtual worlds such as Second Life is the abil-

DOI: 10.4018/978-1-4666-1770-4.ch011

ity to immerse the occupant into an environment that would otherwise be impossible. The ability to interact in learning spaces that do not and cannot exist in the real world offers unique educational opportunities. It was with these concepts in mind that we began to explore the possibilities of using Immersive Learning Environments for medical education.

The use of Second Life for medical and healthcare education has been well documented (Boulos et al., 2007; Boulos et al., 2008; Gorini et al., 2008). Second Life has been used for a wide variety of educational activities, and there are currently several hundred educational institutions using Second Life for teaching and learning (Kemp, 2009). Medical and healthcare education is especially well represented, and Second Life has been used for disaster simulation (Boulos et al., 2008), nursing training (Skiba, 2009), nutrition education (Second Life Nutrition Game, 2009), etc., much of which is referenced by one of the primary in-world sources of healthcare information – HealthInfo Island (Perryman, 2009; Second Life HealthInfo Island, 2009) funded by the National Library of Medicine. In addition to these clinical healthcare education resources, there are several basic medical and biological simulations in Second Life. Genome Island (Clark, 2008) is a richly developed resource for genetic and molecular biological information, and other simulations such as Biome (Greenwood, 2009) and Second Nature (Scott, 2009) provide innovative approaches to exploring biology and nature in a virtual environment. In contrast, due to the inherent difficulty in creating accurate and realistic biological models using the tools available, there are relatively few anatomical simulations in Second Life. As such, our goal in building the virtual testis was not to attempt to re-create an accurate anatomical representation of the testis, but rather to explore novel ways in which we could examine the relationships between the anatomy and physiology to describe various aspects of testicular function.

We chose to model the testis in SL for several reasons: 1) there are key concepts in testicular physiology, such as the blood-testis barrier that lend themselves to a visual explanation of the process, 2) the testis has "moving parts" that could be animated and scripted, and 3) the students could progress through the various parts of the testis and follow a logical progression of how the anatomy and physiology work together to regulate sperm production. We considered other aspects of the reproductive system, including the ovary and uterus, but ultimately decided that the testis was best suited for the opportunities afforded by the Second Life platform (Danforth, 2008).

Design and Development

The Virtual Testis is located above the Ohio State University College of Medicine Island in Second Life; OSU Medicine (Danforth, 2009). It was built in three parts in reverse order, although there was significant overlap during the construction process. One of our primary goals was to make the model large enough so that visitors could "fly into" the testis and see how the testis functions from a "sperm's eye view".

It immediately became clear that the normal building tools available in Second Life would be inadequate for a project of this scale. All objects in Second Life are created from standard building shapes, such as blocks, spheres, tubes, etc. and are called primitives or "prims". Normal objects are limited to a maximum size of 10 meters (m) x 10 m x 10 m. The testis model required objects as large as 150m x 150m x 150m so "giant prim" or "megaprim" were used. However, working with objects of this size was problematic on several levels. First, these giant prims only existed in a few predefined sizes and could not be resized. As such we were limited to the sizes that already existed in-world at the time.

To get around the limitations of using giant prims various other options were explored, including geodesic dome makers, the creation of giant objects using combinations of normal prim, etc., however none were suitable for the project. Figure 1 depicts the overall structure of the model. To the left is the testis, inside of which are numerous seminiferous tubules which are the main functional units responsible for spermatogenesis. In order to provide adequate detail, we created a single, "magnified" tubule that is seen on the right side of the build, coming out of the testis. Note that this is not the correct anatomical representation of the testis in situ – the tubules are never outside the testis and the single tubule is expanded in size. To provide a sense of scale, the author's avatar is denoted by the arrow.

Part 1: The Blood-Testis Barrier

Design and construction of the final component of the build and tour – the blood-testis barrier, was performed first. In the mammalian testis, developing sperm cells are protected from immune attack by a selective barrier that exists within the seminiferous tubule. The seminiferous tubule is an avascular structure - there are no blood vessels inside the tubule where the sperm are located. Therefore all products from the circulatory system, including antibodies, must pass through several cells and structures before entering the tubule. Since sperm cells have only half of the number of chromosomes as all other cells in the body, they would be recognized as foreign cells by the immune system and would be attacked and removed by circulating antibodies. As such, a structure has evolved in the testis to restrict products from the immune system from entering the tubule. This structure is called the blood-testis barrier and its function is sometimes confusing for students. We therefore decided to build a model of the blood-testis barrier so the students could more clearly envision how the anatomy and physiology worked together to protect developing sperm.

Construction of this model was aided tremendously by the incorporation of specialized building objects called sculpted prims into the Second Life client which occurred at this time. Prior to this development, all objects in Second Life were created from standard building shapes as described previously. As such, it was exceedingly difficult to construct organic shapes like organs and cells. Sculpted prims allowed for the creation

Figure 1. Overview of the virtual testis in Second Life. This simulation is located above the Ohio State University College of Medicine Island.

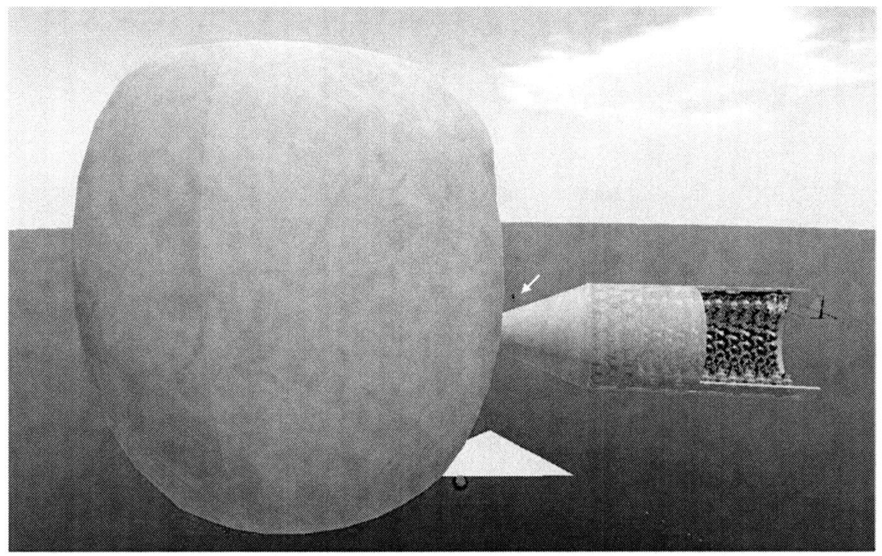

of detailed objects such as the Sertoli cells which more accurately resembled the correct anatomy of the testis structures (Figure 2). Although this is a highly stylized depiction of a Sertoli cell, it relatively closely resembles the standard structure depicted in most physiology textbooks. For the surface image (texture) of the Sertoli cell we utilized a scanning electron micrograph of an actual Sertoli cell from a horse. It revealed somewhat the 3-d structure of the topology of the Sertoli cell and helped add context and contrast to the Second Life version. The image was edited in Adobe Photoshop (Adobe Systems Inc, San Jose CA) to make it more realistic and to add some features necessary to depict components of the blood-testis barrier. Sertoli cells were constructed as large as possible using normal prim – 10m x 10m x 10m. A 40m x 40m x 40m giant cylinder was created for the basal lamina surrounding the Sertoli cells. The sperm cells were simple spheres with some texturing added for contrast.

This part of the build was created so that the students would be able to interact with the system, and could proceed through the various steps at their own pace. As such the components were programmed using the Second Life scripting language to require the students to touch directional signs that caused the sperm to move through the structure and that allowed the components of the blood-testis barrier to be visualized. At each stage the process was explained and the students could repeat the entire demonstration as many times as desired.

Part 2: The Seminiferous Tubule

After completion of the blood-testis barrier simulation, an entire seminiferous tubule was constructed to provide perspective and context for the anatomical relationships between the Sertoli cells and the tubule. This was a relatively simple object to create since it largely involved duplication of the individual Sertoli cells within a giant cylinder. In order to visualize the blood testis barrier the Sertoli cell texture was modified to visualize the tight junction connections. Sertoli

Figure 2. The blood-testis barrier. The image on the left is the model we constructed in Second Life. On the right is a typical drawing of Sertoli cells from Wikipedia.

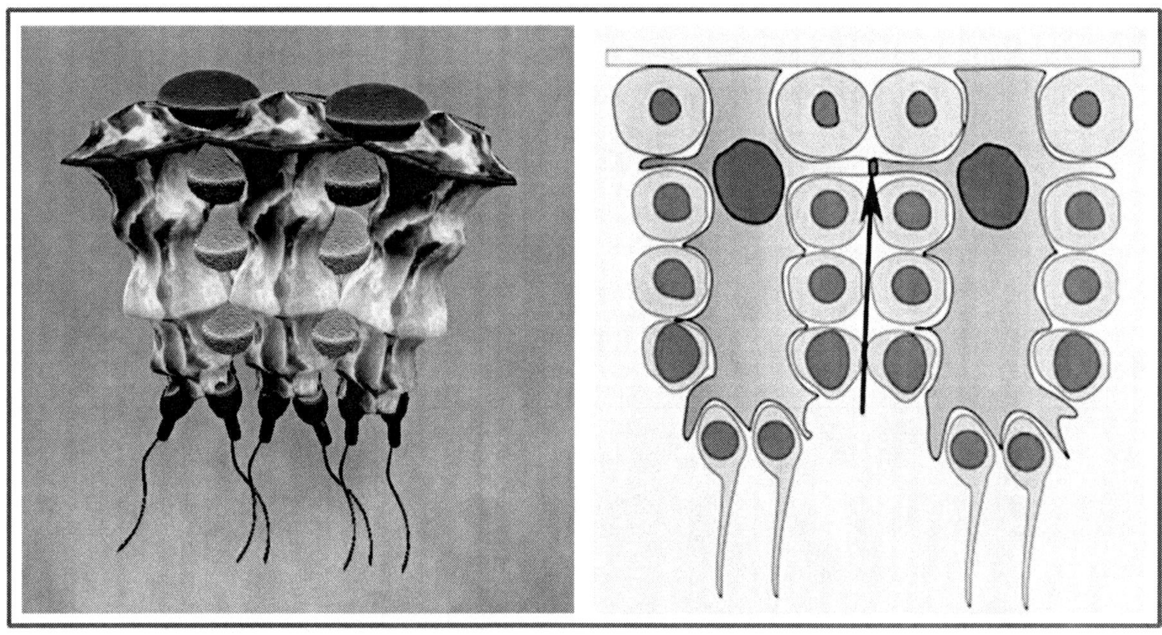

cells were then arranged within the cylinder (Figure 3). Animations were added to depict sperm moving down the length of the tubule.

Part 3: The Testis

The testis itself was constructed from a giant torus (150m x150m x150m) cut and hollowed to the appropriate dimensions (Figure 1). A large number of building tools and shapes were evaluated for this part of the build, and this was the most useful. The testis was created in two halves so that one half could be rendered transparent when necessary in order to visualize the tubules inside the structure.

Inside the testis are numerous "low magnification" versions of the seminiferous tubule described above. For the most part, these consist of hollow pipes twisted together to resemble the tortuous nature of the seminiferous tubule. These individual tubules were duplicated and manually assembled to form a syncytium of tubules within the testis. Since the number of objects allowable in Second Life is limited, the tubule was photographed against a green screen backdrop, and applied as a texture to panels placed behind the actual tubules, thus giving the appearance of many more tubules within the testis than are actually present.

Each tubule was scripted (programmed) to become transparent upon command from the tour vehicle and also to illustrate the path of sperm as they travel down the tubule (Figure 4). One section of the tubule was filled with the tails of developing sperm, so that when the tour vehicle enters the tubule, the occupants are surrounded by developing sperm traveling down the tubule. Outside the testis an epididymis was created using a giant sculpted prim.

The Tour

One of the most important design features of this project was that it had to be easy for novice users of Second Life to use. A very small percentage (< 1% surveyed) of our students had ever used Second Life before so they would have to download the program, create an account, and learn the interface before accessing any resources in world. As such, every effort was made to make the process as simple as possible, and a decision was made to utilize a tour based approach to the simulation. A walking tour was considered, but the size and complexity of the build made that too difficult. The Guided Tour System (Timtam, 2009) in Second Life was purchased for this tour. This touring system is quite sophisticated and allowed for the inclusion of essentially all of the features needed on the tour. The tour had to be very precise in navigating very small spaces such as the inside of the tubules. It also had to be able to communicate and issue commands along the route to get components to become transparent, highlighted, move, etc. These could have been scripted exterior to the tour itself but it was much easier to incorporate the commands as part of the tour. The ability to create a unique tour vehicle was an advantage, as was the ability of several people to take the tour at the same time.

The most difficult aspect of developing the tour was identifying the precise coordinates necessary for the stops along the way, as well as the timing of the commands. Perhaps as much as 10 – 20% of the total time spent on the build was devoted to creating and fine-tuning the tour, including the audio portion of the tour. Initially, a text-based version of the tour was created. Structures and features were explained along the way. It became clear, however, that diverting attention between the text presented and the testis structures was distracting, so an audio version of the tour was added. Adding voice narration proved extremely difficult, and as of the time of publication, is still not implemented with 100% reproducibility. A discussion of the problems and pitfalls encountered throughout the build is included later in this article. A "working" version of voice narration was added approximately six months after the initial completion of the model.

Figure 3. Cross section of the entire seminiferous tubule. The basal lamina is the white structure covering the tubule. The developing sperm cells are colored blue, red, pink, cyan, and green. The Sertoli cells that support and nurture the sperm are gray. Sperm that are being released into the lumen of the tubule are bright green.

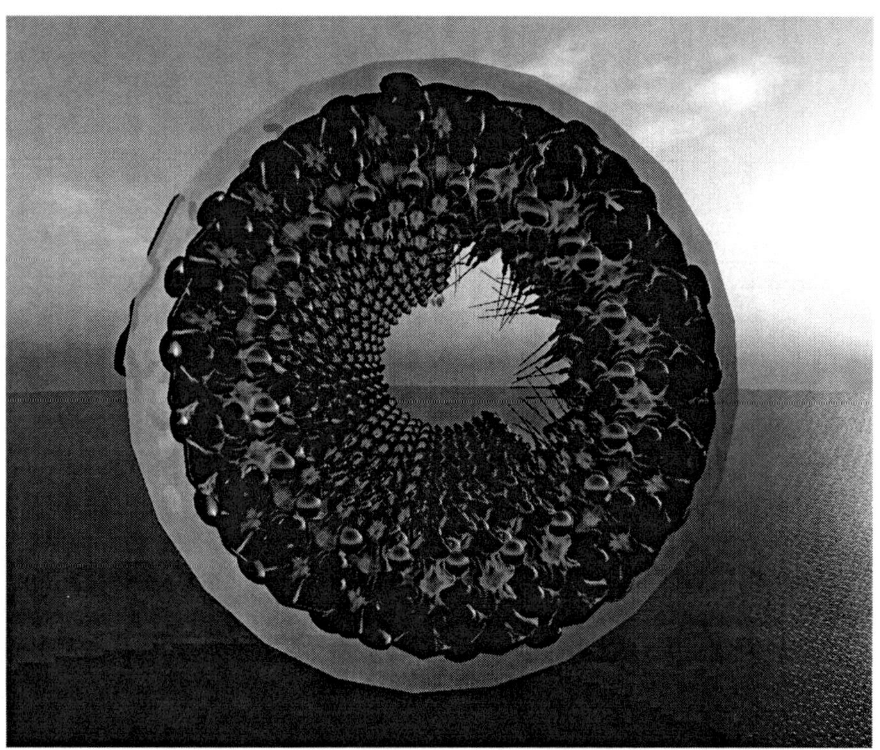

Figure 4. Overview of the testis. Left - The front half has been made transparent in order to visualize the tubule and collecting ducts inside the testis. Right - Sperm are depicted as bright green and move from the tubules, through the collecting ducts (red) and out of the testis into the vas defrens.

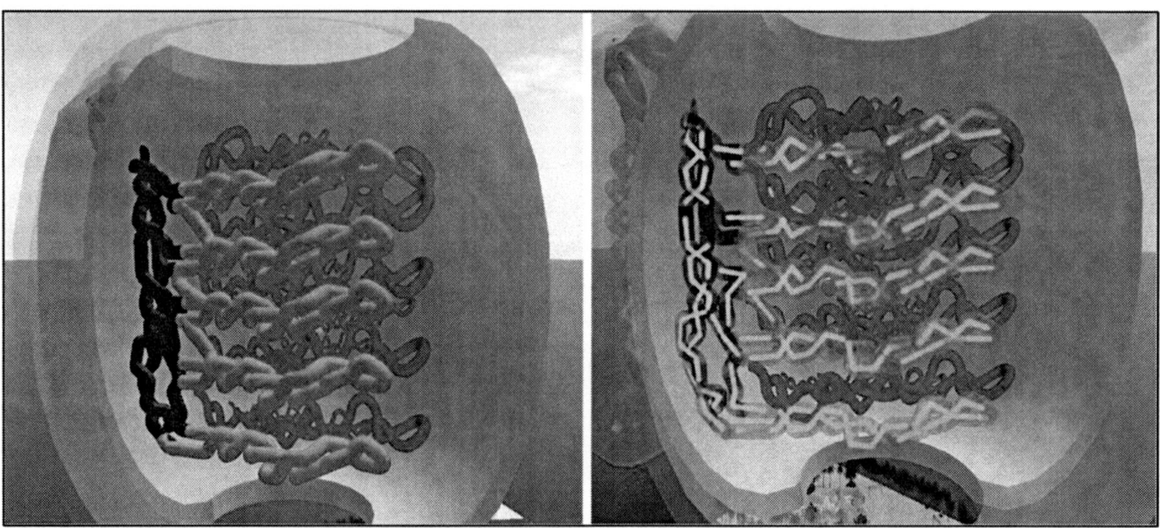

Figure 5. Inside a single seminiferous tubule. Tails of sperm attached to the Sertoli Cells are evident. Released sperm are depicted as fluorescent green and are traveling down the tubule.

The tour begins by taking the students to an overview of the testis and explains the anatomy and physiology of various components. The covering of the testis is then made transparent (see Figure 4) so that internal structures can be visualized. The tour then enters a single low magnification version of the tubule to depict sperm movement through the structure (Figure 5).

The tour then proceeds to a higher magnification depiction of a single seminiferous tubule to examine in detail how the anatomy and physiology interact to regulate sperm production (Figure 6.)

After traveling through the tubule and in between individual Sertoli cells, the tour exits the opposite side to reveal the architecture of the blood vessels and Leydig cells, which are located outside the tubule but play an important role in regulating sperm production (Figure 7).

At the end of the tour the students view the blood-testis barrier model (Figure 2) and then take a second tour vehicle back to the start of the tour. On the way "home" the salient features discussed during the tour are revisited and each student receives a note card with a summary of important points (Figure 8). At the end is a meeting area that contains an in-world feedback assessment tool as well as a self-assessment quiz that each student can take to test his or her knowledge of testicular anatomy and physiology. Whenever possible the students were met as they finished the tour to discuss their experience and answer any questions.

OUTCOMES/STUDENT FEEDBACK

In the spring of 2008, and again in 2009 approximately 100 first and Second year Medical Students took the testis tour and approximately 51 completed the feedback survey. A standard five point Likert Scale was used that ranked their experience on a scale of 1 to 5, with 1 = Strongly Disagree and 5 = Strongly agree. The survey instrument used for the second year was slightly altered from the first year so for the most part, only questions that were asked on both surveys are included. Student participation in this project

Figure 6. High magnification section of the tubule. Top – entering the tubule. Bottom - traveling between individual Sertoli cells. Developing sperm have been removed to illustrate a condition called "Sertoli Cell Only Syndrome", in which developing sperm are absent and patients are infertile.

was approved by our University Institutional Review Board. The survey used for this analysis is included in Appendix 1.

One main concern in using Second Life as an educational tool was whether the students would consider it a valuable use of their time and effort. Medical students are extremely busy and are acutely aware of whether educational technologies and resources are worth the investment of their time. In addition, very few (9/49) had ever used Second Life before. As such, each student was asked how long they spent acquiring an account, logging in, completing orientation, etc. The data from both years indicated that students considered this a valuable use of their time and a useful educational resource. 42 out of 49 students either agreed or strongly agreed that the testis tour was a valuable use of their study time (mean = 4.2). In addition, the students felt that the sign-up process was relatively easy (4.1). After analyzing the 2008 data, however, it was determined that the students who had no previous experience with Second

Figure 7. Outside the tubule. This view illustrated the network of blood vessels surrounding the tubule as well as the Leydig cells which produce testosterone – also outside the tubule.

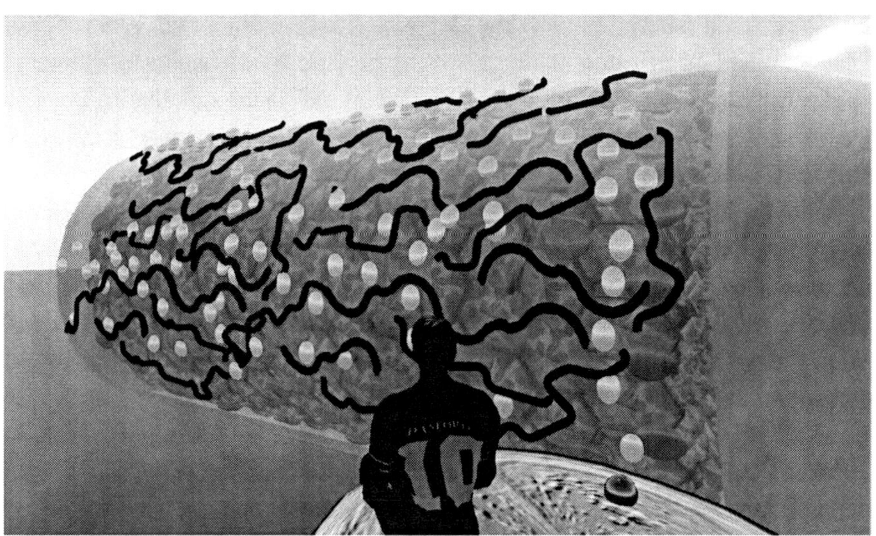

Figure 8. Summary of important points. After completing the blood-testis barrier simulation the students return to the start of the tour and review the important points learned on the tour.

Life were spending an average of 35 minutes acquiring accounts and logging in etc. Although this was considered a reasonable amount of time, several students did encounter difficulties with the orientation experience provided by Linden Lab. As such an orientation experience on OSU Medicine was created for the second class. A primary advantage of this system is that the students never had to leave the island. A URL directly to OSU Medicine was provided and after creating their account, the students logged in directly at the OSU Medicine orientation area as their first experience in Second Life. An additional advantage of creating a dedicated orientation experience was the orientation could be tailored to meet the needs of the students. Although some students will continue utilizing Second Life after finishing with the course, the majority will not return, at least until additional educational resources are developed. Therefore the amount of information provided in the orientation was limited to only that which was necessary for basic navigation and communication. As a result in the second year no students expressed any difficulty with the orientation process and the students felt that the orientation was relatively easy to navigate (4.1). Interestingly however, the amount of time spent completing orientation actually increased slightly (although not significantly) to 40 minutes. This was partly due to the fact that the students spent more time visiting with other students and faculty during the orientation process, which was not the case with the original orientation experience. Nevertheless, the orientation process is being re-designed somewhat to be more efficient and easier to navigate.

The students felt that the tour of the testis was informative (4.3), and 44/47 (94%) felt that Second Life should be used for other medical education experiences. An additional question regarding the testis tour was added to the survey for 2009, "The testis tour helped me understand testicular function", and this class of students also considered this a useful exercise (4.25).

Undergraduate Students

Although the testis tour was designed primarily for first and second year medical students, it can be used for almost any upper level college curriculum. As such, I encouraged students in my Physiology 312 class "Principles of Human Physiology" to take the tour. This is a large class (>200 students/year) consisting of primarily pre-med, pre-vet, and nursing students. Although the feedback we received was positive and generally similar to that received from the medical students, the utilization of this optional resource was limited to a fairly small subset (<15 each year) of students. It is my experience that learning resources not specifically "required" in the syllabus are largely underutilized by undergraduates, at least compared to medical students. As such, in future years, the testis tour will be demonstrated in class to the undergraduates as opposed to having them log in and experience the tour from within Second Life. We recognize that this limits some of the primary affordances of the Second Life platform; namely immersiveness and small group interaction, however exposing all students to this highly visual description if testicular function is perhaps most important for this group.

The General Public

Since its creation in 2008, the "Tour of the Testis" has been experienced by several hundred visitors. We monitor unique visitors to this resource every day. During a recent analysis the total number of visitors to the testis simulation for the period from 2/15 - 3/15 was 162 (5.4/day), with a range of 0 - 23/day. The average time per visit was 7.4 minutes, with a range of 5 - 15 minutes. The visitors do not include the author's staff or students but do not necessarily represent unique visitors. After analyzing the data, approximately 75-80% of the visits are unique visitors. In addition, the average time/visit is a significant under estimate. The visitor detector loses the avatars once they start the testis tour. Assuming all visitors completed the tour, the average time/visit would be approximately 25 minutes.

Challenges

Audio

As previously mentioned, the initial implementation of the tour utilized text to describe the features, structures, and processes that were visualized along the tour. This was relatively easy to implement but required precise adjustment of timing to coordinate the appearance of text with scripted elements. A major drawback to using text-based descriptions was that it required the visitor to constantly shift attention between reading the text descriptions and watching the accompanying animations and structures. Early feedback indicated that this was a considerable distraction. As such, a voice narrated version of the tour was developed after the first group of students completed the exercise. This was much more difficult than initially thought, and as of August 2009, an effective and consistent voice-based narration of the testis tour is still not fully implemented. The primary difficulty with using recorded voice in Second Life stems from difficulties with the Linden Scripting Language, and variability in client computers and internet connections. There are two primary methods for delivering voice narration in Second Life; using 10 second sound snippets and using parcel media commands. The former approach has been implemented and a narrated tour is available using this technique. As expected, however, artificially constructing the "teaching modules" in 10 second increments limits the flexibility of the approach. In addition, it is exceedingly difficult to get the sound files to play reliably when called during the tour. Quality control testing indicates that the tour faithfully delivers all audio files less than 20% of the time, although usually only one or two files get dropped.

Due to these limitations the use of parcel media commands to provide the voice narration of the tour has been investigated. The potential advantages to this approach are that the narrations can be of any duration and the parcel media commands available should provide more precise and reliable control over the delivered speech. Unfortunately limitations within the Linden Scripting Language as well as variability in client internet connection speeds can adversely affect the quality and reliability of the delivered audio. No robust and reliable solution for delivering audio in this fashion has been developed, despite consulting with numerous experts on Second Life and Linden Scripting Language. This is a major goal for the upcoming year.

Client Computing Capability

It was recognized early in the design and building phases of the project that the vast majority of the students would be accessing Second Life using laptop computers over a wireless internet connection. As such, the simulation was designed to be useable and useful under these limitations. Primary considerations were to limit the number and size of the textures and images in the build, as well as minimize the number of objects used in the various sections. One difficulty with this approach was that the size and design of the various components often meant that fairly large textures would be required which might quickly overload the processing capability of the graphics cards in the students' computers. To offset these issues very few textures were utilized in the entire build and textures and images were re-used whenever possible. As such, although the testis build requires that the viewing distance setting in the client software be maximized so that all structures can be visualized (the structures take up the entire island from corner to corner), the number of objects and textures that must be displayed even with the viewing distance set at maximum was far less than required in most Second Life builds. Total objects used for this build are approximately 5,000 and the total number of textures included in all sections of the testis is less than 25.

Interaction

One of the seminal advantages of immersive learning environments such as Second Life is the ability to synchronously work in small group settings and interact with others who are not nearby in the physical world. The original goal was to have the students log into to Second Life from their respective computers and take the tour in groups of 2-4. They would then be met after the tour to review their knowledge and answer questions. Although this did occur to some extent, the majority of the students entered Second Life and took the tour by themselves and most interactions between faculty and students were one to one. As such, the testis tour has become largely an asynchronous learning resource which students utilize individually.

Timeline

A common question that arises after one completes the testis tour is "how long did it take to build?" It is difficult to identify exactly how long was spent building the testis simulation and accompanying tour because a considerable amount of time early on was devoted to learning the idiosyncrasies of Second Life and how it might be useful for Medical Education. Nevertheless, approximately 1-2 hours per day for 6 months were spent completing the basic components. As the beginning of class drew closer 8+ hours per day for 2-3 weeks were needed to complete the project. As previously mentioned, creating the actual tour was much more time consuming than originally anticipated and over 40 hours were devoted to working on that part alone. During the three week course segment most of each weekday evening was spent in Second Life meeting with students and answering questions.

Whereas this time commitment is perhaps not feasible for many educators, it is probably not dramatically greater than many institutions and educational technology departments spend to replicate traditional brick and mortar structures (buildings, classrooms, faculty offices, etc.) in Second Life that sometimes have marginal educational value in immersive learning environments.

FUTURE DEVELOPMENT

Over the next year the testis tour will be upgraded with more reliable audio streaming and the creation of additional interactive simulations along the tour. Additional simulations will be added illustrating hormone secretion and action and depicting the two cell two gonadotropin regulation of testicular steroid production. In addition the effect of various disease conditions on testicular anatomy and physiology will be incorporated.

SUMMARY AND CONCLUSION

The testis tour has been a valuable resource for the students at Ohio State, as well as a popular demonstration of the technology and opportunities afforded by immersive learning environments such as Second Life. It has frequent visitors, perhaps because it highlights a unique educational approach and leverages strengths of the Second Life platform, including immersiveness and small group active learning. It was built as a prototype demonstration to explore the possibilities of immersive learning environments, and has served as the "preliminary data" providing proof of concept for funding of our other educational projects in Second Life including simulations of ovarian function, creation of virtual patients for medical education, and simulated oral exams for Emergency Medicine residents.

Immersive learning environments offer unique opportunities to engage students in interesting and interactive educational experiences. Students can become active participants in their learning, rather than passive recipients of information, as often occurs in traditional didactic approaches. The net generation expects their learning to be active, social, and learner centered. Virtual worlds like Second Life enable students to realize these expectations and immerse themselves in learning spaces not possible in the physical world.

ACKNOWLEDGMENT

Rob Shepherd provided helpful advice on how to best visualize certain aspects of the project. Rebecca Waller provided immeasurable guidance, help, and a place to build the early prototypes of the virtual testis. David Way and The Center for Education and Scholarship at The Ohio State University College of Medicine were instrumental in assisting with the assessment of student feedback. Funding for this project was provided by The Ohio State University College of Medicine, The Ohio State University Teaching Enhancement Program, The Ohio State University Board of Trustees, and Perinatal Resources Inc.

REFERENCES

Bolous, M., Ramloll, R., Jones, R., & Toth-Cohen, S. (2008). Web 3D for public, environmental and occupational health: Early examples from Second Life. *International Journal of Environmental Research and Public Health, 5*, 290–317. doi:10.3390/ijerph5040290

Bonwell, C., & Eison, J. (1991). *Active learning: Creating excitement in the classroom (AEHE-ERIC Higher Education Report No. 1).* Washington, DC: Jossey-Bass.

Boulos, M., Hetherington, L., & Wheeler, S. (2007). Second Life: An overview of the potential of 3-D virtual worlds in medical and health education. *Health Information and Libraries Journal, 24*, 233–245. doi:10.1111/j.1471-1842.2007.00733.x

Clark, M. (2008). Genome Island. *Educause Review, 43*(5). Retrieved June 28, 2009 from http://www.educause.edu/node/163160

Danforth, D. (2008). Development of an interactive virtual 3-D model of the human testis using the Second Life platform. In *Proceedings of the 41st Annual Meeting of the Society for the Study of Reproduction.*

Danforth, D. (2009). *Ohio State University College of Medicine Island – Second Life OSU Medicine*. Retrieved June 28, 2009 from http://slurl.com/secondlife/OSU%20Medicine/69/94/302

Felder, R. M. (1993). Reaching the second tier: Learning and teaching styles in college science education. *Journal of College Science Teaching, 23*, 286–290.

Felder, R. M., & Silverman, L. K. (1988). Learning and teaching styles in engineering education. *English Education, 78*, 674–681.

Gorini, A., Gaggiolo, A., Vigna, C., & Riva, G. (2008). A Second Life for eHealth: Prospects for the use of 3-D virtual worlds in clinical psychology. *Journal of Medical Internet Research, 10*(3), e21. doi:10.2196/jmir.1029

Greenwood, C. (2009). *And it grows and grows*. Retrieved June 17, 2009 from http://simbioticbiome.wordpress.com/

Hansen, M. (2008). Versatile, immersive, creative and dynamic virtual 3-D healthcare learning environments: A review of the literature. *Journal of Medical Internet Research. 10*(3). Retrieved June 30, 2009 from http://www.jmir.org/2008/3/e26/HTML

Kemp, J. (2009). *Sim teach wiki*. Retrieved September 10, 2009 from http://www.simteach.com/wiki/index.php?title=Institutions_and_Organizations_in_SL

Mayer, R. (2004). Should there be a three-strikes rule against pure discovery learning? The case for guided methods of instruction. *The American Psychologist, 59*(1), 14–19. doi:10.1037/0003-066X.59.1.14

Perryman, C. (2009). *HealthInfo Island blog*. Retrieved June 26, 2009 from http://healthinfoisland.blogspot.com/from

Scott, J. (2009). *Second Nature Website*. Retrieved June 26 2009 from http://www.nature.com/secondnature/index.html

Second Life. (2009). *Second Nature Island.* Retrieved June 26, 2009 from http://slurl.com/secondlife/Second%20Nature/218/213/28

Second Life Development Service from the VITAL Lab @ Ohio University. (2009). *Vital Wiki.* Retrieved July 1, 2009 from http://vital.cs.ohiou.edu/vitalwiki/index.php/Nutrition_Game Skiba, D. (2009). Nursing education 2.0: A second look at Second Life. *Nursing Education Perspectives, 30*(2), 129-131.

Second Life Healthinfo Island. (2009). *Healthinfo Island*. Retrieved September 10, 2009 from http://slurl.com/secondlife/Healthinfo%20Island/184/61/22.

Second Life Nutrition Game. (2009). *Nutrition Game*. Retrieved September 10, 2009 from http://slurl.com/secondlife/ohio%25university/161/175/25/

Timtam, B. (2009). Guided tour system user manual. Retrieved September 10, 2009 from http://www.hudbook.net/GTSmanual.pdf

Valkoss, P. (2005). *Why the blank stare? Strategies for visual learners*. Retrieved June 28, 2009 from http://www.phschool.com/eteach/social_studies/2003_05/essay.html

APPENDIX 1

Note: Questions Used for this Paper have been Italicized.

Med 2 Second Life Student Survey: 2008-9
Real Life Name ________________Second Life Name ________________
Was this your first time using Second Life? Yes ___ No ___
If Yes, about how long did you spend in obtaining your account and going through the orientation? ______
If No, about approximately how many hours have you used Second Life prior to class? _____

DIRECTIONS: *Please read the items below! Then circle the response that best represents your opinion. Use the key to the right.*	1= Strongly Disagree 2= Disagree 3= Disagree/ Agree about equally 4= Agree 5= Strongly Agree				
	SD	**D**	**A/ D=**	**A**	**SA**
The sign-up process was easy	1	2	3	4	5
The Orientation was easy to navigate in Second Life	1	2	3	4	5
The Testis and Ovary Simulations were easy to locate in Second Life	1	2	3	4	5
The virtual patients were easy to locate.	1	2	3	4	5
The Testis tour was informative	1	2	3	4	5
The Testis tour helped me understand testicular function	1	2	3	4	5
The Ovary tours/activities were informative	1	2	3	4	5
The Ovary tours/activities helped me understand ovarian function	1	2	3	4	5
Given the investment of time you spent (create account, orientation, tours, etc.) the Second Life experience was worth the effort	1	2	3	4	5
Second Life should be used for other medical education *Experiences*	1	2	3	4	5

What was the most useful activity you participated in on OSU Medicine in Second Life?
Please elaborate on what other medical education experiences that Second Life should be used.

Script for Requesting Participation in the Survey

I am conducting a brief survey about your experiences using Second Life over the past three weeks. I am interested in find out what aspects of the Second Life activities you found most and least useful. Participation in the survey is completely optional as was participation in Second Life itself. The survey will be distributed at the end of your exam for the block. All information obtained in the survey will be kept confidential and will have no impact on your grade for the block. Survey responses will not be examined until all grades for the block are finalized.

This work was previously published in International Journal of Virtual and Personal Learning Environments, edited by Michael Thomas, Volume 1, Issue 2, pp. 45-58, copyright 2010 by IGI Publishing (an imprint of IGI Global).

Chapter 12
Affective Load and Engagement in Second Life:
Experiencing Urgent, Persistent, and Long-Term Information Needs

Diane Nahl
University of Hawaii, USA

ABSTRACT

New users of virtual environments face a steep learning curve, requiring persistence and determination to overcome challenges experienced while acclimatizing to the demands of avatar-mediated behavior. Concurrent structured self-reports can be used to monitor the personal affective and cognitive struggles involved in virtual world adaptation to specific affordances while performing particular tasks and activities with avatars. Examination of user discourse in self-reports reveal that participants focus on micro-management concerns about how to proceed in an activity, replete with intense emotions and uncertainty over how to operate affordances. Concurrent structured self-reports engage users in meta-affective and meta-cognitive reflection and facilitate coping with confusion and negative emotions. As Second Life is a complex virtual world with hundreds of affordances, people experience a continuous stream of information needs. Urgent, persistent, and long-term information needs are associated with differing qualities and intensities of affective load, such as impatience, irritation, anxiety, and frustration. When a particular information need is met, affective engagement results in intensity proportional to the affective load. Constructing user discourse during virtual activities serves as a coping mechanism that facilitates adaptation by raising meta-cognitive and meta-affective awareness.

INTRODUCTION

This article reports an exploratory study that examines information behavior practices of university students new to Second Life (SL), and introduces a framework for studying information needs of students in virtual environments that highlights personal aspects in learning. Today nearly every discipline teaches college and university courses in virtual worlds, a figure predicted to increase rapidly as millions of virtualized tweens enter college (KZERO, 2008, 2009). Librarians represent

DOI: 10.4018/978-1-4666-1770-4.ch012

one of the earliest academic and cultural groups to build a presence, create information collections, and deliver services in Second Life (Bell & Trueman, 2008). The present study contributes to the emerging area of virtual world information behavior (Mon, 2009).

The virtual world Second Life is a collaborative effort of millions of 'residents' to recreate physical and social elements of real life (RL) (Boellstorff, 2008; Castronova, 2005; Castronova, 2007; Grassian & Trueman, 2007; Luo & Kemp, 2008; Ostrander, 2008; Sanchez, 2009). Second Life is a real time telecommunications system constructed collaboratively to facilitate social networking of participants in distributed locations. In this ultra constructivist 3-D immersive environment, participants custom-create buildings, shopping malls, clothes, animations, scripts, creatures, plants, activities, events, etc.

Virtual places are accessible via SLURL coordinates and teleport links from the Web, inworld map, and search engine. Second Life is noted for excellent reproductions of cities, rooms, gardens, and objects. Inworld objects are solid so avatars must go around them to continue walking or flying, permitting collaborative viewing, inspection, manipulation, and navigation. With the exception of flying, such interactive functions are familiar in physical learning environments and facilitate collaborative learning (Dwyer, 2007).

The present study examines streams of discourse generated by people as they moved through the SL environment alone and in company, interacting with objects that provide information. The purpose was to determine whether virtual world user discourse would demonstrate a pattern similar to discourse generated while using Web and application technologies, with particular focus on the affective dimensions of technology use (Nahl, 2007a, 2007b). SL assignments included concurrent self-reports with prompts to be completed at intervals during activities and tasks.

The prompts were designed to generate a form of verbalization known as user discourse (Nahl, 2007a; Rimmer, 2001). Three personal learning aspects were elicited that focus on user feelings, thoughts, and noticings while performing SL activities. Here a framework applied to analyze user discourse in prior studies of information systems was applied to the virtual world (Nahl, 2005, 2007a, 2007b). Analysis of SL user discourse confirmed the applicability of the Information Reception and Engagement model (see Figure 1), and revealed gradations of feelings in relation to three types of information needs experienced while performing SL tasks.

Prior research has demonstrated the presence, varieties, and influence of affect in information behavior (IB), and has examined the relationship between affect and cognition in reading, information seeking, information retrieval, decision-making, and task performance (Nahl & Bilal, 2007). These studies have shown that while affect accompanies every activity and its qualities are manifold, it frequently fluctuates and seldom remains steady. How a student feels while doing a task can determine the quality of work and whether it is completed, e.g., high frustration leads to ending a task early.

METHODOLOGY

The participants in the study were 11 undergraduate and graduate students in psychology and library and information science who were taking one of three elective disciplinary courses with virtual world components in 2009. Students examined Second Life from the perspective of their disciplines and course focus. The four male and seven female students were new to Second Life: two had explored other virtual worlds, and two had some gaming background. During a 16 week term they spent a minimum of eight hours inworld weekly, and generated user discourse by constructing concurrent structured self-reports of their SL experiences while doing their assignments and projects.

Figure 1. Social-biological technology model of information reception and engagement

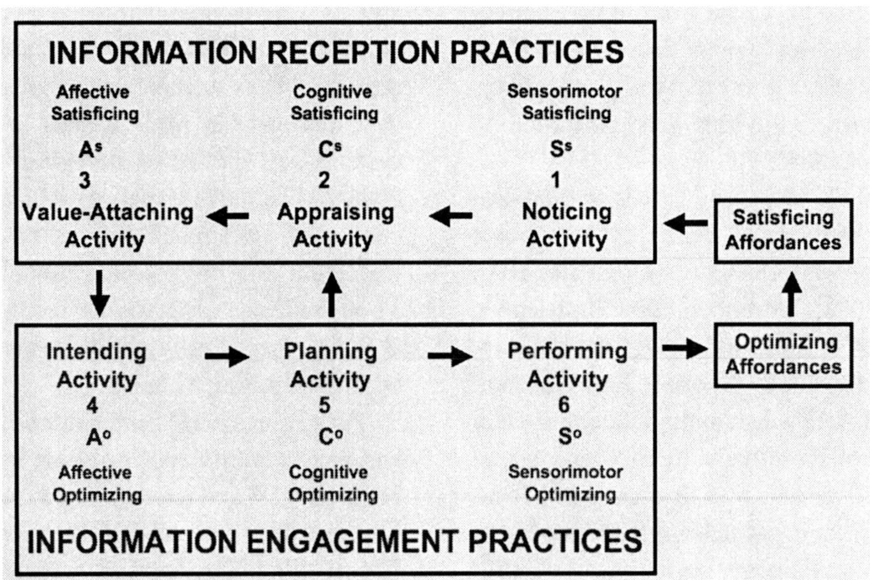

All classes met face-to-face in labs and worked collaboratively inworld during the sessions. In addition, students did virtual world assignments and research individually and in teams. All participants used structured self-report forms tailored to specific course assignments. Students followed instructions to perform inworld tasks, recorded their experience in narrative form, and gave periodic ratings for optimism, self-efficacy, and uncertainty. Averages of formative ratings were not analyzed in this study, but ratings were employed to raise meta-affective and meta-cognitive awareness of SL activities. Students used their self-report data to write papers for their course assignments.

For example, in a task involving acquiring particular items and organizing them in an SL Inventory, students were instructed to mark the same affective scales on a Notecard at five points during the task: before starting the task, after a few steps were completed, after several steps were completed, after several more steps were completed, and at the end. Specific narrative prompts were inserted in the Notecard at these intervals to guide students. Prompts also asked students to record cognitive and sensorimotor facets of experience.

The narrative and numerical prompts served to focus attention on emotional and cognitive aspects of sub-tasks, providing an instrument for eliciting portions of personal reactions that ordinarily remain undocumented. As shown in prior studies of Web search behavior and technology use, individual user discourse obtained during typical tasks, while guided or directed by the researcher, reflects the information behavior practices of discourse communities (Nahl, 2007a, 2007b).

Concurrent and retrospective self-reports provide a versatile method with which to enhance meta-affective and meta-cognitive reflection and increase positive participation in SL. Such process methods have been readily adopted by individuals for recording, logging, blogging, or journaling about their SL activities and reactions. In order to ensure avatars perform well and Chat comments remain socially relevant, each participant performs group practices that can be seen by other group members. Visitors, strangers, or newbies are marked by different information behavior

Box 1.

Comment descriptively on your personal User Experience in terms of Affect (feelings, emotions, values, preferences, expectations), Cognition (confusion, understanding, problem solving, strategy, knowledge acquisition), and Sensorimotor (noticings, performance, actions, procedures, routines, accomplishments). a. How likely is it that you will become good at this particular task? Doubtful 1 2 3 4 5 6 7 8 9 10 Almost Certain Type your number here: Briefly explain your rating: b. How likely is it that the skills you are learning in this task will be useful in your career? Doubtful 1 2 3 4 5 6 7 8 9 10 Almost Certain c. To what extent are you feeling frustrated doing this particular task? Not Frustrated 1 2 3 4 5 6 7 8 9 10 Extremely Frustrated d. To what extent are you feeling irritated doing this particular task? Not Irritated 1 2 3 4 5 6 7 8 9 10 Extremely Irritated The following narrative prompts were inserted at the appropriate points in the task sequence: 1. Copy SLURLs here and describe items you obtained: 2. Describe the Wear process, SL affordances used, and perceived level of success: 3. Describe missing or unnecessary elements and efforts to add or detach them from avatar, and perceived success: 4. Describe your inventory organization strategy and search approach:

practices. User discourse is a productive source of data for identifying and charting the micro-information behavior practices that participants in the virtual world continuously engage in.

PERSONAL INFORMATION RECEPTION AND ENGAGEMENT IN THE VIRTUAL WORLD

User discourse is spontaneously constructed during the process of engaging technological affordances. The overt verbalization that accompanies activity, functions as an embodiment of awareness of what is going on in the stream of micro-events that occupy attention (Ericsson & Simon, 1980, 1993). One can experience this process of awareness embodiment through the 'think aloud' method that has been used to raise conscious awareness of mental states during a task (Nahl, 2005). In technology interactions it is common to construct user discourse (silent or audible) to assist in managing the sequencing of micro-behaviors while creating and searching for files or other computer tasks. Nahl (2007a) has shown that user discourse generated in a variety of technology environments corresponds to the affective, cognitive, and sensorimotor human systems (Norman, 2004).

Nahl (2007b) employs a *social-biological technology* model to show how these three information processing systems are integrated. The model in Figure 1 describes the synergy of the sensorimotor system in interaction with technological affordances designed to display information and enable control through commands and selections. The model shows that each *noticing* of elements on a display and every command entered are sensorimotor outcomes of ongoing cognitive and affective activities. When an element is noticed on a screen (e.g., an avatar name tag) there is a spontaneous adaptive cognitive reaction that attaches some specific meaning to it, and this meaning evokes an emotion or value (e.g., '*That's my good friend*' or '*That's a surprising name!*'). The cognitive meaning and affective value-attachment activities of individuals result from adaptation to social practices. When people function in an information environment, their actions, evaluations, engagement intentions, and plans develop organically, as part of their personal adjustment to the social computing situation, thus technology, biology, and social practices are fused in an interactive synergy.

The realistic humanoid appearance and motion of avatars, fantastical avatar shapes, and iconic 3-D representations of urban and rural environments facilitate an intense emotional and sensorimotor experience. For example, in the following reflection from a self-report, a 'newbie' avatar owner describes how various SL seating types affected her ability to focus attention:

This building has theater seating with comfy looking chairs. I can imagine myself listening to a lecture in this area. I notice there is a large cognitive difference for me when learning in areas in which I like the environment versus when I don't. For example, I've seen some areas with stone seating and feel urgent for the lecture to end. Then there are some places where the seating is mostly pillows on the grass and I find myself way too relaxed in RL to focus on listening to a lecture. So at least in this area there's a nice middle ground. The chairs appear soft without the urgency to find a 'comfortable' chair or to leave ... but also not too soft to the point where I'm falling asleep at my monitor. It's interesting to me that my RL body responds to a virtual environment the same way it would respond in the same RL environment.

Strong feelings and intense reactions frequently accompany experiential learning in SL. For example, consider the analysis of a text fragment from the self-report above.

Micro-analysis of concurrent verbalizations provides a situated, objective indication of what information is noticed, how it is evaluated, and what the person intends to do with it.

Figure 1 represents the social-biological technology model (Nahl, 2007b) specifying two iterative phases involved in the minimal unit of interaction with affordances made available by an interface. One phase involves the reception of information through *satisficing affordances* such as a command menu or a display window. The other phase involves engaging the environment by acting through *optimizing affordances* such as mouse and keyboard, and buttons and links to click on screen. According to the model, the information reception phase involves an organic sequence from sensorimotor to cognitive to affective. First, *noticing* information through a satisficing affordance such as an image or text on screen. This is an activity of the sensorimotor system (S). Second, *appraising* what has been noticed, this involves constructing meaning and implication, an activity of the cognitive system (C). Third, *value-attaching* the appraised noticing (or 'evaluation'), an activity of the affective system (A). For example, a user notices the hovering text in the tree house classroom on the screen (sensorimotor activity – S), figures that it is a clickable object (cognitive activity – C), and feels hopeful clicking it will open the door (affective activity – A). Information reception occurs via satisficing

Box 2.

and
[cognitive planning activity constructing a coherent justification]
I find myself
[sensorimotor noticing activity describing one's physical state at the computer station]
way too relaxed in RL
[affective evaluation activity using a comparative rating procedure]
to focus on listening to a lecture.
[affective motivational activity involving an intention guiding a specific goal]
So at least
[cognitive appraising activity attaching a particular meaning to the situation]
in this area there's
[sensorimotor noticing activity identifying a place on the display screen]
a nice middle ground.
[affective evaluation activity using a comparative rating procedure]

until an acceptable decision is made to act on or abandon information.

Once information has been satisficed through affective value-attachment activities (‘*I want to get into that tree house room. It looks interesting. It will be fun going there*’), the three biological phases proceed in reverse order. Fourth, *forming a motivated intention* is an ‘optimizing’ affective activity that produces an intention to engage the system for the sake of a goal (also called ‘conative’). Fifth, *constructing a plan of execution* is a cognitive activity constrained by the affective intention or goal. Sixth, executing the plan by *performing an action* on an available optimizing affordance, for example, using the mouse and click routine on the virtual door to make it open is an activity of the sensorimotor system. After satisficing with display affordances to determine whether it is worthwhile to proceed, we optimize our actions using control affordances. The minimal interaction unit in social-biological technology integrates the six activity phases: noticing (S), appraising (C), value-attaching (A), intending (A), planning (C), and performing (S). The simple personal act of noticing a link and clicking on it involves all six biological activity phases. When user discourse is analyzed there is clear evidence that these six phases embody the context of activities in information environments.

By filtering user discourse analysis with the three biological information systems, it is possible to produce meaningful segments of user verbalizations that indicate the micro-behavioral information practices of people engaged in information activities with technology. This approach is likely to be useful in the analysis of avatar-mediated user discourse produced in the virtual world. For example, the following sample text from a concurrent self-report of an individual who took on the task of finding various activities to do in Second Life and to describe each while engaged in the activity. This segment describes a visit to a shopping area:

> *Starting to feel a little overwhelmed. [A^s value attaching] I'm deciding to just run through the entire store [C^o planning] looking for certain areas [A^o intending]. Too much shopping is making my brain numb. [A^s value attaching] Also, [C^s appraising] I've begun to notice how people advertise. [S^s noticing] Some pictures I look at [S^s noticing] I get an annoying feeling [A^s value attaching]. For example this yellow picture [S^s noticing] bugs me [A^s value attaching]. I can't quite identify [C^o planning] what about the picture bugs me [C^s appraising]. It has to do with [C^s appraising] the yellow background [S^s noticing] and how it relates to [C^s appraising] the outfit the girl is wearing [S^s noticing]. It gives me a different generational vibe [A^s value-attaching].*

Statistical descriptions of discourse segments by frequency and type of references users practice reveal areas of micro-focus and emphasis. The above concurrent self-report mentions 14 satisficing activities, 4 cognitive, 5 sensorimotor, and 5 affective. Three optimizing activities are mentioned, intending and planning to meet a goal.

By charting the flow of micro-information behaviors in context, it is possible to obtain an empirical representation of rich personal details relating to how people actually receive information via a satisficing affordance (through noticing, appraising, value attaching), and how they engage with information in a moment-by-moment interaction with optimizing affordances (through intending, planning, and engaging) (see Appendix 1 for examples). Individual survival and adaptation in a symbiotic human-computer relationship are marked in the virtual world where feelings, intentions, thoughts, noticings, and interactions are expressed through avatar-mediated information and communication activities. These involve group practices, norms and expectations, such as what to notice on a screen and what to ignore, or how to react to some happening inworld or to a remark by someone in Chat.

The six reception and engagement phases were used as prompts in structured self-report forms to help people become more conscious of their spontaneous avatar-mediated activities. This approach builds personal awareness through meta-cognitive and meta-affective reflection on inworld activities. The following examples from two individuals illustrate this procedure:

Learner 1

1. **Noticing:** *I noticed that I had fallen from flight when I clicked on the stop flying button*
2. **Appraising:** *I noticed because I have seen other people fly and land gracefully so I knew I was doing something wrong.*
3. **Value Attaching:** On a scale from 1-10
   Embarrassing: *10*
   Humiliating: *10*
   Aversiveness: *10*
   Urgency: *8*
   Worry about others: *10*

To be honest it just was more embarrassing than anything else because it singles you out as a newbie. When you aren't graceful in the way you walk and fly it's a sign that you are inexperienced.

4. **Intending:** *I want to change this behavior so that people don't single me out right away. The goal is to look like you know what you are doing even when you don't.*
5. **Planning:** *I planned to ask someone or look up how to fix this problem. I just need to have someone to talk to first.*
6. **Executing:** *By watching the Orientation videos, I found a sign that instructed users on how to land so I utilized this resource and will never have to fall out of the sky again. I found out that I just have to click on the 'c' key and that is how to land gently.*

Learner 2

1. **Noticing:** *After re-spawning to my last location, I noticed a creature thing called 'Digital God.'*
2. **Appraising:** *I saw a chair on top of the head of the 'Digital God' and thought that it would be appropriate to ride it, not realizing or knowing that it was another avatar.*
3. **Value attaching:** *Everyone who witnessed this action was name-calling me and stating how much of a newbie I was.*
   Embarrassing: *10*
   Urgency: *7*
   Humiliation: *9*
   Friendliness: *1*
4. **Intending:** *I want to never make the mistake to ride another avatar. It makes you look like a newbie and makes you look like an ass. It shows the rest of the SL community that you don't know or don't care about their rules.*
5. **Planning:** *I will read the note cards and be aware of my surroundings when I enter an area, whether foreign or visited.*
6. **Executing:** *I will attempt a conversation in order to see if they are indeed another avatar or a part of the area to which I traveled.*

People readily provide useful details of their micro-actions in the six information reception and engagement phases.

PERSONAL INFORMATION NEEDS

Researchers examining information needs and seeking in Second Life (Mon, 2009; Ostrander, 2008; Sanchez, 2009) have derived a variety of question typologies, including:

- Wayfinding of places
- Understanding the virtual world
- Obtaining items

- Living as a resident
- Controlling the avatar
- Understanding society and governance
- Presenting the self
- Shaping the environment (Mon, 2009)
- Social information seeking
- Use of visual, experiential mechanisms
- Serendipitous discovery
- Use of the Second Life search utility
- Play and humor (Ostrander, 2008).

In a study of information providers such as librarians Mon identified how they 'found that when questioners were situated within Second Life, their most immediate questions tended to be about Second Life, and the activities they were trying to accomplish there' (2009, p. 8). The above typologies show that SL is a fully social environment that in normal use generates continuous and urgent information needs. It is often stated that SL has a steep learning curve, and instructors struggle to provide the most effective orientation activities to ease entry and adaptation for students. For example, Jarmon, Traphagan, and Mayrath (2008, p. 168) found in a case study of an interdisciplinary course that 'most (75%) disagreed that SL was easy to use, and all commented that they would like to have more training on how to use SL, in particular on building objects.'

Consequently there is increasing attention being paid to affective aspects of information problem solving with technology, including affective computing (Hudlicka, 2002; Picard, 1997;); emotional design (Norman, 2004); positive affect and decision-making (Isen, 2004); affective load in technology use (Nahl, 2005); experience design and participatory design in HCI (Sharp, Rogers, & Preece, 2007); intrinsic motivation and gaming (Whitton, 2009); and humor agents and positive affect (Dybala, Ptaszynski, Rzepka, & Araki, 2009), among others. Information behavior research in SL reveals that users report a full range of affective experience, from frustration and fear to joy and inspiration. Sanchez (2009) found students described their SL experience variously as frustrating, boring, tedious, overwhelming, addictive, awkward, and too time consuming, as well as fun, interesting, pleasurable, and involving and generative of a sense of accomplishment and pride.

Jarmon et al. (2008, p. 168) conducted pre-post affective assessments including perceptions, attitudes, and reactions of students to SL. Students found the project-based course enjoyable, engaging, a good learning experience, and most wanted to return to SL on their own, while at the same time, some felt SL did not enhance collaboration or communication. Toro-Troconis, Mellstrom, and Partridge (2008, pp. 345-346) gave medical students in SL six statements to explore the 'affective component' including fear, hesitation, avoidance, uneasiness, perceived usefulness, and perceived control. They found that perceived and experienced difficulty exacts an emotional cost and emotional coping skills are needed to remain engaged with complex systems.

Affective load is a theoretical concept that attempts to identify, measure, and chart the cumulative emotional cost involved in personal adaptation and engagement with technological affordances. Affective load refers to the intensity and quality of consummatory value-attaching activities during information reception while interacting with satisficing affordances. The components of affective load in Web-based activities include emotional uncertainty, irritation, anxiety, frustration, rage, low optimism, low self-efficacy, and external locus of control (Nahl, 2005). Biologically, these are affective indications of the struggle to engage the optimizing affordances of the interface.

In the literature definitions of the concept and process of *engagement* are manifold, but all definitions share strong positive affective components. Kappelman (1995) identified affect as a significant factor in engaging with software. Jarmon et al. (2008) considered the level of student motivation in engagement (p. 159) relating to social interaction (p. 160), other communities (p. 162) and the course.

O'Brien and Toms (2008) articulated a process model of engagement based on research with users of four different information systems concluding that, '*Engagement* is sustained when users are able to maintain their attention and interest in the application, and is characterized by positive emotions' (p. 947). They identified several threads contributing to the engagement process, including a Sensual Thread and an Emotional Thread that embody feelings, perceptions and emotions via satisficing (incorporating) and optimizing (acting on and with) information. The Sensual Thread involves satisficing and optimizing: 'At times the application facilitated the engagement with its presentation of information or graphics and multimedia features; at other times it deterred engagement with its inability to meet the customization and communicative needs of participants' (p. 947). In this study, 'The emotional thread accounts for the affective experiences of users' interactions, as well as the motivations that influenced and maintained their use of the application' (p. 947).

Their participants reported affective responses such as interest, enjoyment, satisfaction, sense of accomplishment, and fun; as well as uncertainty, doubt, anxiety, frustration, guilt, boredom, and time pressure. Engagement is primarily affective in nature since without affect there is no engagement, i.e., there is no plan (C) without intention (A) and no understanding (C) without evaluation (A). Preliminary analysis of Chat in Second Life reveals three types of affective information needs experienced inworld, each with particular affective properties when an information need is met (engagement) and not met (load).

Since SL is a complex virtual world replete with **hundreds** of affordances, people experience a continuous and rapid stream of information needs, some of which are immediate and urgent, while others can be postponed. As a result of this complexity, people are constantly engaged in solving information needs that allow them to continue inworld activities, or threaten to disrupt or embarrass them in the process.

URGENT INFORMATION NEEDS

An avatar attempting to enter a classroom in a tree house notices hovering text instructing, 'Touch Me For Door Controls,' and after clicking unsuccessfully a couple of times and not knowing what to do next, typed in Chat, '*What's the Me?*' seeking a solution to an urgent information need. A nearby avatar typed '*Click the door opposite from where you are.*' After repositioning, the avatar opened the door thanking the responder. Such activity indicates that user discourse is a prominent feature of Second Life. People frequently use Chat to ask how to do something or where to find something, and other people readily respond with answers.

Daily life is replete with urgent information needs that must be solved immediately to avert a crisis. In avatar-mediated information behavior one learns basic survival skills such as requesting help from other avatars. At times basic skills fail and a crisis precipitates urgent personal information needs. For example, instead of moving forward the avatar behaves as if there is an invisible barrier it cannot cross, moving sideways along it or reversing direction. This occurs sometimes when teleporting to an area experiencing lag or when parts of the build take longer to 'rez' than others, giving the impression the avatar is free to walk in that direction when there is a yet unseen barrier. It can be puzzling, frustrating, and even alarming to see one's avatar suddenly unable to move. During several seconds of a crisis urgent information needs are activated involving heavy affective load. Box 3, for example, shows an excerpt from a concurrent structured self-report dealing with these issues.

The feeling of being overwhelmed with information is particularly stressful in SL because it consists entirely of information with hundreds of affordances in every locale. The simplest activities in the virtual world are information intense and can incur affective load. The activities of avatars depend on continuous information seeking and management practices and people must adapt to

Box 3.

> To what extent are you feeling frustrated doing this particular task?
> Not Frustrated 1 2 3 4 5 6 7 8 9 10 Extremely Frustrated
> Type your number here: **8** and briefly explain your rating:
> *Knowing the fact that the Reference Desk will be filled with information makes me feel overwhelmed and frustrated. I do not like how information is everywhere in SL. Sometimes note cards and reading instructions give me a headache.*

handle affective load collateral to avatar-mediated interactions.

The following segment from a retrospective self-report illustrates the intensity of affective load associated with urgent information needs:

Lyra sent us IM beforehand saying that we will need pictures. I had plenty of pictures on my desktop so I was not worried at all. But I misunderstood and found out that I needed the pictures to be in my inventory. When one thing goes wrong and [we] cannot move on to the next step, I begin to feel frustrated. My classmate was following her without any problems. Why can't I do it?? Plus, when I do not get it, it slows down the class. I really hate that feeling. When my frustration hit the maximum point, I just wanted to give up. I usually never feel that way even if I faced difficulties. I craved for some immediate help. I wanted someone to show me how to do it from my point of view, but that was impossible.

The specific emotional character of urgent information needs is embodied in the statement, '*When one thing goes wrong and [we] cannot move on to the next step, I begin to feel frustrated.*' Information becomes urgent when it is needed immediately to prevent a crisis ('*when I do not get it, it slows down the class. I really hate that feeling*'). When affective load is high the motivation to quit builds rapidly ('*When my frustration hit the maximum point, I just wanted to give up.*') and the person disengages, shuts down, and quits.

PERSISTENT INFORMATION NEEDS

Not all information needs require immediate resolution. They can be postponed. Activities can proceed with sufficient satisficing and without crisis. The specific information need is on hold, and it revives again in different activities and locations. Information needs that persist increase affective load, though less steeply than urgent information needs. In the following user discourse segment from a retrospective self-report the individual expresses awareness of a persistent information need that curtails her participation in the communicative practices of the group:

I saw people clapping at the end of the lecture. I needed to participate myself more to make the communication become more real. Some people write how they felt and their opinions constantly during the lecture and I was too busy following the directions. I realize that I need to attend more public conferences; events that offer guest speakers to get more used to and witness ways of communication in SL.

Multi-tasking is a common practice in information intense collaborative exchanges. During a talk in Second Life the Local Chat window displays short segments of text pasted or typed by the presenter. Typed user discourse constructions by the audience of attending avatars ('*people write how they felt and their opinions constantly during the lecture*') are inserted between the presenter's text segments. If the presenter uses Voice, Local Chat becomes an active back channel of commentary from the avatar audience. It takes repeated practice to follow the presentation while disentangling several topical threads occurring simultaneously in Chat. The affective load of feeling excluded from communication sparked a new resolve to practice more in the future to develop the skills. This information need will persist until SL chat and gestures in presentation settings have been mastered and become routine.

In the virtual world everything one can do and be is encapsulated in the 'Inventory' folders. After a few months of inworld exploration it is common to accumulate thousands of Inventory items in dozens of folders and sub-folders containing items of clothing, avatar pets, personal animation HUDs, images or textures, interactive scripts, note cards, landmarks, etc. Locating items in the Inventory often becomes an activity marked by intense affective load. Inventory management raises a host of persistent personal information needs. The following (see Box 4) is from a concurrent structured self-report of a student attending an introductory Inventory management class in SL.

During the class activity the person experienced affective load (high frustration), but coped with it through a goal of striving to become an organized person and engaged in inventory management. Meta-affective reflection enables re-prioritization of feelings and emotions so that a higher goal can mitigate negative emotions, the task can be completed successfully, and the persistent information need can be met.

LONG-TERM INFORMATION NEEDS

Information intense environments such as Second Life provide a progressive form of adaptation or acculturation. 'Newbie' avatars are easily recognized by 'Residents' by their stilted appearance and gait, primitive interaction style, and less informed content, apparent in user discourse constructions in Local Chat. Residents and newbies alike constantly face information needs that may not be urgent or persistent because they can be postponed indefinitely. Long-term information needs are embodied in the awareness that in the information environment created by social-biological technology one is in some sense always a newbie.

Inevitably certain information needs are postponed indefinitely for the sake of less convenient and inefficient workarounds, and some are given up altogether. While few might enjoy studying the knowledge filled Second Life Wiki, merely being aware of its existence helps people postpone their long-term information needs (*'I will look this up some day'*). In the following examples participants commented on their long-term information needs as personal goals that stretched into the distant future, e.g.,

'Someday I would like to learn how to make clothes in SL.'

'I wish I could do art in SL, that would be cool, maybe I'll figure it out eventually.'

Box 4.

How likely is it that you will become good at this particular task? (1 to 10)

I give myself 9 because I realized that organizing my inventory is important and by doing it, I improved and became good at it.

How likely is it that the skills you are learning in this task will be useful in your career?

I give it 10 because organizing skill is a skill that most careers would expect you to have.

To what extent are you feeling frustrated doing this particular task?

I give it 9 because when I first looked through my inventory, it was a huge mess.

To what extent are you feeling irritated doing this particular task?

I give it 8 because looking at each item and deciding whether I should keep it or not took some time.

'She's earns money as a DJ in SL, wow I could learn to do that if I had time.'

'I know it would be easier if I memorized the SL keyboard shortcuts.'

'I'd like to take a land management course some day.'

Affective load in long-term information needs is felt as slight irritation distributed over time and easily tolerated.

Activity in SL generates a constant flow of information needs with the concomitant dynamics of affective load and engagement as such learning opportunities flow naturally in the immersive virtual information environment. To avoid disengagement avatars faced with novel information needs must develop coping mechanisms to mitigate high levels of affective load.

AFFECTIVE LOAD AND ENGAGEMENT

Everything in the virtual world depends on managing bits of information to remain engaged. Figure 2 makes theoretical predictions based on the situated experience of a small sample and prior research. It may be useful for categorizing activities during real time avatar-mediated synchronous social and collaborative interactions in a wide variety of settings and situations.

While some information needs in the virtual world can be postponed others cannot. For instance, when trying on hair in a store without a change room, bald avatars can be seen. It is common for users to report feeling 'embarrassed,' even 'humiliated' when other avatars suddenly appear and witness their baldness. The affective information need might be: Where can I put on this Demo hair so no one will see? or, How can I get used to strangers seeing my bald avatar? This is a persistent information need because it recurs while it goes unmet. Persistent information needs like this can be postponed since one can still try on and buy the hair. But postponement bears an affective cost, namely, repeated occasions of embarrassment accompanied by uneasy expectations, even 'alarm,' that becomes associated with the practice of inworld shopping for hair.

Persistent information needs are common in SL and generate moderate to high levels of affective load in ranges of anxiety and frustration. When a persistent information need is eventually resolved, it increases enjoyment and fun in the activity. In contrast, urgent information needs do not tolerate postponement so unless resolved immediately, affective load rapidly overwhelms to the point of disengagement. When solved in time, positive affective engagement is proportional to the affective load. Participants in SL need strategies to mitigate affective load, to adapt to and minimize a sudden lack of crucial information and ability, and to manage their personal SL information environment to accomplish self-directed goals. Remaining engaged is the highest reward. Solving an urgent information need boosts self-efficacy, or the feeling that one can survive in this novel 3-D environment.

Affective load from an unfulfilled information need is more serious and emotionally stressful when the solution cannot be postponed. One participant reported that she logged in several times in one hour and found her avatar in the same position, pinned between a bridge railing and a large sign. Each time she would give up after a few minutes of trying to move her avatar, hoping each new login would start the avatar in a different position. Finally, she managed to move out of the crevice in time to finish a required task of teleporting to a specific location '*At last! That was so frustrating and took way too long but I feel so much better when I can move her and teleport. Ahhhh.*'

The Affective Load and Affective Engagement scales in Figure 2 are derived from the ratings and comments of users discussing their information

Figure 2. Affective load and information needs

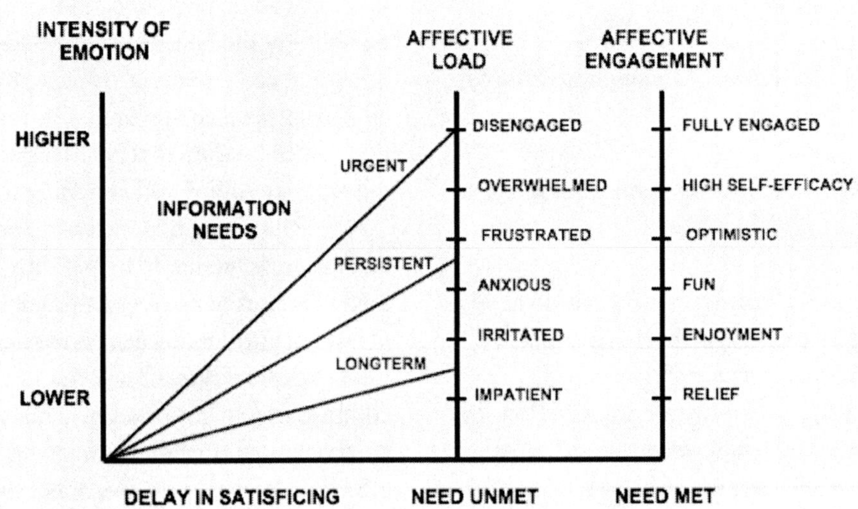

needs under various online conditions (Nahl, 2005, 2007a). Both scales represent cumulative gradations from lower to higher intensities of emotion as reported by users. The intensity of emotion from lower to higher is cumulative, such that a higher intensity emotion incorporates all of the emotions beneath it on the scale. To become disengaged is a compound affective state that involves experiencing a cumulative series of negative emotions such as feeling overwhelmed, frustrated, anxious, irritated, and impatient. To become fully engaged is a compound affective state that involves experiencing a cumulative series of positive emotions such as feeling high self-efficacy, optimistic, fun, enjoyment, and relief.

In Figure 2 if an urgent information need is unmet it cumulates to maximum affective load, disengagement, or quitting. In contrast, a long-term information need has low affective load associated with indefinite postponement. When a long-term information need is eventually met, the felt impatience or irritation about the long-term uncertainty is replaced with enjoyment and relief. When an urgent information need is delayed for a relatively brief time and then met, impatience associated with the brief delay is transformed into relief. When a persistent information need is unmet for a relatively longer time the experience of frustration turns into optimism about solving similar problems in the future. The affective dynamism in Figure 2 shows that lower intensity feelings can be experienced in all three types of information needs with different amounts of delay. With long delays before the need is met, the intensity of feelings increases in proportion to the type of information need. This theoretical model based on prior and present research data needs to be tested with different user groups engaged in a wide variety of SL activities in the future.

CONCLUSION

Behavior in the virtual world consists of information management activities participants practice in their interactions. Each participant succeeds by interacting with interface affordances through information reception and engagement. In this process users experience three types of information needs linked to particular negative and positive emotional dynamics. Analysis of future data on real time information activities of avatars in SL may show that micro-analysis of user discourse offers a useful perspective on the complexity of avatar-mediated interaction, and provides insight for improved instruction and design of immersive collaborative spaces.

Affective load and engagement are dynamic field features of immersive environments that fluctuate according to situational influences including technology, social practices, and human systems. Ultimately the personal achievement of coping with affective load and enabling affective engagement determines whether someone becomes an occasional visitor or a regular participant and full-fledged SL resident.

REFERENCES

Bell, L., & Trueman, R. B. (2008). *Virtual worlds, real libraries: Librarians and educators in Second Life and other multi-user virtual environments*. Medford, NJ: Information Today.

Boellstorff, T. (2008). *Coming of age in Second Life: An anthropologist explores the virtually human*. Princeton, NJ: Princeton University Press.

Castronova, E. (2005). *Synthetic worlds: The business and culture of online games*. Chicago: University of Chicago Press.

Castronova, E. (2007). *Exodus to the virtual world: How online fun is changing reality*. New York: Palgrave Macmillan.

Dwyer, N. (2007). *Incorporating indexicality and contingency into the design of representations for computer-mediated collaboration*. Unpublished doctoral dissertation, University of Hawaii, Honolulu.

Dybala, P., Ptaszynski, M., Rzepka, R., & Araki, K. (2009). Humoroids - conversational agents that induce positive emotions with humor. In *Proceedings of the 8th International Conference on Autonomous Agents and Multiagent Systems (AAMAS 2009)*, Budapest, Hungary (pp. 1171-1172).

Ericsson, K. A., & Simon, H. A. (1980). Verbal reports as data. *Psychological Review*, *87*, 215–251. doi:10.1037/0033-295X.87.3.215

Ericsson, K. A., & Simon, H. A. (1993). *Protocol analysis: Verbal reports as data*. Cambridge, MA: MIT Press.

Grassian, E., & Trueman, R. B. (2007). Stumbling, bumbling, teleporting and flying ... Librarian avatars in Second Life. *RSR. Reference Services Review*, *35*, 84–89. doi:10.1108/00907320710729373

Hudlicka, E. (2002). This time with feeling: Integrated model of trait and state effects on cognition and behavior. *Applied Artificial Intelligence*, *16*(7/8), 1–31.

Isen, A. M. (2004). Positive affect and decision making. In Lewis, M., & Haviland-Jones, J. M. (Eds.), *Handbook of emotions* (pp. 417–435). New York: Guilford Press.

Jarmon, L., Traphagan, T., & Mayrath, M. (2008). Understanding project-based learning in Second Life with a pedagogy, training, and assessment trio. *Educational Media International*, *45*(3), 157–176. doi:10.1080/09523980802283889

Kappelman, L. A. (1995). Measuring user involvement: A diffusion of innovation perspective. *Database Advances*, *26*(2/3), 65–86.

KZERO. (2008). *Virtual worlds registered accounts and virtual worlds by sector Q4*. Retrieved July 20, 2009, from http://www.kzero.co.uk/blog/?page_id=2092

KZERO. (2009). *Kids, tweens, and teens in virtual worlds case study*. Retrieved July 20, 2009, from http://www.kzero.co.uk/blog/?p=2722

Luo, L., & Kemp, J. (2008). Second Life: Exploring the immersive instructional venue for library and information science education. *Journal of Education for Library and Information Science*, *49*(3), 147–166.

Mon, L. (2009). Questions and answers in a virtual world: Educators and librarians as information providers in Second Life. *Journal of Virtual Worlds Research*, *2*(1), 4–21.

Nahl, D. (2005). Affective and cognitive information behavior: Interaction effects in Internet use. In *Proceedings of the 68th Annual Meeting of the American Society for Information Science & Technology*. Medford, NJ: Information Today.

Nahl, D. (2007a). Domain interaction discourse analysis: A technique for charting the flow of micro-information behavior. *The Journal of Documentation*, *63*(3), 323–339. doi:10.1108/00220410710743270

Nahl, D. (2007b). Social-biological information technology: An integrated conceptual framework. *Journal of the American Society for Information Science and Technology*, *58*(13), 2021–2046. doi:10.1002/asi.20690

Nahl, D., & Bilal, D. (Eds.). (2007). *Information and emotion: The emergent affective paradigm in information behavior research and theory*. Medford, NJ: Information Today.

Norman, D. A. (2004). *Emotional design: Why we love (or hate) everyday things*. New York: Basic Books.

Obrien, H. L., & Toms, E. G. (2008). What is user engagement? A conceptual framework for defining user engagement with technology. *Journal of the American Society for Information Science and Technology*, *59*(6), 938–955. doi:10.1002/asi.20801

Ostrander, M. (2008). Talking, looking, flying, searching: Information seeking behaviour in Second Life. *Library Hi Tech*, *26*(4), 512–524. doi:10.1108/07378830810920860

Picard, R. W. (1997). *Affective computing*. Boston: MIT Press.

Rimmer, J. (2001). User discourse and technology design. In Zayas, B., & Gama, C. (Eds.), *Information technologies and knowledge construction: Bringing together the best of two worlds (CSRP 538). Falmer*. UK: University of Sussex.

Sanchez, J. (2009). Implementing Second Life: Ideas, challenges, and innovations. *Library Technology Reports*, *45*(2), 5–39.

Sharp, H., Rogers, Y., & Preece, J. (2007). Affective aspects. In *Interaction design: Beyond human-computer interaction* (pp. 181–215). New York: Wiley.

Toro-Troconis, M., Mellstrom, U., & Partridge, M. (2008). Game based learning in respiratory medicine via Second Life. *Thorax*, *63*, 206.

Whitton, N. (2009). Gaming and the network generation. In Wheeler, S. (Ed.), *Connected minds, emerging cultures: Cybercultures in online learning* (pp. 77–89). Charlotte, NC: Information Age Publishing.

APPENDIX A

Identifying Exemplars for User Discourse Analysis

1. **Noticing Practices (sensorimotor satisficing):** identifying a location; object or avatar; focusing on or ignoring something visible or audible; recognizing something; etc.
2. **Appraising Practices (cognitive satisficing):** assessing; interpreting; categorizing; justifying; giving reasons; attributing cause; comparing; limiting; explaining; listing; etc.
3. **Value-Attaching Practices (affective satisficing):** feeling positive or negative emotions; evaluating; rating; applying reference norms; prioritizing or ranking; finding something acceptable vs. aversive; feeling satisfied vs. not; consummating or fulfilling a need; feeling attracted or interested vs. not; etc.
4. **Intending Practices (affective optimizing):** purpose or goal-setting; regulating or directing; striving or persisting; intending or wanting to; engaging or making use of; implementing or adopting; looking for or searching; etc.
5. **Planning Practices (cognitive optimizing):** predicting or problem solving; designing or scheduling; inventing or extending; imagining or picturing; managing or setting objectives; etc.
6. **Performing Practices (sensorimotor optimizing):** clicking; mouseing; doing something; giving a command; moving the avatar; teleporting; typing in chat; verbalizing; inspecting; reading; buying; building; waiting; sitting; etc.

This work was previously published in International Journal of Virtual and Personal Learning Environments, edited by Michael Thomas, Volume 1, Issue 3, pp. 1-16, copyright 2010 by IGI Publishing (an imprint of IGI Global).

Chapter 13
Investigating Modes of Student Inquiry in Second Life as Part of a Blended Approach

Sheila Webber
University of Sheffield, UK

ABSTRACT

This article discusses activities carried out in the virtual world of Second Life (SL) as part of a compulsory class in the first year of an undergraduate programme. The paper identifies the contribution of SL to the students' learning environment and an Inquiry Based Learning (IBL) approach to programme design. The reasons for taking an IBL approach are explained in relation to institutional and disciplinary goals. The paper reflects on the contribution of the three key learning environments—the classroom, WebCT and SL—to students' learning. SL is evaluated in relation to a conceptual framework of IBL. It is concluded that SL has made a contribution to students' achievement of learning outcomes from the class, and has facilitated the development of students' inquiry skills. In conclusion, further avenues for developing research and teaching are identified.

INTRODUCTION

This article discusses activities carried out in Second Life (SL) and identifies its contribution to students' learning environments and to an Inquiry Based Learning (IBL) approach to programme design, adopting an action research orientation (Levy, 2003). The class in which the SL activities take place is a core (compulsory) module entitled, *Information Literacy*, taken in the first year of an undergraduate programme in the United Kingdom (UK). It is a campus-based class that already has a blended learning approach commonly found in the UK (Sharpe et al., 2006), combining face-to-face sessions with the use of what in the UK is called a Virtual Learning Environment (VLE), WebCT, and interaction with other web-based resources such as e-journals and wikis.

DOI: 10.4018/978-1-4666-1770-4.ch013

The author is the class coordinator. The aim of incorporating the SL learning environment into the class was, firstly, to improve students' engagement with research models of a core subject (Information Behaviour), thus contributing to a key learning outcome of the class. Secondly, she aimed to identify whether SL was synergistic with an IBL approach. The research was supported by an award from the University of Sheffield's Centre for Inquiry Based Learning in the Arts and Social Sciences (CILASS). CILASS also funded the purchase and rent of a SL island, Infolit iSchool, for its first year.

SL is a 3-D virtual world and the trademark of Linden Lab. People are represented within SL by 3-D avatars; via these avatars they can create and trade objects, rent land, and participate in a variety of activities organised by other SL residents.

The paper begins by describing the class in which the learning activities took place, and the characteristics of the teaching-learning environment (TLE). This includes identifying the nature of the blended delivery of this class and the overall pedagogic approach to the programme. The reasons for taking an IBL approach are explained in relation to institutional and disciplinary goals. It goes on to consider SL in relation to IBL, connecting it to a conceptual model derived from a longitudinal research project into students' conceptions of IBL, undertaken by CILASS.

After describing the activities that took place in SL, and their relation to the learning outcomes and assessment of the class, the contribution of SL to students' learning is discussed. The article finishes by evaluating SL in relation to the conceptual framework of IBL presented earlier.

CONTEXT AND AIMS: THE INFORMATION LITERACY CLASS

The context for the research reported here is a class, *Information Literacy*, which is core in the level one (freshman) year of the B.Sc. Information Management (IM) degree offered in the Department of Information Studies at the University of Sheffield. The number of students taking the class is 20-30 each year. The overall aims of the class are to develop students' information literacy skills in key areas and to enhance their understanding of information literacy and information behaviour theories. The class is worth one-third of the credits in the first semester.

Additionally, the class is designed to develop students' inquiry skills so that they can engage with mini research projects carried out the following semester (Cox et al., 2008a), with the ultimate goal of conducting individual research projects in their final year. The *Information Literacy* class also contributes to the progression of other key skills e.g., group work skills.

The author had identified that the teaching and assessment strategy for the class was not enabling students to demonstrate their grasp of information behaviour theory, which had been assessed primarily through an academic essay. This had led to the reproduction of information rather than evidence of ability to apply and understand the models. IBL was seen as a means to engage students more meaningfully with the models. SL provided an environment in which data gathering could take place, providing students with unique data, to which they could apply their understanding of the models. Thus the aims of the action research were to facilitate deeper engagement with the subject matter, and to identify whether SL itself was a viable environment for IBL. This article reports on the delivery of the *Information Literacy* class in the 2007/8 and 2008/9 academic years.

THE TEACHING-LEARNING ENVIRONMENT

Since this paper is concerned with the students' personal learning environment, this section begins by identifying a framework for discussion. Entwistle (2003) notes the many ways in which the term 'environment' is interpreted in educational literature. Entwistle and Smith (2002) developed a conceptual framework to describe influences on the outcomes of learning, amplified through the major project on *Enhancing Teaching-Learning Environments in Undergraduate Courses* (ETL Project, 2003), which investigated the TLE in different disciplines. Entwistle (2003) identifies how these influences combine to determine the quality of learning within the TLE.

Key actors are the students and the teachers. Students bring their existing knowledge and personal characteristics, their approach to learning and their perceptions and expectations of the TLE. Teachers normally determine what students are expected to learn. Major factors are the teachers' approaches to teaching how they select, organise, present and assess course materials, and how they design and implement the TLE. Teachers' approaches will in turn be influenced by their department, university, and the academic community in which they work (Entwistle, 2003, pp. 1-5).

Therefore this section describes the influences that contributed to the TLE of this particular class, starting by outlining the overall pedagogic approach and then articulating the principles adopted for course design. Disciplinary and institutional influences are identified. The section finishes by reflecting on the characteristics of the students taking the programme.

The overarching pedagogic approach for the BSc IM Programme is Inquiry Based Learning (IBL). Khan and O'Rourke (2005) have characterised IBL as involving students in engaging with their discipline through self-directed inquiries, often collaborative. A defining characteristic of IBL is that both the questions and the solutions are open ended (i.e. not determined by the tutor). This distinguishes it from Problem Based Learning (PBL): whereas PBL activities start with a problem set by the tutor (Savin-Baden & Major, 2004), a complete approach to IBL will involve the learner developing his/her own problem, and the range of outcomes will be correspondingly wide ranging.

Where inquiry skills are the goal of a whole programme (as is the case with the BSc Information Management), the IBL strategy may include PBL and other approaches that are used to scaffold learners' development, produce effective inquirers and raise confidence levels.

This focus on IBL partly arises from an institutional focus on IBL. Sheffield University hosts CILASS, one of the Centres for Excellence in Teaching and Learning financed by the Higher Education Funding Council for England (http://www.shef.ac.uk/cilass/). IBL is seen as an appropriate approach in a research-led university such as Sheffield, and IBL skills are identified as being required of a Sheffield graduate (Sheffield University, 2007). CILASS funds IBL projects, and the author was successful in gaining a CILASS award for purchase of a SL island for one year to host IBL activities. In terms of influences from the discipline of IM, the Quality Assurance Agency, which is the body which has responsibility for setting standards for, and evaluating, the quality of teaching in UK Higher Education, requires a subject benchmark statement to be drawn up for each subject taught at the undergraduate level in the UK. These benchmarks are developed by groups of experts in the discipline, and they describe the characteristics of programmes and the capabilities of graduates.

The subject benchmark for librarianship and IM (QAA, 2007) specifies that 'Because of the nature of the subject matter, HEIs [Higher Education Institutions] will be expected to place particular emphasis on inquiry and evidence-based practice, and to foster a high standard of ability to conduct research' (p. 5). Virtual environments are mentioned as possible venues for student learning. Additionally, understanding the use of technology is identified as being part of the discipline itself, including 'The ability to use a range of electronic communication and collaboration tools, including email, discussion lists and virtual environments' (p. 5). Thus both an IBL approach and use of SL follow recommendations for teaching of IM in the UK.

The adoption of an IBL approach from the start of university education is in line with the Boyer Commission's (1998) recommendations for an Inquiry Based freshman year. This is accommodated by the English practice of choosing the major area of university study on entry: in the BSc IM two thirds of the first year consists of compulsory IM classes. Brew (2006) also argues that an IBL approach helps people cope better with today's super-complex world 'we need to work with students to develop approaches to learning which teach both them and us how to live. This suggests a move towards more inclusive, collaborative, inquiry-based models of research, teaching and learning' (p. 15).

A blended learning strategy is used to implement the IBL approach in this campus-based programme, combining face-to-face and online teaching. Sharpe et al. (2006), in their review and study, identify three approaches to blended e-learning:

1. The provision of online supplementary resources (with an online source used to distribute course material);
2. Transformative course level practice underpinned by radical course design: in this approach the principle of constructive alignment (Biggs, 1999) of learning, teaching and assessment is applied, using a mix of technologies to foster learning and stimulate conceptual change;
3. A holistic view of technology used to support learning where 'the whole thing is blended together, any device, anytime, anyplace' (interviewee, quoted Sharpe et al., 2006, p. 26): this is more likely to characterise a whole-institution approach.

The second approach is the one espoused in designing the *Information Literacy* class. The course level teaching practice is transformative in aiming to support development of critical inquiry skills, and to challenge students to develop their own questions and arguments. The author's own conception of 'good' teaching of information literacy is that of facilitating understanding of the value of being information literate in life, study and work. She has been influenced by her own research into UK academics' conceptions of teaching information literacy (Webber & Johnston, 2005).

A constructive alignment approach to assessment is adopted, with learning activities developing skills and knowledge to enable students to tackle assignments more effectively, and the assignments requiring students to use the skills and knowledge gained in class, and to reflect on their learning. 45% of the *Information Literacy* class mark is for a reflective report (with evidence presented in an e-portfolio) on progress towards information literacy. 15% of the mark is for a review of a book or website, and 40% for a report on the student's contribution to a research study in information behaviour, which is described in more detail below.

As already noted, the characteristics, behaviour, expectations and knowledge of the students themselves contribute towards defining the learning environment and the quality of the learning outcomes. There are challenges, however, to engaged learning of the subject. IM is an unfamiliar discipline, not taught at school. It is therefore a contested discipline (Middleton, 2004) with uncertain boundaries. As well as introducing incoming students to theories and practice of IM, teachers also need to support students in identifying their own existing knowledge and skills relevant to IM.

Students are also unfamiliar with the term 'Information Literacy', as has been identified at the start of the class. The first session of *Information Literacy* briefly introduces a model of information literacy (the SCONUL seven pillars model; SCONUL, 1999). Students map their own strengths and weaknesses, individually and in groups, finally sharing this information with the whole class using PowerPoint and WebCT. This exercise identifies the variety of existing skills, and areas for development, and provides a base line for students' reflective e-portfolios on information literacy.

Surveys of students' use of ICT have been carried out in the second semester of the BSc IM programme and from this we know that (Cox, 2008b) most of our first years use Facebook for social networking, but that use of some other Web 2.0 tools, such as weblogs and wikis, is small. In 2007/8 none of the students in the Information Literacy class had used virtual worlds, and in 2008/9 two had used them, but very briefly.

THE BLENDED LEARNING ENVIRONMENT

Sharpe et al. (2006) note the multiplicity of definitions of blended learning, and propose eight dimensions that can be used to capture the ways in which blended learning is interpreted. These eight definitions can be applied to the *Information Literacy* class discussed here as follows:

- *Delivery* is as an on-campus programme;
  - **Chronology:** learner-tutor and peer-to-peer interaction is predominantly synchronous;
  - **Locus:** classroom-based (rather than practice-based);
  - **Roles for the students are:** information literate learner, collaborator (in group activities) and research assistant (in the SL research project); the class coordinator (the author) has the role of teacher, principal investigator (of the SL research project), facilitator of learning and lifelong learner;
- The *Pedagogic approach* has already been described;
  - **Focus is on the learning goals for the class:** these are framed to position the class as contributing to progression within the BSc programme and the student's lifecourse;
  - **Direction** is primarily from the class tutor, although there are activities in which the students need to manage themselves or their group;
  - **Technologies** used are the VLE WebCT, including the discussion board, group, and e-portfolio functions; the virtual world Second Life; Email; External web sites and search engines; and MS Office.

The three key teacher-facilitated learning environments were the physical classroom, WebCT and SL (students also use or create their own learning spaces at home, in the library etc.). The way in which these three key teacher-facilitated environments were used will be discussed further.

The Information Literacy class is taught in the Department's own teaching rooms. Face-to-face lectures are used to introduce the class and key topics within it, and, to explain connections between different activities. Lectures on information literacy and information behaviour are given by research-active academics who can speak eloquently about developments in the field (including their own research). Lectures are seen as valuable in communicating arguments, ideas and passion for the subject.

WebCT is used as a repository for lecture material, a means of communicating and sharing in group activities (with each group allocated a private discussion area), a notice board, a channel for interacting and sharing during class activities and a medium for creating and publishing evidence of information literacy (in the student's e-portfolio).

WebCT is the main educational technology supported by Sheffield University, and all classes in the Department of Information Studies use it to (at a minimum) store lecture materials. WebCT e-portfolios are also used for Personal Development Planning (PDP), maintaining a record of the students' development of employability skills. Therefore students need to feel comfortable with WebCT as a learning space for reflection and time is taken in first year classes to teach students how to use it.

The virtual world SL is used as an environment for carrying out research interviews; students have to develop SL communication skills and collect research data. SL also serves as an exhibition space for a key set of student presentations, bringing them to the attention of the wider world. Students are based on an island, Infolit iSchool that belongs to the University of Sheffield. Webber (2008) has described the island as being conceived for inquiry based and reflective activities.

BLENDING SL INTO THE STUDENTS' LEARNING ENVIRONMENT

SL has been characterised as a virtual world in that it is, for example (Warburton, 2009), persistent, involves embodiment as a three dimensional avatar who interacts with the environment and other avatars in real time, and is similar with the physical world in key ways, for example movement and topography. Jarmon (2008) identifies affordances of SL, including communication through various inworld (within SL) channels, embodied social presence, and the possibility for anyone (willing to develop the skills) to create 3-D objects and script them. This leads to possibilities for immersion in different languages and cultures, creation of learning communities internationally, and applications in work, leisure and education. Since SL is hosted and maintained by its North American creators, Linden Lab, it does not require special technical expertise to start using it, and anyone can sign up and create an avatar for free.

A regular series of surveys of the use of virtual worlds in UK Higher Education (HE) carried out for the Eduserv Foundation (Kirriemuir, 2007a, 2007b, 2008a, 2008c, 2009a, 2009c) has shown that SL is by far the most used virtual world, and is used in a very wide variety of disciplines. Kirriemuir (2009b) has estimated that 90% of UK Higher Education institutions have some kind of SL presence.

The author concurs with Salmon's (2009) view that 'we should not begin at the beginning with [SL] pedagogy, but rather reach back to our most abiding and productive educational models to inform our learning design' (p. 530). Findings from studies such as those of Mayrath et al. (2007) appear to confirm that good course design practice (such as making a clear connection between activities and learning) apply in SL as much as in any other environment. However, advice has emerged on specific ways in which learning to 'be' in SL can be scaffolded (e.g., Savin-Baden et al., 2009).

SL AND IBL

Since the land-cost of the SL island, Infolit iSchool, was funded by CILASS for its first year, the class coordinator was required to identify whether SL had potential as a site for IBL. CILASS has developed a conceptual framework for IBL which is derived from a longitudinal qualitative study of Sheffield University undergraduates' conceptions of learning (CILASS, 2008; Levy, 2008). In this research, a sample of students have been interviewed at regular intervals through all three years of their degree programme. The axes for this framework (see Figure 1) concern the people directing the inquiry (staff- or student-led) and the way in which the students are engaged with disciplinary knowledge (exploring existing knowledge, or building new knowledge). In the context of this matrix, 'Exploring the knowledge-base of the discipline', means searching for, or through, existing knowledge – for example, in journal articles. In the top half of the matrix, learners may be synthesising information to produce new insights, but they are not gathering and analysing new data to add to the knowledge base. In the bottom half of the matrix students are creating new disciplinary knowledge.

All these ways of experiencing IBL are valuable, scaffolding students' skills and knowledge to the point where they can confidently formulate their own meaningful research questions and interrogate the knowledge base effectively (to identify relevant literature to their question and use it to form and discuss their question).

In the first semester of the first year, i.e., the semester in which the Information Literacy class takes place, the emphasis is on the right hand side of the matrix. In the second semester, students move to the left hand side, identifying a new question for a group research project, and inquiry skills are developed to help students undertake their individual IM research project in the final year.

THE INTERVENTION IN SL

Levy (2003) has noted the need for 'thick' contextual descriptions in presenting accounts of action research. For this project, data was gathered in the form of: feedback from students through inworld chat with students and co-tutors (captured in chat transcripts); tutor observation of class activity; examination of student coursework (this coursework included student reflection and research interview transcripts); and tutor reflection (via personal journaling, interview and discussion with co-tutors acting as 'critical friends'). The planning phase of the action research cycle involved setting up the learning environments (SL, WebCT classroom); discussion about goals and activities with tutors and 'critical friends' with experience of SL teaching; preparing documentation and identifying what data would be gathered on the intervention.

In the *Information Literacy class* the goals are that, by the end of the module, students will have learnt how to:

Figure 1. The inquiry based learning model

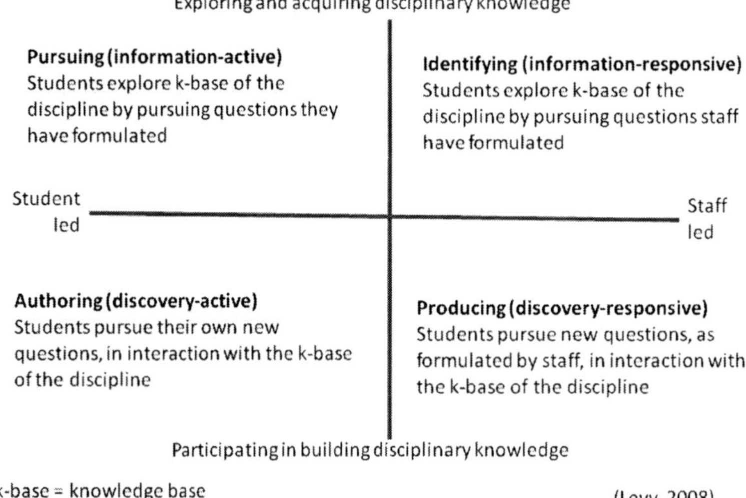
IBL conceptual framework
Exploring and acquiring disciplinary knowledge
Pursuing (information-active)
Students explore k-base of the discipline by pursuing questions they have formulated
Identifying (information-responsive)
Students explore k-base of the discipline by pursuing questions staff have formulated
Student led
Staff led
Authoring (discovery-active)
Students pursue their own new questions, in interaction with the k-base of the discipline
Producing (discovery-responsive)
Students pursue new questions, as formulated by staff, in interaction with the k-base of the discipline
Participating in building disciplinary knowledge
k-base = knowledge base
(Levy, 2008)

1. Analyse their own information behaviour and start to identify ways in which they can become more information literate;
2. Understand some key information literacy models and theories;
3. Plan a strategy for seeking information and search for information;
4. Apply an evaluation framework to information resources;
5. Interact with others to explore their information behaviour and needs;
6. Communicate more effectively orally and in writing.

The activities involving SL relate to goals 1, 5 and 6, and are associated with credit-bearing coursework, worth 40% of the class mark. The coursework requires students to carry out a research interview in SL, analyse transcripts in relation to real life information behaviour research models, and reflect on their performance as interviewers. As will described, scaffolding activities also target goals 1, 3 and 4.

In the following account the SL-related activities (only) will be described sequentially, as they ran in 2008/9. Following this, observations will be made on the relationship between the three learning environments (classroom, WebCT, SL) and between different modes of learning about information behaviour.

Week 1: Students are given a very short introduction to SL, shown how to sign up for an avatar, and told to register and tell the class coordinator their avatar name.

Week 2: A short introduction outlines why SL is relevant to the class, and why virtual world skills are relevant in careers in IM. Articles identifying use in business, especially by target employers, are brought to students' attention (e.g., Swabey, 2007).

Students follow a link to an induction area in SL, outdoors on Infolit iSchool, where they practice communicating with each other through chat, moving around, buying and opening boxes, wearing clothes and 'rezzing' objects.

There are three tutors for the scheduled SL sessions: one of which is the class coordinator, who is based in the lab with the students and is mainly focused on helping students navigate round the screen and encouraging them to help each other. A key aim is to make the initial SL experience non-threatening.

In both years one in-SL-only tutor has been a librarian based at St Andrews University in Scotland with good SL skills, able to collaborate without moving from her desk several hundred miles away. The second tutor varied between a librarian based at Sheffield University (but again based at her desk), a research assistant based elsewhere in the Department, and (to cover one session at a few days notice), a librarian from Edinburgh University, Scotland. This remote collaboration enables a better staff-student ratio in SL than is generally possible outside it.

Week 3: SL development is focused on those skills which are directly relevant to the compulsory task, i.e., research interviewing. In week 3 students pair off and select an island location to chat, instant message an allocated tutor to say where they are, and log their chat. They send the chat to their tutor in a notecard (within SL). Again the class tutor is in the lab with students, since apart from problems with SL, students also generally have issues with the institutional computer setup, which is still new to them.

Week 4: The first lecture introducing the meaning of information and information behaviour is given by a Professor in the field, with an associated exercise in which students explore their understanding of 'information'. Following this, students are briefed on a class (face-to-face) exercise which is phased over three weeks, and is designed to develop their searching, evaluation and presentation skills. The students are given a scenario: in 2007/8 and 2008/9 this was that a friend is thinking of going into SL, but is concerned about possible dangers, including Internet addiction.

The students form groups and each group searches for evidence about this problem to present in week 6. The exercise provides an opportunity for the students to discover more about SL, to start weighing evidence about it, and to raise any worries that they themselves have. The students also work further on developing their SL skills.

Week 5: Students are given a brief introduction to the skills of interviewing, and practice interviewing each other face-to-face in class, in triads (interviewee, interviewer, observer), and giving each other feedback. They then perform the same exercise in SL, with student pairs each observed by a tutor, and recording their text chat. The questions relate to the interviewee's information behaviour, and the script is a shortened version of one that the students use in the real interviews later in the semester. Text chat is used for all the SL sessions. Savin-Baden et al. (2009, p. 21) have noted that 'An experienced group can communicate surprisingly efficiently using text chat, a communication paradigm that is becoming ever more part of our culture.' Conducting interviews in text chat also means that there is a ready-made transcript.

Week 6: Students give their presentations in class and get formative feedback using the form that is used for summative assessment of presentations in the Department. The presentations are uploaded by the tutor into SL, for display in the Department's 'office'.

Week 7: The second session on information behaviour is held. Students learn about three particular models of information encountering (Erdelez, 1999), information seeking (Ellis & Haugan, 1997) and information visibility (Mansourian & Ford, 2007). The students also reflect on their own behaviour by completing survey instruments from Erdelez' and Mansourian's research.

Students are introduced formally to the research exercise that they will be participating in when they conduct their interviews. The research has gone through the University's research ethics approval process, and this process is explained to the students. The research question is 'What types of information behaviour can be identified in searches for information connected with SL activities?' This is a qualitative investigation, using a self-selecting sample of volunteers (mostly educators or librarians) recruited by the class coordinator via discussion lists or through personal contacts. This is justifiable in a novel research area, where there is little existing evidence. The class coordinator matches students with interviewees, provides an information sheet on the research, notifies both parties, and gives the students responsibility for setting up the interview.

The interview questions are designed to enable students to compare their results with findings from existing research into information behaviour in real life, but also to provide scope for further analysis. The students ask a SL resident to remember a time when s/he had an information need relating to a SL activity. The student then asks questions about information behaviour related to that need.

Students are reminded of the need to obtain informed consent, to ensure that the interviewee confirms that s/he has all the information they need about the research, to be well prepared, and to log the chat. The anonymous chatlog also has to be passed to the class coordinator. Each student is sent a second transcript, gathered by a classmate, so that each person analyses two interviews.

Week 8 onwards: Students should have carried out their interviews before week 11, to give them time to analyse their data and reflect on the process before submitting their assignment in week 12.

THE USE OF KEY LEARNING ENVIRONMENTS: WEBCT AND FACE-TO-FACE

All three environments, classroom, WebCT and SL, play a role in these activities. WebCT is primarily used archivally and as a point of interaction during class activities. It is archival, since it is the place where students can find tutor-created material that enables them to carry out their tasks: assignment and activity briefings, lecture PowerPoints, the ethics approval documents for the research, and up-to-date versions of the class schedule. Student feedback (e.g., from staff-student committees) shows that they like us to take a consistent approach in WebCT with this material. WebCT is also an archive for student-created content, in particular their pictures of SL and their presentations.

The formal physical spaces for this class are a small lecture room and two computer labs. WebCT is first encountered in the labs, and the Departmental lab is the place where a good deal of engagement with WebCT takes place, both in class and outside it. WebCT is also used from other labs and libraries on campus, and from home. Most sessions in this class involve using WebCT in some way, usually as part of an in-class activity (such as examining websites and posting evaluations, or commenting on other people's postings, or uploading presentations prior to presenting them to the class).

Private WebCT discussion boards are created for each of the 'SL dangers' presentation groups, and some student groups use these to exchange information on progress and upload their contributions to the joint PowerPoint. Students who miss sessions are also directed to carry out activities and post material in their own time and WebCT tracking shows that many of them do this. However, WebCT discussion boards set up for student questions on assessment and resources are used very little. Students prefer emailing tutors, asking for tutors' advice face-to-face or communicating between themselves in various ways, face-to-face and virtual. Students use some other functions, such as the WebCT blog feature, in activities concerned with creating their e-portfolio of evidence on their information literacy.

WebCT does not enable linkage of SL and web-based activity, and the link between the two environments merely exists in terms of archiving information about SL activity or checking information on activities to be carried out in SL. There is a more fluid link between face-to-face classroom activity and SL. The lab in which the students learn about SL is one in which they learn face-to-face in class, and they also use the lab outside class time as study area, and a site for social interaction. During the SL lab the tutor is interacting with the students inworld and face-to-face, and similarly the students interact with each other in-world and in class, particularly if they are seeking or giving help, or want to share something amusing.

CONTRIBUTION OF SL TO LEARNING

The aim of using SL to help students understand models of information behaviour was judged to be successful, on the basis of the students' performance in the assessed coursework. Students were able to reflect on their interviewing experience, and provided reasonable to excellent analyses of the interview transcripts, showing understanding of existing research models through the way in which they compared and contrasted their own findings.

Since each cohort of students is unique, detailed comparison with the previous year's exercise (an essay) would not have been meaningful. However, the author noted that the SL activity resulted in fewer superficial accounts of models (reproducing notes) since students had to make the effort to compare the research models to their own data. There were a larger number of excellent pieces of work than in previous years, and fewer poor ones. The author noted that the pieces were also easier to mark, since the comparison and analysis made it more evident whether or not students understood what they were writing about. There was also no evidence of plagiarism: incorporating new data meant that it was very difficult to find a copy-and-paste solution.

SL is valuable in mediating access to research participants (interviewees) from varied backgrounds and countries, and in providing opportunities to carry out novel research. In this way it provides a more authentic research experience; students can pursue new research questions and must learn to negotiate with genuine, and unfamiliar, research participants. Good et al. (2008, p. 170) have noted that SL, because of its novelty, is a good venue for setting 'problematic problems'.

The virtual environment also provides students with experiences which they can compare with their 'real life' experiences: notably experiences of interviewing and experiences of information behaviour. There is evidence of this reflective comparison in their coursework assignments, for example student 's' (2008/9) wrote that, 'In Second Life it is always going to be harder to anticipate how much your interviewee plans on saying', and student 'x' (2008/9) observed that 'Abbreviations were used often, but in the environment of a virtual world I believe this was appropriate, as it is acceptable for a meeting in such informal conditions'. Variation theory views learning as occurring when learners are able to discern the object of study in different ways, learning through perceiving and experiencing this variation (Pang & Marton, 2005). It is possible that experiencing the same phenomenon inside and outside a virtual world may enable this kind of discernment, and the author plans to explore the applicability of variation theory in SL further, in 2009/10.

As noted by Edirisingha et al. (2009), the 3-D environment enables interviewee and interviewer to engage in social conversation stimulated by artefacts or avatar movement. An example from a 2008/9 interview transcript demonstrates this:

Interviewee ***11:*** *so this is your university area.*

Interviewer*:* *ya*

Interviewee*:* *looks like a lot of work has been going on.*

This shows that as well as providing a wider range of interviewees (outside the immediate geographical location of Sheffield), SL also provides opportunities for building empathy between interviewer and interviewee, opportunities not available in 2-D online interviewing spaces, such as text chat rooms. Interviews took place in a variety of locations on the home island (from the Underwater Doughnuts to office space) and other locations chosen by interviewees. This freedom of choice provided challenges, for example to the student whose interviewee broke off to chase away griefers (troublemakers), bustling the interviewer along with her. However, these challenges provided opportunities for learning, as demonstrated in the students' reflective accounts of their interviews.

It has already been stated that the espoused approach to blended learning for this class was the second of those identified by Sharpe et al. (2006), namely transformative course level practice underpinned by radical course design which aims to foster learning and stimulate conceptual change. The structure of the learning environment

WebCT was identified as transmissive rather than constructivist or transformative. WebCT privileges the content produced by tutors and course designers, with student-created contributions limited to discussion and chat areas, except when students are creating content in their own e-portfolios. Thus, in terms of the IBL matrix in Figure 1, it provided a repository for disciplinary knowledge provided by the teacher and (to a much more limited extent) discovered by students: thus it engaged them only in 'information responsive' mode

SL appears to offer more opportunities as an environment to stimulate conceptual change in learners' thinking. Savin-Baden et al. (2009, p. 16) suggest that SL, as a Web 2.0 application, is suited to more student-centred approaches, such as intentional course design, in which there are 'multiple models of action, knowledge, reasoning and reflection, along with opportunities for the student to challenge, evaluate and interrogate them'. Bayne (2008) identifies SL as an 'uncanny space', not necessarily comfortable, but provoking reflection on different ways of thinking and being. She cites Barnett's description of his concept of pedagogy for uncertain times which 'itself has to be uncertain. It is open, it is daring, it is risky, it is itself, unpredictable' (Barnett cited in Bayne, 2008, p. 204).

BARRIERS TO ENGAGEMENT WITH SL AS A LEARNING ENVIRONMENT

In addition to the action research data already mentioned, the author contributed brief accounts of the intervention described in this paper to most of the Eduserv surveys of UK HE use of virtual worlds (see contributions from Webber in Kirriemuir 2007a, 2007b, 2008a, 2008b, 2008c, 2009c). These accounts highlight two institutional issues that were barriers to effective pedagogy: namely, computers that could not cope fully with the demands of SL in 2007/8, and, in both years that the module ran, students' limited access to SL on campus. SL had not been made available on the University's 'managed desktop' (so that it could not even be loaded from a memory stick), meaning that students could only use the Departmental computer lab that was open to them on weekdays until 5.30pm. In both years, the majority of students were not able to access SL effectively from their homes, and the wireless laptops that the Department was able to loan to students were not sufficiently high specification to make using SL effective. Warburton (2009) and others have identified technical issues as barriers to engagement with SL.

Herold (2009) notes that his Hong Kong media studies students perceived SL as a game, rather than a social networking tool or learning environment. As with the Hong Kong students, the BSc IM students lacked other friends in SL and did not see it as a place to socialise. The majority of BSc IM students only visited SL when required for class-related activities. Warburton (2009) has identified 'Lack of social persistence' as a characteristic of SL: you cannot see an avatar's social network, in contrast to the way in which a person's network and personal content become visible when you 'friend' them on a social networking site like Facebook. The author has observed new students showing each other Facebook profiles in face-to-face classes, as a way of introducing themselves: when you 'friend' someone on SL you are still restricted to a limited amount of information on their SL profile.

Jarmon (2009) has noted that researchers should distinguish between different levels of participation in SL when interpreting studies of its pedagogic use. These students did carry out an activity independently, but most did not initiate activities on their own. An exception was a student who used SL to stage pictures to illustrate the 'SL dangers' group presentation.

The activities and assessment involving SL can be mapped against the framework presented earlier in Figure 1. Students were 'information responsive' in exploring the knowledge base of the discipline through staff-formulated questions, by investigating the possible dangers of SL (using information from a variety of publications and web sources), and by using survey instruments produced by previous researchers to understand their own information behaviour. They also did this in a limited fashion by 'exploring' a 3-D model of the SCONUL seven pillars of information literacy within SL. Thus SL played a limited role in this mode of IBL, where the focus is on exploring an *existing* knowledge base (embodied in articles, artefacts, presentations etc.), since there is a limited amount of information about IM and IB within SL itself.

It is questionable whether setting up more ways of searching web-based catalogues or linking to web-based articles from within SL would add anything to the learning experience, since students would be using SL simply as a crude graphical interface. The majority of the IM knowledge base is outside SL and students need to develop their ability to identify and evaluate the sources that comprise the knowledge base, and learn to make sense of academic papers. Similarly, since this is a campus-based class with weekly face-to-face sessions, students might well question the value of simple discussion of IM articles in SL, particularly since most of them cannot access SL from home.

In terms of 'discovery responsive' IBL, with students pursuing new questions formulated by staff, students were able to collect data to analyse and to respond to the information behaviour research question formulated by the class coordinator. They interacted with the knowledge base of the discipline outside SL, in comparing their results with existing models of information behaviour. SL enabled movement into this 'discovery responsive' mode by providing the field for new inquiry (information behaviour in the context of a virtual world) and affording access to respondents outside Sheffield (and the UK), making the inquiry a more authentic and challenging experience. A 2007/8 student observed in an email to the course coordinator that 'I'd like to take this opportunity to say I "really" enjoyed doing the interview task - I'd say it made a great use of the advantages of Second Life, connecting to people who might be geographically far, far away, and giving a more personal element to the interaction that plain chat would not have had.'

In the following semester students moved into 'discovery-active' mode, when they identified their own research question in another class, Inquiry in Information Management. In 2008/9 SL was chosen as the subject of research by one group of students, who investigated whether their classmates thought that Second Life would have an impact on IM. It can be noted that the majority of those surveyed thought it would.

CONCLUSION AND FURTHER WORK

The aims of the action research were achieved, in that the quality of student work (judged to be the most important indicator) had improved, and it was easier to determine whether or not students had understood research models of information behaviour. It was also identified that SL was indeed a fruitful environment for IBL. Additionally, taking a blended approach made it easier to engage students with all quarters of the IBL matrix in Figure 1. WebCT ('information responsive') and SL ('discovery active/responsive') were complementary in this respect, while face to face work enabled various modes of IBL, and prepared students for online work.

SL has therefore made a positive contribution to the *Information Literacy* class. It has in turn influenced the TLE. The author has been provoked into reflecting further on pedagogy, discussing teaching and learning with inworld and out of world collaborators. Problems sometimes start discussion, but they result in more talk about teaching. The ability to instant message collaborators during SL teaching sessions also gives possibilities for private (between teachers) real-time debate and banter that is not feasible in face-to-face collaborative teaching. The addition of the new environment to the existing mix changes the ways in which the others are used, particularly face-to-face teaching, and thus the overall student learning experience.

As has already mentioned, the author intends to explore further the use of SL as a facilitator of learning through variation theory: enabling students to experience and reflect on variations in the ways in which subjects of study can be conceived.

Further research is also planned which uses the IBL conceptual framework as a starting point to investigate the extent to which students could engage more with the IM knowledge base within SL. There would be two goals: to deepen understanding of selected portions of the knowledge base, through reflection and critique, and to scaffold engagement with SL itself as a meaningful site for inquiry. The affordances of SL could be exploited through:

- Students spending more time interacting with, or building, models that represent important disciplinary concepts or theories, with the aim of deepening their understanding of the knowledge base. Since models of information literacy have already been constructed on Sheffield's own island and elsewhere, more active and critical use of these will be a first step.
- Students critiquing and comparing contributions to the disciplinary knowledge base that already exists in SL. An interesting issue is the extent to which the students can contribute to building or displaying the knowledge base, for exploration by future groups of students. So far this has happened through displaying the MS PowerPoint slides created about the dangers of SL by the 2008/9 cohort, and by mounting copies of posters presenting results of student mini-projects produced for a real life poster session in semester two of 2007/8. The knowledge base is also embodied in experts. Interacting with professors from other countries is an obvious application of SL, though real life time zone issues are a factor.
- Students locating and tagging the knowledge base as it exists in SL, reflecting on how they can make it retrievable by others. Up until now there has been so little that this would have been a rather fruitless exercise, but it is slowly becoming more worthwhile.

Discovering new worlds brings risks and rewards. Through careful planning of the teaching-learning environment, educators can make riskiness rewarding rather than fatal. The beneficiaries are the educators, the learners, and even the discipline itself.

ACKNOWLEDGMENT

I would like to thank Professor Nigel Ford for his help in revising the article. I would like to dedicate the article to Professor Leslie Jarmon, whose encouragement and support were invaluable and inspiring.

REFERENCES

Bayne, S. (2008). Uncanny spaces for higher education: teaching and learning in virtual worlds. *ALT-J*, *16*(3), 197–205. doi:doi:10.1080/09687760802526749

Biggs, J. (1999). *Teaching for quality learning at university*. Buckingham, UK: SRHE and Open University Press.

Brew, A. (2006). *Research and teaching: Beyond the divide*. London: Palgrave.

Centre for Inquiry Based Learning in the Arts and Social Sciences. (2008). *Inquiry-based learning: A conceptual framework*. Sheffield, UK: CILASS. Retrieved July 20, 2009, from http://www.shef.ac.uk/content/1/c6/07/93/44/Microsoft%20 Word%20-%20CILASS%20IBL%20Conceptual%20Framework%20_Version%202_.pdf

Cox, A., Levy, P., Stordy, P., & Webber, S. (2008a). Inquiry-based learning in the first-year information management curriculum. *Italics, 7*(1). Retrieved July 20, 2009, from http://www.ics.heacademy.ac.uk/italics/vol7iss1/pdf/Paper1.pdf

Cox, A., Tapril, S., Stordy, P., & Whittaker, S. (2008b). Teaching our grandchildren to suck eggs? Introducing the study of communication technologies to the 'Digital generation'. *Italics, 7*(1). Retrieved July 20, 2009, from http://www.ics.heacademy.ac.uk/italics/vol7iss1/pdf/Paper5.pdf

Edirisingha, P., Nie, M., Pluciennik, M., & Young, R. (2009). Socialisation for learning at a distance in a 3-D multi-user virtual environment. *British Journal of Educational Technology, 40*(3), 458–479. doi:doi:10.1111/j.1467-8535.2009.00962.x

Ellis, D., & Haugan, M. (1997). Modelling the information seeking patterns of engineers and research scientists in an industrial environment. *The Journal of Documentation, 53*(4), 384–403. doi:doi:10.1108/EUM0000000007204

Entwistle, N. (2003). *Concepts and conceptual frameworks underpinning the ETL project*. Edinburgh, UK: University of Edinburgh. Retrieved July 10, 2009, from http://www.ed.ac.uk/etl

Entwistle, N., & Smith, C. (2002). Personal understanding and target understanding: Mapping influences on the outcomes of learning. *The British Journal of Educational Psychology, 72*, 321–342. doi:doi:10.1348/000709902320634528

Erdelez, S. (1999). Information encountering: It's more than just bumping into information. *Bulletin of the American Association for Information Science, 25*(3), 25–29.

Good, J., Howland, K., & Thackray, L. (2008). Problem-based learning spanning real and virtual worlds: a case study in Second Life. *ALT-J, 16*(3), 163–172. doi:doi:10.1080/09687760802526681

Herold, D. K. (2009). Virtual education: Teaching media studies in Second Life. *Journal of Virtual Worlds Research, 2*(1), 3-17. Retrieved August 1, 2009, from https://journals.tdl.org/jvwr/article/view/380/454

Jarmon, L. (2008). Pedagogy and Learning in the Virtual World of *Second Life*. In Rogers, P. (Ed.), *Encyclopedia of distance and online learning* (2nd ed., *Vol. 3*, pp. 1610–1619). Hershey, PA: IGI Global.

Jarmon, L. (2009). An ecology of embodied interaction: pedagogy and homo virtualis. *Journal of virtual worlds research, 2*(1). Retrieved July 22, 2009, from https://journals.tdl.org/jvwr/article/view/624/453, Khan, P., & O'Rourke, K. (2005). Understanding Enquiry-based Learning. In T. Barrett, I. Mac Labhrainn, & H. Fallon (Eds.), *Handbook of enquiry and problem based learning.* Galway, Ireland: CELT. Retrieved August 1, 2009, from http://www.aishe.org/readings/2005-2/chapter1.pdf

Kirriemuir, J. (2007a). *A July 2007 'snapshot' of UK higher and further education developments in Second Life*. Bath, UK: Virtual World Watch, for the Eduserv Foundation. Retrieved August 5, 2009, from http://virtualworldwatch.net/wordpress/wp-content/uploads/2009/07/snapshot-one.pdf

Kirriemuir, J. (2007b). *An update of the July 2007 'snapshot' of UK higher and further education developments in Second Life.* Bath, UK: Virtual World Watch, for the Eduserv Foundation. Retrieved August 5, 2009, from http://virtualworldwatch.net/wordpress/wp-content/uploads/2009/07/snapshot-two.pdf

Kirriemuir, J. (2008a). *The autumn 2008 snapshot of UK higher and further education developments in Second Life*. Bath, UK: Virtual World Watch, for the Eduserv Foundation. Retrieved August 5, 2009, from http://virtualworldwatch.net/wordpress/wp-content/uploads/2009/07/snapshot-four.pdf

Kirriemuir, J. (2008b). *'Measuring' the impact of Second Life for educational purposes responses and Second Life meeting transcript.* Bath, UK: Eduserv Foundation. Retrieved August 5, 2009, from http://www.eduserv.org.uk/~/media/foundation/sl/impactreport032008/impactreport%20pdf.ashx

Kirriemuir, J. (2008c). *A spring 2008 'snapshot' of UK higher and further education developments in Second Life May 2008*. Bath, UK: Virtual World Watch, for the Eduserv Foundation. Retrieved August 5, 2009, from http://virtualworldwatch.net/wordpress/wp-content/uploads/2009/07/snapshot-three.pdf

Kirriemuir, J. (2009a). *Early summer 2009 Virtual World Watch snapshot of virtual world activity in UK HE and FE*. Bath, UK: Virtual World Watch, for the Eduserv Foundation. Retrieved August 5, 2009, from http://virtualworldwatch.net/wordpress/wp-content/uploads/2009/06/snapshot-six.pdf

Kirriemuir, J. (2009b, August 9). *Personal communication via email.*

Kirriemuir, J. (2009c). *The Spring 2009 snapshot of virtual world use in UK higher and further education*. Bath, UK: Virtual World Watch, for the Eduserv Foundation. Retrieved August 5, 2009, from http://www.scribd.com/doc/12459921/The-Spring-2009-Snapshot-of-Virtual-World-Use-in-UK-Higher-and-Further-Education

Levy, P. (2003). A methodological framework for practice-based research in networked learning. *Instructional Science*, *31*, 87–109. doi:doi:10.1023/A:1022594030184

Levy, P. (2008). 'I feel like a grown up person': First year undergraduates' experiences of inquiry and research. *Paper presented at a CILASS Research seminar.* Sheffield, UK: Centre for Inquiry Based Learning in the Arts and Social Sciences. Retrieved August 1, 2009, from http://www.shef.ac.uk/cilass/

Mansourian, Y., & Ford, N. (2007). Web searchers' attributions of success and failure: An empirical study. *The Journal of Documentation*, *63*(5), 659–679. doi:doi:10.1108/00220410710827745

Mayrath, M., Sanchez, J., Traphagan, T., Heikes, J., & Trivedi, A. (2007). Using Second Life in an English course: Designing class activities to address learning objectives. In *Proceedings of World Conference on Educational Multimedia, Hypermedia and Telecommunications 2007*. Chesapeake, VA: AACE. Retrieved August 20, 2009, from http://research.educatorscoop.org/EDMEDIA07.proceeding.pdf

Middleton, M. (2004). The way that information professionals describe their own discipline: a comparison of thesaurus descriptors. *New Library World*, *105*(11/12), 429–435. doi:doi:10.1108/03074800410568770

Pang, M. F., & Marton, F. (2005). Learning theory as teaching resource: Enhancing students' understanding of economic concepts. *Instructional Science*, *33*(2), 159–191. doi:doi:10.1007/s11251-005-2811-0

Project, E. T. L. (2003). *ETL Project*. Retrieved August 1, 2009, from http://www.ed.ac.uk/etl

Quality Assurance Agency. (2007). *Librarianship and information management.* Mansfield, UK: The Quality Assurance Agency for Higher Education. Retrieved August 1, 2009, from http://www.qaa.ac.uk/academicinfrastructure/benchmark/statements/Librarianship07.pdf

Salmon, G. (2009). The future for (second) life and learning. *British Journal of Educational Technology*, *40*(3), 526–538. doi:doi:10.1111/j.1467-8535.2009.00967.x

Savin-Baden, M., & Major, C. H. (2004). *Foundations of problem-based learning*. Maidenhead, UK: Open University Press.

Savin-Baden, M., Tombs, C., White, D., Poulton, D., Kavia, S., & Woodham, L. (2009). *Getting started with Second Life*. Bath, UK: JISC. Retrieved August 7, 2009, from http://www.jisc.ac.uk/media/documents/publications/gettingstartedwithsecondlife.pdf

SCONUL. (1999). *Information skills in higher education*. London: Society of College, National and University Libraries.

Sharpe, R., Benfield, G., Roberts, G., & Francis, R. (2006). *The undergraduate experience of blended e-learning: a review of UK literature and practice*. York, UK: Higher Education Academy. Retrieved January 10, 2010, from http://www.heacademy.ac.uk/assets/York/documents/ourwork/archive/blended_elearning_full_review.pdf

Sheffield University. (2007). *Shaping our learning, teaching and assessment future: Our shared vision*. Sheffield, UK: Sheffield University. Retrieved August 1, 2009, from http://www.shef.ac.uk/content/1/c6/08/20/69/SOLTAF%5B1%5D.pdf

Swabey, P. (2007, October). Serious business in virtual worlds. *Information Age*. Retrieved August 16, 2009, from http://www.information-age.com/search/274916/serious-business-in-virtual-worlds.thtml

The Boyer Commission on Educating Undergraduates in the Research University. (1998). *Reinventing undergraduate education: A blueprint for America's research universities*. New York: State University of New York. Retrieved July 20, 2009, from http://naples.cc.sunysb.edu/pres/boyer.nsf/673918d46fbf653e852565ec0056ff3e/d955b61ffddd590a852565ec005717ae/$FILE/boyer.pdf

Warburton, S. (2009). Second Life in higher education: Assessing the potential for and the barriers to deploying virtual worlds in learning and teaching. *British Journal of Educational Technology*, *40*(3), 414–426. doi:doi:10.1111/j.1467-8535.2009.00952.x

Webber, S. (2008). *An exploration of the island*. Retrieved August 20, 2009, from http://infolitischool.pbworks.com/An+exploration+of+the+island

Webber, S., & Johnston, B. (2005, September 6-8). Information literacy in the curriculum: selected findings from a phenomenographic study of UK conceptions of, and pedagogy for, information literacy. In C. Rust (Ed.), *Proceedings of Improving student learning: Diversity and inclusivity: the 11th ISL symposium*, Birmingham, UK (pp. 212-224.) Oxford, UK: Oxford Brookes University.

This work was previously published in International Journal of Virtual and Personal Learning Environments, edited by Michael Thomas, Volume 1, Issue 3, pp. 55-70, copyright 2010 by IGI Publishing (an imprint of IGI Global).

Chapter 14
Low-Cost Virtual Laboratory Workbench for Electronic Engineering

Ifeyinwa E. Achumba
University of Portsmouth, UK

Djamel Azzi
University of Portsmouth, UK

James Stocker
University of Portsmouth, UK

ABSTRACT

The laboratory component of undergraduate engineering education poses challenges in resource constrained engineering faculties. The cost, time, space and physical presence requirements of the traditional (real) laboratory approach are the contributory factors. These resource constraints may mitigate the acquisition of meaningful laboratory experiences by students, which is especially true in developing countries. Virtual laboratories can be used to complement the traditional laboratory to enhance students' laboratory experience. In extreme cases of lack of resources, the virtual lab can be used as an alternative laboratory. Although some research on the implementation of virtual laboratories has occurred, more efforts are required because of the diverse experiential needs and requirements of the engineering curriculum. This paper presents a low-cost, web-based virtual laboratory workbench for use as part of undergraduate electronic engineering courses. Some distinguishing features of the virtual workbench are that students can undertake curriculum-based laboratory activities in a realistic manner; it integrates a Bayesian Network-based assessment structure for the assessment of students' performance; and it affords the instructor flexibility in designing laboratory exercises.

INTRODUCTION

Laboratory activities are crucial components of engineering education. Some of their benefits in engineering education include: helping students to deepen their understanding of taught concepts through relating theory to practice; and motivating students' interest in a subject (Davies, 2008). Computer Aided Learning (CAL) tools can be used to enhance laboratory learning in various ways. Advances in web and computer technologies continue to facilitate the provision of improved

DOI: 10.4018/978-1-4666-1770-4.ch014

laboratory learning and experimentation. CAL tools provide improved environments for laboratory education that are comparable to and in some cases better than the traditional method (Li, 2005).

Virtual laboratories are CAL tools that can provide laboratory learning environments in a wide variety of forms and formats beyond the limitations of the traditional laboratory. Research evidence has proven the effectiveness of virtual laboratories in enhancing students' laboratory learning and performance (Campbell et al., 2002). In some cases, the evidence contradicts popular hypotheses that physical presence and face-to-face instructor-student interactions provide more valuable experiences and produce better learning results.

Although virtual laboratories have proven useful in many areas of education, their use in engineering laboratory education is still a challenge because of numerous experiential requirements. Thus, for various fields of engineering, research is on-going on virtual laboratories that can emulate the traditional laboratory processes. The aim is not to replace the traditional laboratory with virtual laboratories but to complement it (Mannix, 2000). Virtual laboratories provide meaningful laboratory experiences (Davies, 2008) and also serve as alternatives in extreme cases (Budhu, 2002). This is because they can be used to provide meaningful laboratory experiences (Davies, 2008).

Presently, the Internet is widely utilized as a platform for web-based virtual laboratories. This paper presents a web-based virtual laboratory workbench with which electronic engineering undergraduate students can undertake curriculum-based laboratory activities in a realistic manner. The workbench has a wide curriculum scope and is not limited to a single area or level of application, thus affording instructors flexibility in designing laboratory exercises. In addition, the virtual laboratory incorporates a Bayesian network-based laboratory performance assessment model for assessing students' laboratory activities from a holistic perspective.

MOTIVATION

In the early years of Electrical and Electronic Engineering (EEE) degree programmes, undergraduate students face the challenge of grasping the fundamental concepts taught in lectures. In universities offering a 5-year undergraduate EEE programme such as the Federal University of Technology, Owerri (FUTO), Nigeria, all the EEE students offer the same course units in their first three years of study. During this three-year period, the students are exposed to the foundations of science and general studies, fundamental EEE course principles and circuit theory. Laboratory activities are concentrated mainly in the second and third years of study. At the end of the third year, students choose their preferred EEE course options: Communication Engineering (COE), Power Systems Engineering (PSE) and Electronic and Computer Engineering (ECE). As the students enter into their fourth and fifth years of study, they concentrate mainly on course units for their respective options. At this level, they begin to apply the fundamental concepts learnt in their earlier years to specific problem contexts.

Research has shown that students find it difficult to grasp the fundamental concepts taught in the early years of EEE degree programme (Gilbert, 2003). Laboratory activities can be used to enhance students' understanding of concepts taught in lectures. However, laboratory education can present a number of challenges to engineering faculties, especially those in developing countries which often lack meaningful laboratory resources because of resource constraints and students often far outnumber the available laboratory equipment. The severity of these challenges in developing countries is such that some students may graduate without the opportunity for meaningful laboratory experiences. The cost, time, space and physical presence requirements of the traditional engineering laboratory approach are major contributory factors to these challenges. A web-based virtual laboratory has the potential to address most of these militating factors.

Another challenge faced by engineering faculties is the performance assessment of students' laboratory activities. The traditional method of assessing the performance of students' laboratory activities is by marking the written reports of laboratory activities produced by students. This method of assessment can be time consuming, typically 33 working hours per week for classes of around 200 students (Hughes, 2004). Large classes pose the additional problems of fair and consistent assessment of laboratory activities due to human bias. Large student numbers and a decreasing number of instructors make it difficult to continue this approach.

These challenges are the major motivating factors behind the research context addressed in this paper. The objective is to provide both instructor and students with a tool which provides a realistic laboratory environment (albeit virtual) to increase the use of laboratory activities to enhance students' understanding of fundamental engineering concepts. Enhancing the understanding of fundamental engineering concepts will help lay a more solid foundation for students on which to build in later undergraduate and professional years.

RELATED WORK ON VIRTUAL LABORATORIES

There has been considerable research and attempts at implementation vis-à-vis virtual laboratories to date. In this section, the concept of a virtual laboratory is introduced and some work on virtual laboratories that demonstrate the feasibility and benefits of virtual laboratories in engineering education are cited. Throughout the literature, the concept of the virtual laboratory is used in an inconsistent and confusing manner. Online teaching and learning environments and remote laboratories are often referred to as virtual laboratories. In this context, the definition given by Auer (2000) is adopted: Virtual laboratories are software versions of the real laboratory where experimental setups are implemented in software such that a personal computer can take the place of a laboratory workbench. Virtual laboratories differ from remote laboratories in that remote laboratories are characterized by mediated reality (Ma & Nickerson, 2006). Remote laboratories are real laboratories with remote user presence and internet/web mediated access and operations. Laboratory devices are interfaced to and manipulated by a local computer. The device is then remotely controlled over the Internet. This requires the existence of a middleware that will allow remote clients to connect to the local computer, in order to manipulate the device.

There are websites associated with some of them and many more are reported in research literature. For instance, a simulated virtual laboratory for teaching power system dynamics and control was presented by Vanfreti (2007). The laboratory was built by obtaining a customized computer application for laboratory topics using Matlab and Simulink simulation tools. Palop and Teruel (2000) presented a Virtual WorkBench, a collection of simulation tools, for teaching analog to digital conversion, digital signal processing, digital filters and Fourier transforms. The Virtual WorkBench was developed using a combination of tools: LabVIEW, Matlab, Multisim, Spice and Electronic Work Bench (EWB). Other examples include the MATLAB-based electromagnetic fields virtual laboratory reported by de Magistris (2005), and the set of configurable java applets for teaching photonics by Gopalan and Cartwright (2006). The implementation of virtual laboratories is also reported by Zhou and Lo (2007) and Duarte and Mahalingam (2008). The virtual laboratory by Zhou and Lo (2005) is, like that of de Magistris (2005), a set of java simulation applets used for enhancing students' understanding of the concepts taught in a course unit on random signals and noise. The virtual laboratory by Duarte and Mahalingam (2008), intended to provide meaningful laboratory

Figure 1. High-level view of the virtual laboratory workbench

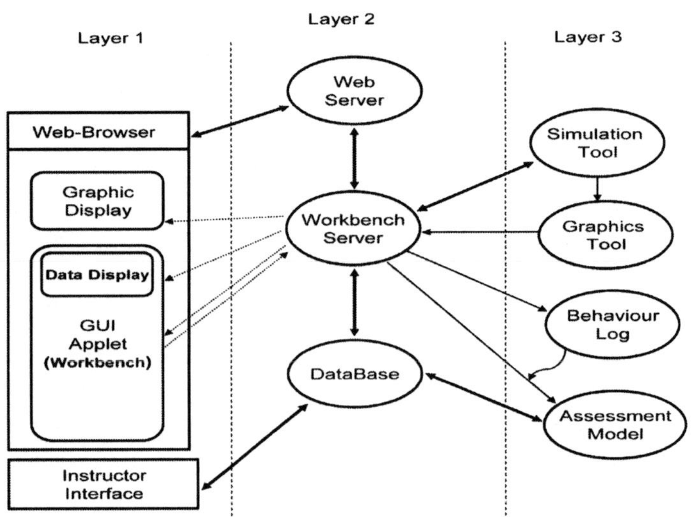

experiences for students with motor disabilities, made intensive use of commercial software tools.

Generally, these virtual laboratory implementations exhibit relative limitations in that they are based on commercial software tools (Matlab, Simulink, PSpice, LabVIEW, Multisim and Authorware, ORCAD) that may be expensive to licence and therefore not suitable for resource constrained faculties. The implementations that employed java applet technology are merely a collection of simulation tools for the demonstration of concepts and therefore not intended for use to perform curriculum-based experiments.

Furthermore, although virtual laboratories can alleviate most of the difficulties and inconveniences associated with the traditional laboratory, they are still not available for the whole spectrum of EEE. Existing virtual laboratories address specific experiments or a group of experiments and the majority are hybrid. Most importantly, the integration of any form of assessment structure (on- or off-line) for the performance assessment of students' laboratory activities is none existent. The virtual laboratory workbench presented in this paper is low cost and can be used to perform curriculum-based experiments. It also incorporates an assessment model for the performance assessment of student's laboratory activities.

SYSTEM ARCHITECTURE

By definition, the virtual laboratory workbench is a virtual learning software environment with which to practically construct and simulate electronic circuits in a realistic manner. The workbench is web-based, meaning that access to its interface is through a web-browser. This section gives a description of the virtual laboratory workbench in terms of its high-level structure as shown in Figure 1.

Essentially, the virtual laboratory workbench is based on the client-server concept and has a three-layer architecture. The client is the workbench applet which runs inside a browser and provides the user with an innovative interactive Graphical User Interface (GUI) with which to realistically construct and simulate circuits. The server facilitates user access to the workbench. The server interfaces between the workbench, circuit simulation, graphic tools and database. The workbench needs to access the database for

Figure 2. The virtual laboratory workbench GUI

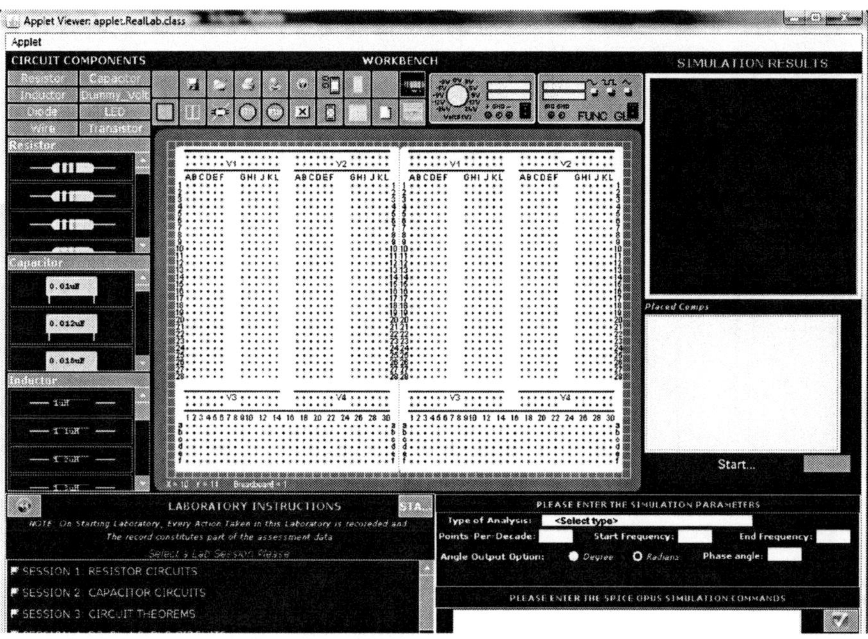

user authentication, access control and logging of user behaviour data. The components and devices required to build a circuit are laid out on the workbench GUI. Communication between the client and the server is achieved using Remote Method Invocation (RMI) technology. Java DataBase Connectivity (JDBC) technology is used for communication with the database. User laboratory attendance records (login and logout times and date, laboratory activity performed, and so on) are recorded on the database.

THE WORKBENCH FRONT-END (THE CLIENT-SIDE)

The virtual workbench front-end, the client application, consists of a java applet that provides a GUI for the user. Figure 2 shows the workbench front-end which provides the user with the facilities and features to perform curriculum-based laboratory activities. The user can select, pick and drop any of the components, place or remove a picked up component on the breadboard, and make connections using wires of assorted colours, among other functions. The user has the option of using either a single breadboard or two cascaded breadboards.

The GUI has eight main panels: the components, tools, bench, laboratory instructions, assessment/simulation commands, simulation result, calculator and placed components panels. The components panel holds all the circuit components required to construct a circuit. The bench panel is used for placing the breadboard(s) in order to undertake circuit construction. The breadboard provides both vertical and horizontal grids numbered A to L and 1 to 28 respectively, with power and ground rails. The tools panel contains two basic input devices: the power supply and the function generator. Square, triangular or sinusoidal signal with different frequencies and amplitude can be selected on the function generator. Also, located in the tools panel is the menu bar which consists of the clickable buttons for clearing the workbench or the breadboard, switching between single and cascaded breadboard, among other functions. The simulation output is displayed on the Simulation results panel. A calculator is pro-

Figure 3. The back-end sequence of events

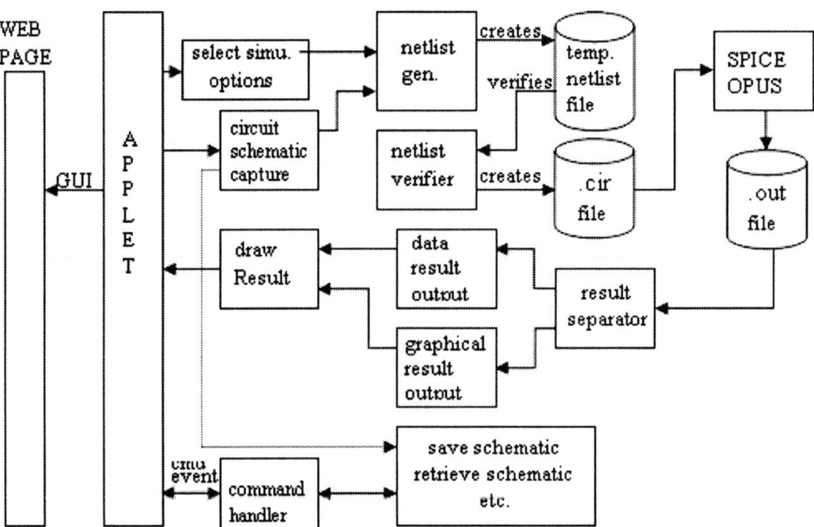

vided on the interface for any calculations as may be necessary. Students are encouraged to do all calculations using the integrated calculator so their actions can be 'observed' and logged. The components placed on the breadboard are numbered in the order in which they are placed, according to their component types, such as R1, R2, R3, for resistors, and displayed in the placed components panel, together with their values and the nodes to which they are connected. This helps the user to identify each component on the breadboard at any point in time and is also used for issuing commands for circuit simulation. Laboratory instructions are displayed in the instruction panel. After circuit construction, simulation is initiated by clicking on the SIM button in the tools panel. This triggers a number of events at the back-end of the virtual workbench.

THE WORKBENCH BACK-END (THE SERVER-SIDE)

The series of events that take place at the back-end, from constructing a circuit to simulating the circuit and generating output is highlighted in Figure 3. At the backend, on the server machine, the server applications and the simulation software package, SpiceOpus, run. The DataBase Management System (DBMS), MySQL, and the web server, Apache, run under XAMPP, an integrated server package. Both SpiceOpus and XAMPP are freeware. Also running on the server is the Netlist Parser developed as part of the virtual workbench project.

On completion of circuit construction, the schematic of the constructed circuit is captured. The netlist generator uses the schematic to create a netlist. The netlist parser verifies the correctness of the generated netlist in order to ensure that it can be simulated. Spice Opus is then invoked to simulate the circuit using the netlist. The netlist generation steps are detailed in the sub-section on netlist generation. The circuit simulator runs the actual simulation process by being invoked through a command line call. When the simulation is finished, the results are returned to the applet for display in the Simulation result panel. Graphs of different vectors can be plotted and visualized in the virtual laboratory environment.

Table 1. Netlist file description of the circuit of Figure 5

```
vcc 1 0 dc 12V
rl 1 2 2.2k
r2 2 3 2.2k
r3 1 4 4.7k
r4 4 3 4.7k
r5 4 5 2k
r6 5 6 2k
r7 3 7 2k
r8 7 6 2k
r9 6 0 2k
```

Figure 4. Sample circuit schematic (Adapted from Harb, 2000)

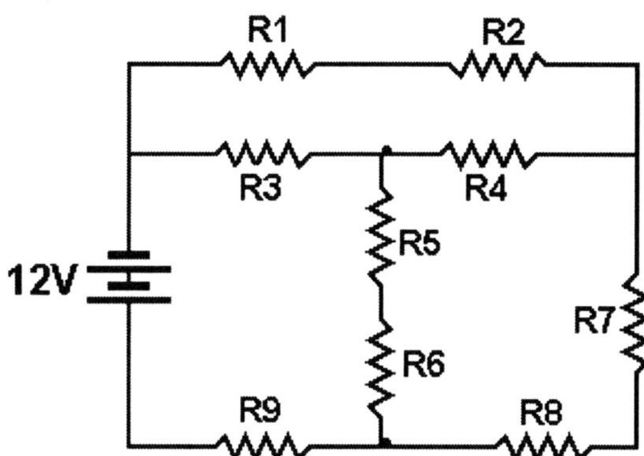

Netlist Generation

A captured circuit schematic contains the list of components used to construct the circuit and their contact positions on the breadboard. Essentially, a schematic is a set of vectors of the form (<ComponentName>, <ComponentValue>, <x1>, <y1>, <x2>, <y2>), where the x1, y1 and x2, y2 pairs indicate the first and second contact positions (coordinates) on the breadboard respectively. One aim of the netlist generation process is to covert the x1, y1 and x2, y2 coordinate pairs to actual node positions on the circuit. Three main steps are involved in the netlist generation process:

- Wire removal (circuit collapse).
- Nodes identification and node number assignment.
- Components' left and right nodes number assignment based on their contact positions on the breadboard.

The output of the process is a netlist which is a set of vectors of the form: (<Component Name> <Node left> <Node right> <Value> <Unit>). The vector contains all the information required by the simulation tool to simulate the circuit. Figure 4 shows a sample circuit schematic and Figure 5 shows the same circuit after the circuit collapse and node assignment steps. The nodes are numbered 0 to 7 with thick black dots indicating the nodes. The netlist file description of the circuit is listed in Table 1. The netlist is passed to Spice-Opus which simulates the circuit and returns the results to the server.

DESIGN AND IMPLEMENTATION ISSUES

The objective of this work was to design and implement a web-based virtual laboratory workbench for EEE undergraduate courses. A number of factors were taken into consideration in the development of the virtual workbench. Cost consideration was a major factor, bearing in mind faculties in developing countries that may be resource constrained and have need for a complement or alternative to the traditional laboratory. The system is implemented using java technologies and freeware software to ensure low cost. The main challenges of using freeware software are twofold: they are offered in their downloaded form without warranty. The user takes responsibility for use as they do not necessarily come with any form of technical support. The user is also reliant on discussion forums and the goodwill of the freeware developers.

Java was chosen for the development of the virtual workbench for a number of reasons. The virtual laboratory is web-based and the Java GUI applet has to be displayed in web-browsers. Java is

Figure 5. Output of the circuit collapse process

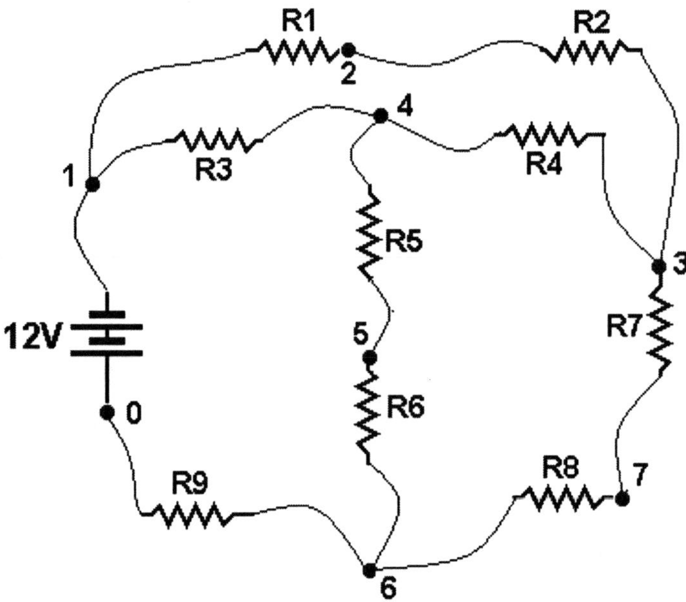

machine-independent which inherently solves the problem of running the code on different platforms, as students will be accessing the virtual laboratory from different computers. In addition, Java applet codes do not reside on the client computer but are downloaded and executed on the fly and therefore make no demand on the client's resources. Java eliminates most of the problems exhibited by codes developed in other languages, such as deceptive interactivity (Hamza, Alhalabi, & Marcovitz, 2000). Java's multithreading feature allows for concurrent executions of a code which makes it possible for many students to access the virtual laboratory and communicate with the workbench server simultaneously. Its object oriented nature facilities system design and development and its RMI technology provides a persistent mode for client/server connection which eliminates extra server overheads thereby improving performance.

Another influencing factor was user interface clustering. Classical (textual and form-based) user interfaces do have some advantages. They can download fast and run reliably on any standard browser. However, classical user interfaces can be intimidating and the desktop is often clustered with multiple frames (del Alamo et al., 2003). Having multiple frames open at once clusters the desktop and may result in confusion. An integrated interface that combines all the necessary panels into a single window with minimum textual components was created. Failing this, a minimum of seven different widows would have been required. This helped avoid clustering and makes the user experience more intuitive. We also avoided the use of popup windows which are considered to be annoying (Mavrikis, 2005). In this particular case of a virtual laboratory where student interactions would be systematically logged, the use of popup windows was not considered desirable. We resorted to the technique of removing panes that were not immediately in use and replacing them with ones that were immediately in use. The removed panes were replaced when required. For example, after a student had finished carrying out a laboratory activity, the simulation commands pane was no longer required. It was removed and replaced with the activity results pane to enable students to enter their laboratory activity results for assessment.

In addition, equipment in the real laboratory are often near-research-grade complex, multi-mode and multi-function instruments. These are often intimidating and difficult for students to understand and use. The instructor ends up providing a laboratory instruction sheet that includes a 'button pushing recipe' that leads the students 'by the nose' to use the equipment, which impinges on the limited laboratory time slot (Siegel, 2002). In view of this, given the students' level and limited experience, only instruments that are no more complex than is necessary to carry out laboratory activities are provided. Namely, power supply and function generator.

Essentially, the design and implementation of the virtual laboratory workbench was driven by need. The first step in the creation of a virtual laboratory is to define the need and it should be ensured that the end product of the implementation process is functionally satisfying.

LABORATORY ACTIVITY PERFORMANCE ASSESSMENT

The critical role of laboratory activities in engineering education makes the ongoing challenge of performance assessment of students' laboratory activities one of the utmost importance. Marking students' laboratory activity reports is time-consuming for instructors, especially for large classes. The performance assessment of laboratory work is further compounded by the proliferation of virtual laboratories. In the virtual laboratory, assessment is no less critical because it is a major driving force for all learning activities and without it, there is no measure of student performance (QAA, 2006).

In view of this, a Bayesian network-based laboratory performance assessment model is incorporated into the virtual workbench environment. Assessment is based on a student's behaviour while interacting with the environment. Behaviour refers to what a student does in terms of key presses, mouse clicks and responses to questions and test items. The behaviour log is analyzed at different levels of granularity in order to generate input data for the assessment model.

There are several ways to capture and log students' interaction events in a laboratory environment. One option is either the use of cameras, tape recorders and/or screen capture software. It is costly and difficult to setup and analyze the recorded data using such tools (Mavrikis, 2005). An alternative is to have the instructor unconstructively observe each student, and record assessment data, while students are interacting with the environment. This technique may be impracticable for large classes as the instructor may not be able to carefully observe each student. Another alternative is to incorporate a software agent that can unconstructively 'observe' students and log the interaction events for analysis. This approach is widely adopted by researchers (Mavrikis, 2005; Stathacoulopous et al., 2007; Vanlehn, 2001). This technique requires that prior decision be made about what interaction events are relevant for the intended analysis because it is necessary that the logged data fits the intended analysis. This data gathering technique is adopted in this work. An agent consisting of an events tracker and recorder is programmed into the virtual workbench. The agent tracks and records key presses, mouse clicks and mouse movement events with respect to the workbench GUI components. The format of each event record is: <time_of_the_event><type_of_event><the_component_involved_in_the_event><value_of_the_component><event_trigger_source_(mouse/keyboard)>.

The events logged include component (such resistor or capacitor) selection, pickup and placement on the breadboard, dropping of picked up components, removal of a component connected on the breadboard and search for a component in a component container. The logged events are transformed and analyzed at different levels of granularity to extract evidential data for input into the assessment model. Transformation involves

Figure 6. High-level diagrammatic representation of the virtual laboratory with integrated assessment model

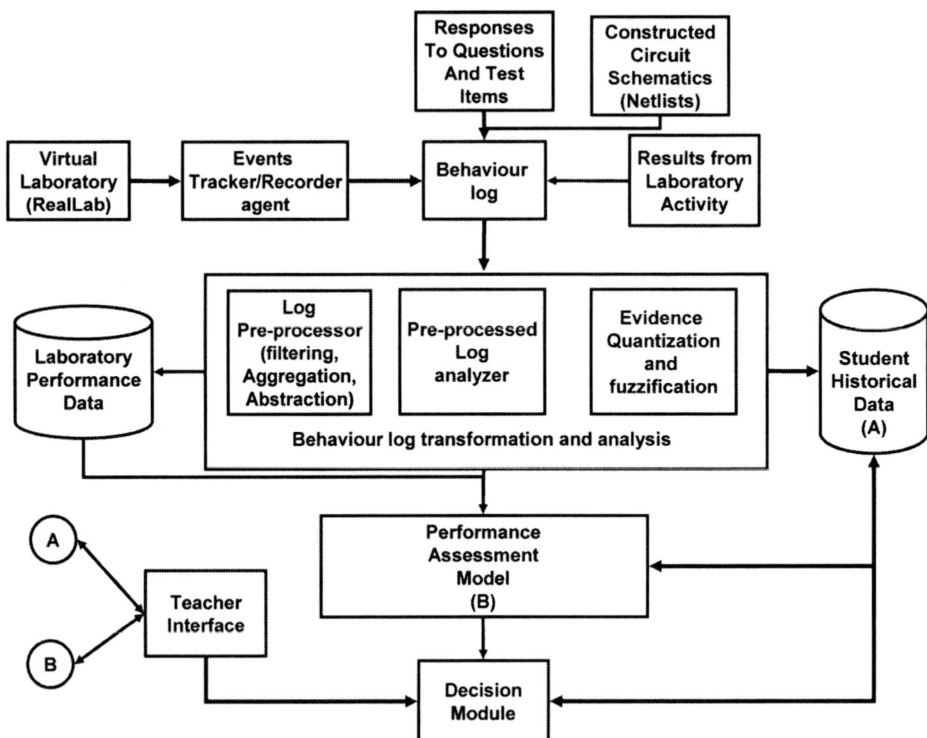

filtering, aggregation and abstraction. Attendance records (login and logout times and date, laboratory activity performed, and so on) are also logged for analysis and information to the instructor.

Detailed description of the assessment model is the subject of another paper but descriptions of its preliminary design issues are given in Chika et al. (2009), while the details of its conceptual foundation can be found in Chika et al. (2008). Figure 6 shows a high-level diagrammatic representation of the virtual laboratory with the integrated performance assessment model.

PEDAGOGICAL APPLICATION

The virtual laboratory workbench can be used to carry out curriculum-based laboratory activities. Therefore, it can be effectively employed by the instructor to enhance students' understanding of fundamental engineering concepts taught in the classroom. It is important that students fully grasp the fundamental engineering concepts in the early undergraduate years. This view is supported by theories of learning and cognitive development. The most accepted and applied theories of learning and cognitive development are those by Jean Piaget (1970) and William G. Perry (1959). Piaget focused on child cognitive development while Perry (1959) focused on university students' cognitive development. Perry's theory postulates that students may not learn a concept if they have not learnt its prerequisite concepts (Wankat & Oreovicz, 1993). An attempt to teach them concepts which they are unable to learn (concepts above their current level of learning) leads to frustration, confusion and memorization without assimilation (Wankat & Oreovicz, 1993). The onus is on the instructor to design laboratory activities that promote students' understanding of specific concepts.

It is not the goal of the virtual laboratory to define the laboratory learning activities and goals. It is left to the instructor to design experiments and ensure that each practical exercise fits in with the overall aims of the course unit. The instructor has to deal with the challenges of designing laboratory learning within electronic engineering curriculum (Davies, 2008). Ideas and practical guides for this have been given by Davies (2008). A poorly designed laboratory activity may offer little added value while a well-designed activity can make an invaluable contribution to students' learning (Edward, 2002).

The contents of a course unit can be grouped into knowledge goals. Each knowledge goal can have a set of outcome concepts and pre-requisite concepts. The prerequisite concepts are those the learner should have prior knowledge of in order to fully understand the outcome concepts. The instructor can design laboratory activities and group them into sessions. Each laboratory session can address a specific knowledge goal. Table 2 highlights an electronic engineering knowledge goal, its outcome concepts and pre-requisite concepts. Laboratory activities can then be designed to address aspects of the outcome concepts, with clear learning objectives. Learning objectives are essential in applying an effective system of assessment (Feisel & Rosa, 2005).

This approach ensures that students carry out concept-based laboratory activities in order to ensure full understanding of knowledge goals whose theories have been learnt in the lectures. Figure 7 is a sample laboratory activity, from the set of activities used for the evaluation of the virtual laboratory workbench. The activity involves a number of tasks: selecting the correct circuit components and connecting them together properly in order to meet functional expectation; loading an electronic circuit; plotting a graph; calculation; measurement; and graph observation and interpretation.

Table 2. A knowledge goal with some outcome and pre-requisite concepts

Knowledge Goal: Filters		
No.	Outcome Concept	Prerequisite Concept
1	Low pass filters	R, L, C circuit components characteristics
2	High pass filters	
3	Band pass filters	
4	All pass filters	
5	Band reject (Notch) filters	

Figure 8 shows the constructed circuit for the laboratory activity of Figure 7, on the virtual laboratory workbench breadboard while Figure 9 shows the graph plotted in the virtual laboratory as part of the laboratory activity of Figure 7.

Obviously, in order to undertake this laboratory activity, the student must know and understand the resistor colour coding scheme in order to select and use the right resistor, as in the case of traditional laboratory. Also, the student has to connect the function generator to the breadboard, switch it on, select the desired signal type (sinusoid, square or triangular) and set the signal amplitude. It also entails that the student has a good understanding of the layout of the breadboard and the interconnections (continuities and discontinuities) of its grid lines, as in the traditional laboratory environment.

This pedagogical approach to engineering laboratory education using the virtual electronic workbench is in conformity with the student-centred learning paradigm (Barr & Tagg, 1995). Student-centred learning emphasises the promotion of experiential learning and enhanced active student participation. The virtual workbench is a tool with which active student participation can be enhanced.

Figure 7. Sample laboratory activity that can be undertaken in the virtual workbench environment

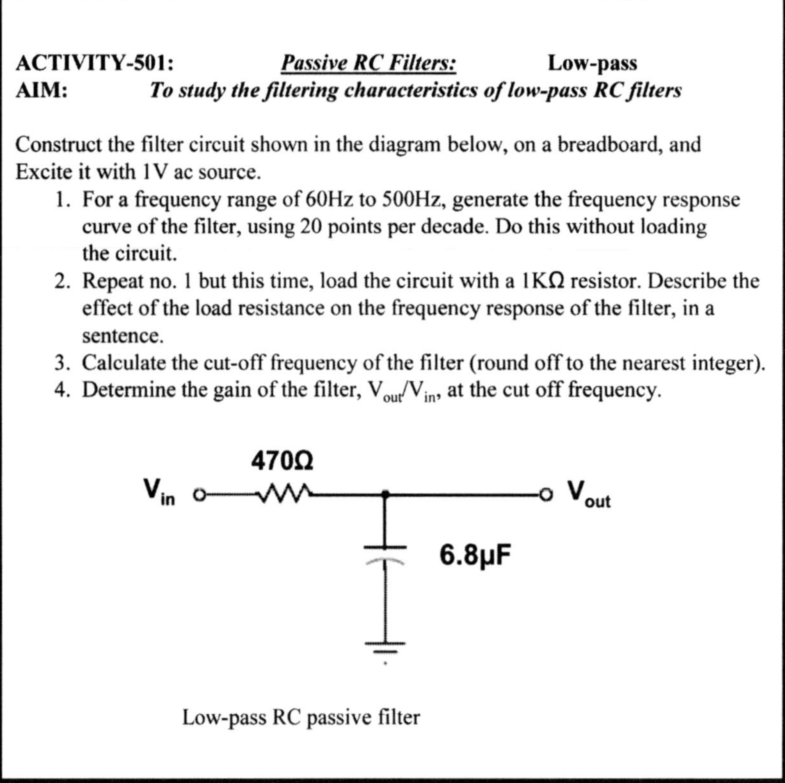

ACTIVITY-501: ***Passive RC Filters:*** **Low-pass**
AIM: ***To study the filtering characteristics of low-pass RC filters***

Construct the filter circuit shown in the diagram below, on a breadboard, and Excite it with 1V ac source.

1. For a frequency range of 60Hz to 500Hz, generate the frequency response curve of the filter, using 20 points per decade. Do this without loading the circuit.
2. Repeat no. 1 but this time, load the circuit with a 1KΩ resistor. Describe the effect of the load resistance on the frequency response of the filter, in a sentence.
3. Calculate the cut-off frequency of the filter (round off to the nearest integer).
4. Determine the gain of the filter, V_{out}/V_{in}, at the cut off frequency.

Low-pass RC passive filter

Figure 8. Constructed circuit of the laboratory activity of Figure 7

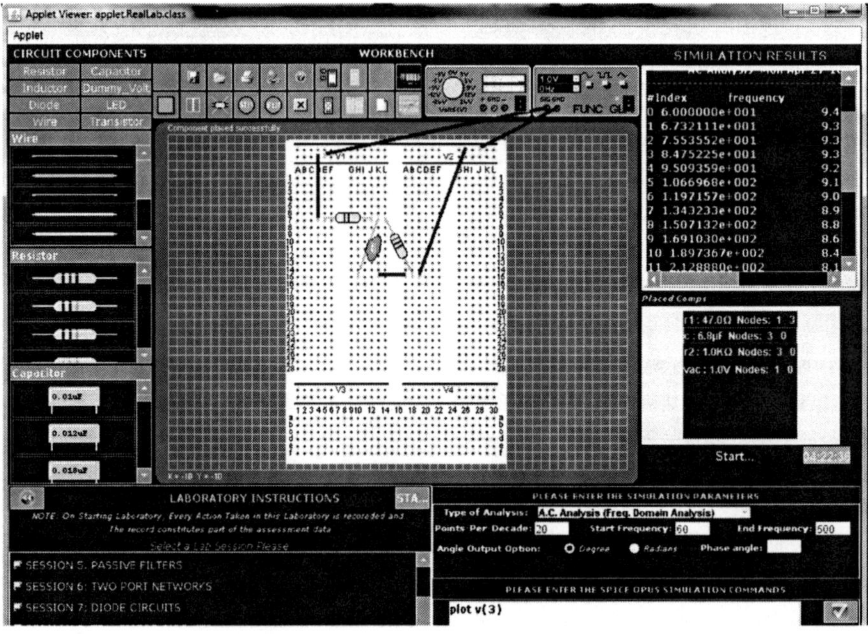

Figure 9. The frequency response curve of the circuit of Figure 7 loaded with a 1KΩ resistor

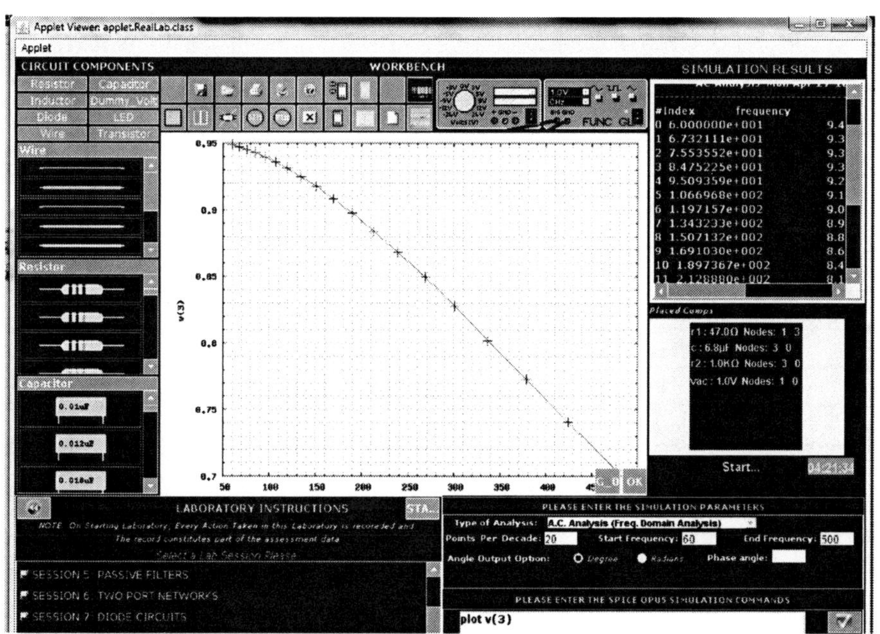

CLASSROOM EVALUATION AND RESULTS

The virtual electronic workbench was used in relation to a second year analogue electronics and circuits engineering course unit in the Electronic and Computer Engineering (ECE) department at the University of Portsmouth, UK. An aspect of the course unit involves the design, building and analysis of passive filter circuits. In a class of 30 students, 50% volunteered to participate in the evaluation exercise and 60% of the volunteers actually participated. The aim of the evaluation process is two-fold. First, to verify that the use of the virtual laboratory workbench can facilitate students' grasp of concepts taught in lectures. The second aim of the evaluation exercise was to generate students' logs of interaction with the virtual workbench for analysis and data extraction. The data is to be used for the evaluation of the performance assessment model.

A total of nine different laboratory activities were given to the students to undertake in the virtual laboratory environment. The first five laboratory activities, addressing the concepts of Ohm's law, Resistors in series, Resistors in parallel, AC circuits, and maximum power transfer theorem, were intended to gradually ease the students into using the virtual electronic laboratory environment. The last four laboratory activities addressed passive RC filter concepts which are the concepts of interest that have been taught in lectures.

The students were given written pre- and post-tests covering the addressed outcome concepts of the knowledge goal, passive filters. The pre-test was intended to assess the prior knowledge state of the students before perusing the workbench while the post-test was intended to assess changes in knowledge state after perusing the workbench. The same set of test items were used for pre- and post-tests without the students knowing they were going to undertake the same test at the end of the evaluation exercise. The difference was that the post-test contained other test items, in addition to the pre-test items but interest was mainly in the students' responses to the pre-test component part of the post-test items. The other component

Table 3. Pre- and post-tests results

S/No	Participant ID	Pre-Test Score (%)	Post- Test Score (%)	% Gain
1	P05	55	82	33
2	P06	64	73	12
3	P07	91	91	0
4	P09	64	82	22
5	P10	64	82	22
6	P11	36	73	51
7	P12	55	45	-22
8	P13	64	82	22
9	P14	64	91	30
	Mean	**61.89**	**77.89**	**18.89**

items were used as mere masks. The test results are shown in Table 3.

The mean percentage score gain of the students (18.89%) is encouraging despite the seemingly knowledge 'loss' by student P12. Using a one-sample, one-tailed t-test, at $\alpha = 0.05$, the post-test and pre-test mean scores were compared in order to verify that the difference between the mean scores is statistically significant. These results, $t(8) = 3.4586$ and $p = 0.0043$ imply that the difference between them is indeed statistically significant. The p-value contains the strength of the evidence. This indicates that the virtual laboratory workbench can be effectively integrated in the practical training of students for the enhancement of their understanding of taught concepts. It is anticipated that the virtual laboratory workbench will further be evaluated, with a larger student sample size, at a university in one of the countries in developmental transition, in order to draw more robust and justifiable conclusions.

FEEDBACK FROM STUDENTS

Results of the pre- and post-tests indicate improvement in students' grasp of the addressed concepts. At the end of the evaluation exercise, participating students filled out anonymous feedback forms. The feedback data indicated an overall positive reaction. The students unanimously agreed that the evaluation activities addressed concepts related to the taught course unit they are undertaking. 85% of the students said the virtual workbench was easy to use and that the use of the virtual workbench enhanced their understanding of the concepts addressed by the laboratory activities. In the words of one of the participants, "It's easier to use than fiddling with real components. Also, (the workbench is) very quick to plot graph of results". The students agreed the virtual workbench is an effective tool with which to understand basic principles. This is reflected in the pre- and post-test results.

Comments about the best aspects of the virtual workbench reflected the ability to construct and simulate circuits realistically without the need for real equipment. All the participants recommended the virtual workbench for use by students and gave it an overall rating of 80%. They all said they enjoyed participating in the evaluation exercise. The response from the teacher of the second year analogue electronics and circuits engineering course unit indicates a positive attitude towards the virtual workbench. The teacher had an earlier opportunity to use the workbench to undertake the laboratory exercises before it was given to the students.

CONCLUSION

The paradigm shift in engineering education from lecturing to student-centred learning emphasises active learning. The evidence and support for active learning is extensive and should stimulate instructors to facilitate students' learning. The level of efforts to facilitate learning can be substantiated by willingness to embed more laboratory activities in taught course units. This requires the adoption of intuitive laboratory learning tools and well-planned laboratory experiences that will facilitate students' grasp of fundamental concepts and stimulate cognitive growth. This has been demonstrated by the evaluation results of the virtual laboratory workbench. The evaluation has shown the effectiveness of the use of well designed laboratory activities and an intuitive laboratory learning tool to improve students' grasp of taught concepts.

The workbench presented in this paper is easy to use and can be used to realistically undertake curriculum-based laboratory activities. Students can do and re-do experiments several times and the instructor has a veritable and flexible platform for integrating theory and practice in order to enhance learning. The instructor can monitor and handle many more students easily. The instructor also has the opportunity to synchronize laboratory activities with lectures and it is possible to achieve a one-to-one student-equipment ratio. There is room for an increase in the number of laboratory activities and the distraction of equipment setup and teardown are eliminated. Students with mobility related issues can easily be accommodated with regards to laboratory activities.

The web-based virtual laboratories alleviate most of the limitations of the traditional laboratory. This will motivate students to challenge themselves with more laboratory activities. The end result of such engagement will be the acquisition of transferable practical skills and cognitive growth.

REFERENCES

Auer, M. E. (2000). *Virtual Lab versus Remote Lab*. Retrieved January 10, 2008, from http://www.online-lab.net/rel/documents/auer_icde.pdf

Barr, R. B., & Tagg, J. (1995). From teaching to learning: A new paradigm for undergraduate education. *Change*, *27*(6), 12–25.

Bloom, B. S. (1956). *Taxonomy of educational objectives. Handbook I: The cognitive domain*. New York: David McKay.

Budhu, M. (2002, August 18). *Virtual laboratories for engineering education*. Paper presented at the International Conference on Engineering Education. Retrieved December 7, 2008, from http://www.ineer.org/Events/ICEE2002/Proceedings/Papers/Index/O334-O337/O334.pdf

Campbell, J. O., Bourne, J., Mosterman, P., & Brodersen, A. J. (2002). Effectiveness of learning simulations for electronic laboratories. *Journal of Engineering Education*, *91*(1), 81–87.

Chika, I. E., Azzi, D., Hewitt, A., & Stocker, J. (2009). A holistic approach to assessing students' laboratory performance using Bayesian networks. In *Proceedings of IEEE Workshop on Computational Intelligence in Virtual Environments (CIVE '09)*, Nashville, TN (pp. 26-32).

Chika, I. E., Azzi, D., & Williams, R. (2008, September 25). *Students' laboratory work performance assessment*. Paper presented at the International Conference on Interactive Computer Aided Learning (ICL2008).

Davies, C. (2008). *Learning and teaching in laboratories: An engineering subject centre guide*. Retrieved May 24, 2008, from http://www.engsc.ac.uk/downloads/scholarart/laboratories.pdf

de Magistris, M. (2005). A MATLAB-based virtual laboratory for teaching introductory quasi-stationary electromagnetics. *IEEE Transactions on Education*, *48*(1), 81–88. doi:10.1109/TE.2004.832872

del Alamo, J. A., Chang, V., Hardison, J., Zych, D., & Hui, L. (2003, July 21). *An online microelectronics device characterization laboratory with a circuit-like user interface*. Paper presented at the International Conference on Engineering Education. Retrieved April 20, 2007, from http://www-mtl.mit.edu/~alamo/pdf/2003/RC-95%20delAlamo%20ICEE%202003%20paper.pdf

Duarte, M., Butz, B. P., Miller, S. M., & Mahalingam, A. (2008). An intelligent universal virtual laboratory (UVL). *IEEE Transactions on Education*, *51*(1), 2–9. doi:10.1109/TE.2006.888902

Edward, N. S. (2002). The role of laboratory work in engineering education: student and staff perceptions. *International Journal of Electrical Engineering Education*, *39*(1), 11–19.

Feisel, D. L., & Rosa, A. J. (2005). The role of the laboratory in undergraduate engineering education. *Journal of Engineering Education*, *94*(1), 121–130.

Gilbert, H. D. (2003, November 5). *Electrical Engineering 215 – A case study in assessment*. Paper presented at the 33rd ASEE/IEEE Frontiers in Education Conference. Retrieved May 18, 2007, from http://fie-conference.org/fie2003/papers/1199.pdf

Ginsburg, H. P., & Opper, S. (1988). *Piaget's theory of intellectual development*. Upper Saddle River, NJ: Prentice Hall.

Gopalan, P., & Cartwright, A. N. (2001). Java enabled opto-electronic learning tools and a supporting framework. In *Proceeding of American Society for Engineering Educational Annual Conference and Exposition,* Albuquerque, NM (pp. 3532-3563).

Hamza, K., Alhalabi, B., & Marcovitz, D. M. (2000, February 8). *Remote labs*. Paper presented at the International Conference of the Society for Information Technology and Teacher Education, Association for the Advancement of Computing in Education. (ERIC Document Reproduction Service No. ED444475)

Harb, S. (2000). *Web-based circuit design simulation package for solving Electrical engineering circuits*. Unpublished master's thesis, University of Central Florida, Orlando, FL.

Hughes, I. (2004). Coping strategies for staff involved in assessment of laboratory write-ups. *Journal of Bioscience Education, 3*(4). Retrieved September 12, 2008, from http://www.bioscience.heacademy.ac.uk/journal/vol3/beej-3-4.htm

Li, S., & Khan, A. A. (2005). Applying IT tools to a laboratory course for measurement, analysis, and design of electric and electronic circuits. *IEEE Transactions on Education*, *48*(4), 520–530. doi:10.1109/TE.2005.852601

Ma, J., & Nickerson, J. V. (2006). Hands-on, simulated, and remote laboratories: A comparative literature review. *ACM Computing Surveys*, *38*(3), 1–24.

Mannix, M. (2000). *The virtues of virtual labs.* Retrieved July 28, 2008, from http://www.highbeam.com/doc/1P3-60667340.html

Mavrikis, M. (2005). Logging, replaying and analyzing students' interactions in a web-based ILE to improve student modelling. In *Proceedings of the 12th International Conference on Artificial Intelligence in Education,* Amsterdam, The Netherlands (pp. 967-972).

Palop, J. M. G., & Teruel, J. M. A. (2000). Virtual workbench for electronic instrumentation teaching. *IEEE Transactions on Education*, *43*(1), 15–18. doi:10.1109/13.825734

Perry, W. (1970). *Forms of intellectual and ethical development in the college years*. New York: Holt, Rinehart and Winston.

QAA. (2006). *Subject benchmark statements: Engineering*. Retrieved November 24, 2007, from http://www.qaa.ac.uk/academicinfrasctructure/benchmark/statements/Engineering06.pdf

Siegel, M. (2002). What to do when the teaching lab instruments are too sophisticated for the students. In *Proceedings of the International Symposium on Virtual and Intelligent Measurement Systems (VIMS2002)* (pp. 123-128).

Stathacopoulou, R., Grigoriadou, M., Samarakou, M., & Mitropoulos, D. (2007). Monitoring students' actions and using teachers' expertise in implementing and evaluating the neural network-based fuzzy diagnostic Model. *Expert Systems with Applications*, *32*(4), 955–975. doi:10.1016/j.eswa.2006.02.023

Vanfreti, L. (2006). *A comprehensive virtual laboratory for teaching power systems dynamics and control at undergraduate level.* Retrieved March 17, 2007, from http://www.rpi.edu/~vanfrl/publications.html

Vanlehn, K. (2001, April). *Olae: A Bayesian performance assessment for complex problem solving*. Paper presented at the Annual Meeting of the National Council on Measurement in Education, Seattle, WA. ED453285

Wankat, P., & Oreovicz, F. (1992), *Teaching Engineering*. Retrieved June 28, 2007, from https://engineering.purdue.edu/ChE/News_and_Events/Publications/teaching_engineering/index.html

Zhou, G. T., & Lo, H. (1999, June). *Developing Java-based virtual laboratory tools for an undergraduate random signals and noise course*. Paper presented at the ASEE Annual Conference & Exposition. Retrieved August 5, 2007, from http://www.succeed.ufl.edu/papers/99/00838.pdf

This work was previously published in International Journal of Virtual and Personal Learning Environments, edited by Michael Thomas, Volume 1, Issue 4, pp. 1-17, copyright 2010 by IGI Publishing (an imprint of IGI Global).

Section 4
Evaluation

Chapter 15
The Development of a Personal Learning Environment in Second Life

Sandra Sutton Andrews
Arizona State University, USA

Angel Jannasch-Pennell
Arizona State University, USA

Mary Stokrocki
Arizona State University, USA

Samuel A. DiGangi
Arizona State University, USA

ABSTRACT

In this qualitative pilot study, the authors report on curriculum field trials within a personal learning environment (PLE) designed by a collaboration of academic researchers and nonprofit volunteers working together in the virtual world of Second Life. The purpose of the PLE is to provide learners less likely to have access to educational opportunities with a means to create a 'new life' in the real world, through a basic web-based curriculum and an advanced Second Life curriculum. Field trials of the Second Life curriculum were held with youth from underserved populations (n=6) to identify participant characteristics that facilitate success with the curriculum. Performance on instructional outcomes was examined in addition to a participatory action research methodology (PAR) that was employed with participants as co-researchers. To protect identities, the authors use a case study approach to track one composite participant/co-researcher through the curriculum.

INTRODUCTION

We report in this paper on *Transitions: a Place for Dreams*, a personal learning environment (PLE) designed by a collaboration of academic researchers, nonprofit volunteers and social action developers, who met and work together in the virtual world of Second Life. In the following sections, we briefly note the project purpose, then outline the research questions, the research approach, the hallmarks of the personal learning environment concept with regard to the project

DOI: 10.4018/978-1-4666-1770-4.ch015

design, and present the results of the Second Life curriculum field trials.

THE TRANSITIONS: A PLACE FOR DREAMS PROJECT

Transitions: A Place for Dreams is first a collaboration of academic researchers working with five core nonprofit and social action organizations located physically in Arizona/Mexico, Canada, Boston, Los Angeles, Seattle, and 'virtually' in the Nonprofit Commons (NPC) in Second Life, a virtual community founded in 2006. Each of the five collaborating partner groups has a focus on issues of homelessness, poverty and disempowerment. All five report the successful use of various technologies with clients, in some cases via computer technology centers or loaned computers. A small but growing percentage of clients own laptops. The *Transitions: A Place for Dreams* PLE builds on the five organizations' experience in seeking to provide accessible, appropriate online instruction to as wide an audience as possible. The primary goal of the instruction is to allow users to design a better life, after individualized mentoring in areas such as technology skills and small business practices. A carefully designed PLE, flexible enough to meet the needs of the individual, was chosen as the vehicle for the instruction.

The PLE includes both web-based and Second Life portions (as not all members of the target population have access to Second Life); this paper focuses on field trials with the Second Life portion of the PLE.

SECOND LIFE CURRICULUM FIELD TRIALS

The purpose of the field trials is twofold: first, to identify user characteristics that may lead to success with the Second Life curriculum, as well as any hindrances to success; and second to monitor efficacy of the program curriculum, by examining performance with regard to instructional outcomes.

RESEARCH QUESTIONS

Within a PLE constructed according to the principles of flexibility, symmetry, and attention to means of coordination (Wilson, Liber, Johnson, Beauvoir, Sharples, & Milligan, 2006), as well as in accordance with features of the online participatory culture (Jenkins, Purushotma, Clinton, Weigel, & Robison, 2006; Seely Brown & Adler, 2008), we ask the following questions:

1. What participant characteristics facilitate success within the curriculum, and what hindrances to learning appear? We seek to identify these participant characteristics and hindrances in order to be able to design and refine scaffolding.

To answer this research question, we observed the paths of pilot users through the curriculum and participatory environment. We then conducted follow-up interviews based on questions arising during these observations.

2. Are the participants able to accomplish the instructional outcomes? Success with completion of outcomes is an initial indicator of the efficacy of the instruction in empowering users to redefine and recreate their lives.

To answer this second research question, we noted outcomes in terms of art making, action plan, participation, technology skills and proposal writing:

Outcome: Art making. To an extent the Second Life curriculum design may be seen as arts-based: students are immersed in a user-created environment and have access to content creation tools. They are introduced to a variety of arts-based making concepts (Irwin, 2004) through interactive examinations of art works, and express these concepts in the building of a series of virtual objects. We examine these virtual objects as outcomes.

Outcome: Action plan. Each student creates an action plan for a business or other initiative; the plan must satisfy a basic rubric. The action plan is modeled on the concept pioneered by Ashoka and entails a plan for a social 'changemaker' venture, as a next step in the student's own life (Ashoka, 2009). The plan need not affect anyone other than the student, although it may do so if the student desires.

Outcome: Participation. The project goes beyond induction into the participatory culture (Jenkins et al., 2006), to include participatory action research, where participants are equally researchers and the stated goal is one of social action toward the social good. We therefore examine our observations in order to contribute to our understanding of participation, including contributions to project design, mentoring, and any relevant characteristics of the action plan.

Outcome: Technology skills acquisition. Acquisition of technology skills is of interest within this project, relying as it does on the PLE concept and on reports by five nonprofit/social good organizations that a sufficient number of their clients can access the PLE. We therefore note which technology skills students are practicing and acquiring.

Outcome: Funding proposal. Future plans for *Transitions: A Place for Dreams* include the hope of distributing micro-loans or grants. While success in finding funding is currently not required, students are asked to locate funding sources for micro-funding and to create a brief proposal according to a basic rubric.

THEORETICAL BACKGROUND

Personal Learning Environments

In designing the *Transitions: A Place for Dreams* PLE, the researchers took into account the PLE literature, in particular Wilson et al. (2006), as well as literature describing participatory culture, including Jenkins et al. (2006) and Seely Brown and Adler (2008).

Early in the development of the Internet, educators took time to learn the markup language of HTML in order to create instructional web pages, experimenting with the ability of the technology to collect data, even creating interactive discussion boards in Perl. In time some educators took development a step farther, creating online tools and infant learning management systems or LMSs (Andrews, DiGangi, Winograd & Jannasch, 1999). Later, corporate, course-based learning management systems replaced homegrown solutions with university-wide applications. Yet, viewed another way, the seemingly *less* dominant, non-corporate development has always been the larger, more coherent one. Indeed, today's course-centric learning management systems may be said to represent an effort to keep pace with technologies evolving so rapidly that special interest groups such as 'education' are driven to stop development long enough to use the technology: this is the LMS as band-aid.

It is the more curious educators who, unsung or even discouraged by educational institutions from further investigation, have continued to test new technologies as these emerge (Wilson et al., 2006). Such educators have helped drive the development of technologies in education by using/combining these in innovative ways, and have prepared the field of education for the emergence again of educator-driven learning solutions, of what we call today, the personal learning environment. It is this alternate development of solutions for online education that Wilson et al. (2006) call upon educators to investigate and improve.

In designing *Transitions: A Place for Dreams* as a PLE, we looked first to Wilson et al. (2006), who offer a set of features and goals to be considered in a personal learning environment. In their 2006 paper, "Personal Learning Environments: Challenging the Dominant Design of Educational Systems," the writers ask educators to imagine replacing the course-centric 'dominant vehicle' with technologies more suited to the individualized needs of teachers and learners, suggesting that many of the elements of an alternate solution already exist. That is to say, that the means of coordination and implementation must still be created, and that it lies in the interests of educators to do so.

Participatory Culture

In designing *Transitions: A Place for Dreams* we have also taken into account elements of the 'participatory culture.' Jenkins, Purushotma, Clinton, Weigel, and Robison (2006) describe the participatory culture in terms of education, noting that media operate in specific cultural and institutional contexts that determine how and why they are used. They suggest that access to the participatory culture functions as a new hidden curriculum, shaping which youth will succeed and which will be left behind as they enter school and the workplace (2006). This participatory culture entails a variety of aspects, not least a tendency towards informal mentorship. This informal mentorship bears a relationship to the concept of reciprocal teaching: reciprocal teaching and cooperative learning are approaches in which students draw on their own strengths to assist other students, such that both mentors and mentees benefit (Brush, 1998; Palincsar & Brown, 1984).

John Seely Brown and Richard Adler (2008) believe that the nature of knowledge itself is changing due to this same participatory culture: when understanding is constructed through conversations and collaborations, the 'how' of learning replaces the 'what.' Brown and Adler go so far as to provide a new dictum, 'We participate, therefore we are.' They also speak of the resulting 'new culture of sharing' created on the Internet, a culture they view as critical to the ability of society to offer sufficient educational opportunities to coming generations.

To a great extent the participatory culture has developed from the interaction of user demand and an inherent, persistent bias toward sharing built into the underlying philosophy and coding of the Internet. Users prioritize those elements of the Internet that facilitate ease of participation, while builders of seminal web technologies have held to a collaborative, consensus-based philosophy (Andrews et al., 1999; Raymond, 1996). This philosophy has in turn furthered the emergence of Web 2.0 technologies.

The concept of the PLE has also been influenced by Weinberger's *Small Pieces Loosely Joined* (2002). Van Harmelen (2008) points out that, although Weinberger's book predates Web 2.0 development, it nonetheless describes important aspects of this development. We note that there is a relationship between design for participation and use of Web 2.0 technologies, as Web 2.0 applications by definition are participatory. We note especially the changing relationships – reflected in the evolution of the highly participatory and customizable Web 2.0 technologies – among devices, applications, and the spaces that they access and create, looking forward for example to the possibility of interactive virtual worlds applications on mobile phones.

The principle of flexibility (Wilson et al., 2006) relates to the participatory culture as well. In terms of flexibility, the shared *spaces* of the PLE are more important than the technologies (hardware, software) used to access them; the technologies can be changed, while the spaces and communities remain stable. Wilson (2008) has further contributed a highly flexible set of instructional patterns and organizational possibilities within a PLE, defining these as elements of a pattern language for a PLE. Following these ideas, it becomes clear that a replacement for the standard learning management system will need to be programmatically as flexible as possible, so that new technologies can replace old ones. That is, the PLE must consider *technologies that are evolving along a number of lines of development*, and *that will continue to evolve*. Fortunately, while devices used to access the Internet will no doubt continue to grow more powerful and more convenient, this is at least in part possible because the web was always conceived of as 'device independent', never computer-centric (W3C, 2003).

Art-Making and Arts-Based Instruction

Working with relatively affluent students, Hayes (2007) noted small but significant contributions to perceived IT proficiencies having to do with experience creating in-game content. She also reported that students were more likely to create in-game content when they spent more than 10 hours per week online. A sufficiently engaging, participatory curriculum may encourage youth to spend more time online, and an arts-based portion of the curriculum that provides opportunities for the creation of in-world content may also contribute to increased technology proficiencies.

There is a precedent in using artmaking with underserved populations and in art therapy, e.g., for self-expression and self-affirmation (Ewald, 2005). We draw here also from Eisner (1991), whose innovative qualitative research work capitalized on examples from the arts as he argued the role and practice of educational critics studying educational settings. Over several years, Irwin (2004) noticed a growth of such arts-based research forms and offers such examples as narrative, autobiography, performative ethnography, readers' theatre, poetic inquiry, self-study, among many other creative forms of inquiry: all with an element of participation in one of the senses defined by Jenkins et al. (2006), in that content is created by users. In short, it may be that in integrating arts-based experiences we can at the same time engage users, prepare users for the participatory future, and provide space for them to develop technology skills.

METHODOLOGY

Participatory Action Research (PAR)

The research group chose a participatory action research (PAR) approach as most appropriate for the targeted populations and issues. In participatory action research, the goal is social action; those taking part in a project are considered co-researchers rather than participants, since they bring their own knowledge and experience to the table (Fine, Boudin et al., 2001; Kemmis, 1993; Sohng, 1996). A social action goal may be introduced by an outside researcher, but can also be further developed by participant co-researchers; the true measure of success lies in whether social action goals agreed upon by the group are met. PAR research incorporates equality of voice among outside researchers and participant co-researchers: 'Nothing about us without us.' Participant/co-researcher privacy and dignity are prioritized. Labeling is avoided, along with any language to which co-researchers object. In a PAR project, 'helping' participants is not the purpose, but rather shared progress towards a larger goal. This approach is practical as well as idealistic, as co-researchers possess local expertise without which a grassroots project, for example, may not succeed.

The social action goal for *Transitions: a Place for Dreams* is the creation of a learning community for those seeking a new life, whether the desire is for shelter, for job training, for educational opportunities, for an opportunity to mentor, or any combination of these; the Second Life curriculum provides the more advanced elements. Co-researcher expertise is important and, in the field trials, includes knowledge of what it is like to live and to use technology on the road, on the street, 'out of a car,' or with a disability.

In keeping with the PAR approach, while we first target under-resourced populations, the project is not limited to these, for the expectation is that users will succeed and will themselves become mentors. In using 'mentor/instructor' and 'mentee/student' interchangeably, we remind ourselves that mentees can become mentors, and that the teaching relationship here is one of equality.

Records of an early organizing Second Life conversation for *Transitions: a Place for Dreams* illustrate the delicate nature of the language strategies put into play. Use of the word 'homeless' in the project name was considered and rejected, as it would apply a label to persons who might not wish that label to be used.

February 8, 2008

[10:30] A: I think many [participant co-researchers] would love the 'In Transition' name. It is open ended. Hopeful.

[10:30] B: yes.

[10:30] C: In Transition is most approachable.

[10:31] B: yes and less offensive.

[10:31] C: for those who are living in cars, for instance, but do not want to call themselves homeless.

[10:31] C: or couchsurfing, monastics like me ;-)

[10:31] C: i'm a total friar.

[10:31] A: we use Floaters - Japanese word for homeless, floating from couch to couch.

[10:31] C: Floaters is a great name.

Participant Co-Researchers

With Jenkins et al. (2006), we identify at-risk and low-income youth as a group in need of induction into the participatory culture in order to attain future success. As Second Life is currently available free to educators only for those working with students aged eighteen and upwards, field trials were restricted to youth who were at least eighteen.

Six youths took part in the field trials, making up a theoretical sample that included two 'street kids,' two mobile youth living in vehicles, and two youths with a disability. All were male and between the ages of 18 and 27. The participant co-researchers were recruited by one of the five core nonprofit organizations called Floaters, a technology outreach group for homeless/formerly homeless and persons with disabilities, along with its sister group, the Homeless Peoples Network, a longstanding electronic mailing list. It is from Floaters that the research approach was drawn as well, with support contributed by the Arizona State University Applied Learning Institute alt^I and the Arizona State University Art Education Department.

The project was presented to prospective participant co-researchers as one with a particular social action goal – a learning community that could provide scaffolding, a 'way up', to those seeking a new life. The six were invited to take part in the curriculum trials as co-researchers, equal in voice to the outside researchers, contributing specialized knowledge having to do with their life experience.

Gaining Access

It is an absolute priority to preserve the equality of participant as co-researcher in terms of the PAR research methodology, for it is via this approach that access is gained to the 'homeless'. Trust is gained through the PAR approach. If participants are to be treated as equals, they must be depicted in a way that is in harmony with their view of themselves. The researchers must further take care to ensure and to make clear that there is no hidden agenda.

The nature of the mobile youth population served may be described in a number of ways. In one view, such transient youth are living a romantic life, perhaps making and selling their own jewelry as they travel to fairs and concerts; in this view, these youths are simply making alternate lifestyle choices. In another view, 'street kids' and 'road dogs' live on the edge. Alcoholism is common as they grow older; supports such as healthcare are few. Neither view describes their situation precisely. The youths who come into the project may mix practicality with spirituality, and disillusionment with a faith in a benign, accessible universe. They may drink, perhaps a great deal. They are fiercely independent, want to meet us on their own terms, and would like mentoring and assistance based on those terms rather than out of pity. In some ways this is a deeply spiritual lifestyle: they express hope that an idealistic point of view might actually work and want to know whether they might be able to succeed in life without compromising their principles. As with other underserved youthful populations, their altruism is a means for us to provide them with opportunities (Martinek, Schilling, & Hellison, 2006). As they mentor others, they learn, and their life choices expand.

In addition to mobile youth, those with a disability are a second population in the current curriculum trials. Learning disabilities in particular disproportionately affect people living in poverty (Cortiella, 2009) and 38.7% of those with a learning disability do not graduate from high school (Lissner, 2009). Learning disabilities are often an 'invisible' disability and, in terms of accessible features of technology-based instruction, have only recently begun to benefit from a level of research and resources long available to the more visible disabilities (WebAim, 2009).

SETTING THE TRANSITIONS: A PLACE FOR DREAMS PLE

Face-to-Face Setting

In the field trials, face-to-face mentors were used in order to obtain a greater range of observations. The youths were individually mentored in Second Life, with the academic researchers acting as mentors, for up to eight sessions per youth. These sessions variously took place on the university campus, at Wi-Fi enabled fast food restaurants and truck stops, or in homes, at the co-researchers' convenience.

At times, an additional researcher was present only in Second Life; at these times, text rather than voice communication was used, as text requires fewer resources in terms of bandwidth and hardware.

PLE Setting

The *Transitions: A Place for Dreams* PLE is the setting of interest, particularly since some users will not have access to a face-to-face mentor. The PLE is therefore described here in some detail with regard to the design principles mentioned earlier.

Flexibility and the Transitions: A Place for Dreams PLE

We have indicated that flexibility of the technologies used is an important feature of the PLE. To illustrate the dynamic nature of the set of spaces used, we note that early plans included Google's Lively, another virtual world. Lively was to be used as a virtual meeting space only, easy to access although offering little opportunity for content creation. When Google stopped support of this entry-level virtual world, the pedagogical focus on shared spaces rather than on the supporting technology allowed the *Transitions: A Place for Dreams* project to absorb the change within the PLE (Figure 2).

Symmetry and Asymmetry in the Transitions: A Place for Dreams PLE

In describing hallmarks of the personal learning environment, Wilson et al. (2006) suggest 'symmetric' relationships wherein students and instructors have equal ability to create content. Under the prevailing LMS structure, use of such a design may be hampered by the definition of roles within the LMS, whereas the Second Life learning spaces diagrammed in Figure 1 provide a variety of types of highly symmetric access. The first of these spaces is the Aloft meeting space, envisioned as a virtual 'squat' (in street terminology, any space appropriated as shelter). The meeting space consists of two stories connected by stairs that visually, and metaphorically, display the steps between the lowest project level (the need for shelter) and the highest (service and mentoring). At the top of the stairs is a comfortable outdoor seating area with sun umbrella and rattan rug. At ground level are a broken couch, with one leg missing; orange crates; an oil drum for a fireplace; and sleeping bags. Neither students nor mentors build in these meeting areas: thus there is mentor/student symmetry (Figure 3).

In keeping with the PAR approach of 'nothing about us without us,' the space was implemented only after first checking with members of the mobile population, to make certain it would not be viewed as offensive or clichéd. The space was approved as being realistic, although it was pointed out that in a real-world setting, someone would have improved the space to the extent possible by leveling the couch, either by taking off the remaining legs or by substituting a sturdy object for the missing leg.

The second symmetric learning space is the Floaters Gallery, offering interactive instruction in the form of questions about displayed art. Though only project curators have the ability to hang virtual artwork, both mentors and students have the option of becoming curators: by volunteering, members of both groups can achieve 'build' status

Figure 1. The four Second Life instructional spaces include three smaller spaces as well as the 'nurturing' NonProfit Commons space, which provides a variety of opportunities for networking with other project members as well as with other nonprofit representatives. The NPC provides a buffer between the PLE and other Second Life communities

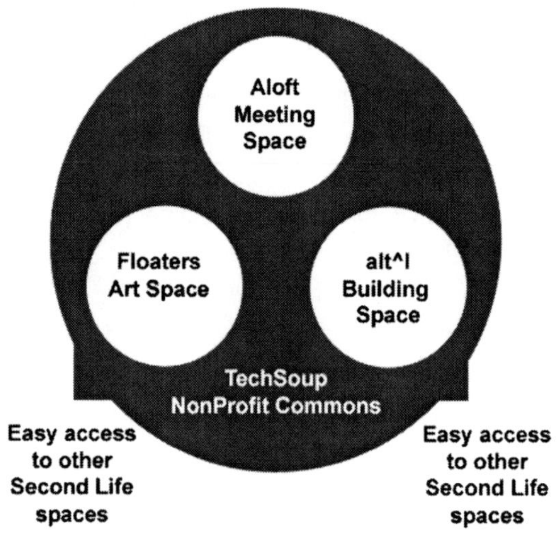

in this second area. Thus the relationship between mentor and student is symmetric here (Figure 4).

The third area is a 'sandbox' provided by Arizona State University **alt^I**. After investigating the artworks in the gallery, students integrated the concepts learned by building a house in the sandbox. As students and teachers alike can build here, and as constructions remain until the builder takes them down, the mentor/student relationship in terms of content creation in this third instructional space is symmetric (Figure 5).

In addition to these three learning spaces, the Nonprofit Commons serves as an element of the

Figure 2. Transitions: A Place for Dreams 'Treehouse' space in Google Lively, 2008, with instructional videos inside the tree trunks

Figure 3. A two-story 'squat' on Aloft Nonprofit Commons island. Stairs are labeled with the Transitions: A Place for Dreams program levels; the upper steps represent the Second Life curriculum

Figure 4. Floaters Gallery space on Plush Nonprofit Commons island. Students learn about the artwork through 'notecards' attached to the images

Figure 5. Arizona State University Applied Learning Technologies Institute **alt^I**: *'sandbox' where participants build virtual homes*

Figure 6. May 7, 2009 'dance' at the Nonprofit Commons: weekly social events provide networking opportunities. The Commons is a nurturing space functioning as a frame for, and as a part of, the PLE.

PLE. The nurturing role of the Nonprofit Commons towards participating nonprofit organizations extends to the provision of a variety of safe spaces and networking opportunities open to all *Transitions: a Place for Dreams* co-researchers, as NPC residents. Here as well, instructor-mentors and student-mentees have equal access and hence symmetry is observed (Figure 6).

Coordination and Organization in Transitions: A Place for Dreams

A third design point chosen from Wilson et al. (2006) is the consideration of coordination and organization. We have noted the relationship between Weinberger's *Small Pieces Loosely Joined* (2002) and the PLE concept. The *Transitions: A Place for Dreams* PLE can indeed be described as a set of interchangeable 'small pieces'. The immediate issue is therefore that of coordination and organization versus transparency: how can Weinberger's 'small pieces loosely joined' be so integrated as to offer choices and exploration, while still providing clear paths and sufficient scaffolding? For *Transitions: A Place for Dreams,* the PLE elements are coordinated in a number of ways. The first is vertical coordination: seven instructional spaces (three web-based, and four in Second Life) represent a hierarchy of program levels that are also steps along the way to designing and implementing a new future. Within Second Life, organization is place-based, in the form of the set of four virtual offices and collaborative spaces described. A centralized 'home' - a web-based portal accessible either within or outside of Second Life – is an additional site of coordination.

The mentoring process is key in terms of organization and coordination. We have noted the identification by Jenkins et al. (2006) of informal mentorship as an aspect of the participatory culture. As they progress, students in the Second Life curriculum are asked to 'give back' by mentoring others before moving on to the next level. This simultaneously adds a layer of record keeping (portfolios created by the student are shared with mentors) and to the sustainability of the project. Mentoring is also pedagogically appropriate: as was mentioned, benefits to both mentor and mentee have been shown in the seminal work done by Palincsar and Brown (1984) as well as by researchers such as Brush (1998).

Reciprocity

Reciprocity is particularly important in working with vulnerable populations. In this project, participant co-researchers contribute directly to a goal to which they have a personal connection, and benefit by gaining skills. Small stipends were also made available, as appropriate in return for the insider knowledge contributed.

Data Sources

Our data collection methods are primarily observational, with two researchers, when possible, working together. In some cases, as noted previously, an additional researcher was present in Second Life to add virtual observational data. Additional data include the curriculum outcomes generated by the students, follow-up interviews, and lists of games with which each student was familiar.

Procedure

The six participant co-researchers were first provided with a verbal introduction in which they were asked to contribute to the building of a project for the social good, while also working on a design for their own future. Second Life was described as a 'playground' for designers rather than a game, or as a 'virtual Lego kit', descriptions provided by Linden Lab staff (P. Rosedale, personal communication, August 13, 2009). Following the introduction, the youths were given access to the Second Life curriculum within the PLE.

The curriculum is individualized and flexible, but with specific instructional objectives; it is presented here in order to show the nature of the work expected of the participant co-researchers. Eight sets of initial educational experiences are included:

1. Introductory and exploratory exercises: orientation, avatar creation, and individualized exploration of the environment, culminating in art exploration in the Gallery.
2. Basic content creation, including simple scripting.

   3.- 4. Dreaming a future, with two sets of tasks to be accomplished simultaneously: the design of a home, and the planning of a virtual business or similar initiative, followed by the building of the home and the creation of the 'action plan' for the business.

In this, the heart of the instruction, participant co-researchers select the areas in which they wish to be mentored. In designing the dual 'dreaming a future' project we drew our inspiration in part from the concept of reteaching, a teaching strategy that can involve the transformation of previous knowledge, here by using similar principles in two different ways (Kowalski, 2004). The instructional design for the project also reinterprets the concept of universal design for learning, a concept furthered by David Rose of the Center for Applied Special Technology (CAST, located at http://cast.org) that specifically calls for multiple means of *representation, action/expression* and *engagement* (Rose & Meyer, 2006).

5. Business ethics and small business practices.
6. Creating a poster to advertise the business.
7. Giving back to the project through unique contributions, which may include mentoring, suggestions for project improvement, and an action plan that targets a larger issue.
8. Seeking funding opportunities.

Expected outcomes of the curriculum, as stated in the second research question, include the avatar; a virtual home; a poster; an action plan; evidence of participation in program design and mentoring; an increase in technology skills; and a proposal towards obtaining micro-funding.

The Case of Albert

We report here on our observations of one user called 'Albert', as he moved through the curriculum. Albert is a composite participant constructed in order to protect the identities of the participant co-researchers. Ensuring privacy beyond what is required in other research situations is an integral part of the PAR agreement with users. It is only by rigorous adherence to this policy that access is maintained. As more published articles become available on the web, it may become difficult to assure participant co-researchers that information cannot be traced back to specific users; hence the decision to construct a composite user.

Albert is 19 years old, of middle height and with unruly brown hair; he had graduated from high school in the previous year. School had been difficult for him even after a learning disability was diagnosed and an IEP (Individualized Education Program) prepared. Fortunately he was able to attend an alternative high school that focused on technology, an area in which he excelled. Nevertheless, his grades were low. After high school he traveled for nearly a year, as college seemed an unlikely possibility. An aunt with an extensive import business provided him with a small inventory of handmade jewelry to sell on commission, to which he added stones that he wrapped in silver wire. In so doing he became part of a small community of young artists who are loosely linked to one of the five participating nonprofit groups, a technology outreach organization. Following this, and with the encouragement of the outreach organization, he returned home to take advantage of a summer technology program in his home city.

Figure 7. Albert changed the look of his avatar several times, trying out every option

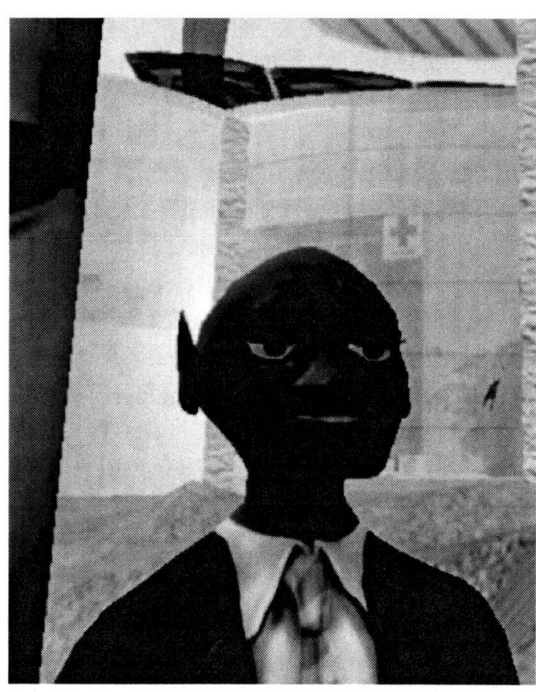

The researchers began by giving Albert an overview of the project, inviting him to participate as a co-researcher who would help create the *Transitions: a Place for Dreams* curriculum as a program for social change, while selecting and moving towards his own goals. He was asked to participate by offering suggestions and, as he advanced, by mentoring. In the second part of the introduction he was given an overview of the nature of Second Life: as a virtual world, playground for designers and virtual Lego kit.

Albert selected an avatar name and entered a standard orientation tutorial provided by Linden Lab, makers of Second Life. He began by testing each of the avatar creation features. Expressing surprise at the number of options in comparison to games, he spent a full twenty minutes trying each feature and ended by creating a tall, dark avatar (Figure 7).

Albert moved quickly through the tutorial options during his first session with the researchers, opting out of the orientation process as soon as he discovered a way to leave the island, in the form of a 'Click Here to Teleport' sign. He next spent some time searching for elements of traditional gaming, before asking where he could learn to build. At this point the instruction moved to the Floaters Gallery, with an introduction to design principles and the basic building tools.

In subsequent sessions, while continuing on occasions to look for gaming elements, Albert refined his building skills as well, becoming far more skillful at building than the researchers. As he built, he commented without being prompted on ideas that the researchers might use with other youth. When building his virtual home, he became a mentor for the researchers, who watched with fascination as he produced an innovative, asymmetrical one-piece hollow structure.

As he taught himself increasingly complex building skills, Albert was asked to design a small business, to create an action plan towards this goal, and to create a poster that would both incorporate good art principles and advertise his business. Albert planned a Second Life architecture business. For the required poster, he used Adobe Photoshop to create the image, then uploaded it as a texture to Second Life for display, a process that involved the acquisition of further technology skills. In this he deconstructed a task into discrete steps in ways similar to Hayes' and King's *The Sims 2* players, who, as Hayes and King point out, are learning by tinkering – an important part of software creation and use (Hayes & King, in press).

Participant co-researchers are also asked to locate funding sources and to construct a brief sample proposal, as at some point funding may allow the project to offer microloans. Going beyond the project's expectations, Albert sought, and quite unexpectedly received, one thousand dollars in the form of a grant, based on an action plan submission. In submitting to this competition, he revised his original action plan. In this second, award-winning action plan he moved from a virtual world business to one that combines web technologies and real-world expression, while allowing him to mentor others.

In his follow-up interview, Albert directly attributed his success to his gaming experience, explaining that such features of Second Life as the inventory and the avatar creation process appeared to be derived from videogames. Asked which games he had played, he easily covered two sheets of paper with scrawled lists of videogames played in his lifetime (Figure 8).

RESULTS AND CONCLUSION

In the first research question, we sought to identify participant characteristics that contributed to ease of use and success with the curriculum, as well as any hindrances.

In follow-up interviews, five of the six participant co-researchers spoke of fairly extensive gaming experience, as evidenced by the fact that each was able to create a lengthy list of games he had played; the sixth, while lacking gaming experience, had previously used another virtual world. All six were able to acquire skills in the Second Life environment with little instruction from the researcher mentors.

It may be that gaming experience and/or experience in another virtual world will impact both speed of entry, and paths that students follow in learning to use the virtual world. As an example of impact on learning paths, the participants agreed in the follow-up interviews that they expected to begin with an avatar creation process (Appearance mode in Second Life) and further expected this process to resemble that which they had experienced in games or in another virtual world. The young men with gaming experience expressed surprise at the many options in comparison to games they had played, and most were highly engaged in the process, as evidenced by length of time spent and number of options tried. Participants without gaming experience may be less likely to spend time on the avatar creation process. On the other hand, all

Figure 8. Albert created a practice action plan for a Second Life architectural firm along with a poster advertising his building skills

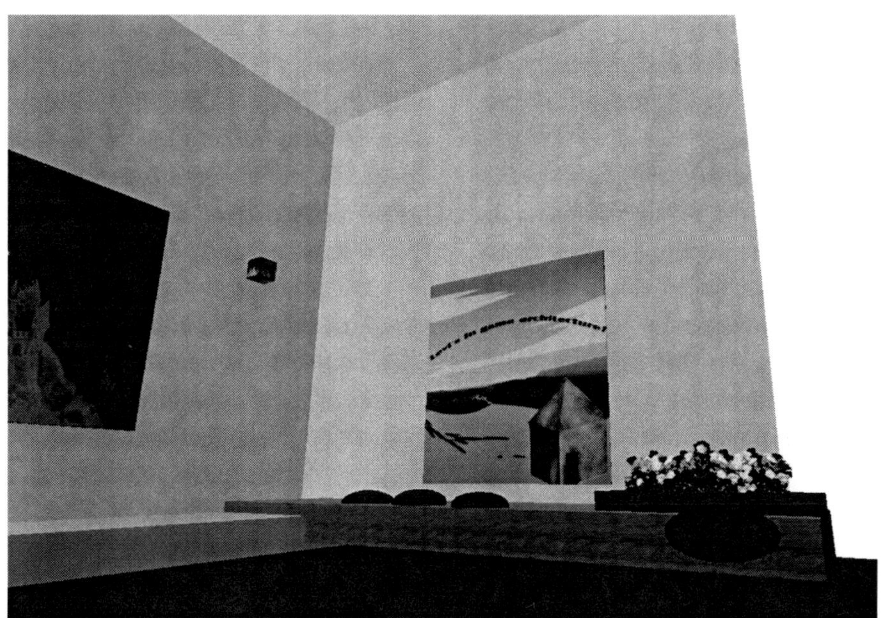

five of the youths with gaming experience skipped most of the orientation tutorial, explaining variously in follow-up interviews that they did not foresee any difficulties with the environment, or expected to be able to learn later. 'I'll learn it as I go along,' one said.

Certainly gaming experience is likely to be one of the participant characteristics associated with success in the curriculum; those who lack such experience may require scaffolding in the form of a slower-paced entry experience.

The expectation of gaming features within the virtual world may also act as hindrance. Follow-up interviews made it clear that to a greater or lesser extent the pilot users fully expected to find gaming features such as dragons to fight, in spite of an introduction in which the researchers clarified that Second Life is not a game. This impression is not easily modified; Tom Hale of Linden Lab reported that in early tests of a Second Life portal that allowed users to select their primary virtual worlds interest, '*play*' was chosen by the largest number of persons (Hale, 2009).

Outcomes and objectives. In the second research question, we sought evidence that the users were able to accomplish the instructional objectives.

Given basic rubrics, mentors and individualized instruction, our users accomplished the instructional objectives with little difficulty. The patterns followed by the six participant co-researchers as they navigated through the early steps of Second Life usage were similar in spite of disparate levels of education, literacy, disability, technology experience, and housing stability: they were able to create and modify their avatars, follow the orientation tutorials, and seek out experiences that included dragon fighting and horseback riding.

Each constructed the artmaking objectives, although not always in the manner expected. Avatar creation, as mentioned, went well beyond what was expected in most cases; but so did homebuilding. Rather than creating the simple cubes or attempts at mansions that the researchers expected, the students envisioned cones and cylinders reaching into the sky, or springboards into watery homes, and some added professional-appearing textures.

With the posters, further mentoring was at times required to remind students of design principles. The brief action plans and funding proposals were easily completed.

In terms of giving back to the program we also saw success. Each took the requirement to participate as a co-researcher seriously and, with no further prompting beyond the initial introduction, contributed ideas for the curriculum. In building: 'Make sure you show them that they can build with different shapes.' On having fun: 'Monsters!' These ideas have been incorporated into the curriculum. As indicated, some were able to mentor their mentors; in two cases, we noted spontaneous mentoring among the participant co-researchers. We note as well that while most action plans were individual in nature, the young men took pains to find a way to bring consideration of the social good into their plans. Although 'Albert's' initial action plan, for example, was not a social action plan, he later modified it.

Finally, our users added to their technology and technology-related skills, learning specific Second Life skills and acquiring principles of design to embody in virtual artmaking. As stated, funding proposals were easily completed, although only one participant submitted his to an agency.

NEXT STEPS

In order to fully serve the targeted populations with a Second Life and web-based learning community, *Transitions: a Place for Dreams* will require volunteer programmers and/or funding. Rapid completion of the social action goal would be gratifying. However, participatory action research often moves slowly, and we can certainly continue to build out the environment, expand the pilot group, and train mentors. With minimal funding, we can extend the curriculum to further trials with populations served by the other groups that make up *Transitions: a Place for Dreams,* e.g. the women survivors of domestic violence served by Bridges for Women, or the homeless served by Community VoiceMail. Amoration in Los Angeles and the Vesuvius Group in Boston respectively have ties to 'street kids' and low-income youth projects, and both can contribute pilot users. It is also important that we test virtual mentoring, that is, without a face-to-face mentor.

We note that age, gender and gaming experience, or experience in another virtual world, were the common participant characteristics in this group of successful Second Life users. While we cannot conclude that most at-risk or indeed other youth will have gaming experience, we do suspect that a larger percentage of these in comparison to our other target groups (such as older low income persons) will have such experience. All six of the participant co-researchers engaged in the pilot program is young men. Young women from similar populations are being recruited.

Other questions remain as well. Our users' commitment to the curriculum, and their creativity as expressed in home building, raise questions as to which features of the environment and the curriculum most engaged them. We will need further trials in order to determine whether arts-based instruction and the creation of inworld content might contribute to technology proficiencies. With our current participant co-researchers we can also now begin to examine the relationship between building a virtual life, and building a new life in the real world.

The process of building a virtual home may be particularly important to those who may not have a home, as reflected in the enormous creativity seen in these trials. The process of building a home is likewise important symbolically with regard to the social action goal of developing a permanent, participatory community of learners and mentors within *Transitions: a Place for Dreams.* In *Ritual House* (2006), Knowles states that sheltering is not merely about the physical structure, but also about repeated actions that take place in the structure. If 'classes' do not meet regularly, we can still incorporate repeated actions. Home building, participation in dances, lectures and other collaborative activities, as well as acts of giving back, may all contribute to the development of the community.

ACKNOWLEDGMENT

The authors gratefully acknowledge the contributions to this paper by the following representatives of partnering nonprofit and social good organizations: Joyce Bettencourt with the Vesuvius Group; Buffy Bye of Bridges for Women; Jessica Dally of Community VoiceMail; Evonne Heyning of Amoration; and Susan Tenby of TechSoup Global. Additional thanks go to Global Kids.

REFERENCES

Andrews, S., DiGangi, S., Winograd, D., & Jannasch, A. (1999). Designing online instruction using multidisciplinary procedures. In *Proceedings of the 21st Annual Selected Research and Development Papers.* Columbus, OH: AECT. Retrieved from http://is.asu.edu/research/AECT1999b/aect99b.rtf

Ashoka. (2009). Youth Venture. Retrieved July 1, 2009, from http://www.ashoka.org/youthventure

Brown, J. S., & Adler, R. P. (2008). Minds on fire: Open education, the long tail, and learning 2.0. *EDUCAUSE Review, 43*(1), 16–32. Retrieved from http://www.educause.edu/EDUCAUSE+Review/EDUCAUSEReviewMagazineVolume43/MindsonFireOpenEducationtheLon/162420.

Brush, T. (1998). Embedding cooperative learning into the design of Integrated Learning Systems: Rationale and guidelines. *Educational Technology Research and Development, 46*(3), 5–18. doi:10.1007/BF02299758

Cortiella, C. (2009). *The state of learning disabilities 2009.* Washington, DC: National Center for Learning Disabilities. Retrieved from http://www.ncld.org/stateofld

Eisner, E. W. (1991). *The enlightened eye: Qualitative inquiry and the enhancement of educational practice.* New York: Macmillan.

Ewald, W. (2005). *In peace and harmony: Carver portraits.* Richmond, VA: Hand Workshop Art Center.

Fine, M., Boudin, K., Bowen, I., Clark, J., Hylton, D., Migdalia, M., et al. (2001, June). *Participatory action research: From within and beyond prison bars.* Paper presented at the Bridging the Gap: Feminisms and Participatory Action Research Conference, Boston College, MA. Retrieved from http://www.wnum.org/gap/fine.htm

Hale, T. (2009). *Second Life roadmap.* Paper presented at the Second Life Community Convention (SLCC), San Francisco, CA.

Hayes, E. (2007). Game content creation and IT proficiency: An exploratory study. *Computers & Education, 51*(1), 97–108. doi:10.1016/j.compedu.2007.04.002

Hayes, E., & King, E. (in press). Not just a dollhouse: What *The Sims 2* can teach us about women's IT learning. *New Horizons (Baltimore, Md.).*

Irwin, R. L. (2004). A/r/tography: A metonymic métissage. In Irwin, R. L., & de Cosson, A. (Eds.), *A/r/tography: Rendering self through arts-based living inquiry* (pp. 27–38). Vancouver, BC: Pacific Educational Press.

Jenkins, H., Purushotma, R., Clinton, K., Weigel, M., & Robison, A. (2006). *Confronting the challenges of participatory culture: Media education for the 21st century.* Chicago, IL: The John D. and Catherine T. MacArthur Foundation, Digital Media and Learning Initiative. Retrieved from http://www.newmedialiteracies.org

Kemmis, S. (1993). Action research and social movement: A challenge for policy research. *Education Policy Analysis Archives*, *1*(1). Retrieved from http://epaa.asu.edu/epaa/v1n1.html.

Knowles, R. (2006). *Ritual house: Drawing on nature's rhythms for architecture and urban design*. Washington, DC: Island Press.

Kowalski, C. (2004). Getting classes in GEAR: A lesson planning model for English reteaching. *The Language Teacher, 28*(5), 19-24. Retrieved 2009, from http://www.jalt-publications.org/tlt/articles/2004/05/kowalski

Lissner, L. S. (2009). *Transition to college: Strategic planning to ensure success*. Washington, DC: National Center for Learning Disabilities. Retrieved from http://www.ncld.org/publications-a-more/parent-aamp-advocacy-guides/transition-to-college-strategic-planning

Martinek, T., Schilling, T., & Hellison, D. (2006). The development of compassionate and caring leadership among adolescents. *Physical Education and Sport Pedagogy*, *11*(2), 141–157. doi:10.1080/17408980600708346

Palincsar, A. S., & Brown, A. L. (1984). Reciprocal teaching of comprehension-fostering and comprehension-monitoring activities. *Cognition and Instruction*, *1*(2), 117–175. doi:10.1207/s1532690xci0102_1

Raymond, E. S. (1996). *New hacker's dictionary*. Cambridge, MA: MIT. Retrieved December 10, 2009, from http://www.ccil.org/jargon/jargon_toc.html

Rose, D. H., & Meyer, A. (Eds.). (2006). *A practical reader in universal design for learning*. Boston: Harvard Education Press.

Sohng, S. S. (1996). Participatory research and community organizing. *Journal of Sociology and Social Work*, *23*(4), 77–97.

Van Harmelen, M. (2008). Design trajectories: Four experiments in PLE implementation. *Interactive Learning Environments*, *16*(1), 35–46. doi:10.1080/10494820701772686

WebAim. (2009). *Overview of Steppingstones cognitive research.* Retrieved from http://webaim.org/projects/steppingstones/cognitiveresearch

Weinberger, D. (2002). *Small pieces loosely joined.* New York: Perseus Books Group.

Wilson, S. (2008). Patterns of personal learning environments. *Interactive Learning Environments*, *16*(1), 17–34. doi:10.1080/10494820701772660

Wilson, S., Liber, O., Johnson, M., Beauvoir, P., Sharples, P., & Milligan, C. (2006). Personal learning environments: Challenging the dominant design of educational systems. In *Proceedings of the 2nd International Workshop on Learner-oriented Knowledge Management and KM-oriented Learning*, Crete, Greece (pp. 67-76).

World Wide Web Consortium. (W3C). (2003). *Device Independence Working Group*. Retrieved from http://www.w3.org/2001/di/

This work was previously published in International Journal of Virtual and Personal Learning Environments, edited by Michael Thomas, Volume 1, Issue 3, pp. 36-54, copyright 2010 by IGI Publishing (an imprint of IGI Global).

Chapter 16
A Framework for the Assessment of Wiki-Based Collaborative Learning Activities

Hagit Meishar-Tal
Open University of Israel, Israel

Mat Schencks
Open University, UK

ABSTRACT

This paper discusses the pedagogical and technological aspects of assessing wiki-based collaborative learning activities. The first part of the paper presents a general framework of collaborative learning assessment. The framework is based on four aspects of assessment, characterized by four questions: who, what, how and by whom. The second part of the paper concentrates on the analysis of the applicability of the assessment framework in wikis. A systematic analysis of MediaWiki's reports is conducted in order to discuss the requisite information required for a well-balanced and effective assessment process. Finally, a few suggestions are raised for further improvements of the wiki's reports.

INTRODUCTION

Educational institutions and individual educators are adopting social software tools (often called Web 2.0 tools) such as wikis and blogs to support learning and teaching (Alexander, 2006; Downes, 2005; Franklin & van Harmelen, 2007). Although there are several examples of the effective use of social software tools (e.g., Minocha, 2009), there is currently little (formal) guidance for educators to assist them vis-à-vis the design and assessment of learning activities. Furthermore, designing assessment can be extremely challenging (see Cubric, 2007; MacDonald, 2005). On the one hand, counting the number of students' contributions may not be an effective indicator of their students' work if the contributions are not insightful enough. On the other hand, ignoring the interaction and collaboration within the group as indicators for assessment could overlook an important goal of

DOI: 10.4018/978-1-4666-1770-4.ch016

collaborative learning: achieving collaboration between the learners.

Wikis are considered to be suitable for collaborative authoring activities. Wikis enable the co-production of content at a distance (Aguar et al., 2004; Bruns & Humphreys, 2005; Lamb, 2004). However, in educational settings, the assessment of wiki activities is quite challenging from both the technological and pedagogical perspectives. From the technical perspective, wikis are designed and configured around the content rather than the users (Bruns & Hamphreys, 2005). The content created by a particular student is fragmented and distributed; therefore tracing a particular student's contributions in a wiki can be challenging and time-consuming for the assessor. Pedagogically, being a collaborative learning activity, the assessment of the activities involves several considerations. These include having a balance between the assessment of the group work and the students' individual contributions, and between the assessment of the product of collaboration (the outcomes) and the process of collaboration itself (MacDonald, 2003; Tal-Elhasid & Meishar-Tal, 2009). This makes the task of designing criteria for assessment and evaluation of student performance quite onerous for the assessor or educator.

This paper reveals the complexity of designing assessment criteria for online collaborative learning activities in a wiki and proposes pedagogical and technological solutions for overcoming obstacles related to the assessment of collaborative wiki assignments.

THE CHALLENGE OF ASSESSING COLLABORATIVE LEARNING ACTIVITIES

Assessment is a key component in the design of a learning activity. Effective assessment can enhance learning satisfaction, and it helps to set expectations of the students and to shape their learning process accordingly (Angelo, 1995; Shepard, 2000). Therefore, the assessment criteria should be clear to the students from the outset. The criteria should be related to the learning outcomes and reflect the goals of the task or learning activity (Angelo, 1995). The assessment should also include feedback and guidance and not just marks or grades (Shepard, 2000). Assessment should be related to the skills and performance of the students, instead of just measuring the learning products (Huba & Freed, 1999).

The assessment of online collaborative learning activities is even more complicated and hence, more difficult to design, as stated by Swan et al. (2006):

The assessment of collaboration requires a radical rethinking of assessment methodologies. Three issues are involved: the variety and kinds of goals for online collaboration, the complexity of assessing both individual and group behaviours, and collaboration on assessment itself (p. 46).

Another way of describing the three issues stated by Swan et al. (2006) is by asking three fundamental questions:

1. Who is the entity which we ought to assess? Is the entity the group or the individual within the group?
2. What is the object of assessment? (that is, what is being assessed?). Is the object of assessment the product/outcomes of learning or should it also be connected to the collaborative process itself? One of the goals of collaborative learning activities should be to achieve collaboration among the group members. If learning is achieved but in a non-collaborative way, would we be able to say that the activity was fully successful?
3. By whom? Who should be the assessor? Should the assessment be conducted by the educator or maybe the students themselves can conduct peer assessment?

The assessment of collaborative learning can be based on several factors, some of which are quantitative, such as the number of contributions, while others are qualitative, such as the quality of the contributions. Thus, a fourth question should be asked:

4. How should we conduct the assessment? Qualitatively? Quantitatively? Related to this are considerations of which tools are available to help us assess the final product, and to assess the learning process if collaboration is taking place at a distance and asynchronously.

We will now address each of these questions in turn.

WHO TO ASSESS?

The assessment of collaborative learning activities can be related to either the group or the individual within the group. When the assessment is based on individual performance only, and does not take group work into account, there is a risk that collaborative activities will turn into competitive activities (Johnson & Johnson, 1989). On the other hand, when the assessment is based on group work rather than on individual endeavour, the students are unsatisfied with the assessment method, as 'they would have preferred more marks for the individual contribution to collaborative work' (MacDonald, 2003, p. 387).

Therefore, a good collaborative learning activity would have to assure each individual within the group that he would have the opportunity to express himself and contribute to the group. At the same time, the group will need to work together as a 'unit' and not as a collection of individuals. Therefore, the assessment of collaborative activities should be designed in a way that values both individual and group effort (Swan et al., 2006).

WHAT TO ASSESS?

The problem with the assessment of the collaborative activities in online learning is that some of the process that contributes towards collaborative activity may not be visible to the assessor. Unlike a real-time synchronous setting of a physical classroom, the students learning online are working from different locations and most likely at different times. They may be using different and diverse communication tools such as a discussion forum, instant messenger, Skype, or phone calls to plan the process of collaboration. If the communication is spread over different tools and if there is no formal record of the discussions or group decisions, the assessor will only be able to see the final product of collaboration and not the *process* of collaboration. In such a situation, it will be difficult for the assessor to separate each individual's contribution from the final product and to understand how well that individual had participated and contributed during the process of collaboration.

There are some ways to overcome this problem, for example, by keeping a diary of the group work or maintaining an e-portfolio of the individual's learning process which logs their contribution in the collaborative work (Swan et al., 2006). Students could also be asked to reflect on the collaboration process and their personal experiences, and report these reflections as part of the formal assessment. There are examples in the literature where reflective accounts have been part of the assessment (e.g., Mason et al., 2004; Minocha & Thomas, 2007). The problem with these solutions is that they might be biased and would not reflect the true situation. Students tend not to be critical in the case of self-assessment or peer assessment (Pimentel et al., 2005).

There is another way by which an assessor can keep track of the process of collaboration. The individual groups could be asked to keep all the discussions in one place such as a forum within the virtual learning environment for example. The assessor will then be able to look through these discussions and gain some insight into the process of collaboration and even track down the decisions, individual workloads and actions performed by individual participants (MacDonald, 2005). Such discussion records are authentic, first-hand accounts of what actually happened and are not reflective or perceived descriptions.

WHO IS THE ASSESSOR?

Online learning environments are the appropriate place for implementing alternative assessment methods, such as self-assessment and peer assessment (Luca & McLoughlin, 2002). Self-assessment is a process in which students are involved in and responsible for assessing their own piece of work. Self-assessment can be used for the sake of helping students to develop their ability to examine and think critically about their own learning. Peer assessment is where students are involved in the assessment of the work of other students. It can be employed in order to develop students' ability to work cooperatively, to be critical of others' work and receive critical appraisals and feedback on their own work (Swan et al., 2006).

The problem with self-assessment is that unskilled people tend to hold overly favourable views of their abilities in many social and intellectual domains, and therefore tend not to be critical (Kruger & Dunning, 1999). In the case of peer assessment, as Pimentel et al. (2005, p. 498) explain, 'learners fear criticizing other learners' work' and this can lead to 'inappropriate behaviour' in which reciprocal favours of high grades are expected.

Therefore, educators, more often than not, utilize self-assessment and peer assessment as methods of learning, but not as a method of marking, namely, self-assessment and peer assessment are embedded in the activity, but these activities are assessed by the educators and not by the students themselves.

HOW TO ASSESS?

The assessment of online collaborative learning activities should preserve balance between qualitative and quantitative measurements (Piementel et al., 2005). The qualitative assessment criteria should be related to the quality of the materials, which have been submitted to the learning environment; for example, the quality of content of messages submitted to discussion forums. In addition, the assessment can also contain some quantitative requirements, such as the number of contributions or the length of the final product (number of words).

The quantitative assessment can encourage active participation and collaboration. Providing the rubric (assessment criteria) in advance can shape student behaviour in the learning environment and lead to more interaction and collaboration among the students (Swan et al., 2007).

Quantitative assessment can serve as a way to balance the activity among students, and to ensure that each student has an equal opportunity to express himself. By setting expectations, indicating clearly what amount of work is expected from each student (in terms of minimum or maximum number of contributions), the educator can attempt to reduce the likelihood of one student taking over the activity and not leaving any opportunity for others to contribute (Tal-Elhasid & Tal-Meishar, 2009).

Quantitative assessment can also be used to measure the intensity of collaboration within the group (Meishar-Tal & Tal-Elhasid, 2008). The intensity of collaboration reflects the process of collaboration between the members of the study group. The number of interactions between members of the group can indicate whether or not the group worked collaboratively. If each member of a group participated only once, the level of interaction would be suspected to be low, but if each member had participated many times, in editing peers' work or commenting on peers' work and in reacting to feedback from peers, then the intensity of collaboration among the group members would be higher. For measures such as this to be accurate it is essential that all interactions are documented online and for there to be no 'invisible' interactions (for example by e-mail or by telephone) that are not visible to the assessor.

The problem with quantitative assessment is that it could be subject to manipulations by the students. If the students know that they are assessed based on quantitative measurements only, for example, by the number of contributions they provide, they can manipulate their records by submitting more contributions that are lacking in quality content. To prevent this, additional qualitative assessment is therefore important.

Qualitative assessment should be based on evaluating the quality of the content that has been uploaded to the learning environment by the learners. This information is open-ended and therefore more fully reflects the knowledge constructed by the learner or the group, especially when constructivist pedagogy is employed (Kendle & Northcote, 2000).

Qualitative assessment has been frequently considered impractical and time-consuming, because it places a tremendous burden on the assessor, who has to read all the students' contributions in a fragmented and non-linear way (Fujitani et al., 2003). To reduce the burden on the assessor, online reports that accumulate and organize the users' contributions and the group work are invaluable. A combination of quantitative and qualitative approaches can help make assessment of the individual's and the group work more practical and feasible.

ASSESSMENT CRITERIA FOR COLLABORATIVE LEARNING ACTIVITIES

The educators who design collaborative learning activities should design the assessment criteria in a balanced way: by combining process assessment with product assessment, individual criteria with group criteria, using qualitative methods of assessments with quantitative methods, and by engaging the students themselves in the assessment, either by using self-assessment or peer assessment as part of the process. Such a design process also needs to be aligned with the learning goals of the assignment to ensure high levels of participation and collaboration among the learners.

Designing assessment criteria is a work of combination and aggregation. Each criterion contains the four aspects of assessment discussed above. For example: consider an activity which aims to develop a glossary through collaboration. This activity should be assessed in several ways. The first is the group's product: assessing the content of the final glossary. It should use qualitative measurements, evaluating the content of the terms in the co-built glossary, but it should also use quantitative measurements, counting the number of terms in the glossary (the size of the glossary) that the group has built, and the extent of collaboration among the group members. The second way is the individual level. Here the assessment should concentrate on quantitative measurements, connected to the level of individual's participation and involvement in the process. In this case, the number of contributions to the final product, in relation to new terms or the extent to which learners took part in the improvement of existing terms in the glossary, should be counted for each participant. The individual's contributions can also be assessed qualitatively, by reading all the contributions related to an individual. The individual assessment can be enhanced by self-assessment, in which the students would have to write an account, by way of reflection on their own learning processes, about the group work they participated in.

This example above can be translated into a table (Table 1). The table that we have developed can serve as a tool for the course designers to plan the assessment criteria and to assure the checks and balances of the assessment framework. The number of combinations possible for assessment criteria is 24: 2x (who) x2 (what) x2 (how) x3 (by whom).

ASSESSMENT OF COLLABORATIVE LEARNING ACTIVITIES IN WIKIS

A wiki is one of the best online tools to facilitate collaborative writing assignments. A wiki enables the creation of collaborative documents from a distance, by enabling all the users not only to share, but also to edit a shared document together, adding to it, deleting parts of it or rephrasing it. All previous versions of the document can be accessed and thus, any unwanted changes in the wiki can be reinstated and every change that was made can be related to a specified user (Schwartz, Clark, Cossarin, & Rudolph, 2004).

Wikis are often provided with 'Talk' pages or 'Comments' in which the collaborators can discuss and negotiate changes they make in their co-edited document. This feature enables the collaborators to concentrate their work in one environment only, without needing to use more communication tools for their collaboration. From the assessment perspective, this feature guarantees that the process of collaboration is well documented.

Another advantage of wikis lies in the fact that the environment is organized thematically, as distinguished from chronologically, as online discussion forums are. This feature ensures that important information that was uploaded to the wiki will stay accessible for a long time and would not be 'buried' under the new information that is added to the environment (Bruns & Hamphreys, 2005). These are some of the reasons that explain the fact that most higher education institutions are adopting wikis as a platform for collaborative learning (Aguar, Reitman, & Zhou, 2004; Parker & Chao, 2007).

Some wikis have useful features in the software that provide the assessor with the important information for assessment. In the following paragraphs, a detailed analysis of the features of MediaWiki will show how the information accumulated on the server can be utilised for assessment purposes.

Table 1. Assessment criteria for the glossary example

Criteria	Who	What	How	By whom	% from grade
Number of contributions per person	Individual	Process	Quantitatively	Tutor	
Number of terms in the Glossary	Group	Product	Quantitatively	Tutor	
Quality of student work	Individual	Product/ process	Qualitatively	Self assessment/ Tutor	
Quality of terms in the glossary	Group	Product	Qualitatively	Tutor	
Quality of group work	Group	Process	Qualitatively	Peer assessment/ Tutor	
Intensity of group work	Group	Process	Quantitatively	Tutor/peer	

QUALITATIVE ASSESSMENT (GROUP AND INDIVIDUALS)

The qualitative assessment of the group produced final product is the easiest and most time-efficient approach. Instead of reading 'more of the same' individual assignments, the assessor has to read only the final version of the co-authored article and assess the content: Is it relevant for the task? Does it cover all the relevant issues? Is the content accurate or are there any mistakes and misconceptions? Some quantitative measurements can be relevant as well: Is it long/short enough? Are there enough references or links to relevant websites? This information can be obtained from the server, but it is not presented in such a way that is best suited to the needs of the assessor unless a specific report is designed for this purpose.

The qualitative assessment of the individual contributions is also available through the 'Compare Versions' screen (Figure 1). Each page on the wiki has a history page, which contains all the old versions of the page; thus, by choosing 'changes' on the history list, the assessor can compare two versions of the same page. The differences between the versions are highlighted, and it is easy to identify the changes that were made by a specific user in this page. This tool is a powerful one for assessing the individual's contributions qualitatively. The 'Compare Versions' screen allows the assessor to connect changes in the shared documents to specific users; this being so, this option enables instructors to assess each contribution separately and with relation to a specific user.

QUANTITATIVE ASSESSMENT (GROUP, PROCESS)

The advantage of wikis is their ability to provide the assessor with valuable quantitative information which can support the assessment of the process of learning. All actions in the environment, including views only, are documented and can be analyzed for assessment purposes. All actions are related to users and therefore can assist in separating individual work from group work.

The 'History' view of a page is one example of a report that can support quantitative assessment of group work (Figure 2). This provides an abundance of information about the collaborative process that has or has not occurred on it. It reflects the most important components in the measurement of collaborative work: the number of collaborators and the number of versions.

The number of collaborators can be easily detected, since every version is related to a specified user. By counting the number of con-

Figure 1. Compare Versions view

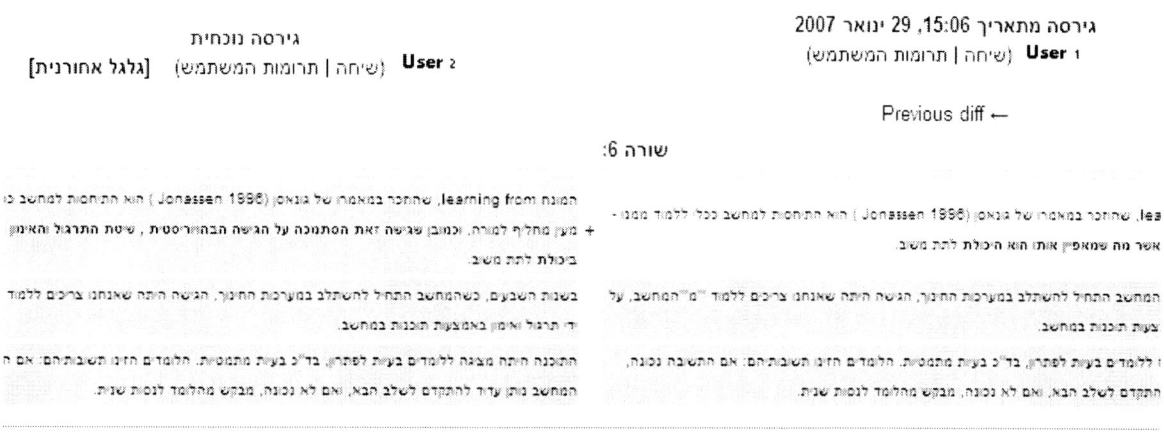

Figure 2. History view

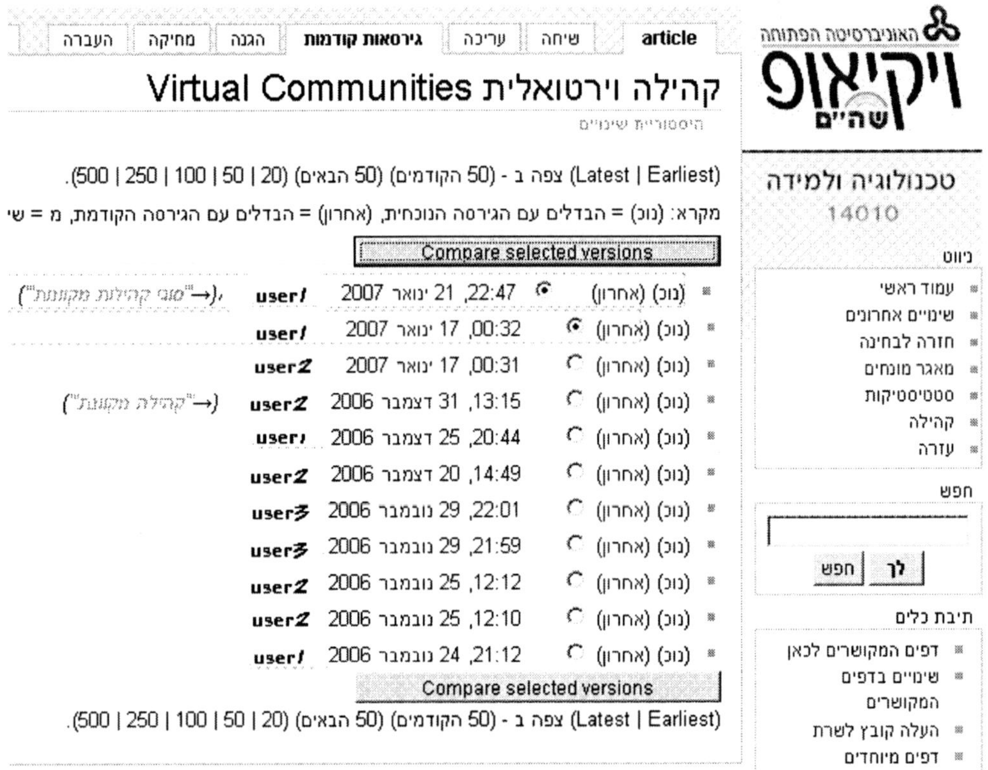

tributors and dividing this total by the number of potential contributors (number of students on the course), the level of participation can be measured (Meishar-Tal & Tal-Elhasid, 2008).

The number of versions or edits should be treated carefully and critically. It can indicate the amount of work and the attention invested in a specific page, but it depends on the way in which the students are used to saving their work. If a student saves their work every minute, as opposed to once at the end of the work, then the list of versions will be very long. Versions that are created sequentially by the same editor should therefore be considered as one (Meishar-Tal & Tal-Elhasid, 2008).

Furthermore, by looking at the history report of a page, it is possible to analyze the extent of collaboration. The meaning of extent or intensity of collaboration in this setting is not just the number of edits in the page, but the number of times a user returns to, and adds or edits information on a page in response to changes by others (Meishar-Tal & Tal-Elhasid, 2008). Assuming all interactions between the learners are conducted on the wiki and not by other means of communication, if a user edits a page once and never returns to see what other students have been doing, collaboration is considered to be 'weak'. However, if a user edits a page, then another user changes his version and the first user returns and continues to change the page in response to the former change, it may be a sign that a more intensive form of collaboration has occurred.

Another way of looking at the process of collaboration is through the types of actions that have been taking place in the wiki. If the users only add to each other's work without deleting or rephrasing, it can reflect a lower level of collaboration. If there are many deletions and revisions, it might indicate that an 'edit war' has taken place (Viegas, Wattenberg, & Dave, 2004); conversely, if there were many instances of rephrasing, formatting and changes in content, it might signify a high level of collaboration.

QUANTITATIVE ASSESSMENT (GROUP, PRODUCT)

Quantitative data can also support the assessment of the group product of learning. By providing statistical data about the number of words/lines or links added to a page, the assessor can get some preliminary information about the adequacy of the assignment to the formal requirements. This information is not generated automatically in MediaWiki and the assessor must calculate it manually.

QUANTITATIVE ASSESSMENT (INDIVIDUAL PRODUCT AND PROCESS)

Since every change in the wiki is recorded and related to a user, a user report can be produced easily. MediaWiki's user contributions report provides information for quantitative assessment, by presenting a list of all the activity relating to a specific user (Figure 3).

Simply counting the number of contributions is a misleading action as it was explained earlier. The way to overcome this at the level of the individual is by counting 'clear' edits – only counting those edits on the same page if the time between the edits is greater than a decided time interval. For example, if two edits occurred sequentially, but in a time interval of two hours, then they should be counted as two actions; however, if the two occurred within five minutes of each other, then they should be counted as one (Voss, 2005).

Further information provided by the user report relates to the number of edited pages by user. This can serve as an indication for the level of engagement in the assignment. By counting the number of edited pages the user contributions are not biased by the number of edits and this can better reflect the amount of work invested in the in the final product.

These two numerical measurements are not available in the standard reports that MediaWiki provides, and they need to be calculated manually by the assessor. Choosing the right measurement for the user contributions depends heavily on the nature of the task and the structure of the wiki. If the students were asked to add pages or to edit existing pages in a wiki, then the number of the pages that they have edited would be a satisfactory measure. However, if the students were asked to work on a specific page and edit it together, then the number of clear edits would reflect more accurately the amount of work the students have invested.

WHO CONDUCTS THE WIKI ASSESSMENT AND HOW?

The question of who conducts the assessment is closely related to the architecture of the permission system. MediaWiki is an open system in which all the information is open and accessible to all users, including the users' contribution reports. This is a pre-condition for peer assessment. The educator can use the wiki not only for summative but also for formative assessment (Cubric, 2007) by leaving his comments and feedbacks in the 'Discussion' page. In this way, s/he provides opportunities for improvements and corrections by the individual students and by the group as a whole.

Figure 3. User contribution report

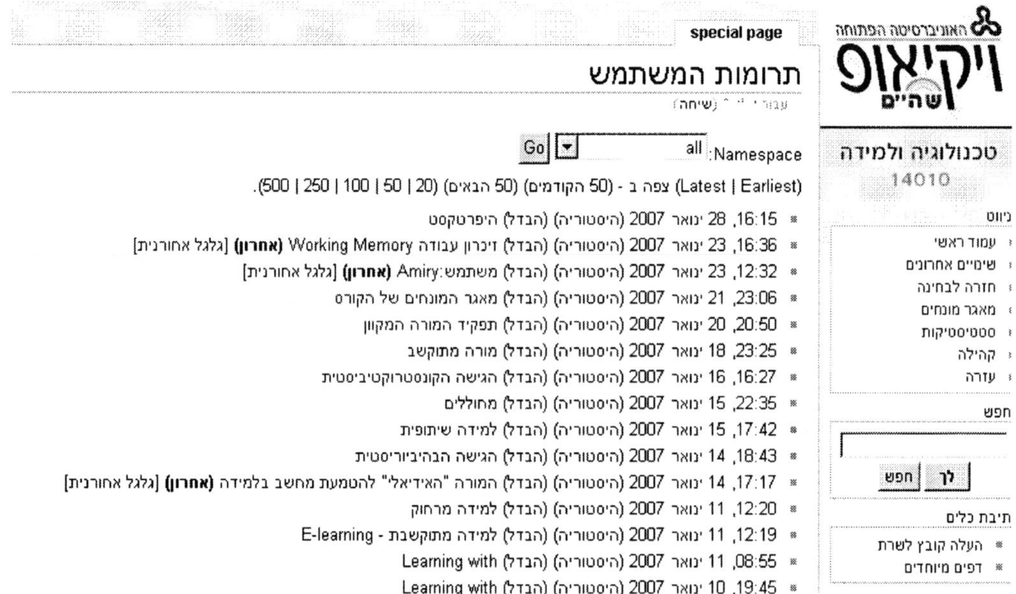

BACK TO THE GLOSSARY EXAMPLE

Returning to the glossary activity example that was described earlier in this paper, the MediaWiki Reports assist the assessor in a number of ways. The 'History' report provides information on the number of editors per page and the intensity of collaboration between the participants. This report therefore supports the assessor in assessing collaboration between the group members.

The 'User Contribution' report organizes all the information on a particular learner in one place, making it possible for the assessor to get a full picture of the learner's work during the activity. Used in combination with the 'Compare Version' view it supports the assessor in evaluating the quality of each learner's contributions.

Needless to say, the assessor will have to read the glossary terms at the end of the activity in order to assess their quality.

Some crucial information is still difficult to retrieve from MediaWiki: summative information on the group work (number of pages in a wiki, total number of participants, intensity of group work etc.) as well as on the individual (number of active days, number of pages edited, number of 'clear edits' etc.). This information is not provided by the reports and the assessor will have to gather it manually.

CONCLUSION

This paper suggests a framework for assessing collaborative learning activities. The framework contains four aspects of assessment that are characterised by the questions: who, what, how and by whom. These four aspects can formulate all kinds of combinations; moreover, they can be translated into assessment criteria. The educator should design the assessment criteria in a well-balanced way and refer to all aspects of assessment in order to achieve effective assessment.

In this paper, we have applied the framework and evaluated it in the MediaWiki environment. MediaWiki offers the assessor diverse information that can be helpful in assessing the learning activity from a wide range of perspectives and cover the four aspects of collaborative learning assessment. The reports that are provided within MediaWiki are powerful and support most of the requirements of collaborative learning assessment. They offer the assessor a wide variety of information that can help to assess both the learning process as well as the end-product from a wide range of perspectives in addition to covering the four aspects of collaborative learning assessment. Educators who are using MediaWiki as an environment for collaborative learning activities should be aware of these tools and try to utilise them for assessment purposes.

Nevertheless, some information is still not easily or automatically available for the assessor: the analysis of the 'History report' and the 'User Contributions report' that were described in detail in this paper show a lack of fundamental summative information, such as the number of editors, the number of edits, and the number of participation days. There is a need for developers of educational wikis to design more 'assessment oriented reports', in order to ease the work of educators who have to cope with complex sets of assessment criteria within distributed learning environments.

REFERENCES

Alexander, B. (2006, March/April). Web 2.0: A new wave of innovation for teaching and learning? *EDUCAUSE Review, 41*(2), 32–44.

Angelo, T. A. (1999). Doing assessment as if learning matters most. *AAHE Bulletin*. Retrieved May 11, 2009, from http://www.umd.umich.edu/casl/natsci/faculty/zitzewitz/curie/TeacherPrep/38.pdf

Augar, N., Raitman, R., & Zhou, W. (2004, December 5-8). Teaching and learning online with wikis. In R. Atkinson, C. McBeath, D. Jonas-Dwyer, & R. Phillips (Eds.), In *Proceedings of Beyond the comfort zone: the 21st ASCILITE Conference*, Perth, Australia (pp. 95-104). Retrieved May 11, 2009, from http://www.ascilite.org.au/conferences/perth04/procs/augar.html

Bruns, A., & Humphreys, S. (2005). *Wikis in Teaching and Assessment: The M/Cyclopedia Project*. Retrieved February 28, 2009 from http://snurb.info/files/Wikis%20in%20Teaching%20and%20Assessment.pdf

Cubric, M. (2007, October 21-23). Wiki-based process framework for blended learning, In *Proceedings of the 2007 international symposium on Wikis*, Montréal, Québec, Canada.

De Pedro Puente, X. (2007, October 21-23). New method using wikis and forums to evaluate individual contributions in cooperative work while promoting experimental learning: Results from preliminary experience. In *Proceedings of Wikisym 2007*, Quebec, Canada.

Downes, S. (2005). E-Learning 2.0. *eLearn Magazine, 10*, 1.

Duffy, P. D., & Bruns, A. (2006). The use of blogs, wikis and RSS in education: A conversation of possibilities. In *Proceedings Online Learning and Teaching Conference 2006*, Brisbane, Australia (pp. 31-38).

Franklin, T., & van Harmelen, M. (2007). *Web 2.0 for Learning and Teaching in Higher Education Report*. London: The observatory of borderless higher education. Retrieved May 11, 2009, from http://www.jisc.ac.uk/media/documents/programmes/digital_repositories/web2-content-learning-and-teaching.pdf

Fugitani, S., Mochizuki, T., Koto, H., Isshiki, Y., & Yamauchi, Y. (2003). *Development of collaborative learning assessment tool with multivariate analysis applied to electronic discussion forums*. Paper presented at *the World Conference on E-Learning in Corp., Govt., Health., & Higher Ed. (ELEARN)*, Phoenix, AZ.

Huba, M. E., & Freed, J. E. (2000). *Learner-centered assessment on college campuses: Shifting the focus from teaching to learning*. Boston: Allyn & Bacon.

Johnson, D. W., & Johnson, R. T. (1989). *Cooperation and competition: Theory and research*. Edina, MN: Interaction Book Company.

Krueger, J., & Mueller, R. A. (2002). Unskilled, unaware, or both? The better-than-average heuristic and statistical regression predict errors in estimates of own performance. *Journal of Personality and Social Psychology, 82*, 180–188. doi:10.1037/0022-3514.82.2.180

Lamb, B. (2004). Wide open spaces: Wikis, ready or not. *EDUCAUSE Review, 39*(5), 36–48.

Luca, J., & McLoughlin, C. (2002, December 8-11). A question of balance: using self and peer assessment effectively in teamwork. Wind of change in the sea of learning. In *Proceedings of the Annual Conference of the Australasian Society for Computers in Learning in Tertiary Education (ASCILITE 2002)*, New Zealand.

MacDonald, J. (2003). Assessing online collaborative learning: process and product. *Computers & Education, 40*(4), 337–391. doi:10.1016/S0360-1315(02)00168-9

Mason, R., Pegler, C., & Weller, M. (2004). E-portfolios: an assessment tool for online courses. *British Journal of Educational Technology, 35*(6), 717–727. doi:10.1111/j.1467-8535.2004.00429.x

McLoughlin, C., & Luca, J. (2001, December 9-12). Quality in online delivery: What does it mean for assessment in e-learning environments? In *Proceedings of the 18th Annual Conference of the Australasian Society for Computers in Learning in Tertiary Education: Meeting at the Crossroads (ASCILITE 2001)*, Melbourne, Australia.

Meishar-Tal, H., & Tal-Elhasid, E. (2008). Measuring collaboration in educational wikis: a methodological discussion. *International Journal of Emerging Technologies in Learning, 3*, 46–49.

Minocha, S. (2009). *A study on the effective use of social software to support student learning and engagement*. Retrieved May 11, 2009, from http://www.jisc.ac.uk/whatwedo/projects/socialsoftware08.aspx

Minocha, S., & Thomas, P. G. (2007). Collaborative Learning in a Wiki Environment: Experiences from a software engineering course. *New Review of Hypermedia and Multimedia, 13*(2), 187–209. doi:10.1080/13614560701712667

Northcote, M., & Kendle, A. (2000). The Struggle for Balance in the Use of Quantitative and Qualitative Online Assessment Tasks. In *Proceedings of the 17th Annual Conference of the Australasian Society for Computers in Learning in Tertiary Education*, Coffs Harbour, NSW, Australia.

Parker, K. R., & Chao, J. T. (2007). Wiki as a teaching tool. *Interdisciplinary Journal of Knowledge and Learning Objects, 3*, 57–72.

Pimentel, M., Gerosa, M. A., Fuks, H., & De Lucena, C. J. P. (2005). Assessment of collaboration in online courses. In *Proceedings of the 2005 conference on Computer support for collaborative learning: learning 2005: the next 10 years!* Taipei, Taiwan.

Schwartz, L., Clark, S., Cossarin, M., & Rudolph, J. (2004). Educational wikis: Features and selection criteria. *The International Review of Research in Open and Distance Learning, 5*(1). Retrieved May 11, 2009, from http://www.irrodl.org/index.php/irrodl/article/viewArticle/163

Shepard, L. A. (2000). The role of assessment in a learning culture. *Educational Researcher, 29*(7), 4–14.

Swan, K., Schenker, J., Arnold, S., & Kuo, C.-L. (2007). Shaping online discussion: assessment matters. *E-mentor, 1*(18), 78-82. Retrieved May 11, 2009, from http://www.e-mentor.edu.pl/_xml/wydania/18/390.pdf.

Swan, K., Shen, J., & Hiltz, R. (2006). Assessment and collaboration in online learning. *Journal of Asynchronous Learning Networks, 10*(1), 45–62.

Tal Elhasid, E., & Meishar-Tal, H. (2006). Wiki as an online collaborative learning environment at the Open University. Human Resources. *Mashabei Enosh, 225*(6), 48–53.

Tal-Elhasid, E., & Meishar-Tal, H. (2009). Models of activity, collaboration and assessment in wikis in academic courses. In Szücs, A., Tait, A., Vidal, M., & Bernat, U. (Eds.), *Distance and e-learning in transition - Learning innovation, technology and social challenges* (pp. 745–756). New York: Wiley-ISTE.

Viegas, F. B., Wattenberg, M., & Dave, K. (2004). Studying cooperation and conflict between authors with history flow visualizations. In *Proceedings of the CHI conference on Human factors in computing systems*, Vienna, Austria (pp. 575-582).

Voss, J. (2005). Measuring Wikipedia. In *Proceedings of International Conference of the 10th International Society for Scientometrics and Informetrics*, Stockholm, Sweden. Retrieved May 11, 2009, from http://eprints.rclis.org/3610/1/MeasuringWikipedia2005.pdf

This work was previously published in International Journal of Virtual and Personal Learning Environments, edited by Michael Thomas, Volume 1, Issue 3, pp. 71-82, copyright 2010 by IGI Publishing (an imprint of IGI Global).

Chapter 17
Evaluating Games-Based Learning

Thomas Hainey
University of the West of Scotland, Scotland

Thomas Connolly
University of the West of Scotland, Scotland

ABSTRACT

A highly important part of software engineering education is requirements collection and analysis, one of the initial stages of the Software Development Lifecycle. No other conceptual work is as difficult to rectify at a later stage or as damaging to the overall system if performed incorrectly. As software engineering is a field with a reputation for producing graduate engineers who are ill-prepared for real-life software engineering contexts, this paper suggests that traditional educational techniques (e.g. role-play, live-through case studies and paper-based case studies) are insufficient in themselves. In an attempt to address this problem we have developed a games-based learning application to teach requirements collection and analysis at the tertiary education level. One of the main problems with games-based learning is that there is a distinct lack of empirical evidence supporting the approach. This paper will describe the evaluation of the requirements collection and analysis process using a newly developed framework for the evaluation of games-based learning and will focus on evaluation from a pedagogical perspective.

INTRODUCTION

Requirements collection and analysis is a highly important early stage of the Software Development Lifecycle (Sommerville, 2007). According to Brooks (1987) no other conceptual work is as difficult to rectify at a later stage of a software project or as damaging to the overall system if performed incorrectly. Games-based learning (GBL) could potentially overcome some of the problems associated with traditional approaches to teaching requirements collection and analysis, as it is perceived to be a highly engaging form of supplementary learning by some educationalists. A primary question of this research is to ascertain if a GBL intervention can act as a suitable supplement for different learning experiences such as role-play and paper-based case studies.

DOI: 10.4018/978-1-4666-1770-4.ch017

One of the main problems associated with the field of games-based learning is the distinct lack of empirical evidence supporting the approach (Connolly, Stansfield & Hainey, 2007; de Freitas, 2006). This paper will make a contribution to the empirical evidence in the games-based learning field by conducting 3 experiments comparing a games-based learning approach to role-playing and paper-based approaches for teaching requirements collection and analysis. Two studies were performed at the University of the West of Scotland, the first in May 2008 and the second as part of a serious games module in April 2009. A third study was also conducted at Glasgow Caledonian University in April 2009. This paper will discuss some of the problems associated with teaching requirements collection and analysis, the advantages and disadvantages of traditional teaching approaches, and how and in what ways GBL can act as a suitable supplement to these traditional approaches. The problem of the lack of empirical evidence and general evaluation frameworks will then be discussed, leading to the introduction of a new evaluation framework for games-based learning. The requirements collection and analysis game will then be described in more detail. Finally, the results of the three individual experiments will be presented followed by discussion and a conclusion.

PROBLEMS IN TEACHING REQUIREMENTS COLLECTION AND ANALYSIS AND SOFTWARE ENGINEERING

The problems associated with teaching software engineering have been discussed in detail in a previous study (Connolly et al., 2007). Problems specifically associated with teaching requirements collection and analysis are deeply rooted in the lack of definitional conformity to what a requirement is.

Software Requirements

The IEEE defines a requirement as "a condition or capability needed by a user to solve a problem or achieve an objective" or "a condition or capability that must be possessed by a system to satisfy a contract standard, specification or other formally imposed document." A requirement is a statement specifying part of the required functionality of the system. One of the primary reasons that requirement capture and analysis is so problematic and complex is that a requirement can be expressed in different levels of abstraction or complexity. Sommerville (2007) emphasizes "the term requirement is not used in the software industry in a consistent way. In some cases, a requirement is simply a high-level, abstract statement of a service that the system should provide or a constraint on the system. At the other extreme, it is a detailed, formal definition of a system function" (p. 118). To combat the complication encountered by the different levels of abstraction, Sommerville (2007) distinguishes between user requirements and system requirements:

- User requirements (requirements of a high level of abstraction) are "statements, in a natural language plus diagrams, of what services the system is expected to provide and the constraints under which it must operate." (p. 118)
- System requirements (requirements of a highly detailed nature describing what the system should do) "set out the system's functions, services and operational constraints in detail. The system requirements document (sometimes called a functional specification) should be precise. It should define exactly what is to be implemented. It may be part of the contract between the system buyer and the software developers." (p. 118)

Advantages and Disadvantages of Traditional Teaching Techniques

Some of the advantages and disadvantages of traditional techniques are displayed in Table 1, adapted from Bonwell (1996), Cashin (1985), Wehrli and Nyquist (2003) and Davis (2001), the ADPRIMA Instructional Methods information website (2009) and Connolly et al. (2004).

Games-Based Learning can potentially help with some of the shortcomings as games enable meaning to be *situated* (Lave & Wegner, 1991), *anchored* (Bransford et al., 1990) and support "conceptual interaction" (Laurillard, 1996). Situated learning is important as GBL is at its most powerful when it is "personally meaningful, experimental, social, and epistemological all at the same time" (Shaffer, Squire, Halverson & Gee, 2004, p. 3). Games provide experiential learning where knowledge is created through the transformation of experience (Kolb, 1984) providing the four stages of the experiential learning cycle: concrete experience, reflective observation, abstract conceptualization, and active experimentation. Healy and Connolly (2007) compared the difference between traditional methods and GBL. Some of the main differences concern the passivity of traditional methods as opposed to the interactive and active learning strategies evident in GBL. Traditional methods are viewed as out-

Table 1. Advantages and disadvantages

Teaching Technique	Advantages	Disadvantages
Lectures	• Lecturers have full control of the learning experience. • Intrinsic interest of a subject can be communicated through the lecturer's enthusiasm. • Large amounts of information can be tailored and presented to large audiences containing material not otherwise available to students. • Lectures can provide a model of how professionals address problems and questions. • Appeal to students who learn by listening and present very little risk for students.	• Lecturer is required to be an effective speaker and become a 'sage on stage'. • No mechanism exists to ensure that students are intellectually engaged, meaning that they are often passive recipients resulting in information being quickly forgotten. • Student's attention begins to wane after a short period (approximately 15 to 25 minutes). • Lectures are not suited for teaching abstract, complex subjects, or higher order thinking skills such as values, motor skills, analysis and application etc. • Assumes that all students are at the same level of understanding and learn at the same pace. • Students who have different optimal learning styles other than listening are at a disadvantage.
Role-Play	• Participants are actively involved in the exercise. • Enhances the learning experience by adding elements of variety, reality and specificity. • Provides a safe environment to increase practice experience when real life experiences are unavailable. • Immediate feedback is provided and can give new perspectives on situations. • Likelihood of transfer from the classroom to the real world is improved.	• Puts pressure on learner to perform and can result in embarrassment if learners are too self conscious. • Can be time consuming as good practice usual requires a debriefing session. • The role-play has to be well planned, monitored and orchestrated otherwise it may lack focus. • Puts mental pressure on the acting participants if questions are asked that deviate from the script. • Requires appropriate monitoring by a knowledgeable person to provide appropriate feedback.
Paper-based Case-Studies	• Students can apply new skills. • Develops analytical problem solving skills. • Can be relatively self-pacing if it is in the form of a coursework as participants can study in their own time. • Useful method for finding a large number of solutions for complex issues.	• The case study must be carefully prepared and defined. • It may be difficult for the students to see the relevance of the case study for their own situation. • Inappropriate results may occur if the case-study has insufficient information. • Approach is not suitable to elementary education.

dated and based on an instructivist methodology. GBL, on the other hand, is considered more up-to-date and underpinned by students actively seeking information and knowledge. A further and significant difference is that where traditional methods are proven, GBL has yet to attract a great deal of empirical research (Connolly, Stansfield & Hainey, 2007; de Freitas, 2006).

LACK OF EMPIRICAL EVIDENCE AND EVALUATION FRAMEWORKS IN GBL

O'Neil, Wainess, and Baker. (2005) believe that an essential element missing is the ability to properly evaluate games for education and training purposes. If games are not properly evaluated and concrete empirical evidence is not obtained in individual learning scenarios that can produce generalisable results, then the potential of games in learning can always be dismissed as unsubstantiated optimism. In the O'Neil study, a large amount of literature was collected and analysed from the PsycINFO, EducationAbs, and SocialAciAbs information systems. Out of several thousand articles, 19 met the specified criteria for inclusion and had empirical data that was either qualitative, quantitative or both. The literature was then viewed through Kirkpatrick's four levels for evaluating training and the augmented CRESST model. The majority of the studies analysed performance on game measurements. Other studies included the observation of military tactics used, time to complete the game, transfer test of position location, flight performance and a variety of questionnaires including exit, stress and motivation. The review of empirical evidence on the benefit of games and simulations for educational purposes is a recurring theme in the literature and can be traced even further back. For example, Randel, Morris, Wetzel, and Whitehill (1992) examined 68 studies from 1963 comparing simulations/games approaches and conventional instruction in direct relation to student performance. Some of the following findings were made:

- 38 (56%) of the studies found no difference; 22 (32%) of the studies found a difference that favoured simulations/games; 5 (7%) of studies favoured simulations/games however control was questionable; 3 (5%) found differences that favoured conventional instruction.
- With regard to retention, simulations/games induced greater retention over time than conventional techniques.
- With regard to interest, out of 14 (21%) studies, 12 (86%) showed a greater interest in games and simulations over conventional approaches.

Dempsey, Rasmassen and Lucassen (1994) performed a literature review ranging from (but not limited to) 1982 to 1994 and discovered 91 sources (most of them journal papers). The main findings of this study were that majority of the articles discovered were discussion based (n = 43) i.e. "articles which state or describe experiences or opinions with no empirical or systematically presented evidence" (p. 4). Thirty-three research articles, nine literature review, seven theoretical and a very small number of development articles (n = 4) were discovered. The study acknowledged that it had unsystematically sampled a very small amount of the literature as a whole but expected the literature to follow the trend of being dominated by discussion articles. The current state of the literature certainly follows this trend as discussion papers are simpler to write than research or empirical studies. Although lack of empirical evidence supporting GBL is not a new issue, the growing popularity of computer games in conjunction with recent advances in games and hardware technology, and the emergence of virtual worlds and massively multiplayer online games (MMOGs), reinforces the need for more empirical-based research. The following section examines previous proposals for evaluation frameworks before proposing an extended framework that we will subsequently apply to our game for requirements collection and analysis.

PREVIOUS EVALUATION FRAMEWORKS

When developing an evaluation framework for GBL, it seems logical to design the framework from a pedagogical perspective as the entire ideology of GBL is based on using games/simulations to motivate and engage learners, resulting in more effective learning even at a supplementary level. There are very few evaluation frameworks in the literature that specifically address the effectiveness of GBL from this perspective and ask questions such as: Does the GBL environment increase knowledge acquisition? Does it improve learner performance? Does it assist in the formation of metacognitive strategies? The majority of available frameworks are focused on either eLearning or commercial games such as World of Warcraft. Two examples of these frameworks are based on Nielsen's Heuristic Evaluation developed in 1990 (Nielsen & Molich, 1990). Heuristic Evaluation consists of ten recommended heuristics and is supposed to be performed by a small team of evaluators. It is a Human Computer Interaction (HCI) technique that focuses on finding interface usability problems and has been extended with additional heuristics to encompass website specific criteria. The technique has also been expanded and developed to produce a framework for Web-based learning (Ssemugabi & de Villiers, 2007) and a framework for heuristic evaluation of Massively Multi-player On-Line Role Playing Games (MMORPGs) (Song & Lee, 2007). One of the main difficulties associated with frameworks developed from Heuristic Evaluation is that the quality of a Heuristic Evaluation is dependent on the knowledge of the expert reviewer. By extending frameworks to encompass web-based learning and MMORPGs, suitable reviewers would have to have sufficient knowledge of HCI and games to perform a high-quality evaluation. In addition, from a GBL perspective the main difficulty is that these frameworks do not specifically focus on pedagogy.

Tan, Ling and Ting (2007) reviewed four GBL frameworks and models including: the design framework for edutainment environments, the adopted interaction cycle for games, the engaging multimedia design model for children and the game object model. According to their results one framework significantly addressed pedagogy and game design, namely the game object model (GOM) (Amory, Naicker, Vincent & Adams, 1999). GOM has been further developed using theoretical constructs and developments in the literature to become the game object model version II framework (GOM II) (Amory, 2006). This particular framework can be used from both a game design and an evaluation perspective. Kirkpatrick's four-level framework takes pedagogy into account (1994). It was originally developed in 1994 as a framework for evaluating training but it has also been proposed for the evaluation of business simulations as educational tools (Schumann, Anderson, Scott & Lawton, 2001).

The CRESST model of learning is composed of five families of cognitive demands and can be used in a motivational learning view for the evaluation of games and simulations (Baker & Mayer, 1999). Each family in the CRESST model is composed of a task that can be used as a skeletal design for testing and instruction. The CRESST model is divided into content specific and content independent variables. Content specific variables include: content understanding and problem solving. Content independent variables include: collaboration/teamwork, communication and self-regulation. A further framework specifically for games and simulations that addresses pedagogy is the Four Dimensional Framework (FDF) (de Freitas & Oliver, 2006). The FDF is "designed to aid tutors selecting and using games in their practice. The framework includes: context, learner specification, pedagogy used and representation as four key aspects for selecting the correct game for use in learning practice" (de Freitas, 2006, p. 69).

New Framework for GBL evaluation

Connolly, Stansfield and Hainey (2009) reviewed the literature and formulated a new evaluation framework for GBL (Figure 1). The purpose of the framework is to identify the main potential evaluation categories of games-based learning available in the scientific literature. The categories do not necessarily have to be viewed in isolation but as a collective whole depending on what is to be evaluated. The framework can be used in both a developmental sense to inform design during the implementation and embedding of a GBL environment for formative assessment, as well as to point to examples of individual analytical measurements already present in the literature for summative evaluation.

A brief description will be provided for each category:

- **Learner performance:** Encompasses pedagogy from the perspective of the learner and is concerned with evaluating aspects of learner performance. It is primarily associated with identifying improvements in learner performance.
- **Motivation:** The particular motivations of the learner using the intervention, the level of interest in participating in the intervention, participation over a period of time and determining what particular motivations are most important.
- **Perceptions:** Covers perceptions associated with the learner such as overview of time, how real the game is, its correspondence with reality, whether the games-based learning intervention represents a holistic view of a particular organization or process, game complexity, advice quality and level of self reported proficiency at playing games etc.
- **Attitudes:** Learner and instructor attitudes towards various elements that may alter the effectiveness of the games-based learning intervention. Elements include: learner attitudes towards the taught subject, learner attitudes towards games, and instructor attitudes towards the incorporation of games into the curricula etc.
- **Preferences:** Considers learner and instructor preferences during a GBL intervention. There are different learning styles (Kolb, 1984) therefore different learners have different preferences, for example,

Figure 1. Evaluation framework for effective games-based learning

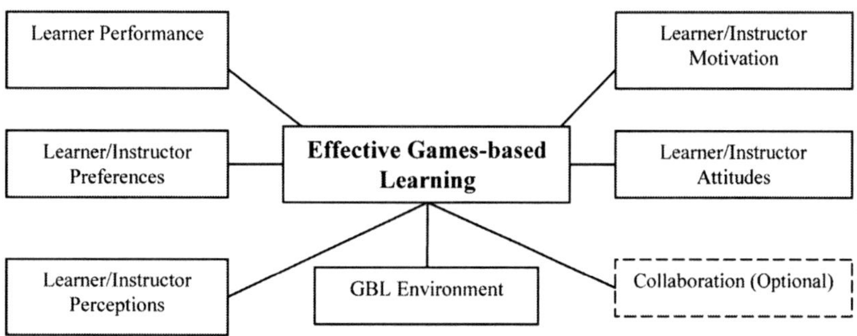

the preference for the medium used when teaching the material.

- **Collaboration:** Collaboration is optional for GBL depending on whether the game is played on an individual level, cooperative group level, or competitive group level etc. The main ways of evaluating collaboration are through log files monitoring interaction, mapping team aspects to learner comments, measuring the regularity and level of collaboration and learner group reflection essays.
- **GBL environment:** Encompasses all aspects that could potentially be evaluated about the games-based learning environment. It is one of the most complicated categories as it can be divided into five subcategories: environment, scaffolding, usability, level of social presence and deployment.

The framework was highly instrumental in formulating the pre- and post-tests for the evaluation of our game. We have also successfully used the framework to evaluate an Alternate Reality Game (ARG) for motivating secondary school students to learn a second language (Hainey et al., in print).

SIMULATING REQUIREMENTS COLLECTION AND ANALYSIS USING A GBL APPROACH

Gameplay

The basic idea of the game we have developed is for the team (comprising one or more players) to manage and deliver a number of software development projects. Each player has a specific role, such as project manager, systems analyst, systems designer or team leader. A bank of scenarios have been created based on case studies the authors have been using for many years in teaching and learning; for example, the *DreamHome* Estate Agency, the *StayHome* Online DVD Rentals company, the *PerfectPets* Veterinary Clinic, the Blackwood Library and the Fair Winds Marina. Each scenario has an underlying business model; for example, there will be a budget for the delivery of the project, a set timescale for the delivery of the project and a set of resources (at present, staff with specified technical specializations) that can be used on the project. Additional resources can be brought in for a project although this will have a cost and timescale (delay) associated with it. The project manager has overall responsibility for the delivery of each project on budget and on time and is given a short brief for each project. Communication is one of the key aspects of the game and the project manager must communicate relevant details of the project to the other players. This is done using a message metaphor – any player can communicate with any other player(s) by sending a message. Players have a message board that indicates whether there are any unread messages.

The player(s) assigned to the system analyst role have to identify the requirements for the project. To do this, the player must move through the game and 'talk' to the non-player characters (NPCs) in the game, as illustrated in Figure 2(a). In addition, there are objects in the game that can also convey relevant information when found (for example, a filing cabinet may convey requirements). For the prototype game we are using written transcripts in place of NPC speech. We hope shortly to use lip-synching within the game to have the NPCs 'talk' to the system analyst. Each NPC's 'speech' will contain some general background details and a number of requirements (the analyst has to distinguish the requirements from the general details). Visiting the same NPC may generate the same speech or a new speech. Each speech will generate a transcript that the analyst can visit at any point in the game (see Figure 2(b)). The transcript is presented as a numbered list of requirements. During the play, the analyst can use the transcripts to produce an initial 'wish-list' of requirements, which can be refined until the analyst believes all requirements have been identified, at which point the analyst can send the completed requirements to the project manager. The project manager now has two choices: send the requirements to the designer to produce an outline high-level design or consider the requirements to be incorrect and ask the analyst to rework the requirements (asking for rework will have a 'cost' associated with it).

EVALUATION OF THE REQUIREMENTS COLLECTION AND ANALYSIS GAME

The requirements collection and analysis game will be evaluated using the previously discussed evaluation framework. For the purposes of this paper the reported results will focus in particular on pedagogy, technical aspects of the game and student perceptions.

Methodology

The general experimental designs of studies evaluating games-based learning are experimental as opposed to quasi-experimental and are typically based on the pre-test/post-test approach (Maguire et al., 2006). The experimental designs producing the most impressive results associated with pedagogy used the standard pre-test → post-test, experimental - control group design, in which a particular group is exposed to the intervention and a particular group is not.

Evaluation Procedures

In the experimental game group, each participant was presented with a pre-test designed to collect some demographic and learner type information, assess the level of knowledge the participant already possessed about requirements collection and analysis and collect additional qualitative information, such as the most important technical aspects that they believe a game should possess. The participant was then presented with a summary information screen that could be referred to at any point during game play. The summary information screen detailed how to operate within the game environment. The participant was allowed to play the game for as long as it took to produce a requirements specification that the player believed to be satisfactory, which generally took between 15 and 40 minutes. Upon completion of the game the participant completed a post-test designed to test knowledge of requirements collection and analysis to analyse whether there was a knowledge gain. The questions were not identical to the pre-test but very similar. It also collected information about positive and negative aspects of the game,

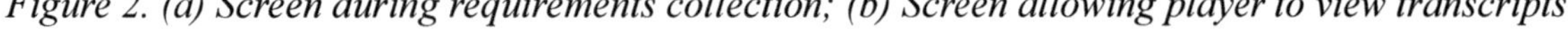

Figure 2. (a) Screen during requirements collection; (b) Screen allowing player to view transcripts

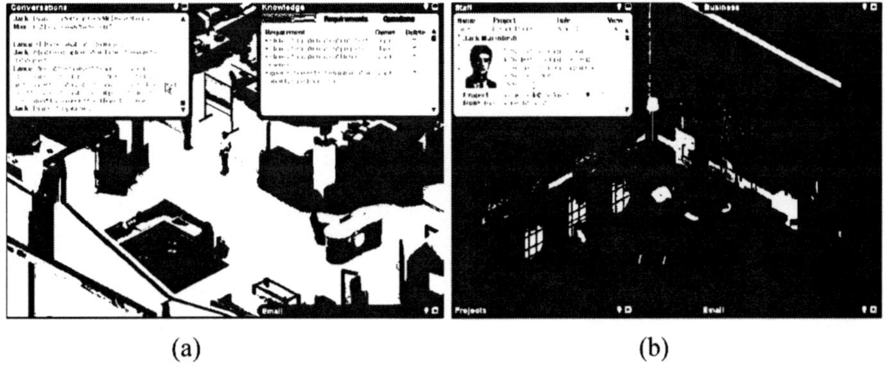

(a) (b)

technical aspects ratings, perceptions and preferences of the learners.

In the control role-play group, each participant was presented with a pre-test similar to those in the game group collecting demographic information and learner type information and assessing the level of knowledge of requirements collection and analysis. The knowledge test was identical to the experimental game group. The participants were then provided with a summary for the role-playing exercise similar to the summary screen for the game but with all the game elements removed in paper-based format. As in the game exercise, participants were provided with questions to start the role play. Members of staff and students acted out the parts of the characters in the game using the exact same case study and script that was incorporated into the game. Participants were told to note down any requirements and any additional questions they asked that were not included in the script. The role-play exercises took approximately 15 minutes and 90 minutes respectively and proceeded until all characters were interviewed to the satisfaction of the participants. Participants then completed the post-test to assess whether there was an identifiable knowledge gain. Again the questions were not completely identical to those in the pre-test but there were some similarities. It also collected information about the positive and negative aspects of the activity, aspect ratings, perceptions and preferences of the learners.

In the control paper-based group each participant was presented with the pre-test collecting demographic information, learner type information and assessing the level of knowledge similar to the other two groups. The participants were then presented with the same summary information excluding game and role-play elements. The script for the role-play and the game was provided to the participants and they were asked to underline all requirements. They were also asked to note down any additional questions that they believed to be necessary to fulfil this task. Participants were then presented with the post-test similar to those used in the other two groups but tailored for a paper-based study. The knowledge test questions were the same as in the other two groups.

Study One

Participants

Study 1 involved 39 participants from the University of the West of Scotland with a mean age of 28 (SD, 6.913) and a range from 19 to 44 years. 16 participants were assigned to the game group, 13 participants were assigned to a role-playing group and 10 participants were assigned to a paper-based group. The participants in the game group were a mixture of 10 (62.5%) undergraduate and 6 (37.5%) postgraduate Computer Networking, Information Technology and Multimedia Technology students. 14 participants were male and 2 were female. The mean age of participants was 25.13 years (SD, 5.572) with a range from 19 to 36. The participants in the role-playing group were a mixture of 8 (61.5%) postgraduate students and 5 (38.5%) undergraduate students studying Computer Games Technology, Networking, Information Technology and Multimedia and Web Authoring. The mean age of the participants was 29.31 (SD, 7.962) with a range from 19 to 44 years. All participants in the game and role-play groups were undertaking a module called *Introduction to Database Systems*. The paper-based group consisted of 10 PhD research students outside the field of computing who had never been taught requirements collection and analysis before. 8 (80%) were female and 2 (20%) were male. The mean age was 30.90 (SD, 6.244) with a range from 24 to 44 years.

Results

The mean score on the pre-test for the game group was 3.94 (SD = 1.34) and on the post-test was 5.00 (SD = 1.26). A paired samples t-test revealed that the increase in scores between the pre- and post-test was significant ($t(15) = -3.437$, $p = 0.004$). For the role-playing group the pre-test mean on the knowledge score was 3.69 (SD = 1.032) and on the post-test 4.62 (SD = 1.193). A paired samples t-test shows that the increase in knowledge was significant t(12) = -2.984, p = 0.011. The mean score for the pre-test in the paper-based case study group was 3.60 (SD = 1.71) and 4.50 (SD = 1.08) on the post-test. The paired sample t-test showed that the result of the knowledge increase in this group was not significant t(9) = -1.445, p = 0182. A mixed-design ANOVA (Analysis of variance) revealed no significant differences in knowledge levels between the three groups (F(2) = 0.053, p = 0949) indicating that the game is just as an effective form of supplementary learning experience.

Participants' mean ratings of the technical aspects of the game-based learning environment (from very good, scored as 5 to very bad, scored as 1) were generally positive. The aspects rated from highest to lowest were environmental realism (4.00, SD = 0.82), graphics (3.75, SD = 0.86), environmental navigation (3.75, SD = 0.93), character customisation (3.38, SD = 0.89), realism of the characters in the environment (3.31, SD = 1.01) and clear goal structure (3.31, SD = 1.08). The lowest ratings were for collaboration (2.37, SD = 1.75) and sound (1.19, SD = 1.47). This suggested that participants were generally satisfied with the game interface as very few marks of 2 or less were observed.

Participants' ratings of the aspects of the paper-based case study (from very good, scored as 5 to very bad, scored as 1) were not particularly positive. The aspects rated from highest to lowest were: narrative and dialog (4.20, SD = 0.63), realism of the scenario (3.70, SD = 1.41) and realism of characters in the dialog (3.40, SD = 1.51), clear goal structure (2.70, SD = 1.83), help and scaffolding facilities (2.20, SD = 1.75), collaboration (2.00, SD = 1.70), and ability to improvise (2.00, 1.63). The realism of narrative, dialog and characters being rated highly is an encouraging occurrence as the paper-based script is a direct representation of the dialog in the game, indicating that the case study is acceptable regardless of what format it is delivered in.

Participants' ratings of the aspects of the role-play activity (from very good scored as 5 to very bad scored as 1) were generally positive. The aspects rated from highest to lowest were: collaboration (3.77, SD = 0.832), clear goal structure (3.54, SD = 1.13), narrative and dialog (3.54, SD = 0.78), ability to improvise (3.46, SD = 0.88), realism of the scenario (3.31, SD = 0.95), realism of the characters and the dialog (3.00, SD 1.15). Help and scaffolding facilities rated the lowest (2.85, SD = 1.14). One possible explanation for this is that the role-play was conducted in a traditional classroom with members of staff and researchers playing the parts, so that the participants possibly did not realize that they had access to help and scaffolding for the duration of the role-play with regards to members of staff being present.

Students' Perceptions of the Game

The students were generally supportive of the use of the game in learning. 15 of the 16 participants agreed or strongly agreed that the game could be used in the intended domain in the future and 14/16 felt that the game fitted well into its intended context. 12 agreed that the game was engaging, 9 agreed that the game sustained their engagement, 9 would like to play the game again and 12 believed that the game could increase their skills at Higher Education level.

Positive Features of the Game

Several students picked up on the graphics as a positive feature of the game, while several liked the interaction and the conversational nature of the requirements collection:

The interaction.

Conversation, collection of data.

It shows the user how and from where s/he could collect the required data.

Different people to ask i.e. advisor, manager.

One participant identified the real world setting of the game as useful in making links between being a student and working:

It is good that it feels like you work in a company and have to solve a 'real' job.

One student commented on the game as useful in learning:

Makes you think so helps you learn.

Negative Features of the Game

Participants also offered useful feedback about how to improve the game:

No 'end game' to reach a result/resolution.

Speed of character, how all the questions piled up/ difficulty of organisation. Information overload at the beginning/no back story.

It was too repetitive.

No real control of the characters.

I couldn't find the right persons for solving the conflicts I found.

I think it must have more controls and more questions to ask.

Study Two

Participants

8 participants from an honours year module called Serious Games at the University of the West of Scotland were randomly divided into two groups. 4 were assigned to a game group and 4 assigned to a role-playing group. All participants were male. The mean age was 21.50 (SD = 0.756) with a range from 21 to 23.

Results

Participants' scores on the knowledge requirements tests before and after both interventions were compared. The mean score on the pre-test for the game group was 6.25 (SD = 1.5) and on the post-test 11.25 (SD = 1.708). A paired sample t-test showed that the increase in knowledge was significant ($t(3) = -3.576$, $p = 0.030$) in the game group. The mean score in the pre-test for the role-play was 6.25 (SD = 1.5) and on the post-test 8.50 (SD = 1.00). A paired sample t-test showed that the increase in knowledge was significant ($t(3) = -3.576$, $p = 0.037$). A mixed design ANOVA between the knowledge scores of the pre- and post-tests of the two groups was not significant ($F(1) = 1.580$; $p = 0.255$ indicating that the game group and role-play group were similarly effective.

Study Three

Participants

8 participants from a Computer Games Software Development Course at Glasgow Caledonian University were randomly divided into two groups. 4 were assigned to the game group and 4 were

assigned to a role-playing group. All participants were male. The mean age was 19.125 (SD, 1.885) with a range from 12 to 22.

Results

Participants' scores on the knowledge requirements tests before and after both interventions were compared. The mean score on the pre-test for the game group was 4.50 (SD=3.109) and on the post-test was 9.75 (SD = 1.258). A paired samples t-test indicated that the increase in knowledge in the game group was significant (t(3) = -2.458, p = 0.04). The mean score in the pre-test for the role-play group was 6.75 (SD = 0.957) and on the post-test was 9.75 (SD=0.957). A mixed design ANOVA between the knowledge scores of the pre-tests and post-tests of the two groups was not significant (F(1)=3.423; p=0.114) indicating that the game group and role-play group were equally effective.

Study 2 and 3 Combined Results

The technical rating aspects of the game for study 2 and 3 were generally good. The highest rated aspects were: navigation inside the environment (4.25, SD=0.46), control mechanism and interface (4.13, SD = 0.83), graphics (3.88, SD = 0.64), realism of characters in the environment (3.88, SD = 0.35), character customization (3.88, SD = 0.35), realism of the environment (3.75, SD = 0.46), help and scaffolding (3.62, SD = 0.51), narrative and dialog (3.50, SD = 0.76) and clear goal structure (3.50, SD = 1.20). The lowest rating aspect was collaboration (1.75, SD = 1.67). The role playing aspects for study 2 and 3 were in some ways consistent with those of study 1. Higher ratings were observed for collaboration, ability to improvise and narrative and dialog. All other ratings were significantly more negative.

Positive features of the game were:

Graphics, script.

Good graphics, well thought out.

Good graphics, navigation, very well planned dialog. Interactivity.

Negative features of the game were:

Too much text. Not as fun as a commercial game.

A little slow.

The majority of the students who took part in the two studies agreed that they would be willing to play the game as part of a computing course and that the game was engaging. All participants either agreed or strongly agreed that the game would fit well into its intended context for teaching requirements collection and analysis.

Discussion

An observation made about the advantages of each technique by the researchers involved was rooted in the identification of requirements in all of the groups. The game group would always manage to identify significantly more requirements in general and more requirements that were either conflictual or required some form of clarification. In the role-playing group it was observed that while collaboration, help and scaffolding and improvisation were considered better, due to the fact that the requirements were not specifically highlighted in the exercise, then significantly less were discovered. The paper-based exercise gave the participants the ability to study the script at greater length; however, it became apparent that the participants were becoming overly analytical and highlighting all of the text the majority of the time without specifically identifying the requirements that were more easily identifiable in the game. One of the major advantages highlighted in the role-playing activity was the ability to improvise, however the fact that a game is a "closed, formal system" (Crawford, 1982, p. 7) meant that the participants in the game group were not permitted to deviate from the programmed script. While reducing improvisation, this is also a mechanism to stop the participant deviating into irrelevancies. When additional questions were asked outside the script, it put mental pressure on the academic or researcher to come up with a sensible answer that adhered to the case study as a whole. This may indicate that GBL is more of an adaptive platform for teaching subjects that are highly textual and abstract in nature.

In terms of the game's effectiveness at providing a supplementary learning experience, the ANOVAs presented no significant difference, indicating that the game was just as effective as traditional techniques for getting participants to learn the material. The major strength of the game was its ability to get participants to identify a significantly higher number of confliction and clarification requirements.

The comparison of the game with the paper-based case study and role-play groups has verified that the case study is sufficiently complex and well structured for future experiments. It also shows that the game and paper-based case study aspects were viewed as generally positive whereas the role-play was not perceived as favourable. This is possibly due to the fact that the role-play activities put the participants on the spot in a more direct manner. The participants have to interact with tutors and ask questions, and as a result may feel pressured to produce solutions. This may suggest that the game and the paper-based case study are more familiar territory and put the participants more at ease.

CONCLUSION

In terms of future directions, we have established that the GBL approach to teaching requirements collection and analysis is just as effective as traditional techniques in terms of learning and in some cases more suitable. Further analysis of the results collected in this study will attempt to determine if the game is more intrinsically motivating and more engaging than the traditional techniques. The purpose of the studies was to ensure that valid and analysable results would be collected by running the evaluation. The studies revealed a number of improvements that could be made to the evaluation instruments entailing removal of some redundant questions, addition of questions and slight alteration to others questions to eliminate ambiguity. Future iterations of the evaluation will be conducted with an external group to test if the findings of the study evaluations are consistent.

REFERENCES

Amory, A. (2006). Game object model version II: A theoretical framework for educational game development. *Educational Technology Research and Development*, *55*(1), 51–77. doi:10.1007/s11423-006-9001-x

Amory, A., Naicker, K., Vincent, J., & Adams, C. (1999). The use of computer games as an educational tool: 1. Identification of appropriate game types and game elements. *British Journal of Educational Technology*, *30*, 311–322. doi:10.1111/1467-8535.00121

Baker, E. L., & Mayer, T. E. (1999). Computer-based assessment of problem solving. *Computers in Human Behavior*, *15*, 269–282. doi:10.1016/S0747-5632(99)00023-0

Bonwell, C. C. (1996). Enhancing the lecture: Revitalizing a traditional format. In T. E. Sutherland & C.C. Bonwell (Eds.), *Using active learning in college classes: A range of options for faculty, New Directions for Teaching and Learning No. 67.* (pp. 31 - 44). Place: Wiley Periodicals Inc., A Wiley Company.

Bransford, J., Sherwood, R., Hasselbring, T., Kinzer, C., & Williams, S. (1990). Anchored instruction: Why we need it and how technology can help. In D. Nix & R. Spiro (Eds.), *Cognition, education and multimedia: Exploring ideas in high technology* (pp. 163-205). Hillsdale, NJ: Lawrence Erlbaum Associates.

Brooks, F. (1987). No silver bullet: Essence and accidents of software engineering. *IEEE Computer*, *20*(4), 10–19.

Cashin, W. E. (1985). *Improving lectures idea paper No. 14.* Manhattan: Kansas State University, Center for Faculty Evaluation and Development.

Connolly, T. M., Stansfield, M. H., & Hainey, T. (2007). An application of games-based learning within software engineering. *British Journal of Educational Technology*, *38*(3), 416–428. doi:10.1111/j.1467-8535.2007.00706.x

Connolly, T. M., Stansfield, M. H., & Hainey, T. (2009) Towards the development of a games-based learning evaluation framework. In T. M. Connolly, M. Stansfield, & L. Boyle (Eds.), *Games-based learning advancements for multisensory human computer interfaces: Techniques and effective practices.* Hershey PA: IGI Global.

Connolly, T. M., Stansfield, M. H., McLellan, E., Ramsay, J., & Sutherland, J. (2004, November). Applying computer games concepts to teaching database analysis and design. In *Proceedings of the International Conference on Computer Games, AI, Design and Education*, Reading, UK.

Crawford, C. (1982). *The art of computer game design.* Berkeley, CA: McGraw-Hill.

Davis, B. G. (2001). *Tools for teaching*. San Francisco: Jossey-Bass Publishers.

de Freitas, S. (2006). Learning in immersive worlds. *Joint Information Systems Committee.* Retrieved May 27, 2009, from http://www.jisc.ac.uk/media/documents/programmes/elearninginnovation/gamingreport_v3.pdf de Freitas, S., & Oliver, M. (2006). How can exploratory learning with games and simulations within the curriculum be most effectively evaluated. *Computers & Education. 46*(3), 249-264.

Dempsey, J. V., Rasmussen, K., & Lucassen, B. (1994, February 16-20). Instructional gaming: Implications for instructional technology. In *Proceedings of the Annual Meeting of the Association for Educational Communications and Technology*, Nashville, TN.

Hainey, T., Connolly, T. M., Stansfield, M. H., Boyle, L., Josephson, J., O'Donovan, A., et al. (in print). ARGuing for multilingual motivation in Web 2.0: An evaluation of a large-scale European pilot. In *Proceedings of the 3rd European Conference on Games-based Learning (ECGBL)*, October 2009, Graz, Austria.

Healy, A., & Connolly, T. M. (2007, October 25-26). Does games-based learning, based on a constructivist pedagogy, enhance the learning experience and outcomes for the student compared to a traditional didactic pedagogy? In *Proceedings of 1st European Conference on Games-Based Learning. (ECGBL)*, Paisley, Scotland.

Instructional Methods Information Website, A. D. P. R. I. M. A. (2009). Retrieved 21 May, 2009, from http://www.adprima.com/teachmeth.htm

Kirkpatrick, D. L. (1994). *Evaluating training programs: The four levels.* San Francisco: Berrett-Koehler.

Kolb, D. A. (1984). *Experiential learning*, Englewood Cliffs, NJ: Prentice Hall.

Laurillard, D. (1996, June). *Keynote speech at the ACM SIGCSE/SIGCUE Conference,* Barcelona.

Lave, J., & Wenger, E. (1991). *Situated learning: Legitimate peripheral participation.* UK: University of Cambridge Press.

Maguire, M., Elton, E., Osman, Z., & Nicolle, C. (2006). Design of a virtual learning environment for students with special needs. *Human Technology: An Interdisciplinary Journal on Humans in ICT Environments*, *2*(1), 119–153.

Nielsen, J., & Molich, R. (1990, April 1-5) Heuristic evaluation of user interfaces. Seattle, WA. In *Proceedings of the ACM HI'90 Conference* (pp. 249-256).

O'Neil, H. F., Wainess, R., & Baker, E. L. (2005). Classification of learning outcomes: evidence from the computer games literature. *Curriculum Journal*, *16*(4), 455–474. doi:10.1080/09585170500384529

Randel, J. M., Morris, B. A., Wetzel, C. D., & Whitehill, B. V. (1992). The effectiveness of games for educational purposes a review of research. *Simulation & Gaming*, *23*(3), 261–276. doi:10.1177/1046878192233001

Schumann, P. L., Anderson, P. H., Scott, T. W., & Lawton, L. (2001). A framework for evaluating simulations as educational tools. *Developments in Business Simulations and Experiential Learning, 28.*

Shaffer, D. W., Squire, K. T., Halverson, R., & Gee, J. P. (2004). Video games and the future of learning, *Phi Delta Kappan*. Retrieved 6 December, 2008 from http://www.academiccolab.org/resources/gappspaper1.pdf

Sommerville, I. (2007). Software engineering, 8th ed. Harlow: International Computer Science, Addison Wesley.

Song, S., & Lee, J. (2007). Key factors of heuristic evaluation for game design: Towards massively multi-player online role-playing game. *International Journal of Human-Computer Studies*, *65*, 709–723. doi:10.1016/j.ijhcs.2007.01.001

Ssemugabi, S., & de Villiers, R. (2007, October 2-3). A comparative study of two usability evaluation methods using a web-based e-learning application. In *Proceedings of the 2007 Annual Research Conference of the South African Institute of Computer Scientists and Information Technologists on IT Research in Developing Countries*, Fish River Sun, Sunshine Coast, South Africa.

Tan, P.-H., Ling, S.-W., & Ting, C.-Y. (2007) Adaptive digital game-based learning framework. In *Proceedings of the 2nd international conference on Digital interactive media in entertainment and arts* 07 Perth, Western Australia.

Wehrli, G., & Nyquist, J. G. (2003). Creating an educational curriculum for learners at any level. *AABB Conference.* Retrieved May 27, 2009, from http://www.nhchc.org/UNMSOM/Resources-forDevCurr_Teaching_LearningActivities.pdf

This work was previously published in International Journal of Virtual and Personal Learning Environments, edited by Michael Thomas, Volume 1, Issue 1, pp. 51-71, copyright 2010 by IGI Publishing (an imprint of IGI Global).

Chapter 18
Challenges Facing the Semantic Web and Social Software as Communication Technology Agents in E-Learning Environments

Bolanle A. Olaniran
Texas Tech University, USA

ABSTRACT

The semantic web describes the process whereby information content is made available for machine consumption. With increased reliance on information communication technologies, the semantic web promises effective and efficient information acquisition and dissemination of products and services in the global economy, in particular, e-learning. Despite the semantic web's promises, certain challenges face the realization of these goals. In this paper, the author addresses key challenges, including technological and socio-cultural issues, in addition to discussing specific implications relating to the direction of the semantic web.

INTRODUCTION

The concept of the semantic web focuses on the new generation of World Wide Web (W3) architecture platforms that enhance content delivery within formal semantics. The semantic web also describes the process where information content is made readily available for machine consumption (Stojanovic, Staab, & Studer, 2001). However, with the increased reliance on technologies, in particular the semantic web for information dissemination and product and service delivery in the global economy, there are key communication challenges that include technology and socio-cultural implications that must be addressed. From the founder of the Internet's standpoint, the semantic web provides an environment in which human and machine agents communicate on a semantic basis (Berners-Lee, 2000). For this reason, the foundation for the semantic web is based on

DOI: 10.4018/978-1-4666-1770-4.ch018

ontology. Ontology represents the organization of information about products, services, and other materials around a small domain of semantically enriched objects. Ontology thus, consists of semantic networks of concepts, relations, and rules that define the meaning of information resources (de Moor, 2005; Lytras & Naeve, 2006). From this perspective, information and materials can be organized into customized databases and delivered to end-users on demand according to the users' preferred needs.

The goal of the semantic web is to develop a basis for intelligent applications enabling more efficient information use through collections of repository knowledge and information databases (Schoop, Moor, & Dietz, 2006). The organization of the semantic web holds significant implications for information delivery, culture, marketing, and communication about products or services. How people search for information is important and it is also exacerbated by non-local users, an issue that is rarely addressed in the research literature. It is the goal of the proposed article to explore how the semantic web enables the dissemination and acquisition of information and e-learning collaboration to address both technical and socio-cultural challenges.

The rise of the World Wide Web (W3) has significantly influenced the way people conduct research, commerce, politics, and the way they learn or receive education in the global world. Internet use has grown significantly in recent years and continues to grow rapidly in non-English speaking regions. Data suggest that between 2000-2007, Internet use in Latin America and the Middle East grew by 577% and 920% respectively (Miniwats International, 2007; Wang, 2008). Access to the Internet and the W3 allows users to search information on billions of topics and in variety of ways. The impact, however, is not limited to information searches alone, rather the W3 has evolved as a means for building a sense of community, for learning, products and services, along with agenda setting. However, in spite of the advantages that the web brings, one of the problems or challenges that results from this copious amount of data is *information overload*. It is not uncommon for one query to produce hits ranging from hundreds to millions of results when searching for information online (de Moor, 2005). As Gozzi (2007) puts it, "there may be billions of web pages in existence, but if we can't find what we are looking for, these pages are useless" (p. 276). For learners and users alike, the challenge shifts from finding information to deciphering the usefulness and relevance of that information. Therefore, for the semantic web to have the intended impact and continued relevance for users, much needs to be done regarding its complex, changing, and imperfect sources of meaning. Therefore, great confusion and debate remains as to how to model context in the semantic web in order to achieve its practical usefulness (de Moor, 2005; Mey, 2003; Stojanovic et al., 2001).

Primarily, the semantic web makes its greatest contribution by making the W3 more relevant by adding structure (i.e., reasoning rules) and logic (i.e., the most common form of meaning) (Berners-Lee, Hendler, & Lassila, 2001). The semantic web creates structure by establishing rules for reasoning and organizing web content in a way that they can be shared, used, and distributed by communication agents and end users (i.e., learners). The semantic web is about making people's life easier by answering a host of familiar "ready-reference queries" (Adams, 2002). The key to the semantic web is ontology (i.e., shared meanings and services), which can be used to improve the accuracy of web searches and service discovery and delivery (Adams, 2002; Giles, 2008). The underlying assumption of ontology is that by selecting the right concept for a given task or shared knowledge, in theory, the task should become more effective, efficient, and accessible. However, this is precisely the challenge. In theory, an ontological concept should drive efficiency and accessibility, while in reality, there are several factors that hinder the accuracy and performance of ontology within the semantic web. Furthermore, in practice, the semantic web needs to take into account issues of semantics and pragmatics of the web (e.g., de Moor, 2005; Giles, 2008; Kim & Dong, 2002; Reppenning & Sullivan, 2003; Singh, 2002; Spyns & Meersman, 2003; Stojanovic et al., 2001). To further understand these concepts, the next section examines the technical challenges presented by the semantic web.

TECHNICAL CHALLENGES

In an attempt to make the semantic web a reality, one begins with extensible markup language (XML) which provides structure and syntax rules. In addition to the XML, challenges remain with the notion of a resource description framework (RDF), which addresses the additional architectural layer that focuses on actual semantics, or meanings. Problems exist in deciding how much XML would accomplish and to what degree functionalities of the semantic web must be relegated to RDF (Stojanovic et al., 2001; Veltman, 2004). The interface used to ask questions in some versions of the semantic web (i.e., DBPedia) is presumed to frighten less web-savvy users, while at the same time, other software that can be used to search a broader range of online semantic information is not suitable for the average user (Giles, 2008). Furthermore, the detail of what RDF content looks like in a semantic web context is always in question, thus, adding to the difficulty.

One of the primary challenges with the semantic web is that the platform or architecture layer is always changing. For instance, the fundamentals of the semantic web shifted from standard generalized markup language (SGML) to XML, to Unicode plus uniform resource identifiers (URI) (Veltman, 2004). Without getting overly technical, *ontology* enters the picture to speak to the difficulties in sense-making (i.e., meaning creation and sharing). However, among these various types of platforms, the issue of meaning was never really addressed by an ontological perspective. As a matter of fact, platform designers have relegated ontology to the idea of logic-meaning language, which continues to remain the most common interpretation associated with a given idea or concept. However, the problem persists because meanings are deemed subjective and often perceived as irrelevant or unimportant within the semantic web. The limitation of associating meaning to logic creates pragmatic and contextual challenges. These problems of pragmatic and contextual challenge are otherwise referred to as semantic primitives (Sowa, 2000).

The logic structure often fails as different disciplines, communities, and cultures have different terminologies and meanings for similar words (Olaniran, 2007a, 2007b). Furthermore, while it is true that logic may be ideal and perhaps solve some of the challenges with computer-to-computer communication and interactions, and may even offer solutions to science and technology, there remains the challenge of individual needs and contextual differences in the determination of meaning, and consequently, in interactions where human-human, human-computer, and other instances of human-computer-human interactions are intertwined (i.e., Veltman, 2004).

It has been suggested that the semantic web goes beyond mere access to information to one that accesses different methods of knowing (Berners-Lee, 2000). However, implementing this suggestion varies according to different point of views, whether the semantic web belongs to that of an educational technologist or an artificial intelligence researcher (Veltman, 2004). Gruber claims that the goal for computer scientists involved in the semantic web is to agree upon an authorized set of ontologies that can be used and re-used across multiple disciplines and settings (as cited in Giles, 2008). This problem is illustrated in an analogy where computer scientists and programmers are concerned with how software and machines interact with ontologies, whereas, librarians (or end users), on the other hand, are mostly concerned with how patrons retrieve information with the aid of taxonomies (Giles, 2008). Complicating the integration between computer scientists or developers and end users is the fact that an application domain rarely describes its semantics (Kobielus, 2007). Specifically, developers often find relational data structures difficult to fathom when they are trying to associate a complex set of linked data, such as tables with a coherent business-level conceptual model. Whereas integration specialists often have to infer semantics from non-detailed project documents and attempt to create cross-application data maps that are based on those inferences (Adams, 2002; Gasevic & Hatala, 2006; Kobielus, 2007).

As the semantic web gains prominence in e-learning for disseminating knowledge, its proponents tout its ability to adapt to learners' needs. For instance, e-learning within the context of the semantic web enabled focus on constructing context, and the re-use of learning objects (including information that can be re-used or referenced), and the execution of collaborative tasks (Snae & Brueckner, 2007).

This re-use of e-learning resources, such as those offered through the semantic web, depends on the fit as determined by the language, culture curriculum, computer-use practices and philosophies of teachers and potential users/learners (Collis & Strijker, 2004). However, creating a fit between technology and users' practices is difficult. Collis and Strijker (2004) contend that the reason for this difficulty includes the way in which learning objects are used in reality and practice, which also involves organizational or contextual settings of individuals that create, label, and offer learning objects in some respect and those that select and use them. Collis and Strijker (2004) emphasize the differences in e-learning contexts based on three different scenarios including: academic, corporate, and military (see Collis & Strijker, 2004).

Another area of concern with technology in e-learning involves the degree to which technology tools help address user learning styles. For instance, it is argued that not all users have the same motivation to learn, goals, background, interests, and needs (Alfonseca, et al., 2006; Olaniran, 2007a; Olaniran, Burley, Chang, Kuo, & Agnello, 2009). Consequently, semantic web tools, or learning resources, based upon these factors may be easy to navigate or use by certain users while remaining difficult for others. Alfonseca et al. (2006) argues that there remains a need to make sure that learning technologies become adaptive and more importantly adapt these resources to individual learners within e-learning contexts. From there we can take into account the cognitive structures and contexts of learning materials (see also Collis & Strijker, 2004).

While some attempts have been made in semantic web applications to be more responsive to learner's needs, some challenges remain (Collis & Strijker, 2006). For example Collis and Strijker (2004) identified some of these attempts which include the personal reader, ACTT - a design time tool allowing a course developer to create adaptive-activated oriented courses. Notwithstanding, the need for the semantic web to become adaptive is contingent on its ability to gather and store information about learners (e.g., goals, preferences, knowledge, etc.). However, this information is often difficult to collect. For instance, individuals may be reluctant to provide information about themselves especially in an open web. Consequently, without knowledge about the user, a system would act in the same manner for all learners or users (Koch, 2001).

Furthermore, the concepts of universals and particulars take center stage when oral knowledge begins to shift to written knowledge (Veltman, 2004). Universals focus on the attempt to standardize information possibly for multiple uses. Particulars, on the other hand, focus on the unique nature of information for specific contextual use. The technology trend demands an increased need to digitize information in an attempt to make information more readily available to people as evident through the semantic web. However, there is tension between universals and particulars that creates a challenge for e-learners and semantic web users; in that both concepts of universals and particulars entail logical rules, in particular the notion of relations. For instance, logical rules such as: 'relations with,' 'relations to,' and 'in comparison to,' allow people to develop an understanding and definition of concepts. Within the contexts of universals and particulars, there is a logical but rather imperfect method of understating a concept that involves the definition in terms of what a concept may represent (Lytras & Naeve, 2006; Veltman, 2004). Therefore, arriving at a particular meaning depends on the category of definition one is using. For example, four semantic definition categories were offered, including: 1. *Abstraction* (something is a), 2. *Partition* (something is a part of), 3. *Opposition* (something is not), and 4. *function* (something is about) (Dahlberg, 1995). Unfortunately, no one particular dictionary offers a comprehensive definition at these four levels of distinctions. Thus, the problem of an acceptable definition persists and is germane to content on the semantic web. In essence, to assume that facts and logical rules are adequate is problematic because of the impossibility of describing data enough for various users at the semantic level (Braun & Schmidt, 2006; Schoop et al., 2006; McCool, 2005).

The universal conceptual approach is considered static and can easily be incorporated into machine language or metaphors (Veltman, 2004). On the other hand, the particular conceptual approach is constantly changing. When considering services or knowledge dissemination via electronic platforms, it makes sense to separate the changing from the static. More importantly, the universals or the unchanging aspects are more amenable to a machine program as objective elements that can be easily assessed than the particulars or subjective information. This problem creates a challenge in the sense that by separating or not accounting for the different particulars, the target audience for whom the semantic web is designed becomes limited at best, or are removed altogether (Anderson, 2004; Koch, 2001; Olaniran, 2007a; Olaniran et al., 2009; Veltman, 2004). Although a solution might be to establish a new set of particulars that all context can relate to, unfortunately, this approach is not feasible. It would be impossible to understand and preserve past classification schemes from different contexts. Similarly, creating new classification schemes is believed to be insufficient to understand *how* and *why* some contexts use different methods of organizing knowledge (Veltman, 2004).

The idea of particulars have been addressed in the literature as learning styles which consist of a learner's or user's preferences as to how people acquire and process information (Alfonseca et al., 2006; Felder & Silverman, 1996). Thus, all learners have a unique way of learning. The Myers-Briggs type indicators, for example, specifically place people on a certain criteria of: thinking/feeling, extrovert/introvert, sensation/intuit, and judgment/perception (Briggs & Myers, 1977); however, there remain many varieties of learning style models (for a brief description see Alfonseca et al., 2006). For instance, Felder and Silverman (1996) offer five learning styles including:

- **Active/reflective**: where active learners prefer to learn by doing, while reflective learners prefer observation.
- **Sensing/intuitive**: where sensing learners learn by facts and procedures, while intuitive learners focus on conceptual information about theories and meanings.
- **Sequential/global**: sequential learners prefer an information structure that focuses on step by step processes, while global learners prefer to build knowledge maps by looking at information in a flexible manner.
- **Visual/verbal**: visual learners obtain information through graphs, pictures, and

diagrams, while verbal learners prefer oral information or lectures.

- **Inductive/deductive**: inductive learners prefer material focusing on principles and theories by inferences, while deductive learners prefer to focus on effects and uses from general information.

Alfonseca et al. (2006) argue that the above model is more flexible than most bipolar models of learning. In spite of its complexity, it is fair to argue that the model is not comprehensive or complete. For instance, it has been shown that Thai students prefer learning that is based upon rote, memorization and games (Snae & Brueckner, 2007). Consequently, the interaction of e-learners depends on the features and capabilities of the semantic web, while the needs and preferences of e-learners, with regards to these tools, would vary from student to student (Alfonseca et al., 2006).

SOCIO-CULTURAL CHALLENGES

The issue of culture is especially problematic to the semantic web and, in essence, one that information technology (IT) designers and theorists fail to consider adequately. The inattention to social issues such as culture by semantic web proponents emanates from too much focus on the technical aspects of the platform (Giles, 2008, Stojanovic et al., 2001; Veltman, 2004). Culture, however, is the essence of human existence and development. Significant bodies of literature have identified the need for understanding culture and its implications in knowledge-based and e-learning, and in the world of globalization and technologies (Hofstede, 1980, 1996; Gudykunst & Kim, 1997; Olaniran, 2007a, 2007b). Since all cultures focus on some aspects of knowledge and ignore others, history is essential for understanding different sources of meanings and the limitations of worldviews that we use in presenting them (Veltman, 2004).

More specific to the issue of the semantic web is the need to explore how social factors and culture influence knowledge management and learning, such that mere access, which has a challenge of its own as far as the semantic web is concerned, is not the sole determinant of content and knowledge management as a whole. For instance, Olaniran (2007a) illustrates the effect of culture on e-learning using Hofstede's dimensions of cultural variability (see also Van Dam & Rogers, 2002). In particular, the uncertainty avoidance dimension and e-learning identifies security and risk as primary concerns in some cultures. For instance, while e-learning is expected to be seen in high-risk or innovative cultures (i.e., low uncertainty avoidance) as something intriguing and potentially fun, motivational, and interesting; in a low risk cultural environment (i.e., high uncertainty avoidance), the same technology can be perceived as dangerous or a counter-culture altogether (Olaniran, 2007a; Van Dam & Rogers, 2002). From another standpoint, certain cultures view authority or power distance differently (Hall, 1976; Hofstede, 1980). For instance, in a high power distance culture (i.e., a measure of inequality in a culture), contrary to low power distance culture, knowledge is never shared equally nor is it expected to be shared equally across the society and people. High power distance culture recognizes the uneven distribution of power in the society, and thus, influences how information is viewed and consequently, disseminated among people across professions and organizations (Olaniran, 2008).

The different approach to power, in essence, becomes contradictory to the aim of information and knowledge management and the semantic web technologies that power it. For instance, different learning styles surface within different cultures. In particular, technology architecture such as the semantic web is seen as a convenient way to accomplish the aim of a constructivist idea (e.g., Weigel, 2003) of making learning fun, easy, and for giving greater control to users about the learning and knowledge management processes.

However, in some power distant cultures, such an approach is counter to cultural demands, many times confusing, and often frowned upon (Olaniran & Agnello, 2008). Thus, a learning style that emphasizes the hierarchical transfer of skills (i.e., telling) from an authoritative power to students and technology users is the norm (Olaniran, 2007a; Richards & Nair, 2007).

Furthermore, it has been suggested that it might be difficult to get people to use certain technology in power distant cultures where status dictates every aspect of interpersonal communication (e.g., Devereaux & Johansen, 1994; Olaniran, 2007b). For instance, Japanese designers address the challenge with culture and technology use by acknowledging that not all types of communication can be supported by communication technology systems (e.g., Internet or semantic web). Furthermore, the use of technology for supporting collaborative projects in Japan demands that groups must first meet physically to establish a trusting environment before interacting via technology medium (see also Barron, 2000; Olaniran, 2007a).

The role of culture on e-learning and the semantic web can be drawn from an explanation provided by Kawachi (1999), who argues that the Japanese do not embrace e-learning as a result of their language structure. Specifically, he indicates that the Japanese language, developed early in life, is more susceptible to the right brain learning mode (i.e., visual and memorization skills) when compared to the left brain (i.e., analytic and argumentation skills). As a result, the web is primarily used for searching and printing-out information for reading or translating, and secondarily for entertainment and games (Kawachi, 1999).

In essence, when there is no fit between technology and culture the diffusion and eventual acceptance of the technology will be seriously handicapped, regardless of whether it is the semantic web or not (e.g., Green & Ruhledder, 1995, Mesdag, 2000; Olaniran, 2007a, 2007b). He also identified that e-learning presents challenges because the tools and opportunities for discovering learners' perceptions and cultural predispositions are constrained by bandwidth that limits the view of body language and paralinguistic cues which, in turn, influence the effectiveness of communication (see also Alfonseca et al., 2006; Snae & Brueckner, 2007). This control is more conducive to universals. Thus, the semantic web is designed with the goal of having content applied universally such that individuals, irrespective of contexts, cultures and/or unique preferences, are able to use it.

However, different societies have developed their own vocabularies to meet their unique needs. The different vocabularies, however, lack formal semantics. Semantics are essential because regardless of the time and money put into creating databases and training materials, the content is useless if it cannot be indexed or searched with ease (Giles, 2008; Stojanovic et al., 2001). A similar idea indicates that semantic web ontology lacks semantics and is centrally structured with a universal ideology (Cayzer, 2004). Consequently the semantic web is believed to be better served by precise, local and domain specific vocabularies than that of a universal one-size-fits-all (Cayzer, 2004; Tennis & Sutton, 2008). After all, machines can not use partial information and they do not know what is inside an image. Ultimately, they are not good at making analogies or combining information from disparate sources, thus, they cannot make an accurate assessment of how meaning is negotiated and how information will be interpreted or understood (Adams, 2002; Kay, 2006).

OTHER FACTORS

Another factor contributing to the adoption and acceptance of any technology, including the semantic web, is access (Olaniran, 2007a; Vaughan & McVicar, 2004; Wahid, 2007). The level of access to technology, especially in less economically developed countries (LEDCs), has been written about extensively and continues to reinforce the digital divide between economically developed countries (EDCs) and the LEDCs. An erroneous assumption often made about technology especially by designers and programmers, is the fact that individuals around the world regardless of contexts have similar and easy access to technology. Also, the lack of proficiency in English, for example, creates a hindrance to information communication technology (ICT) adoption in certain countries (Olaniran, 2007b; Wahid, 2007). Consequently, content providers create content for the semantic web and knowledge management systems without regard to the issue of access and/or bandwidth (Olaniran, 2007a, 2008; Olaniran & Edgell, 2008; Wahid, 2007). Currently, there are no universally accepted browsers for the semantic web. Different software and platforms currently power queries within the semantic web unbeknownst to the user (Giles, 2008).

When addressing the issue of access within e-learning, or the semantic web in general, one must also contend with security. The heavy reliance on ICT within the distributed and collaborative environments necessitate knowledge externalization that requires digitalized taxonomies and rules that can be stored and transferred (Lee et al., 2005). Therefore, the semantic web and e-learning systems can capture more organizational knowledge that traditionally resides within an individual. The externalized, once–tacit knowledge can be easily transferred to collaborators while also being more open to theft by hackers (Lee et al., 2005). Therefore, strategic and proprietary knowledge and competence must be safeguarded now more so than before. Knowledge in the semantic web world resides in metadata, which is located in different databases created by organizations to preserve their competitive advantage, but also the knowledge remains machine accessible. Thus, when two or more agents or web services communicate to share information, it is imperative that they ensure all parties involved are permitted to request data. Extensible Access Control Markup Language (XACML) is one way to specify how to control access to a given data and ensure authorization. XACML provides an appropriate response to third party requests to certain data based on specified rules and policies to evaluate a requester's credentials, the type of request activity, and the range of possible inputs. Additionally, a related issue is the role allocation between IT staff and non-IT staff. Although role based access-control creates a separation of roles and rules for assigning security permissions, there are times that this role separation is not quite clear within organizations. For instance, the inferred/reconstructed knowledge becomes problematic, where more than two individuals share knowledge base, or 'nuggets of knowledge' each of which do not undermine confidentiality (Bertino et al., 2006; Lee et al., 2005).

RESEARCH IMPLICATIONS

Given the issues raised in this paper, the semantic web needs to be pragmatic in order to be effective and useful. Specifically, the semantic web must also be sophisticated enough to address how different people and cultures categorize, classify, and organize their worlds and interactions that exist within them. The globalization trend, which stresses increased universality, or a move towards it, is not helping the situation because we live in a world where developed countries with populations less than one third of the world control technologies and resources, and transplant these resources to the rest of the world. Consequently, traditional and *particular* distinctions are constantly overlooked and eroded (Hovy, 2002).

One way, by which the semantic web is attempting to resolve the challenge of the distinctions, is ontology. Ontology is usually attributed to generic meaning and knowledge that can be used in different applications (de Moor, 2005; Lytras & Naeve, 2006). However, to be effective, it is argued that ontology needs to be less restrictive or tightly linked to a particular purpose or group of user (Spyns, Meersman, & Jarrar, 2002). The challenge, however, is that ontology is not an end in itself.

One of the purposes of the semantic web is to provide access to web services through varieties of autonomous communication agents - small computer programs that navigate the web and act on information based on their assigned task (Anderson, 2004). Services or content cannot be described without paying attention to how it will be used (i.e., pragmatics) because a ‘community of service’ almost always uses services in novel and unintended ways. To this end, the ideas of pragmatics have been proposed, which entail the notion of making the semantic web adapt to users and specific contexts (Anderson, 2004; Kim & Dong, 2002; Lytras & Naeve, 2006). Anderson (2004) specifically argues for the role of teachers in developing their skills in a way that they are able to respond to student and curriculum needs by developing online learning activities that are adaptable to diverse student needs and learning styles. He proposes how the semantic web affordances can guide e-learning. For instance, these systems can increase their effectiveness by creating content that changes in response to individual learner preferences, or through the creation of agents for personalizing and re-using content, translating and monitoring community interactions, and offering timely feedback. However, the extent to which the issue of pragmatics can overcome the challenges of the semantic web for e-learners depends on the comprehensiveness of the data collected from users.

The ecological approach is another idea that has been offered as a way for moving semantics forward. The ecological approach is based on two ideas including: the belief that e-learning systems and the semantic web should be adaptive to users and also that technology, especially artificial intelligence, should help accomplish the adaptation (McCalla, 2004). Again, with the ecological approach, the emphasis is on capturing sufficient information about how learners use a system in an attempt to make the system respond to their respective need. In essence, the approach involves creating models of learners or users and then mining the models for the information that learners interact with (McCalla, 2004). According to McCalla (2004), “the information and the data mining algorithm interact with one another in an ecosystem where the relevance and usefulness of information is always being adjusted to suit the changing needs of learners and teachers to fit changes in the external environment and the system’s perception” (pp. 2-3). Of course, there are many technologies that are needed to make the ecological approach feasible and successful. They include data clustering, data mining, collaborative filtering, and learner modeling. By McCalla’s (2004) admission, apart from the learner modeling, few if any of these techniques are in use in e-learning. As a matter of fact, a very limited number of e-learning teachers are competent in these techniques creating additional challenges for teachers and learners in mastering these technologies. There appears to be a significant amount of research to be done in identifying the best way to incorporate these strategies and programs into e-learning. However, one thing is paramount, there needs to be social mechanisms for evaluating specific contexts and interactions in semantic web learning environments (de Moor, 2005; Kim & Dong, 2002; Lytras & Naeve, 2006; Mey, 2003; Olaniran, 2004, 2008; Singh, 2002).

It is true that for the semantic web to accomplish its claims and potentials, more work must be done on its pragmatics. For instance, the keyword query is inadequate. What is needed rather is a query that can answer specific questions and bypass useless data. Due to the wealth of information available, this added functionality remains essential. Similarly, the languages developed by the W3 consortium to describe data semantically are quite complex for web site owners to the extent that web developers may opt for simpler semantic processes, such as meta data tags, which are already in use. However, these meta tags used to describe shared bookmarks (e.g., del.icio.us, stumbleupon.com), in themselves limit the potential for identifying certain types of data, therefore, making the semantic web and more complex programming options more appealing (Bleicher, 2006; Giles, 2007; Kobielus, 2007).

Furthermore, a semantic web that recognizes the viewpoints and the knowledge levels of both content developers and end users in e-learning systems is required (Stojanovic et al., 2001). For instance, simple keyword queries do not always pick up synonyms, abbreviations, different languages (i.e., house & haus), or even morphological variations within the query context. The context of use for extracting meanings stored in ontology would still need to be understood. Thus, one way of overcoming such challenges is to establish and define corresponding relations in keywords in the domain ontology (Stojanovic et al., 2001*)*. Furthermore, determining how the meaning negotiation process works can be helpful for the pragmatics of the web and for creating automated or support systems for these negotiations (de Moor, 2005). This approach would help in network applications where individuals or communities of users are able to immerse themselves by tapping into their full collaborative potential. For example, the idea of multiple knowledge neighborhoods (i.e., locations in cyberspace), where specific users and groups can meet with the goal of learning about certain topics is suggested (Stutt & Motta, 2004).

The semantic web can be aimed at supporting different communities by providing specific ontologies for them either through topics, tasks, practices, and other means. The semantic web can aim at providing acceptable definitions or vocabularies for each community. Consequently, the targeted ontologies could result in fewer problems in developing, negotiating, and sharing understandings than when offering global ontology (Stutt & Motta, 2004). The advantage of this approach is that it allows a knowledge neighborhood (i.e., organization or work group) to address its own specific requirements, while maintaining the option for sharing content with other communities. Communicating across boundaries of different communities cannot solve the cultural and cross-cultural challenges; however, it can offer a buffer where members from different communities may help synthesize and translate information or concepts to other community members. In other words, membership in different communities can allow learning objects or ontologies to be flexible in addressing local (intra) and outside (inter) community needs, such that the particular data are able to take on different meanings in multiple domains and to a certain degree, cultural settings (Singh, Iyer, & Salam, 2005; Stutt & Motta, 2004; Tallman, Jenkins, Henry, & Pinch, 2004).

At the same time, ongoing work in semantic web browsers to augment successful knowledge navigation needs to be rolled out sooner than later. A case in point is the 'Magpie' semantic browser, which originated as a means of assisting in sense-making for users and to provide access via contextual menus for complementary databases or sources of knowledge that can be used in contextualizing and interpreting information on web pages.

CONCLUSION

The semantic web is an idea to remove chaos in the current data structure of the web. However, there is still much left to be done for this goal to become a reality. This paper raises some challenges that need to be addressed and offers suggestions with regard to what needs to be done and how it might be accomplished. Therefore, while semantic web opts to revolutionize knowledge management systems, it is still too early to determine what the future holds for this idealistic endeavor. Proponents of the semantic web have jumpstarted the process, but it remains to be seen whether others will follow their lead, or whether the phenomenon will become the norm in the not-so-distant future.

REFERENCES

Adams, K. (2002). The semantic web: Differentiating between taxonomies and ontologies. *Online, 26*(4), 20-33. Retrieved January 22, 2009, from http://www.online mag.net

Alfonseca, E., Carro, R. M., Martín, E., Ortigosa, A., & Paredes, P. (2009). The impact of learning styles on student grouping for collaborative learning: A case study. *User Modeling and User-Adapted Interaction, 16*, 377–401..doi:10.1007/s11257-006-9012-7

Barron, T. (2000). E-learning's global migration. *Learning Circuits.* Retrieved August 26, 2005, from http://www.astd.org/LC/2000/0900_barron.htm

Berners-Lee, T. (1998). *What the semantic web isn't but can represent.* The World Wide Web Consortium. Retrieved January 22, 2009, from http://www.w3.org/DesingnIssues/RDFnot.html

Berners-Lee, T., Hendler, J., & Lassila, O. (2001). The semantic web. *Scientific American*, 35–43.

Bertino, E., Khan, L., Sandhu, R., & Thuraisingham, B. (2006). Secure knowledge management: Confidentiality, trust, and privacy. *IEEE Transactions on Systems. Man & Cybernetics: Part A, 36*(3), 429–438..doi:10.1109/TSMCA.2006.871796

Bleicher, P. (2006). Getting to a semantic web on the internet. *Applied Clinical Trials Magazine,* 42-43. Retrieved January 22, 2009, from http://appliedclinicaltrialsonline.findpharma.com/appliedclinicaltrials/article/articleDetail.jsp?id=310806

Braun, S., & Schmidt, A. (2006). Socially-aware informal learning support: Potentials and challenges of the social dimension. In *Proceedings of the Joint International Workshop on Professional Learning, Competence Development and Knowledge Management-LOKMOL and L3NCD, 1st European Conference on Technology Enhanced Learning,* Crete, Greece. Retrieved December 20, 2009, from http://cnm.open.ac.uk/projects/ectel06/pdfs/ECTEL06WS68d.pdf#page=25

Briggs, K. C., & Myers, I. B. (1977). *Myers-Briggs type indicator*. Palo Alto, CA: Consulting Psychologist Press, Inc.

Cayzer, S. (2004). Semantic blogging and decentralized knowledge management. *Communications of the ACM, 47*(12), 47–52. doi:10.1145/1035134.1035164

Chung, W. (2008). Web searching in a multilingual world. *Communications of the ACM, 51*(5), 32–40. doi:10.1145/1342327.1342335

Collis, B., & Strijker, A. (2004). Technology and human issues in reusing learning objects. *Journal of Interactive Media in Education, 4*, 1-32. Retrieved May 1, 2009, from http://www-jime.open.ac.uk/2004/4/collis-2004-4.pdf

Dahlberg, I. (1995). Conceptual structures and systematization. *International Forum on Information and Documentation, 20*(3), 9–24.

de Moor, A. (2005). Patterns for the pragmatic web. In *Proceedings of the 13th International Conference on Conceptual Structures,* Kassel, Germany (LNAI 3596, pp. 1-18).

Felder, R. M., & Silverman, L. K. (1988). Learning and teaching styles in engineering education. *English Education, 78*, 674–681.

Gasevic, D., & Hatala, M. (2006). Ontology mappings to improve learning resource search. *British Journal of Educational Technology, 37*(3), 375–389. doi:10.1111/j.1467-8535.2006.00611.x

Giles, J. (2008). The semantic web will make finding answers online as simple as asking the right question. *New Scientist, 198*(2658), 26–27. doi:10.1016/S0262-4079(08)61363-9

Gozzi, R. Jr. (2007). Searching for search engine metaphors. *Etc.; a Review of General Semantics*, 276–279.

Green, C., & Ruhleder, K. (1995). Globalization, borderless worlds, and the tower of Babel: Metaphors gone awry. *Journal of Organizational Change Management, 8*(4), 55–68. doi:10.1108/09534819510090213

Gudykunst, W. B., & Kim, Y. Y. (1997). *Communicating with strangers: An approach to intercultural communication* (3rd ed.). New York: McGraw-Hill.

Hall, E. T. (1976). *Beyond culture*. New York: Doubleday.

Hofstede, G. (1980). *Culture's consequences*. Beverly Hills, CA: Sage.

Hofstede, G. (1996). *Cultures and organizations: Software of the mind*. New York: McGraw Hill.

Hovy, E. (2002). Comparing sets of semantic relations in ontologies. In Green, R., Bean, C., & Myaeng, S. H. (Eds.), *The semantics of relationships*. Dordrecht, The Netherlands: Kluwer Academic Publishers.

Kawachi, P. (1999). *When the sun doesn't rise: Empirical findings that explain the exclusion of Japanese from online global education*. Retrieved January 12, 2008, from http://www.ignou.ac.in/Theme-3/Paul%20%20KAWACHI.html

Kay, R. (2006). Semantic web. *Computerworld*, 32.

Kim, H., & Dong, A. (2002). *Pragmatics of the semantic web*. Paper presented at the Semantic Web Workshop.

Kobielus, J. (2007). The semantic web: Meaning and SOA. *Business Communications Review*, 30-36.

Koch, N. (2001). *Software engineering for adaptive hypermedia applications. Reihe Softwaretechnik, 12*. Munich, Germany: Uni-Druck Publishing Company.

Lee, J., Upadhyaya, S. J., Rao, H. R., & Sharman, R. (2005). Secure knowledge management and the semantic web. *Communications of the ACM, 48*(12), 49–54. doi:10.1145/1101779.1101808

Lytras, M., & Naeve, A. (2006). Semantic e-Learning: Synthesizing fantasies. *British Journal of Educational Technology, 37*(3), 479–491. doi:10.1111/j.1467-8535.2006.00617.x

McCalla, G. (2004). The ecological approach to the design of e-learning environments: Purpose-based capture and use of information about learners. *Journal of Interactive Media in Education, 7*. Retrieved April 18, 2009, from http://www-jime.open.ac.uk/2004/7/mccalla-2004-7.pdf

McCool, R. (2005). Rethinking the semantic web: Part I. *IEEE Internet Computing*, 86–88.

Mesdag, M. V. (2000). Culture-sensitive adaptation or global standardization - the duration of usage hypothesis. *International Marketing Review, 17*, 74–84. doi:10.1108/02651330010314722

Mey, J. L. (2003). Context and (dis)ambiguity: A pragmatic view. *Journal of Pragmatics, 35*, 331–347. doi:10.1016/S0378-2166(02)00139-X

Miniwats International. (2007). *Internet usage statistics: The internet big picture.* Retrieved April 20, 2008, from www.Internetworldstats.com/stats.htm

Olaniran, B. A. (2004). Computer-mediated communication in cross-cultural virtual groups. In Chen, G. M., & Starosta, W. J. (Eds.), *Dialogue among diversities* (pp. 142–166). Washington, DC: National Communication Association.

Olaniran, B. A. (2007a). Challenges to implementing e-learning in lesser-developed countries. In Edmundson, A. (Ed.), *Globalized e-learning cultural challenges* (pp. 18–34). Hershey, PA: Idea Group.

Olaniran, B. A. (2007b). Culture and communication challenges in virtual workspaces. In St-Amant, K. (Ed.), *Linguistic and cultural online communication issues in the global age* (pp. 79–92). Hershey, PA: Idea Group.

Olaniran, B. A. (2008). Group decision making in computer-mediated communication as networked communication: Understanding the technology and implications. In Raisinghani, M. S. (Ed.), *Handbook of research on global information technology management in digital economy.* Hershey, PA: IGI Global.

Olaniran, B. A., & Agnello, M. F. (2008). Globalization, educational hegemony, and higher education. *Journal of Multicultural Educational Technology, 2*(2), 68–86. doi:10.1108/17504970810883351

Olaniran, B. A., & Edgell, D. (2008). Cultural implications of collaborative information technologies (CITs) in international online collaborations and global virtual teams. In Zemliansky, P., & St-Amant, K. (Eds.), *Handbook of global virtual workspaces* (pp. 118–133). Hershey, PA: Idea Group.

Patil, B., Maetzel, K., & Neuhold. (2003). *Creating digital opportunities in IT education: An inclusive framework.* Retrieved January 29, 2008, from http://ecommerce.lebow.drexel.edu/eli/2003Proceedings/docs%5C093Patil.pdf

Repenning, A., & Sullivan, J. (2003). The Pragmatic web: Agent-based multimodal web interaction with no browser in sight. In *Proceedings of the 9th International Conference on Human-Computer Interaction,* Zurich, Switzerland (pp. 212-219).

Richards, C., & Nair, G. (2007). 21st century knowledge-building in the Asia Pacific: Towards a multidisciplinary framework for linking ICT-based social and personal contexts of education and development. *The Electronic Journal on Information Systems in Developing Countries, 32*(7), 1–11.

Schoop, M., de Moor, A., & Dietz, J. L. G. (2006). The pragmatic web: A manifesto. *Communications of the ACM, 49*(5), 75–76. doi:10.1145/1125944.1125979

Singh, M. P. (2002). The Pragmatic Web. *IEEE Internet Computing,* 4–5. doi:10.1109/MIC.2002.1003124

Singh, R., Iyer, L., & Salam, A. F. (2005). The semantic e-business vision. *Communications of the ACM, 48*(12), 38–41. doi:10.1145/1101779.1101806

Snae, C., & Brueckner, M. (2007). Ontology-driven e-learning system based on roles and activities for Thai learning environment. *Interdisciplinary Journal of Knowledge and Learning Objects, 3.* Retrieved April 18, 2009, from http://ijklo.org/Volume3/IJKLOv3p001-017Snae.pdf

Sowa, J. (2000). *Knowledge representation.* Pacific Grove, CA: Brooks/Cole.

Spyns, P., & Meersman, R. A. (2003). *From knowledge to interaction: From the semantic to the pragmatic web.* Brussels, Belgium: STARLab.

Spyns, P., Meersman, R. A., & Jarrar, M. (2002). Data modeling versus ontology engineering. *SIGMOD Record*, *31*(4), 12–17. doi:10.1145/637411.637413

Stojanovic, L., Staab, R., & Studer, R. (2001). *eLearning based on semantic web*. Paper presented at World Conference on the WWW and Internet (WebNet), Orlando, Florida.

Stutt, A., & Motta, E. (2004). Semantic learning webs. *Journal of Interactive Media in Education*, *10*. Retrieved October 15, 2008, from http://www-jime.open.ac.uk/2004/10

Tallman, S., Jenkins, M., Henry, N., & Pinch, S. (2004). Knowledge clusters and competitive advantage. *Academy of Management Review*, *29*(2), 258–271. doi:10.2307/20159032

Tennis, J. T., & Sutton, S. A. (2008). Extending the simple knowledge organization system for concept management in vocabulary development applications. *Journal of the American Society for Information Science and Technology*, *59*(1), 25–37. doi:10.1002/asi.20702

Van Dam, N., & Rogers, F. (2002, May). E-Learning cultures around the world: Make your globalized strategy transparent. *E-learning*, 28–33. Retrieved February 12, 2008 from http://www.elearningmag.com.

Vaughan, K., & MacVicar, A. (2004). Employees' pre implementation attitudes and perceptions to e-learning: A banking case study analysis. *Journal of European Industrial Training*, *28*(5), 400–413. doi:10.1108/03090590410533080

Veltman, K. H. (2004). Towards a semantic web for culture. *Journal of Digital Information*, *4*(4), 3–15.

Wahid, F. (2007). Using the technology adoption model to analyze Internet adoption and use among men and women in Indonesia. *The Electronic Journal on Information Systems in Developing Countries*, *32*(6), 1–8.

Weigel, V. (2003). *Deep learning for a digital age*. San Francisco, CA: Jossey-Bass.

This work was previously published in International Journal of Virtual and Personal Learning Environments, edited by Michael Thomas, Volume 1, Issue 4, pp. 18-30, copyright 2010 by IGI Publishing (an imprint of IGI Global).

Compilation of References

A'Herran, A. (2000, June 12-17). Research and evaluation of online systems for teaching and learning. *AusWeb2k-The Sixth Australian World Wide Web Conference*, Rihga Colonial Club Resort, Cairns. Retrieved April 30, 2009, from http://ausWeb.scu.edu.au/aw2k/papers/a_herran/paper.html

Adams, K. (2002). The semantic web: Differentiating between taxonomies and ontologies. *Online, 26*(4), 20-33. Retrieved January 22, 2009, from http://www.onlinemag.net

Adams, P. C. (2005). *The boundless self: Communication in physical and virtual spaces*. NY: Syracuse UP.

Akrich, M. (1992). The description of technical objects. In Bijker, W., & Law, J. (Eds.), *Shaping technology/building society: Studies in sociotechnical change* (pp. 205–224). Cambridge, MA: MIT Press.

Alexander, B. (2006, March/April). Web 2.0: A new wave of innovation for teaching and learning? *EDUCAUSE Review*, *41*(2), 32–44.

Alfonseca, E., Carro, R. M., Martín, E., Ortigosa, A., & Paredes, P. (2009). The impact of learning styles on student grouping for collaborative learning: A case study. *User Modeling and User-Adapted Interaction*, *16*, 377–401.. doi:10.1007/s11257-006-9012-7

Allen, I. E., & Seaman, J. (2008). Staying the course: online education in the United States, 2008. *Sloan-C*. Retrieved June 22, 2009 from http://www.sloan-c.org/publications/survey/pdf/staying_the_course.pdf

Alvardo, P. (2004, January). Seven steps to selecting a learning management system. *Chief Learning Officer*. Retrieved April 30, 2009, from http://www.clomedia.com/content/templates/clo_Webonly.asp?articleid=365&zoneid=78

Amichai-Hamburger, Y., & McKenna, K. (2006). The contact hypothesis reconsidered: Interacting via the Internet. *Journal of Computer-Mediated Communication*, *11*(3), 825–843. doi:doi:10.1111/j.1083-6101.2006.00037.x

Amory, A. (2006). Game object model version II: A theoretical framework for educational game development. *Educational Technology Research and Development*, *55*(1), 51–77. doi:10.1007/s11423-006-9001-x

Amory, A., Naicker, K., Vincent, J., & Adams, C. (1999). The use of computer games as an educational tool: 1. Identification of appropriate game types and game elements. *British Journal of Educational Technology*, *30*, 311–322. doi:10.1111/1467-8535.00121

Anderson, T. (2006). *PLEs versus LMS: Are PLEs ready for prime time?* Retrieved April 1, 2010, from http://terrya.edublogs.org/2006/01/09/ples-versus-lmsare-ples-ready-for-prime-time/

Anderson, C. (2006). *The long tail: Why the future of business is selling less of more*. Hyperion.

Andrews, S., DiGangi, S., Winograd, D., & Jannasch, A. (1999). Designing online instruction using multidisciplinary procedures. In *Proceedings of the 21st Annual Selected Research and Development Papers*. Columbus, OH: AECT. Retrieved from http://is.asu.edu/research/AECT1999b/aect99b.rtf

Andrews, T., & Schwarz, G. (2002). Preparing students for the virtual organisation: An evaluation of learning with virtual learning technologies. *Educational Technology and Society*, *5*(3), 54–65.

Angelo, T. A. (1999). Doing assessment as if learning matters most. *AAHE Bulletin*. Retrieved May 11, 2009, from http://www.umd.umich.edu/casl/natsci/faculty/zitzewitz/curie/TeacherPrep/38.pdf

Antonacci, D., & Modaress, N. (2008). Envisioning the educational possibilities of user-created virtual worlds. *AACE Journal*, *16*(2), 115–126.

Armbrust, M., Fox, A., Griffith, R., Joseph, A. D., Katz, R. H., Konwinski, A., et al. (2009). *Above the clouds: A Berkeley view of cloud computing*. University of California at Berkeley. Retrieved May 25, 2009, from http://www.eecs.berkeley.edu/Pubs/TechRpts/2009/EECS-2009-28.html

Arver, C. (2007). Are you willing to have your students join Ralph, Jack, and Piggy? *English Journal*, *97*(1), 37–42.

Ashoka. (2009). Youth Venture. Retrieved July 1, 2009, from http://www.ashoka.org/youthventure

Aspin, D. N., & Chapman, J. D. (2000). Lifelong learning: Concepts and conceptions. *International Journal of Lifelong Education*, *19*(1), 2–19. doi:doi:10.1080/026013700293421

Atkinson, R. K., Mayer, R. E., & Merrill, M. M. (2005). Fostering social agency in multimedia learning: Examining the impact of an animated agent's voice. *Contemporary Educational Psychology*, *30*(1), 117–139. doi:doi:10.1016/j.cedpsych.2004.07.001

Attwell, G. (2007). The personal learning environments - the future of elearning? *eLearning Papers*, *2*(1). Retrieved April 1, 2010, from http://www.elearningeuropa.info/files/media/media11561.pdf

Attwell, G. (2007). Personal learning environments for creating, consuming, remixing and sharing. In *Proceedings of the 2nd TENCompetence Open Workshop* (pp. 36-41). Bolton, UK: Institute of Educational Cybernetics.

Auer, M. E. (2000). *Virtual Lab versus Remote Lab*. Retrieved January 10, 2008, from http://www.online-lab.net/rel/documents/auer_icde.pdf

Augar, N., Raitman, R., & Zhou, W. (2004, December 5-8). Teaching and learning online with wikis. In R. Atkinson, C. McBeath, D. Jonas-Dwyer, & R. Phillips (Eds.), In *Proceedings of Beyond the comfort zone: the 21st ASCILITE Conference*, Perth, Australia (pp. 95-104). Retrieved May 11, 2009, from http://www.ascilite.org.au/conferences/perth04/procs/augar.html

Baker, E. L., & Mayer, T. E. (1999). Computer-based assessment of problem solving. *Computers in Human Behavior*, *15*, 269–282. doi:10.1016/S0747-5632(99)00023-0

Baker, S. (2007). Google and the wisdom of clouds. *Business Week*, , 4064.

Barab, S., Scott, B., Ingram-Goble, A., Goldstone, R., Zuiker, S., & Warren, S. (2007). Situative embodiment as a curricular scaffold: using videogames to support science education. In *Proceedings of the American Education Research Association*, Chicago, IL. Retrieved June 22, 2009 from http://inkido.indiana.edu/research/onlinemanu/papers/emb_lab_study.pdf

Barab, S. A., Hay, K. E., Barnett, M., & Squire, K. (2001). Constructing virtual worlds: Tracing the historical development of learner practices. *Cognition and Instruction*, *19*(1), 47–94. doi:10.1207/S1532690XCI1901_2

Barab, S., Sadler, T., Heiselt, C., Hickey, D., & Zuiker, S. (2007). Relating narrative, inquiry, and inscriptions: Supporting consequential play. *Journal of Science Education and Technology*, *16*(1), 59–82. doi:10.1007/s10956-006-9033-3

Barker, S. B., & Ansorge, J. (2007). Robotics as means to increase achievement scores in an informal learning environment. *Journal of Research on Technology in Education*, *39*(3), 229–243.

Barlow, K., & Lane, J. (2007). Like technology from an advanced alien culture: Google Apps for education at ASU. In *Proceedings of the 35th Annual ACM SIGUCCS Conference on User Services* (pp. 8-10). New York: ACM.

Barron, T. (2000). E-learning's global migration. *Learning Circuits*. Retrieved August 26, 2005, from http://www.astd.org/LC/2000/0900_barron.htm

Barr, R. B., & Tagg, J. (1995). From teaching to learning: A new paradigm for undergraduate education. *Change*, *27*(6), 12–25.

Bateson, M. (1993). Joint performance across cultures: Improvisation in a Persian garden. *Text and Performance Quarterly*, *13*(2), 113–121. doi:doi:10.1080/10462939309366037

Baumgartner, P., Hfele, H., & Maier-Hfele, K. (2004). *Content Management Systems in e-Education. Auswahl, Potenziale und Einsatzmglichkeiten*. Innsbruck-Wien, Germany: StudienVerlag.

Bayne, S. (2008). Uncanny spaces for higher education: teaching and learning in virtual worlds. *ALT-J*, *16*(3), 197–205. doi:doi:10.1080/09687760802526749

Beard, L., & Harper, C. (2000). Student perceptions of online versus campus instruction. *Education*, *122*(4), 658–664.

Beffa-Negrini, P., Miller, B., & Cohen, N. (2002). Factors related to success and satisfaction in online learning. *Academic Exchange Quarterly*, *6*(3), 105–114.

Beichner, R. J. (1990). The effects of simultaneous motion presentation and graph generation in a kinematics lab. *Journal of Research in Science Teaching*, *27*(8), 803. doi:10.1002/tea.3660270809

Bell, L., & Trueman, R. B. (2008). *Virtual worlds, real libraries: Librarians and educators in Second Life and other multi-user virtual environments*. Medford, NJ: Information Today.

Bennett, S., Maton, K., & Kervin, L. (2008). The 'digital natives' debate: A critical review of the evidence. *British Journal of Educational Technology*, *39*(5), 775–786. doi:doi:10.1111/j.1467-8535.2007.00793.x

Berg, Z. (2008). Multi-user virtual environments for education and training? A critical review of Second Life. *Educational Technology Magazine: The Magazine for Managers of Change in Education*, *48*(3), 27–31.

Berners-Lee, T. (1998). *What the semantic web isn't but can represent.* The World Wide Web Consortium. Retrieved January 22, 2009, from http://www.w3.org/DesingnIssues/RDFnot.html

Berners-Lee, T., Hendler, J., & Lassila, O. (2001). The semantic web. *Scientific American*, 35–43.

Bertino, E., Khan, L., Sandhu, R., & Thuraisingham, B. (2006). Secure knowledge management: Confidentiality, trust, and privacy. *IEEE Transactions on Systems. Man & Cybernetics: Part A*, *36*(3), 429–438..doi:10.1109/TSMCA.2006.871796

Bickley, D. (2009). *NMU Speech-Language & Hearing Virtual Clinic: Project news/updates*. Retrieved June 23, 2009 from http://www.donbickley.com/nmuspeech-pathPN.html

Biggs, J. (1999). *Teaching for quality learning at university*. Buckingham, UK: SRHE and Open University Press.

Blaisdell, M. (2006). All the right MUVEs. *T.H.E. Journal*, *33*(14), 28–38.

Bleicher, P. (2006). Getting to a semantic web on the internet. *Applied Clinical Trials Magazine*, 42-43. Retrieved January 22, 2009, from http://appliedclinicaltrialsonline.findpharma.com/appliedclinicaltrials/article/articleDetail.jsp?id=310806

Bloom, B. S. (1956). *Taxonomy of educational objectives. Handbook I: The cognitive domain*. New York: David McKay.

Boellstorff, T. (2008). *Coming of age in Second Life: An anthropologist explores the virtually human*. Princeton, NJ: Princeton University Press.

Bolous, M., Ramloll, R., Jones, R., & Toth-Cohen, S. (2008). Web 3D for public, environmental and occupational health: Early examples from Second Life. *International Journal of Environmental Research and Public Health*, *5*, 290–317. doi:10.3390/ijerph5040290

Bonk, C., & Thomas, H. (1997). Learner-centered web instruction for higher-order thinking, teamwork, and apprenticeship. In Khan, B. H. (Ed.), *Web-Based Instruction* (pp. 167–178). Englewood Cliffs, NJ: Educational Technology Publications.

Bonwell, C. C. (1996). Enhancing the lecture: Revitalizing a traditional format. In T. E. Sutherland & C.C. Bonwell (Eds.), *Using active learning in college classes: A range of options for faculty, New Directions for Teaching and Learning No. 67.* (pp. 31 - 44). Place: Wiley Periodicals Inc., A Wiley Company.

Bonwell, C., & Eison, J. (1991). *Active learning: Creating excitement in the classroom (AEHE-ERIC Higher Education Report No. 1).* Washington, DC: Jossey-Bass.

Boulos, M., Hetherington, L., & Wheeler, S. (2007). Second Life: An overview of the potential of 3-D virtual worlds in medical and health education. *Health Information and Libraries Journal, 24*, 233–245. doi:10.1111/j.1471-1842.2007.00733.x

Bourke, P. (2008). Evaluating Second Life as a tool for collaborative scientific visualization. In *Proceedings of the Computer Games and Allied Technology*, Singapore. Retrieved June 30, 2009 from http://local.wasp.uwa.edu.au/~pbourke/papers/cgat08/index.html

Bransford, J., Sherwood, R., Hasselbring, T., Kinzer, C., & Williams, S. (1990). Anchored instruction: Why we need it and how technology can help. In D. Nix & R. Spiro (Eds.), *Cognition, education and multimedia: Exploring ideas in high technology* (pp. 163-205). Hillsdale, NJ: Lawrence Erlbaum Associates.

Braun, S., & Schmidt, A. (2006). Socially-aware informal learning support: Potentials and challenges of the social dimension. In *Proceedings of the Joint International Workshop on Professional Learning, Competence Development and Knowledge Management-LOKMOL and L3NCD, 1st European Conference on Technology Enhanced Learning,* Crete, Greece. Retrieved December 20, 2009, from http://cnm.open.ac.uk/projects/ectel06/pdfs/ECTEL06WS68d.pdf#page=25

Brew, A. (2006). *Research and teaching: Beyond the divide*. London: Palgrave.

Briggs, K. C., & Myers, I. B. (1977). *Myers-Briggs type indicator*. Palo Alto, CA: Consulting Psychologist Press, Inc.

British Library. (2008). *Information behaviour of the researcher of the future*. Retrieved April 30, 2009, from http://www.bl.uk/news/pdf/googlegen.pdf

Brooke, J. (1996). SUS: a "quick and dirty" usability scale. In Jordan, P. W., Thomas, B., Weerdmeester, B. A., & McClelland, A. L. (Eds.), *Usability Evaluation in Industry*. London: Taylor and Francis.

Brooks, F. (1987). No silver bullet: Essence and accidents of software engineering. *IEEE Computer, 20*(4), 10–19.

Brouchoud, J. (2006). *The arch*. Retrieved May 1, 2009, from http://archsl.wordpress.com/2007/08/30/open-source-scripts-reflexive-virtual-architecture/

Brown, E., Gordon, M., & Hobbs, M. (2008). Second Life as a holistic learning environment for problem-based learning and transferable skills. In *Proceedings of the Researching Learning in Virtual Environments International Conference* (pp. 39-48). Retrieved May 8, 2009 from http://www.open.ac.uk/relive08/documents/ReLIVE08_conference_proceedings_Lo.pdf

Brown, A. L. (1992). Design experiments: theoretical and methodological challenges in creating complex interventions in classroom settings. *Journal of the Learning Sciences, 2*(2), 141–178. doi:10.1207/s15327809jls0202_2

Brown, J. S., & Adler, R. P. (2008). Minds on fire: Open education, the long tail, and learning 2.0. *EDUCAUSE Review, 43*(1), 16–32.

Brown, J., Collins, A., & Duguid, P. (1989). Situated cognition and the culture of learning. *Educational Researcher, 18*(1), 32–42.

Bruns, A., & Humphreys, S. (2005). *Wikis in Teaching and Assessment: The M/Cyclopedia Project*. Retrieved February 28, 2009 from http://snurb.info/files/Wikis%20in%20Teaching%20and%20Assessment.pdf

Brush, T. (1998). Embedding cooperative learning into the design of Integrated Learning Systems: Rationale and guidelines. *Educational Technology Research and Development, 46*(3), 5–18. doi:10.1007/BF02299758

Buchanan, R. (1999). Design Research and the New Learning. *Design Issues, 17*(4), 3–23. doi:doi:10.1162/07479360152681056

Budhu, M. (2002, August 18). *Virtual laboratories for engineering education*. Paper presented at the International Conference on Engineering Education. Retrieved December 7, 2008, from http://www.ineer.org/Events/ICEE2002/Proceedings/Papers/Index/O334-O337/O334.pdf

Burden, D., Conradi, E., Woodham, L., Poulton, T., Savin-Baden, M., & Kavia, S. (2008). Creating and assessing a virtual patient player in Second Life. In *Proceedings of the Researching Learning in Virtual Environments International Conference* (pp. 49-62). Retrieved May 8, 2009 from http://www.open.ac.uk/relive08/documents/ReLIVE08_conference_proceedings_Lo.pdf

Burke, K. (1935). *Permanence and change: An anatomy of purpose*. NY: New Republic.

Buyya, R., Yeo, C. S., & Venugopal, S. (2008, September). Market-oriented cloud computing: Vison, hype, and reality for delivering IT services as computing utilities. In *Proceedings of the 10th IEEE International Conference on High Performance Computing and Communications*. Los Alamitos, California: IEEE CS Press.

Byrne, C. (2009). *Water on tap: The use of virtual reality in education*. Retrieved June 30, 2009 from http://www.hitl.washington.edu/publications/dissertations/Byrne/

Byrne, C., & Bricken, M. (1992). *Summer students in virtual reality: A pilot study on educational applications of virtual reality technology*. Retrieved June 30, 2009 from http://ftp.hitl.washington.edu/projects/education/psc/psc.html

Calongne, C. M. (2008). Educational frontiers: Learning in a virtual world. *EDUCAUSE Review, 43*(5), 36-48. Retrieved June 1, 2009 from http://net.educause.edu/ir/library/pdf/ERM0852.pdf

Camilleri, V., & Montebello, M. (2008). SLAVE–Second Life assistant in a virtual environment. In *Proceedings of the Researching Learning in Virtual Environments International Conference* (pp. 72-82). Retrieved May 8, 2009 from http://www.open.ac.uk/relive08/documents/ReLIVE08_conference_proceedings_Lo.pdf

Campbell, J. O., Bourne, J., Mosterman, P., & Brodersen, A. J. (2002). Effectiveness of learning simulations for electronic laboratories. *Journal of Engineering Education, 91*(1), 81–87.

Candlin, C. (1987). Toward task-based learning. In C. Candlin & D. Murphy (Eds.), *Language Learning Tasks* (pp. 5-22). Englewood Cliffs, N.J: Prentice Hall.

Carmean, C., & Haefner, J. (2003). Next-generation course management systems. *EDUCAUSE Quarterly, 26*(1), 10–13.

Carnevale, D. (2008). Colleges get out of e-Mail business. *The Chronicle of Higher Education, 54*(18).

Carr, N. G. (2003). IT doesn't matter. *Harvard Business Review, 81*(5), 41–49.

Cashin, W. E. (1985). *Improving lectures idea paper No. 14*. Manhattan: Kansas State University, Center for Faculty Evaluation and Development.

Castronova, E. (2005). *Synthetic worlds: The business and culture of online games*. Chicago: University of Chicago Press.

Castronova, E. (2007). *Exodus to the virtual world: How online fun is changing reality*. New York: Palgrave Macmillan.

Cayzer, S. (2004). Semantic blogging and decentralized knowledge management. *Communications of the ACM, 47*(12), 47–52. doi:10.1145/1035134.1035164

Centre for Inquiry Based Learning in the Arts and Social Sciences. (2008). *Inquiry-based learning: A conceptual framework*. Sheffield, UK: CILASS. Retrieved July 20, 2009, from http://www.shef.ac.uk/content/1/c6/07/93/44/Microsoft%20Word%20-%20CILASS%20IBL%20Conceptual%20Framework%20_Version%202_.pdf

Chatti, M. A., Jarke, M., & Frosch-Wilke, D. (2007). The future of elearning: A shift to knowledge networking and social software. *International Journal of Knowledge and Learning, 3*(4/5), 404–420. doi:doi:10.1504/IJKL.2007.016702

Cheal, C. (2007). Second Life: hype or hyperlearning? *Horizon, 15*(4), 204–210. doi:10.1108/10748120710836228

Chika, I. E., Azzi, D., & Williams, R. (2008, September 25). *Students' laboratory work performance assessment*. Paper presented at the International Conference on Interactive Computer Aided Learning (ICL2008).

Chika, I. E., Azzi, D., Hewitt, A., & Stocker, J. (2009). A holistic approach to assessing students' laboratory performance using Bayesian networks. In *Proceedings of IEEE Workshop on Computational Intelligence in Virtual Environments (CIVE '09)*, Nashville, TN (pp. 26-32).

Childress, M., & Braswell, R. (2006). Role-playing games for online learning. *Distance Education, 27*(2), 187–196. doi:10.1080/01587910600789522

Chohan, N. (2001). VLE procurement. *JISC briefing paper, 2*. Retrieved April 30, 2009, from http://www.jisc.ac.uk/mle/reps/briefings/bp2.html

Choi, I. L., & Turgeon, A. J. (2005). Scaffolding peer-questioning strategies to facilitate metacognition during online small group discussion. *Instructional Science, 33*(5-6), 483–511. doi:10.1007/s11251-005-1277-4

Chomsky, N. (1957). *Syntactic structures*. The Hague, Paris: Mouton.

Chung, W. (2008). Web searching in a multilingual world. *Communications of the ACM, 51*(5), 32–40. doi:10.1145/1342327.1342335

Clark, A. (2009). *Natural born cyborgs? Edge: The third culture*. Edge Foundation, Inc. Retrieved February 21, 2009, from http://www.edge.org/3rd_culture/clark/clark_index.html

Clark, M. (2008). Genome Island. *Educause Review, 43*(5). Retrieved June 28, 2009 from http://www.educause.edu/node/163160

Cochrane, K. (2006). Case study: International Spaceflight Museum. In D. Livingstone & J. Kemp (Eds.), *Proceedings of the Second Life Education Workshop at the Second Life Community Convention 2006* (pp. 2-5). Retrieved May 5, 2009 from http://www.simteach.com/SLCC06/slcc2006-proceedings.pdf

Collis, B., & Strijker, A. (2004). Technology and human issues in reusing learning objects. *Journal of Interactive Media in Education, 4*, 1-32. Retrieved May 1, 2009, from http://www-jime.open.ac.uk/2004/4/collis-2004-4.pdf

Conner, M. L. (1997). *Informal learning*. Retrieved September 15, 2009 from http://www.marciaconner.com/intros/informal.html

Connolly, T. M., Stansfield, M. H., & Hainey, T. (2009) Towards the development of a games-based learning evaluation framework. In T. M. Connolly, M. Stansfield, & L. Boyle (Eds.), *Games-based learning advancements for multisensory human computer interfaces: Techniques and effective practices.* Hershey PA: IGI Global.

Connolly, T. M., Stansfield, M. H., McLellan, E., Ramsay, J., & Sutherland, J. (2004, November). Applying computer games concepts to teaching database analysis and design. In *Proceedings of the International Conference on Computer Games, AI, Design and Education*, Reading, UK.

Connolly, T. M., Stansfield, M. H., & Hainey, T. (2007). An application of games-based learning within software engineering. *British Journal of Educational Technology, 38*(3), 416–428. doi:10.1111/j.1467-8535.2007.00706.x

Conole, G. (2008). New schemas for mapping pedagogies and technologies. *Ariadne, 56*. Retrieved April 30, 2009, from http://www.ariadne.ac.uk/issue56/conole/

Conrad, D. (2002). Engagement, excitement, anxiety, and fear: Learners' experiences of starting an online course. *American Journal of Distance Education, 16*(4), 205–226. doi:10.1207/S15389286AJDE1604_2

Corbit, M. (2002). Building virtual worlds for informal science learning (SciCentr and SciFair) in the Active Worlds Educational Universe (AWEDU). *Presence: Tele-operators & Virtual Environment, 11*(1), 55–67. doi:10.1162/105474602317343659

Cortiella, C. (2009). *The state of learning disabilities 2009*. Washington, DC: National Center for Learning Disabilities. Retrieved from http://www.ncld.org/stateofld

Cox, A., Levy, P., Stordy, P., & Webber, S. (2008a). Inquiry-based learning in the first-year information management curriculum. *Italics, 7*(1). Retrieved July 20, 2009, from http://www.ics.heacademy.ac.uk/italics/vol7iss1/pdf/Paper1.pdf

Cox, A., Tapril, S., Stordy, P., & Whittaker, S. (2008b). Teaching our grandchildren to suck eggs? Introducing the study of communication technologies to the 'Digital generation'. *Italics, 7*(1). Retrieved July 20, 2009, from http://www.ics.heacademy.ac.uk/italics/vol7iss1/pdf/Paper5.pdf

Craig, E. (2007, June). *Meta-perspectives on the Metaverse: A blogsphere debate on the significance of Second Life.* Paper presented at ED-MEDIA World Conference on Educational Multimedia, Hypermedia & Telecommunications, Vancouver, Canada.

Crawford, C. (1982). *The art of computer game design*. Berkeley, CA: McGraw-Hill.

Cross, J. (2006). *Informal learning: rediscovering the natural pathways that inspire innovation and performance*. Pfeiffer.

Cuban, L. (1992). Curriculum stability and change. In P.W. Jackson (Ed.), *Handbook of research on curriculum* (pp. 216-247). New York: Macmillan.

Cubric, M. (2007, October 21-23). Wiki-based process framework for blended learning, In *Proceedings of the 2007 international symposium on Wikis*, Montréal, Québec, Canada.

CUELC. (2008). *Cairo University eLearning Center*. Retrieved April 1, 2010, from http://elearning.eng.cu.edu.eg

Dahlberg, I. (1995). Conceptual structures and systematization. *International Forum on Information and Documentation, 20*(3), 9–24.

Damer, B. (2008). Meeting in the ether: A brief history of virtual worlds as a medium for user-created events. *Journal of Virtual Worlds Research, 1*(1). Retrieved June 5, 2009 from http://journals.tdl.org/jvwr/article/view/285/239

Dancy, M. H., & Beichner, R. (2006). Impact of animation on assessment of conceptual understanding in physics. *Physical Review Special Topics-Physics Education Research, 2*(1), 010104. doi:10.1103/PhysRevST-PER.2.010104

Danforth, D. (2008). Development of an interactive virtual 3-D model of the human testis using the Second Life platform. In *Proceedings of the 41st Annual Meeting of the Society for the Study of Reproduction.*

Danforth, D. (2009). *Ohio State University College of Medicine Island – Second Life OSU Medicine*. Retrieved June 28, 2009 from http://slurl.com/secondlife/OSU%20 Medicine/69/94/302

Davies, C. (2008). *Learning and teaching in laboratories: An engineering subject centre guide.* Retrieved May 24, 2008, from http://www.engsc.ac.uk/downloads/scholar-art/laboratories.pdf

Davis, B. G. (2001). *Tools for teaching*. San Francisco: Jossey-Bass Publishers.

de Freitas, S. (2006). Learning in immersive worlds. *Joint Information Systems Committee.* Retrieved May 27, 2009, from http://www.jisc.ac.uk/media/documents/programmes/elearninginnovation/gamingreport_v3.pdf

de Freitas, S., & Oliver, M. (2006). How can exploratory learning with games and simulations within the curriculum be most effectively evaluated. *Computers & Education. 46*(3), 249-264.

de Freitas, S. (2008). *Serious virtual worlds: A scoping study*. JISC publications. Retrieved March 14, 2009, from http://www.jisc.ac.uk/publications/publications/seriousvirtualworldsreport.aspx

de Freitas, S., & Griffiths, M. (2008). The convergence of gaming practices with other media forms: what potential for learning? A review of the literature. *Learning, media and technology, 33*(1), 11-20.

De Lucia, A., Francese, R., Passero, I., & Tortora, G. (2009). Development and evaluation of a virtual campus on Second Life: the case of SecondDMI. *Computers & Education, 52*(1), 220–233. doi:10.1016/j.compedu.2008.08.001

de Magistris, M. (2005). A MATLAB-based virtual laboratory for teaching introductory quasi-stationary electromagnetics. *IEEE Transactions on Education, 48*(1), 81–88. doi:10.1109/TE.2004.832872

de Moor, A. (2005). Patterns for the pragmatic web. In *Proceedings of the 13th International Conference on Conceptual Structures,* Kassel, Germany (LNAI 3596, pp. 1-18).

de Nood, D., & Attema, J. (2006). *Second Life: The second life of virtual reality*. The Hague: Electronic Highway Platform.

De Pedro Puente, X. (2007, October 21-23). New method using wikis and forums to evaluate individual contributions in cooperative work while promoting experimental learning: Results from preliminary experience. In *Proceedings of Wikisym 2007*, Quebec, Canada.

Dede, C., Clarke, J., Ketelhut, D., Nelson, B., & Bowman, C. (2005). *Fostering motivation, learning, and transfer in multi-user virtual environments*. Paper presented at the American Educational Research Association Conference, Montreal, Canada.

Dede, C., Salzman, M., & Bowen Loftin, R. (1996a). ScienceSpace: Virtual realities for learning complex and abstract scientific concepts. In *Proceedings of the Virtual Reality Annual International Symposium* (pp. 246-252, 271). Washington, DC: IEEE.

Dede, C. (1995). The evolution of constructivist learning environments: Immersion in distributed, virtual worlds. *Educational Technology, 35*(5), 46–52.

Dede, C. (2009). Immersive Interfaces for Engagement and Learning. *Science, 323*(5910), 66. doi:10.1126/science.1167311

Dede, C. J., Salzman, M., & Loftin, R. B. (1996b)... *Lecture Notes in Computer Science, 1077*, 87.

del Alamo, J. A., Chang, V., Hardison, J., Zych, D., & Hui, L. (2003, July 21). *An online microelectronics device characterization laboratory with a circuit-like user interface*. Paper presented at the International Conference on Engineering Education. Retrieved April 20, 2007, from http://www-mtl.mit.edu/~alamo/pdf/2003/RC-95%20delAlamo%20ICEE%202003%20paper.pdf

Deleuze, G., & Guattari, F. (1988). *A Thousand plateaus: Capitalism and schizophrenia*. Minneapolis: University of Minnesota Press.

Delwiche, A. (2006). Massively multiplayer online games (MMOs) in the new media classroom. *Educational Technology & Society, 9*(3), 160–172.

DeMers, M. (2008). Inside the metaverse: A Second Life for GIS education. *GIS Educator*, Winter, 3. Environmental Systems Research Institute (ESRI), Redlands: California. Retrieved September 6, 2009 from http://www.esri.com/library/newsletters/giseducator/gised-winter08.pdf

Dempsey, J. V., Rasmussen, K., & Lucassen, B. (1994, February 16-20). Instructional gaming: Implications for instructional technology. In *Proceedings of the Annual Meeting of the Association for Educational Communications and Technology*, Nashville, TN.

Derrington, M., & Homewood, B. (2008). Get real - this isn't real, it's Second Life: Teaching ESL in a virtual world. In *Proceedings of the Researching Learning in Virtual Environments International Conference* (pp. 106-120). Retrieved May 8, 2009 from http://www.open.ac.uk/relive08/documents/ReLIVE08_conference_proceedings_Lo.pdf

Di Nitto, E., Mainetti, L., Monga, M., Sbattella, L. M., & Tedesco, R. (2006). Supporting interoperability and reusability of learning objects: The virtual campus approach. *Educational Technology & Society, 9*(2), 33–50.

Di Paolo, E. A. (2009). Extended life. *Topoi, 28*, 9–21. doi:doi:10.1007/s11245-008-9042-3

Downes, S. (2005). E-Learning 2.0. *eLearn Magazine, 10*, 1.

Downes, S. (2006). *Learning networks and connective knowledge*. Retrieved April 1, 2010, from http://it.coe.uga.edu/itforum/paper92/paper92.html

Dresang, E., & McClelland, K. (1999). Radical change: Digital age literature and learning. *Theory into Practice, 38*(3), 160–167.

Duarte, M., Butz, B. P., Miller, S. M., & Mahalingam, A. (2008). An intelligent universal virtual laboratory (UVL). *IEEE Transactions on Education, 51*(1), 2–9. doi:10.1109/TE.2006.888902

Duffy, P. D., & Bruns, A. (2006). The use of blogs, wikis and RSS in education: A conversation of possibilities. In *Proceedings Online Learning and Teaching Conference 2006*, Brisbane, Australia (pp. 31-38).

Dufresne, R. J., Gerace, W. J., Mestre, J. P., & Leonard, W. J. (2005). *Ask-it/a2l: Assessing student knowledge with instructional technology*. Retrieved June 30, 2009 from http://www.citebase.org/abstract?id=oai:arXiv.org:physics/0508144

Dunleavy, M., Dede, C., & Mitchell, R. (2009). Affordances and limitations of immersive participatory augmented reality simulations for teaching and learning. *Journal of Science Education and Technology, 18*, 7–22. doi:10.1007/s10956-008-9119-1

Dwyer, N. (2007). *Incorporating indexicality and contingency into the design of representations for computer-mediated collaboration*. Unpublished doctoral dissertation, University of Hawaii, Honolulu.

Dybala, P., Ptaszynski, M., Rzepka, R., & Araki, K. (2009). Humoroids - conversational agents that induce positive emotions with humor. In *Proceedings of the 8th International Conference on Autonomous Agents and Multiagent Systems (AAMAS 2009)*, Budapest, Hungary (pp. 1171-1172).

Eckstein, R., Loy, M., & Wood, D. (1998). *Java Swing*. Sebastopol, CA: O'Reilly Media.

Edirisingha, P., Nie, M., Pluciennik, M., & Young, R. (2009). Socialisation for learning at a distance in a 3-D multi-user virtual environment. *British Journal of Educational Technology, 40*(3), 458–479. doi:doi:10.1111/j.1467-8535.2009.00962.x

Edward, N. S. (2002). The role of laboratory work in engineering education: student and staff perceptions. *International Journal of Electrical Engineering Education, 39*(1), 11–19.

Eisner, E. W. (1991). *The enlightened eye: Qualitative inquiry and the enhancement of educational practice*. New York: Macmillan.

Ellis, D., & Haugan, M. (1997). Modelling the information seeking patterns of engineers and research scientists in an industrial environment. *The Journal of Documentation, 53*(4), 384–403. doi:doi:10.1108/EUM0000000007204

Energy Information Administration (2009). *Average retail price of electricity to ultimate customers by end-use sector, by state.*

Entwistle, N. (2003). *Concepts and conceptual frameworks underpinning the ETL project.* Edinburgh, UK: University of Edinburgh. Retrieved July 10, 2009, from http://www.ed.ac.uk/etl

Entwistle, N., & Smith, C. (2002). Personal understanding and target understanding: Mapping influences on the outcomes of learning. *The British Journal of Educational Psychology, 72*, 321–342. doi:doi:10.1348/000709902320634528

Erdelez, S. (1999). Information encountering: It's more than just bumping into information. *Bulletin of the American Association for Information Science, 25*(3), 25–29.

Ericsson, K. A., & Simon, H. A. (1980). Verbal reports as data. *Psychological Review, 87*, 215–251. doi:10.1037/0033-295X.87.3.215

Ericsson, K. A., & Simon, H. A. (1993). *Protocol analysis: Verbal reports as data.* Cambridge, MA: MIT Press.

Ewald, W. (2005). *In peace and harmony: Carver portraits.* Richmond, VA: Hand Workshop Art Center.

Faiola, A. (2007). The Design enterprise: Rethinking the HCI education paradigm. *Design Issues, 23*(3), 30–45. doi:doi:10.1162/desi.2007.23.3.30

Feisel, D. L., & Rosa, A. J. (2005). The role of the laboratory in undergraduate engineering education. *Journal of Engineering Education, 94*(1), 121–130.

Felder, R. M. (1993). Reaching the second tier: Learning and teaching styles in college science education. *Journal of College Science Teaching, 23*, 286–290.

Felder, R. M., & Silverman, L. K. (1988). Learning and teaching styles in engineering education. *English Education, 78*, 674–681.

Feldon, D., & Kafai, Y. (2008). Mixed methods for mixed reality: Understanding users' avatar activities in virtual worlds. *Educational Technology Research and Development, 56*(5/6), 575–593. doi:10.1007/s11423-007-9081-2

Fetscherin, M., & Lattemann, C. (2007). *User acceptance of virtual worlds: An explorative study about Second Life.* Rollins College: University of Potsdam.

Fine, M., Boudin, K., Bowen, I., Clark, J., Hylton, D., Migdalia, M., et al. (2001, June). *Participatory action research: From within and beyond prison bars.* Paper presented at the Bridging the Gap: Feminisms and Participatory Action Research Conference, Boston College, MA. Retrieved from http://www.wnum.org/gap/fine.htm

Fisher, C. (2006). *Small pieces versus Moodle.* Retrieved April 30, 2009, from http://remoteaccess.typepad.com/remote_access/2006/10/small_pieces_ve.html

FitzGerald, S. (2007, June). *Virtual worlds - What are they and why do educators need to pay attention to them?* Paper presented at E-learning Networks June Online Event. Retrieved July 18, 2009, from http://seanfitz.wikispaces.com/virtualworldsenetworks07

Foster, A. (2005). The avatars of research. *The Chronicle of Higher Education, 52*(6), A35.

Fox, H. (1994). *Listening to the world: Cultural issues in academic writing.* Urbana, IL: National Council of Teachers of English.

Franklin, T., & van Harmelen, M. (2007). *Web 2.0 for Learning and Teaching in Higher Education Report.* London: The observatory of borderless higher education. Retrieved May 11, 2009, from http://www.jisc.ac.uk/media/documents/programmes/digital_repositories/web2-content-learning-and-teaching.pdf

Free Software Foundation. (2009). *The gnu general public license.* Retrieved June 30, 2009 from http://www.gnu.org/copyleft/gpl.html.

Freire, P. (1976). *Education, the practice of freedom.* London: Writers and Readers Publishing Cooperative.

Fugitani, S., Mochizuki, T., Koto, H., Isshiki, Y., & Yamauchi, Y. (2003). *Development of collaborative learning assessment tool with multivariate analysis applied to electronic discussion forums.* Paper presented at *the World Conference on E-Learning in Corp., Govt., Health., & Higher Ed. (ELEARN)*, Phoenix, AZ.

Fuller, I., Gaskin, S., & Scott, I. (2003). Student perceptions of geography and environmental science fieldwork in the light of restricted access to the field, caused by foot and mouth disease in the UK in 2001. *Journal of Geography in Higher Education, 27*(1), 79–102. doi:10.1080/0309826032000062487

Gallese, V., Eagle, M., & Migone, P. (2007). Intentional attunement: Mirror neurons and the neural underpinnings of interpersonal relations. *Journal of the American Psychoanalytic Association, 55*(1), 131–176.

Gasevic, D., & Hatala, M. (2006). Ontology mappings to improve learning resource search. *British Journal of Educational Technology, 37*(3), 375–389. doi:10.1111/j.1467-8535.2006.00611.x

Gee, J. P. (2003). *What videogames have to teach us about learning and literacy.* New York: Palgrave Macmillan.

Gee, J. P. (2007). Are video games good for learning? In de Castell, S., & Jenson, J. (Eds.), *Worlds in play* (pp. 323–336). New York: Lang.

Gibson, J. J. (1977). The theory of affordances. In Shaw, R. E., & Bransford, J. (Eds.), *Perceiving, acting, and knowing.* Hillsdale, NJ: Lawrence Erlbaum Associates.

Gibson, J. J. (1979/1986). *The ecological approach to visual perception.* Mahwah, NJ: Erlbaum.

Gilbert, H. D. (2003, November 5). *Electrical Engineering 215 – A case study in assessment.* Paper presented at the 33rd ASEE/IEEE Frontiers in Education Conference. Retrieved May 18, 2007, from http://fie-conference.org/fie2003/papers/1199.pdf

Gilbert, J. K., Watts, D. M., & Osborne, R. J. (1982). *Physics Education, 17*(2), 62. Retrieved June 30, 2009 from http://stacks.iop.org/0031-9120/17/62

Gilbert, J. K., Reiner, M., & Nakhleh, M. (Eds.). (2008). *Visualization: Theory and practice in science education.* New York: Springer Verlag. doi:10.1007/978-1-4020-5267-5

Giles, J. (2008). The semantic web will make finding answers online as simple as asking the right question. *New Scientist, 198*(2658), 26–27. doi:10.1016/S0262-4079(08)61363-9

Ginsburg, H. P., & Opper, S. (1988). *Piaget's theory of intellectual development.* Upper Saddle River, NJ: Prentice Hall.

Gitomer, J. (2006). *Little black book of connections – 6.5 ASSETS for networking your way to RICH relationships.* Austin, TX: Bard Press.

Goffman, E. (1956). *The presentation of self in everyday life.* New York: Doubleday.

Goldstein (2008). The tower, the cloud, and the IT leader and workforce. In R. Katz (Ed.), *The tower and the cloud* (pp. 238-260). Boulder, CO: Educause.

Gollub, R. (2007). Second Life and education. *Crossroads: The ACM Student Magazine, 14(1).* Retrieved June 12, 2009 from http://www.acm.org/crossroads/xrds14-1/secondlife.html

Good, J., Howland, K., & Thackray, L. (2008). Problem-based learning spanning real and virtual worlds: a case study in Second Life. *ALT-J, 16*(3), 163–172. doi:10.1080/09687760802526681

Google (2009). *LMS and Google Apps – first comes love... Official Google enterprise blog.* Retrieved May 29, 2009, from http://googleenterprise.blogspot.com/2009/02/lms-and-google-apps-first-comes-love.html

Google (2009). *Google wave.* Retrieved May 29, 2009, from http://wave.google.com/

Google. (2009). *OpenSocial: The Web is better when it's social.* Retrieved May 25, 2009, from http://code.google.com/apis/opensocial/

Gopalan, P., & Cartwright, A. N. (2001). Java enabled opto-electronic learning tools and a supporting framework. In *Proceeding of American Society for Engineering Educational Annual Conference and Exposition,* Albuquerque, NM (pp. 3532-3563).

Gorini, A., Gaggiolo, A., Vigna, C., & Riva, G. (2008). A Second Life for eHealth: Prospects for the use of 3-D virtual worlds in clinical psychology. *Journal of Medical Internet Research, 10*(3), e21. doi:10.2196/jmir.1029

Gozzi, R. Jr. (2007). Searching for search engine metaphors. *Etc.; a Review of General Semantics*, 276–279.

Grassian, E., & Trueman, R. B. (2007). Stumbling, bumbling, teleporting and flying... Librarian avatars in Second Life. *RSR. Reference Services Review*, *35*, 84–89. doi:10.1108/00907320710729373

Green, C., & Ruhleder, K. (1995). Globalization, borderless worlds, and the tower of Babel: Metaphors gone awry. *Journal of Organizational Change Management*, *8*(4), 55–68. doi:10.1108/09534819510090213

Greenwood, C. (2009). *And it grows and grows*. Retrieved June 17, 2009 from http://simbioticbiome.wordpress.com/

Groff, L., & Smoker, P. (1997). *Introduction to futures studies*. Retrieved October 1, 2007, from http://www.csudh.edu/global_options/IntroFS.HTML

Grove, P., & Steventon, G. (2008). Exploring community safety in a virtual community: using Second Life to enhance structured creative learning. In *Proceedings of the Researching Learning in Virtual Environments International Conference* (pp. 154-171). Retrieved May 8, 2009 from http://www.open.ac.uk/relive08/documents/ReLIVE08_conference_proceedings_Lo.pdf

Gruson, E., Staal, G., & St. Joost, A. (2000). *Copy proof: A new method for design and education*. Rotterdam, The Netherlands: 010 Publishers.

Gudykunst, W. B., & Kim, Y. Y. (1997). *Communicating with strangers: An approach to intercultural communication* (3rd ed.). New York: McGraw-Hill.

Guidugli, S., Gauna, C. F., & Benegas, J. (2005). *The Physics Teacher, 43*(6), 334. Retrieved June 30, 2009 from http://link.aip.org/link/?PTE/43/334/1

Gunawardena, C., & Zittle, F. (1997). Social presence as a predictor of satisfaction within a computer-mediated conferencing environment. *American Journal of Distance Education*, *11*(3), 8–26. doi:10.1080/08923649709526970

Guzdial, M., Jochen, R., & Kehoe, C. (2001). Beyond adoption to invention: Teacher-created collaborative activities in higher education. *Journal of the Learning Sciences*, *10*(3), 265–279. doi:10.1207/S15327809JLS1003_2

Haigh, M., & Gold, J. R. (1993). The problems with fieldwork: a group based approach towards integrating fieldwork into the undergraduate geography curriculum. *Journal of Geography in Higher Education*, *17*(1), 21–32. doi:10.1080/03098269308709203

Hainey, T., Connolly, T. M., Stansfield, M. H., Boyle, L., Josephson, J., O'Donovan, A., et al. (in print). ARGuing for multilingual motivation in Web 2.0: An evaluation of a large-scale European pilot. In *Proceedings of the 3rd European Conference on Games-based Learning (ECGBL)*, October 2009, Graz, Austria.

Hale, T. (2009). *Second Life roadmap.* Paper presented at the Second Life Community Convention (SLCC), San Francisco, CA.

Hall, E. T. (1976). *Beyond culture*. New York: Doubleday.

Hamza, K., Alhalabi, B., & Marcovitz, D. M. (2000, February 8). *Remote labs*. Paper presented at the International Conference of the Society for Information Technology and Teacher Education, Association for the Advancement of Computing in Education. (ERIC Document Reproduction Service No. ED444475)

Hansen, M. (2008). Versatile, immersive, creative and dynamic virtual 3-D healthcare learning environments: A review of the literature. *Journal of Medical Internet Research. 10*(3). Retrieved June 30, 2009 from http://www.jmir.org/2008/3/e26/HTML

Hara, N., & Kling, R. (1999). Students' frustrations with a web-based distance education course. *First Monday, 4*(12). Retrieved June 1, 2009 from http://www.uic.edu/htbin/cgiwrap/bin/ojs/index.php/fm/article/view/710/620

Harb, S. (2000). *Web-based circuit design simulation package for solving Electrical engineering circuits*. Unpublished master's thesis, University of Central Florida, Orlando, FL.

Hargis, J. (2008). Second Life for distance learning. *Turkish Online Journal of Distance Education, 9*(2), 57–63.

Hart, J. (2008). *Top 100 Tools for Learning 2008.* Retrieved April 30, 2009, from http://www.c4lpt.co.uk/recommended/top100.html

Hayes, B. (2008). Cloud computing. *Communications of the ACM, 51*(7). New York: ACM.

Hayes, E. (2007). Game content creation and IT proficiency: An exploratory study. *Computers & Education, 51*(1), 97–108. doi:10.1016/j.compedu.2007.04.002

Hayes, E., & King, E. (in press). Not just a dollhouse: What *The Sims 2* can teach us about women's IT learning. *New Horizons (Baltimore, Md.)*.

Healey, M., & Jenkins, A. (2000). Learning cycles and learning styles: the application of Kolb's experiential learning model in higher education. *The Journal of Geography, 99*, 185–195. doi:10.1080/00221340008978967

Healey, M., Kneale, P., & Bradbeer, J. (2005). Learning styles among geography undergraduates: an international comparison. *Area, 37*(1), 30–42. doi:10.1111/j.1475-4762.2005.00600.x

Healy, A., & Connolly, T. M. (2007, October 25-26). Does games-based learning, based on a constructivist pedagogy, enhance the learning experience and outcomes for the student compared to a traditional didactic pedagogy? In *Proceedings of 1st European Conference on Games-Based Learning. (ECGBL)*, Paisley, Scotland.

Hermans, H., & Verjans, S. (2009). *Developing a sustainable, student centred VLE: The OUNL case*. Retrieved May 29, 2009, from http://dspace.ou.nl/bitstream/1820/1894/1/Hermans_Verjans_ICDE2009_V4.pdf

Herold, D. K. (2009). Virtual education: Teaching media studies in Second Life. *Journal of Virtual Worlds Research, 2*(1), 3-17. Retrieved August 1, 2009, from https://journals.tdl.org/jvwr/article/view/380/454

Herwig, A., & Parr, P. (2002). Game engines: tools for landscape visualization and planning. Trends in GIS and virtualization. In *Environmental Planning and Design* (pp. 161–172). Heidelberg, Germany: Wichmann Verlag.

Hiltz, S. (1997). Impacts of college-level courses via asynchronous learning networks: Some preliminary results. *Journal of Asynchronous Learning Networks, 1*(2). Retrieved May 3, 2008 from http://www.aln.org/alnweb/journal/issue2/hiltz.htm

Hofstede, G. (1980). *Culture's consequences*. Beverly Hills, CA: Sage.

Hofstede, G. (1996). *Cultures and organizations: Software of the mind*. New York: McGraw Hill.

Hogg, R. V. (1991). Statistical education: improvements are badly needed. *The American Statistician, 45*, 342–343. doi:10.2307/2684473

Hollins, P., & Robbins, S. (2008). The educational affordances of multi user virtual environments (MUVE). In *Proceedings of the Researching Learning in Virtual Environments International Conference* (pp. 172-180). Retrieved May 8, 2009 from http://www.open.ac.uk/relive08/documents/ReLIVE08_conference_proceedings_Lo.pdf

Honan, W. (1994, March 23). Academic disciplines increasingly entwine, recasting scholarship. *New York Times*, 19.

Honebein, P. C. (1996). Seven goals for the design of constructivist learning environments. In B. Wilson (Ed.), *Constructivist learning environments: Case studies in instructional design.* (pp. 3-8). Englewood Cliffs, NJ: Educational Technology Publications.

Hovy, E. (2002). Comparing sets of semantic relations in ontologies. In Green, R., Bean, C., & Myaeng, S. H. (Eds.), *The semantics of relationships*. Dordrecht, The Netherlands: Kluwer Academic Publishers.

Huba, M. E., & Freed, J. E. (2000). *Learner-centered assessment on college campuses: Shifting the focus from teaching to learning*. Boston: Allyn & Bacon.

Hudlicka, E. (2002). This time with feeling: Integrated model of trait and state effects on cognition and behavior. *Applied Artificial Intelligence, 16*(7/8), 1–31.

Hughes, I. (2004). Coping strategies for staff involved in assessment of laboratory write-ups. *Journal of Bioscience Education, 3*(4). Retrieved September 12, 2008, from http://www.bioscience.heacademy.ac.uk/journal/vol3/beej-3-4.htm

Iacoboni, M. (2008). *Mirroring people: The new science of how we connect with others*. New York: Farrar, Straus & Giroux.

IBM. (2005). *On demand learning: Blended learning for today's evolving workforce*. Retrieved September 15, 2009 from http://www935.ibm.com/services/uk/index.wss/executivebrief/igs/a1022918?cntxt=a1006794

IBM. (2009). *About IBM*. Retrieved September 9, 2009 from http://www.ibm.com/ibm/us/en/

Information Society Technologies. (2009). *Presence research pro-active initiative*. Retrieved February 20, 2009, from www.cordis.lu/ist/fet/pr.htm.

Instructional Methods Information Website, A. D. P. R. I. M. A. (2009). Retrieved 21 May, 2009, from http://www.adprima.com/teachmeth.htm

Irwin, R. L. (2004). A/r/tography: A metonymic métissage. In Irwin, R. L., & de Cosson, A. (Eds.), *A/r/tography: Rendering self through arts-based living inquiry* (pp. 27–38). Vancouver, BC: Pacific Educational Press.

Isen, A. M. (2004). Positive affect and decision making. In Lewis, M., & Haviland-Jones, J. M. (Eds.), *Handbook of emotions* (pp. 417–435). New York: Guilford Press.

Iversen, J. S. (n.d). *Futures thinking methodologies – Options relevant for "schooling for tomorrow"*. Retrieved March 14, 2009, from http://www.oecd.org/dataoecd/41/57/35393902.pdf

Jafari, A., McGee, P., & Carmean, C. (2006). Managing courses, defining learning: What faculty, students, and administrators want. *EDUCAUSE Review, 41*(4), 50–71.

Jarmon, L. (1996). *An ecology of embodied interaction: Turn-taking and interactional syntax in face-to-face encounters*. Unpublished doctoral dissertation on CD-ROM, University of Texas at Austin.

Jarmon, L. (2009). An ecology of embodied interaction: pedagogy and homo virtualis. *Journal of virtual worlds research, 2*(1). Retrieved July 22, 2009, from https://journals.tdl.org/jvwr/article/view/624/453,

Jarmon, L., & Sanchez, J. (2008b, October 24-29). The educators coop: A virtual world model for real world collaboration. In *Proceedings of the 2008 Annual Convention of the American Society for Information Science and Technology (ASIS&T)*, Columbus, OH.

Jarmon, L., & Sanchez, J. (2009). The Educators Coop: A model for collaboration and LSI communication research in the virtual world. *Electronic Journal of Communication, 9*(1/2).

Jarmon, L., Lim, K., & Carpenter, S. (Eds.). (2009). *Special Issue*: Pedagogy, education and innovation in virtual worlds. *Journal of Virtual Worlds Research*. Retrieved July 18, 2009, from http://www.jvwresearch.org/v2n1.html

Jarmon, L. (2008). Pedagogy and Learning in the Virtual World of *Second Life*. In Rogers, P. (Ed.), *Encyclopedia of distance and online learning* (2nd ed., *Vol. 3*, pp. 1610–1619). Hershey, PA: IGI Global.

Jarmon, L. (2009). *Homo Virtualis*: Virtual worlds, learning, and an ecology of embodied interaction. *International Journal of Virtual and Personal Learning Environments, 1*(1), 38–56.

Jarmon, L. (2009). Learning in virtual world environments: Social-presence, engagement & pedagogy. In Rogers, P., Berg, G., Boettcher, J., Howard, C., Justice, L., & Schenk, K. (Eds.), *Encyclopedia of distance and online learning* (pp. 1610–1619). Hershey, PA: IGI Global.

Jarmon, L., & Sanchez, J. (2008). The educators coop experience in Second Life: A model for collaboration. *The Journal of the Research Center for Educational Technology, 4*(2), 66–82.

Jarmon, L., & Sanchez, J. (in press). The educators coop: A model for collaboration and LSI communication research in the virtual world. *Electronic Journal of Communication. CIOS*.

Jarmon, L., Traphagan, T., & Mayrath, M. (2008). Understanding project-based learning in Second Life with a pedagogy, training, and assessment trio. *Educational Media International*, *45*(3), 157–176. doi:10.1080/09523980802283889

Jarmon, L., Traphagan, T., & Mayrath, M. (2008). Understanding project-based learning in Second Life with a pedagogy, training, and assessment trio. *Educational Media International*, *45*(3), 157–176. doi:doi:10.1080/09523980802283889

Jarmon, L., Traphagan, T., Mayrath, M., & Trivedi, A. (2009a). Virtual world teaching, experiential learning, and assessment: An interdisciplinary communication course in Second Life. *Computers & Education*, *53*, 169–182. doi:doi:10.1016/j.compedu.2009.01.010

Jarmon, L., Traphagan, T., Traphagan, J., & Jones-Eaton, L. (in press). Aging, lifelong learning, and the virtual world of Second Life. In Wankel, C., & Kingsley, J. (Eds.), *Higher Education in Second Life*. Charlotte, NC: Information Age Publishing.

Jeffery, C. (2008). Using non-player characters as tutors in virtual environments. In *Proceedings of the Researching Learning in Virtual Environments International Conference* (pp. 181-188). Retrieved May 8, 2009 from http://www.open.ac.uk/relive08/documents/ReLIVE08_conference_proceedings_Lo.pdf

Jenkins, H., Purushotma, R., Clinton, K., Weigel, M., & Robison, A. (2006). *Confronting the challenges of participatory culture: Media education for the 21st century*. Chicago, IL: The John D. and Catherine T. MacArthur Foundation, Digital Media and Learning Initiative. Retrieved from http://www.newmedialiteracies.org

Jennex, M., Olfman, L., Panthawi, P., & Park, Y. (1998). An organizational memory Information Systems success model: An extension of DeLone and McLean's I/S success model. In *Proceedings of the Thirty-First Annual Hawaii International Conference on System Sciences* (p. 157).

Jigsaw Networking. (2009). *Cloud computing*. Retrieved May 29, 2009, from http://www.jigsawnetworking.com/articles/cloud-computing-for-creatives.aspx

Jimoyiannis, A., & Komis, V. (2001). Computer simulations in physics teaching and learning: A case study on students' understanding of trajectory motion. *Computers & Education*, *36*(2), 183–204. doi:10.1016/S0360-1315(00)00059-2

Johnson, L., Levine, A., & Smith, R. (2009). *The 2009 horizon report*. Austin, TX: The New Media Consortium.

Johnson, D. W., & Johnson, R. T. (1989). *Cooperation and competition: Theory and research*. Edina, MN: Interaction Book Company.

Johnson, J. L. (2000). Learning communities and special efforts in the retention of university students: what works, what doesn't, and is the return worth the investment? *Journal of College Student Retention: Research. Theory into Practice*, *2*(3), 219–238.

Johnson, L., & Levine, A. (2008). Virtual worlds: Inherently immersive, highly social learning spaces. *Theory into Practice*, *47*(2), 161–170. doi:10.1080/00405840801992397

Jonassen, D. H., & Land, S. M. (2000). *Theoretical foundations of learning environments*. Mahwah, N.J: Lawrence Erlbaum Associates.

Kappelman, L. A. (1995). Measuring user involvement: A diffusion of innovation perspective. *Database Advances*, *26*(2/3), 65–86.

Katz, R., Goldstein, P., & Yanosky, R. (2009). *Research Bulletin (Sun Chiwawitthaya Thang Thale Phuket)*, 2009.

Kawachi, P. (1999). *When the sun doesn't rise: Empirical findings that explain the exclusion of Japanese from online global education*. Retrieved January 12, 2008, from http://www.ignou.ac.in/Theme-3/Paul%20%20KAWACHI.html

Kay, R. (2006). Semantic web. *Computerworld*, 32.

Kearney, D. J., & Miller, D. C. (2008). VandalMail live: Bringing a campus into the Microsoft @EDU program. In *Proceedings of the 36th Annual ACM SIGUCCS Conference on User Services* (pp. 107-112). New York: ACM.

Kelton, A. J. (2007). Second Life: Reaching into the virtual world for real-world learning. *Educause Center for Applied Research (ECAR) Research Bulletin*, (17), 1-13. Retrieved May 12, 2009 from http://net.educause.edu/ir/library/pdf/ERB0717.pdf

Kemmis, S. (1993). Action research and social movement: A challenge for policy research. *Education Policy Analysis Archives, 1*(1). Retrieved from http://epaa.asu.edu/epaa/v1n1.html.

Kemp, J. (2009). *Sim teach wiki*. Retrieved September 10, 2009 from http://www.simteach.com/wiki/index.php?title=Institutions_and_Organizations_in_SL

Kemp, J., & Livingstone, D. (2006). Putting a Second Life 'metaverse' skin on learning management systems. In D. Livingstone & J. Kemp (Eds.), *In Proceedings of the Second Life Education Workshop at the Second Life Community Convention 2006* (pp. 13-18). Retrieved May 5, 2009 from http://www.simteach.com/SLCC06/slcc2006-proceedings.pdf

Ketelhut, D. (2007). The impact of student self-efficacy on scientific inquiry skills: an exploratory investigation in "River City," a multi-user virtual environment. *Journal of Science Education and Technology, 16*(1), 99–111. doi:10.1007/s10956-006-9038-y

Kim, H., & Dong, A. (2002). *Pragmatics of the semantic web*. Paper presented at the Semantic Web Workshop.

Kirkpatrick, D. L. (1994). *Evaluating training programs: The four levels*. San Francisco: Berrett-Koehler.

Kirriemuir, J. (2007). *A July 2007 'snapshot' of UK higher and further education developments in Second Life*. Bath, UK: Virtual World Watch, for the Eduserv Foundation. Retrieved August 5, 2009, from http://virtualworldwatch.net/wordpress/wp-content/uploads/2009/07/snapshot-one.pdf

Kirriemuir, J. (2007). *An update of the July 2007 'snapshot' of UK higher and further education developments in Second Life*. Bath, UK: Virtual World Watch, for the Eduserv Foundation. Retrieved August 5, 2009, from http://virtualworldwatch.net/wordpress/wp-content/uploads/2009/07/snapshot-two.pdf

Kirriemuir, J. (2008). *The autumn 2008 snapshot of UK higher and further education developments in Second Life*. Bath, UK: Virtual World Watch, for the Eduserv Foundation. Retrieved August 5, 2009, from http://virtualworldwatch.net/wordpress/wp-content/uploads/2009/07/snapshot-four.pdf

Kirriemuir, J. (2008). *'Measuring' the impact of Second Life for educational purposes responses and Second Life meeting transcript*. Bath, UK: Eduserv Foundation. Retrieved August 5, 2009, from http://www.eduserv.org.uk/~/media/foundation/sl/impactreport032008/impactreport%20pdf.ashx

Kirriemuir, J. (2008). *A spring 2008 'snapshot' of UK higher and further education developments in Second Life May 2008*. Bath, UK: Virtual World Watch, for the Eduserv Foundation. Retrieved August 5, 2009, from http://virtualworldwatch.net/wordpress/wp-content/uploads/2009/07/snapshot-three.pdf

Kirriemuir, J. (2009). *Early summer 2009 Virtual World Watch snapshot of virtual world activity in UK HE and FE*. Bath, UK: Virtual World Watch, for the Eduserv Foundation. Retrieved August 5, 2009, from http://virtualworldwatch.net/wordpress/wp-content/uploads/2009/06/snapshot-six.pdf

Kirriemuir, J. (2009, August 9). *Personal communication via email.*

Kirriemuir, J. (2009). *The Spring 2009 snapshot of virtual world use in UK higher and further education*. Bath, UK: Virtual World Watch, for the Eduserv Foundation. Retrieved August 5, 2009, from http://www.scribd.com/doc/12459921/The-Spring-2009-Snapshot-of-Virtual-World-Use-in-UK-Higher-and-Further-Education

Klamma, R., Chatti, M. A., Duval, E., Hummel, H., Hvannberg, E. H., & Kravcik, M. (2007). Social software for life-long learning. *Journal of Educational Technology & Society, 10*(3), 72–83.

Knowles, R. (2006). *Ritual house: Drawing on nature's rhythms for architecture and urban design*. Washington, DC: Island Press.

Kobielus, J. (2007). The semantic web: Meaning and SOA. *Business Communications Review*, 30-36.

Koch, N. (2001). *Software engineering for adaptive hypermedia applications. Reihe Softwaretechnik, 12*. Munich, Germany: Uni-Druck Publishing Company.

Kolb, A. Y., & Kolb, D.A. (2008). The learning way: Meta-cognitive aspects of experiential learning. *Simulation & Gaming*, OnlineFirst, published on October 10, 2008 as doi:10.1177/1046878108325713.

Kolb, D. A. (1984). *Experiential learning: Experience as the source of learning and development.* Englewood Cliffs, N.J: Prentice-Hall.

Kolb, A. Y., & Kolb, D. A. (2005). *The Kolb learning style inventory—version 3.1: Technical Specifications.* Boston, MA: Hay Resources Direct.

Kowalski, C. (2004). Getting classes in GEAR: A lesson planning model for English reteaching. *The Language Teacher, 28*(5), 19-24. Retrieved 2009, from http://www.jalt-publications.org/tlt/articles/2004/05/kowalski

Krueger, J., & Mueller, R. A. (2002). Unskilled, unaware, or both? The better-than-average heuristic and statistical regression predict errors in estimates of own performance. *Journal of Personality and Social Psychology, 82*, 180–188. doi:10.1037/0022-3514.82.2.180

KZERO. (2008). *Virtual worlds registered accounts and virtual worlds by sector Q4.* Retrieved July 20, 2009, from http://www.kzero.co.uk/blog/?page_id=2092

KZERO. (2009). *Kids, tweens, and teens in virtual worlds case study.* Retrieved July 20, 2009, from http://www.kzero.co.uk/blog/?p=2722

L2P. (2008). *Lehr- und Lernportal (L2P).* Retrieved April 1, 2010, from http://www.cil.rwthaachen.de/L2P.htm

Lamb, G. M. (2006, October 5). Real learning in a virtual world. *The Christian Science Monitor.* Retrieved October 6, 2006, from http://www.csmonitor.com/2006/1005/p13s02-legn.html

Lamb, B. (2004). Wide open spaces: Wikis, ready or not. *EDUCAUSE Review, 39*(5), 36–48.

Latour, B. (1990). Drawing things together. In Lynch, M., & Woolgar, S. (Eds.), *Representation of Scientific Practice* (pp. 19–68). Cambridge, MA: MIT Press.

Laurillard, D. (1996, June). *Keynote speech at the ACM SIGCSE/SIGCUE Conference,* Barcelona.

Lave, J., & Wenger, E. (1991). *Situated learning: Legitimate peripheral participation.* New York: Cambridge University Press.

Lee, J., Upadhyaya, S. J., Rao, H. R., & Sharman, R. (2005). Secure knowledge management and the semantic web. *Communications of the ACM, 48*(12), 49–54. doi:10.1145/1101779.1101808

Leslie, S. (2005). *The good thing about bad presentations, or how I came to love social software.* Retrieved April 30, 2009, from http://www.edtechpost.ca/wordpress/2005/11/17/the-good-thing-about-bad-presentations-or-how-i-came-to-love-social-software/

Levy, P. (2008). 'I feel like a grown up person': First year undergraduates' experiences of inquiry and research. *Paper presented at a CILASS Research seminar.* Sheffield, UK: Centre for Inquiry Based Learning in the Arts and Social Sciences. Retrieved August 1, 2009, from http://www.shef.ac.uk/cilass/

Levy, P. (2003). A methodological framework for practice-based research in networked learning. *Instructional Science, 31*, 87–109. doi:doi:10.1023/A:1022594030184

Liber, O., & Holyfield, S. (Eds.). (2006). Creating a managed learning environment. *JISC InfoNet.* Retrieved April 30, 2009, from http://www.jiscinfonet.ac.uk/InfoKits/InfoKits/creating-an-mle/index_html

Life, S. in Education (n.d.). *Educational uses of Second Life.* Retrieved July 18, 2009, from http://sleducation.wikispaces.com/educationaluses

Linden Research Inc. (2009). *llapplyimpulse.* Retrieved June 9, 2009 from http://wiki.secondlife.com/wiki/LlApplyImpulse

Linden Research Inc. (2009). *llgetmass.* Retrieved June 9, 2009 from http://wiki.secondlife.com/wiki/LlGetMass

Linden Research Inc. (2009). *llrezatroot.* Retrieved June 9, 2009 from http://wiki.secondlife.com/wiki/LlRezAtRoot

Linden Research Inc. (2009). *llsetbuoyancy.* Retrieved June 9, 2009 from http://wiki.secondlife.com/wiki/LlSetBuoyancy

Linden Research Inc. (2009). *llsetforce.* Retrieved June 9, 2009 from http://wiki.secondlife.com/wiki/LlSetForce

Linden Research Inc. (2009). *llsettimerevent.* Retrieved June 9, 2009 from http://wiki.secondlife.com/wiki/LlSetTimerEvent

Linden Research Inc. (2009). *Lsl portal*. Retrieved June 9, 2009 from http://wiki.secondlife.com/wiki/LSL Portal

Linden Research Inc. (2009). *Pi*. Retrieved June 9, 2009 from http://wiki.secondlife.com/wiki/PI

Linden Research Inc. (2009). *State entry*. Retrieved June 9, 2009 from http://wiki.secondlife.com/wiki/State entry

Linden Research Inc. (2009). *timer*. Retrieved June 9, 2009 from http://wiki.secondlife.com/wiki/Timer

Li, S., & Khan, A. A. (2005). Applying IT tools to a laboratory course for measurement, analysis, and design of electric and electronic circuits. *IEEE Transactions on Education*, *48*(4), 520–530. doi:10.1109/TE.2005.852601

Lissner, L. S. (2009). *Transition to college: Strategic planning to ensure success*. Washington, DC: National Center for Learning Disabilities. Retrieved from http://www.ncld.org/publications-a-more/parent-aamp-advocacy-guides/transition-to-college-strategic-planning

Lowe, C., & Clark, M. A. (2008). Student perceptions of learning in a virtual world. In *Proceedings of the 24th Annual Conference on Distance Teaching and Learning*. Retrieved June 30, 2009 from http://www.uwex.edu/disted/conference/Resource_library/proceedings/08_13442.pdf

Lubensky, R. (2006). *The present and future of Personal Learning Environments (PLE)*. Retrieved April 1, 2010, from http://members.optusnet.com.au/rlubensky/2006/12/presentand-future-of-personal-learning.html

Luca, J., & McLoughlin, C. (2002, December 8-11). A question of balance: using self and peer assessment effectively in teamwork. Wind of change in the sea of learning. In *Proceedings of the Annual Conference of the Australasian Society for Computers in Learning in Tertiary Education (ASCILITE 2002)*, New Zealand.

Luo, L., & Kemp, J. (2008). Second Life: Exploring the immersive instructional venue for library and information science education. *Journal of Education for Library and Information Science*, *49*(3), 147–166.

Lynch, M. A., & Tunstall, R. J. (2008). When worlds collide: Developing game-design partnerships in universities. *Simulation & Gaming*, *39*(3), 379–398. doi:doi:10.1177/1046878108319275

Lytras, M., & Naeve, A. (2006). Semantic e-Learning: Synthesizing fantasies. *British Journal of Educational Technology*, *37*(3), 479–491. doi:10.1111/j.1467-8535.2006.00617.x

MacDonald, J. (2003). Assessing online collaborative learning: process and product. *Computers & Education*, *40*(4), 337–391. doi:10.1016/S0360-1315(02)00168-9

Maguire, M., Elton, E., Osman, Z., & Nicolle, C. (2006). Design of a virtual learning environment for students with special needs. *Human Technology: An Interdisciplinary Journal on Humans in ICT Environments*, *2*(1), 119–153.

Ma, J., & Nickerson, J. V. (2006). Hands-on, simulated, and remote laboratories: A comparative literature review. *ACM Computing Surveys*, *38*(3), 1–24.

Mannix, M. (2000). *The virtues of virtual labs*. Retrieved July 28, 2008, from http://www.highbeam.com/doc/1P3-60667340.html

Mansourian, Y., & Ford, N. (2007). Web searchers' attributions of success and failure: An empirical study. *The Journal of Documentation*, *63*(5), 659–679. doi:doi:10.1108/00220410710827745

Martinek, T., Schilling, T., & Hellison, D. (2006). The development of compassionate and caring leadership among adolescents. *Physical Education and Sport Pedagogy*, *11*(2), 141–157. doi:10.1080/17408980600708346

Martin, S., & Vallance, M. (2008). The impact of synchronous inter-networked teacher training in information and communication technology integration. *Computers & Education*, *51*, 34–53. doi:10.1016/j.compedu.2007.04.001

Mason, H. (2007, August 24-26). *Experiential education in Second Life*. Paper presented at the Second Life Education Workshop at Second Life Community Convention, Chicago Hilton, Chicago, USA.

Mason, R., Pegler, C., & Weller, M. (2004). E-portfolios: an assessment tool for online courses. *British Journal of Educational Technology*, *35*(6), 717–727. doi:10.1111/j.1467-8535.2004.00429.x

Mavrikis, M. (2005). Logging, replaying and analyzing students' interactions in a web-based ILE to improve student modelling. In *Proceedings of the 12th International Conference on Artificial Intelligence in Education*, Amsterdam, The Netherlands (pp. 967-972).

Mayer, R. (2003). Learning environments: The case for evidence-based practice and issue-driven research. *Educational Psychology Review*, *15*(4), 359–366. doi:doi:10.1023/A:1026179332694

Mayer, R. (2004). Should there be a three-strikes rule against pure discovery learning? The case for guided methods of instruction. *The American Psychologist*, *59*(1), 14–19. doi:10.1037/0003-066X.59.1.14

Mayrath, M., Sanchez, J., Traphagan, T., Heikes, J., & Trivedi, A. (2007, June). *Using Second Life in an English course: Designing class activities to address learning objectives.* Paper presented at ED-MEDIA World Conference on Educational Multimedia, Hypermedia & Telecommunications, Vancouver, Canada.

Mayrath, M., Traphagan, T., Jarmon, L., Trivedi, A., & Resta, P. (2009). *Teaching with virtual worlds: Factors to consider for instructional use of Second Life*. Paper presented to 2009 Annual Convention of the American Educational Research Association, San Diego, CA.

McAlpine, I. (2000). Collaborative learning online. *Distance Education*, *21*(1), 66–80. doi:10.1080/0158791000210105

McCalla, G. (2004). The ecological approach to the design of e-learning environments: Purpose-based capture and use of information about learners. *Journal of Interactive Media in Education, 7.* Retrieved April 18, 2009, from http://www-jime.open.ac.uk/2004/7/mccalla-2004-7.pdf

McCarthy, S., & Crossette, A. (2007). *University of Texas at Austin unites project in East Austin with virtual reality world.* Retrieved June 5, 2009 from http://www.utexas.edu/news/2007/12/03/architecture_alley_flat/

McCool, R. (2005). Rethinking the semantic web: Part I. *IEEE Internet Computing*, 86–88.

McDermott, L. C. (2001). Students knowledge and learning. In Tiberghien, A., Jossem, E. L., Barojas, J., & Deardorff, D. (Eds.), *Connecting research in physics education with teacher education.* Melville, NY: American Institute of Physics.

McGee, P. (2007, June). *Extreme learning in a virtual (world) learning environment: Who needs pedagogy anyway?* Paper presented at ED-MEDIA World Conference on Educational Multimedia, Hypermedia & Telecommunications, Vancouver, Canada.

McLoughlin, C., & Luca, J. (2001, December 9-12). Quality in online delivery: What does it mean for assessment in e-learning environments? In *Proceedings of the 18th Annual Conference of the Australasian Society for Computers in Learning in Tertiary Education: Meeting at the Crossroads (ASCILITE 2001)*, Melbourne, Australia.

McLoughlin, C., & Luca, J. (2002, June 24-29). Experiential learning on-line: the role of asynchronous communication tools. In *Proceedings of the 14th ED-MEDIA World Conference on Educational Multimedia, Hypermedia & Telecommunications,* Denver, CO.

McVey, M. (2008). Observations of expert communicators in immersive virtual worlds: implications for synchronous discussion. *Research in Learning Technology*, *16*(3), 173–180.

Meishar-Tal, H., & Tal-Elhasid, E. (2008). Measuring collaboration in educational wikis: a methodological discussion. *International Journal of Emerging Technologies in Learning*, *3*, 46–49.

Mesdag, M. V. (2000). Culture-sensitive adaptation or global standardization - the duration of usage hypothesis. *International Marketing Review*, *17*, 74–84. doi:10.1108/02651330010314722

Mey, J. L. (2003). Context and (dis)ambiguity: A pragmatic view. *Journal of Pragmatics*, *35*, 331–347. doi:10.1016/S0378-2166(02)00139-X

Mical, T. (2002). The stealth landscape of Tokyo. *NEH Summer Institute 2002*. Retrieved August 15, 2005, from http://www.usc.edu/dept/LAS/ealc/Mical.pdf

Middleton, M. (2004). The way that information professionals describe their own discipline: a comparison of thesaurus descriptors. *New Library World, 105*(11/12), 429–435. doi:doi:10.1108/03074800410568770

Mikropoulos, T. (2001). Brain activity on navigation in virtual environments. *Journal of Educational Computing Research*, *24*(1), 1–12. doi:10.2190/D1W3-Y15D-4UDW-L6C9

Miniwats International. (2007). *Internet usage statistics: The internet big picture.* Retrieved April 20, 2008, from www.Internetworldstats.com/stats.htm

Minocha, S. (2009). *A study on the effective use of social software to support student learning and engagement.* Retrieved May 11, 2009, from http://www.jisc.ac.uk/whatwedo/projects/socialsoftware08.aspx

Minocha, S., & Tingle, R. (2008). Socialisation and collaborative learning of distance learners in 3-D virtual worlds. In *Researching Learning in Virtual Environments International Conference Proceedings* (pp. 216-227). Retrieved May 8, 2009 from http://www.open.ac.uk/relive08/documents/ReLIVE08_conference_proceedings_Lo.pdf

Minocha, S., & Thomas, P. G. (2007). Collaborative Learning in a Wiki Environment: Experiences from a software engineering course. *New Review of Hypermedia and Multimedia, 13*(2), 187–209. doi:10.1080/13614560701712667

Moll, L. C. (1992). *Vygotsky and education: Instructional implications and applications of sociohistorical psychology*. UK: Cambridge University Press.

Mon, L. (2009). Questions and answers in a virtual world: Educators and librarians as information providers in Second Life. *Journal of Virtual Worlds Research, 2*(1), 4–21.

Moreno, R., Mayer, R., Spires, H., & Lester, J. (2001). The case for social agency in computer-based teaching: Do students learn more deeply when they interact with animated pedagogical agents? *Cognition and Instruction, 19*(2), 177–213. doi:doi:10.1207/S1532690XCI1902_02

Mullen, L., Beilke, J., & Brooks, N. (2007). Redefining field experiences: Virtual environments in teacher education. *International Journal of Social Sciences, 2*(1), 22–28.

Murphy, K., & Collins, M. (1997). Communication conventions in instructional electronic chats. *First Monday, 2*(11). Retrieved June 1, 2009 from http://www.uic.edu/htbin/cgiwrap/bin/ojs/index.php/fm/article/view/558/479

Murphy, K., & Cifuentes, L. (2001). Using web tools, collaborating, and learning online. *Distance Education, 22*(2), 285–305. doi:10.1080/0158791010220207

Nahl, D. (2005). Affective and cognitive information behavior: Interaction effects in Internet use. In *Proceedings of the 68th Annual Meeting of the American Society for Information Science & Technology*. Medford, NJ: Information Today.

Nahl, D. (2007). Domain interaction discourse analysis: A technique for charting the flow of micro-information behavior. *The Journal of Documentation, 63*(3), 323–339. doi:10.1108/00220410710743270

Nahl, D. (2007). Social-biological information technology: An integrated conceptual framework. *Journal of the American Society for Information Science and Technology, 58*(13), 2021–2046. doi:10.1002/asi.20690

Nahl, D., & Bilal, D. (Eds.). (2007). *Information and emotion: The emergent affective paradigm in information behavior research and theory*. Medford, NJ: Information Today.

Nardi, B. A. (2005). Beyond bandwidth: Dimensions of connection in interpersonal communication. *Computer Supported Cooperative Work, 14*(2), 91–130. doi:doi:10.1007/s10606-004-8127-9

National Center for Education Statistics (NCES). (1999). Distance education at postsecondary education institutions: 1997-1998. *U.S. Department of Education, NCES 2000-013*. Retrieved June 1, 2009 from http://nces.ed.gov/pubs2000/2000013.pdf

National Center for Education Statistics (NCES). (2008). Distance education at degree-granting postsecondary institutions: 2006-07. *U.S. Department of Education.* Retrieved June 1, 2009 from http://nces.ed.gov/pubsearch/pubsinfo.asp?pubid=2009044

Neustaedter, C., & Fedorovskaya, E. (2009). Capturing and sharing memories in a virtual world. In *Proceedings of ACM CHI 2009 Conference on Human Factors in Computing Systems* (pp. 1161-1170). Retrieved June 4, 2009 from http://portal.acm.org/citation.cfm?doid=1518701.1518878

New Media Consortium. (2009). *The Horizon Report.* Retrieved July 18, 2009, from http://www.nmc.org/publications/2009-horizon-report

Nielsen, J., & Molich, R. (1990, April 1-5) Heuristic evaluation of user interfaces. Seattle, WA. In *Proceedings of the ACM HI'90 Conference* (pp. 249-256).

Niemitz, M., Slough, S., Peart, L., Klaus, A. D., Leckie, R. M., & St. John, K. (2008). Interactive virtual expeditions as a learning tool: the school of rock expedition case study. *Journal of multimedia and hypermedia, 17*(4), 561-580.

Nonaka, I., & Takeuchi, H. (1995). *The knowledge-creating company: How Japanese companies create the dynamics of innovation*. New York: Oxford University.

Norman, D. (2008). *On eduglu – part 1: Background.* Retrieved April 30, 2009, from http://www.darcynorman.net/2008/02/16/on-eduglu-part-1-background/

Norman, D. A. (1990). *The design of everyday things*. New York: Doubleday.

Norman, D. A. (2004). *Emotional design: Why we love (or hate) everyday things*. New York: Basic Books.

Northcote, M., & Kendle, A. (2000). The Struggle for Balance in the Use of Quantitative and Qualitative Online Assessment Tasks. In *Proceedings of the 17th Annual Conference of the Australasian Society for Computers in Learning in Tertiary Education*, Coffs Harbour, NSW, Australia.

Notar, C., Wilson, J., & Ross, K. (2002). Distant learning for the development of higher-level cognitive skills. *Education, 122*(4), 642–648.

Nulty, D. D., & Barrett, M. A. (1996). Transitions in students' learning styles. *Studies in Higher Education, 21*(3), 333–345. doi:10.1080/03075079612331381251

O'Neil, H. F., Wainess, R., & Baker, E. L. (2005). Classification of learning outcomes: evidence from the computer games literature. *Curriculum Journal, 16*(4), 455–474. doi:10.1080/09585170500384529

O'Reilly, T. (2007). What is Web 2.0: Design patterns and business models for the next generation of software. *International Journal of Digital Economics, 65*, 17–37.

Obrien, H. L., & Toms, E. G. (2008). What is user engagement? A conceptual framework for defining user engagement with technology. *Journal of the American Society for Information Science and Technology, 59*(6), 938–955. doi:10.1002/asi.20801

OECD. (2005). E-learning in tertiary Education: Where do we stand? *Education & Skills, 4*, 1–293.

Olaniran, B. A. (2004). Computer-mediated communication in cross-cultural virtual groups. In Chen, G. M., & Starosta, W. J. (Eds.), *Dialogue among diversities* (pp. 142–166). Washington, DC: National Communication Association.

Olaniran, B. A. (2007). Challenges to implementing e-learning in lesser-developed countries. In Edmundson, A. (Ed.), *Globalized e-learning cultural challenges* (pp. 18–34). Hershey, PA: Idea Group.

Olaniran, B. A. (2007). Culture and communication challenges in virtual workspaces. In St-Amant, K. (Ed.), *Linguistic and cultural online communication issues in the global age* (pp. 79–92). Hershey, PA: Idea Group.

Olaniran, B. A. (2008). Group decision making in computer-mediated communication as networked communication: Understanding the technology and implications. In Raisinghani, M. S. (Ed.), *Handbook of research on global information technology management in digital economy*. Hershey, PA: IGI Global.

Olaniran, B. A., & Agnello, M. F. (2008). Globalization, educational hegemony, and higher education. *Journal of Multicultural Educational Technology, 2*(2), 68–86. doi:10.1108/17504970810883351

Olaniran, B. A., & Edgell, D. (2008). Cultural implications of collaborative information technologies (CITs) in international online collaborations and global virtual teams. In Zemliansky, P., & St-Amant, K. (Eds.), *Handbook of global virtual workspaces* (pp. 118–133). Hershey, PA: Idea Group.

Olsen, D. R., & Goodrich, M. A. (2003). *Metrics for evaluating human-robot interactions.* Retrieved March 14, 2009, from http://icie.cs.byu.edu/Papers/RAD.pdf

Omale, N., Hung, W., Luetkehans, L., & Cooke-Plagwitz, J. (2009). Learning in 3-D multiuser virtual environments: exploring the use of unique 3-D attributes for online problem-based learning. *British Journal of Educational Technology, 40*(3), 480–495. doi:10.1111/j.1467-8535.2009.00941.x

Ostrander, M. (2008). Talking, looking, flying, searching: Information seeking behaviour in Second Life. *Library Hi Tech, 26*(4), 512–524. doi:10.1108/07378830810920860

Palincsar, A. S., & Brown, A. L. (1984). Reciprocal teaching of comprehension-fostering and comprehension-monitoring activities. *Cognition and Instruction, 1*(2), 117–175. doi:10.1207/s1532690xci0102_1

Palop, J. M. G., & Teruel, J. M. A. (2000). Virtual workbench for electronic instrumentation teaching. *IEEE Transactions on Education*, *43*(1), 15–18. doi:10.1109/13.825734

Pang, M. F., & Marton, F. (2005). Learning theory as teaching resource: Enhancing students' understanding of economic concepts. *Instructional Science*, *33*(2), 159–191. doi:doi:10.1007/s11251-005-2811-0

Parker, K. R., & Chao, J. T. (2007). Wiki as a teaching tool. *Interdisciplinary Journal of Knowledge and Learning Objects*, *3*, 57–72.

Patil, B., Maetzel, K., & Neuhold. (2003). *Creating digital opportunities in IT education: An inclusive framework.* Retrieved January 29, 2008, from http://ecommerce.lebow.drexel.edu/eli/2003Proceedings/docs%5C093Patil.pdf

Peña, J., McGlone, M., Jarmon, L., & Sanchez, J. (2009). *The automatic effects of avatar appearance and role labels in language use in a virtual environment.* Paper to be presented at the November 2009 Annual Convention of the National Communication Association, Chicago, Ill.

Pena, C. M., & Alessi, S. M. (1999). Promoting a qualitative understanding of physics. *Journal of Computers in Mathematics and Science Teaching*, *18*(4), 439–457.

Perryman, C. (2009). *HealthInfo Island blog*. Retrieved June 26, 2009 from http://healthinfoisland.blogspot.com/from

Perry, W. (1970). *Forms of intellectual and ethical development in the college years*. New York: Holt, Rinehart and Winston.

Peters, T. (2007). *A report on the first year of operation of the Alliance Second Life Library 2.0 project also known as the Alliance Information Archipelago*. April 11, 2006 through April 18, 2007. Retrieved June 8, 2009 from http://www.alliancelibrarysystem.com/pdf/07sllreport.pdf

Phet. (2009). *Interactive simulations*. Retrieved June 30, 2009 from http://phet.colorado.edu

Phillips, A. (2008, January 15). Asperger's therapy hits Second Life: Experts express concern about applying online actions to real life. *ABC News*. Retrieved June 8, 2009 from http://abcnews.go.com/Technology/OnCall/story?id=4133184&page=1

Picard, R. W. (1997). *Affective computing*. Boston: MIT Press.

Pimentel, M., Gerosa, M. A., Fuks, H., & De Lucena, C. J. P. (2005). Assessment of collaboration in online courses. In *Proceedings of the 2005 conference on Computer support for collaborative learning: learning 2005: the next 10 years!* Taipei, Taiwan.

Pitcher, J. (2007). *Class management*. Retrieved June 4, 2009 from http://jpitcher.edublogs.org/2007/11/14/class-management/

Polanyi, M. (1967). *The tacit dimension*. New York: Anchor Books.

Prensky, M. (2001). Digital natives, digital immigrants. *On the Horizon*, *9*(5). NCB University Press. Retrieved April 30, 2009, from http://www.marcprensky.com/writing/Prensky%20-%20Digital%20Natives,%20Digital%20Immigrants%20-%20Part1.pdf

Prensky, M. (2006). *Don't bother me, Mom, I'm learning! How computer and video games are preparing your kids for 21st century success and how you can help!*St. Paul, MN: Paragon House.

Project, E. T. L. (2003). *ETL Project*. Retrieved August 1, 2009, from http://www.ed.ac.uk/etl

QAA. (2006). *Subject benchmark statements: Engineering.* Retrieved November 24, 2007, from http://www.qaa.ac.uk/academicinfrasctructure/benchmark/statements/Engineering06.pdf

Quality Assurance Agency. (2007). *Librarianship and information management.* Mansfield, UK: The Quality Assurance Agency for Higher Education. Retrieved August 1, 2009, from http://www.qaa.ac.uk/academicinfrastructure/benchmark/statements/Librarianship07.pdf

Ramondt, L. (2008). Towards the adoption of Massively Multiplayer Educational Gaming. In *Proceedings of the Researching Learning in Virtual Environments International Conference Proceedings* (pp. 258-268.) Retrieved May 8, 2009 from http://www.open.ac.uk/relive08/documents/ReLIVE08_conference_proceedings_Lo.pdf

Randel, J. M., Morris, B. A., Wetzel, C. D., & Whitehill, B. V. (1992). The effectiveness of games for educational purposes a review of research. *Simulation & Gaming*, *23*(3), 261–276. doi:10.1177/1046878192233001

Raymond, E. S. (1996). *New hacker's dictionary*. Cambridge, MA: MIT. Retrieved December 10, 2009, from http://www.ccil.org/jargon/jargon_toc.html

Repenning, A., & Sullivan, J. (2003). The Pragmatic web: Agent-based multimodal web interaction with no browser in sight. In *Proceedings of the 9th International Conference on Human-Computer Interaction,* Zurich, Switzerland (pp. 212-219).

Richards, C., & Nair, G. (2007). 21st century knowledge-building in the Asia Pacific: Towards a multidisciplinary framework for linking ICT-based social and personal contexts of education and development. *The Electronic Journal on Information Systems in Developing Countries*, *32*(7), 1–11.

Rimmer, J. (2001). User discourse and technology design. In Zayas, B., & Gama, C. (Eds.), *Information technologies and knowledge construction: Bringing together the best of two worlds (CSRP 538). Falmer*. UK: University of Sussex.

Riva, G., Anguera, M., Wiederhold, B., & Mantovani, F. (Eds.). (2006). *From communication to presence: Cognition, emotion and culture towards the ultimate communicative experience*. Amsterdam: IOS Press. Retrieved February 20, 2009, from http://www.emergingcommunication.com/volume8.html

Rose, D. H., & Meyer, A. (Eds.). (2006). *A practical reader in universal design for learning*. Boston: Harvard Education Press.

Rowlands, S., Graham, T., Berry, J., & McWilliams, P. (2007). Conceptual change through the lens of Newtonian mechanics. *Science & Education*, *16*, 21–42. doi:10.1007/s11191-005-1339-7

Ryan, M. (2008). 16 ways to use virtual worlds in your classroom: Pedagogical applications of Second Life. In *Proceedings of the Researching Learning in Virtual Environments International Conference* (pp. 269-277). Retrieved May 8, 2009 from http://www.open.ac.uk/relive08/documents/ReLIVE08_conference_proceedings_Lo.pdf

Salmon, G. (2009). The future for (second) life and learning. *British Journal of Educational Technology*, *40*(3), 526–538. doi:doi:10.1111/j.1467-8535.2009.00967.x

Sanchez, J. (2007, June). *A sociotechnical systems analysis of Second Life in an undergraduate English course*. Paper presented at ED-MEDIA World Conference on Educational Multimedia, Hypermedia & Telecommunications, Vancouver, Canada.

Sanchez, J. (2009). Student Second Life event: under water fun. Retrieved June 9, 2009 from http://educatorscoop.org/blog/?p=171

Sanchez, J. (2009). Implementing Second Life: Ideas, challenges, and innovations. *Library Technology Reports*, *45*(2), 5–39.

Sanders, C. A. (2008). Coming down the e-mail mountain, blazing a trail to Gmail. In *Proceedings of the 36th Annual ACM SIGUCCS Conference on User Services Conference* (pp. 101-106). New York: ACM.

Savin-Baden, M., Tombs, C., White, D., Poulton, D., Kavia, S., & Woodham, L. (2009). *Getting started with Second Life*. Bath, UK: JISC. Retrieved August 7, 2009, from http://www.jisc.ac.uk/media/documents/publications/gettingstartedwithsecondlife.pdf

Savin-Baden, M., & Major, C. H. (2004). *Foundations of problem-based learning*. Maidenhead, UK: Open University Press.

Scherer, D. (2009). Vpython. Retrieved June 30, 2009 from http://vpython.org/

Schneiderman, B. E. (2008). Creating a learning space that is virtual and experiential. *Journal of Aesthetic Education*, *42*(2), 38–50. doi:10.1353/jae.0.0003

Schoop, M., de Moor, A., & Dietz, J. L. G. (2006). The pragmatic web: A manifesto. *Communications of the ACM*, *49*(5), 75–76. doi:10.1145/1125944.1125979

Schumann, P. L., Anderson, P. H., Scott, T. W., & Lawton, L. (2001). A framework for evaluating simulations as educational tools. *Developments in Business Simulations and Experiential Learning, 28*.

Schwartz, L., Clark, S., Cossarin, M., & Rudolph, J. (2004). Educational wikis: Features and selection criteria. *The International Review of Research in Open and Distance Learning, 5*(1). Retrieved May 11, 2009, from http://www.irrodl.org/index.php/irrodl/article/viewArticle/163

Sclater, N. (2007). *Downside of the small pieces model.* Retrieved April 30, 2009, from http://sclater.com/blog/?p=45

Sclater, N. (2008). Web 2.0, personal learning environments and the future of learning management systems. Boulder, CO: Educause Center for Applied Research. *Research Bulletin (Sun Chiwawitthaya Thang Thale Phuket)*, 13.

SCONUL. (1999). *Information skills in higher education.* London: Society of College, National and University Libraries.

SCORM. (2009). *The Sharable Content Object Reference Model (SCORM), Advanced Distributed Learning.* Retrieved April 1, 2010, from http://www.adlnet.org/Technologies/scorm/default.aspx

Scott, J. (2009). *Second Nature Website*. Retrieved June 26 2009 from http://www.nature.com/secondnature/index.html

Second Life Development Service from the VITAL Lab @ Ohio University. (2009). *Vital Wiki*. Retrieved July 1, 2009 from http://vital.cs.ohiou.edu/vitalwiki/index.php/Nutrition_Game Skiba, D. (2009). Nursing education 2.0: A second look at Second Life. *Nursing Education Perspectives, 30*(2), 129-131.

Second Life Healthinfo Island. (2009). *Healthinfo Island.* Retrieved September 10, 2009 from http://slurl.com/secondlife/Healthinfo%20Island/184/61/22.

Second Life Nutrition Game. (2009). *Nutrition Game*. Retrieved September 10, 2009 from http://slurl.com/secondlife/ohio%25university/161/175/25/

Second Life. (2009). *Second Nature Island*. Retrieved June 26, 2009 from http://slurl.com/secondlife/Second%20Nature/218/213/28

Senge, P. (1994). *The fifth discipline: The art and practice of a learning organization.* New York: Doubleday Publishers.

Shaffer, D. W., Squire, K. T., Halverson, R., & Gee, J. P. (2004). Video games and the future of learning, *Phi Delta Kappan*. Retrieved 6 December, 2008 from http://www.academiccolab.org/resources/gappspaper1.pdf

Shanbhag, R. (2008). *Open source Moodle heads to the Amazon cloud.* Retrieved May 29, 2009, from http://asterisk.tmcnet.com/topics/open-source/articles/34257-open-source-moodle-heads-the-amazon-cloud.htm

Sharpe, R., Benfield, G., Roberts, G., & Francis, R. (2006). *The undergraduate experience of blended e-learning: a review of UK literature and practice.* York, UK: Higher Education Academy. Retrieved January 10, 2010, from http://www.heacademy.ac.uk/assets/York/documents/ourwork/archive/blended_elearning_full_review.pdf

Sharp, H., Rogers, Y., & Preece, J. (2007). Affective aspects. In *Interaction design: Beyond human-computer interaction* (pp. 181–215). New York: Wiley.

Sheffield University. (2007). *Shaping our learning, teaching and assessment future: Our shared vision.* Sheffield, UK: Sheffield University. Retrieved August 1, 2009, from http://www.shef.ac.uk/content/1/c6/08/20/69/SOLTAF%5B1%5D.pdf

Shepard, L. A. (2000). The role of assessment in a learning culture. *Educational Researcher, 29*(7), 4–14.

Siegel, M. (2002). What to do when the teaching lab instruments are too sophisticated for the students. In *Proceedings of the International Symposium on Virtual and Intelligent Measurement Systems (VIMS2002)* (pp. 123-128).

Siemens, G. (2004). *Learning management systems: The wrong place to start learning.* Retrieved April 1, 2010, from http://www.elearnspace.org/Articles/lms.htm

Siemens, G. (2006). *Knowing knowledge.* Retrieved April 1, 2010, from http://ltc.umanitoba.ca/KnowingKnowledge/index.php/Main_Page

Singh, M. P. (2002). The Pragmatic Web. *IEEE Internet Computing*, 4–5. doi:10.1109/MIC.2002.1003124

Singh, R., Iyer, L., & Salam, A. F. (2005). The semantic e-business vision. *Communications of the ACM, 48*(12), 38–41. doi:10.1145/1101779.1101806

Skehan, P. (1998). *A cognitive approach to language learning.* UK: Oxford University Press.

Sloan-C. (2008). *Staying the course: Online education in the United States, 2008*. Retrieved May 8, 2009 from http://www.sloan-c.org/publications/survey/pdf/staying_the_course.pdf

Snae, C., & Brueckner, M. (2007). Ontology-driven e-learning system based on roles and activities for Thai learning environment. *Interdisciplinary Journal of Knowledge and Learning Objects, 3*. Retrieved April 18, 2009, from http://ijklo.org/Volume3/IJKLOv3p001-017Snae.pdf

Sohng, S. S. (1996). Participatory research and community organizing. *Journal of Sociology and Social Work, 23*(4), 77–97.

Sommerville, I. (2007). Software engineering, 8th ed. Harlow: International Computer Science, Addison Wesley.

Song, S., & Lee, J. (2007). Key factors of heuristic evaluation for game design: Towards massively multi-player online role-playing game. *International Journal of Human-Computer Studies, 65*, 709–723. doi:10.1016/j.ijhcs.2007.01.001

Soukup, C. (2004). Multimedia Performance in a Computer-Mediated Community: Communication as a Virtual Drama. *Journal of Computer-Mediated Communication, 9*(4). Retrieved July 26, 2009, from http://jcmc.indiana.edu/vol9/issue4/soukup.html

Sowa, J. (2000). *Knowledge representation*. Pacific Grove, CA: Brooks/Cole.

Spyns, P., & Meersman, R. A. (2003). *From knowledge to interaction: From the semantic to the pragmatic web.* Brussels, Belgium: STARLab.

Spyns, P., Meersman, R. A., & Jarrar, M. (2002). Data modeling versus ontology engineering. *SIGMOD Record, 31*(4), 12–17. doi:10.1145/637411.637413

Ssemugabi, S., & de Villiers, R. (2007, October 2-3). A comparative study of two usability evaluation methods using a web-based e-learning application. In *Proceedings of the 2007 Annual Research Conference of the South African Institute of Computer Scientists and Information Technologists on IT Research in Developing Countries*, Fish River Sun, Sunshine Coast, South Africa.

Stahl, G., Koschmann, T., & Suthers, D. (2006). Computer-supported collaborative learning: An historical perspective. In Sawyer, R. K. (Ed.), *Cambridge handbook of the learning sciences* (pp. 409–426). UK: Cambridge University Press.

Stathacopoulou, R., Grigoriadou, M., Samarakou, M., & Mitropoulos, D. (2007). Monitoring students' actions and using teachers' expertise in implementing and evaluating the neural network-based fuzzy diagnostic Model. *Expert Systems with Applications, 32*(4), 955–975. doi:10.1016/j.eswa.2006.02.023

Steed, A., Slater, M., Sadagic, A., Bullock, A., & Tromp, J. (1999, March 13-17). Leadership and collaboration in shared virtual environments. In *Proceedings of the IEEE Virtual Reality*, VR. IEEE Computer Society, Washington, DC, 112.

Stein, R. (2007, October 6). Real hope in a virtual world. *Washingtonpost.com,* p. A01. Retrieved February 28, 2009, from http://www.washingtonpost.com/wp-dyn/content/article/2007/10/05/AR2007100502391.html

Steinkuehler, C., & Williams, D. (2006). Where everybody knows your (screen) name: Online games as 'third places.' *Journal of Computer-Mediated Communication, 11*(4). Retrieved July 26, 2009, from http://jcmc.indiana.edu/vol11/issue4/steinkuehler.html

Stojanovic, L., Staab, R., & Studer, R. (2001). *eLearning based on semantic web.* Paper presented at World Conference on the WWW and Internet (WebNet), Orlando, Florida.

Stutt, A., & Motta, E. (2004). Semantic learning webs. *Journal of Interactive Media in Education, 10*. Retrieved October 15, 2008, from http://www-jime.open.ac.uk/2004/10

Suchman, L. (1987). *Plans and situated actions: The problem of human-machine communication*. New York: Cambridge University Press.

Suchman, L. (2002). Practice-based design of information systems: Notes from the hyperdeveloped world. *The Information Society, 18*, 139–144. doi:doi:10.1080/01972240290075066

SUMI. (2008). *SUMI-The de facto industry standard evaluation questionnaire for assessing quality of use of software by end users*. Retrieved April 1, 2010, from http://sumi.ucc.ie/

Surowiecki, J. (2004). *The wisdom of crowds: Why the many are smarter than the few and how collective wisdom shapes business, economies, societies, and nations*. New York: Doubleday.

Swabey, P. (2007, October). Serious business in virtual worlds. *Information Age*. Retrieved August 16, 2009, from http://www.information-age.com/search/274916/serious-business-in-virtual-worlds.thtml

Swan, K., Schenker, J., Arnold, S., & Kuo, C.-L. (2007). Shaping online discussion: assessment matters. *E-mentor, 1*(18), 78-82. Retrieved May 11, 2009, from http://www.e-mentor.edu.pl/_xml/wydania/18/390.pdf.

Swan, K. (2001). Virtual interaction: Design factors affecting student satisfaction and perceived learning in asynchronous online courses. *Distance Education, 22*(2), 306–331. doi:10.1080/0158791010220208

Swan, K., Shen, J., & Hiltz, R. (2006). Assessment and collaboration in online learning. *Journal of Asynchronous Learning Networks, 10*(1), 45–62.

Tal Elhasid, E., & Meishar-Tal, H. (2006). Wiki as an online collaborative learning environment at the Open University. *Mashabei Enosh, 225*(6), 48–53.

Tal-Elhasid, E., & Meishar-Tal, H. (2009). Models of activity, collaboration and assessment in wikis in academic courses. In Szücs, A., Tait, A., Vidal, M., & Bernat, U. (Eds.), *Distance and e-learning in transition - Learning innovation, technology and social challenges* (pp. 745–756). New York: Wiley-ISTE.

Tallman, S., Jenkins, M., Henry, N., & Pinch, S. (2004). Knowledge clusters and competitive advantage. *Academy of Management Review, 29*(2), 258–271. doi:10.2307/20159032

Tan, P.-H., Ling, S.-W., & Ting, C.-Y. (2007) Adaptive digital game-based learning framework. In *Proceedings of the 2nd international conference on Digital interactive media in entertainment and arts* 07 Perth, Western Australia.

Tao, P. K. (2001). Developing understanding through confronting varying views: The case of solving qualitative physics problems. *International Journal of Science Education, 23*, 1201–1218. doi:10.1080/09500690110038602

Tao, P. K., & Gunstone, R. F. (1999). Conceptual change in science through collaborative learning at the computer. *International Journal of Science Education, 21*, 39–57. doi:10.1080/095006999290822

Taylor, A. (2009). Virtual worlds, social networks provide brave new world for emergency training. *Idaho State University Magazine, 39*(2). Retrieved June 10, 2009 from http://www.isu.edu/magazine/spring09/play2train.shtml

Taylor, T. L. (2006). Play between worlds: exploring online game culture. MIT Press: Cambridge, MA. In T. Boellstorff (2008). *Coming of Age in Second Life.* NJ: Princeton University Press.

Taylor, K. (2006). Social networks and presence in Second Life. *Cyberpsychology & Behavior, 12*(1), 721–722.

Tennis, J. T., & Sutton, S. A. (2008). Extending the simple knowledge organization system for concept management in vocabulary development applications. *Journal of the American Society for Information Science and Technology, 59*(1), 25–37. doi:10.1002/asi.20702

Terry, N. (2001). Assessing enrollment and attrition rates for the online MBA. *Technological Horizons in Education Journal, 28*(7), 64.

Thaden-Koch, T. C. (2003). *A coordination class analysis of college students: Judgments about animated motion* (Tech. Rep. No. AAI3104628). Nebraska, USA: ETD collection for University of Nebraska-Lincoln. Retrieved June 20, 2009 from http://digitalcommons.unl.edu/dissertations/AAI3104628

The Boyer Commission on Educating Undergraduates in the Research University. (1998). *Reinventing undergraduate education: A blueprint for America's research universities.* New York: State University of New York. Retrieved July 20, 2009, from http://naples.cc.sunysb.edu/pres/boyer.nsf/673918d46fbf653e852565ec0056ff3e/d955b61ffddd590a852565ec005717ae/$FILE/boyer.pdf

The Peak. (2009). *Opinions: Editor's voice: SFU online voice sucks, 132*(4). Retrieved May 25, 2009, from http://www.the-peak.ca/article/18222

Thomas, S. (2006). Pervasive learning games: Explorations of hybrid educational gamescapes. *Simulation & Gaming, 37*(1), 41–55. doi:doi:10.1177/1046878105282274

Thornburg, D. (2002). *The new basics: Education and the future of work in the telematic age*. Virginia: ASCD.

Timtam, B. (2009). Guided tour system user manual. Retrieved September 10, 2009 from http://www.hudbook.net/GTSmanual.pdf

Tobin, D. R. (2000). *All learning is self-directed: How organizations can support and encourage independent learning*. ASTD Press.

Toro-Troconis, M., Mellstrom, U., & Partridge, M. (2008). Game based learning in respiratory medicine via Second Life. *Thorax, 63*, 206.

Trindade, J., Fiolhais, C., & Almeida, L. (2002). Science learning in virtual environments: a descriptive study. *British Journal of Educational Technology, 33*(4), 471–488. doi:10.1111/1467-8535.00283

Trotter, A. (2006). Educators get a "Second Life.". *Education Week, 27*(42), 1.

Truelove, I., & Hibbert, G. (2008). Learning to walk before you know your name: Pre-Second Life scaffolding for noobs. In *Proceedings of the Researching Learning in Virtual Environments International Conference* (pp. 362-368). Retrieved May 8, 2009 from http://www.open.ac.uk/relive08/documents/ReLIVE08_conference_proceedings_Lo.pdf

Tu, C., & Corry, M. (2001). A paradigm shift for online community research. *Distance Education, 22*(2), 245–263. doi:10.1080/0158791010220205

Valkoss, P. (2005). *Why the blank stare? Strategies for visual learners*. Retrieved June 28, 2009 from http://www.phschool.com/eteach/social_studies/2003_05/essay.html

Vallance, M., & Wiz, C. (2007, March). *Virtual collaborative spaces.* Keynote paper and Podcast presented at North Zone Online ICT Symposium, Singapore. Retrieved March 14, 2009, from http://www.mshs.moe.edu.sg/symposium2007/keynote.htm

Vallance, M. (2007). An information and communications technology (ICT)-enabled method for collecting and collating information about pre-service teachers' pedagogical beliefs regarding the integration of ICT. *ALT-J, 15*(1), 51–65. doi:10.1080/09687760601129851

Van Assche, F., Duval, E., Massart, D., Olmedilla, D., Simon, B., & Sobernig, S. (2006). Spinning interoperable applications for teaching & learning using the simple query interface. *Journal of Educational Technology & Society, 9*(2), 51–67.

Van Dam, N., & Rogers, F. (2002, May). E-Learning cultures around the world: Make your globalized strategy transparent. *E-learning*, 28–33. Retrieved February 12, 2008.

Van Harmelen, M. (2008). Design trajectories: Four experiments in PLE implementation. *Interactive Learning Environments, 16*(1), 35–46. doi:10.1080/10494820701772686

Van Schaik, L. (2008). *Spatial intelligence*. Chichester, UK: John Wiley & Sons, Ltd.

Vanfreti, L. (2006). *A comprehensive virtual laboratory for teaching power systems dynamics and control at undergraduate level.* Retrieved March 17, 2007, from http://www.rpi.edu/~vanfrl/publications.html

Vanlehn, K. (2001, April). *Olae: A Bayesian performance assessment for complex problem solving*. Additional information about the document that does not fit in any of the other fields; not used after 2004.Paper presented at the Annual Meeting of the National Council on Measurement in Education, Seattle, WA. (ERIC Document Reproduction Service No. A unique accession number assigned to each record in the database; also referred to as ERIC Document Number (ED Number) and ERIC Journal Number (EJ Number).ED453285)

Vaquero, L., Rodero-Merino, L., Caceres, J., & Lindner, M. (2009). A break in the clouds: Towards a cloud definition. New York: ACM. *Computer Communication Review, 39*(1), 50–55. doi:10.1145/1496091.1496100

Vaughan, K., & MacVicar, A. (2004). Employees' pre implementation attitudes and perceptions to e-learning: A banking case study analysis. *Journal of European Industrial Training*, *28*(5), 400–413. doi:10.1108/03090590410533080

Veltman, K. H. (2004). Towards a semantic web for culture. *Journal of Digital Information*, *4*(4), 3–15.

Viegas, F. B., Wattenberg, M., & Dave, K. (2004). Studying cooperation and conflict between authors with history flow visualizations. In *Proceedings of the CHI conference on Human factors in computing systems*, Vienna, Austria (pp. 575-582).

Voss, J. (2005). Measuring Wikipedia. In *Proceedings of International Conference of the 10th International Society for Scientometrics and Informetrics*, Stockholm, Sweden. Retrieved May 11, 2009, from http://eprints.rclis.org/3610/1/MeasuringWikipedia2005.pdf

Vygotsky, L. (1986). *Thought and language.* Cambridge, MA: MIT Press.

Vygotsky, L. S. (1978). *Mind and society: The development of higher mental processes*. Cambridge, MA: Harvard University Press.

Wagner, C. (2008). Learning experience with virtual worlds. *Journal of Information Systems Education*, *19*(3), 263–266.

Wahid, F. (2007). Using the technology adoption model to analyze Internet adoption and use among men and women in Indonesia. *The Electronic Journal on Information Systems in Developing Countries*, *32*(6), 1–8.

Wang, Y., & Braman, J. (2009). Extending the classroom through Second Life. *Journal of Information Systems Education*, *20*(2), 235–247.

Wankat, P., & Oreovicz, F. (1992), *Teaching Engineering*. Retrieved June 28, 2007, from https://engineering.purdue.edu/ChE/News_and_Events/Publications/teaching_engineering/index.html

Warburton, S. (2009). Second Life in higher education: Assessing the potential for and the barriers to deploying virtual worlds in learning and teaching. *British Journal of Educational Technology*, *40*(3), 414–426. doi:10.1111/j.1467-8535.2009.00952.x

Ward, A. (2008). The power of connections. *The American School Board Journal*, *195*(9), 52–54.

Warschauer, M. (1999). *Electronic literacies: language, culture, and power in online education.* Mahwah, N.J: Lawrence Erlbaum Associates.

Weasenforth, D., Biesenbach-Lucas, S., & Weasenforth, C. (2002). Realizing constructivist objectives through collaborative technologies: Threaded discussions. *Language Learning & Technology*, *6*(3), 58.

WebAim. (2009). *Overview of Steppingstones cognitive research.* Retrieved from http://webaim.org/projects/steppingstones/cognitiveresearch

Webber, S. (2008). *An exploration of the island.* Retrieved August 20, 2009, from http://infolitischool.pbworks.com/An+exploration+of+the+island

Webber, S., & Johnston, B. (2005, September 6-8). Information literacy in the curriculum: selected findings from a phenomenographic study of UK conceptions of, and pedagogy for, information literacy. In C. Rust (Ed.), *Proceedings of Improving student learning: Diversity and inclusivity: the 11th ISL symposium,* Birmingham, UK (pp. 212-224.) Oxford, UK: Oxford Brookes University.

Wehrli, G., & Nyquist, J. G. (2003). Creating an educational curriculum for learners at any level. *AABB Conference.* Retrieved May 27, 2009, from http://www.nhchc.org/UNMSOM/ResourcesforDevCurr_Teaching_LearningActivities.pdf

Weigel, V. (2003). *Deep learning for a digital age*. San Francisco, CA: Jossey-Bass.

Weinberger, D. (2002). *Small pieces loosely joined.* New York: Perseus Books Group.

Weiss, A. (2007). Computing in the clouds. *netWorker, 11*(4), 16-25. New York: ACM.

Weller, M. (2007). *The VLE/LMS is dead.* Retrieved April 30, 2009, from http://nogoodreason.typepad.co.uk/no_good_reason/2007/11/the-vlelms-is-d.html

Weller, M. (2006). *Virtual learning environments: Using, choosing and developing your VLE.* London, New York: Routledge.

Wenger, E. (1998). *Communities of practice: Learning, meaning, and identity*. UK: Cambridge University Press.

Whitton, N. (2009). Gaming and the network generation. In Wheeler, S. (Ed.), *Connected minds, emerging cultures: Cybercultures in online learning* (pp. 77–89). Charlotte, NC: Information Age Publishing.

Wilson, S., Liber, O., Johnson, M., Beauvoir, P., Sharples, P., & Milligan, C. (2007). Personal learning environments: Challenging the dominant design of educational systems. *Journal of e-Learning and Knowledge Society, 3*(2), 27-38.

Wilson, S., Sharples, P., & Griffiths, D. (2009). Distributing education services to personal and institutional systems using Widgets. In *Proceedings of the First International Workshop on Mashup Personal Learning Environments* (pp. 25-32). Maastricht, Netherlands.

Wilson, S. (2008). Patterns of personal learning environments. *Interactive Learning Environments, 16*(1), 17–34. doi:10.1080/10494820701772660

Winn, W. (2002). Learning in artificial environments: Embodiment, embeddedness and dynamic adaptation. Retrieved March 12, 2009 from http://depts.washington.edu/edtech/ticl.htm

World Wide Web Consortium. (W3C). (2003). *Device Independence Working Group*. Retrieved from http://www.w3.org/2001/di/

Ye, E., Liu, C., & Polack-Wahl, J. (2007). Enhancing software engineering education using teaching aids in 3-D online virtual worlds. In *Proceedings of the 37th ASEE/IEEE Frontiers in Education Conference* (pp. T1E-8-T1E-13).

Yee, N., & Balilenson, J. (2007). The Proteus effect: The effect of transformed self-representation on behavior. *Human Communication Research, 33*, 271–290. doi:doi:10.1111/j.1468-2958.2007.00299.x

Yellowlees, P., & Cook, J. (2006). Education about hallucinations using an Internet virtual reality system: a qualitative survey. *Academic Psychiatry, 30*(6), 534–539. doi:10.1176/appi.ap.30.6.534

Yeo, S., Loss, R., Zadnik, M., Harrison, A., & Treagust, D. (2004). What do students really learn from interactive multimedia? A physics case study. *American Journal of Physics, 72*(10), 1351–1358. doi:10.1119/1.1748074

Zhou, G. T., & Lo, H. (1999, June). *Developing Java-based virtual laboratory tools for an undergraduate random signals and noise course*. Paper presented at the ASEE Annual Conference & Exposition. Retrieved August 5, 2007, from http://www.succeed.ufl.edu/papers/99/00838.pdf

About the Contributors

Michael Thomas, Ph.D., is Senior Lecturer in Language Learning Technologies at the University of Central Lancashire, UK. He has taught at universities in the UK, Germany and Japan. His research interests are in task-based learning and CALL and distance and online learning. He is editor of two book series, '*Digital Education and Learning*' (with James Paul Gee and John Palfrey) and '*Advances in Digital Language Learning and Teaching*' (with Mark Peterson and Mark Warschauer) and editor or author of over ten books. Among his recent publications are *Handbook of Research on Web 2.0 and Second Language Learning* (2009), *Task-Based Language Learning & Teaching with Technology* (with H. Reinders) (2010), *Digital Education* (2011), *Deconstructing Digital Natives* (2011) and *Online Learning* (2011). He is also founding Editor-in-Chief of the *International Journal of Virtual and Personal Learning Environments* (IJVPLE). Dr Thomas is a Fellow of the Higher Education Academy.

* * *

Ifeyinwa E. Achumba received a B.Sc degree in Computer Science from the University of Nigeria, Nsukka and an M.Sc degree in Computer Engineering, from the Federal University of Technology, Owerri (FUTO). Currently, she is a Ph.D. student in the Electronic and Computer Engineering Department of the University of Portsmouth, UK. The research programme is funded by the Schlumberger Foundation under its Faculty For The Future (FFTF) Scholarship programme aimed at encouraging women in Sciences, Technology and Engineering (STE) in their pursuit of academic excellence. Ifeyinwa is also a tenured academic at the Electrical and Electronic Engineering Department at the Federal University of Technology, Owerri, Nigeria.

Mohammad Ridwan Agustiawan obtained his bachelor's degree from Institut Teknologi Bandung, Indonesia in 2003 and his master's degree in Software Systems Engineering from RWTH Aachen University, Germany in 2008.

Sandra Sutton Andrews teaches a variety of related graduate courses in the Mary Lou Fulton College of Education in the USA. Her research interests center on the use of emerging technologies in education, while simultaneously ensuring equal accessibility of technologies and opportunities for all learners, regardless of economic situation, gender or disability. This dual focus necessitates fieldwork on a grassroots level, most recently in the virtual world of Second Life. Dr. Andrews' participatory research has led to initiatives in several Arizona cities as well as in Massachusetts, Mexico, and among several highly mobile populations. Within her work in the Arizona State University's Applied Learning Technologies Institute alt^I, she currently leads the ARISE program, a virtual learning community for middle school science teachers.

Robert L. Appelman Ph.D. is a clinical professor at Indiana University in the USA. He is Coordinator of the Undergraduate Instructional Technology program within the IST Department, which includes responsibility for technology integration courses for the Teacher Education Program. It also includes a Cognate in Instructional Technology covering The Impact of Games in IT, Applications of Multimedia in IT, Video in the Classroom, and a general introduction to IT. Other responsibilities include teaching graduate research in the area of virtual learning environments and directing the VX Lab (Virtual Xperience Lab) that focuses on Game Play Analysis.

Djamel Azzi received an Ingenieur D'Etat degree in electronics from the Universite de Constantine Algeria in 1988, an M.Sc, degree in control technology (1991) and his Ph.D, degree in control engineering (1993) from the University of Manchester Institute of Science and Technology (UMIST) in the U.K. Currently, he is a Principal Lecturer in the Department of Electronic and Computer Engineering at the University of Portsmouth U.K. His research interests include all aspects of AI but in particular its application to robotics, wireless sensor networks and assisted living.

Kelly Black is an Associate Professor of Mathematics at Clarkson University. His primary research interests are in the numerical approximation of partial differential equations. He has examined a wide range of application areas including biology, laser physics, and computational fluid dynamics. Kelly's teaching interests are varied, and he has taught courses ranging from statistics, calculus, and graduate level numerical analysis courses. He is particularly interested in bringing different disciplines together in the classroom and helping the students make connections to different topics that are explored.

Mohamed Amine Chatti has a diploma degree in Computer Science from the Technical University of Kaiserslautern, Germany. He is currently working as a research assistant and Ph.D. student at the Chair of Computer Science 5 Information Systems, RWTH Aachen University, Germany. His research interests include Web information systems, technology enhanced learning, professional learning, knowledge management, personal learning environments, and knowledge ecologies.

Alice Chik is an Assistant Professor in the Department of English, City University of Hong Kong. Her research interests include language education in popular culture. She is currently conducting a research project on the digital gaming pattens of second language learners.

Thomas Connolly is Chair of the ICT in Education Research Group at the University of the West of Scotland, the Director of the Scottish Centre for Enabling Technologies and Director for the Centre of Excellence in Games-based Learning. His specialisms are online learning, games-based learning and database systems. Professor Connolly has published papers in a number of international journals as well as authoring the highly acclaimed books, *Database Systems: A Practical Approach to Design, Implementation*, and *Management, Database Solutions* and *Business Database Systems*, all published by Addison Wesley Longman. Professor Connolly also serves on the editorial boards of many international journals, as well as managing several large-scale externally funded research projects.

Douglas Danforth received his Ph.D in Physiology from the University of Arizona in 1984 and is currently Associate Professor of Obstetrics and Gynecology at Ohio State University and Director of the College of Medicine Independent Study Program. Dr. Danforth has received more than $2,000,000 in research and educational grants, and has published more than 75 abstracts, 48 manuscripts, and 22 book chapters or invited articles. He has received numerous awards for teaching and research including, The American College of Obstetricians and Gynecologists Purdue Frederick Award for Excellence in Medical Research, The American Professors of Gynecology and Obstetrics Outstanding Teaching Award, The Ohio State University College of Medicine Excellence in Teaching Award, Distinguished Educator Award, and Preclinical Professor of the Year Award. Dr. Danforth was named a Distinguished Ohio Educator by Ohio Magazine and was elected as Faculty Member of Alpha Omega Alpha Medical Honor Society.

Michael DeMers is Associate Professor of geography at New Mexico State University. Dr. DeMers is the author of four GIS books including GIS for Dummies, and co-editor of the GIS&T Body of Knowledge, published jointly by the University Consortium for Geographic Information Science (UCGIS) and the Association of American Geographers (AAG). Mike's research involves GIS applications and design, GIS curriculum development, and online GIS education. DeMers is the Vice Chair of the AAG Geography Education Specialty Group and a member of the board of the Applied Geography Specialty Group. Besides his traditional university teaching duties he is also a mentor and teaches Intermediate Second Life for Educators for Sloan-C. He has served on the board of the Biogeography Specialty Group and as the Secretary of the US-International Association for Landscape Ecology.

Samuel Digangi is Associate Vice President University Technology and Associate Professor of Education specializing in technology integration. Dr DiGangi is executive director of alt^I ASU's Applied Learning Technologies Institute. His research activities focus on infusing effective components of instructional design with emerging technology in education. In addition to extensive use of computer-mediated instruction in his teacher preparation courses Dr. DiGangi directs several sponsored research projects examining implementation of high technology telecommunications and international networking in the classroom. He has taught numerous courses devoted to evaluation and assessment of the impact of technology on education. His focus includes classical quantitative methodology as well as Exploratory Data Analysis techniques. He has developed and delivered courses and training addressing research design methodology and evaluation, placing emphasis on data-based decision-making and continuous monitoring of performance.

Anne Fox is a teacher of English and teacher trainer based in Denmark. She teaches both face-to-face, in blended mode and exclusively online. She has coordinated and been a partner and external evaluator in several international projects dealing with e-learning, intercultural education and teacher training. She is the co-host of the Absolutely Intercultural podcast.

Tom Hainey is a final year PhD candidate in the School of Computing at the University of the West of Scotland researching evaluation frameworks for games-based learning. His research also covers using games-based learning for requirements analysis.

Charles Hamilton (Longg Weeks in Second Life) leads Virtual World Strategy for the IBM Center for Advanced Learning. For the previous two years Chuck led the Learning and New Media Program for the IBM 3D Internet Group as well as, IBM's IBM@PLAY program. With over 11 years in IBM's learning community Chuck's passion lies in connecting people and technology. Examples of Chuck's work in virtual spaces have been published in Fast Company, Talent Management Magazine, Computer World, Meetings and Incentive Magazine, the Wall Street Journal, Canadian Business and The Globe & Mail.

Angel Jannasch-Pennell is Assistant Vice President, University Technology at Arizona State University and Director of the Applied Learning Technologies Institute alt^I, where she directs Research and Outreach initiatives. Her focus brings an applied, research driven focus to the Institute, coordinating teams of researchers, faculty, and technical experts toward the proposal, development and implementation of technology innovation - in collaborative projects across Colleges and Centers, to community-based endeavors and University partnerships.

Matthias Jarke is Professor of Information Systems at RWTH Aachen University and Director of the Fraunhofer FIT Institute of Applied IT in Sankt Augustin, Germany. In his research, he investigates IS support for knowledge-intensive cooperative processes in business, engineering, and culture. As president of the German computer society (GI), he was responsible for the definition of Germany's IT accreditation guidelines. Both his university group and Fraunhofer FIT have been involved in numerous eLearning activities, ranging from the high school level to entrepreneurship training. Jarke serves on a number of national and international advisory boards.

Leslie Jarmon is a Senior Lecturer at the University of Texas at Austin where she has designed and taught graduate courses since 1998. She is a leader in the university's entry into virtual world environments, specifically Second Life (SL), and has published research and presented at numerous conferences including Best Practices in Education in SL, the American Sociological Association, and the New Media Consortium Symposium on Creativity. Dr. Jarmon's current research focuses on virtual embodiment issues and on virtual environments as new sites for collaboration and communities of learners on an international scale. She is a co-founder of the Educators Coop in Second Life, a 3-D virtual residential community of interdisciplinary educators, researchers, and librarians from around the world. Jarmon served as Community Outreach Officer for the Science, Technology, & Society (STS) Program and as Coordinator for the STS Civic Forum on the Societal Implications of Nanotechnology.

Jessica Knott is a producer for Michigan State University's Virtual University Design and Technology department, helping professors learn to effectively integrate technology into their teaching. She holds a Bachelor of Arts in Journalism with a specialization in public relations and a Master of Arts in

Education, focusing on educational technology and K-16 leadership. She has worked in higher education information technology for nine years and her educational interests include student engagement and literacy in the online realm and the potential of social networking in higher education.

Kristen Langlois (Krissy Bechir in SL) is a Learning Program Manager in IBM Canada's Learning (Human Resources) organization. She has extensive experience developing and facilitating classroom learning programs and in the past two years has successfully delivered learning programs for IBM in Second Life. These programs focus on employee development and dive into topics such as career planning, IBM Career planning tools and resources, mentoring, resume writing, interview skills and speed mentoring activities.

John Paul Loucky, Associate Professor in Kyushu, Japan, has taught all levels and communication skill areas of TESOL/EFL for nearly 20 years. He has written extensively on L2 reading and vocabulary in journals and online encyclopedias. His Homepage-www.CALL4All.us provides an extensive clearinghouse of CALL organizations and a Virtual Encyclopedia of language education sites worldwide.

Stewart Martin is a former secondary school headmaster whose academic and research interests have developed from over thirty years experience in mainstream education. He has acted as an educational consultant to organizations in both the public and private sectors in the UK, the Netherlands and Canada and was for some years a company CEO. He writes and researches in the fields of education, digital technology, citizenship, leadership and educational achievement and has published software and books to support independent learning. His research has been funded by the European Commission (Comenius programme); the Teacher Development Agency; the Higher Education Funding Council (HEFCE); and the Prime Minister's Initiative (PMI2) stream from the British Council.

Lorri Mon is an Assistant Professor at Florida State University's College of Communication and Information. She received the 2007 ASIS&T SIG-USE Elfreda A. Chatman Research Award for study of information providers in the virtual world of Second Life. Since 2007, she has been bringing classes of graduate students into Second Life as part of an FSU School of Library and Information Studies course exploring the provision of information services in a variety of virtual environments. She also is a co-principal investigator on a 3-year Institute of Museum and Library Services grant, "A Virtual Learning Laboratory for Digital Reference: Transforming the Internet Public Library," which has included development of a virtual learning community.

Diane Nahl is Professor in the Library and Information Science Program in the Department of Information and Computer Sciences at the University of Hawaii. She teaches courses in virtual world librarianship, reference and information services, human-system interaction, and information literacy instructional design. Her Second Life avatar is Adra Letov, founder of the LIS Student Union, orientation and instruction coordinator and board member for the Community Virtual Library, and council member for University of Hawaii System Island where she supervises undergraduate and graduate students in virtual world projects and producing educational events. She conducts and publishes research on the role of emotion in information behaviour, and has worked on and presented research in virtual world conferences including Virtual Worlds Best Practices in Education (VWBPE) 2009 and Libraries in Virtual Worlds 2010. Her current research involves collaborating with several geographically dispersed co-researchers studying academic librarians in SL.

Bolanle A. Olaniran (Ph.D) is a Professor and Interim Chairperson in the Department of Communication Studies at Texas Tech University. His areas of research include: Communication technologies and Computer-Mediated Communication, Organizational, Cross-cultural, and Crisis Management Communication. He has authored several articles in discipline focus and interdisciplinary focus Journals (i.e., Regional, National, and International) and edited book chapters in each of these areas. He has edited a book on e-learning. He serves as consultant to organizations at local, national and government level. His works have gained recognition such as the American Communication Association's "Outstanding Scholarship in Communication field," among others. He is also the recipient of the TTU 2006 Office of the President's Diversity Award; 2007 President's Excellence in Teaching Award; and was nominated for the 2007 TTU Chancellor's Distinguished Teaching Award.

Jonathon Richter, EdD is a Research Associate for the Center for Advanced Technology in Education (CATE) at the University of Oregon, USA, where he coordinates research on online teaching. Dr. Richter completed his doctorate at the University of Montana in 2003 and served as Assistant Professor of Education at Montana State University-Northern from 2002-2005. His research and futurist thinking has been featured at The American Educational Research Association, The World Future Society's Annual Conference, The National Educational Computing Conference, and The Pan-American Symposia on ePortfolios.

Sarah "Intellagirl" Robbins is a Ph.D. Candidate at Ball State University where she has been teaching using Second Life since 2005. Her research focuses on the communication mechanics of virtual worlds and how those mechanics contribute to the social and learning aspects of these worlds. Her dissertation will be a study of 75 different virtual worlds. Sarah is also the coauthor of *Second Life for Dummies* and a consultant to higher education institutions around the United States and the globe. Her research has been featured in The New York Times, the Chronicle of Higher Education, and Educause Review. Sarah currently serves as the Senior Director of Emerging Technologies at the Kelley School of Business at Indiana University.

Mat Schencks is a Media Project Manager working in Learning Teaching Solutions at the Open University in the UK working to produce innovative distance learning materials with the Faculty of Social Science. Mat was previously the Business Project Leader for Online Communication and Collaboration tools in the Open University's Virtual Learning Environment programme and holds an MA in Online and Distance Learning.

Niall Sclater is Director of Learning Innovation at the Open University and previously directed the OU's virtual learning environment programme. Before October 2005 Niall was Head of eLearning at the University of Strathclyde. He has been involved in the research, development and implementation of learning technology since 1990. He co-founded and managed Clyde Virtual University and the Scottish Computer Assisted Assessment Network. He set up the CETIS Assessment Special Interest Group and ran the Web-Supported Learning initiative of the European Consortium of Innovative Universities. He was also founder and Director of the €4m EU-funded Mediterranean Virtual University. Further information is available at sclater.com.

Maria Elena Solares-Altamirano holds an MA degree in Education (TESOL) and a Post-graduate Diploma in TESOL from the Institute of Education, University of London. She is an Associate Professor in the Department of Applied Linguistics of the Foreign Language Teaching Center (CELE), Universidad Nacional Autónoma de México nd has broad experience in teaching English and Spanish as foreign languages. She is a teacher educator, course and materials designer, online tutor and academic coordinator of the online diploma course ALAD (Actualización en Lingüística Aplicada a Distancia) at CELE, UNAM.

Marcus Specht is Professor for Advanced Learning Technologies at the Open University of the Netherlands and is currently involved in several national and international research projects on competence based lifelong learning, personalized information support and contextualized learning. From 2005 he was Associate Professor at the Open University of the Netherlands and worked on competence-based education, learning content engineering and management, and the personalization for learning. Currently, he is working on Mobile and Contextualized Learning Technologies, Learning Network Services, and Social and Immersive Media for Learning.

James Stocker received a first class degree in Computer Engineering from the University of Portsmouth, in 2007. He was then selected for and started a postgraduate degree at the same university in Cognitive Computing and Machine Learning. He suspended his studies in 2008 to participate in a joint knowledge transfer (Business+) project between the University of Portsmouth and Smart-e Ltd. (high end audio visual switching equipment manufacturer) writing control software for video matrix control and IP connectivity. James currently holds a full time position with Smart-e Ltd. as a graduate software engineer.

Mary Stokrocki is Professor of Art at Arizona State University. She was won numerous awards including: 2007 College of Arts & Architecture Alumni Award, Pennsylvania State University; 2007 Women's Caucus June King McFee Award presented at the National Art Education; 2005 Lowenfeld Award, and the 1995 Manual Barkan award for outstanding research article. Her qualitative research focuses on multicultural teaching/learning in Cleveland, Rotterdam, Ankara, Sao Paulo, Warsaw, Barcelona, Portugal, and the Yaqui, Pima/Maricopa, Ak-Chin, Apache and Navajo Reservations in Arizona. Her recent research involves explorations in empowering students and disenfranchised people in virtual worlds.

Riley Triggs is a Lecturer in Design at the University of Texas at Austin. He received a bachelor's degree in architecture from the University of Texas at Austin and a master's degree in architecture from Rice University where he explored the intersection of humans and architecture through the emotions of characters in horror films. Currently he is working on smoothing the interstitial space between virtual and physical environments using information as a medium in persistent online environments such as Second Life and Blue Mars, as well as in augmented reality applications for personal computing devices such as the Apple iPhone.

Frank Tuzi, Ph.D., Professor and Chair of the TESL Department at Nyack College, New York, has taught ESL, TESL, English composition and computer courses for nearly 15 years. His research interests include SLA, e-learning, education, and program development. His research site (http://www.ituzi.net) houses courses, developed materials, research projects, and selected flashed presentations.

Michael Vallance is a Professor at Future University, Japan. He has a Doctorate in Education from Durham University and a Masters Degree in Computer Assisted Learning from Stirling University, UK. He is the co-author of *Using IT in the Language Classroom* and is widely published in educational technology journals. He is involved in a number of ICT research projects such as Task Design for Web 2.0, Podmaps for iPods, and Virtual Collaborative Spaces. His current funding is from the Prime Minister's Initiative (PMI2). His Second Life avatar is Dafydd Beresford. His Website is available at http://web.mac.com/mvallance/

Paul van Schaik is a Professor of Psychology at the University of Teesside and a National Teaching Fellow, with a special interest in Human-Computer Interaction (HCI). His research focuses on interaction experience ('user experience') and information architecture as well as technology acceptance, web-site usability, electronic performance support and decision-making. His work has been published in leading HCI journals.

Tracy A. Villareal is a Biological Oceanographer in the Department of Marine Science, University of Texas at Austin. He received a B.S. and M.S. from Texas A&M University and a Ph.D. (1989) from the University of Rhode Island. After a post-doc at SUNY, Stony Brook and Woods Hole Oceanographic Institution, he joined the faculty at the University of Massachusetts, Boston. He moved to the Marine Science Institute in Port Aransas, Texas in 1997. He has published over 80 papers, focusing primarily on the ecology of marine phytoplankton.

Henry Watson (Watty Berkson in Second Life) is an Application Consultant with 15 years experience delivering software solutions at IBM. Since 2006, Henry has been helping clients understand the potential of virtual worlds and how to leverage them effectively for business purposes. During this time Henry has managed the design and delivery of many successful virtual world solutions for clients and IBM's own internal use.

Sheila Webber is Senior Lecturer in the Department of Information Studies at the University of Sheffield, UK, in which she is Director of Learning and Teaching and Director of the Centre for Information Literacy Research. Her key area for teaching and research is information literacy: she is an internationally invited speaker on this topic and a member of the International Federation of Library Associations and Institutions Information Literacy Section committee. She is also a Fellow of the Chartered Institute of Library and Information Professionals, a Fellow of the Higher Education Academy and an Academic Fellow in the Centre for Inquiry Based Learning in the Arts and Social Sciences. In Second Life she is Sheila Yoshikawa, owner of Sheffield University's InfolitiSchool island.

Martin Weller is a Professor in Educational Technology at the Institute for Educational Technology at the UK Open University. Among his publications are *Delivering Learning on the Net: The Why, What and How of Online Education* (2002) and *Virtual Learning Environments: Using, Choosing and Developing Your VLE* (2007). His research interests are in e-learning, learning design, VLEs, open content, Web 2.0 emerging technologies and artificial intelligence.

Charles Wiz is a Lecturer in the English Education Department at Yokohama National University, Japan. He has a B.A. in English literature and an M.Ed. in Applied Linguistics. His research interests include exploring virtual realities as learning environments, the vocabulary of the Internet and MMORPGs, and second language vocabulary acquisition.

Index

A

affective activity 172-173
Affordance Design 115
Alternate Reality Game (ARG) 256
Augmented Reality 42, 45, 132
avatar 46, 49, 59, 61-63, 65-67, 69, 71-72, 76, 79-80, 83-86, 91, 103-104, 108, 116, 121, 123-124, 126-128, 132, 140, 155, 171-172, 174-176, 178-179, 183, 189, 191, 194-195, 230-233

B

Bayesian Networks 201, 215
Blackboard 7, 13-15, 18, 22, 33
blood-testis barrier 154-156, 159, 161

C

centralised model 3, 8
Chatbot 126
Cloud Computing 10-12, 16-18
cognitive activity 172-173
Collaborative Authoring 237-238
Communication Engineering (COE) 202
Compare Version 246
Computer Aided Learning (CAL) 201
Conversational Framework 43
Co-Presence 58-59, 61, 64, 71, 73

D

Data Sources 230
decentralised model 1, 3-4, 7-8
default PLE (DPLE) 3
discovery responsive 196
Distance Education 91, 121, 131-135

E

economically developed countries (EDCs) 272
Electrical and Electronic Engineering (EEE) 202
Electronic and Computer Engineering (ECE) 202, 213
electronic learning (e-learning) 1-2, 7-11, 13-18, 22, 33, 39-40, 74, 110, 187, 200, 247-249, 254, 264-266, 268, 270-278
Empirical Evidence 250-251, 253
English as a second language (ESL) 126
experiential learning 43, 53, 57, 62-63, 68, 75, 77-78, 80, 89-92, 95-96, 103, 110, 128, 133, 172, 211, 252, 263-264
Extensible Access Control Markup Language (XACML) 272

F

falling monkey 149
Floaters Gallery 226, 228, 232
Four Dimensional Framework (FDF) 254

G

game object model (GOM) 254
Games-based learning (GBL) 250
Geographic Education 77
Girlstart 60, 62
Google Apps for Education 7, 10, 12, 14-15, 18
Graphical User Interface (GUI) 204

H

Hilde Hullabaloo's Cancerland 125
Homo Virtualis 58-61, 63-67, 69, 71-73, 110, 198
human-computer interaction (HCI) 96

I

Immersive Learning Environments 153-154, 163-164
Individualized Education Program (IEP) 231
Informal Learning 20-21, 24, 39, 56, 112, 119, 275
information behavior (IB) 169
Information Literacy 184-185, 187-188, 190-191, 193, 196-197, 200
Information Literacy class 185, 187-188, 190, 196
information responsive 195-196
Inquiry Based Learning (IBL) 184, 186
Interaction Effort (IE) 45-46, 49, 52
intrinsic motivation 175

J

Java DataBase Connectivity (JDBC) technology 205

K

Kinematics 137, 148-150
Kolb's Experiential Learning Theory 80

L

Learning Content Management Systems (LCMS) 22
learning object repositories (LOR) 23
LEGO Mindstorms 44-45
LEGO robots 42, 50, 52
less economically developed countries (LEDCs) 271
Lifelong learning 15, 20-21, 24, 39, 62, 75
Linden dollars 85, 126-127
Linden Scripting Language (LSL) 129
llRezAtRoot command 148

M

machinima 129
Mars Living Module Station 59
Mashups 20-21, 25-27, 38
massively multiplayer online games (MMOGs) 253
MediaWiki 237, 242, 245-247
Mercator-800 81-82
Microsoft Live@edu 13
Model-View-Controller (MVC) 27
Moodle 7, 9, 13-15, 18-19, 22, 33
Multi-User Virtual Environment (MUVE) 77, 79

N

National Oceanic and Atmospheric Administration (NOAA) 125
nearest neighbor 84-85
Nielsen's Heuristic Evaluation 254
non-player characters (NPCs) 256
NXT Mindstorms 42, 44, 46-49, 52

O

OLLI program 62
openID 6, 27, 29-30, 35, 37
Open University 1, 10, 16-17, 20, 39, 197, 200, 237, 249
Ortho-Prosthetic 65, 67

P

Participatory Action Research (PAR) 219, 223
Pedagogic approach 185-186, 188
personal adaptation 175
Personal Knowledge Networks (PKN) 25
Personal Learning Environments (PLE) 1, 40
personal learning network (PLN) 3
Physics Engine 137, 141-142, 149
planimetric distance 88
Play2Train 127, 135
PLEF Architecture 28
Power Systems Engineering (PSE) 202
Problem Based Learning (PBL) 186

Q

Quest Atlantis 122, 126

R

Reciprocity 230
Remote Method Invocation (RMI) technology 205
Resource-Constrained Faculties 201
Runescape 126

S

sage on the stage 121, 123
sandbox 47, 59, 226, 228
Science Metrics 42
Second Life Nutrition Game 154, 166
Second Life (SL) 58-59, 94, 168, 184

sensorimotor activity 172
sensorimotor facets 170
sensorimotor system 171-173
Sertoli cells 156, 158-160
Simple Query Interface (SQI) 23
Skype 79, 239
Smooth Space 98, 109
social-biological technology 170-173, 178
Speed Mentoring 112-118
standard generalized markup language (SGML) 267

T

Task Effectiveness (TE) 45-46, 49, 52
teacher learner environment (TLE) 3
technology-enhanced learning (TEL) 20-22
The Cloud 10-18

U

uncanny space 195

V

virtual learning environments (VLE) 1, 22
Virtual Self-Representations 61
Virtual Testis 154-155, 165

W

Web 2.0 1, 3, 7, 10-11, 17, 19, 22, 40, 112, 188, 195, 222, 237, 247, 263
World Wide Web (W3) 265-266

Z

Zone of Proximal Development 71, 125

CPSIA information can be obtained at www.ICGtesting.com
Printed in the USA
BVOW051950230412

288424BV00002B/6/P